ED-B

TENTH EDITION

Strategies for
Successful Writing
A Rhetoric, Research Guide, Reader, and Handbook

James A. Reinking

Robert von der Osten

D1497444

PEARSON

Boston   Columbus   Indianapolis   New York   San Francisco   Upper Saddle River
Amsterdam   Cape Town   Dubai   London   Madrid   Milan   Munich   Paris   Montréal   Toronto
Delhi   Mexico City   São Paulo   Sydney   Hong Kong   Seoul   Singapore   Taipei   Tokyo

Senior Acquisitions Editor: Lauren A. Finn
Senior Development Editor: David B. Kear
Senior Supplements Editor: Donna Campion
Senior Marketing Manager: Sandra McGuire
Senior Media Producer: Stefanie Snajder
Production Manager: Denise Phillip
**Project Coordination, Text Design,
  and Electronic Page Makup:** PreMediaGlobal
Cover Design Manager: Wendy Ann Fredericks

Cover Designer: Nancy Sacks
Photo Researcher: Jorgensen Fernandez
Text Permissions Researcher: Glenview
Senior Manufacturing Buyer: Roy Pickering
Printer and Binder: R. R. Donnelley/Crawfordsville
Cover Printer: Lehigh-Phoenix Color/Hagerstown
Exercises Icon: Lightpoet/Shutterstock
Purpose of Synthesis Icon: Pling/Shutterstock

This text was typeset in: ITC New Baskerville Std

For permission to use copyrighted material, grateful acknowledgment is made to the copyright holders appearing on the appropriate page within text and on page 720, which are hereby made part of this copyright page.

Library of Congress Cataloging-in-Publication Data

Reinking, James A., author.
   Strategies for Successful Writing: A Rhetoric, Research Guide, Reader, and Handbook / James A. Reinking,
Robert von der Osten.—[Tenth Edition]
      pages cm
   Includes bibliographical references and index.
   ISBN-13: 978-0-205-88311-0 (pbk.)
   ISBN-10: 0-205-88311-7 (pbk.)
   1. English language—Rhetoric—Handbooks, manuals, etc.   2. English language—Grammar—Handbooks, manuals, etc.
3. Report writing—Handbooks, manuals, etc.   4. College readers.   I. Von der Osten, Robert, author. II. Title.
   PE1408.R426 2013
   808'.0427—dc23
                                                                                          2012042485

Student Edition ISBN-13: 978-0-205-88311-0
Student Edition ISBN-10:   0-205-88311-7

1 2 3 4 5 6 7 8 9 10—DOC—16 15 14 13

Instructor's Review Copy ISBN-13: 978-0-205-88378-3
Instructor's Review Copy ISBN-10:   0-205-88378-8

A la Carte Edition ISBN-13: 978-0-205-88379-0
A la Carte Edition ISBN-10:   0-205-88379-6

Contents

v

Reader 461

Rhetorical Table of Contents

Narration

Description

Process Analysis

Illustration

Classification

Comparison

Cause and Effect

Definition

Argument

Mixing the Writing Strategies

Thematic Table of Contents

Life's Changes

Who We Are

Our Relationship to Nature

Health

Popular Culture and the Arts

Science and Technology

Diversity in Our Lives

American Borders

Language Use and Abuse

Struggling with Ethical Issues

Handbook   607

Sentence Elements

Editing to Correct Sentence Errors

Editing to Correct Faulty Punctuation and Mechanics

Spelling and Word Usage

Preface

The tenth edition of *Strategies for Successful Writing: A Rhetoric, Research Guide, Reader, and Handbook* is a comprehensive textbook that offers ample material for a full-year composition course. Instructors teaching a one-term course can make selections from Chapters 1 to 17, from whatever types of specialized writing suit the needs of their students, and from appropriate essays in the Reader.

Because we strongly believe that an effective composition textbook should address the student directly, we have aimed for a style that is conversational yet clear and concise. We believe that our style invites students into the book, lessens their apprehensions about writing, and provides a model for their own prose. This style complements our strong student-based approach to writing, and together they help create a text that genuinely meets student needs.

Changes in the Tenth Edition

The enthusiastic response to the nine previous editions both by teachers and students has been very gratifying. The tenth edition retains the many popular features of the previous editions and incorporates a number of improvements suggested by users and reviewers that should considerably enhance the utility of the text. Among the changes the following are noteworthy.

- More of the information in the Rhetoric chapters is presented using visual strategies:
  - Color highlighting of key passages in sample texts identifies different writing strategies in action.
  - Graphic organizers provide guidelines for developing essays.
  - Sample Student Essays are annotated to draw students' attention to writers' strategies.
- New learning objectives frame each chapter's content to guide both instructors and students to the goals of the chapter.
- One-third of the short sample texts have been updated with newer and more engaging samples.

- Half of the professional selections in the Reader have been replaced with essays on current topics that include social media, immigration, citizen policing videos, education, and more.
- Expanded coverage of thesis statements starts in Chapter 3 (with more examples of effective and ineffective thesis statements, analysis of them, and a list of strategies for developing effective ones) and continues through Chapters 8 to 16 with brief sections on developing thesis statements for each rhetorical mode.
- A new discussion of writing for media describes how to extend the principles of writing to changing online environments such as blogs, Web sites, and social media (Chapter 1).
- Chapter 21 on "Documenting Sources" has been divided into two new chapters that handle MLA and APA style separately to make it easier for students to find content consistent with the style they are expected to use.
- Updated discussion of research methods now emphasizes electronic research, including refining online searches and evaluating sources, more accurately reflecting how students conduct research today (Chapter 20).
- The revised Stepping Up to Synthesis feature in each modes chapter helps students integrate source material regardless of which type of rhetorical strategy they are using. The section includes guidelines for prewriting, evaluating sources, planning, and drafting a source-based paper for each of the writing strategies.
- Chapter 7 has been rewritten to make more active recommendations for students and to be more student friendly in its tone.
- A section on visual argumentation has been added to Chapter 16 "Argument: Convincing Others".
- The flowcharts on the writing process for each strategy at the end of the chapters have been simplified and made consistent both with each other and the text to make them easier for students to use.
- Most of the Connected Discourse exercises have been changed so that the topic of the exercises is more current.

Assorted updates and additions throughout the text, too numerous to mention individually, should help make the text even more effective.

The Rhetoric

In addition to these improvements, the text offers many other noteworthy features. The Rhetoric consists of 19 chapters, grouped into four parts. The first part includes four chapters. Chapter 1 introduces students to the purposes of writing; the need for audience awareness, which includes a discussion of discourse communities; and the qualities of good writing. Chapter 2 offers suggestions for effective reading. Chapter 3 looks at the planning and drafting stages. Chapter 4 takes students through the various revision stages, starting with a systematic procedure for revising the whole essay and then moving to pointers for revising its component parts. Sets of checklists pose key questions for students to consider. Chapters 3 and 4 are unified by an unfolding case history that includes the first draft of a student paper, the initial revision marked with changes, and the final version. Notes in the margin highlight key features of the finished paper. Students can relate the sequence of events to their own projects as they work through the various stages. Both chapters offer suggestions for using word-processing programs, and Chapter 4 explains peer evaluation of drafts, collaborative writing, and maintaining and reviewing a portfolio.

In the second part, we shift from full-length essays to the elements that make them up. Chapter 5 first discusses paragraph unity; it then takes up the topic sentence, adequate development, organization, coherence, and finally introductory, transitional, and concluding paragraphs. Throughout this chapter, as elsewhere, carefully selected examples and exercises form an integral part of the instruction.

Chapter 6 focuses on various strategies for creating effective sentences. Such strategies as coordinating and subordinating ideas and using parallelism help students to increase the versatility of their writing. The concluding section offers practical advice on crafting and arranging sentences so that they work together harmoniously. Some instructors may wish to discuss the chapters on paragraphs and sentences in connection with revision.

Chapter 7, designed to help students improve their writing style, deals with words and their effects. We distinguish between abstract and concrete words as well as between specific and general terms, and we also discuss the dictionary and thesaurus. Levels of diction—formal, informal, and technical—and how to use them are explained, as are tone, various types of figurative language, and irony. The chapter concludes by pointing out how to recognize and avoid wordiness, euphemisms, clichés, mixed metaphors, and sexist language.

The 10 chapters in the third part (Chapters 8–17) feature the various strategies, or modes, used to develop papers. These strategies, which follow a general progression from less to more complex, are presented as natural ways of thinking, as problem-solving strategies, and therefore as effective ways of organizing writing. One chapter is devoted to each strategy. This part concludes with a chapter on "Mixing the Writing Strategies", which explains and shows that writers frequently use these patterns in assorted combinations for various purposes. Planning and writing guidelines are presented for problem/solution and evaluation reports, two common types that rely on a combination of strategies.

Except for Chapter 17, the discussion in each chapter follows a similar approach: First explaining the key elements of the strategy; next pointing out typical classroom and on-the-job applications to show students its practicality; and then providing specific planning, drafting, and revising guidelines. Practical heuristic questions are also posed. A complete student essay, accompanied by questions, follows the discussion section. These essays represent realistic, achievable goals and spur student confidence, while the questions reinforce the general principles of good writing and underscore the points we make in our discussions. Twenty carefully chosen writing suggestions follow the questions in most chapters. All chapters conclude with a section entitled "Stepping Up to Synthesis." These sections explain and illustrate how students can advance their writing purpose by synthesizing material from various sources. Synthesis, of course, helps students develop and hone their critical reading and thinking skills. Furthermore, *Teaching Composition with Strategies for Successful Writing* includes suggestions for using the Reader essays and writing strategies to build assignments around themes.

The fourth and final part of the Rhetoric concentrates on three specialized types of college and on-the-job writing. Chapter 18 offers practical advice on studying for exams, assessing test questions, and writing essay answers. To facilitate student comprehension, we analyze both good and poor answers to the same exam question and provide an exercise that requires students to perform similar analyses.

Chapter 19 uses Stephen Crane's "The Bride Comes to Yellow Sky" as a springboard for its discussion. The chapter focuses on plot, point of view, character, setting, symbols, irony, and theme—the elements students will most likely be asked to write about. For each element, we first present basic features and then offer writing guidelines. Diverse examples illustrate these elements. The chapter ends with sections that detail the development of a student paper and explain how to include the views of others when writing about literature.

An expanded chapter on "Business Writing" is now available in the e-Book.

The Research Guide

The Research Guide consists of four chapters. Chapter 20 is a thorough and practical guide to writing library research papers. A sample pacing schedule not only encourages students to plan their work and meet their deadlines but also enables them to track their progress. As in Chapters 3 and 4, a progressive case history gradually evolves into an annotated student paper, which includes the results of a personal interview, thus demonstrating that primary research can reinforce secondary research. The chapter also includes a detailed account of how to handle a variety of quotations and avoid plagiarism.

Chapter 21 details and illustrates the correct formats for bibliographical references and in-text citations for the MLA style and Chapter 22 does the same for the APA systems of documentation. Guidelines are based on the 2009 edition of the *Publication Manual of the American Psychological Association* and current online updates as well as the 2009 edition of *The MLA Style Manual*. Our detailed treatment in Chapters 20, 21, and 22 should make supplemental handouts or a separate research-paper guide unnecessary.

Chapter 23 offers an in-depth discussion of interview, questionnaire, and direct-observation reports. After pointing out the nature, usefulness, and requirements of primary research, we explain how to plan and write each report, concluding with an annotated student model that illustrates the guidelines.

The Reader

The Reader, sequenced to follow the order of the strategies presented in the Rhetoric, expands the utility of the text by providing a collection of 38 carefully selected professional models that illustrate the various writing strategies and display a wide variety of style, tone, and subject matter and from a wide range of sources. These essays, together with the nine student models that accompany the various strategy chapters, should make a separate reader unnecessary.

Supplementing the chapter on reading strategies, the Reader comes with reading suggestions for each strategy that detail how to read the essays of a given type, how to read essays critically, and how to read the essays as a writer.

Each essay clearly illustrates the designated pattern, each has been thoroughly class-tested for student interest, and each provides a springboard for a stimulating discussion. In making our selections we have aimed for balance and variety:

1. Some are popular classics by acknowledged prose masters; some, anthologized for the first time, are by fresh, new writers.
2. Some are straightforward and simple, some challenging and complex.
3. Some adopt a humorous, lighthearted approach; some a serious, thoughtful one.
4. Some take a liberal stance, some a conservative one; and some address ethnic, gender, and cultural diversity.
5. A few are rather lengthy; most are relatively brief.

The first essay in each strategy section is annotated in the margin to show which features of the strategy are included. These annotations not only facilitate student understanding but also help link the Rhetoric and Reader into an organic whole. A brief biographical note about the author precedes each selection, and stimulating questions designed to enhance student understanding of structure and strategy follow it. In addition, a segment entitled "Toward Key Insights" poses one or more broad-based questions prompted by the essay's content. Answering these questions, either in discussion or writing, should help students gain a deeper understanding of important issues. Finally, we include a writing assignment suggested by the essay's topic.

The Handbook

The comprehensive Handbook, which features tab indexing on each page for easy access to all material, consists of four parts: "Sentence Elements," "Editing to Correct Sentence Errors," "Editing to Correct Faulty Punctuation and Mechanics," and "Spelling and Word Usage." Explanations skirt unneeded grammatical terminology and are reinforced by sets of sentence exercises in the first three sections. The section on "Sentence Elements" explains how students can use these elements to improve their writing skills. We also include connected-discourse exercises—unfolding narratives that engage and retain student interest and therefore facilitate learning—in the "Sentence Errors" and "Punctuation and Mechanics" sections. Extra sets of 20-item exercises that parallel those in the Handbook are available upon request to instructors who adopt the book. The "Spelling and Word Usage" unit presents four useful spelling rules and offers similarly comprehensive coverage of troublesome usages. Instructors can use the Handbook either as a reference guide or as a basis for class discussion.

Supplements

Teaching Composition with *Strategies for Successful Writing*

The *Teaching Composition with Strategies for Successful Writing*, Tenth Edition (ISBN 0-205-88376-1), supplement offers various suggestions for teaching first-year composition, a sample syllabus for a sequence of two 15-week semesters, numerous guidelines for responding to student writing, and a detailed set of grading standards. This new edition has added for each chapter teaching strategies, classroom activities, suggested readings, and answers to the exercises. In addition, it contains an extra set of 20-item exercises that parallel those in the Handbook section of *Strategies*. The exercises can be used either in the classroom or as assignments.

PowerPoints to Accompany *Strategies for Successful Writing*

Ideal for hybrid or distance learning courses, the PowerPoint presentation deck offers instructors slides to adapt to their own course needs.

Online Resources for Instructors and Students

Pearson MyLabs

The Pearson English MyLabs empower students to improve their skills in writing, grammar, research, and documentation with market-leading instruction, multimedia tutorials, exercises, and assessment tools. Students can use the MyLab on their own, benefiting from self-paced diagnostics and extra practice in content knowledge and writing skills. Instructors can use MyLabs in ways that best complement their courses and teaching styles. They can work more efficiently and more closely with students by creating their own assignments and using time-saving administrative and assessment tools. The marginal icons found in this book link students to enhanced online resources and assessment through the Pearson eText, which is also available in an iPad version. To learn more, visit www.pearsonhighered.com/englishmylabs or ask your Pearson representative.

Pearson eText

An interactive online version of *Strategies for Successful Writing* is available as an eText bringing together the many resources of the MyLab with the instructional content of this successful book to create an enhanced learning experience for students. Marginal icons in the Pearson eText link to a wealth of online resources:

👁 Video tutorials illustrate key concepts, offering tips and guidance on critical reading, evaluating sources, avoiding plagiarism, and many other topics.

- ((•〔 Audio podcasts discuss common questions about grammar, usage, punctuation, and mechanics.
- ▤ •〔 Sample documents illustrate the range of writing students do in composition classes, their other courses, the workplace, and the community.
- ⚙⚙ •〔 Additional exercises help students assess their understanding of concepts before applying them in their own writing.

Accelerated Composition

Support for acceleration or immersion courses focuses on three fundamental areas: reading, writing, and grammar. Additional questions for professional and student readings help students understand, analyze, and evaluate the strategies writers employ. For each of the text's major writing assignments, additional activities and prompts encourage students to break down the tasks involved in writing a paper into manageable chunks. Grammar support includes diagnostic, practice, instruction, and mastery assessment. Contact your Pearson representative for access through our English MyLab and for ordering information.

Michelle Zollars, Associate Professor and Coordinator of the Accelerated Learning Program at Patrick Henry Community College, has used Strategies *for Successful Writers* for ten years and authors the reading and writing support for accelerated courses. She has been teaching the accelerated composition model for over five years; has presented on acceleration at National Association for Developmental Education, the Council on Basic Writing conferences, and the Conference on Acceleration; and has served on the Developmental English Curriculum Team of the Virginia Community College System.

CourseSmart eTextbook

Students can subscribe to *Strategies for Successful Writing* at CourseSmart.com. The format of the eText allows students to search the text, bookmark passages, save their own notes, and print reading assignments that incorporate lecture notes.

Android and iPad eTextbooks

Android and iPad versions of the eText provide the complete text and the electronic resources described above.

Acknowledgments

Like all textbook writers, we are indebted to many people. Our colleagues at Ferris State University and elsewhere, too numerous to mention, have assisted us in several ways: critiquing the manuscript; testing approaches, essays, and exercises in their classrooms; and suggesting writing models for the text.

We would like to thank all those faculty members who forwarded student work to be considered for the 9th edition and which have been continued in the 10th. These essays are powerful evidence of the effective teaching of all of the contributors and their tremendous impact on student lives. David Burlingame, Heald College; Sandra Cusak, Heald College & Reedley College; Ruth Dalton, Montgomery College; Linda Gary, Tyler Junior College; Vicki Holmes, University of Nevada Las Vegas; Theresa Mlinarcik, Macomb Community College; Emily Moorer, Hinds Community College; Carol Osborne, Coastal Carolina University; Roseann Shansky, Ferris State University; Efstathia Siegel, Montgomery College; Geraldine Yap, Cosumnes River College.

In addition, we thank our reviewers, whose many suggestions have greatly improved our text: Linda Brender, Macomb Community College; Joann Bruckwicki, Tyler Junior College; Jim Brueggeman, Western Technical College; Kimberley Carter, Virginia College; Scott Contor, Oakland Community College; Edwin Cummings, Bryant and Stratton College; Anthony Gancarski, Virginia College; Suzanne Martens, Grand Rapids Community College; Arch Mayfield, Wayland Baptist University; Robin McGinnis, Daymar College Bowling Green; Summerlin Page, Central Carolina Community College; Sarah Peters, Collin College; Philip Poulter, Texas State Technical College; Nancy Risch, Caldwell Community College; Kevin Sanders, University of Arkansas–Pine Bluff; Andrea Serna, National American University; Josh Woods, Kaskaskia College.

Special thanks are also due to the outstanding team at Pearson, whose editorial expertise, genial guidance, and promotional efforts have been vital to this project: Phil Miller, former President of Humanities and Social Sciences Division, who first saw the potential in our approach; Joe Opiela, Editorial Director for English, and Lauren Finn, Senior Acquisitions Editor, whose efficiency, knowledge, and understanding of authors' concerns have enhanced our pleasure in preparing this edition; David Kear, Senior Development Editor; Denise Phillip, our Production Editor; and Sandra McGuire, whose marketing expertise will help our book find its way.

Special thanks goes to Kyra Hunting and Elyse Glass who have provided the personal support that have made both the work of teaching as well as the editing of this book possible.

J.A.R.
R.v.d.O.

To the Student

No matter what career you choose, your ability to communicate clearly and effectively will directly affect your success. In the classroom, your instructor will often evaluate your mastery of a subject by the papers and examinations you write. Prospective employers will make judgments about your qualifications and decide whether to offer you an interview on the basis of your job application letter and résumé. On the job, you will be expected to write clear, accurate reports, memorandums, and letters.

There is nothing mysterious about successful writing. It does not require a special talent, nor does it depend on inspiration. It is simply a skill, and like any other skill, it involves procedures that can be learned. Once you understand them and the more you practice, the easier writing becomes.

Strategies for Successful Writing will help you become a successful writer. And after you graduate it can serve as a useful on-the-job reference. The first, third, and fourth chapters explore the fundamentals of writing and the general steps in planning, drafting, and revising papers. Chapter 2 will help you read more effectively for college and show you how to read like a writer. The next three chapters zero in on paragraphs, sentences, and writing style. The next 10 explain the basic writing strategies you can use for most writing projects. The final six turn to specialized writing—essay examinations, papers about literature, library research papers, and papers based on your own original research results. The book concludes with a Reader and, if you are using the complete version of the text, a Handbook.

From time to time you have probably had the unpleasant experience of using textbooks that seemed to be written for instructors rather than students. In preparing this book, we have tried never to forget that you are buying, reading, and using it. As a result, we have written the text with your needs in mind. The book uses simple, everyday language and presents directions in an easy-to-follow format. The chapters on writing strategies provide examples of student essays that supplement the professional essays in the Reader. These student examples represent realistic, achievable goals. When you compare them to the professional examples, you'll see that students can indeed do excellent work. We are confident that by learning to apply the principles in this text, you will write well too.

Here's wishing you success!

Rhetoric

CHAPTER 1 Writing: A First Look

In this chapter, you will learn how to:

1.1 Establish the purpose for your writing.

1.2 Determine the audience for your writing.

1.3 Identify the qualities of good writing.

1.4 Apply writing techniques to changing media.

1.5 Write ethically and avoid plagiarism.

Why write? Aren't texting, e-mail, voice mail, and cellular phones dooming ordinary writing? Not long ago, some people thought and said so, but events haven't supported those predictions. In fact, much electronic media, such as blogging and tweeting, have increased the amount of writing people do. Although devices such as cell phones have made some writing unnecessary, the written word still flourishes both on campus and in the world of work.

Writing offers very real advantages to both writers and readers:

- It gives writers time to reflect on and research what they want to communicate and then lets them shape and reshape the material to their satisfaction.
- It makes communication more precise and effective.
- It provides a permanent record of thoughts, actions, and decisions.
- It saves the reader's time; we absorb information more swiftly when we read it than when we hear it.

What kind of writing will people expect you to do?

- At college you may be asked to write lab reports, project proposals, research papers, essay exams, marketing plans.
- Job hunting requires application letters.
- On the job, you might describe the advantages of new computer equipment, report on a conference you attend, explain a new procedure, suggest a new security system, or present a marketing plan.
- Personally, you may need to defend a medical reimbursement, request a refund for a faulty product, or find a solution to a personal problem.

Here is the raw truth: the ability to write will help you earn better grades, land the job you want, and advance in your career. Writing will help you create the future you want in a competitive world.

When we write, it is often in response to a situation that shapes the purpose and audience of our writing. We rarely write in isolation, but instead write to others who have an interest in our message.

The Purposes of Writing

Whenever you write, some clear purpose should guide your efforts. If you don't know why you're writing, neither will your reader. Fulfilling an assignment doesn't qualify as a real writing purpose. Faced with a close deadline for a research paper or report, you may tell yourself, "I'm doing this because I have to." An authentic purpose requires you to answer this question: What do I want this piece of writing to do for both my reader and for me?

Purpose, as you might expect, grows out of the writing situation. You explore the consequences of the greenhouse effect in a report for your science instructor. You write an editorial for the college newspaper to air your frustration over inadequate campus parking. You propose that your organization replace an outdated piece of equipment with a state-of-the-art model.

Following are four common *general writing purposes*, two or more of which often join forces in a single piece:

1.1

Establish the purpose for your writing.

To Inform   We all have our areas of expertise and often share that information with each other. A student in computer science could post a blog on a class instructional site on how to create a web page. A medical researcher shares her research in her publications with other doctors and other research professionals.

To Persuade   You probably have strong views on many issues, and these feelings may sometimes impel you to try swaying your reader. In a letter to the editor, you might attack a proposal to establish a nearby chemical waste dump. Or, alarmed by a sharp jump in state unemployment, you might write to your state senator and argue for a new job-training program.

To Express Yourself   When you text a friend, you choose words and phrases to show off who you are. By your topic, word choice, example, or turn of phrase, you display a bit of yourself whether in e-mails, journals, poetry, essays, or fiction.

To Entertain   Some writing merely entertains; some writing couples entertainment with a more serious purpose. A lighthearted approach can help your reader absorb dull or difficult material.

Watch the Animation on the **Purposes of Writing**

More Specific Purposes

Besides having one or more *general purposes*, each writing project has its own *specific purpose*. Consider the difference in the papers you could write about solar homes. You might explain how readers could build one, argue that readers should buy one, express the advantages of solar homes to urge Congress to enact a tax credit for them, or satirize the solar home craze so that readers might reevaluate their plans to buy one.

Having a specific purpose assists you at every stage of the writing process. It helps you define your audience; select the details, language, and approach that best suit their needs; and avoid going off in directions that won't interest them. The following example from the Internet has a clear and specific purpose.

Turn Down Your iPod Volume (or Go Deaf)

Marianne Halavage

1   I have had a Walkman, CD Walkman or iPod surgically attached to my ears via headphones since about the age of about five (anatomically strange. But true).

2   So chances are that I'm a case in point for the recent LA Times article. It says that one in every five teens has at least a slight hearing loss. Many experts think the culprit is the use of headphones to listen to portable music.

3   LA Times said:

Most teens think they are invulnerable and for most of them, the hearing loss is not readily perceptible so they are not aware of the damage. But the bottom line is, "Once there, the damage is irreversible," said Dr. Gary C. Curhan of Brigham and Women's Hospital.

4   Irreversible, you HEAR him. Gone. NEVER to return.

5   The idea of losing my hearing, even a little bit, terrifies me. Struggling to hear my music: my first love, my passion and my therapist; unable to hear my family and friends. I don't even want to think about it.

6   But for my hearing's sake in the future, I will. I'm 28, long out of teeniedom, so no doubt some damage has been done. But I will, from now on, keep the volume on my iPod at an ear-friendly level, as the experts advise:

"The message is, we've got to stop what we are doing," said Dr. Tommie Robinson Jr., president of the American Speech-Language-Hearing Assn. "We have to step back and say: OK, turn down the volume on iPods and earbuds and MP3 players. Wear ear protection at rock concerts or when you are exposed to loud noises for long periods of time," like when using a lawn mower.

7   Um, not so sure that many teens will take to wearing ear protection at concerts. They'd probably rather lose their hearing than have their pals laugh at them for looking a bit naff in it.

8   But, no ear protection now, hearing aid later…

9   Suddenly ear protection never sounded so good.

To grab her reader in a busy Internet environment, Marianne Halavage announces her purpose boldly in her title. The remainder of the paragraphs provide, alternately, statements by authority arguing that listening to loud music is likely to result in hearing loss with her own personal reaction where she identifies with her audience. The last two single-sentence paragraphs provide the reader with a stark choice and reaffirms the essay's purpose.

Now examine this paragraph, which does *not* have a specific purpose:

> Imagine people so glued to their computers that they forget to eat or sleep and even miss work. It is like a strange version of a zombie movie. What could have eaten their brains? Video games can be addictive as players struggle to get to the next level. Still, this negative effect is exaggerated. But there are a number of qualities that make a video game player want to keep coming back to the game and any good game designer needs to know those qualities.

Is the paper for game addicts to get them to quit, a humorous analogy, or a serious recommendation to game designers? Once the writer decides on a purpose, the paragraph can be focused.

> The stereotype of gamers is that they are so glued to their computers that they forget to eat, sleep, or work. While this is a gross exaggeration, game designers do want their players to be hooked on their games. There are in fact a number of qualities that make video players want to keep returning to a favorite game, and any good game designer needs to know those qualities.

The Audience for Your Writing

Everything you write is aimed at some audience—a person or group you want to reach. The ultimate purpose of all writing is to have an effect on a reader (even if that reader is you), and therefore purpose and audience are closely linked. You would write differently about your college experience to a young relative, your best friend, your parents, your advisor, or a future employer.

1.2

Determine the audience for your writing.

- School is fun and I am learning a lot.—to a young relative to reassure
- I went to the greatest party.—to your best friend to entertain
- I am working hard.—to your parents to persuade them to send extra support
- I have learned many things that will help me contribute to your company.—to an employer to persuade them to consider you for a job

It is important to recognize that writing, even texting, is very different from face to face conversations.

Face to Face	Writing
You can observe body language and vary what you are saying in response.	You don't get to see how people are responding.
You can respond to immediate questions.	It would be hard for people to get questions to you.
There is little record of what you say.	Readers can reread your text.

Once written work has left your hands, it's on its own. You can't call it back to clear up a misunderstanding or adjust your tone. What this means is that as a writer, you need to be able to anticipate your readers' needs and responses.

Establishing rapport with your audience is easy when you're writing for your friends or someone else you know a great deal about. You can then judge the likely response to what you say. Often, though, you'll be writing for people you know only casually or not at all: employers, customers, fellow citizens, and the like. In such situations, you'll need to assess your audience before starting to write and/or later in the writing process.

◉ Watch the Animation on **Developing an Audience Profile**

A good way to size up your readers is to develop an audience profile. This profile will emerge gradually as you answer the following questions:

1. What are the educational level, age, social class, and economic status of the audience I want to reach?
2. Why will this audience read my writing? To gain information? Learn my views on a controversial issue? Enjoy my creative flair? Be entertained?
3. What attitudes, needs, and expectations do they have?
4. How are they likely to respond to what I say? Can I expect them to be neutral? Opposed? Friendly?
5. How much do they know about my topic? (Your answer here will help you gauge whether you're saying too little or too much.)
6. What kind of language will communicate with them most effectively? (See "Level of Diction" in Chapter 7.)

College writing assignments sometimes ask you to envision a reader who is intelligent but lacking specialized knowledge, receptive but unwilling to put up with boring or trite material. Or perhaps you'll be assigned, or choose, to write for a certain age group or readers with particular interests. At other times, you'll be asked to write for a specialized audience—one with some expertise in your topic. This difference will affect what you say to each audience and how you say it.

The Effect of Audience on Your Writing

Let's see how audience can shape a paper. Suppose you are explaining how to take a certain type of X-ray.

If your audience is a group of lay readers who have never had an X-ray, you might

- Avoid technical language.
- Compare an X-ray to a photograph.
- Explain the basic process, including the positioning of patient and equipment.
- Comment on the safety and reliability of the procedure.
- Indicate how much time it would take.

If, however, you were writing for radiology students, you might

- Consistently use the technical language appropriate for this audience.
- Emphasize exposure factors, film size and required view.
- Provide a detailed explanation of the procedure, including how to position patients for different kinds of X-rays.
- Address your readers as colleagues who want precise information.

Audience shapes all types of writing in a similar fashion, even your personal writing. Assume you've recently become engaged, and to share your news you write two e-mails: one to your minister or rabbi and the other to your best friend back home. You can imagine the differences in details, language, and general tone of each e-mail. Further, think how inappropriate it would be if you accidentally sent the e-mail intended for one to the other. Without doubt, different readers call for different approaches.

Discourse Communities

Professionals often write as members of specific communities. For example, biologists with similar interests often exchange information about their research. The members of a community share goals, values, concerns, background information, and expectations, and this fact in turn affects how they write. Because such writing is closely tied to the interests of the community, professional articles often start with a section linking their content to previous research projects and articles. Often custom dictates what information must be included, the pattern of organization and the style the paper should follow. Throughout college, you will discover that part of learning to write is becoming familiar with the values and customs of different discourse communities. To do this, you'll need to read carefully in your major field, acquainting yourself with its current issues and concerns and learning how to write about them. As you start reading in any professional area, ask yourself these questions:

1. What are the major concerns and questions in this field?
2. What seems to be common knowledge?

3. To what works do writers regularly refer?
4. How do those in the field go about answering questions?
5. What methods do they follow?
6. Which kinds of knowledge are acceptable? Which are not?
7. What values seem to guide the field?
8. What kinds of information must writers include in papers?
9. How are different writing projects organized?
10. What conventions do writers follow?

We all, of course, belong to many different communities. Furthermore, a community can involve competing groups, conflicting values, differing kinds of writing projects, and varying approaches to writing. But as part of your growth as a writer and professional, you'll need to understand the goals and rules of any community you enter.

EXERCISE

The following three excerpts deal with the same subject—nanotechnology— but each explanation is geared to a different audience. Read the passages carefully; then answer the following questions:

1. **What audience does each author address? How do you know?**
2. **Identify ways in which each author appeals to a specific audience.**

1. Nanotechnology is the creation of functional materials, devices and systems through control of matter on the nanometer length scale (1–100 nanometers) and exploitation of novel phenomena and properties (physical, chemical, biological, mechanical, electrical…) at that length scale. For comparison, 10 nanometers is 1,000 times smaller than the diameter of a human hair. A scientific and technical revolution has just begun based upon the ability to systematically organize and manipulate matter at nanoscale. Payoff is anticipated within the next 10–15 years.

    CNT Center for Nanotechnology

2. Today's manufacturing methods are very crude at the molecular level. Casting, grinding milling and even lithography move atoms in great thundering statistical herds.

    It's like trying to make things out of LEGO blocks with boxing gloves on your hands. Yes, you can push the LEGO blocks into great heaps and pile them up, but you can't really snap them together the way you'd like.

    In the future, nanotechnology (more specifically, *molecular nanotechnology* or MNT) will let us take off the boxing gloves. We'll be able to snap together the fundamental building blocks of nature easily, inexpensively and in most of the ways permitted by the laws of nature. This will let us continue the revolution in computer hardware to its ultimate limits: molecular computers made from molecular logic gates connected by molecular wires. This new pollution free manufacturing technology will also let us inexpensively fabricate a cornucopia of new products that are remarkably light, strong, smart, and durable.

    Dr. Ralph Merkle, *Nanotechology*

3. **Nanotechnology** is a general term used to refer to technological research and developments on the nanometer scale, with one nanometer equal to one millionth of a millimeter. An important aspect of nanotechnology is the belief that as tools get smaller, the physical forces acting on them will produce differing effects than what we currently observe. It is expected that gravity would play a lesser role in the interaction of nanotools and that surface tension and van der Waals forces would play greater roles.

Sage Reference Online, Encyclopedia of Governance

Just as you would not dial a telephone number at random and then expect to carry on a meaningful conversation, so you should not expect to communicate effectively without a specific audience in mind.

One other note: As you shape your paper, it is important that the writing please you as well as your audience—that it, satisfy your sense of what good writing is and what the writing task requires. You are, after all, your own first reader.

The Qualities of Good Writing

Good writing is essential if you want your ideas to be taken seriously. Just as you would have trouble listening to someone with his shirt on backwards and wearing two different kinds of shoes, most readers dismiss out of hand writing that is disorganized, poorly worded or marred by errors in grammar and spelling. In a world where most people are drowning under an information overload, few have the time or inclination to hunt through bad writing to search for quality ideas. Employers discard job seekers with poorly worded cover letters; badly written proposals are rejected; and few bother to read poorly written articles.

1.3

Identify the qualities of good writing.

Three qualities—fresh thinking; a sense of style including the use of correct grammar and punctuations; and effective organization—help to ensure that a piece of prose will meet your reader's expectations.

Fresh Thinking   You don't have to astound your readers with something never before discussed in print. Unique ideas and information are rare. You can, however, freshen your writing by exploring personal insights and perceptions. Using your own special slant, you might show a connection between seemingly unrelated items, as does a writer who likens office "paper pushers" to different kinds of animals. Keep the expression of your ideas credible, however; far-fetched notions spawn skepticism.

Sense of Style   Readers don't expect you to display the stylistic flair of Maya Angelou. Indeed, such writing would impair the neutral tone needed in certain kinds of writing, such as technical reports and legal documents. Readers do, however, expect you to write in a clear style. And if you strengthen it with vivid, forceful words, readers will absorb your points with even greater interest.

Readers also expect you to use standard grammar, spelling, and punctuation. The chapters ahead show you how to use language in ways that project your views and personality. Chapters 6 and 7, in particular, will help you develop a sense of style, as will the many readings throughout the book.

Effective Organization   All writing should be organized so it is easy to follow. A paper should have a beginning, a middle and an end; that is, an introduction, a body, and a conclusion. The introduction sparks interest and acquaints the reader with what is to come. The body delivers the main message and exhibits a clear connection between ideas so that the reader can easily follow your thoughts. The conclusion ends the discussion so the reader feels satisfied rather than suddenly cut off. Overall, your paper should follow a pattern that is suited to its content and will guide the reader. Organizational patterns, or strategies of development, are the subject of Chapters 8–17. Chapter 5 discusses introductions and conclusions.

Freshness, style and organization are weighted differently in different kinds of writing. A writer who drafts a proposal to pave a city's streets will probably attach less importance to fresh thinking than to clear writing and careful organization. On the other hand, fresh thinking can be very important in a description of an autumn forest scene. You will learn more about these qualities throughout this book.

Writing and Changing Media

1.4

Apply writing techniques to changing media.

Listen to the Podcast on **Communicating with Electronic Media**

At college and on the job, you will e-mail, text message, tweet, blog and write text for web pages. The processes and principles in this book apply to any media for which you may write. Regardless of the media, you need to employ effective writing processes, consider your purpose and audience, and employ effective organizational strategies. If you are texting your boss to let him know why you will be late to work, you know you will have to be polite and clear about the reasons you are delayed. Clearly, "Dude, traffic-jam," won't do. If you are creating a web site that presents your restaurant, you are likely to write a description of the restaurant, revising the text several times to make it as effective as possible. If you are writing a blog on your favorite rock group, you might identify what has caused them to be successful or compare them with other groups. Throughout college, instructors may encourage you to use other media to complete assignments. Almost every career will expect you to know a wide range of communication media. What follows are a few points you might consider.

E-Mail   While in college, you will e-mail faculty and advisors. E-mail has the advantage of giving both you and your reader a written record of the exchange. If you ask a faculty member for permission to vary an assignment, it might be better to ask using an e-mail. A conversation will soon fade from each of your memories. However, an e-mail provides you with a written record of your request and, hopefully, the permission you received.

Though e-mail is often informal, you should still follow good writing practices when writing e-mail. The following e-mail to a professor is clearly too informal and incomplete. It also establishes the wrong tone.

Prof,

Sorry missed class. Car trouble. I'll turn my paper in Monday when I see ya, OK.

Thanks tons.

Who is writing the message? Was the car trouble sufficient for an extension on the paper? Is the person simply using the car trouble to stall for extra time? Why didn't she jump the car or get a ride to campus? The informal tone makes it seem that the student does not take the class or the professor seriously.

A more formal communication sensitive to the situation and the audience would be much better.

Professor von der Osten

I am very sorry I missed class today. I live in Cadillac, an hour's drive from campus; unfortunately, this morning my car would not start because the distributor is broken. This is my first absence, and I notice from the syllabus we are allowed five unexcused absences. If you wish, I can bring in the estimate from the garage. I have e-mailed Tim Sullivan for notes from today's class.

Attached you will find a copy of the paper due today, Friday, September 25. Thank you for allowing us to submit our papers electronically in case of an emergency. I will also bring in a hard copy on Monday in case that would assist you.

I look forward to seeing you in class on Monday.

Susan Miller

ENGL 150: 9:00 A.M.

This more complete e-mail recognizes the formality of the situation, uses an appropriate form of address, provides a clearer explanation, indicates a serious attitude about the work in question, takes clear steps to meet the demands of the situation, and clearly identifies the writer in a way that recognized the reader may have many classes and students.

Your e-mail, like all writing, should be appropriate to the situation and the audience. An e-mail in response to a formal situation or to an important audience should be appropriately formal and serious. Since you and your readers are busy, try to write clearly and completely so that follow-up exchanges are unnecessary. Use a subject line that clearly identifies what the e-mail is about. Avoid abbreviations, slang, emoticons or other informal devices except with close friends.

Be sure to clearly identify who you are, your position and why you are writing; not all e-mail addresses clearly identify the writer. Most important of all, remember that your e-mail can be forwarded to other readers, so make sure your messages reflect well on you.

Below are sample e-mails one of the authors received in a single semester. In each case, indicate what the problem with the e-mail is and how could it be written to be more effective for the audience.

1. Here (The only message on an e-mail that submitted an attached paper).
2. Hey teach, Sorry I won't be in class. Family trouble. (A student with excessive absences.)
3. Do you mind writing a letter of recommendation for me? The position I am applying for is attached. (A colleague looking for another job.)
4. Can I drop my chemistry class? The teacher sucks. (An e-mail from an advisee to her advisor.)
5. I really don't understand this assignment. Can I do it differently. I have go lots of ideas. (From a student beginning a class assignment.)

Text Messaging   Text messaging has some dangers. It is easy to respond too quickly to a question and so provide an incomplete answer. Because messages are necessarily short, they can often be too incomplete or lack the necessary context. Since people text from their phones, it is easy to be excessively informal or make careless mistakes in spelling or grammar. Text messages should reflect on you professionally.

As with all writing, you should know your audience and person. If you are writing to your BFF you can LOL ☺. If you are writing to someone you don't know well or with whom you have a professional relationship, however, avoid abbreviations and symbols. Crafting a short message can be harder than writing at length since it takes skill to be clear and concise. The short text message "Go ahead with 3 copies to Madison" will be confusing unless the context is clear. If you can't assume the context, and many people are too busy to recall the assumed details, you need to be more complete. "Please send 3 copies each of the editions of FemSpec from 4.1 to 10.2 to our Madison address, 324 Blakemore Road, Madison, WI 43432." A complete message may require more typing, but it will save time in the long run.

Twitter   There are some fields, such as media studies or business, where you may be required to follow the Twitter Feed for an industry or area. Twitter is simply a system for sharing short messages of 140 characters. Most tweets are not very consequential. However, if you are writing or responding to a tweet, the goal is to have an interesting message in a very few words. Wordiness is out. You must assume some context. *Bring four copies of writing assignment 1 rough draft to class Monday for peer response.*

Rewrite the following messages so that they would be suitable as a tweet.

1. Katherine Briggs has done it again and in *River Marked* produced another compelling Mercy Thompson story with magic, mystery, and romance. She is on her honeymoon with husband, a werewolf, but their getaway doesn't last long as she ends up in a battle for her life with a river monster that threatens humankind. (Create a tweet for Katherine Briggs fans.)

2. This semester our online registration system will allow interested students to sign up for two semesters instead of just one, locking in their schedule for not just the Fall but also the Spring semester. Students are not required to schedule the second semester. If they do so, they will have to do an online drop and add process to change schedules. However, students who do not register for two semesters may find the classes they want closed for the Spring semester. (Create a tweet that could go to students.)

Blogs   Sometimes it seems as if almost everyone has a blog. There is nothing fancy about a "blog," a term which is simply a blending of the words Web Log. A blog is a web based statement of the writer's idea, a web essay. Many learning platforms allow you to blog to share your ideas with your class. Some teachers have students create blogs using a common blog-based program, such as Wordpress or Blogger, which are very easy to use.

Blogs let you make an argument, share an enthusiasm, review a movie and more. A blog needs to follow many of the strategies of writing explained in this text. However, in addition a blog let's you link your blog to other blogs or sites that might relate to or develop an idea; it also allows you to use images or video files. Ideally blogs are the length of a single page, though they can be longer. In a blog you are competing on a very busy Internet, so it is very important to grab your reader's attention quickly and have something interesting to say with vivid language.

Writing for a Web Page   Increasingly students applying for jobs provide on their resume an address to their Web pages. A web page lets them post more information about their experience, show samples of their work and shape the kind of professional impression that they make. Employers often look for the web site of applicants because it not only lets them have more information about a job candidate but demonstrates whether or not the prospective employee has initiative and the necessary skills. In many careers, writing for a web page can be a regular responsibility. A nurse might write for a hospital web page on standard post-operative care. An engineer may write technical information about the company's product line. To help you get ready for your web-based future, a number of college courses have students work on a web-based project.

Web pages need to be attractive, easy to use, clear and meet the needs of multiple users. Web design is an important skill beyond the scope of this book, but following are a few key ideas you should know.

- Keep the information clear and simple.
- Recognize that you need to grab and hold your reader's attention, so you need to make it immediately clear what information the web site is providing.
- Use hyper-text strategies. That means that you can provide a simpler statement to meet the need of most audiences and then provide links from key words to additional information for the reader who is seeking more.
- Make it easy for the reader to process information. Where appropriate, you should use visual strategies such as headings, sub-headings, and bullets to guide your reader. Use pictures or other visuals that clearly make your point and make the site attractive.

Because web pages are public documents, you want to make certain that your document is very well proofread.

Analyze the Interactive Document on **Using Graphics**

✓ **Using Graphics and Text**   Increasingly, writers combine graphics with text to make their point. There are books that use a comic style to explain complex philosophical ideas. Graphic novels are an art form that many take seriously. New computer programs make it easy to create an illustrated storyboard with text to make your point or use pictures and add text.

Writing for such a graphic form requires several distinct techniques:

1. The images need to clearly make the point or support the point.
2. The writing needs to be very clear and concise.
3. Shorter sentences and precise vocabulary are needed to make certain that the reader doesn't get confused.
4. The graphic needs to fit the available space without overrunning the text.

Writing and Ethics

1.5

Write ethically and avoid plagiarism.

Think for a minute about how you would react to the following situation. You decide to vacation at a resort after reading a brochure that stressed its white-sand beach, scenic trails, fine dining and peaceful atmosphere. When you arrive, you find the beach overgrown with weeds, the trails littered and view unappealing, and the restaurant a greasy-spoon cafeteria. Worse, whenever you go outside, swarms of vicious black flies attack you. Wouldn't you feel cheated? Closer to home, think how you'd react if you decided to attend a college because of its distinguished faculty members only to discover upon arrival that they rarely teach on campus. The college counts on their reputations to attract students even though they are usually unavailable. Hasn't the college done something unethical?

As these examples show, good writing is also ethical writing. Like you, readers expect that what they read will be dependable information. Few, if any, would bother with a piece of writing that they realized was intended to deceive. A good test of the ethics of your writing is whether you would read your own work and act on the basis of it. Would you feel comfortable with it, or would you feel cheated, manipulated, deceived, or harmed in some way? By learning and practicing the principles of ethical writing, you will help ensure that your writing meets the standards that your readers expect.

The Principles of Ethical Writing

- **Truthful**   Writing perceived as truthful should *be* truthful. Granted, a writer may use humorous exaggeration to make us laugh, and some sales pitches may stretch the truth a bit in order to entice buyers. ("Try Nu-Glo toothpaste and add sparkle to your life.") But most readers recognize and discount such embellishments which, unlike major distortions, harm nobody. Deliberate, serious falsehoods, however, may harm not only the reader but sometimes the writer as well. Angered by the misrepresentations in the vacation brochure, you would certainly warn your friends against the resort and might even take some legal action against it.

- **Complete**   Writing meant to be perceived as truthful should tell the whole truth, omitting nothing the reader needs to know in order to make informed decisions. The text should not be deliberately incomplete so as to mislead. Suppose that a university's recruitment brochures stress that 97 percent of its students get jobs upon graduation. What the brochures don't say is that only 55 percent of the jobs are in the graduates' chosen fields despite strong employer demand for graduates in those areas. Clearly these brochures are deceptive, perhaps attracting students who would otherwise choose schools with better placement records.

- **Clear**   Writing should be clear to the reader. All of us know the frustration of trying to read a crucial regulation that is impossible to comprehend. A person who writes instructions so unclear that they result in harmful mistakes is partially responsible for the consequences. Readers have a right to expect understandable, accurate information. Thus, it would be deceptive for a group of state legislators to call a proposed bill the Public Education Enhancement Act when it would in fact bar teachers from belonging to unions.

- **No Harm**   Writing should not be intended to harm the reader. Certainly it is fair to point out the advantages of a product or service that readers might not need. Most people understand the nature of this type of advertising. But think how unethical it would be for a writer to encourage readers to follow a diet that the writer knew was not only ineffective but harmful. Think of the harm a writer might cause by attempting, deliberately, to persuade readers to try crack cocaine.

Plagiarism

Often our writing draws on the work of others. We get information from an article, summarize what they have to say, perhaps paraphrase their wording, or use quotes that really help make a point. There are techniques for using information

Watch the Video on Avoiding Plagiarism

from sources discussed. which you should review if you are drawing information from sources. Still, pivotal to ethics in writing is avoiding plagiarism. When you turn in a piece of writing, you designate it as your own work in your own words. If you have taken material from sources (including the Internet) without using the proper documentation, even if it is in your own words, it is plagiarism, an unacceptable practice for any writer. If you use another writer's language, even in part, without using quotation marks, you are also engaging in plagiarism. Most faculty members check carefully for plagiarism and many automatically fail a paper for academic dishonesty. Some even give the student an F for the entire course.

Why is this an important issue?

1. Other people have worked hard to develop ideas, do research and write effectively. They deserve credit for their work when someone else uses it; it is their property. The authors of this text, for example, pay fees to use the essays of others. You would probably not like it if others used material from your papers without giving you credit.
2. Proper documentation strengthens your work since the source, often written by an expert, can add credibility to your claims if properly recognized.
3. If you take some material from a source and use it in your paper without documentation or quotation, you are falsely presenting another writer's work as your own. It is not much different from cheating and simply presenting an entire paper purchased from the Internet as your own work.
4. You are in the process of being trained in college to be professionals. Professionals need to be ethical. You wouldn't want someone to take credit for the computer program you wrote, charge you for repairs they didn't make, or write you a ticket for a traffic violation you didn't commit. Journalists have been fired, politicians have lost elections, and companies have been sued because they have been involved in plagiarism.
5. You certainly cannot develop as a writer if your writing isn't mostly your own work.

How can you avoid plagiarism and the failing grade that often comes with it?

1. Be committed to honesty. You should make certain your writing is your own work.
2. If an assignment does not ask you to use sources but you believe information from sources would be useful, talk to your teacher. There may be a reason that you are not asked to use sources. If sources are acceptable, you may be asked to follow a specific procedure for that assignment, such as turning in copies of your sources.
3. Be meticulous in documenting your sources, even if the material is in your own words, and in quoting and documenting any language that comes from another writer, even if it is only part of a sentence.
4. Carefully double-check to make certain that all the content in your text is your own and that if you used a source at all, it is documented.
5. Carefully double-check to make certain that all of your text uses your own language and that if you did use another writer's language, you used quotation marks.

6. If you are not sure about whether documentation or quotation marks are necessary, check with your teacher.

7. Make clear decisions about what counts as common knowledge. No one is expected to document what a reasonably educated person would know: that George Washington was our first president, that water consists of H_2O or that the Supreme Court rules on constitutional issues. As you proceed in college, your stock of common knowledge will grow. Yet, be careful that you don't sweep too many things under the common knowledge rug. One good rule of thumb is that if you didn't know it before you read the source, you probably should not count it as common knowledge and should document the information.

You must make a conscious effort to avoid plagiarism. Ignorance and carelessness are rarely accepted as an excuse by professors trying hard to make certain that students are graded fairly and no one gets credit for work that is not their own. If you follow the guidelines in this text and ask your teacher for help when you are confused, you will easily avoid the embarrassment and the often dire consequences of being accused of plagiarism.

Complete additional exercises and practice in your MyLab

A First Look at Your Writing

Know your discourse community.

- Read works in a community and talk to participants to discover shared questions.
- Determine what counts as knowledge.
- Look at sample writing to determine conventions.

Know your purpose.

- Decide if you are going to inform, persuade, express yourself, entertain.
- Identify the specific purpose.

Know your audience.

- List what you think your writer already knows.
- Identify the reasons they will read your writing.
- Try to read as your audience to anticipate their response.

Apply principles of good writing.

- Write with fresh thinking that offers your own slant. Being honest about your observations will help this.
- Write with a clear style in your own voice; don't overly inflate your language.
- Use the techniques in this text to create effective organization.

Make certain your writing is ethical!

- Write in a way that is truthful, unslanted, complete, clear, and helpful, rather than harmful.
- Make your writing your own, and avoid plagiarism.

2

Strategies for Successful Reading

In this chapter, you will learn how to:

2.1 Read for different purposes.

2.2 Employ different strategies for a first and second reading.

2.3 Overcome reading challenges.

2.4 Use reading techniques to develop your writing.

2.5 Write a summary.

2.6 Write a critique.

Good writing requires good reading. You get ideas, information, a feel for language, and ideas for writing from what you read. As a writer, you are a part of a knowledge community that learns from reading and responds to the texts of others. Effective reading is not the passive process that many people imagine. On the contrary, it requires the ongoing interaction of your mind and the printed page. Bringing your knowledge and experience to bear on a piece of writing can help you assess its events, ideas, and conclusions. For example, an understanding of marriage, love, and conflict, as well as experience with divorce, can help readers comprehend an essay that explores divorce. As you read, you must also understand each point that's made, consider how the various parts fit together, and try to anticipate the direction the writing will take. Successful reading requires work. Fortunately, you can follow specific strategies to help yourself read better.

Orienting Your Reading

Different purposes require different approaches to reading. When reading for pleasure, you can relax and proceed at your own pace, slowing down to savor a section you especially enjoy, speeding up when you encounter less

2.1

Read for different purposes.

19

interesting material, and breaking off when you wish. Reading for information, for solid understanding, or to critique an argument calls for a more methodical approach. Sometimes, you read specifically for material or arguments that you can use in your own writing. Below are some useful questions to guide your reading:

- **Why am I reading this material?** Is it for long-term use, as a reference for a project, or as a building block to understanding more material?
- **How well do I need to know the material in the article?** Can you look back to the article as a reference? Is there only one main point you need to know? Are you going to be tested on much of the material in depth?
- **Is some material in the article more important to me than other material?** Sometimes in doing research you may be looking for a specific bit of information that is only a paragraph in a long article. If so, you can skim for the information. In most things you read, some sections are more important than others. Often you can read to get the main points of the article and not focus on all the details. Sometimes, of course, you need to know the material in depth.
- **What will I need to do with the material from the article?** If you are looking for ideas for your own writing, you might read quickly. If you will be responsible for writing a critique of the article, you will need to read carefully and critically.
- **What kind of reading does the material suggest?** The significance, the difficulty, and the nature of the writing all can influence how you read. An easy humorous narrative can be read in a more leisurely fashion. A careful argument on an important issue merits careful attention to the main points and the evidence and may even require you to outline the argument.

EXERCISE

Look briefly at "The Appeal of the Androgynous Man" on page 28. Identify three purposes you could have for reading this essay. Identify how these purposes would affect how you would read the essay and what you would look for in the essay.

A First Reading

2.2

Employ different strategies for a first and second reading.

You don't just jump in your car and take off. Usually you take a few minutes to think about where you want to go. Sometimes you even have to check your route. The same is true of effective reading. Because of the challenging nature of most college-level reading assignments, you should plan on more than one reading. A good first reading should orient you to the material.

Orient Yourself to the Background of the Essay   Before you begin, scan any accompanying biographical sketch and try to determine the writer's expertise and views on the topic. Henry Jenkins' background as a university professor along with his numerous publications on popular culture give additional weight to his article on video games, "Art Form for the Digital Age" (in The Reader). Sometimes there is material by the author or the editor on the writing of the essay. Professional essays often start with an abstract that provides a brief summary of the article. At this point you may want to judge the credibility of the source.

Use the Title as a Clue   Most titles identify the topic and often the viewpoint as well. Thus, "If You're Happy and You Know It, Must I Know, Too?" (in the Reader) suggests that the author seems to be somewhat skeptical of the need to show our feelings, in this case through emoticons. Some titles signal the writer's primary strategy, whether it is a comparison, definition, or argument. "Grant and Lee: A Study in Contrasts" (in the Reader) is clearly a comparison.

Skim to Get the Gist of the Article   Sometimes you can just read the introductory and concluding paragraphs and the topic sentences (often the first or last sentences of paragraphs). Other times you will need to read the whole essay quickly. Try to gain an idea of the essay's main thrust, the key ideas that support it, and the ways that they are organized. In your first reading, you can skim the more difficult sections without trying to understand them fully.

Make Connections with What You Have Read   When you've finished skimming the essay, and before you reread the essay, think about what you've learned and then, either by saying it to yourself or jotting it down, express it *in your own words.* You can hardly be said to understand what you've read, and you will be less likely to remember it, until you can state its essence in your own words. Go back and underline the thesis statement (a statement of the main point of the essay) or, if one is not included, try to formulate one in your own words. Try to identify the strategy used by the writer. Also, stop and identify what you already know about the topic and your connection to the issue. You will read more effectively if you can connect what you read to your own knowledge and interests. Jot down questions that the first reading has raised in your mind. Try to identify the strategies used by the writer; if any were effective, write those strategies down for your own possible use.

Watch the Animation on **Active Reading**

EXERCISE

Reading Activities

1. Identify what you can about the background of the article, "The Appeal of the Androgynous Man," from the statement about the author.
2. Write what you expect based on the title.
3. Skim the essay and then write down what you identify as the main points of the essay. Identify the essay's thesis. Jot down at least two questions you have.

Additional Readings

If the material was difficult or you need to know it well, a second or even third reading may be necessary. On the second reading, which will take more time than the first, you carefully absorb the writer's ideas.

Read Carefully and Actively   Read at a pace suitable to the material. Underline significant topic sentences as well as other key sentences and ideas or facts that you find important, but keep in mind that underlining in itself doesn't ensure comprehension. Restating the ideas in your own words is more effective. Depending on your purposes, you may want to write down the main points in your own words or jot down the ideas in the margins. As you proceed, examine the supporting sentences to see how well they back up the main idea. Keep an eye out for how the essay fits together.

Consider Reading as a Kind of Conversation with the Text   Develop the habit of asking questions about facts, reasons, and ideas—practically anything in the essay. Jot your queries and their answers in the margins. (On page 28 you can see how a student interacted with the first page of Amy Gross's essay, "The Appeal of the Androgynous Man.") Good writers anticipate your questions and answer them; and because you have posed the questions yourself, you are more likely to see the connections in the text. If the author hasn't answered your questions, there may be problems with the work. It can help to keep a reading log in a notebook or as a computer file where you jot down your ideas as you are reading. Your notes or questions on your reading can be the basis for a writing project, or it can offer material you can use in a later research paper."

Master Unfamiliar Words   At times, unfamiliar words can hinder your grasp of the material. Whenever you encounter a new word, circle it, use context to help gauge its meaning, check the dictionary for the exact meaning, and then record it in the margins or some other convenient place. If the writing is peppered with words you don't know, you may have to read the whole piece to figure out its general drift; then, look up key words, and finally reread the material. A word list from your reading can help you enhance the vocabulary in your writing. Sometimes unfamiliar vocabulary, such as "derivatives," is part of the professional vocabulary you will need to know to discuss the issues involved.

Take Conscious Steps to Understand Difficult Material   When the ideas of a single section prove difficult, restate the points of those sections you do understand. Then experiment by stating in your own words different interpretations of the problem section and see which one best fits the writing as a whole.

Sometimes large sections or entire texts are extremely difficult. Following are several strategies you can use to help yourself:

- State the ideas that are easier for you to understand and use them as keys to unlock meanings that are difficult but not unintelligible. Save the most difficult sections until last. Don't think you have to understand everything completely. Some works take a lifetime to fully understand.

- Discuss a difficult essay with others who are reading it.
- Read simpler material on the topic.
- Go to your teacher for help. He or she may help you find background material that will make the selection easier.

Pull the Entire Essay Together   Whenever you finish a major section of a lengthy essay, express your sense of what it means. Speak it out loud or write it down. If you have trouble seeing the connections between ideas, try visually representing them. You might make an outline that states the main points followed by subpoints. For a comparison, you might create a table with the main points of the comparison side by side. You can make a drawing connecting the main ideas in a network, list the steps in an instruction, or write out the main facts.

To strengthen your grasp of material you'll need to remember for some time, try restating its main points a couple of days after the second reading. Sometimes it is helpful to explain the material to a sympathetic listener. If anything has become hazy or slipped your mind, reread the appropriate section(s). If you really must know the material, try making up your own test and giving it to yourself. Writing in your own words about what an essay meant can give you ideas for an essay that develops the reading, contradicts it, or takes a part of it and launches in a new direction.

Mastering Reading Problems

Many factors are important to effective reading. If your environment is too noisy, you are too tired, or you have something on your mind, you can have trouble reading. Do your reading at the time of day when you are most alert. Be sure you are in an environment that lets you concentrate and that is well lit. Try to be rested and comfortable. If you get tired, take a break for a specific time period; perhaps go for a short walk. If something else is bothering you, try to resolve the distraction or put it out of your mind. If you find the material uninteresting, try to find a connection between the topic and your interests and goals; read more actively. Of course, all these principles apply to your writing as well.

2.3

Overcome reading challenges.

In turn, this broadened perspective can supply you with writing ideas.

- Write down new perspectives, insights, or ways of viewing the world.
- Keep a reading/writing journal where you summarize what you've read and jot down writing ideas.
- Take down specific ideas, facts, and even quotes that you might use.
- Always note the source so you can document it properly to avoid plagiarism.

Such a rich treasure trove will provide a powerful resource for writing ideas, writing strategies, and material to strengthen your essays.

If you have extensive problems reading for college, you can get help. Most colleges have courses in reading and tutors. College often requires a lot of reading, so take the steps necessary to be the most effective reader possible.

Reading Activities

1. Read "The Appeal of the Androgynous Man" a second time, continuing to write your own questions and notes in the margin.
2. Create a table with two columns comparing the all-man and the androgynous man.
3. Identify three words that you might find relatively new and find their definitions from the context and a dictionary.
4. Try explaining the article to a friend or your roommate.

Reading to Critique

In college you usually read not only to understand but also to evaluate what you read. Your instructors will want to know what you think about what you've read. Often you'll be asked whether you agree or disagree with a piece of writing. Sometimes you will be asked to write an explicit critique of what you read.

Merely because information and ideas are in print does not mean that they are true or acceptable. An essay, for example, might include faulty logic, unreasonable ideas, suspect facts, or unreliable authorities. Don't hesitate to dispute the writer's information.

- Does it match your experience?
- Do the pieces of evidence support the claim?
- Do the ideas appear reasonable?
- Are there other pieces of evidence or other works that contradict these claims?
- Do the ideas connect in a logical way?

Knowledge of the principles of argumentation and various reasoning fallacies can help you critique a piece of writing. These issues are discussed in the chapter on argumentation.

Reading Activities

Prepare your critique of "The Appeal of the Androgynous Man" by doing the following:

1. Identify where and how the claims don't match your experience.
2. Indicate where the evidence does not support the claims.
3. Indicate at least a few places where the ideas do not appear reasonable.
4. Identify any evidence that seems to contradict the author's claims.
5. Evaluate whether the ideas connect in a logical way.

Reading Assignments Carefully

Many students could get better grades by simply reading their assignments more carefully. In assignments, professors often indicate possible topics, suggest readers, identify the kinds of information that should and **should not** be included, set expectations on style and format, and establish procedures for the assignment such as the due date. You should read the assignment several times. Carefully note any specifications on topic, audience, organizational strategy, or style and format. Be sure to jot down procedures, such as due dates, in an assignment log or your calendar. Do not make assumptions. If you are not clear about a part of the assignment, ask your instructor.

Below is a very specific assignment; read it over carefully to determine what it requires.

Objective Description Short Assignment (50 points)

Typed final draft following the class format guide is due in class September 12. This assignment page should be turned in with your completed description:

The corner of Perry and State Street, near the Starr building has been the scene of a terrible accident. The insurance company has asked you to write a brief objective description (approximately two pages double spaced) of the intersection for a report for possible use in court. Your description should not try to take a position about the relative danger of the intersection but rather provide as clear a picture as possible of the situation. The description should include the arrangement of the streets including the number of lanes, the businesses located immediately around the intersection, traffic and pedestrian flow, and the timing of the lights and the effect of that timing on traffic.

Checklist:

The description should:

1. Provide the general location of the intersection.
2. Indicate their traffic function—i.e., major route from 131 into downtown Big Rapids.
3. Describe the actual roads.
4. Identify the businesses and their locations.
5. Describe traffic and pedestrian flow.
6. Detail the timing of the lights.
7. Maintain objective language.
8. Use clear, nontechnical language.

The assignment specifies the topic (a specific intersection), an audience (a court of law and an insurance company), key elements that are required as part of the description, a general style of writing (objective without taking a stance), and procedures including a deadline and format constraints. Clearly a short paper about the accident would not be acceptable since the assigned topic is the actual structure of the intersection. A style of writing that stressed the "horribly short lights that force students to scurry across like mice in front of a cat" would lose points since it takes a position and is not objective. Any description that left out any of the required elements (such as the timing of the lights) would also lose points.

Reading as a Writer

2.4

Use reading techniques to develop your writing.

All of us who write can use reading as a springboard for improving our writing. You can do several things to make your reading especially useful.

As you read, the views of others, the experiences they relate, and the information they present often deepen your understanding of yourself, your relationships, and your surroundings. In turn, this broadened perspective can supply you with writing ideas. When possibilities surface, be sure to record them. Some writers keep a reading journal in which they summarize what they've read and jot down writing ideas that come to mind. In addition, you can take down specific ideas, facts, and perhaps even a few particularly telling quotations that you discover. You may want to incorporate this material into your writing at a later time. Carefully record the source so that you can document it properly in order to avoid plagiarism.

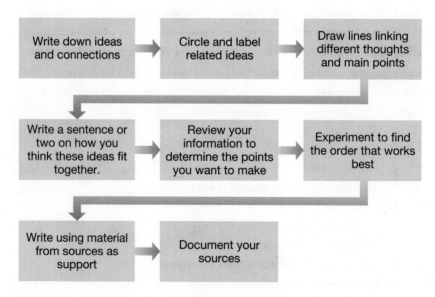

When you read various sources that explore the same topic or related topics, you may notice connections among their ideas. Let's see how you might use synthesis in writing an actual essay. Suppose, for example, you've read Amy Gross's

"The Appeal of the Androgynous Man," "Sound and Furry" by Dan Greenberg, and Chris Lee's "Invasion of the Bodybuilders" (in the Reader).

How do you use this to write an essay?

All of these ideas and examples could help you build an essay that points out how men can sometimes become desensitized or trapped, even victimized, by living according to stereotypes of masculinity. If you will be writing a paper that synthesizes material from various sources, review how to document your sources properly.

Because writers solve problems, you'll want to pay attention to the techniques and strategies that other writers use. If you find an introduction, an organizational pattern, a transition, a certain description or a comparison unusually engaging, study the writer's technique. Perhaps you can use it yourself. Similarly, observe when a piece of writing fails and try to determine why.

EXERCISE

Reading Activities

1. Identify at least two strategies that the author used that you would find useful.
2. Identify at least two phrases that you found effective.
3. Identify at least two ideas that could spark your own writing.

AMY GROSS

both male and female in one

The Appeal of the Androgynous Man

Amy Gross, a native of Brooklyn, New York, earned a sociology degree at Connecticut College. Upon graduation, she entered the world of fashion publishing and has held writing or editorial positions at various magazines, including Talk, Mademoiselle, Good Housekeeping, Elle, *and* Mirabella. *She is the newly appointed editor-in-chief of* O, the Oprah Magazine. *In our selection, which first appeared in* Mademoiselle, *Gross compares androgynous men favorably to macho "all-men."*

1   James Dean was my first androgynous man.[1] I figured I could talk to him. He was anguished and I was 12, so we had a lot in common. With only a few exceptions, all the men I have liked or loved have been a certain kind of man: a kind who doesn't play football or watch the games on Sunday, who doesn't tell dirty jokes featuring broads or chicks, who is not contemptuous of conversations that are philosophically speculative, introspective, or otherwise foolish according to the other kind of man. He is more self-amused, less inflated, more quirky, vulnerable and responsive than the other sort (the other sort, I'm visualizing as the guys on TV who advertise deodorant in the locker room). He is more like me than the other sort. He is what social scientists and feminists would call androgynous: having the characteristics of both male and female.

2   Now the first thing I want you to know about the androgynous man is that he is neither effeminate nor hermaphroditic. All his primary and secondary sexual characteristics are in order and I would say he's all-man, but that is just what he is not. He is more than all-man.   _both male and female sex organs_

3   The merely all-man man, for one thing, never walks to the grocery store unless the little woman is away visiting her mother with the kids, or is in the hospital having a kid, or there is no little woman. All-men men don't know how to shop in a grocery store unless it is to buy a 6-pack and some pretzels. Their ideas of nutrition expand beyond a 6-pack and pretzels only to take in steak, potatoes, scotch or rye whiskey, and maybe a wad of cake or apple pie. All-men men have absolutely no taste in food, art, books, movies, theatre, dance, how to live, what are good questions, what is funny, or anything else I care about. It's not exactly that the all-man's man is an uncouth illiterate. He may be educated, well-mannered, and on a first-name basis with fine wines. One all-man man I knew was a handsome individual who gave the impression of being gentle, affectionate, and sensitive. He sat and ate dinner one night while I was doing something endearingly feminine at the sink. At one point, he mutely held up his glass to indicate in a primitive, even ape-like, way his need for a refill. This was in 1967, before Women's Liberation. Even so, I was disturbed. Not enough to break the glass

[1]James Dean (1931–1955) was a 1950s film star who gained fame for his portrayals of restless, defiant young men.

Margin annotations:

Does she favor androgynous men? What kind of appeal?

She will give a woman's perspective. She writes for and edits women's magazines.

Seems like she is going to talk about the advantages of androgynous men as compared to other men. Sees them as better.

Attempt to counter stereotype? Can't androgynous men also be effeminate?

over his handsome head, not even enough to mutely indicate the whereabouts of the refrigerator, but enough to remember that moment in all its revelatory clarity. No androgynous man would ever brutishly expect to be waited on without even a "please." (With a "please," maybe.)

4   The brute happened to be a doctor—not a hard hat—and, to all appearances, couth. But he had bought the whole superman package, complete with that fragile beast, the male ego. The androgynous man arrives with a male ego too, but his is not as imperialistic. It doesn't invade every area of his life and person. Most activities and thoughts have nothing to do with masculinity or femininity. The androgynous man knows this. The all-man man doesn't. He must keep a constant guard against anything even vaguely feminine (i.e., "sissy") rising up in him. It must be a terrible strain.

5   Male chauvinism is an irritation, but the real problem I have with the all-man man is that it's hard for me to talk to him. He's alien to me, and for this I'm at least half to blame. As his interests have not carried him into the sissy, mine have never taken me very far into the typically masculine terrains of sports, business and finance, politics, cars, boats and machines. But blame or no blame, the reality is that it is almost as difficult for me to connect with him as it would be to link up with an Arab shepherd or Bolivian sandalmaker. There's a similar culture gap.

6   It seems to me that the most masculine men usually end up with the most feminine women. Maybe they like extreme polarity. I like polarity myself, but the poles have to be within earshot. As I've implied, I'm very big on talking. I fall in love for at least three hours with anyone who engages me in a real conversation. I'd rather a man point out a paragraph in a book—wanting to share it with me—than bring me flowers. I'd rather a man ask what I think than tell me I look pretty. (Women who are very pretty and accustomed to hearing that they are pretty may feel differently.) My experience is that all-men men read books I don't want to see paragraphs of, and don't really give a damn what I or any woman would think about most issues so long as she looks pretty. They have a very limited use for women. I suspect they don't really like us. The androgynous man likes women as much or as little as he likes anyone.

7   Another difference between the all-man man and the androgynous man is that the first is not a star in the creativity department. If your image of the creative male accessorizes him with a beret, smock and artist's palette, you will not believe the all-man man has been seriously short-changed. But if you allow as how creativity is a talent for freedom, associated with imagination, wit, empathy, unpredictability, and receptivity to new impressions and connections, then you will certainly pity the dull, thick-skinned, rigid fellow in whom creativity sets no fires.

8   Nor is the all-man man so hot when it comes to sensitivity. He may be true-blue in the trenches, but if you are troubled, you'd be wasting your time trying to milk comfort from the all-man man.

9   This is not blind prejudice. It is enlightened prejudice. My biases were confirmed recently by a psychologist named Sandra Lipsetz Bem, a professor at Stanford University. She brought to attention the fact that high masculinity in males (and high femininity in females) has been "consistently correlated with lower overall intelligence and lower creativity." Another psychologist, Donald W. MacKinnon, director of the Institute of Personality Assessment and Research at the University of California in Berkeley, found that "creative males give more expression to the feminine side of their nature than do less creative men.... [They] score relatively high on femininity, and this despite the fact

Suggests "all-men" men reject behaviors and interests they consider feminine, but isn't she stereotyping? Are all these men like this? She seems to be exaggerating.

that, as a group, they do not present an effeminate appearance or give evidence of increased homosexual interests or experiences. Their elevated scores on femininity indicate rather an openness to their feelings and emotions, a sensitive intellect and understanding self-awareness and wide-ranging interests including many which in the American culture are thought of as more feminine...."

10   Dr. Bem ran a series of experiments on college students who had been categorized as masculine, feminine, or androgynous. In three tests of the degree of nurturance—warmth and caring—the masculine men scored painfully low (painfully for anyone stuck with a masculine man, that is). In one of those experiments, all the students were asked to listen to a "troubled talker"—a person who was not neurotic but simply lonely, supposedly new in town and feeling like an outsider. The masculine men were the least supportive, responsive or humane. "They lacked the ability to express warmth, playfulness and concern," Bem concluded. (She's giving them the benefit of the doubt. It's possible the masculine men didn't express those qualities because they didn't possess them.)

11   The androgynous man, on the other hand, having been run through the same carnival of tests, "performs spectacularly. He shuns no behavior just because our culture happens to label it as female and his competence crosses both the instrumental [getting the job done, the problem solved] and the expressive [showing a concern for the welfare of others, the harmony of the group] domains. Thus, he stands firm in his opinion, he cuddles kittens and bounces babies and he has a sympathetic ear for someone in distress."

12   Well, a great mind, a sensitive and warm personality are fine in their place, but you are perhaps skeptical of the gut appeal of the androgynous man. As a friend, maybe, you'd like an androgynous man. For a sexual partner, though, you'd prefer a jock. There's no arguing chemistry, but consider the jock for a moment. He competes on the field, whatever his field is, and bed is just one more field to him: another opportunity to perform, another fray. Sensuality is for him candy to be doled out as lure. It is a ration whose flow is cut off at the exact point when it has served its purpose—namely, to elicit your willingness to work out on the field with him.

13   Highly masculine men need to believe their sexual appetite is far greater than a woman's (than a nice woman's). To them, females must be seduced: Seduction is a euphemism for a power play, a con job. It pits man against woman (or woman against man). The jock believes he must win you over, incite your body to rebel against your better judgment: in other words—conquer you.

14   The androgynous man is not your opponent but your teammate. He does not seduce: he invites. Sensuality is a pleasure for him. He's not quite so goal-oriented. And to conclude, I think I need only remind you here of his greater imagination, his wit and empathy, his unpredictability, and his receptivity to new impressions and connections.

Writing About What You Read

Often in college you will be asked to write about what you read. This culminates in the Research Paper. However, sometimes you will have to write shorter summaries and critiques.

Writing a Summary

A summary states the main points of an essay in *your own words*. It is a useful way to learn what you read. It is also how you share what you read. Instructors sometimes have students read different books and articles and share the results. Many readers summarize their favorite books online as a service to others searching for something good to read. Businesses and professionals will have employees summarize articles to share with their colleagues. The art of summarizing is the backbone of research writing.

2.5

Write a summary.

A good summary lets someone who hasn't read the essay understand what it says. A summary can be one or more paragraphs. It should

- provide a context for the essay,
- introduce the author of the essay,
- and state the thesis, (these first three elements often form the introduction of a multiparagraph summary)
- then state the main points of the essay (sometimes but not always based on the topic sentences),
- and conclude by pulling the essay together.

To prepare to write a summary, follow the steps in effective reading.

- Underline the main points of the essay.
- Write in the margins or a separate sheet of paper those main points in your own words.
- Decide the order that would make sense for your reader.
- Prepare a brief outline.
- Use your own words; if you use the author's words, quote and document to avoid plagiarism.
- Don't insert your own views, since a summary is about the author's position.

◉ **Watch** the Animation on **Writing a Summary**

A Sample Single Paragraph Summary of "The Appeal of the Androgynous Man"

What kind of man should appeal to women? According to Amy Gross, the editor-in-chief of *O* magazine, in "The Appeal of the Androgynous Man," her ideal is and the ideal of women should be the "androgynous man," a man who shares the personality characteristics of both male and female. To make her point, Amy Gross contrasts the all-man man and the androgynous man. She believes that the all-man man does not share in activities like shopping, has no taste in the arts, is imperialistic, resists anything feminine, and is interested in only exclusively male topics. Worse, she points to studies that show that more masculine men are less creative. Further, she argues that the all-man tends to see women as something to conquer rather than as partners. The androgynous man, by comparison, is very different. He does not resist things that are feminine and so shares in domestic activities, is comfortable with the arts, and can share interests with women. He is shown by studies to be more creative. Further, according to Gross, "The androgynous man is not your opponent but your teammate." As a result, she concludes that the androgynous man has the qualities that women should really look for in a man.

Writing a Critique

2.6

Write a critique.

Often you will be asked to give your views on an essay, indicating where you agree and disagree with the author's position. A faculty member may ask students to critically respond to an article. Employers may want your response to someone else's report or a professional article affecting your field. In general, writing a critique is a vital part of building an argument or a critical research paper. Remember you can always agree with part of what a person says and disagree with other parts. A critique combines a summary of the article with your thoughtful reaction. Most critiques consist of several paragraphs. A critique usually includes:

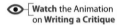
Watch the Animation on **Writing a Critique**

- a context for the essay
- an introduction to the author
- a statement of the essay's thesis
- the thesis for your critique
- a summary of the essay
- a statement of the points with which you agree
- a statement with reasons and evidence for your disagreement
- a conclusion

You are well prepared to write a critique if you follow the steps for reading effectively and reading critically.

- In addition to the summarizing comments, jot down whether you agree or disagree and why.
- It may be helpful to create a table that lists the major claims of the essay and your response, including whether you agree or disagree and why, including reasons or facts you have at your disposal.
- Determine an organizational pattern that works.
- Write your draft and revise.

A Sample Multiparagraph Critique of "The Appeal of the Androgynous Man"

1   What kind of man should appeal to women? According to Amy Gross, the editor-in-chief of O magazine, in "The Appeal of the Androgynous Man," her ideal is and the ideal of women should be the "androgynous man," a man who shares the personality characteristics of both male and female. But matters are not so simple. Amy Gross falsely divides men into two stereotyped categories. In fact, real men are much more complex.

2   To make her point, Amy Gross contrasts the all-man man and the androgynous man. She believes that the all-man man does not share in activities like shopping, has no taste in the arts, is imperialistic, resists anything feminine, and is interested in only exclusively male topics. Worse, she points to studies that show that more masculine men are less creative. Further, she argues that the all-man tends to see women as something to conquer rather than as partners. The androgynous man, by

comparison, is very different. He does not resist things that are feminine and so shares in domestic activities, is comfortable with the arts, and can share interests with women. He is shown by studies to be more creative. Further, according to Gross, "The androgynous man is not your opponent but your teammate." As a result, she concludes that the androgynous man has the qualities that women should really look for in a man.

3   She is right that if the all-man male were like she said, he would truly be undesirable. No woman should want a partner who takes her for granted, doesn't share her interests, or treats her simply as someone to conquer. But is that really what men are like? My brother plays football and loves to watch it on television. He also hunts and fishes. But that isn't all he does. He plays with kittens, loves to cook, plays the guitar and sings, and secretly likes "chick flicks." As far as I can tell, he treats his girlfriend well. He seems genuinely concerned about her, will spend hours shopping with her, goes to events that interest her, and generally seems sensitive to her needs. Is he an "all-man" or an "androgynous man"? Equally a man can write poetry, love Jane Austen, cook gourmet meals, and still take women for granted. From what I have read, Pablo Picasso treated women dreadfully, even if he was a great artist. Was he an "all-man" man or an "androgynous man"?

4   Ms. Gross seems to present evidence from psychological studies that show that more masculine men are less creative than more feminine men. Maybe so, but she doesn't give us the evidence we need to make up our own minds. How did they actually measure masculinity and femininity? How many people were tested? What did they count as creativity? Personally I have my doubts. Writers such as Ernest Hemingway and Norman Mailer were pretty masculine men and yet were still very creative. I know a lot of men who have feminine characteristics who aren't any more creative than the average person.

5   The mistake Ms. Gross makes is that she believes that women should select types of men. They shouldn't. Women date, love, and marry individual men. As a result, a woman should really be concerned about whether the man shares her interests, treats her well, has qualities she can love, and will be faithful. Where the man fits on Ms. Gross's little chart is far less important than the kind of man he is, regardless of whether he is "androgynous."

Complete additional exercises and practice in your MyLab

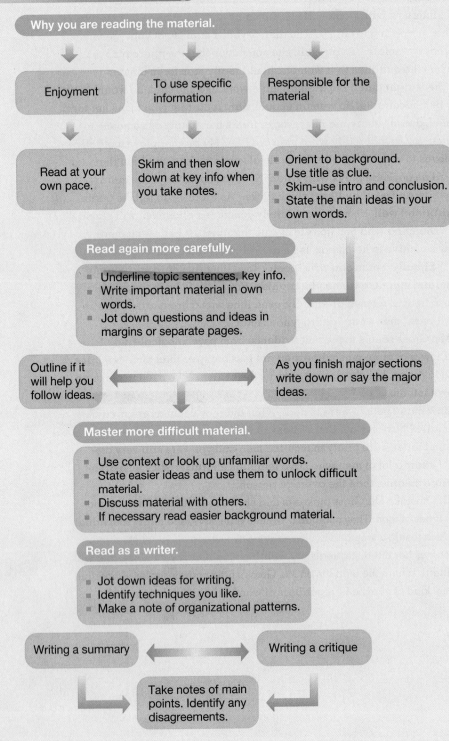

Successful Reading

Why you are reading the material.

| Enjoyment | To use specific information | Responsible for the material |

Read at your own pace.

Skim and then slow down at key info when you take notes.

- Orient to background.
- Use title as clue.
- Skim-use intro and conclusion.
- State the main ideas in your own words.

Read again more carefully.

- Underline topic sentences, key info.
- Write important material in own words.
- Jot down questions and ideas in margins or separate pages.

Outline if it will help you follow ideas.

As you finish major sections write down or say the major ideas.

Master more difficult material.

- Use context or look up unfamiliar words.
- State easier ideas and use them to unlock difficult material.
- Discuss material with others.
- If necessary read easier background material.

Read as a writer.

- Jot down ideas for writing.
- Identify techniques you like.
- Make a note of organizational patterns.

Writing a summary

Writing a critique

Take notes of main points. Identify any disagreements.

CHAPTER 3 Planning and Drafting Your Paper: Exploration

In this chapter, you will learn how to:

3.1 Analyze the assignment to understand its goals.

3.2 Use different strategies to find and develop a topic.

3.3 Gather information to support your topic.

3.4 Organize and outline your paper.

3.5 Develop an effective thesis statement.

3.6 Write a first draft of your paper.

Many students believe that good essays are dashed off in a burst of inspiration by born writers. Some boast that they cranked out A papers in an hour. Perhaps. But for most of us, writing is a process that takes time and work. It is also a messy process. Don't confuse your planning and drafting with a final version. If your grammar and spell check slow you down, turn it off until you are revising a later draft or proofreading your work.

Writing is a flexible process. No one approach works for every writer. Some writers establish their purpose and draft a plan for carrying it out at the start of every project. Others begin with a tentative purpose or plan and discover their final direction as they write.

Regardless of how it unfolds, the writing process consists of the following stages. Advancing through each stage will guide you if you have no plan or if you've run into snags with your approach. Once you're familiar with these stages, you can combine or rearrange them as needed.

- Understanding the assignment
- Zeroing in on a topic
- Gathering information
- Organizing the information
- Developing a thesis statement
- Writing the first draft

Types of Writers

Planners	Explorers
Start with a focused idea. Usually have a clear plan. Tend to develop existing plan.	Discover ideas while writing. Often follow out inspirations. Can develop tangents. Usually write more than final.
Can write like an outline. May tend to underdevelop. Can miss possible ideas.	Can go off on tangents. May initially lack obvious organization. Usually have more than needed.
Can benefit from additional brainstorming. May need additional development. May need to explore ideas outside plan.	May need to plan after drafting. Might need several revisions. Might need to refocus and cut.

Understanding the Assignment

3.1

Analyze the assignment to understand its goals.

Instructors differ in how they approach writing assignments. Some specify the topic; some give you several topics to choose from; and still others offer you a free choice. Likewise, some instructors dictate the length and format of the essay, whereas others don't. Whatever the case, be sure you understand the assignment before you go any further.

Think of it this way: If your boss asked you to report on ways of improving the working conditions in your office and you turned in a report on improving worker benefits, would you expect the boss's approval? Following directions is crucial, so ask your instructor to clear up any questions you might have about the assignment. Don't be timid; it's much better to ask for directions than to receive a low grade for failing to follow them.

Once you understand the assignment, consider the project *yours.* If you are asked to describe a favorite vacation spot for a local newspaper, here is your chance to inform others about a place that is special to you. By asking yourself what the assignment allows you to accomplish, you can find your own purpose.

Zeroing in on a Topic

A subject is a broad discussion area: sports, college life, culture, and the like. A topic is one small segment of a subject, such as testing athletes for drug use, Nirvana College's academic probation policy, or texting . If you choose your own topic, pick one that is narrow enough so that you can develop it properly. Avoid sprawling, slippery issues that lead to a string of trite generalities.

3.2

Use different strategies to find and develop a topic.

In addition, choose a familiar topic or one you can learn enough about in the time available. Avoid overworked topics such as arguments about the death penalty or the legal drinking age, which generally repeat the same old points. Instead, select a topic that lets you draw upon your unique experiences and insights and offer a fresh perspective to your reader.

Strategies for Finding a Topic

Whenever your instructor assigns a general subject, you'll need to stake out a limited topic suitable for your paper. If you're lucky, the right one will come to mind immediately. More often, though, you'll need to resort to some special strategy. Following are six proven strategies that many writers use. Not all of them will work for everyone, so experiment to find those that produce a topic for you.

Tapping Your Personal Resources   Over the years, you've packed your mind with memories of family gatherings, school activities, movies, concerts, plays, parties, jobs, books you've read, TV programs, dates, discussions, arguments, and so on. All these experiences can provide suitable topics. Suppose you've been asked to write about some aspect of education. Recalling the difficulties you had last term at registration, you might argue for better registration procedures. Or if you're a hopeless TV addict who must write on some advertising topic, why not analyze TV advertising techniques?

Anything you've read in magazines or journals, newspapers, novels, short stories, or textbooks can also trigger a topic. Dan Greenburg's "Sound and Fury" (in The Reader), in which a potentially explosive situation is defused, might suggest a paper on some dangerous encounter in your past. An article reviewing the career of a well-known politician might stir thoughts of a friend's experience in running for the student council.

EXERCISE

Select five of the subjects listed below. Tapping your personal resources, name one topic suggested by each. For each topic, list three questions that you might answer in a paper.

Life on a city street
A particular field of work
Some branch of the federal bureaucracy

Some aspect of nature
Contemporary forms of dancing
Youth gangs

Concern for some aspect of the environment
Saving money
Home ownership
Schools in your town
Leisure activities
Trends in technology
A best-selling book

Fashions in clothing
Trendiness
Human rights
Public transportation
Childhood fears
A new scientific discovery
A religious experience

Watch the Animation on
Keeping a Journal

Keeping a Journal   Many writers record their experiences in a journal. A journal provides a number of possible writing topics as well as valuable writing practice.

In a journal you have the freedom to explore thoughts, feelings, responses, attitudes, and beliefs without reservation and without concern for "doing it right." *You* control the content and length of the entry. Furthermore, depending on your instructor's preference, you usually don't have to worry about correct spelling or grammar. Journal writing does not represent a finished product but rather an exploration.

A few simple guidelines ensure effective journal entries:

1. Write on the computer or in any kind of notebook that appeals to you; the content, not the package, is the important thing.
2. Write on a regular basis—at least five times a week, if possible. In any event don't write by fits and starts, cramming two weeks' of entries into one sitting.
3. Write for 10 to 20 minutes, longer if you have more to say. Don't aim for uniform entry length, such as three paragraphs or a page and a half. Simply explore your reactions to the happenings in your life or to what you have read, heard in class, or seen on television. The length will take care of itself.
4. If you have multiple pages of journals in your word processor, you can use Find to search key words to discover related ideas.

Let's examine a typical journal entry by Sam, a first-year composition student.

> Last week went back to my hometown for the first time since my family moved away and while there dropped by the street where I spent my first twelve years. Visit left me feeling very depressed. Family home still there, but its paint peeling and front porch sagging. Sign next to the porch said house now occupied by Acme Realtors. While we lived there, front yard lush green and bordered by beds of irises. Now an oil-spattered parking lot. All the other houses on our side of the street gone, replaced by a row of dumpy buildings housing dry cleaner, bowling alley, hamburger joint, shoe repair shop, laundromat. All of them dingy and rundown looking, even though only a few years old.
>
> Other side of the street in no better shape. Directly across from our house a used-car dealership with rows of junky looking cars. No trace left of the Little League park that used to be

there. Had lots of fun playing baseball and learned meaning of sportsmanship. To left of the dealer-
ship my old grade school, now boarded and abandoned. Wonder about my fifth-grade teacher
Mrs. Wynick. Is she still teaching? Still able to make learning a game, not a chore? Other side of
dealership the worst sight of all. Grimy looking plant of some sort pouring foul smelling smoke into
the air from a discolored stack. Smoke made me cough.

     Don't think I'll revisit my old street again.

This journal entry could spawn several essays. Sam might explore the causes of
residential deterioration, define sportsmanship, explain how Mrs. Wynick made
learning a game, or argue for stricter pollution control laws.

*Write journal entries over the next week or two for some of the follow-
ing items that interest you. If you have trouble finding a suitable topic
for a paper, review the entries for possibilities.*

Encounters with technology	Developing relationships
Single or married life	Parents
Financial or occupational considerations	Ideas gained through reading

Sorting Out a Subject   All of us sort things. We do it whenever we tackle the ✓
laundry, clear away a sinkful of dishes, or tidy up a basement or garage. Sorting
out a subject is similar. First, we break our broad subject into categories and
subcategories and then allow our minds to roam over the different items and
see what topics we can turn up. The chart on page 40 shows what one student
found when she explored the general topic of internet communication. It is easy
to create a table in your software program or use a SmartGraphic that helps you
highlight a relationship.

    As you'll discover for yourself, some subjects yield more topics than others;
some, no topics at all.

*Select two of the following subjects and then subdivide those two into
five topics.*

Advertising	Movies	The space program
Dwellings	Occupations	Sports
Fashions	Popular music	Television programs
Magazines	Social classes	Vacations

Results of Sorting out the subject of Internet Communication					
Personal		Community		Large Community of Followers	
Texting	Chat	Discussion Boards	Face Book	Blogs	Tweeting
The reasons texting is replacing E-mail

The style of texting

The extent to which texting influences language use

The dangers of texting and driving; the effects of texting on attention. | The growing use of chat for online support.

The role of Chat in higher education and online classes.

The comparison of online chat and phone calls. | Fan Boards

Professional Discussion Boards

Discussion Boards in the classroom

Frequently Asked Questions

The problem of civility in discussion boards

The growing use of discussion boards with online news media | Why FB became so popular.

The challenges of keeping FB profitable.

Effects FB has on the social relations of college students.

≈ | Political Blogs
Corporate Blogs
Personal Blogs

How to write a successful blog

The way blog may keep us in our personal information bubble.

The extent to which blogs give average citizens a political voice. | Celebrity tweets
Political tweets
Tweeting Friends
Product Tweets

The ways tweeting is increasingly used in political campaigns.

The ways tweets are used to manage a celebrity's image.

A classification of the different kinds of people who tweet and follow tweets. |

√ **Asking Questions**   Often, working your way through these basic questions will lead you to a manageable topic:

1. Can I define my subject?
2. Does it break into categories?
3. If so, what comparisons can I make among these categories?
4. If my subject is divided into parts, how do they work together?
5. Does my subject have uses? What are they?
6. What are some examples of my subject?
7. What are the causes or origins of my subject?
8. What impact has my subject had?

Let's convert these general questions into specific questions about telescopes, a broad general subject:

1. What is a telescope?
2. What are the different kinds of telescopes?
3. How are they alike? How do they differ?
4. What are the parts of each kind of telescope, and how do they work together?

5. What are telescopes used for?
6. What are some well-known telescopes?
7. Who invented the telescope?
8. What impact have telescopes had on human life and knowledge?

Each of these questions offers a starting point for a suitably focused essay. Question 3 might launch a paper comparing reflecting and refracting telescopes; question 6 might be answered in a paper about the Hubble Space Telescope and the problems with it.

Select two of the following subjects. Create general questions and then convert them into specific questions. Finally, suggest two essay topics for each of your two subjects.

Astrology	Games	Shopping malls
Books	Microorganisms	Stars
Colleges	Plays	Television
Emotions	Religions	Warships

Freewriting   The freewriting strategy snares thoughts as they race through your mind, yielding a set of sentences that you then look over for writing ideas. To begin, turn your pen loose and write for about five minutes on your general subject. Put down everything that comes into your head, without worrying about grammar, spelling or punctuation. What you produce is for your eyes alone. If the thought flow becomes blocked, write "I'm stuck, I'm stuck…" until you break the mental logjam. When your writing time is up, go through your sentences one by one and extract potential topic material. If you draw a blank, write for another five minutes and look again. A useful strategy is to take key ideas or phrases from your freewriting and then in a separate page or file do additional freewriting on each of those ideas or phrases.

Watch the Animation on Freewriting

The following example shows the product of one freewriting session. Drew's instructor had assigned a two- or three-page paper on technology; and since Drew is a business major, he considers a more personal technology with which he has experience, the cell phone.

> Technology, huh. What do I know about technology? Cell phones are technology? What about them? There are so many kinds. Razors, Blackberries. I love my new iPhone. It does everything, plays music, lets me text, check out YouTube, e-mail, take pictures and store them. They change people lives. But how? Well, we are always on them talking to friends, to anybody, and parents and teachers never get it. But why do we talk on them so much. Stuck, stuck, stuck. Well, I keep in

touch with friends. Some are away at college. My girlfriend is always calling me. We also get lots of stuff done, like checking out my stupid bills.

This example suggests at least three papers. For people shopping for a new cell phone, Drew could identify the advantages of different types. He could write to people who are considering buying an iPhone about the features of the phone. He could write to those perplexed by student behavior to explain why students use cell phones so extensively.

√ **Brainstorming**   Brainstorming, a close cousin of freewriting, captures fleeting ideas in words, fragments and sometimes sentences, rather than in a series of sentences. Brainstorming garners ideas faster than the other strategies do. But unless you move immediately to the next stage of writing, you may lose track of what some of your fragmentary jottings mean.

To compare the results of freewriting and brainstorming a topic, we've converted our freewriting example into this list, which typifies the results of brainstorming:

Types of cell phones	stores pictures
Razors	text message
Blackberries	e-mails
iPhones	why people use e-mail
plays music	to coordinate life
view YouTube	to get things done
takes pictures	to keep in touch

EXERCISE   *Return to the five subjects you selected for the exercise on page 37. Freewrite or brainstorm for five minutes on each one and then choose a topic suitable for a two- or three-page essay. State your topic, intended audience, and purpose.*

Narrowing a familiar subject may yield not only a topic but also the main divisions for a paper on it. Drew's freewriting session uncovered several possible cell phone topics as well as a way of approaching each: classifying types of cell phones and writing about the strengths and weaknesses of each or identifying the different features of an iPhone and describing each feature and how it works or explaining each of the reasons college students use cell phones so frequently. Ordinarily, though, the main divisions will emerge only after you have gathered material to develop your topic. Drew, on considering his options, decides he doesn't know enough about types of cell phones and might get carried away when writing about the iPhone. He decides to write about the reasons college students are so attached to their cell phones.

Identifying Your Audience and Purpose

You can identify your purpose and audience at several stages in the writing process. Sometimes both are set by the assignment and guide your selection of a topic. For example, you might be asked to write the college president to recommend improvements in the school's registration system. At other times, you may have to write a draft before you can determine either. Usually, though, the selection of audience and purpose goes hand in hand with determining a topic. Think of the different types of information Drew would gather if he wrote for (1) college students to break them of their cell phone habits, (2) college professors and parents to make cell phone use seem less peculiar (3) or a sociology professor to demonstrate how common behaviors can be explained through sociological theories.

Gathering Information

Once you have a topic, you'll need things to say about it. This supporting material can include facts, ideas, examples, observations, sensory impressions, memories and the like. Without the proper backup, papers lack force, vividness and interest and may confuse or mislead readers. The more support you can gather, the easier it will be for you to write a draft. Time spent gathering information is never wasted.

3.3

Gather information to support your topic.

Strategies for Gathering Information

If you are writing on a familiar topic, much of your supporting material may come from your own head. Brainstorming is the best way to retrieve it. With unfamiliar topics, brainstorming won't work. Instead, you'll have to do some background reading. Whatever the topic, familiar or unfamiliar, talking with friends, parents, neighbors or people knowledgeable about the topic can also produce useful ideas.

Brainstorming   Brainstorming a topic, like brainstorming a subject, yields a set of words, fragments and occasionally sentences that will furnish ideas for the paper. Drew has decided that he wants to demonstrate to professors and parents that there are good reasons for student cell phone use. He generated the following list through brainstorming.

students open cell phones after class	weather updates
coordinating life	sending e-mails
meeting friends for study sessions	sending pictures by e-mail
arranging a lunch date	holding up a phone at a concert
getting a ride	calling when something funny happens
coordinating a team project	keeping in touch
getting things done	old friends in different colleges
resolving bill disputes	boyfriends or girlfriends
scheduling car repairs	text messaging
finding babysitters	playing music

You can see how some thoughts have led to others. For example, the first jotting, "arranging a lunch date," leads naturally to the next one, "getting a ride." And "keeping in touch" leads to "old friends in different colleges."

Branching is a helpful and convenient extension of brainstorming that allows you to add details to any item on your list. Here's how you might use this technique to approach "cell phone use":

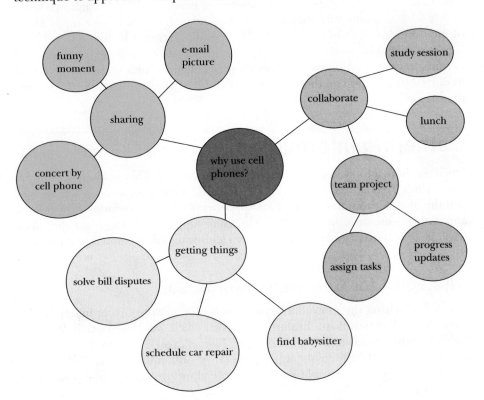

Don't worry if your brainstorming notes look chaotic and if some seem irrelevant. Sometimes the most unlikely material turns out to be the freshest and most interesting. As you organize and write your paper, you'll probably combine, modify and omit some of the notes, as well as add others. Drew decides from his brainstorming that "playing music," "sending e-mails," and "getting weather updates" are too specific to only a few kinds of cell phones and should not be part of his paper. There are now a number of brainstorming software programs such as the TheBrain and MindMeister that let you brainstorm on your computer on the web, and even allow you to include images in your brainstorming. You can also use existing graphic programs on your computer.

Prepare a brainstorming sheet of supporting details for one of the topics you developed for the exercise on page 39.

Reading   When you have to grapple with an unfamiliar topic, look in the library for material to develop it. Once you have a list of references, start searching for the books or articles. Look through each one you find and jot down information that looks useful, either as direct quotations or in your own words.

Whenever you use a direct quotation or rephrased material in your paper, you must give proper credit to the source. If you don't, you are guilty of plagiarism, a serious offense that can result in a failing grade for the course or even expulsion from college.

Talking with Others   You can expand the pool of ideas gained through brainstorming or reading by talking with some of the people around you. Imagine you're writing a paper about a taxpayers' revolt in your state. After checking the leading state newspapers at the library, you find that most of the discontent centers on property taxes. You then decide to supplement what you've read by asking questions about the tax situation in your town.

Your parents and neighbors tell you that property taxes have jumped 50 percent in the last two years. The local tax assessor tells you that assessed valuations have risen sharply and that state law requires property taxes to keep pace. She also notes that this situation is causing some people on fixed incomes to lose their homes. A city council member explains that part of the added revenue is being used to repair city streets, build a new library wing, and buy more fire-fighting equipment. The rest is going to the schools. School officials tell you they're using their extra funds to offer more vocational courses and to expand the program for learning-disabled students. As you can see, asking questions can broaden your perspective and provide information that will help you to write a more worthwhile paper.

Social Media is a powerful tool for getting ideas and information.

- Post your issue and ideas on Facebook to get information and possible reading from friends.
- Conduct a survey using Facebook.
- E-mail friends, family or even experts.
- Log on to discussion boards on the Internet.

Organizing the Information

If you have ever listened to a rambling speaker spill out ideas in no particular order, you probably found it hard to pay attention to the speech, let alone make sense of it. So, too, with disorganized writing. A garbled listing of ideas serves no one; an orderly presentation highlights your ideas and helps communication succeed.

3.4

Organize and outline your paper.

Your topic determines the approach you take. In narrating a personal experience, such as a mishap-riddled vacation, you'd probably trace the events in the order they occurred. In describing a process, say caulking a bathtub, you'd take the reader step by step through the procedure. To describe a hillside view near your home, you might work from left to right. Or you could first paint a word picture of some striking central feature and then fan out in either direction. Other topics dictate other patterns, such as comparison and contrast, cause and effect, and illustration.

You can best organize long pieces of writing, such as library research papers, by following a formal outline. For shorter papers, however, a simple, informal system of *flexible notes* will do nicely.

The Flexible Notes System

To create a set of flexible notes, write each of your key points at the top of a separate page, computer file, or sheet of paper. If you have a thesis statement (see page 48), refer to it for your key points. Next, list under each heading the supporting details that go with that heading. Drop details that don't fit and expand points that need more support. It can be handy to save each new page with a number, such as "topic3", so if you discover that you cut something useful, you can retrieve it. When your points are finished, arrange them in the order you expect to follow in your essay. Your computer allows you to readily pull material from different pages and even files onto a single page. Do not hesitate to cut and paste to try out different organizational patterns. Drew's notes for the cell phone paper look like this:

Coordinating Activities

Meeting friends for a study session
Arranging a lunch date
Getting a ride
Coordinating a team project

Getting Things Done

Resolving bill disputes
Scheduling car repairs
Finding babysitters

Sharing

Sending pictures by e-mail
Holding up phone at concert
Call about something funny happening

Keeping in Touch

Old friends in different colleges
Boyfriends and girlfriends
Text messaging

Since coordinating activities, getting things done, sharing, and keeping in touch are equivalent reasons, this listing arranges them according to their probable importance—starting with the most important reason from the point of view of the audience.

Now you're ready to draft a plan showing how many paragraphs you'll have in each part of the essay and what each paragraph will cover. Sometimes the number of details will suggest one paragraph; other times you'll need a paragraph block—two or more paragraphs. Here's a plan for Drew's cell phone essay:

Coordinating Activities

Meeting for study session
Arranging a lunch date
Getting a ride
Coordinating a team project

Getting Things Done

Resolving bill disputes
Scheduling car repairs
Finding a babysitter

Sharing

Sending pictures by e-mail
Holding up phone at concert
Calling about a funny event

Keeping in Touch

Old friends in different colleges
Boyfriends and girlfriends   } By voice
Text messaging   } By text

These groupings suggest one paragraph about coordinating activities, one about getting things done, one about sharing, and two about keeping in touch.

Organize into flexible notes the supporting details that you prepared for the exercise on page 44. Arrange your note pages in a logical sequence and draft a plan showing the number and content of the paragraphs in each section.

Creating an Outline

With longer essays or if it fits your organizational style, it can be helpful to develop an outline. An outline can show you how to organize and develop your paragraphs. In an outline, you organize your essay into major units using Roman numerals (I, II, III), letters (A, B, C) and numbers to show the structure you will

Watch the Animation on **Outlining**

use in the paper. Introductions and conclusions are not usually included in the outline. Most word processing programs have an outline function that lets you easily create an outline. In Word, you simply click on the outline icon in the bottom left of the page. There are two kinds of outlines. A topic outline simply states the main topic to be addressed in a section.

I. Coordinating Activities
  A. Meeting friends for study sessions
    1. Setting the time
    2. Making certain everyone gets there
  B. Arranging a lunch date
    1. Deciding where everyone is meeting
    2. Arranging a ride to lunch
II. Getting Things Done
  A. Coordinating a team project
    1. Assign tasks
    2. Monitor progress
  B. Resolving bill disputes
    1. Call during business hours

Topic outlines will quickly let you know if you have enough information for a paragraph. If under one major heading, you only have one letter or under a letter only one number, as in II B, you may need to do more brainstorming.

In a sentence outline, you make full statements or sentences that can often be used in your paper. A sentence outline makes you think about what you really want to say.

I. Cell phones can be used to coordinate activities that would be otherwise difficult to coordinate given students' busy schedules.
  A. Cell phones can help students find out where a study session is being held.
  B. Often there is a complex schedule of classes, work, meals and meetings to organize.
  C. Cell phones can let members of a team project keep the project on track.

To develop your outline, you take your brainstorming or notes and mark the major units as I, II, III based on the main ideas they demonstrate. Then you start to develop your outline, identifying the major points for each major heading (I, II…) and the next major points (A, B, C). You can use your outline as a goad to additional planning as you see the holes. You should rarely have an A without a B or a 1 without a 2.

Developing a Thesis Statement

3.5

Develop an effective thesis statement.

A thesis statement presents the main idea of a piece of writing, usually in one sentence. The thesis statement points you in a specific direction, helping you to stay on track and out of tempting byways. In addition, it tells your reader what to expect.

Thesis statements can emerge at several points in the writing process. If ✓ an instructor assigns a controversial topic on which you hold strong views, the statement may pop into your head right away. At other times it may develop as you narrow a subject to a topic. Occasionally, you even have to write a preliminary draft to determine your main idea. Usually, though, the thesis statement emerges after you've gathered and examined your supporting information.

As you examine your information, search for the central point and the key points that back it up; then use these to develop your thesis statement. Converting the topic to a question may help you to uncover backup ideas and write a thesis statement.

<u>**For example:**</u>

Topic:	The commercial advantages of computerized data storage systems.
Question:	What advantages do computerized data storage systems offer business?
Thesis statement:	Computerized data storage systems offer business enormous storage capacity, cheap, instant data transmission almost anywhere, and significantly increased profits.

The thesis statement stems from the specifics the student unearthed while answering the question.

Following are some key strategies that can help you develop a thesis statement.

- Identify your main topic.
- Review your notes or research and identify the specific, major claims you want to make about your topic.
- Select those claims that will be the focus and organizational structure of the paper. You may need to outline first.
- Combine the major claim or claims with the topic in a statement that represents the main point of your paper.

Requirements of a Good Thesis Statement

Unless intended for a lengthy paper, a thesis statement *focuses on just one central point or issue.* Suppose you prepare the following thesis statement for a two- or three-page paper:

⊙─⟨Watch the Animation on **Developing of a Thesis Statement**

> Centerville College should reexamine its policies on open admissions, vocational programs and aid to students.

This sprawling statement would commit you to grapple with three separate issues. At best, you could make only a few general remarks about each one.

To correct matters, consider each issue carefully in light of how much it interests you and how much you know about it. Then make your choice and draft a narrower statement. The following thesis statement would do nicely for a brief paper. It shows clearly that the writer will focus on *just one issue:*

> Because of the rising demand among high school graduates for job-related training, Centerville College should expand its vocational offerings.

A good thesis statement also *tailors the scope of the issue to the length of the paper.* No writer could deal adequately with "Many first-year college students face crucial adjustment problems" in two or three pages. The idea is too broad to yield more than a smattering of poorly supported general statements. Paring it down to "Free time is a responsibility that challenges many first-year college students," however, results in an idea that could probably be developed adequately.

A good thesis statement further provides *an accurate forecast of what's to come.* If you plan to discuss the effects of overeating, don't say, "Overeating stems from deep-seated psychological factors and the easy availability of convenience foods." Such a statement, incorrectly suggesting that the paper will focus on causes, would only mislead and confuse your reader. On the other hand, "Overeating leads to obesity, which can cause or complicate several serious health problems" accurately represents what's to follow.

Finally, a good thesis statement is *precise, often previewing the organization of the paper.* Assertions built on fuzzy, catchall words like *fascinating, bad, meaningful* and *interesting*, or statements like "My paper is about…" tell neither writer nor reader what's going on. To illustrate:

- New York is a fascinating city.
- My paper is about no-fault divorce.
- The United States budget deficit is complex and involves the amount of revenue collected, discretionary and non-discretionary spending, the long-term prospects of entitlement programs, as well as interest rates and the value of the dollar.
- In this paper I will discuss the dangers of texting.

These examples raise a host of questions. Why does the writer find New York fascinating? Because of its skyscrapers? Its night life? Its theaters? Its restaurants? Its museums? Its shops? Its inhabitants? And what about no-fault divorce? Will the writer attack it, defend it, trace its history or suggest ways of improving it? To find out, we must journey through the paper, hoping to find our way without a road-map sentence. How can the writer tackle all of these questions concerning the deficit without writing a book? What will actually be the focus? Besides starting with a cliché, we are left to wonder what kinds of danger of texting the writer is going to address.

Now look at the rewritten versions of those faulty thesis statements:

- New York's art museums offer visitors an opportunity to view a wide variety of great paintings.

- Compared to traditional divorce, no-fault divorce is less expensive, promotes fairer settlements and reflects a more realistic view of the causes of marital breakdown.
- While currently the United States borrows money at historically low rates, the current deficit could easily be made worse by an increase in the rate for U.S. treasuries or a more general increase in interest rates.
- The evidence is clear. Texting while driving is almost as dangerous as drinking and driving.

These statements tell the reader not only what points the writer will make but also the order they will follow.

In brief, your thesis statement should

- focus on just one central point or issue.
- narrow the scope of the issue to what is manageable.
- provide an accurate forecast of what is to come.
- often preview the organization of the paper.

Your thesis statement should **not**

- be too vague or general.
- include more than you can reasonably manage in a paper.
- suggest a different focus or organization than you follow in your paper.
- use clichéd and excess wording like "In this paper I will discuss...."

Omission of Thesis Statement

Not all papers have explicit thesis statements. Narratives and descriptions, for example, sometimes merely support some point that is unstated but nevertheless clear, and professional writers sometimes imply their thesis rather than state it openly. Nonetheless, a core idea underlies and controls all effective writing. Usually it is best to state that core idea in a thesis statement.

Changing Your Thesis Statement

Before your paper is in final form, you may need to change your thesis statement several times. If you draft the thesis statement during the narrowing stage, you might change it to reflect what you uncovered while gathering information. Or you might amend it after writing the first draft so that it reflects your additions and deletions. In his first rough draft, Drew thought "In the end this cell phone mania is a necessary part of college life" was an adequate thesis statement. In revising his draft, however, he realized that it was not precise enough to direct his readers. He added a more precise statement that identified the main reasons addressed in his paper to serve as his thesis: "They use cell phones to coordinate the day's activities, to get some business done, to share life's events, and to keep in touch."

Tentative or final, formulated early or late, the thesis statement serves as a beacon that spotlights your purpose.

1. Write a thesis statement for the flexible notes that you developed for the exercise on page 47.
2. Reread "Requirements of a Good Thesis Statement" and then explain why each of the following does or does not qualify as an effective thesis statement for a two- or three-page essay.
   a. My paper discusses the problem of employee absenteeism in American industry.
   b. Living on a small island offers three advantages: isolation from city problems, the opportunity to know your neighbors, and the chance to go fishing whenever you want.
   c. Although I don't know much about running a college, I know that Acme College is not run well.
   d. Increasing federal outlays for education will help us construct needed school buildings and create a better-trained workforce.
   e. Many people, wanting simpler and slower-paced lives, have abandoned high-paying executive positions for lower-paying, less stressful jobs.
   f. Vacationing in Britain is a nice way to spend a summer.
   g. Extending Middletown's intracity transit system will save consumers money, reduce pollution and increase city revenues.
   h. Most cable TV companies provide subscribers with several specialized-program channels.
3. Revise the following five weak thesis statements.
   a. The first year of college can be hard.
   b. Facebook offers lots of features.
   c. My paper discusses the importance of writing for college students.
   d. Global warming is changing the weather.
   e. In this paper I will talk about how wireless phones do more than ever.

Writing the First Draft

3.6

Write a first draft of your paper.

Now on to the first draft of your essay. The writing should go rather quickly. After all, you have a topic you're qualified to write about, a thesis statement that indicates your purpose, enough information to develop it, and a written plan to follow. But sometimes when you sit down to write, the words won't come, and all you can do is doodle or stare at the blank page. Perhaps the introduction is the problem. Many writers are terrified by the thought of the opening paragraph. They want to get off to a good start but can't figure out how to begin. If this happens to you, additional brainstorming or freewriting can make you more comfortable and may suggest an opening. Keep in mind that any lead-in you write now can be changed later. If these suggestions don't solve your problem, skip the introduction for the time being. Once you have drafted the body of the paper, an effective opening should come more easily. Always remember how easy it is to revise on a computer, adding material, cutting things don't work and moving material around.

Following are some suggestions for writing a first draft:

1. Reread your thesis statement, notes, brainstorming and written plan. They will start you thinking.
2. Rewrite your thesis statement at the top of your first page to break the ice and build momentum.
3. **If it helps, just start writing without worrying about anything but getting ideas down; you can reshape everything later.**
4. Write quickly; capture the drift of your thoughts. Concentrate on content and organization, but recognize that you can easily move the organization around later. Don't spend time correcting grammatical or punctuation errors, improving your language or making the writing flow smoothly. You might lose your train of thought and end up doodling or staring again.
5. If you have ideas that may not fit the flow, you can open another page to jot down those ideas so they are not lost and save the page under a different file name. If you don't know what to say about a section, you can mark that place xxxxx and fill it in later.
6. If you have ideas while writing for earlier sections, you can either go back and write them or keep a separate page you can open to jot down the additional ideas that come to you.
7. Take breaks at logical dividing points, such as when you finish discussing a key point. Before you start to write again, scan what you've written.

Now for some specific suggestions that will help you with the actual writing:

1. Write your first paragraph, introducing your essay and stating your thesis. If you get stuck here, move on to the rest of the paper.
2. Follow your plan as you write. Begin with your first main point and work on each section in turn.
3. Look over the supporting details listed under the first heading in your flexible notes. Write a topic sentence stating the central idea of the paragraph.
4. Turn the details into sentences; use one or more sentences to explain each one. Add other related details, facts or examples if they occur to you.
5. When you move from one paragraph to the next, try to provide a transitional word or sentence that connects each paragraph.
6. Write your last paragraph, ending your essay in an appropriate fashion. If you get stuck, set your conclusion aside and return to it later.

Writing a draft isn't always so systematic. If you are inspired, you may want to abandon your plans and simply use your first draft to explore ideas. You can always revise, so don't be overly concerned if you get off track. You might uncover some of your best material during this type of search.

EXERCISE

Using the plan you prepared for the exercise on page 47, write the first draft of an essay.

Drew now uses his thesis statement and paragraph-by-paragraph plan to write the following draft. Notice that Drew, like many writers, gets off track. That is a common occurrence at this stage and can even be a step in generating new ideas. It isn't something to reject. Drew knows even as he writes that he will need to make significant revisions. We will focus on the revision process and Drew's revisions in the next chapter.

CASE HISTORY   Cell Phone Use
Rough Draft

Students open their cell phones almost before they are out of the room. It confuses professors and parents. My parents complain that young people are so wrapped up in their cell conversations that they completely miss the world around them. Why are students such non-stop cell phone users? It looks ridiculous when large numbers of college students wander around talking into their phones, ignoring the people around them. In the end this cell phone mania is a necessary part of college life.

It is hard to imagine how people managed their lives without cell phones since there seems to be so much to get done. Weren't friends going to meet after class for a study session? Where is everybody? Life in college can be crazy. We juggle complex schedules, work, meals. A quick phone call can organize it all. We arrange study sessions, confirm a lunch date, get a ride, coordinate a team project for class, and maybe even make time for a date.

Students, like everyone else, need to call about possible jobs, resolve disputes over bills, arrange to have theirs car fixed, find out the results of medical tests, and even, in some cases, find babysitters. Sometimes walking back to the dorm from a night class, students are on the phone simply to feel safer so that if anything happens they can let someone else know and perhaps get help. Cell phones let them get all this done.

Cell phones let us be together at the same time, even if we are in different places. Part of the reason for such widespread cell phone use is that instead of having to wait, a quick phone call has one person getting out of bed while another is getting out of class. Two friends seated at different ends of a stadium can enjoy the blow by blow of the action at the same time.

Everyone likes to share. Cell phones let people share. Many phones even let you take a picture and send it by e-mail to a friend. It is because of this practice that cell phones are banned in some locker rooms and why it is dangerous to be caught in an embarrassing situation at a party. You never know what can be e-mailed to your friends or even posted to the Internet. At concerts some in the audience call up friends and then hold up the phone so that they can hear part of a concert. When something really funny is happening, anyone can, with a quick call, share it with someone else who would appreciate the moment. L.O.L. Cell phones allow an instant connection, a voice instant messenger.

Cell phone calls let people reach out and touch each other. Most phone calls are very short. "Hey, what's up"? "What are you doing"? "How are you"? Little information is exchanged. "Nothing much," in fact, is a common answer. What do such phone calls accomplish? They let people keep in touch with each other.

Text messaging is really a very handy way to keep in touch. Even if you can't reach the other person, you can leave a message to let him know that you are thinking about him. Other people keep in touch through MySpace or Facebook, which lets friends know what is going on with each others lives, even long lost friends. Facebook can even be a great space for sharing since you can post pictures, blog your ideas, identify your favorite group and more. If anything, college students of today can be considered the in-touch generation.

It must have been weird to wait an entire day before bragging to friends and family about getting the only A on a Chemistry test. It is almost impossible to imagine that students managed the complex schedule of their days before cell phones. It should not be surprising that students talk on their cell phones over nothing.

Complete additional exercises and practice in your MyLab

Planning and Drafting Your Paper

Understand the assignment.

- Understand the topic.
- Identify key expectations.
- Make the project yours.

Find your topic.

- Talk with others.
- Keep a journal.
- Sort out the subject into categories.
- Brainstorm.

Identify audience, purpose.

Develop details.

Read, talk to others, and brainstorm.

Organize the information.

- Create labeled flexible notes.
- Develop a rough plan—a list of points in order.
- Write a quick draft to find your focus and pattern.

Develop a focused thesis.

- Focus on just one central point or issue.
- Provide an accurate forecast of what is to come.

Draft to capture your thoughts—expect to revise.

CHAPTER 4

Revising and Editing Your Paper: Courageous Transformations

In this chapter, you will learn how to:

4.1 Approach your writing to effectively revise.

4.2 Use the F.A.C.T. strategy to guide your revision.

4.3 Revise at the paragraph and sentence level.

4.4 Participate in peer evaluation and use peer responses in your own revision.

4.5 Write collaboratively with others using many media.

4.6 Assemble and maintain a portfolio of your writing.

Good writers don't express themselves perfectly on the first try; they revise until their writing is effective.

Just what is revision? Don't confuse it with proofreading or editing, the final stage of the writing process, where you carefully inspect your word choice, spelling, grammar and punctuation. Revision is much more drastic, often involving an upheaval of your draft as you change its content and organization in order to communicate more effectively.

Most of what you read, including this book, has been altered considerably and improved as the writers progressed through early drafts. This fact shouldn't surprise you. After all, a rough draft is merely a first attempt to jot down some ideas. No matter how well you gather and organize your material, you can't predict the outcome until you've prepared a draft. Sometimes only touch-up changes are required. More often, though, despite your efforts this version will be incomplete, unclear in places and possibly disorganized. You might even discover an entirely different idea, focus or approach buried within it. During revision you keep changing things—your focus, approach to the topic, supporting material and thesis statement—until the results satisfy you.

Inexperienced writers often mistakenly view initial drafts as nearly finished products rather than as experiments to alter, or even scrap, if need be. To revise successfully, you need to control your ego and your fear and become your own first critical reader. Set aside natural feelings of accomplishment ("After all, I've put a great deal of thought into this") and dread ("Actually, I'm afraid of what I'll find if I look too closely"). Instead, recognize that revision offers an opportunity to upgrade your strong features, strengthen your weak ones, or explore entirely new directions.

Preparing to Revise

4.1

Approach your writing to effectively revise.

To distance yourself from your writing and sharpen your critical eye,

- Set your draft aside for at least half a day, longer if possible.
- Write down your purpose and audience for your essay.
- Write down possible alternate directions for your essay.
- Write down any ideas or phrases that have come to you in writing the essay.
- Read your essay at least three times, once for each of the following reasons:
  - To improve the development of the essay as a whole.
  - To strengthen paragraph structure and development.
  - To sharpen sentences and words.

The right attitude is vital to effective revision. Far too many students hastily skim their essays to reassure themselves that "Everything sounds O.K." Avoid such a quick-fix approach. If your draft appears fine on first reading, probe it again with a more critical eye. Try putting yourself in your reader's place. Will your description of a favorite getaway spot be clear to someone who has never seen it? Will your letter home asking for money really convince parents who might think they've already given you too much? Remember: If you aren't critical now in anticipating confusion and objections, then your reader certainly will be later.

When you finish reading your paper for content, make a final, meticulous sweep to search for errors and problems that mar your writing. Use the Personal Revision Checklist on the inside back cover of this book to note your own special weaknesses, perhaps some problem with punctuation or a failure to provide specific support. Later chapters discuss paragraphs, sentences and words in detail. Check these chapters for more information about the points introduced here.

Considering the Whole Essay

4.2

Use the F.A.C.T. strategy to guide your revision.

If you inspect your draft only sentence by sentence, you can easily overlook alternative directions for your work, gaps in the text, or how the parts work together. A better approach is to step back and view the overall essay rather than its separate parts, asking questions such as "Is there any entirely new direction to take the paper, perhaps following up on a section that works especially well?" "Does the beginning mesh with the end?" "Does the essay wander?" "Has anything been left out?" In this way you can find new approaches and gauge how part and whole relate.

Use the acronym *FACT* to guide this stage of your revision.

Watch the Video on **Revising Your Paper**

F. Ask yourself first whether the whole essay *FITS* together, presenting a central point for a specific audience. Have you delivered what the thesis statement promises? First drafts often include paragraphs, or even large sections, that have little bearing on the main point. Some drafts contain the kernels of several different essays. One section of a draft might be geared to one audience (parents, for example) and another section to an entirely different audience (students, perhaps). As you read each part, verify its connection to your purpose and audience. Don't hesitate to chop out sections that don't fit, redo stray parts so they accord with your central idea or alter your thesis statement to reflect better your supporting material. Occasionally, you might even expand one small, fertile section of your draft into an entirely new essay.

A. Whenever we write first drafts, we unwittingly leave out essential material. We often produce text based on our own knowledge and assume far too much, leaving large holes and resulting in "writer-based prose." We need to revise these drafts to produce much more complete texts that meet the needs of our readers, resulting in "reader-based prose." As we revise, we need to identify and fill these inevitable gaps. Ask yourself: "Where will the reader need more information or examples to understand my message?" "Where do I need to explain things more fully?" "What major ideas have I left out?" It can be helpful to reread your notes or do some additional brainstorming. *ADD* the appropriate sentences, paragraphs or even pages.

C. First drafts often contain material that fits the thesis but doesn't contribute to the essay. Writing quickly, we tend to repeat ourselves, include uninteresting or uninformative examples and crank out whole paragraphs when one clear sentence would suffice. As you revise, *CUT* away this clutter with a free hand. Such paring can be painful, especially if you're left with a skimpy text, but your message will emerge with much greater clarity. As you've probably guessed, revising a draft often requires both adding and cutting.

T. Carefully *TEST* the organization of your essay. The text should flow smoothly from point to point with clear transitions between the various ideas. Test the organization by outlining your major and minor points and then check the results for logic and completeness. Alternatively, read the draft and note its progression. Look for spots where you can clarify connections between words and thus help your readers.

Chapters 8–16 explain nine different writing strategies, each concluding with revision questions geared specifically to that strategy. Use these questions, together with the *FACT* of revision, to help you revise more effectively.

It is crucial that you view revision not as a hasty touch-up job or as a quick sweep through your draft just prior to handing it in. Instead, revision should be an ongoing process that often involves an upheaval of major sections as you see your draft through your reader's eyes and strive to write as well as you can.

Decide if you revise better from the computer screen or using a printout. Sometimes essays look different when read in print and you can benefit from a printed copy of your draft, even if you directly revise your computer version. As you read your own essay, note on a separate sheet of paper or computer page problems to solve, ideas to add, and changes to try. You can insert ideas directly into your draft by using a symbol such as <> or a different color font. Some writers use post-it notes, either a software program on a computer or on actual paper, to paste revision ideas where they apply. If you are revising directly on the computer, you should use the Markup feature of your program and track your changes so that you do not lose them. Always keep a backup copy of everything. Accidentally erasing a file or losing your work to an electrical power surge is not uncommon. In addition, consider saving copies of your earlier drafts either as printouts or on disk; selected parts may prove useful later, and new papers sometimes sprout from old drafts. Regardless of the medium you use, be willing to write three or more versions of the same idea to find out which works best. When you approach the actual essay, make your job easier by using these simple techniques.

1. To delete something, cut it and track the changes or cross it out lightly; you may decide to resurrect it later.
2. If you are revising on a computer, simply insert the new material. You can try two or more versions in the same draft or open a new page to try different options. To add a section of text in a print copy, place a letter (*A, B, C, D*) at the appropriate spot and write the new material on a separate sheet, keyed to the letter. Make changes within sections by crossing out what you don't want and writing the replacement above it or nearby.
3. On the computer, you can simply cut and move sections to rearrange the organization. After you have moved material, you will need to make certain it fits into the new context. The cut and paste feature, when abused, can result in a paper that seems very disjointed. To rearrange the organization on a print copy, draw arrows showing where you want things to go, or cut up your draft and rearrange the sections by taping them on new sheets of paper. Use whatever method works best for you.

When you finish revising your draft, you might want to team up with one or more classmates and read one another's work critically. The fresh eye you bring to the task can uncover shortcomings that would otherwise go unnoticed. Pages 71–77 discuss peer editing in detail.

Drew carefully reconsiders his rough draft, which you read on pages 54–55. As we indicated there, the draft needs extensive work.

FIT. While most of Drew's paper fits his audience and thesis, the material concerning the misuses of the cell phone to e-mail pictures and instant messenger slang like L.O.L. doesn't match his audience or purpose. It is offtrack, raises unnecessary suspicion about cell phone use and is too informal for the audience.

ADD. If Drew really wishes to convince a skeptical audience that student cell phone use is necessary, he needs to make his examples more detailed. The material on using cell phones to be together at the same time and to keep in touch are especially scanty, but each paragraph could be more fully explained with more detailed examples.

CUT. The paragraph on text messaging may fit the topic, but it is different in kind from voice communication. Cutting that paragraph will allow the paper to be more focused on a single type of cell phone use.

TEST. If the paper is going to be organized according to the order of importance to the audience, it would make sense to put a paragraph on sharing after "getting business done" and "keeping in touch" before "together at the same time." A careful review of the flow of the paragraphs shows that the third paragraph lacks a clear transitional topic sentence.

EXERCISE

1. *List Drew's other options for revising this draft; indicate the necessary changes if he had decided to write for fellow college students.*
2. *Use the FACT acronym to revise the draft you prepared for the exercise on page 54.*

CASE HISTORY) **Cell Phone Use**
Rough Draft Marked Up

At the end of their class,
Students open their cell phones almost before they are out of the room. It
                flip   are greatly confused by this practice and
confuses professors and parents. My parents complain that young people
                                        Some
are so wrapped up in their cell conversations that they completely miss the
                Most wonder   are compulsive.
world around them. why students such non-stop cell phone users? It looks
            The
ridiculous when large numbers of college students wander around talk-
                                                  ing
                                            may seem ridiculous to
ing into their phones, ignoring the people around them. In the end this cell
outsiders. However,
phone mania is a necessary part of college life.
        There are many reasons students wander around campus talking into the air.
        They use cell phones to coordinate the day's activities, to get some business done,
        to share life's events, and to keep in touch.

    It is hard to imagine how people managed their lives without cell phones

since there seems to be so much to get done. Weren't friends going to meet after
                                            Add (A)   hectic as students
class for a study session? Where is everybody? Life in College can be crazy. We

Continued on next page

Continued from previous page

juggle complex schedules, ^of classes^ work, ~~meals.~~ ^and a social life.^ A quick phone call can organize it all. We arrange study sessions, confirm a lunch date, get a ride, coordinate a team project for class, and maybe even make time for a date.

Add Ⓑ Students, like everyone else, need to call about possible jobs, resolve disputes over bills, arrange to have theirs car fixed, find out the results of

^There is often a lot to get done that has to be squeezed into a busy day.^ medical tests, and even, in some cases, find babysitters. Sometimes walking back to the dorm from a night class, students are on the phone simply to feel safer so that if anything happens they can let someone else know and perhaps get help. Cell phones let them get all this done. ^in the time between classes or even while walking back to their dorm, leaving them with more time for other things like studying or going out with friends.^

~~Cell phones let us be together at the same time, even if we are in different places.~~ Part of the reason for such widespread cell phone use is that instead of having to wait. ^We can be part of the immediate now.^ A quick phone call has one person getting out of bed while another is getting out of class. Two friends seated at different ends of a stadium ^Anyone can know what almost anyone else their call list is doing at any moment.^ can enjoy the blow by blow of the action at the same time.

Everyone likes to share. Cell phones let people share. Many phones ^moments of delight, success, and even failures with others who care.^ even let you take a picture and send it by e-mail to a friend. ~~It is because of this practice that cell phones are banned in some locker rooms and why it is~~ ^When a baby is expected, the soon to be grandparents can't wait for the call.^ ~~dangerous to be caught in an embarrassing situation at a party. You never know what can be e-mailed to your friends or even posted to the internet.~~ At concerts some in the audience call up friends and then hold up the phone so that they can hear part of a concert. When something really funny is happening, anyone can with a quick call share it with someone else who would appreciate the moment. L.O.L. Cell phones allow an instant connection, ~~a voice~~ ^to let people experience what you are experiencing, whether it is excitement over a success, an^ ~~instant messenger.~~ ^idea, the finals of a sporting event, or a newscast.^

Add Ⓒ Cell phone calls let people reach out and touch each other. Most phone calls are very short. "Hey, what's up?" "What are you doing?" "How are you?" Little information is exchanged. "Nothing much," in fact, is a common answer. What do such phone calls accomplish? They let people keep in touch with each other.

~~Text~~ Messaging is really a very handy way to keep in touch. Even if ~~you~~ can't reach the other person, you can leave a message to let ~~you~~ know that you are thinking about them. Other people keep in touch through MySpace or Face Book which lets friends know what is going on with each others lives, even long lost friends. Face Book can even be a great space for sharing since you can post pictures, blog your ideas, identify your favorite group or more. If anything, college students of today can be considered the in touch generation.

It must have been weird to wait an entire day before bragging to friends and family about getting the only A on a Chemistry test. It is almost ~~im-~~
incomprehensible
~~possible~~ that students managed the complex schedule of their days before cell
                                                              at the
phones.   It should not be surprising that students ~~talk~~ on their cell phones
       snap open
~~over nothing.~~
drop of almost anything. The surprise would be if they kept their cell phones in their pockets
and waited. Add Ⓓ

What did a student do if a ride didn't show up? How did a couple share the excitement of a concert in the moment or a good joke if they had to wait days? Earlier generations who seem puzzled by the cell phone fever that has hit college campuses might wonder how they might have felt without a phone, having to wait for weeks for the mail or longer for a visit.

A   A quick cell phone call to a friend reveals that the study session was moved to the student center. Does everyone have his or her part ready for the presentation speech class at 3:00 p.m.? A flurry of cell phone calls makes certain everyone is ready. Will Collin be able to meet his girlfriend this afternoon? He needs to call to see if she is still free. Where is Jennifer since she said she was picking me up in front of the Science Building?

B   Sometimes cell phone calls get important business done. Heather needs to convince her parents that she really, really needs more money to cover the cost of books. Tim needs to contact his advisor so he can schedule for the next semester.

C   If you got an A on a paper that you thought would get an F, you can quickly spread the celebration to anyone who would echo your joy while the feeling was still hot. Sometimes a cell phone call can make the sharing very concrete, getting someone to go outside to look at a spectacular meteor shower,

Continued on next page

Continued from previous page

getting a friend to change channels so they can see an interview with a favorite rock star, or letting family know about a terrible earthquake in China.

D   Contact is what helps keep people close. Parents like their children to visit. Couples need to make time for each other. When people keep in touch, it lets them know that others care, lets them keep each other as important parts of their lives. Some students call their parents every day keeping the family ties tight, getting the emotional reassurance of those loving connections. Sometimes it seems like couples seem to be holding electronic hands as they walk across campus, with little room for some interloper to break up their relationships. Friends may not be able to see each other since they are going to different colleges, but a simple cell phone lets them each know the others are still friends.

CASE HISTORY   Cell Phone Use Second Draft

Clarified classroom by adding class.

At the end of their class, students flip open their cell phones almost before they are out of the room. Professors and parents are confused by this practice. Some complain that young people are so wrapped up in their cell conversations that they completely miss the world around them. Most wonder why students are compulsive cell phone users. There are many reasons students wander around campus talking into the air. They use cell phones to coordinate the day's activities, to get some business done, to share life's events, and to keep in touch. The large number of college students wandering around talking into their phones, ignoring the people around them, may seem ridiculous to outsiders. However, in the end this cell phone mania is a necessary part of college life.

Added thesis statement that outlines paper order.

Provided more detailed account of cell phone use helped.
Placed academic material first for audience.

It is hard to imagine how people managed their life without cell phones since there is so much to coordinate. Weren't friends going to meet after class for a study session? Where is everybody? A quick cell phone call to a friend reveals that the study session was moved to the student center. Does everyone have his or her part ready for the presentation in Speech class at 3:00 P.M.? A flurry of cell phone calls makes certain everyone is ready. Will Collin be able to meet his girlfriend this afternoon? He needs to call to see if she is still free. Where is Jennifer since she said she was picking me up in front of the Science Building? Life in College can be hectic as students juggle complex schedules of classes, work, meal times, and a social life. A quick phone call can organize it all; arrange study sessions, confirm a lunch date, arrange a ride, coordinate a team project for class, and maybe even make time for a date.

> Clarified what was complex.

Sometimes cell phone calls get important business done. Heather needs to convince her parents that she really, really needs more money to cover the cost of books. Tim needs to contact his advisor since he needs to lift his holds so he can schedule for the next semester. Students, like everyone else, need to call about possible jobs, resolve disputes over bills, arrange to have their car fixed, find out the results of medical tests, and even, in some cases, find baby-sitters. There is often a lot to get done that has to be squeezed into a busy day. Sometimes walking back to the dorm from a night class, students are on the phone simply to feel safer so that if anything happens they can let someone else know and perhaps get help. Cell phones let them get all this done in the time between classes or even while walking back to their dorm, leaving them with more time for other things like studying or going out with friends.

> Added a transitional thesis statement. Added more specific examples to appeal to audience.

Everyone likes to share moments of delight, success, and even failure with others who care. When a baby is expected, the soon to be grandparents can't wait for the call. Cell phones let people share. Many phones even let you take a picture and send it by e-mail to a friend. At concerts some in the audience call up friends and then hold up the phone so that they can hear part of a concert. When something really funny is happening, anyone can with a quick call share it with someone else who would appreciate the moment. If you got an A on a paper that you thought would get an F, you can quickly spread the celebration to anyone who would echo your joy while the feeling was still hot. Sometimes a cell phone call can make the sharing

> Added context that relates to understanding of reader. Moved sharing paragraph up to make order of material. Cut material on inappropriate use of phone picture that might offend audience. Added more concrete examples appropriate to target audience.

Continued on next page

Continued from previous page

very concrete, getting someone to go outside to look at a spectacular meteor shower, getting a friend to change channels so they can see an interview with a favorite rock star, or letting family know about a terrible earthquake in China. Cell phones allow an immediate connection to let people experience what you are experiencing, whether it is excitement over a success, an idea, the finals of a sporting event, or a news event.

Cell phone calls let people stay in touch with each other. Most phone calls are very short, over before students have gotten from the classroom to the door of the building. "Hey, what's up?" "What are you doing?" "How are you?" Little information is exchanged and little is really shared. "Nothing much," in fact, is a common response. What do such phone calls accomplish? They let people keep in touch with each other. Contact is what helps keep people close. Parents like their children to visit. Couples need to make time for each other. When people keep in touch, it lets them know that others care, lets them keep each other as important parts of their lives. Some students call their parents every day keeping the family ties tight, getting the emotional reassurance of those loving connections. Sometimes it seems like couples seem to be holding electronic hands as they walk across campus, with little room for some interloper to break up their relationships. Friends may not be able to see each other since they are going to different colleges, but a simple cell phone lets them each know the others still are friends.

Part of the reason for such widespread cell phone use is that instead of having to wait, we can be part of the immediate now. A quick phone call has one person getting out of bed while another is getting out of class. Two friends seated at different ends of a stadium can enjoy the blow by blow of the action at the same time. Anyone can know what almost anyone else in their call list is doing at any moment.

It must have been lonely to wait an entire day before bragging to friends and family about getting the only A on a Chemistry test. It is almost incomprehensible that students managed the complex schedule of their days before

---

Margin notes:

Adds more detailed examples appropriate to target audience.

Cut paragraph on text messages.

This paragraph still needs improvement.

cell phones. What did a student do if a ride didn't show up? How did people share the excitement of a concert in the moment or a good joke if they had to wait days? Earlier generations who seem puzzled by the cell phone fever that has hit college campuses might wonder how they might have felt without a phone, having to wait for weeks for the mail or longer for a visit. It should not be surprising that students snap open their cell phones at the drop of almost anything. The surprise would be if they kept their cell phones in their pockets and waited.

Strengthening Paragraph Structure and Development

Once you finish considering the essay as a whole, examine your paragraphs one by one, applying the *FACT* approach that you used for the whole paper. Make sure each paragraph *FITS* the paper's major focus and develops a single central idea. If a paragraph needs more support or examples, *ADD* whatever is necessary. If a paragraph contains ineffective or unhelpful material, *CUT* it. *TEST* the flow of ideas from paragraph to paragraph and clarify connections, both between and within paragraphs, as necessary. Ask the basic questions in the checklist that follows about each paragraph, and make any needed revisions.

4.3

Revise at the paragraph and sentence level.

REVISION CHECKLIST FOR PARAGRAPHS

- Does the paragraph have one, and only one, central idea?
- Does the central idea help to develop the thesis statement?
- Does each statement within the paragraph help to develop the central idea?
- Does the paragraph need additional explanations, examples, or supporting details?
- Would cutting some material make the paragraph stronger?
- Would reorganization make the ideas easier to follow?
- Can the connections between successive sentences be improved?
- Is each paragraph clearly and smoothly related to those that precede and follow it?

Don't expect to escape making changes. Certain paragraphs may be stripped down or deleted, others beefed up, still others reorganized or repositioned. Chapter 5 contains more information on writing effective paragraphs.

Following are three sample student paragraphs. Evaluate each according to the Revision Checklist for Paragraphs and suggest any necessary changes.

1. I can remember so many times when my father had said that he was coming to pick me up for a day or two. I was excited as a young boy could be at the thought of seeing my father. With all the excitement and anticipation raging inside of me, I would wait on the front porch. Minutes would seem like hours as I would wait impatiently.

2. Going to high school for the first time, I couldn't decide if I should try out for the cheerleading team or wait a year. Since I had time and had been on other squads, I decided "why not?" I had nothing to lose but a lot to gain. Tryouts were not as hard as I thought, but I just knew I had to be on the squad. The tryout consisted of learning the routine they made up, making up your own routine, doing splits, and making a chant. Yet although these things were not that hard, I still was not sure whether I would make the team or not. The time came for the judges to make their decisions on who made the squad. Totaling the votes, they handed the results to the coach. She gave her speech that all coaches give. We were all good, but only a few could be picked for the team. As she started to read the names, I got hot. When she called my name, I was more than happy.

3. For hours we had been waiting under the overhang of an abandoned hut. None of us had thought to bring ponchos on our short hike through the woods. Soon it would be dark. Earlier in the day it had been a perfectly clear day. We all agreed that we didn't want to stand here all night in the dark, so we decided to make a dash for it.

Sharpening Sentences and Words

Next, turn your attention to sentences and words. You can improve your writing considerably by finding and correcting sentences that convey the wrong meaning or are stylistically deficient in some way. Consider, for example, the following sentences:

> Just Mary was picked to write the report.
> Mary was just picked to write the report.
> Mary was picked to write just the report.

The first sentence says that no one except Mary will write the report; the second says that she was recently picked for the job; and the third says that she will write nothing else. Clearly, each of these sentences expresses a different meaning.

Now let's look at a second set of sentences:

> Personally, I am of the opinion that the results of our membership drive will prove to be pleasing to all of us.
> I believe the results of our membership drive will please all of us.

The wordiness of the first sentence slows the reader's pace and makes it harder to grasp the writer's meaning. The second sentence, by contrast, is much easier to grasp.

Like your sentences, your words should convey your thoughts precisely and clearly. Words are, after all, your chief means of communicating with your reader. Examine the first draft and revised version of the following paragraph, which describe the early morning actions of the writer's roommate. The highlighted words identify points of revision.

First Draft

Coffee cup in hand, she moves toward the bathroom. The coffee spills noisily on the tile floor as she reaches for the light switch and turns it on. After looking briefly at the face in the mirror, she walks toward the bathtub.

Revised Version

Coffee cup in hand, she stumbles toward the bathroom. Spilled coffee slaps on the tile floor as she gropes for the light switch and flips it on. After squinting briefly at the face in the mirror, she shuffles toward the bathtub.

Note that the words in the first draft are general and imprecise. Exactly how does she move? With a limp? With a strut? With a spring in her step? And what does "noisily" mean? A thud? A roar? A sharp crack? The reader has no way of knowing. Recognizing this fact, the student revised her paragraph, substituting vivid, specific words. As a result, the reader can visualize the actions more sharply.

Don't confuse vivid, specific words with "jawbreaker words"—those that are complex and pretentious. Words should promote communication, not block it.

Reading your draft aloud will force you to slow down, and you will often hear yourself stumble over problem sections. You'll be more likely to uncover errors such as missing words, excessive repetition, clumsy sentences and sentence fragments. Be honest in your evaluation; don't read in virtues that aren't there or that exaggerate the writing quality. You can easily try different versions of your sentences and word choice by typing them directly in your document. Sometimes it is helpful to try several different versions on a new page or on a sheet of paper and insert the version that works best.

- What sentences are not clearly expressed or logically constructed?
- What sentences seem awkward, excessively convoluted or lacking in punch?
- What words require explanation or substitution because the reader may not know them?
- Where does my writing become wordy or use vague terms?
- Where have I carelessly omitted words or mistakenly used the wrong word?

REVISION CHECKLIST FOR SENTENCES

*Reread exercise paragraph 1 on page 68 and revise the sentence struc-
ture and word choice to create a more effective paragraph.*

Writing the Introduction and Conclusion

If you've put off writing your introduction, do it now. Generally, short papers begin with a single paragraph that includes the previously drafted
thesis statement, which sometimes needs to be rephrased so that it meshes
smoothly with the rest of the paragraph. The introduction acquaints the
reader with your topic; it should clearly signal your intention as well as spark
the reader's interest. Pages 97–99 discuss and illustrate effective introductions. Consider drafting two or more versions of an introduction to see
which works best.

The conclusion wraps up your discussion. Generally a single paragraph in
short papers, a good ending summarizes or supports the paper's main idea.
Pages 100–102 discuss and illustrate effective conclusions. Be willing to experiment as well with different conclusions.

Selecting a Title

Watch the Animation on
Selecting a Title

Most essays require titles. Unless a good title unexpectedly surfaces while you
are writing, wait until you finish the paper before choosing one. Since the reader
must see the connection between what the title promises and what the essay delivers, a good title must be both accurate and specific.

Titling the essay "Cell Phone Use" would mislead the reader since this would
seem to suggest that the essay is on how to use a cell phone. A specific title suggests the essay's focus rather than just its topic. For example, "The Reasons for
College Cell Phone Fever" is a clearer and more precise title than simply "Cell
Phone Use." The essay is about why cell phones are so extensively used, not
about how they are to be used.

To engage your reader's interest, you might try your hand at a clever or
catchy title, but don't get so carried away with creativity that you forget to relate
the title to the paper's content. Following are some examples of common and
clever titles:

Common	"Handling a Hangover"
Clever	"The Mourning After"
Common	"Selecting the Proper Neckwear"
Clever:	"How to Ring Your Neck"

Use a clever title only if its wit or humor doesn't clash with the overall purpose
and tone of the paper.

Peer Evaluation of Drafts

At various points in the writing process, your instructor may ask you and your classmates to read and respond to one another's papers. Peer response often proves useful because even the best writers cannot always predict how their readers will react to their writing. For example, magazine articles designed to reduce the fear of AIDS have, in some cases, increased anxiety about the disease. Furthermore, we often have difficulty seeing the problems with our own drafts because so much hard work has gone into them. What seems clear and effective to us can be confusing or boring to our readers. Comments from our peers can frequently launch a more effective essay.

Just as the responses of others help you, so will your responses help them. You don't have the close, involved relationship with your peers' writing that you do with your own. Therefore, you can gauge their drafts objectively. This type of critical evaluation will eventually heighten your awareness of your own writing's strengths and weaknesses. Knowing how to read your own work critically is one of the most important writing skills you can develop.

4.4

Participate in peer evaluation and use peer responses in your own revision.

Responding to Your Peers' Drafts

Responding to someone else's writing is easier than you might imagine. It's not your job to spell out how to make the draft more effective, how to organize it, what to include and what language to use. The writer must make these decisions. Your job is to *identify* problems, not *solve* them. You can do that best by responding honestly to the draft.

Some responses are more helpful than others. You don't help the writer by casually observing that the draft "looks O.K." Such a response doesn't point to problem areas; rather it suggests that you didn't read the paper carefully and critically. Wouldn't you inform a friend who was wearing clothes that looked terrible *why* they looked terrible? The same attitude should prevail about writing, something that makes a statement just as clothes do. Nor is a vague comment helpful, such as "The introduction is uninteresting." Point out *why* it is uninteresting. For instance, you might note that "The introduction doesn't interest me in the paper because it is very technical, and I get lost. I ask myself why I should read on." Following are two more examples of ineffective responses and their more effective counterparts.

Watch the Video on **Responding to Your Peer's Drafts**

Ineffective

The paper was confusing.

Effective

Paragraphs 2, 3, and 4 confused me. You jumped around too much. First you wrote about your experience on the first day of college, then you went on to how much you enjoyed junior high school, and finally you wrote about what you want to do for a career. I don't see how these ideas relate or why they are in the order that they are.

Ineffective

More examples would help.

Effective

When you indicate that college is a scary place, I get no real idea of why or how. What are the things that you think make college scary? I would like some examples.

Here are some steps to follow when responding to someone else's draft. First, read the essay from beginning to end without interruption. On a separate sheet of paper, indicate what you consider to be the main idea. The writer can then see whether the intended message has come through. Next, identify the biggest problem and the biggest strength. Writers need both negative and positive comments. Finally, reread the paper and write either specific responses to each paragraph or your responses to general questions such as the ones that follow. In either case, don't comment on spelling or grammar unless it really inhibits your reading.

PEER RESPONSE CHECKLIST

- What is the main point of this essay?
- What is the biggest problem?
- What is the biggest strength?
- What material doesn't seem to fit the main point or the audience?
- What questions has the author not answered?
- Where should more details or examples be added? Why?
- At what point does the paper fail to hold my interest? Why?
- Where is the organization confusing?
- Where is the writing unclear or vague?

As you learn the various strategies for successful writing, new concerns will arise. Questions geared to these concerns appear in the revision section that concludes the discussion of each strategy.

An Example of Peer Response in Response to "Cell Phone Use"

What is the main point of this essay?

There are many reasons students use cell phones so extensively, including to coordinate activities, get business done, share with others, keep in touch.

What is the biggest problem?

I didn't really know what was meant by this idea of the immediate now. Where did this idea come from? In what ways do we share the same now. Is this different from keeping in touch?

What is the biggest strength?

The reasons in the paper ring true to my experience, especially with the examples that are used.

What doesn't seem to fit the main point or the audience?

The material on the babysitter doesn't seem to fit or seem likely for most college students. Is walking back to the dorm getting something done? How many students really do that? Doesn't it make you even more vulnerable?

Where should more details or examples be added? Why?

The introduction is kind of boring. An example would make it more real. Also, more details about the now paragraph would make it clearer. Isn't the paper missing something about a really important reason which is simply that everyone is doing it?

Where is the writing unclear or vague?

The writing is pretty clear. But some places could be clearer in the intro. Which "some" and "most" do you mean? Some sentences could be tightened up like "Jim needs to contact his advisor . . ." Your pronouns jump around. Sometimes you use "we" and sometimes "students" and "they."

Acting on Your Peers' Responses

Sometimes you need strong nerves to act on a peer response. You can easily become defensive or discount your reader's comments as foolish. Remember, however, that as a writer you are trying to communicate with your readers, and that means taking seriously the problems they identify. Of course, you decide which responses are appropriate, but even an inappropriate criticism sometimes sets off a train of thought that leads to good ideas for revision.

As you read the final version of Drew's paper on cell phones, carefully examine the margin notes, which highlight key features of the revision. Drew added an example to the introduction to make it more interesting, added a section on how the common use of cell phones has an impact, and clarified the paragraph on "the now." He has cut the material on babysitters and walking across campus that his readers found inappropriate. He has tightened his language by sharpening his sentences and his word choice in a few places and using more consistent pronouns.

CASE HISTORY **The Reasons for College Cell Phone Fever
Final Draft**

Changed title to make it more focused.

At the end of their college classes, students flip open their cell phones almost before they are out of the room.

Continued on next page

Continued from previous page

Added short
conversation to make
more interesting.

"Hey, just got out of English."

"What ya goin' to do?"

"Get some coffee and study before Biology. You?"

"Got Intro to Business in ten minutes."

"Well, see ya."

Added sentence with
more active verbs to
capture scene.

Clarified the "some."

These conversations seem far from necessary. Yet students plow their way from class to class with their cell phones glued to their ears. Professors and parents are confused by this practice. Some parents complain that young people are so wrapped up in their cell conversations that they completely miss the world around them. Many wonder why students are compulsive cell phone users. There are many reasons students wander around campus talking into the air. They use cell phones to coordinate the day's activities, to get business done, to share life's events, and to keep in touch. Part of this trend, undeniably, is that many others are also doing it. The large number of college students who wander around talking into their phones, ignoring the people around them, may seem ridiculous to an outsider. However, in the end this cell phone mania is a reasonable, pleasurable and vital part of college life.

Added trend that is a
later paragraph.

Clarified the word
necessary by expanding
idea.

Simplifies language
since calls are obvious
cell phones. Through
out, changes language
so consistently student
and they, not we.

It is hard to imagine how people managed their lives without cell phones since there is so much to coordinate. Weren't friends going to meet after class for a study session? Where is everybody? A quick call reveals that the study session was moved to the student center. Does everyone have his or her part ready for the presentation in Speech class at 3:00 P.M.? A flurry of calls makes certain everyone is ready. Will Collin be able to meet his girlfriend this afternoon? He needs to call to see if she is still free. Where is Jennifer since she said she was picking me up in front of the Science Building? College life can be hectic as students juggle classes, work, meal times and a social life. A quick phone call can organize it all: arrange study sessions, confirm a lunch date, arrange a ride, coordinate a team project for class and maybe even make time for a date.

Changed language to
tighten life in college
to college life.

Tightened sentence by
cutting wordiness.

Sometimes cell phone calls get important business done. Heather needs to convince her parents that she really, really needs more money to cover the cost of books. Tim needs to ask his adviser to lift his holds so he can schedule next semester's classes. Students, like everyone else, need to call about possible jobs, resolve bill disputes, arrange to have theirs car repaired and find out medical test results. Cell phones let them get all this done in the time between classes or while walking back to their dorms, leaving them with more time for other things like studying or going out with friends.

Everyone likes to share moments of delight, success and even failure with others who care. When a baby is expected, the expectant grandparents can't wait for the call. Cell phones let people share. At concerts, some in the audience call up friends and then hold up the phone so that they can hear part of a concert. When something really funny is happening, anyone can with a quick call share it with someone else who would appreciate the moment. If students get an unexpected A, they can quickly spread the celebration to those who would echo their joy. Sometimes a cell phone call can make the sharing very concrete, getting someone to go outside to look at a spectacular meteor shower, getting a friend to change channels to see an interview with a favorite rock star, or letting family know about a terrible earthquake in China. Cell phones allow an immediate connection to let people experience what callers are experiencing, whether it is excitement over a success, a great idea, the finals of a sporting event or a news event.

Cell phone calls can let people stay in touch with each other. Most phone calls are very short, over before students have gotten from the classroom to the door of the building. "Hey, what's up?" "What are you doing?" "How are you?" Little information is exchanged and little is really shared. "Nothing much," in fact, is a common answer. What do such phone calls accomplish? They let people keep in touch with each other. Contact is what helps keep people close. Parents like their children to visit. Couples need to make time for each other. When people keep in touch, it lets them know that others care, lets them keep each other as important parts of their lives. Some students call their parents

Continued on next page

Tightened language.

Cut the line about walking across campus at night.

Changed pronouns to be consistent.

Cut unnecessary phrase "while the feeling was still hot."

Changed from any idea to a great idea, more likely to be shared.

"Answer" is chosen as a better word than "response."

Continued from previous page

every day to maintain family ties while getting the emotional reassurance of those loving connections. Couples hold electronic hands as they walk across campus. Friends may not be able to see each other since they are going to different colleges, but a simple cell phone confirms their continued friendship.

Provided a context for the paragraph. Reworded to be clearer.

A sociology professor told her class that she thought that the cell phone "created a virtual society of now." Cell phones create a feeling that all are in it together at the same time, even if in different places. Instead of having to wait to find out what might be happening, students can be part of the same now. A quick phone call has one person getting out of bed while another is getting out of class. Two friends seated at different ends of a stadium can enjoy the blow by blow of the action at the same time. Anyone can know what almost anyone else in their call list is doing at any moment. A clip from a news story on television about cosmetic surgery conveyed this perfectly. A woman is talking on her cell phone while she is undergoing liposuction. "Yeh," she declares, "I am undergoing surgery right now. No, I don't feel much, maybe just a tickle." It is hard to get more immediate than that.

Added a very specific example to make the idea clearer.

All of this is made possible because others are doing it. Teenagers are notorious for doing what others are doing. Parents ask, "If your friends jumped off a bridge, would you do it too?" The answer is an embarrassing "yes," especially if the jumpers were attached to bungee cords. It would be embarrassing not to have a cell phone, ideally an Android or an iPhone or whatever is the latest trend. Everyone else seems to be talking while walking. So using cell phones right after class, between classes, during lunch, or at a concert just seems to be normal behavior—and most people want to be normal. Besides, if students are lucky enough to have good friends, their friends are probably calling them; and if friends are calling, it is important to call them back.

Added section on how everyone is doing this has an impact in response to peers.

Added a phrase to be memorable.

Added specific idea to explain concept.

It must have been lonely to wait an entire day before bragging to friends and family about getting the only A on a Chemistry test. It is almost incomprehensible that students managed their complex schedules before cell phones. What did a student do if a ride didn't show up? How did people share the excitement of a concert in the moment or a good joke if they had to wait days? Earlier generations who seem puzzled by the cell phone fever that has hit college campuses might wonder how they might have felt without a phone, having to wait for weeks for the mail or longer for a visit. It should not be surprising that students snap open their cell phones at the end of class. The surprise would be if they kept their cell phones in their pockets and waited.

Of course, you decide which responses are appropriate, but even an inappropriate criticism sometimes sets off a train of thought that leads to good ideas for revisions.

ACTING ON PEER RESPONSE CHECKLIST

- Did the readers understand my main point? If not, how can I make it clearer?
- What did they see as the main problem? Can I solve it?
- What strengths did they identify that I can keep?
- What didn't fit that I need to cut or make clearer?
- Which reader's questions should I answer more completely?
- Where should I add details or examples?
- How could I make sections that lose my reader's interest more engaging, or should I cut those sections?
- Why did my readers find some sections confusing? How could I reorganize those sections?
- Where could I rewrite sections to make them clearer?

Proofreading Your Draft

After revising your draft, proofread or edit it to correct errors in grammar, punctuation and spelling. Effective proofreading is essential since even a few errors quickly detract from the credibility of your work. Since we often overlook our own errors simply because we know what we meant, proofreading can be difficult. Even after you have checked your paper using spell and grammar check, inch through your draft deliberately, moving your finger along slowly under every word. Remember spell check does not catch if you have used the wrong word such as "there" for "their." Grammar check still requires you to make decisions; it does not catch awkward sentences that are grammatical. Ideally follow the above process several times, looking first for errors in grammar, then for sentence errors and problems in punctuation and mechanics, and finally for mistakes in spelling. Be especially alert for problems that have plagued your writing in the past.

Watch the Animation on Proofreading

Effective proofreading calls for you to assume a detective role and probe for errors that weaken your writing. If you accept the challenge, you will certainly improve the quality of your finished work.

Collaborative Writing

4.5

Write collaboratively with others using many media.

In many careers you'll have to work as part of a group to produce a single document. Recognizing this fact, many instructors assign collaborative writing projects. Writing as part of a group offers some advantages and poses some challenges. You can draw on many different perspectives and areas of expertise, split up the work and enjoy the feedback of a built-in peer group. On the other hand, you must also coordinate several efforts, resolve conflicts over the direction of the project, deal with people who may not do their fair share and integrate different styles of writing.

Even though you write as part of a group, the final product should read as though it were written by one person. Therefore, take great pains to ensure that the paper doesn't resemble a patchwork quilt. You can help achieve this goal by following the principles of good writing discussed throughout this book. Following are some suggestions for successful collaborative work:

1. Select a leader with strong organizational skills.
2. Make sure each person has every other group member's phone number and e-mail address.
3. Analyze the project and develop a work plan with clearly stated deadlines for each step of the project.
4. Assign tasks on the basis of people's interests and expertise.
5. Schedule regular meetings to gauge each person's progress.
6. Encourage ideas and feedback from all members at each meeting.
7. If each member will develop a part of the paper, submit each one's contribution to the other members of the group for peer evaluation. This can be done electronically.
8. To ensure that the finished product is written in one style and fits together as a whole, give each member's draft to one person and ask him or her to write a complete draft.
9. Allow plenty of time to review the draft so necessary changes can be made.

Collaborative writing provides an opportunity to learn a great deal from other students. Problems can arise, however, if one or more group members don't do their work or skip meetings entirely. This irresponsibility compromises everyone's grade. The group should insist that all members participate, and the leader should immediately contact anyone who misses a meeting. If a serious problem develops despite these efforts, contact your instructor.

Collaboration Using Electronic and Social Media

Many college students and professionals use social media (including e-mail, chat rooms, Facebook and even text-messaging) to collaborate on writing process. To illustrate:

1. Post a general idea on Facebook so others can add comments on possible topics.
2. E-mail each other information you find, possibly as an attachment in an agreed upon version such as Word.
3. Use a chat room to discuss ideas for the project.
4. Text message your thesis statement to friends to see if it is effective and get feedback.
5. Copy sections of the project into Notes in Facebook or e-mail the sections in an attachment.
6. Share the final document as an attachment.
7. MindMeister and other web programs allows you to build mind maps and brainstorms with others.
8. Google Docs allows participants to share documents for free and edit them just like a word document, only online. This is a common tool of most professions.
9. Wikis, such as wikispaces.com or the Wikis spaces that comes with many electronic learning environments, provides a common space where writers can post brainstorming, add visuals or information, post entire text on line and edit each others work. Wikis are especially easy to use.

Whenever you use available media for collaborative writing, it's a good idea to designate a project leader who will ensure that all members participate and who will receive and distribute all materials. Your instructor may request copies of the e-mail exchanges or access to your web-based collaboration in order to follow your work.

Maintaining and Reviewing a Portfolio

A portfolio is an organized collection of your writing, usually kept in a three-ring binder or folder. It's a good idea to retain all your work for each class, including the assignment sheet, your prewriting, and all your drafts. Organize this material either in the order the papers were completed or by type of assignment.

4.6

Assemble and maintain a portfolio of your writing.

Why assemble a portfolio? Not only can a portfolio be a source of ideas for future writing, but it also allows you to review the progress of your current papers. In addition, should any confusion arise about a grade or an assignment, the contents of your portfolio can quickly clarify matters.

Some instructors will require you to maintain a portfolio. They will probably specify both what is to be included and how it is to be organized. They may use the portfolio to help you gain a better understanding of your strengths and weaknesses. Furthermore, portfolios give your instructor a complete picture of your work. Some departments collect student portfolios to assess their writing program; by reviewing student progress, instructors can determine what adjustments will make the program even more effective. Increasingly, colleges may have you maintain a portfolio using a Web-based program. If your school has you maintain an electronic portfolio, you will receive clear instructions about the process. Do not be afraid to ask questions about this process.

You can review your own portfolio to gain a better understanding of your writing capabilities. Answer these questions as you look over your materials:

1. With what assignments or topics was I most successful? Why?
2. What assignments or topics gave me the most problems? Why?
3. How has my prewriting changed? How can I make it more effective?
4. How has my planning changed? How can I make it more effective?
5. What makes my best writing good? How does this writing differ from my other work?
6. What are the problem areas in my weakest writing? How does this writing differ from my other work?
7. Did I use the checklists in the front of this text to revise my papers? Do I make significant changes on my own, in response to peer evaluation, or in response to my instructor's comments? If not, why not? What kinds of changes do I make? What changes would improve the quality of my work?
8. What organizational patterns have I used? Which ones have been effective? Why? Which ones have given me trouble? Why?
9. What kinds of introductions have I used? What other options do I have?
10. What kinds of grammar or spelling errors mar my writing? (Focus on these errors in future proofreading.)

Complete additional exercises and practice in your MyLab

Revising Your Paper

Prepare to revise.

- Distance yourself from your writing.
- Jot down your initial plans for your writing and ideas that came to mind.
- Talk about your paper with others.
- Read peer response and judge what makes sense.

Revise your whole essay.

- To discover new directions.
- Find what *FITS* and doesn't.
- *ADD* to develop and clarify.
- *CUT* what doesn't help.
- *TEST* the organization and restructure and add transitions.

Revise your paragraphs.

- Read out loud if it is helpful.
- Pay attention to where you stumble and what doesn't sound good.
- Slow down your reading to revise so you don't skim.

- Fit the thesis.
- Focus on central idea.
- Add detail as necessary.
- Cut what doesn't fit.
- Reorganize for easier flow.

Strengthen words and sentences.

- Use more precise and vivid words.
- Make sure sentences mean what you want.
- Cut excess wordiness.

Repeat entire process or parts as needed.

Proofread your paper.

CHAPTER 5   **Paragraphs**

In this chapter, you will learn how to:

5.1 Create effective paragraphs that have unity.

5.2 Apply different strategies for the placement of topic sentences.

5.3 Write paragraphs that are well developed.

5.4 Use a variety of paragraph organizational patterns.

5.5 Achieve coherence in your paragraphs.

5.6 Write introduction, conclusion, and transition paragraphs using a variety of strategies.

Imagine the difficulty of reading a magazine article or book if you were faced with one solid block of text. How could you sort its ideas or know the best places to pause for thought? Paragraphs help guide readers through longer pieces of writing.

- Some break lengthy discussions of one idea into segments of different emphasis, thus providing rest stops for readers.
- Others consolidate several briefly developed ideas. Yet others begin or end pieces of writing or link major segments together.
- Most paragraphs, though, include a number of sentences that develop and clarify one idea.

Throughout a piece of writing, paragraphs relate to one another and reflect a controlling purpose. To make paragraphs fit together smoothly, you can't just sit down and dash them off. Instead, you first need to reflect on the entire essay, then channel your thoughts toward its different segments. Often you'll have to revise your paragraphs after you've written a draft.

Characteristics of Effective Paragraphs

Unity

5.1

Create effective paragraphs that have unity.

A paragraph with unity develops one, and only one, key controlling idea. To ensure unity, edit out any stray ideas that don't belong and fight the urge to take interesting but irrelevant side trips; they only create confusion about your destination. The following paragraph *lacks unity:*

Watch the Animation on **Unity**

> The Montessori Method for teaching math in the earliest grades builds on the child's natural link to physical objects and concrete learning. Spelling and reading are also taught with special materials. It was the psychologist Piaget who recognized that there were different kinds of cognition from the concrete to the more abstract. Maria Montessori was a pioneer in applying insights into how children actually think to the classroom.

What exactly is this writer trying to say? We can't tell. Each sentence expresses a different, undeveloped idea:

1. The use of concrete materials to teach math.
2. The use of special materials to teach spelling and reading.
3. Piaget's contribution in identifying levels of intelligence.
4. Maria Montessori's contribution to education.

In contrast, the following paragraph develops and clarifies only one central idea, the Montessori Method's use of concrete materials to teach math:

> The Montessori Method for teaching math in the earliest grades builds on the child's natural link to physical objects and concrete learning. Children count out unit beads. When they reach 10 unit beads, they can exchange them for a ten-bar, a line of 10 linked beads. Ten ten-bars can be exchanged for one one-hundred square. By physically placing unit beads, ten-lines, and hundred-squares on a mat, children quickly learn about the units, tens, and hundreds place and how to carry. These concrete tools can also help children learn addition and subtraction. Children lay out a number like 236 on a mat as well as the number 165. They add them together, counting up the five and the six to get eleven and exchanging 10 unit-beads for the ten-bar leaving one unit bead, adding up the now 10 ten-bars and exchanging them for a hundred-square and then reading out the resulting number of 401. While the description of the procedure may sound complicated, the actual process of using these concrete materials to understand addition and carrying is easy for children to grasp.
>
> Diane Honegger

Because no unrelated ideas sidetrack the discussion, the paragraph has unity. To check your paragraphs for unity, ask yourself what each one aims to do and whether each sentence helps that aim.

After reading the next two paragraphs, answer the questions that follow.

1. The legend—in Africa—that all elephants over a large geographical area go to a common "graveyard" when they sense death is approaching led many hunters to treat them with special cruelty. Ivory hunters, believing the myth and trying to locate such graveyards, often intentionally wounded an elephant in the hopes of following the suffering beast as it made its way to the place where it wanted to die. The idea was to wound the elephant seriously enough so that it thought it was going to die but not so seriously that it died in a very short time. All too often, the process resulted in a single elephant being shot or speared many times and relentlessly pursued until it either fell dead or was killed when it finally turned and charged its attackers. In any case, no wounded elephant ever led its pursuers to the mythical graveyard with its hoped-for booty of ivory tusks.

   Kris Hurrell

2. It is not surprising that the sales figures for CDs keep slumping since it is easier and more convenient to download the music buyers want from the Internet. The online music stores, such as iTunes, are very easy to use with simple instructions for searching for music and making purchases. Music fans can quickly find the performers or albums of their choice, even obscure works, from the convenience of their living room without having to drive from store to store. Then they can buy either the songs or entire albums that interest them. Once downloaded, they can either burn a CD to play on more traditional stereos or copy the music to an mp3 player of some kind. The effects have been devastating on the music retail industry. Major stores such as Tower Records went out of business. Barnes and Noble has cut back on the number of CDs that the chain sells. The shift to online distribution of music has had the added advantage of allowing alternative groups to present their music that they would have had trouble getting made into CDs and distributed through major chains. This also ends the potential impact of major chains such as Wal-Mart on what music is sold.

   Annonymous

1. Which of these paragraphs lacks unity? Refer to the paragraphs when answering.
2. How would you improve the paragraph that lacks unity?

The Topic Sentence

5.2

Apply different strategies for the placement of topic sentences.

The topic sentence states the main idea of the paragraph. Think of the topic sentence as a rallying point, with all supporting sentences developing the idea it expresses. A good topic sentence helps you gauge what information belongs in a paragraph, thus ensuring unity. At the same time, it informs your reader about the point you're making.

Placement of the topic sentence varies from paragraph to paragraph, as the following examples show. As you read each, note how supporting information develops the topic sentence, which is highlighted.

Topic Sentence Stated First   Many paragraphs open with the topic sentence. The writer reveals the central idea immediately and then builds from a solid base.

It has long been my belief that everyone's library contains an Odd Shelf. On this shelf rests a small, mysterious corpus of volume whose subject matter is completely unrelated to the rest of the library, yet which, upon close inspection, reveals a good deal about its owner. George Orwell's Odd Shelf held a collection of bound sets of ladies' magazines from the 1860's, which he liked to read in his bathtub. Philip Larkin had an especially capacious Odd Shelf crammed with pornography, with an emphasis on spanking. Vice Admiral James Stockdale, having heard that Frederick the Great had never embarked on a campaign without his copy of *The Encheiridion*, brought to Vietnam the complete works of Epictetus, whose Stoic philosophy was to sustain him through eight years as a prisoner of war.

Anne Fadiman, *Ex Libris: Confessions of a Common Reader*

Topic Sentence Stated Last   In order to emphasize the support and build gradually to a conclusion, a topic sentence can end the paragraph. This position creates suspense as the reader anticipates the summarizing remark.

One of the biggest of the Big Questions of existence is, Are (sic) we alone in the universe? Science has provided no convincing evidence one way or the other. It is certainly possible that life began with a bizarre quirk of chemistry, an accident so improbable that it happened only once in the entire observable universe, and we are it. On the other hand, maybe life gets going wherever there are Earthlike planets. We just don't know, (sic) because we have a sample of only one. However, no known scientific principle suggests an inbuilt drive from matter to life. No known law of physics or chemistry favors the emergence of the living state over other states. Physics and chemistry are, as far as we can tell, "life blind."

Paul C. W. Davies, *What We Believe But Cannot Prove*

Topic Sentence Stated First and Last   Some paragraphs lead with the main idea and then restate it, usually in different words, at the end. This technique allows the writer to repeat an especially important idea.

If schoolchildren ever learn anything about this far-flung place, it is usually no more than the events on Signal Hill. From the ordinary square-mile of granite, the modern world seemed to launch itself. First, Guglielmo Marconi clambered up there in 1901, and received the first radio-waves skittering over the ocean. Then came Alcock and Brown in their preposterous aeroplane, and Charles Lindbergh, en route from New York. But this isn't Newfoundland's story, more the history of passers-by. As to what happened in the other 41,999 square miles of Newfoundland, or in Labrador, this is a blank that most children will carry into adulthood.

John Gimlett, *Theater of Fish: Travels Through Newfoundland and Labrador*

Topic Sentence Stated in the Middle　On occasion, the topic sentence falls between one set of sentences that provides background information and a follow-up set that develops the central idea. This arrangement allows the writer to shift the emphasis and at the same time preserve close ties between the two sets.

> Priming people with suggestions can be useful in certain cases. For older folks, it can help them recover real memories. So many elderly people seem unable to "put their finger on" a past experience. But often this is not because the memory has been erased; it's just that the person can't initiate the process of retrieving it. Give such people a beginning—some fact to organize around—and they can then pull all the pieces together. They can remember the word, the name, and the action, and then feel very much relieved. Aging is the most common factor that compromises the memory of us all, and its effects are being studied intensively.
>
> John J. Tratey, M.D., *A User's Guide to the Brain*

Topic Sentence Implied　Some paragraphs, particularly in narrative and descriptive writing, have no topic sentence. Rather, all sentences point toward a main idea that readers must grasp for themselves.

> [Captain Robert Barclay] once went out at 5 in the morning to do a little grouse shooting. He walked at least 30 miles while he potted away, and then after dinner set out on a walk of 60 miles that he accomplished in 11 hours without a halt. Barclay did not sleep after this but went through the following day as if nothing had happened until the afternoon, when he walked 16 miles to a ball. He danced all night, and then in early morning walked home and spent a day partridge shooting. Finally he did get to bed—but only after a period of two nights and nearly three days had elapsed and he had walked 130 miles.
>
> John Lovesey, "A Myth Is As Good As a Mile"

The details in this paragraph collectively suggest a clear central idea: that Barclay had incredible physical endurance. But writing effective paragraphs without topic sentences challenges even the best writers. Therefore, control most of your paragraphs with clearly expressed topic sentences.

EXERCISE

Identify the topic sentences in each of the following paragraphs and explain how you arrived at your decisions. If the topic sentence is implied, state the central idea in your own words.start student font

1. Last winter, while leafing through the <u>Guinness Book of World Records</u>, I came across an item stating that the tallest sunflower ever had been grown by G. E. Hocking, an Englishman. Fired by a competitive urge, I planted a half acre of sunflower seeds. That half acre is now a magnificent 22,000 square feet of green and gold flowers. From the elevated rear deck of my

apartment, I can look out over the swaying mass of thick, hairy green stalks and see each stalk thrusting up through the darker heart-shaped leaves below and supporting an ever-bobbing imitation of the sun. In this dwarf forest, some of the flower heads measure almost a foot in diameter. Though almost all my plants are now blooming, none will top the sixteen feet, two inches reached by Hocking's plant. My tallest is just thirteen feet even, but I don't think that's too bad for the first attempt. Next year, however, will be another matter. I plan to have an automatic watering system to feed my babies.

Joseph Wheeler

2. What my mother never told me was how fast time passes in adult life. I remember, when I was little, thinking I would live to be at least as old as my grandmother, who was dynamic even at ninety-two, the age at which she died. Now I see those ninety-two years hurtling by me. And my mother never told me how much fun sex could be, or what a discovery it is. Of course, I'm of an age when mothers really didn't tell you much about anything. My mother never told me the facts of life.

Joyce Susskind, "Surprises in a Woman's Life"

3. At the most fundamental level, scientific explanation of the world is akin to the process of reading and writing. Whether studying skull structures, geological layers, or bird populations, scientists were deciphering sign systems and interpreting texts. Both the geologist Charles Lyell and the neurobiologist Santiago Ramón y Cajal compared themselves with the linguist Jean François Champollion, who decoded the Egyptian hieroglyphics on the Rosetta stone. Highly conscious of their roles as communicators, scientists did not need critics like Arnold to point out their affinity to ordinary writers. They illustrated it themselves in their own text.

Laura Otis, *Literature and Science in the Nineteenth Century*

4. The first hostage to be brought off the plane was a dark little man with a bald head and a moustache so thick and black that it obliterated his mouth. Four of the masked terrorists were guarding him closely, each with a heavy rifle held ready for fire. When the group was about fifty feet from the plane, a second hostage, a young woman in flowered slacks and a red blouse, was brought out in clear view by a single terrorist, who held a pistol against the side of her head. Then the first four pushed the dark little man from them and instructed him to kneel on the pavement. They looked at him as they might an insect. But he sat there on his knees, seemingly as indifferent as if he had already taken leave of his body. The shots from the four rifles sounded faintly at the far end of the field where a group of horrified spectators watched the grisly proceedings.

Bradley Willis

EXERCISE

1. Develop one of the ideas below into a topic sentence. Then write a unified paragraph that is built around it.

    a. The career (or job or profession) I want is _____ .
    b. The one quality most necessary in my chosen field is _____.
    c. The most difficult aspect of my chosen field is _____.
    d. One good example of the American tendency to waste is _____.
    e. The best (or worst) thing about fast-food restaurants is _____.
    f. The college course I find most useful (or interesting) is _____.
    g. Concentration (or substitute your own term here) is an important part of a successful golf game (or substitute your own sport) _____.
    h. The one place where I feel most at home is _____.
    i. More than anything else, owning a pet (or growing a garden) involves _____.

2. Write a topic sentence that would control a paragraph on each of the following:

    a. Preparations for traveling away from home
    b. Advantages of having your own room
    c. Some landmark of the community in which you live
    d. The price of long-distance telephone calls
    e. Registering for college courses
    f. A cherished memento or souvenir
    g. High school graduation
    h. New Year's resolutions

Adequate Development

5.3

Write paragraphs that are well developed.

Students often ask for guidelines on paragraph length: "Should I aim for fifty to sixty words? Seven to 10 sentences? About one-fourth of a page?" The questions are natural, but the approach is wrong. Instead of targeting a particular length, ask yourself what the reader needs to know. Then supply enough information to make your point clearly. Developing a paragraph inadequately is like inviting guests to a party but failing to tell them when and where it will be held. Skimpy paragraphs force readers to fill in the gaps for themselves, a task that can both irritate and stump them. On the other hand, a paragraph stuffed with useless padding dilutes the main idea. In all cases, the reader, the information being presented, and the publication medium determine the proper amount of detail. A newspaper might feature short paragraphs including only key facts, whereas a scientific journal might have lengthy paragraphs that offer detailed development of facts.

The details you supply can include facts, figures, thoughts, observations, steps, lists, examples and personal experiences. Individually, these bits of information may mean little, but together they clearly illustrate your point. Keep in mind, however, that development isn't an end in itself but instead advances the purpose of the entire essay. Still, less experienced writers often produce underdeveloped paragraphs. Look for places where you can specifically add a clarifying explanation, a detailed example, or a more complete account of an already provided example. You might want to take weak paragraphs and brainstorm for additional details.

Following are two versions of a paragraph, the first inadequately developed:

Underdeveloped Paragraph

Most of the delegates to the Constitutional Convention of 1787 feared too much democracy. As a result, they drafted the Constitution as a document outlining a limited democracy. Indeed, some of the provisions were simply undemocratic. But despite reflecting the delegates' distrust of popular rule, the Constitution did provide a framework in which democracy could evolve.

Adequately Developed Paragraph

Most of the delegates to the Constitutional Convention of 1787 feared too much democracy. As a result, they drafted the Constitution as a document outlining a limited democracy. Indeed, some of the provisions were simply undemocratic: universal suffrage was denied; voting qualifications were left to the states; and women, blacks, and persons without property were denied the federal franchise. Until the passage of the Seventeenth Amendment in 1913, senators were not popularly elected but were chosen by state legislators. But despite reflecting the delegates' distrust of popular rule, the Constitution did provide a framework in which democracy could evolve.

The first paragraph lacks examples of undemocratic provisions, whereas the second one provides the needed information.

Readability also helps set paragraph length. Within a paper, paragraphs signal natural dividing places, allowing the reader to pause and absorb the material presented up to that point. Too little paragraphing overwhelms the reader with long blocks of material. Too much creates a choppy effect that may seem simplistic, even irritating. To counter these problems, writers sometimes use several paragraphs for an idea that needs extended development, or they combine several short paragraphs into one.

 EXERCISE

1. **Indicate where the ideas in this long block of material divide logically; explain your choices.**

    During the summer following graduation from high school, I could hardly wait to get to college and "be on my own." In my first weeks at State University, however, I found that independence can be tough and painful. I had expected raucous good times and a carefree collegiate life, the sort depicted in old beach movies and suggested by the selective memories of sentimental alumni. Instead, all I felt at first was the burden of increasing responsibilities and the loneliness of "a man without a country." I discovered that being independent of parents who kept at me to do my homework and expected me to accomplish certain household chores did not mean I was free to do as I pleased. On the contrary, living on my own meant that I had to perform for myself all the tasks that the family used to share. Studying became a full-time occupation rather than a nightly duty to be accomplished in an hour or two, and my college instructors made it clear that they would have little sympathy for negligence or even for my inability to do an assignment. But what was more troubling about my early college life than having to do laundry, prepare meals and complete stacks of homework was the terrifying sense of being entirely alone. I was independent, no longer a part of the world that had seemed to confine me, but I soon realized that confinement had also meant security. I never liked the feeling that people were watching over me, but I knew that my family and friends were also watching out for me—and that's a good feeling to have. At the university no one seemed particularly to be watching, though professors constantly evaluated the quality of my work. I felt estranged from people in those first weeks of college life, desperately needing a confidant but fearful that the new and tenuous friendships I had made would be damaged if I were to confess my fears and problems. It was simply too early for me to feel a part of the university. So there I was, independent in the fullest sense, and thus "a man without a country."

2. **The following short, choppy units are inadequately developed. List some details you could use to expand one of them into a good paragraph.**

I like living in a small town because the people are so friendly. In addition, I can always get the latest gossip from the local busybody.

In a big city, people are afraid to get too friendly. Everything is very private, and nobody knows anything about anybody else.

3. **Scan the compositions you have written in other classes for paragraphs that are over- or underdeveloped. Revise any you find.**

Organization

5.4

Use a variety of paragraph organizational patterns.

An effective paragraph unfolds in a clear pattern of organization so that the reader can easily follow the flow of ideas. Usually when you write your first draft, your attempt to organize your thoughts will also organize your paragraphs. Writers do not ordinarily stop to decide on a strategy for each paragraph. But when you revise or are stuck, it's useful to understand the available choices. Here are some options:

1. The strategies discussed in Chapters 8–16
2. Order of climax

The choice you make depends upon your material and purpose in writing.

Writing Strategies   These include all of the following patterns:

Time sequence (narration)	Comparison
Space sequence (description)	Cause and effect
Process analysis	Definition
Illustration	Argument
Classification	

Four example paragraphs follow. The first, organized by *time sequence*, traces the sequence of a horrifying failed rescue attempt at sea.

● Watch the Animation on **Chronological Order**

> I once read a story about a sailor who was washed overboard while round the Horn on a clipper ship. His shipmates immediately lowered a boat, and a few of them rowed to the rescue while the remainder of the crew dropped sail and brought the ship into the wind. The boat crew plucked the hapless sailor out of the sea, but the small boat broached on a steep breaking wave and capsized. As the men clung to the upturned keel, a flock of albatrosses circled overhead. The lookout on the main ship watched with horror as one of the birds dove, landed on a man's head, and plucked out his eyes. Then a second bird dove, and a third. Another rescue boat was dispatched, but the lines became tangled in the davits as the mother ship drifted downwind. The lost time was fatal. Blinded and bloody, the men in the water untied their life vests and one by one dove to their deaths rather than face the continued assaults.
>
> Jon Turk, *Cold Oceans: Adventures in Kayaks, Rowboat, and Dogsled*

The next paragraph, organized by *space sequence*, describes a ceramic elf, starting from the bottom and working up to the top. Other common spatial arrangements include top to bottom, left to right, right to left, nearby to far away, far away to nearby, clockwise, and counterclockwise.

● Watch the Animation on **Spacial Organization**

> The ceramic elf in our family room is quite a character. His reddish-brown slippers, which hang over the mantel shelf, taper to a slender point. Pudgy, yellow-stockinged legs disappear into a wrinkled tunic-style, olive-green jacket, gathered at the waist with a thick, brown belt that fits snugly around his roly-poly belly. His short, meaty arms hang comfortably, one hand resting on the knapsack at his side and the other clutching the bowl of an old black pipe. An unkempt, snow-white beard, dotted by occasional snarls, trails patriarch-fashion from his lower lip to his belt line. A button nose capped with a smudge of gold dust, mischievous black eyes, and an unruly snatch of hair peeking out from under his burnt-orange stocking cap complete Bartholomew's appearance.
>
> Maria Sanchez

Although descriptive paragraphs, like those developed by narration, often lack topic sentences, our example leads off with the central idea.

Here is a paragraph showing *process* development.

> Making beer nuts is a quick, simple procedure that provides a delicious evening snack. You'll need six cups of raw peanuts, three cups of sugar, and one-and-one-half cups of water. To begin, combine the sugar and water in a two-quart saucepan and stir to dissolve the sugar. Next, add the peanuts and stir again until all of the peanuts are covered by the sugar-water solution. Leave the pan, uncovered, on a burner set at

medium-high heat for ten to twelve minutes, until the sugar crystallizes and coats the peanuts thoroughly. Stay at the stove during the heating process and stir the mixture every two or three minutes to ensure even coating of the nuts. When the peanuts are thoroughly coated, pour them onto an ungreased cookie sheet and bake at 350 degrees for about thirty minutes, stirring and lightly salting at ten-minute intervals. Serve your beer nuts fresh out of the oven or eat them at room temperature.

Kimberlee Walters

Again, the topic sentence comes first.

The final example illustrates development by *comparison* and also proceeds from an opening topic sentence.

Taken together, we found that both intoxicated drivers and cell phone drivers performed differently from baseline and that the driving profiles of these two conditions differed. Drivers using a cell phone exhibited a delay in their response to events in the driving scenario and were more likely to be involved in a traffic accident. Drivers in the alcohol condition exhibited a more aggressive driving style, following closer to the vehicle immediately in front of them, necessitating braking with greater force. With respect to traffic safety, the data suggest that the impairments associated with cell phone drivers may be as great as those commonly observed with intoxicated drivers.

David L. Strayer, Frank A. Drews, and Dennis J. Crouch,
A Comparison of the Cell Phone Driver and the Drunk Driver

Order of Climax   Climactic order creates a crescendo pattern, starting with the least emphatic detail and progressing to the most emphatic. The topic sentence can begin or end the paragraph, or it can remain implied. This pattern holds the reader's interest by building suspense. On occasion, writers reverse the order, landing the heaviest punch first; but such paragraphs can trail off, leaving the reader dissatisfied.

Here is a paragraph illustrating climactic order:

The speaking errors I hear affect me to different degrees. I'm so conditioned to hearing "It don't make any difference" and "There's three ways to solve the problem" that I've almost accepted such usage. However, errors such as "Just between you and I, Arnold loves Edna" and "I'm going back to my room to lay down" still offend my sensibility. When hearing them, I usually just chuckle to myself and walk away. The "Twin I's"—<u>irrevelant</u> and <u>irregardless</u>—are another matter. More than any other errors, they really grate on my ear. Whenever I hear "that may be true, but it's irrevelant" or "Irregardless of how much I study, I still get <u>C</u>'s," I have the urge to correct the speaker. It's really surprising that more people don't clean up their language act.

Valerie Sonntag

From a magazine or newspaper article, select four paragraphs that illustrate different patterns of organization. Identify the topic sentence in each case; or if it is implied, state it in your own words. Point out the organization of each paragraph.

Coherence

Coherent writing flows smoothly and easily from one sentence and paragraph to another, clarifying the relationships among ideas and thus allowing the reader to grasp connections. Because incoherent writing fails to do this, it confuses, and sometimes even irritates, the reader.

5.5

Achieve coherence in your paragraphs.

Here is a paragraph that lacks coherence:

> I woke up late. I had been so tired the night before that I had forgotten to set the alarm. All I could think of was the report I had stayed up until 3 A.M. typing, and how I could possibly get twenty copies ready for next morning's 9 o'clock sales meeting. I panicked and ran out the door. My bus was so crowded I had to stand. Jumping off the bus, I raced back up the street. The meeting was already under way.
> Mr. Jackson gestured for me to come into the conference room. Inserting the first page of the report into the copier, I set the dial for twenty copies and pressed the print button. The sign started flashing CALL KEY OPERATOR. The machine was out of order. Mr. Jackson asked whether the report was ready. I pointed to the flashing red words. Mr. Jackson nodded grimly without saying anything. He left me alone with the broken machine.

This paragraph has some degree of unity: most of its sentences relate to the writer's disastrous experience with the sales report. Unfortunately, though, its many gaps in logic create rather than answer questions, and in very bumpy prose, at that. Note the gap between the third and fourth sentences. Did the writer jump out of bed and rush right out the door? Of course not, but the reader has no real clue to the actual sequence of events. Another gap occurs between the next two sentences, leaving the reader to wonder why the writer had to race up the street upon leaving the bus. And who is Mr. Jackson? The paragraph never tells, but the reader will want to know.

Now read this rewritten version, additions highlighted:

> I woke up late because I had been so tired the night before that I had forgotten to set the alarm. All I could think of was the report I had stayed up until 3 A.M. typing, and how I could possibly get twenty copies ready for next morning's 9 o'clock sales meeting. When I realized it was 8:30, I panicked. Jumping out of bed, I threw on some clothes, grabbed the report, and ran out the door. My bus was so crowded I had to stand and could not see out the window. Two blocks beyond my stop, I realized I should have gotten off. "Stop!" I cried and, jumping off the bus, raced back up the street. When I reached the office, it was 9:15, and the meeting was already under way. Mr. Jackson, the sales manager, saw me and gestured for me to come into the conference room. "One moment," I said as calmly as I could and hurried to the copier. Inserting the first page of the report into it, I set the dial for twenty copies and pressed the print button. Immediately, the sign started flashing CALL KEY OPERATOR. The machine was out of order. The next thing I knew, Mr. Jackson was

at my side asking whether the report was ready. I pointed to the flashing red words, and Mr. Jackson nodded grimly without saying anything. Turning on his heel, he walked away and left me alone with the broken machine.

As this example shows, correcting an incoherent paragraph may call for anything from a single word to a whole sentence or more.

Coherence derives from a sufficient supply of supporting details and your firm sense of the way your ideas go together. If you brainstorm your topic thoroughly and think carefully about the relationships between sentences, incoherence isn't likely to haunt your paragraphs.

As you write, and especially when you revise, signal connections to the reader by using *transitions*—devices that link sentences to one another. These are the most common transitional devices:

1. Connecting words and phrases
2. Repeated key words
3. Pronouns and demonstrative adjectives
4. Parallelism

You can use them to furnish links both within and between paragraphs.

Connecting Words and Phrases   Connectors clarify relationships between sentences. The following list groups them according to function:

Showing similarity: in like manner, likewise, moreover, similarly

Showing contrast: at the same time, but, even so, however, in contrast, instead, nevertheless, still, on the contrary, on the other hand, otherwise, yet

Showing results or effects: accordingly, as a result, because, consequently, hence, since, therefore, thus

Adding ideas together: also, besides, first (second, third…), furthermore, in addition, in the first place, likewise, moreover, similarly, too

Drawing conclusions: as a result, finally, in brief, in conclusion, in short, to summarize

Pointing out examples: for example, for instance, to illustrate

Showing emphasis and clarity: above all, after all, again, as a matter of fact, besides, in fact, in other words, indeed, nonetheless, that is

Indicating time: at times, after, afterward, from then on, immediately, later, meanwhile, next, now, once, previously, subsequently, then, until, while

Conceding a point: granted that, of course, to be sure, admittedly

Don't overload your paper with connectors. In well-planned prose, your message flows clearly with only an occasional assist from them.

In the following excerpt, which clarifies the difference between workers and workaholics, the connectors are highlighted:

My efforts to define workaholism and to distinguish workaholics from other hard workers proved difficult. While workaholics do work hard, not all hard workers are

Watch the Animation on **Coherence**

workaholics. Moonlighters, for example, may work 16 hours a day to make ends meet, but most of them will stop working when their financial circumstances permit. Accountants, too, seem to work non-stop, but many slow down after the April 15 tax deadline. Workaholics, on the other hand, always devote more time and thought to their work than their situation demands. Even in the absence of deadlines to meet, mortgages to pay, promotions to earn, or bosses to please, workaholics still work hard. What sets them apart is their attitude toward work, not the number of hours they work.

Marilyn Machlowitz, "Workaholism: What's Wrong with
Being Married to Your Work?"

Discussion Questions

    1. What ideas do each of the highlighted words and phrases connect?
    2. What relationship does each show?

Repeated Key Words   Repeating key words, especially those that help convey a paragraph's central idea, can smooth the reader's path. The words may appear in different forms, but their presence keeps the main issues before the reader. In the following paragraph, the repetition of *majority, minority,* and *will* aids coherence, as does the more limited repetition of *government* and *interests.*

    Whatever fine-spun theories we may devise to resolve or obscure the difficulty, there is no use blinking the fact that the will of the majority is not the same thing as the will of all. Majority rule works well only so long as the minority is willing to accept the will of the majority as the will of the nation and let it go at that. Generally speaking, the minority will be willing to let it go at that so long as it feels that its essential interests and rights are not fundamentally different from those of the current majority, and so long as it can, in any case, look forward with confidence to mustering enough votes within four or six years to become itself the majority and so redress the balance. But if it comes to pass that a large minority feels that it has no such chance, that it is a fixed and permanent minority and that another group or class with rights and interests fundamentally hostile to its own is in permanent control, then government by majority vote ceases in any sense to be government by the will of the people for the good of all, and becomes government by the will of some of the people for their own interests at the expense of the others.

Carl Becker, *Freedom and Responsibility in the American Way of Life*

EXERCISE

Write a paragraph using one of the following sentences as your topic sentence. Insert the missing key word and then repeat it in your paragraph to help link your sentences.

1. _____ is my favorite relative.

2. I wish I had (a, an, some, more) _____.

3. _____ changed my life.

4. _____ is more trouble than it's worth.

5. A visit to _____ always depresses me.

6. Eating _____ is a challenge.

7. I admire _____.

Pronouns and Demonstrative Adjectives   Pronouns stand in for nouns that appear earlier in the sentence or in previous sentences. Mixing pronouns and their nouns throughout the paragraph prevents monotony and promotes clarity. We have highlighted the pronouns in the following excerpt from an article about the writer's first visit to a gambling casino.

> There are three of us on this trip, two veterans of Atlantic City and I, a neophyte, all celebrating the fact that we have recently become grandmothers. One of my companions is the canny shopper in our crowd; as a bargain-hunter she knows the ways of the world. I have followed her through discount shops and outlet stores from Manhattan's Lower East Side to the Secaucus, New Jersey, malls....Without saying a word, she hands me a plastic container of the kind that might hold two pounds of potato salad, and takes one herself. She drags me off to the change booth, where she exchanges bills for tubes of silver, careful not to let me see just how much. I do the same. Then she leads me to a clattering corner, where a neon sign winks on and off, *Quartermania*. "Let's try to find a couple of machines that only have handles," she says. . . .
>
> Eileen Herbert Jordan, "My Affair with the One-Armed Bandit"

All the pronouns in the excerpt refer to the writer, her bargain-hunting friend, or the whole group.

Four demonstrative adjectives—*this, that, these* and *those*—also help hook ideas together. Demonstratives are special adjectives that identify or point out nouns rather than describe them. Here is an example from the Declaration of Independence:

> We hold these truths to be self-evident, that all men are created equal, that they are endowed by their Creator with certain unalienable Rights, that among these are Life, Liberty, and the pursuit of Happiness. That to secure these rights, Governments are instituted among Men, deriving their just powers from the consent of the governed. That whenever any Form of Government becomes destructive of these ends, it is the Right of the People to alter or to abolish it, and to institute new Government, laying its foundation on such principles and organizing its power in such form, as to them shall seem most likely to effect their Safety and Happiness.

EXERCISE   *In a magazine, newspaper, textbook or some other written source, find two paragraphs that use pronouns and demonstrative adjectives to increase coherence. Copy the paragraphs, underline the pronouns and demonstrative adjectives, and explain what each refers to.*

Parallelism   Parallelism uses repetition of grammatical form to express a series of equivalent ideas. Besides giving continuity, the repetition adds rhythm and balance to the writing. Note how the following highlighted constructions tie together the unfolding definition of poverty:

> Poverty is staying up all night on cold nights to watch the fire, knowing one spark on the newspaper covering the walls means your sleeping children die in flames. In summer poverty is watching gnats and flies devour your baby's tears when he cries.

The screens are torn and you pay so little rent you know they will never be fixed. Poverty means insects in your food, in your nose, in your eyes, and crawling over you when you sleep. Poverty is hoping it never rains because diapers won't dry when it rains and soon you are using newspapers. Poverty is seeing your children forever with runny noses. Paper handkerchiefs cost money and all your rags you need for other things. Even more costly are antihistamines. Poverty is cooking without food and cleaning without soap.

Jo Goodwin Parker, "What Is Poverty?"

Paragraphs with Special Functions

Special-function paragraphs include introductions, transitional paragraphs, and conclusions. One-paragraph introductions and conclusions appear in short, multiparagraph essays. Transitional paragraphs occur primarily in long compositions.

5.6

Write introduction, conclusion, and transition paragraphs using a variety of strategies.

👁 **Watch** the Animation on **Introductions**

Introductions

A good introduction acquaints and coaxes. It announces the essay's topic and may directly state the thesis. In addition, it sets the tone—somber, lighthearted, angry—of what will follow. An amusing anecdote would not be an appropriate opening for a paper about political torture.

With essays, as with people, first impressions are important. If your opening rouses interest, it will draw the reader into the essay and pave the way for your ideas. If, instead, you'd like to try your hand at turning the reader away, search for a beginning that is mechanical, plodding and dull. Your success will astonish you. Here are some bad openings:

> In this paper I intend to…
>
> Wars have always afflicted humankind.
>
> As you may know, having too little time is a problem for many of us.
>
> In the modern world of today…

How would you respond to these openings? Ask yourself that same question about every opening you write.

Gear the length of the introduction to that of the essay. Although longer papers sometimes begin with two or more introductory paragraphs, generally the lead-in for a short essay is a single paragraph. Here are some possibilities for starting an essay. The type you select depends on your purpose, subject, audience and personality.

A Directly Stated Thesis   This is a common type of opening, orienting the reader to what will follow. After providing some general background, the writer of our example narrows her scope to a thesis that previews the upcoming sections of her essay.

> An increasing number of midlife women are reentering the workforce, pursuing college degrees, and getting more involved in the public arena.

Several labels besides "midlife" have been attached to this type of person: the mature woman, the older woman, and, more recently, the re-entry woman. By definition, she is between thirty-five and fifty-five years old and has been away from the business or academic scene anywhere from fifteen to thirty years. The academic community, the media, marketing people, and employers are giving her close scrutiny, and it is apparent that she is having a greater impact on our society than she realizes.

Jo Ann Harris

A Definition   This kind of introduction works particularly well in a paper that acquaints the reader with an unfamiliar topic.

You are completely alone in a large open space and are struck by a terrifying, unreasoning fear. You sweat, your heart beats, you cannot breathe. You fear you may die of a heart attack, although you do not have heart disease. Suppose you decide you will never get yourself in this helpless situation again. You go home and refuse to leave its secure confines. Your family has to support you. You have agoraphobia— a disabling terror of open spaces.

"Controlling Phobias Through Behavior Modification"

A Quotation   A beginning quotation, particularly from an authority in the field, can be an effective springboard for the ideas that follow. Make sure any quote you use relates clearly to your topic.

The director of the census made a dramatic announcement in 1890. The Nation's unsettled area, he revealed, "has been so broken into by isolated bodies of settlement that there can hardly be said to be a frontier line." These words sounded the close of one period of America's history. For three centuries before, men had marched westward, seeking in the forests and plains that lay beyond the settled areas a chance to begin anew. For three centuries they had driven back the wilderness as their conquest of the continent went on. Now, in 1890, they were told that a frontier line separating the settled and unsettled portions of the United States no longer existed. The west was won, and the expansion that had been the most distinctive feature of the country's past was at an end.

Ropropay Allen Billington, "The Frontier Disappears"

An Anecdote or Personal Experience   A well-told personal anecdote or experience can lure readers into the rest of the paper. Like other introductions, this kind should bear on what comes afterward. Engle's anecdote, like the stories she reviews, demonstrates that "women also have dark hearts."

My mother used to have a little china cream and sugar set that was given to her by a woman who later killed her children with an axe. It sat cheerfully in the china cabinet, as inadequate a symbol as I have ever seen of the dark mysteries within us. Yet at least it was there to remind us that no matter how much Jesus wanted us for a sunbeam, we would still have some day to cope with a deeper reality than common sense could explain. It stood for strange cars not to get into, running shoes to wear when you were out alone at night and the backs of Chinese restaurants you were not supposed to go into.

> Marian Engle, review of *The Goddess and Other Women* by Joyce Carol Oates.

An Arresting Statement   Sometimes you can jolt the reader into attention, using content, language, or both, particularly if your essay develops an unusual or extreme position.

> It's like Pearl Harbor. The Japanese have invaded, and the U.S. has been caught short. Not on guns and tanks and battleships—those are yesterday's weapons—but on mental might. In a high-tech age where nations increasingly compete on brainpower, American schools are producing an army of illiterates. Companies that cannot hire enough skilled workers now realize they must do something to save the public schools. Not to be charitable, not to promote good public relations, but to survive.
>
> Nancy Perry, "Saving the Schools: How Business Can Help"

Interesting Details   These details pique curiosity and draw the reader into the paper.

> Cher, the pretty sixteen-year-old protagonist of Amy Heckerling's *Clueless* (1995), is a rich dumb blonde who is a mediocre student at best, and is obsessed with the pleasures of fashion, beauty culture, and shopping. A coy daddy's girl, is riddled with girly slang. Her universe is filtered entirely through popular culture: she prefers watching cartoons to the news, and she takes pride in the fact that her mother named her after the legendary goddess of pop schlock and excess. (77)
>
> Kathleen Rowe Karlyn, *Unruly Girls Unrepentant Mothers:*
> *Redefining Feminism on Screen*

A Question   A provocative question can entice the reader into the essay to find the answer.

> How does the biggest pop star on the planet reward herself after she's spent the past year touring the world, performing for President Bill Clinton, opening her own boutique in Barneys, releasing a high-fashion picture book, and prepping for her appearance on "Dick Clark's New Year's Rockin' Eve?"
>
> Maureen Callahan, "Lady Gaga Gives 50 Percent of Her Earnings to Her Father"

EXERCISE

1. Explain why each of the preceding introductions interests or does not interest you. Does your response stem from the topic or the way the author introduces it?
2. Find magazine articles with effective introductory paragraphs illustrating at least three different techniques. Write a paragraph explaining why each impresses you.

Transitional Paragraphs

In the midst of a lengthy essay, you may need a short paragraph that announces a shift from one group of ideas to another. Transitional paragraphs summarize previously explained ideas, repeat the thesis, or point to ideas that follow. In our example, Bruno Bettelheim has been discussing a young boy named Joey who has turned into a kind of human machine. After describing Joey's assorted delusions, Bettelheim signals his switch from the delusions to the fears that caused them.

> What deep-seated fears and needs underlay Joey's delusional system? We were long in finding out, for Joey's preventions effectively concealed the secret of his autistic behavior. In the meantime we dealt with his peripheral problems one by one.
>
> Bruno Bettelheim, "Joey: 'A Mechanical Boy'"

The following transitional paragraph looks back as well as ahead:

> Certainly these three factors—exercise, economy, convenience of shortcuts—help explain the popularity of bicycling today. But a fourth attraction sometimes overrides the others: the lure of the open road.
>
> Mike Bernstein

Conclusions

 Watch the Animation on **Conclusions**

A conclusion rounds out a paper and signals that the discussion has been completed. Not all papers require a separate conclusion; narratives and descriptions, for example, generally end when the writer finishes the story or concludes the impression. But many essays benefit from a conclusion that drives the point home a final time. To be effective, a conclusion must mesh logically and stylistically with what comes earlier. A long, complex paper often ends with a summary of the main points, but any of several other options may be used for shorter papers with easy-to-grasp ideas. Most short essays have single-paragraph conclusions; longer papers may require two or three paragraphs.

Following are some cautions about writing your conclusion:

1. Don't introduce new material. Draw together, round out, but don't take off in a new direction.
2. Don't tack on an ending in desperation when the hour is late and the paper is due tomorrow—the so-called midnight special. Your reader deserves better than "All in all, skiing is a great sport" or "Thus we can see that motorcycle racing isn't for everyone."
3. Don't apologize. Saying that you could have done a better job makes a reader wonder why you didn't.
4. Don't moralize. A preachy conclusion can undermine the position you have established in the rest of your composition.

The following examples illustrate several common types of conclusion.

Restatement of the Thesis   The following conclusion reasserts Jordan's thesis that "a mood of antisocial negativism is creeping through the structure of American life, corroding our ideals, and suffocating the hopes of poor people and minorities."

> There is room for honest differences about each of these key issues, but the new negativism's overt greed and the implicit racism of its loud "No" to minority aspirations indicate that this is a poisonous movement that denies the moral ideals and human values that characterize the best in America's heritage.
>
> Vernon E. Jordan, Jr., "The New Negativism"

A Summary   A summary draws together and reinforces the main points of a paper.

> There are, of course, many other arguments against capital punishment, including its high cost and its failure to deter crime. But I believe the most important points against the death penalty are the possibility of executing an innocent man, the discriminatory manner in which it is applied, and the barbaric methods of carrying it out. In my opinion, capital punishment is, in effect, premeditated murder by society as a whole. As the old saying goes, two wrongs don't make a right.
>
> Diane Trathen

A Question   The paragraph below concludes an argument that running should not be elevated to a religion; that its other benefits are sufficient. A final question often prompts the reader to think further on the topic. If your essay is meant to be persuasive, be sure to phrase a concluding question so that the way a reasonable person would answer emphasizes your point of view.

> Aren't those gifts enough? Why ask running for benefits that are plainly beyond its capacity to bestow?
>
> James Fixx, "What Running Can't Do for You"

A Quotation   A quotation can capture the essence of your thought and end the essay with authority.

> If you catch yourself ruminating on why that colleague ignored you in the hall, let it go. "You might never know the reason behind a person's laughter or his look in your direction, so why waste time trying to find an answer?" Freeman says. "Ambiguity is all around us. Don't let it keep you from doing the things you enjoy"
>
> Stephanie Booth, "A Slew of Suspects"

Ironic Twist or Surprising Observation   These approaches prompt the reader to think further about a paper's topic. The following paragraph points out the ironic refusal of the government to confront poverty that exists a mere 10 blocks away from its offices:

> Thus, a stark contrast exists between the two cultures of 14th Street, which appears to be like an earthworm with half of its body crushed by poverty but the other half still alive, wriggling in wealth. The two are alike only in that each communicates little with the other because of the wide disparity between the lives of the people and the conditions of the environments. The devastating irony of the situation on 14th Street lies in the fact that only ten blocks away sit the very government institutions that could alleviate the poverty—the Senate, the House of Representatives, and the White House.
>
> Student Unknown

Arresting Statement A powerfully worded unexpected statement can promote thought about the paper's issue. The final sentence here stops most readers in their tracks.

> Unfortunately, as the situation in large parts of the world at the end of the millennium demonstrates, bad history is not harmless history. The sentences typed on apparently innocuous keyboards may be sentences of death.
>
> Eric Hobsbawm, *On History*

Personal Challenge A challenge often prompts the reader to take some action.

> And therein lies the challenge. You can't merely puff hard for a few days and then revert to the La-Z-Boy recliner, smugly thinking that you're "in shape." You must sweat and strain and puff regularly, week in and week out. They're your muscles, your lungs, your heart. The only caretaker they have is you.
>
> Monica Duvall

Hope or Recommendation Both a hope and a recommendation may restate points already made in the essay or suggest actions to take in order to arrive at a solution.

> This journey to a tragic past will be inextricably bound up with the uplifting sight of the future. Having reached the formal memorial, the quiet pathways marking the foundations of the Twin Towers, visitors may realize that they have, in fact, just walked alongside the true memorial: the living, human building blocks of a future New York.
>
> Max Page and Sigrid Miller Pollin, "Proposal for a Landscape of Learning"

> No one can predict the transformations of twenty-first century society during the information technology revolution. We certainly cannot afford to continue teaching our students only the literacies of the mid-twentieth century, or even to simply lay before them the most advanced and diverse literacies of today. We must help this next generation learn to use these literacies wisely, and hope they will succeed better than we have.
>
> J. L. Lemke, "Metamedia Literacy: Transforming Meanings and Media"

 Complete additional exercises and practice in your MyLab

 EXERCISE

1. Explain why each of the foregoing conclusions does or does not interest you. Does your response stem from the topic or from the author's handling of it?
2. Copy effective concluding paragraphs, illustrating at least three different techniques, from magazine articles. Then write a paragraph explaining why each impresses you.

Paragraphs with Special Functions

Writing Paragraphs.

- Aim for the purpose of the whole paper.
- Use paragraphing to show your paper's organization.
- Focus paragraphs around main ideas.
- Use your writing plan to decide on paragraphs.

Developing your introduction.

- Have a draft thesis statement.
- Choose a strategy based on your audience and purpose.
- Chose a strategy including a definition, a directly stated thesis, a quotation, a personal experience, an arresting statement, a question.

Developing the body paragraphs.

- Build paragraphs around main idea.
- State or imply a topic sentence that provides that main idea.
- Develop main idea with details, explanations, or examples.
- Use a strategy and order for developing the paragraph.
- Provide clear transitions.

Enhancing your paragraphs.

- Check to see if everything in each paragraph fits the topic of the paragraph. Cut or move what doesn't fit.
- Determine if additional details, examples, or explanations are necessary to make your point and add if necessary.
- Make certain that the topic sentence of each paragraph is clear and fits the paragraph.
- Strengthen coherence and cohesion by making certain sentences relate in an order and that repeated words or phrases help show relationships.

Writing a conclusion.

- Aim at pulling the paper together for the reader.
- Determine a strategy based on the paper.
  - Restate thesis in a new way
  - Offer a summary of paper
  - Leave the reader with an important question
  - Offer a personal challenge, hope, or recommendation
  - Use a telling quotation
- Check again to determine that the conclusion fits the paper in tone, content, and approach, and does not raise new issues.

CHAPTER 6 Effective Sentences

In this chapter, you will learn how to:

6.1 Write sentences that avoid unnecessary wordiness.

6.2 Write sentences that are varied in complexity and length.

6.3 Vary the word order of sentences.

6.4 Vary the positioning of movable modifiers.

6.5 Use parallelism to present equivalent ideas.

6.6 Choose the right verb voice for your sentences.

Sentences take many forms, some straightforward and unadorned, others intricate and ornate, each with its own stylistic strengths. Becoming familiar with these forms and their uses gives you the option to:

- emphasize or deemphasize an idea.
- combine ideas into one sentence or keep them separate in more than one sentence.
- make sentences sound formal or informal.
- emphasize the actor or the action.
- achieve rhythm, variety, and contrast.

Effective sentences bring both exactness and flair to your writing. You may wish to read your handbook for review if you are not familiar with the sentence elements or how to identify and correct sentence errors effectively.

Sentence Strategies

Effective sentences are not an accident; they require work. There are several strategies you can employ, including avoiding unnecessary wordiness; varying sentence length, complexity, and word order; building a rhythm for your reader; and selecting the right verb voice. Usually it's best to work on these different strategies as you revise rather than pause to refine each sentence after you write it.

Avoiding Unnecessary Wordiness

Sometimes in first drafts we write flabby sentences.

6.1

Write sentences that avoid unnecessary wordiness.

- It is my considered opinion that you will make an excellent employee.
- Joan will give a presentation on our latest sales figures to the CEO.
- Mr. Headly, who was my seventh-grade biology teacher, recently was honored for the research he had done over the years with his classes.
- My neighbor's Subaru that was old and rusty still could navigate the winter streets better than most other cars.

Although there may be stylistic reasons for these sentences, such as creating variety or adding a particular emphasis, a writer could sharpen them by reordering the sentence structure and eliminating unnecessary words.

- You will make an excellent employee. (The fact that you write it makes it clear that it is your opinion.)
- Joan will present our latest sales figures to the CEO. (Many times we use verbs as nouns with a filler verb—"have a meeting," "give a talk," "go running." Change these nouns back to verbs and dragging sentences can be energized.)
- Mr. Headly, my seventh-grade biology teacher, recently was honored for the research he had done over the years with his classes. (The rules of English let you delete some redundant phrases, even repeated subjects, to tighten your language.)
- My neighbor's rusty, old Subaru still could navigate the winter streets better than most other cars. (Changing a relative clause to simple adjectives makes this sentence crisper.

How do most writers do it? Cut out words that seem unnecessary, organize sentences different ways, and let verbs bear the brunt of the burden.

Watch the Animation on **Avoiding Wordiness**

EXERCISE

Rewrite the sentences to avoid unnecessary wordiness.

1. The principal will give a talk to the parents at the PTA meeting about how important it is for their children to get to school on time.
2. I would like to say that no playwright has ever used language as effectively as Shakespeare.
3. Mozart, who was a musical prodigy, is best known for his operas.
4. The jewelry store sold me a watch that was stolen.
5. The meeting that was scheduled for 3 P.M. was cancelled because Mr. Rushton, the consultant who was giving the presentation about the results on our computer security, was arrested for creating computer viruses that were very destructive.

Varying Sentence Complexity and Length

6.2

Write sentences that are varied in complexity and length.

 Watch the Animation on **Varying Sentence Structure**

Sentences that are all the same length yield a repetitive, tedious prose.

> Janice hated pain. She had her nose pierced. She had her bellybutton pierced. She had her tongue pierced. She wanted to be different. She ended up just like her friends.

This string of simple sentences unnecessarily repeats word phrases and gives the reader a bumpy ride. Combining these sentences results in a smoother and more varied prose style.

> Although Janice hated pain, she had her nose, bellybutton, and tongue pierced in order to be different. She ended up, however, just like her friends.

Simple sentences of one subject and predicate—"The audience was young"—can be combined through coordinate and subordinate conjunctions, as well as the use of relative clause structures and other techniques. The result is not only a smoother style but a combination that more effectively shows the relationship of your ideas.

Coordination Coordinating conjunctions include *and, but, or, nor, for, yet*, and *so*, and you can combine clauses or phrases in a way that makes them equal.

- The audience was young, friendly, and responsive; so it cheered for each speaker.
- Either we hang together or we hang separately.
- A tornado ripped through our town but fortunately it spared our house.

Subordination Subordinate conjunctions such as *because, since, while, before, during, after*, and *instead of* can link dependent clauses to the main independent clause in a way that shows logical relationship.

- Millicent swam 400 laps today **because** she was feeling unusually strong.
- Arthur collapsed on the sofa **after** the dance was over.
- **Once** they had reached the lakeshore, the campers found a level spot **where** they could pitch their tent.

Relative Clauses Nouns can often be modified by relative clauses, which use a **relative pronoun** that substitutes for a noun and binds ideas together.

- Students **who** work hard usually succeed.
- The books on the history of Crete **that** you ordered have finally arrived.

There are other ways to combine sentences and vary sentence length, including the use of prepositional phrases, participle phrases, and infinitive phrases.

- The crook raced **around** the corner, **down** the alley, **into** the arms **of** the waiting police officers. (prepositional phrases)
- Some people handle a crisis by avoiding it, **ignoring** the problem until someone else solves it. (participle phrase)
- The early settlers moved west **to escape** an unsavory or difficult past, **to forge** a new life, **to realize** dreams. (infinitive phrases)

The point is to find ways to vary your sentences to increase interest and rhythm.

Intentional Fragments   A fragment is a part of a sentence that is capitalized and punctuated as if it were a complete sentence.

Although fragments are seldom used in formal prose, they form the backbone of most conversations. Here's how a typical bit of dialogue might go:

"Where are you going tonight?" (*sentence*)
"To Woodland Mall." (*fragment*)
"What for?" (*fragment*)
"To buy some shoes." (*fragment*)

As with most conversations, the sprinkling of complete sentences makes the fragments clear.

Writers of nonfiction use fragments to create special effects. In the following passage, the fragments focus the reader on the urgency of the situation.

> Failed banks. Panicked markets. Rising unemployment. For students of history, or people of a certain age, it all has an all-too-familiar ring. Is this another Great Depression? Not yet.
>
> John Waggoner, "Is Today's Economic Crisis Another Great Depression"

Before using any fragment, think about your intended effect. Unless only a fragment will serve your needs, don't use one; fragments are likely to be viewed as unintentional—and thus errors—in the work of inexperienced writers.

EXERCISE

The following passage includes one or more fragments. Identify each and explain its function.

> He [Richard Wagner] wrote operas; and no sooner did he have the synopsis of a story, but he would invite—or rather summon—a crowd of his friends to his house and read it aloud to them. Not for criticism. For applause. When the complete poem was written, the friends had to come again, and hear *that* read aloud. Then he would publish the poem, sometimes years before the music that went with it was written.
>
> Deems Taylor, "The Monster"

Working together, these techniques provide varied sentences that create interest. In the following paragraph, the sentences differ considerably in length.

> In a city of half a million I still really look at every face, anticipating recognition, because I grew up in a town where every face meant something to me. I have trouble remembering to lock the doors. Wariness of strangers I learned the hard way. When I was new to the city, I let a man into my house one hot afternoon because he seemed in dire need of a drink of water; when I turned from the kitchen sink I found sharpened steel shoved against my belly. And so I know, I know. But I cultivate suspicion with as much difficulty as I force tomatoes to grow in the drought-stricken hardpan of my strange backyard. No creek runs here, but I'm still

listening to secret tides, living as if I belonged to an earlier place: not Kentucky, necessarily, but a welcoming earth and a human family. A forest. A species.

Barbara Kingsolver, *High Tide in Tucson: Essays from Now or Never*

Here Kingsolver uses longer sentences to anticipate her more relaxed sense of the world contrasted with a shorter sentence tied to her experience of the potential of violence. The paragraph ends with two short fragments to focus on those interior spaces.

Varying sentence length can help you emphasize a key idea. If a key point is submerged in a long sentence, highlight it as a separate thought, giving it the recognition it deserves.

Original Version

Employers find mature women to be valuable members of their organizations. They are conscientious, have excellent attendance records, and stay calm when things go awry, but unfortunately many employers exploit them. Despite their desirable qualities, most remain mired in clerical, sales, and elementary teaching positions. On the average they earn two-thirds as much as men.

Revised Version

Employers find mature women to be valuable members of their organizations. They are conscientious, have excellent attendance records, and stay calm when things go awry. Unfortunately, many employers exploit them. Despite their desirable qualities, most remain mired in clerical, sales, and elementary teaching positions. On the average they earn two-thirds as much as men

EXERCISE

Using coordination and subordination, rewrite the following passages to reduce words and/or improve smoothness.

1. He played the piano. He played the organ. He played the French horn. He did not play the viola.
2. The weather was icy cold and windy. Lee was wearing only a T-shirt and athletic shorts.
3. Life on Venus may be possible. It will not be the kind of life we know on Earth. Life on Mars may be possible. It will not be the kind of life we know on Earth.
4. He felt his classmates were laughing at his error. He ran out of the room. He vowed never to return to that class.
5. Albert lay in bed. He stared at the ceiling. Albert thought about the previous afternoon. He had asked Kathy to go to dinner with him. She is a pretty, blond-haired woman. She sits at the desk next to his. They work at Hemphill's. She had refused.

Word Order in Independent Clauses

6.3

Vary the word order of sentences.

What other tools do you have to create more interesting prose? One powerful technique is to vary word order in a sentence. Most independent clauses follow a similar arrangement. First comes the subject, then the verb, and finally any other element needed to convey the main message.

> Barney blushed. (*subject, verb*)
> They built the dog a kennel. (*subject, verb, indirect object, direct object*)
> Samantha is an architect. (*subject, verb, subject complement*)

This arrangement puts the emphasis on the subject, right where it's usually wanted.

But the pattern doesn't work in every situation. Occasionally, a writer wants to emphasize some element that follows the verb, create an artistic effect, or give the subject unusual emphasis. Enter inverted order and the expletive construction.

Inverted Order   To invert a sentence, move to the front the element you want to emphasize. Sometimes the rest of the sentence follows in regular subject-then-verb order; sometimes the verb precedes the subject.

> Lovable he isn't. (*subject complement, subject, verb*)
> This I just don't understand. (*direct object, subject, verb*)
> Tall grow the pines in the mountains. (*subject complement, verb, subject*)

Sentences that ask questions typically follow an inverted pattern.

> Is this your coat? (*verb, subject, subject complement*)
> Will you let the cat out? (*verb, subject, verb, direct object*)

Most of your sentences should follow normal order: Readers expect it and find it easier to read. Don't invert a sentence if the result would sound unnatural. A sentence like "Fools were Brett and Amanda for quitting college" will only hinder communication.

Expletives   An expletive fills a vacancy in a sentence without contributing to the meaning. English has two common expletives, *there* and *it*. Ordinarily, *there* functions as an adverb, *it* as a pronoun, and either can appear anywhere in a sentence. As expletives, however, they alter normal sentence order by beginning sentences and anticipating the real subjects or objects.

Expletives are often used unnecessarily, as in the following example:

> There were twenty persons attending the sales meeting.

This sentence errs on two counts: Its subject needs no extra emphasis, and it is very clumsy. Notice the improvement without the expletive and the unneeded words:

> Twenty persons attended the sales meeting.

When the subject or object needs highlighting, leading off with an expletive will, by altering normal order, call it more forcefully to the reader's attention.

> *Normal order:*   *A fly is in my soup.*
> *He seeks her happiness.*
>
> *Expletive construction:*   *There is a fly in my soup.* (*expletive anticipating subject*)
> *It is her happiness he seeks.* (*expletive anticipating object*)

Once in a while you'll find that something just can't be said unless you use an expletive.

There is no reason for such foolishness.

EXERCISE

Indicate which of these sentences follow normal order, which are inverted and which have expletive constructions. Rewrite so that all will be in normal order.

1. Dick Lewis is a true friend.
2. It was her car in the ditch.
3. May I go to the movie with you?
4. There are many dead fish on the beach.
5. The instructor gave the class a long reading assignment.
6. The Willetts have bought a new house.
7. It is Marianne's aim to become a lawyer.

Positioning of Movable Modifiers

6.4

Vary the positioning of movable modifiers.

Movable modifiers can appear on either side of the main statement or within it.

Modifiers after Main Statement   Sentences that follow this arrangement, frequently called *loose sentences*, occur more commonly than either of the others. They mirror conversation, in which a speaker first makes a statement and then adds further thoughts. Often, the main statement has just one modifier.

Our company will have to file for bankruptcy *because of this year's huge losses.* (*phrase as modifier*)

Or it can head up a whole train of modifiers.

He burst suddenly into the party, loud, angry, obscene. (*words as modifiers*)

The family used to gather around the hearth, doing such chores as polishing shoes, mending ripped clothing, reading, chatting, always warmed by one another's presence as much as by the flames. (*words and phrases as modifiers*)

A sentence may contain several layers of modifiers. In the following example, we've indented and numbered to show the different layers.

1. The men struggled to the top of the hill,
    2. thirsty,
    2. drenched in sweat,
    2. and cursing in pain
        3. as their knapsack straps cut into their raw, chafed shoulders
            4. with every step.

In this sentence, the items numbered 2 refer to *men* in the item numbered 1. Item 3 is linked to *cursing* in the preceding item 2, and item 4 is linked to *cut* in item 3.

The modifiers-last arrangement works well for injecting descriptive details into narratives and also for qualifying, explaining, and presenting lists in other kinds of writing.

Modifiers before Main Statement   Sentences that delay the main point until the end are called *periodic.* In contrast to loose sentences, they lend a formal note to what is said, slowing its pace, adding cadence, and making it more serious.

If you can keep your head when everyone around you is panicking, you probably don't understand the situation. (*clauses as modifiers*)

The danger of sideswiping another vehicle, the knowledge that a hidden bump or hole could throw me from the dune buggy, both of these things added to the thrill of the race. (*noun plus phrase and noun plus clause as modifiers*)

1. *When the public protests,*
2. *confronted with some obvious evidence of the damaging results of pesticide applications,* it is fed little tranquilizing pills of half truth. (*clause and phrase as modifiers*)

Rachel Carson, Silent Spring

As shown in the example, periodic sentences can also have layers of modifiers.

Positioning the modifiers before the main point throws the emphasis to the end of the sentence, adding force to the main point. The delay also lets the writer create sentences that, like the first example, carry stings, ironic or humorous, in their tails.

Modifiers within Main Statement   Inserting one or more modifiers into a main statement creates a sentence with *interrupted order.* The material may come between the subject and the verb or between the verb and the rest of the predicate.

The young girl, wearing a tattered dress and looking anything but well-off herself, gave the beggar a ten-dollar bill. (*phrases between subject and verb*)

The evolutionists, piercing beneath the show of momentary stability, discovered, hidden in rudimentary organs, the discarded rubbish of the past. (*one phrase between subject and verb, another between verb and rest of predicate*)

By stretching out the main idea, inserted modifiers slow the forward pace of the sentence, giving it some of the formality and force of a periodic sentence.

EXERCISE   *Identify each sentence as loose, periodic, or interrupted. Rewrite each as one of the other kinds.*

1. Victoria, rejected by family and friends, uncertain where to turn next, finally decided to start a new life in Chicago.
2. When told that she had to have her spleen removed, the woman gasped.

3. The first graders stood in line, talking and giggling, pushing at one another's caps and pencil boxes and kicking one another's shins, unmindful of the drudgery that awaited them within the old schoolhouse.
4. Good health, warm friends a beautiful summer evening—the best things cannot be purchased.
5. A customer, angry and perspiring, stormed up to the claims desk.
6. Stopping just short of the tunnel entrance, the freight train avoided a collision with the crowded commuter train stalled inside.
7. The new kid hammered away at the fading champ, determination in his eyes and glory in his fists.

Building Rhythm

Effective sentences have patterns of organization that help convey meaning while assisting the readers in following the text. Poor organization, even if grammatical, is usually awkward.

Using Parallelism

6.5

Use parallelism to present equivalent ideas.

👁 ⎡ **Watch the Animation**
   ⎣ on **Using Parallelism**

Parallelism presents equivalent ideas in grammatically equivalent form. Dressing them in the same grammatical garb calls attention to their kinship and adds smoothness and polish. The following sentence pairs demonstrate the improvement that parallelism brings:

Nonparallel:	James's outfit was *wrinkled, mismatched,* and *he needed to wash it.* (*words and independent clause*)
Parallel:	James's outfit was *wrinkled, mismatched,* and *dirty.* (*words*)
Nonparallel:	Oscar likes *reading books, attending plays,* and *to search for antiques.* (*different kinds of phrases*)
Parallel:	Oscar likes *reading books, attending plays,* and *searching for antiques.* (*same kind of phrases*)
Nonparallel:	Beth performs her tasks *quickly, willingly,* and *with accuracy.* (*words and phrase*)
Parallel:	Beth performs her tasks *quickly, willingly,* and *accurately.* (*words*)

As the examples show, revising nonparallel sentences smooths out bumpiness, binds the ideas together more closely, and lends them a more finished look.

Parallelism doesn't always stop with a single sentence. Writers sometimes use it in a series of sentences:

He had never lost his childlike innocence. He had never lost his sense of wonder. He had never lost his sense of joy in nature's simplest gifts.

Balance, a special form of parallelism, positions two grammatically equivalent ideas on opposite sides of some pivot point, such as a word or punctuation mark.

Hope for the best, and prepare for the worst.
Many are called, but few are chosen.
When I'm right, nobody ever notices; when I'm wrong, nobody ever forgets.

Like regular parallel sentences, balanced sentences sometimes come in series:

> The tension in this city is not between white people and Negro people. The tension is, at bottom, between justice and injustice, between the forces of light and the forces of darkness. And if there is a victory, it will be a victory not merely for fifty thousand Negroes, but a victory for justice and the forces of light.
>
> Martin Luther King, Jr., "Pilgrimage to Nonviolence"

Balance works especially well for pitting contrasting or clashing ideas against each other. It sharpens the difference between them while achieving compactness and lending an air of insight to what is said.

Identify each sentence as nonparallel, parallel, or balanced; then rewrite each nonparallel sentence to make it parallel.

1. Professor Bartlett enjoys helping students, counseling advisees, and participation in faculty meetings.
2. I can still see Aunt Alva striding into the corral, cornering a cow against a fencepost, try to balance herself on a one-legged milking stool, and butt her head into the cow's belly.
3. The city plans on building a new fishing pier and on dredging the channel of the river.
4. Elton plans on vacationing in New York, but Noreen wants to raft down the Colorado River.
5. You can take the boy out of the country, but you can't take the country out of the boy.
6. Joe's problem is not that he earns too little money but spending it foolishly.
7. The room was dark, gloomy, and everything was dusty.

Choosing the Right Verb Voice

A sentence's verb voice derives from the relationship between the subject and the action. A sentence in the *active voice* has a subject that does something plus a verb that shows action.

> The boy hit the target.
>
> The girl painted the garage.

This pattern keeps the key information in the key part of the sentence, making it strong and vigorous and giving the reader a close-up look at the action.

The *passive voice* reverses the subject–action relationship by having the subject receive, rather than perform, the action. It is built around a form of the verb *to be*; for example, *is, are, was,* or *were*. Some sentences identify the actor by using a prepositional phrase; others don't mention the actor at all.

> The target was hit by the boy. (*actor identified*)
>
> The federal debt limit is to be increased. (*actor unidentified*)

Demoting or banishing the actor dilutes the force of the sentence, puts greater distance between the action and the reader, and almost always adds extra words to the message.

6.6

Choose the right verb voice for your sentences.

👁— **Watch the Animation on Active and Passive Voice**

Most writers who overuse the passive voice simply don't realize its effects on their writing. Read the following section, written mainly in the passive voice:

> Graft becomes possible when gifts are given to police officers or favors are done for them by persons who expect preferential treatment in return. Gifts of many kinds may be received by officers. Often free meals are given to them by the owners of restaurants on their beats. During the Christmas season, they may be given liquor, food, or theater tickets by merchants.

This impersonal, wordy passage plods across the page and therefore lacks any real, persuasive impact. Now note the livelier tone of this rewritten version.

> Graft becomes possible when police officers accept gifts or favors from persons who expect preferential treatment in return. Officers may receive gifts of many kinds. Restaurant owners often provide free meals for officers on the beat. During the Christmas season, merchants may give them liquor, food, or theater tickets.

Don't misunderstand: The passive voice does have its uses. It can mask identities—or at least try to. A child may try to dodge responsibility by saying, "Mother, while you were out, the living room lamp got broken." Less manipulatively, reporters may use it to conceal the identity of a source.

Technical and scientific writing customarily uses the passive voice to explain processes.

> In the production of steel, iron ore is first converted into pig iron by combining it with limestone and coke and then heating the mixture in a blast furnace. Pig iron, however, contains too many impurities to be useful to industry, and as a result must be refined and converted to steel. In the refining process, manganese, silicon, and aluminum are heated with the pig iron in order to degas it; that is, to remove excess oxygen and impurities from it.

Putting such writing in the passive voice provides a desirable objective tone and puts the emphasis where it's most important: on the action, not the actor. On occasion, everyday writing also uses the passive voice.

The garbage is collected once a week, on Monday.

These caves were formed about 10 million years ago.

In the first case, there's no need to tell who collects the garbage; obviously, garbage collectors do. In the second, the writer may not know what caused the formation, and saying "Something formed these caves about 10 million years ago" would sound ridiculous. In both situations, the action, not the actor, is paramount. Unless special circumstances call for the passive voice, however, use the active voice.

EXERCISE

After determining whether each sentence below is in active or passive voice, rewrite the passive sentences as active ones.

1. Mary's parents gave her a sports car for her sixteenth birthday.
2. Fires were left burning by negligent campers.

3. The new ice arena will be opened by the city in about two weeks.
4. Harry left the open toolbox out in the rain.
5. Corn was introduced to the Pilgrims by friendly American Indians.
6. We have just installed a new computer in our main office.
7. Objections were raised by some members of the legislature to the ratification of the proposed amendment.

Beyond the Single Sentence

Your sentences need to work together to produce the desired effect. Your content and purpose will guide you in determining how your sentences will work together. You will need to vary sentence length, word order, and rhythms to produce your desired effect, but in a way that is not obvious or clumsy. A good place to start is by studying the essays in the Reader to see what kinds of combinations they use—a series of questions that are then answered; long sentences with modifiers that lead to a short sentence that gains emphasis; a series of fragments followed by a long sentence. In your own writing, keep an eye on what kind of sentences you are creating and how those sentences create a pattern.

EXERCISE

Revise the following passages to improve their style.

1. Andrew Carnegie came to America from Scotland. He worked as a factory hand, a telegrapher, and a railway clerk to support himself. His savings from these jobs were invested in oil and later in the largest steel works in the country. Historians do not agree in their assessments of Carnegie. Some have considered him a cruel taskmaster and others a benevolent benefactor. His contributions to American society, however, cannot be denied. He established public libraries all across the country and spent much time in promoting peace. Good or bad, he ranks as one of our most noteworthy nineteenth-century immigrants.
2. She went to the seashore. She found some seashells. She picked up the seashells. She put the seashells into a basket. She had a whole basketful of seashells. She went home with the basket. She took the shells out of the basket. She put the shells on a dinette table. She brought jeweler's tools to the table. She pierced holes in the shells. She strung the shells on small chains. The chains were gold and silver. She made twenty necklaces. The selling price of the necklaces was $10 apiece. She earned $175 profit. She used her profits to go to the shore again. She could afford to stay for a week this time.

Complete additional exercises and practice in your MyLab

Sentence Strategies

Focus on the sentence.

- Don't excessively focus on the sentence when drafting if it interrupts in generating ideas.
- Focus on sentences during the revision cycle.
- Work to make your sentences as sharp as possible.

Sharpen your sentences.

- Cut unneeded words.
- Reword lengthy phrases ("The dull speech" instead of "The speech that was dull".

Create sentence variety.

- Make certain sentences are of different lengths and show logical relationships through coordination, subordination, and relative clauses.
- Vary word order so you don't use the same pattern using inverted order, moving modifiers, and varying sentence types.

Strengthen your sentences further.

- Use the right voice. Only use the passive deliberately; otherwise, change passive sentences to an active voice.
- Use patterns in your sentences to build rhythm. It is possible to repeat sentence type and order if it builds a rhythm for an effect.
- Use parallelism within sentences with lists of words or phrases and with multiple sentences when it builds a point and rhythm.
- Read you paper out loud to see if your paper moves consistently from one paragraph to another.
- Proofread to make certain that your sentences avoid common grammatical and punctuation errors. Avoid sentence fragments unless they are used deliberately and with great care.

CHAPTER 7

Achieving Effective Style and Tone Through Word Choice

In this chapter, you will learn how to:

7.1 Select the kinds of words that will have the most impact in your writing.

7.2 Use the best level of diction and tone for your writing situation.

7.3 Enhance your writing with figurative language and irony.

7.4 Avoid using flawed diction in your writing.

You probably don't wear a tuxedo or formal gown to class. It is as much the wrong style for the classroom as shorts and a torn tee shirt are wrong for a business interview. The way we dress, walk, and talk are part of our style for the situations that confront us. Few would wear a three-piece business suit to a casual beach party or even to most offices. The same is true of writing. Writing like "Hey. Wake yourself up reader. I am giving you truth now" would fit a pop song or informal writing to friends but would horrify teachers or professionals in the workplace. Similarly, a sentence like, "It is of the greatest imperative that we deliberate with the greatest care about the matters of profound destiny that should most trouble our conscience" sounds inflated to almost everyone. How do you shape your writing style so it accomplishes what you want? Using effective sentence strategies is part of the story. The other tool you have is your word choice, sometimes called diction. The words you use in the context of your writing, sometimes called diction, can make as much a difference as putting on a tie or a baseball cap.

Selecting the Right Words

Grab a dictionary, or look at the multiple volume of the Oxford English Dictionary, and you realize how many choices you have for every word you write. You get the most impact by selecting words with the precise meaning you need that also have the right level of abstraction and generality. Reading a lot, studying how words work, and using tools like dictionaries and thesauruses can help you make the best

7.1

Select the kinds of words that will have the most impact in your writing.

choices. It is a lot to ask, but your writing will get better if you learn to love words and even write in a notebook the ones you would like to use later.

Choosing Words with the Meaning You Want

Danny Ozark, a baseball team manager, infamously said, "It is beyond my apprehension." Such malapropisms, or mistaken uses of a word, are usually funny and we all are guilty of them. Obviously writers need to know what a word means and how it is used before sticking it into their writing.

Such errors occur most often when we reach for large words that we don't fully understand. They also occur with common words as well. Imagine you were told that you were "excepted from the job" for which you applied. What are you to think? *Except* means to "exclude or omit" while the intended word *accept* means "to approve." If you demonstrate your popularity by declaring, "My phone rings *continuously*," the implication is that you never answer your phone since *continuously* means "uninterrupted." What you probably meant was that your phone rang *continually*, which means "frequently or regularly repeated." There is a Glossary of Common Troublesome Words ( ). You may want to skim them to identify your own demons.

Even avoiding mistakes, you need to choose the words that communicate what you intend. Do you take class in "a classroom," "a building," at "a school," "a college," "a community college," "a technical institute," "a university," or "an institution of higher education." If you were in New York City, the important point might be that your English class was held on the 23rd floor of a skyscraper. If you were writing generally about education in America, you would want to discuss "institutions of higher education" because that would cover everything after high school. However, if you were addressing your specific situation, you might need a more precise term such as "a community college," or "liberal arts college." Don't let words master you; choose the one that does what you need.

Deciding on Concrete and Abstract Words

Watch the Animation on **Using Concrete Words**

"Live Free or Die." This powerful rallying cry of the American Revolution and the state motto of New Hampshire has punch. It depends on abstract words that name general concepts that don't immediately point to something we can experience with our senses. "Freedom" is pretty abstract, as are words like "love," "patriotism," "conservatism," or even "family." Such words used judiciously can motivate powerful responses; in excess, they can leave writing vague and confusing.

Concrete words evoke precise, vivid mental images and thus help convey a message. A thing is concrete if we can weigh it, hold it, photograph it, smash into it or borrow it from our neighbors. Abstract terms can create different images for different people. Ask your friends to describe what comes to mind when they think of "joy," "patriotism," "freedom" or other abstract terms. Some may think of "freedom" as a shopping mall, others a church service, others a newspaper free to criticize the president. Concrete terms often add to the precision of our writing and certainly make it juicier.

In the following passage, the concrete diction is highlighted:

> To do without self-respect . . . is to be an unwilling audience of one to an interminable documentary that details one's failings, both real and imagined, with fresh footage spliced in for every screening. There's the glass you broke in anger, there's the hurt on X's face; watch now, this next scene, the night Y came back from Houston, see how you muff this one. To live without self-respect is to lie awake some night, beyond the reach of warm milk, phenobarbital, and the sleeping hand on the coverlet, counting up the sins of commission and omission, the trusts betrayed, the promises subtly broken, the gifts irrevocably wasted through sloth or cowardice or carelessness. However long we postpone it, we eventually lie down alone in that notoriously uncomfortable bed, the one we make ourselves. Whether or not we sleep in it depends, of course, on whether or not we respect ourselves.
>
> Joan Didion, "On Self-Respect"

Now note how vague and colorless the passage becomes without the concrete diction:

> To do without self-respect is to be continuously aware of your failings, both real and imagined. Incidents stay in your mind long after they are over. To live without self-respect means being bothered by intentional or unintentional failings, trusts betrayed, promises subtly broken, and gifts irrevocably wasted through sloth or cowardice or carelessness. However long we postpone it, we eventually must come to terms with who we are. How we respond to this situation depends, of course, on whether or not we respect ourselves.

EXERCISE

Underline the concrete terms in the following passage:

> Gluttony wallowed in its nauseous excess at tables spread in the halls of the mighty. The everyday dinner of a man of rank ran from fifteen to twenty dishes; England's earl of Warwick, who fed as many as five hundred guests at a sitting, used six oxen a day at the evening meal. The oxen were not as succulent as they sound; by tradition, the meat was kept salted in vats against the possibility of a siege, and boiled in a great copper vat. Even so, enormous quantities of it were ingested and digested. On special occasions a whole stag might be roasted in the great fireplace, crisped and larded, then cut up in quarters, doused in a steaming pepper sauce, and served on outsized plates.
>
> William Manchester, *A World Lit Only by Fire: The Medieval Mind and the Renaissance: Portrait of an Age*

Deciding How Specific or General Words Should Be

If you tell your friends that you are dating "an animal," there are likely to be some titters, both because of the ambiguity and the odd generality of the word choice. When we decide on words, we decide on how concrete or general a word should be. As we move from *Lassie* to *collie* to *dog* to *mammal* and finally to *animal*, we become less and less specific, ending with a term that encompasses every animal on earth. With each step we retain only those features that fit the more general term. Thus, when we move from *collie* to *dog*, we leave out everything that makes collies different from terriers, greyhounds, and other breeds.

Ask yourself how specific you need to be. If, for instance, you're describing a wealthy jet setter, noting that he drives a Ferrari, not just a car, helps establish his character. If, however, you are writing about celebrating Mardi Gras in New Orleans, your readers don't need to know that you drove a rented Ford Focus from the airport.

EXERCISE

1. **Arrange each set of words from less specific to more specific.**

   a. man, ex-president, human being, George W. Bush, American
   b. Forest Hills Apartments, building, structure, condominium, dwelling

2. **Expand each of the following words into a series of four or more that become progressively more specific. Use 1a or 1b as a pattern.**

   a. activity
   b. event
   c. political party
   d. institution
   e. device
   f. reading matter

Using Dictionaries and Thesauruses

Vocabulary is power, and it is easier than ever to enhance your vocabulary. You can have a word of the day downloaded to your computer or smart phone. Dictionaries and thesauruses are available online. These are powerful tools to strengthen your vocabulary and help you select the most effective word for your writing. Don't overdo it, however. If you look up most words while writing a draft, you will lose your flow; and papers written from a dictionary or thesaurus in a vain attempt to impress the reader often end up comically distorted.

Watch the Animation on **Using a Dictionary**

Dictionaries Dictionaries are storehouses of word meanings, spelling, pronunciation, and even word origins and history. Dictionary makers avoid dictating how words should be used. Instead, they record current and past meanings. When a word gains or loses a meaning or a newly minted word enjoys wide circulation, dictionary makers observe and record. Most users, however, regard dictionaries as authorities on correctness.

Dictionaries supply much more than word meanings. Figure 7.1, an annotated entry from a college-level dictionary, shows what they can provide. Some dictionary entries include idioms, irregular forms of words, usage labels, and supplementary information as well.

Idioms Idioms express meanings that differ from those of the words that make them up. Here are two examples.

I won't *put up with* any foolishness.
The dowager *gave me the cold shoulder.*

Put up with means "tolerate"; *gave me the cold shoulder* means "snubbed me." Looking up the most prominent word of an unfamiliar idiom may lead you to a listing and a definition.

Spelling, Syllabication. When a word has variant spellings, some dictionaries indicate a preferred version. Alphabetically close variants appear in the same entry. Dots or hyphens separate syllables and tell where to divide a word written on two lines.

Parts of Speech. Each word is classified by grammatical function. Usually, abbreviations such as *n* (noun), *adj.* (adjective), and *vt.* (transitive verb) identify the part of speech.

Pronunciation. Dictionaries indicate preferred as well as secondary pronunciations. Accent marks (') show which syllable gets the primary stress and which the secondary stress, if any. To determine the pronunciation, follow the key at the bottom of the page.

Etymology. This term means the origin and development of words. Most college dictionaries limit the entry to the root (original) word and an abbreviation for the original language. The abbreviation key near the front of the dictionary identifies the language.

man-i-fold (man´ ə fōld´) *adj.* [ME. < OE. *manigfeald:* see MANY & -FOLD] 1. having many and various forms, features, parts, etc. *[manifold wisdom]* 2. of many sorts; many and varied; multifarious: used with a plural noun *[manifold duties.]* 3. being such in many and various ways or for many reasons *[a manifold villain]* 4. comprising, consisting of, or operating several units or parts of one kind: said of certain devices —*n.* 1. something that is manifold 2. a pipe with one inlet and several outlets or with one outlet and several inlets, for connecting with other pipes, as, in an automobile, for conducting exhausts from each cylinder into a single exhaust pipe —*vt.* 1. to make manifold; multiply 2. to make more than one copy of *[to manifold a letter with carbon paper]* —*SYN.* see MANY — **man´i-fold´er** *n.* —**man´i-fold´ly** *adv.* —**man´i-fold´ness** *n.*

MANIFOLD
(A. manifold; B. cylinders)

Additional Word Formations. These are words derived from the one being defined. Their parts of speech are also indicated. Because they have the same basic meaning as the parent word, definitions are omitted.

Meanings. Meanings are grouped by parts of speech. Sometimes usage is briefly illustrated (*manifold* duties). Some dictionaries list meanings in historical order, others according to frequency of use. The front part of the dictionary specifies the arrangement.

Synonyms. These are words close in meaning to the one being defined. Although no synonym carries exactly the same meaning as the original, the two may be interchangeable in some situations.

Figure 7.1 From *Webster's New World Dictionary of the American Language*, Third College Edition

Irregular Forms   Any irregular forms are indicated. In *Webster's New World Dictionary*, the entry for the verb *spring* notes that the other forms are *sprang*, *sprung*, and *springing*. This information helps you use correct forms in your writing.

Usage Labels   Usage labels help you determine whether a word suits the circumstances of your writing. Here are the most common labels:

Label	Meaning
Colloquial	Characteristic of informal writing and speaking; should not be considered nonstandard.
Slang	Informal, newly coined words and expressions or old expressions with new meanings.
Obsolete	No longer in use but found in past writing.
Archaic	Still finds restricted use, such as in legal documents; otherwise not appropriate.
Poetic	Used only in poetry and in prose with a poetic tone.
Dialect	Used regularly only in a particular geographical location such as the southeastern United States or the Scottish Lowlands.

Supplementary Information   While focusing primarily on individual words, college-level dictionaries often provide several other kinds of information. They may include a history of the language, lists of standard abbreviations and of colleges and universities, biographical notes on distinguished individuals, and geographical notes on important locations.

Any dictionary is better than none, and often an online dictionary such as Miriam Webster's is most convenient. Many excellent dictionaries, including the Oxford English Dictionary and many specialty dictionaries, are available online, though some require a subscription either by the individual or the university. Online dictionaries often offer entertaining ways to explore words, such as an e-mailed word of the day. When the going gets tough, you might need to head to excellent desk-sized dictionaries such as the following:

The American Heritage Dictionary
Funk and Wagnall's Standard College Dictionary
The Random House Dictionary of the English Language
Merriam-Webster's Collegiate Dictionary
Webster's New World Dictionary of the American Language

Unabridged (complete) dictionaries such as *Webster's Third New International Dictionary* and the *Oxford English Dictionary* can be found in college and public libraries. There you'll also find a variety of specialized dictionaries. Your librarian can direct you to dictionaries that list terms in particular fields.

Use a good desk dictionary to look up the specified information for each of the following lists of words:

1. Variant spellings:

airplane	aesthete	gray	tornadoes
color	gaily	theater	usable

2. Syllabication and the syllable that receives the main stress:

anacrusis	cadenza	harbinger	misanthrope
baccalaureate	exclamation	ionize	sequester

3. Parts of speech:

before	fair	separate	to
deep	here	then	where

4. Etymology:

carnival	Icarian	phenomenon	supercilious
fiduciary	lethargy	sabotage	tawdry

5. Idiomatic phrases:

beat	get	jump	put
eat	high	make	set

6. Synonyms:

attack	ghastly	mercy	plot
distress	keep	object	range

Thesauruses   Thesauruses list synonyms for words but omit the other elements in dictionary entries. There are easy-to-use online Thesauruses like Merriam-Webster's that let you simply enter a word and search. Figure 7.2 shows a typical entry. Note that the items are grouped according to parts of speech, and some are cross-indexed.

A thesaurus will help you find a word with just the right shade of meaning or a synonym when you want to avoid repetition. But synonyms are never exactly equal, nor are they always interchangeable. To illustrate, *old* means "in existence or use for a long time;" *antiquated* conveys the notion that something is old-fashioned or outdated. Therefore, use the thesaurus along with the dictionary. Only then can you tell which synonym fits a specific sentence.

Excellent guides to synonyms include the following:

Roget's International Thesaurus
Webster's New Dictionary of Synonyms
Modern Guide to Synonyms and Related Words

formless *adjective*

1 having no definite or recognizable form <a *formless* mass
of clay that the potter transformed into an attractive
bowl>

Synonyms amorphous, shapeless, unformed, unshaped,
unstructured

Related Words characterless, featureless, nondescript;
chaotic, disorganized, incoherent, systemless, unordered,
unorganized; dim, fuzzy, hazy, inchoate, indefinite,
indeterminate, indistinct, indistinguishable, murky,
nebulous, obscure, unclear, undefined, undetermined,
vague

Near Antonyms coherent, ordered, orderly, organized;
clear, decided, definite, distinct

Antonyms formed, shaped, shapen, structured

2 not composed of matter <from this *formless* void the
universe was supposed to have been created>

Synonyms bodiless, ethereal, formless, incorporeal,
insubstantial, nonmaterial, nonphysical, spiritual,
unbodied, unsubstantial

Related Words metaphysical, psychic (*also* psychical),
supernatural; impalpable, insensible, intangible, invisible;
airy, diaphanous, gaseous, gossamery, tenuous, thin,
vaporous, wispish

Figure 7.2   From the Merriam-Webster online thesaurus.

Achieving the Desired Rhetorical Effect

7.2

Use the best level of
diction and tone for your
writing situation.

What kind of response do you want from your reader based on your writing
style? That response generated by the manner of writing rather than the message is the rhetorical effect. Successful writers create a desired effect through
the level of their diction and the tone of their writing. In many cases, both diction level and tone are also established by the expectations of the writing community. All developing writers struggle with consistently maintaining the right
level of diction. Often your teacher's comments about vocabulary and sentence
variety will also be intended to help you maintain the level of diction your readers will expect.

Selecting the Best Level of Diction

What level of diction is best? The answer depends on the writer's audience and
purpose as well as the expectations of the discourse community. Think about a
safety engineer who investigates a serious industrial accident on which she must
write two reports, one for the safety director of the company, who represents
a technical audience, and another for the local newspaper, read by a general
audience. Although the two accounts would deal with the same matter, clearly
they would use very different language: specialized and formal in the first case,

everyday and more relaxed in the second. In each case, the language would reflect the background of the audience. As you write, always choose language suited to your audience and purpose.

Edited American English follows the familiar grammatical rules maintained in most formal and academic writing. Generally, everything you write for college courses or on the job should be in edited American English. *Nonstandard English* refers to any version of the language that deviates from these rules. Following is an example from Mark Twain's famous novel *The Adventures of Huckleberry Finn:*

> You don't know about me without you have read a book by the name of *The Adventures of Tom Sawyer,* but that ain't no matter. That book was made by Mr. Mark Twain, and he told the truth, mainly. There was things which he stretched, but mainly he told the truth. That is nothing. I never seen anybody but lied one time or another, without it was Aunt Polly, or the widow, or maybe Mary.

Nonstandard English does have a place in writing. Fiction writers use it to narrate the talk of characters who, if real, would speak that way. Journalists use it to report eyewitness reactions to accidents and crimes, and people who compile oral histories use it to record the recollections of people they interview.

Edited American English includes four levels of usage: formal, informal, formal–informal, and technical. Another commonly recognized category is colloquial language and slang.

Formal Level   The formal level, dignified and serious, is suitable for important political, business, and academic occasions. Its vocabulary is marked by many abstract and multisyllabic words but no slang or contractions. Long sentences and deliberately varied sentence patterns help give it a strong, rhythmic flow. Sentences are often periodic, and many have parallel or balanced structures. (See pages 112–113.) Overall, formal prose impresses the reader as authoritative, stately, and graceful.

The following excerpts from John F. Kennedy's inaugural address illustrate the formal level:

> Now the trumpet summons us again—not as a call to bear arms, though arms we need; not as a call to battle, though embattled we are; but a call to bear the burden of a long twilight struggle, year in and year out, "rejoicing in hope, patient in tribulation," a struggle against the common enemies of man: tyranny, poverty, disease, and war itself.
>
> In the long history of the world, only a few generations have been granted the role of defending freedom in its hour of maximum danger. I do not shrink from this responsibility; I welcome it.

The first sentence opens with parallelism to show contrast: "not as a call to bear arms, though arms we need" and "not as a call to battle, though embattled we are." In the second paragraph, parallelism in the second sentence shows contrast. Except for the second sentence in the second paragraph, all of the sentences are periodic rather than loose. Thus, not until the end of the opening sentence do we learn the nature of the "long twilight struggle" to which "the trumpet summons us." Time and again Kennedy uses elevated diction—polysyllabic words like *embattled, rejoicing, tribulation, tyranny, poverty,* and *generations,* along with shorter abstract words like *hope and freedom.* These carefully controlled sentence patterns, along with this wording, lend rhythmical dignity to the whole passage.

Informal Level   Informal writing resembles orderly, intelligent conversation. Earmarked by relatively ordinary words, loose sentences, and numerous shorter, less varied sentence structures than formal prose, informal writing may include contractions or even slang, and it is more likely than formal writing to use the pronouns *I, me, my, you,* and *yours.* Following is an example:

> There was a distressing story in the paper a few months ago. I wish I'd clipped it out and saved it. As it is, I can only hope I remember it fairly accurately. There was a group of people who wanted a particular dictionary removed from the shelves of the local library because it contained a lot of obscenity. I think they said there were sixty-five or so dirty words in it. Some poor woman who was acting as a spokesman for the group had a list of offending words, which she started to read aloud at a hearing. She managed to read about twenty of them before she started sobbing uncontrollably and couldn't continue.
>
> Thomas H. Middleton, "The Magic Power of Words"

Unlike the Kennedy excerpt, this one has relatively uncomplicated sentences. Three of them—the fourth, sixth, and seventh—are loose rather than periodic. The passage includes two contractions, *I'd* and *couldn't,* one casual expression, *a lot of,* and the pronoun *I.* Most of the words are very short, and none would be out of place in an ordinary conversation.

Formal–Informal Level   As life has become less formal, informal diction has become increasingly widespread. Today many articles and books, even ones on relatively serious topics, mix informal and formal elements. Following is an example:

> A lot of people like really loud music. Concertgoers talk about a special state of consciousness, a sense of thrills and excitement, when the music is really loud—over 115 dB. We don't yet know why this is so. Part of the reason may be related to the fact that loud music saturates the auditory system, causing neurons to fire at their maximum rate. When many, many neurons are maximally firing, this could cause an emergent property, a brain state qualitatively different from when they are firing at normal rates. Still, some people like loud music, and some people don't.
>
> Daniel J. Levitin, *This is Your Brain on Music: The Science of a Human Obsession.*

The sentence structure is varied, with most sentences loose. Phrases like "many, many," "really loud music," and "thrills and excitement" suggest a more informal style. Yet phrases like "saturates," "auditory system, "causing neurons to fir at their maximum rate" indicate a formal and possibly technical diction. The last sentence uses parallel phrases that feel formal but are offset by informal language like "still" and "loud music."

Mixing formal and informal diction can result in some ridiculous sentences, as in the following example. "*The national debt poses extraordinary political challenges for a nation too long use to 'cruising easy street.'*" The slang at the end is jarring and undercuts the seriousness of the rest of the sentence. Mixed levels need to be used carefully.

Technical Level   A specialist writing for others in the same field or for sophisticated nonspecialists writes on the technical level. Technical language uses specialized words that may be unfamiliar to a general audience. Its sentences tend to be long and complex, but unlike formal diction it doesn't lean toward periodic sentences, parallelism, and balance. Read this example on neurotransmitters.

> Once the neurotransmitter is released from the neurotransmitter vesicles of the presynaptic membrane, the normal movement of molecules should be directed to receptor sites located on the postsynaptic membrane. However, in certain disease states, the flow of the neurotransmitter is defective. For example, in depression, the flow of the inhibitory neurotransmitter serotonin is defective, and molecules flow back to their originating site (the presynaptic membrane) instead of to receptors on the postsynaptic membrane that will transmit the impulse to a nearby neuron.
>
> Encyclopedia of Mental Disorders, "Neurotransmitters"

Note the specialized vocabulary—*vesicles, presynaptic membrane, postsynaptic, serotonin, receptors*—as well as the length and complexity of the sentences.

Every field has *jargon*, specialized terms or inside talk that provides convenient shorthand for communication among its members. For an audience of biologists, you may write that two organisms have a *symbiotic relationship*, meaning "mutually beneficial;" for psychology majors, you might use *catalepsy* instead of "a temporary loss of consciousness and feeling, often accompanied by muscular rigidity." As a general rule, use technical terms only if your audience will know their meanings. If you must use unfamiliar words when writing for a general audience, define them the first time they appear.

EXERCISE   *Identify the level of diction in each of the following passages. Support your answers with examples from the passages. Point out slang or colloquial expressions.*

1. We may now recapitulate the reasons which have made it necessary to substitute "space-time" for space and time. The old separation of space and time rested upon the belief that there was no ambiguity in saying that two events in distant places happened at the same time; consequently it was thought that we could describe the topography of the universe at a given instant in purely spatial terms. But now that simultaneity has become relative to a particular observer, this is no longer possible.

   Bertrand Russell, *The ABC of Relativity*

2. In some ways I am an exceptionally privileged woman of thirty-seven. I am in the room of a private, legal abortion hospital, where a surgeon, a friend of many years, is waiting for me in the operating room. I am only five weeks pregnant. Last week I walked out of another hospital, unaborted, because I had suddenly changed my mind. I have a husband who cares for me. He yells because my indecisiveness makes

him anxious, but basically he has permitted the final choice to rest in my hands: "It would be very tough, especially for you, and it is absolutely insane, but yes, we could have another baby." I have a mother who cares. I have two young sons, whose small faces are the most moving arguments I have against going through with this abortion. I have a doctorate in psychology which, among other advantages, assures me of the professional courtesy of special passes in hospitals, passes that at this moment enable my husband and my mother to stand in my room at a nonvisiting hour and yell at each other over my head while I sob.

Magda Denes, In Necessity and Sorrow: Life and Death in an Abortion Hospital

3. I have just spent two days with Edward T. Hall, an anthropologist, watching thousands of my fellow New Yorkers short-circuiting themselves into hot little twitching death balls with jolts of their own adrenalin. Dr. Hall says it is overcrowding that does it. Overcrowding gets the adrenalin going, and the adrenalin gets them queer, autistic, sadistic, barren, batty, sloppy, hot-in-the-pants, charred-in-the-flankers, leering, puling, numb—the usual in New York, in other words, and God knows where else. Dr. Hall has the theory that overcrowding has already thrown New York into a state of behavioral sink. Behavioral sink is a term from ethology, which is the study of how animals relate to their environment. Among animals, the sink winds up with a "population collapse" or "massive die-off." O rotten Gotham.

Tom Wolfe, The Pump House Gang

◉━ Watch the Video on Tone

Establishing the Intended Tone

"That paperback sucked." "That tome was a real page turner." "The novel lacked engaging characters." These three sentences may have the same evaluation of a novel, but they vary significantly in their tone and the probable impact they will have on readers. Tone reveals the author's attitude toward the topic and the reader. All writing has a tone that stems from the meaning and connotation of words, the sentence patterns, and the rhythm of the prose.

Managing Denotation and Connotation   "PoPo," "fuzz," "cop," "police officer," and "law enforcement officer," all may refer to the person giving you a ticket, but you know that the last two terms might be the better form of address for the situation. The words have the same denotation but differ in their connotation.

The denotation of a word is its direct, essential meaning: what the word always stands for. The word *book*, for example, denotes "a set of printed or blank sheets bound together along one edge to form a volume." This definition is objective and neutral. It does not assign any special value or convey any particular attitude toward the word or what the word stands for. Connotations are the values and emotional associations that accompany a word. When the self-made man snorts "book learnin'" at his better-educated junior partner, he assigns a value and an attitude—that he ranks experience higher than the knowledge gained from books.

Some words—*death*, for instance—almost always carry strong connotations or emotional associations. *Webster's Tenth New Collegiate Dictionary* defines it as "a permanent cessation of all vital functions" or "the end of life," but it means much more. All of us have hopes, fears, and memories about death, feelings that color our responses whenever we hear or read the word. Likewise, we have personal responses to words like *sexy, cheap, radical, politician,* and *mother*. Experience, to a considerable extent, conditions how we think and feel about a word. To an Olympic swimmer who has won a gold medal, *swimming* may stir pleasant memories of the victory and the plaudits that went with it. The victim of a near-drowning, however, might react to the same word with something approaching horror.

Nonetheless, cultural connotations are more important than personal ones. Cultural connotations develop the way individual ones do, but on a much larger scale, growing out of the common experiences of many speakers and writers and changing with usage and circumstances.

Context, the parts of a passage that precede and follow a word, also affects connotation. Note, for instance, the different associations of *dog* in these sentences:

That movie is a real dog.

I sure am putting on the dog!

It's a dog-eat-dog world.

Your dog-in-the-manger attitude makes you very unpopular.

Denotation is sometimes called the language of science and technology; connotation, the language of art. But we need both to communicate effectively. Denotation allows us to convey precise, essential meanings. Connotation adds richness, warmth, and bite.

Objective Tone   An objective tone keeps the writer's personality and opinions out of the message. Following is an example:

> Myopia is a condition of the eye that makes distant vision blurry. In brief, the myopic individual is nearsighted. When the eye is normal, rays of light pass through it and come to focus on the retina, located at the back of the eye. In the myopic eye, however, the rays of light come together a little in front of the retina. As a result, the distant image is not seen clearly.
>
> Janine Neumann

This tone suits a popular explanation of a medical condition. The prose is businesslike and authoritative, the sentence patterns uncomplicated, and nothing reveals the person behind the words.

Other Attitudes   Sometimes you write merely to inform, sometimes to persuade. In persuasive writing, let your attitude toward your topic set the tone. Decide how subtle, flamboyant, or formal your writing should be and what special tone—satiric, cynical, serious, mock pompous, bawdy, playful—will win your reader over.

Every essay has combined characteristics that give it a special tone. The following excerpts illustrate some of tone's many dimensions:

> Unless you have led an abnormally isolated adulthood, the chances are excellent that you know many people who have at one time or another committed an act, or consorted with someone who was committing an act, for which they might have been sent to prison. We do not consider most of these people, or ourselves, criminals; the act is one thing, the criminality of it quite something else. Homicide, for example, is in our law not a crime; murder only is proscribed. The difference between the two is the intention, or to be more accurate, society's decision about the nature of that intention.
>
> Bruce Jackson, "Who Goes to Prison: Caste and Careerism in Crime"

Here we have a sophisticated and rather formal tone. Terms like *consorted* and *proscribed*, while exactly suited to Jackson's meaning, do not form part of most people's word kits. The complexity of the first sentence and the varied patterns of the others add to the air of sophistication. The emphatic *quite*, meaning "entirely," is cultivated usage; and along with *society's decision*, it lends the tone a wry touch.

> Cans. Beer cans. Glinting on the verges of a million miles of roadways, lying in scrub, grass, dirt, leaves, sand, mud, but never hidden. Piels, Rheingold, Ballantine, Schaeffer, Schlitz, shining in the sun or picked by moon or the beams of headlights at night; washed by rain or flattened by wheels, but never dulled, never buried, never destroyed. Here is the mark of savages, the testament of wasters, the stain of prosperity.
>
> Who are these men who defile the grassy borders of our roads and lanes, who pollute our ponds, who spoil the purity of our ocean beaches with the empty vessels of their thirst?
>
> Marya Mannes, "Wasteland"

Rhythm and word choice contribute equally to the tone of this passage. The excerpt opens with imagistic sentence fragments that create a panoramic word picture of our littered roadways. Then complete sentences and somber commentary follow. Words and patterns are repeated, mixing the dignified language of epic and religion with common derogatory terms—*testament, purity, vessels,* and *fruitful* set against *savages, wasters and defile*—to convey the contradictions Mannes deplores. The rhetorical questions, used instead of accusations, add a sense of loftiness to her outrage, helping create a tone both majestic and disdainful.

> *Erethizon dorsatus,* an antisocial character of the Northern U.S. and Canadian forest, commonly called a porcupine, looks like an uncombed head, has a grumpy personality, fights with his tail, hides his head when he's in trouble, attacks backing up, retreats going ahead, and eats toilet seats as if they were Post Toasties. It's a sad commentary on his personality that people are always trying to do him in.
>
> R. T. Allen, "The Porcupine"

The tone of this passage is affectionately humorous. Allen sets this tone by noting the porcupine's tousled appearance, testy personality, and peculiar habits, such as eating outdoor toilet seats (for their salt content, as Allen later explains).

The net effect is to personify porcupines, making them seem like the eccentric reprobate human that others regard with amused toleration.

The final passage begins by referring to a "promissory note:" the Constitution and the promise of life, liberty, and the pursuit of happiness spelled out in the Declaration of Independence.

> It is obvious today that America has defaulted on this promissory note in so far as her citizens of color are concerned. Instead of honoring this sacred obligation, America has given the Negro people a bad check; a check which has come back marked "insufficient funds." But we refuse to believe that the bank of justice is bankrupt. We refuse to believe that there are insufficient funds in the great vaults of opportunity of this nation. And so we've come to cash this check, a check that will give us upon demand the riches of freedom and the security of justice.
>
> Martin Luther King, Jr., "I Have a Dream"

This writing speaks passionately for freedom and justice. Its most obvious rhetorical strategy is metaphor, first the extended one of the promissory note, then brief separate metaphors that make the same point. Eloquence comes through parallelism, repetition, and words like *sacred* and *hallowed*, vividness through figures of speech like "vaults of opportunity." Like George Orwell, Mark Twain, Joseph Conrad, and other masters of tonal effects whose work appears in this book, King uses both rhythm and diction to create a tone that infuses and invigorates his message.

EXERCISE

Characterize the tone of each of the following paragraphs. Point out how word choice, sentence structure, rhythm, and other elements contribute to it.

1. When I awoke, dimly aware of some commotion and outcry in the clearing, the light was slanting down through the pines in such a way that the glade was lit like some vast cathedral. I could see the dust motes of wood pollen in the long shaft of light, and there on the extended branch sat an enormous raven with a red and squirming nestling in its beak.

   The sound that awoke me was the outraged cries of the nestling's parents, who flew helplessly in circles around the clearing. And he, the murderer, the black bird at the heart of life, sat there, glistening in the common light, formidable, unperturbed, untouchable. The sighing died. It was then I saw the judgment. It was the judgment of life against death. I will never see it again so forcefully presented. I will never hear it again in notes so tragically prolonged. For in the midst of protest, they forgot the violence. There, in that clearing, the crystal note of a song sparrow lifted hesitantly in the hush. And, finally, after painful fluttering, another took the song, and then another, the song passing from one bird to another, doubtfully at first, as though some evil thing was being slowly forgotten. Till suddenly they took heart and sang from many throats joyously together as birds are known to sing. They sang under the brooding shadow of the raven. In simple truth they had forgotten the raven, for they were the singers of life, and not of death.

   Loren Eiseley, "The Judgment of the Birds"

2. America, which leads the world in almost every economic category, leads it above all in the production of schlock. Christmas toys broken before New Year's, wash-n-wear suits that neither wash well nor wear well, appliances that expire a month after the guarantee, Barbie dolls, frozen pizza—these are but a few of the shoddy goods whose main contribution to our civilization, apart from a momentary satisfaction to the purchaser, is to swell the sanitary-fill schlock heaps that are the feces of our Gross (and how!) National Product.

> Robert Claiborne, "Future Schlock"

3. Nelson is known as a blues shouter. But it's a misnomer. "Shouter" gives the impression of a singer who attracts attention by uncontrolled screaming. That's not T99. Nelson brings the whole package. He can be as smooth as Jackie Wilson, as nuanced as his friend Percy Mayfield and urgent as Wynomie Harris. Nelson earned his stripes singing a variety of styles, from straight blues and jump blues to big band and swing to R&B and soul crooner. "It all depended on the audience, man," Nelson told me. "Back then some of those white cats couldn't really understand the blues. You had to sing them something they could relate to."

> Jeffrey St. Clair, "Seduced by a Legend."

Special Stylistic Techniques

7.3

Enhance your writing with figurative language and irony.

The style of a piece of writing is its character or personality. Like people, writing can be many things: dull, stuffy, discordant, sedate, lively, flamboyant, eccentric, and so on. Figurative language and irony can contribute to your own distinctive writing style.

Figurative Language

Figurative language uses concrete words in a nonliteral way to create sharply etched sensory images that catch and hold the reader's attention. Besides energizing the writing, figurative language strengthens the reader's grip on the ideas. Five figurative devices are especially important: simile, metaphor, personification, overstatement, and understatement.

Simile and Metaphor   A *simile* directly compares two unlike things by the use of *like* or *as*. "Todd is as restless as an aspen leaf in a breeze" and "Her smile flicked on and off like a sunbeam flashing momentarily through a cloud bank" are similes. A *metaphor* also compares unlike things, but without using *like* or *as*. Some metaphors include a linking verb (*is, are, were*, and so on); others do not. "The moon was a wind-tossed bark" and "The curtain of darkness fell over the land" are both metaphors. Following is an excerpt that contains similes and metaphors:

> The field is a sea of deep, dark green, a sea made up of millions
> of small blades of grass blended together as one. Each blade is a dark
> green spear, broad at the bottom and narrowing to a needle point at the
> tip. Its full length is arched so that, viewed from one end, it looks like a

shallow trough with paper-thin sides. On the inner side of this trough, small ridges and shallow valleys run from base to tip. To a finger rubbed across them, they feel like short, bristly hairs.

Daniel Kinney

Discussion Questions

1. Locate the similes in this passage and explain how they help the reader.
2. Locate the metaphors and point out how each heightens the sensory impact of the writing.

Writers too often snatch hastily at the first similes and metaphors that come to mind and end up strewing their pages with overused and enfeebled specimens. Johnny is "as blind as a bat," Mary runs around "like a chicken with its head cut off"—and the writing slips into trite gear. Other comparisons link items that are too dissimilar. For example, "The wind whistled through the trees like a herd of galloping horses" would only puzzle a reader.

Personification   This is a special sort of metaphor that assigns human qualities or traits to something nonhuman: a plant, an abstraction, a nonliving thing. Following are some examples:

The vine clung stubbornly to the trunk of the tree.

May fortune smile upon you.

The waves lapped sullenly against the base of the cliff.

Each of these sentences assigns its subject a different emotional quality—stubbornness, friendliness, gloom—each figurative rather than literal: Vines aren't stubborn, fortune doesn't smile, and waves aren't sullen.

Personification sometimes extends beyond a single sentence. To illustrate, the following passage carries a single image through two paragraphs:

> "I figured when my legislative program passed the Congress," [Lyndon] Johnson said in 1971, "that the Great Society had a real chance to grow into a beautiful woman. And I figured her growth and development would be as natural and inevitable as any small child's. In the first year, as we got the laws on the books, she'd begin to crawl. Then in the second year, as we got more laws on the books, she'd begin to walk, and the year after that, she'd be off and running, all the time growing bigger and healthier and fatter. And when she grew up, I figured she'd be so big and beautiful that the American people couldn't help but fall in love with her, and once they did, they'd want to keep her around forever, making her a permanent part of American life, more permanent than the New Deal."
>
> Doris Kearns, "Who Was Lyndon Baines Johnson?"

Through personification, Johnson expresses affection for his social program.

Personification works best when it is used in moderation and doesn't make outrageous comparisons. Dishes don't run away with spoons except in nursery rhymes.

Overstatement   Overstatement, sometimes called hyperbole, deliberately and drastically exaggerates in order to make a point. An example is "Wilfred is the world's biggest fool."

One of the best examples of sustained overstatement is Mark Twain's essay "Fenimore Cooper's Literary Offences." In it, Twain claims, "In one place in *Deerslayer,* and in the restricted space of two-thirds of a page, Cooper has scored 114 offences against literary art out of a possible 115." Twain also asserts, "There have been daring people in the world who claimed that Cooper could write English, but they are all dead now." Through such exaggerations, Twain mocks the shortcomings of Cooper's novels.

Used sparingly, overstatement is emphatic, adding real force to an event or situation. Writers who consistently exaggerate, however, risk losing their credibility.

Understatement   Understatement makes an assertion in a humble manner without giving something its due, as when a sportscaster calls a team's 23–2 record "pretty fair." By drawing attention to the thing it appears to slight, this soft-spoken approach offers writers an effective strategy. Here is an example:

> To assume that Heidi Mansfield lacks the qualifications for this position is not unwarranted.

Without ever actually calling Mansfield unqualified, the statement suggests that she is. Similarly, when a meat company executive says, "It is not unlikely that beef prices will jump ten cents a pound in the next two months," we might as well count on spending another dime. As these statements show, understatement not infrequently has an ulterior motive.

EXERCISE

Identify the similes, metaphors, personifications, overstatements, or understatements in these sentences.

1. The old table greedily sucked up the linseed oil.
2. Russia's social and economic system is a giant staircase that leads nowhere.
3. Stanley has the bile of human meanness by the quart in every vein.
4. Their music sounds like the drumming of an infant's fists against the sides of a crib.
5. You're the world's biggest liar!
6. "Fashion, though folly's child, and guide of fools, Rules e'en the wisest, and in learning rules."
7. Einstein's theories have had some impact on modern science.
8. I'm as tired as a farm horse at sunset.

Irony

Irony occurs when a writer intentionally states one thing but actually means something different or even opposite. A certain point is thus highlighted. The sportswriter who refers to the "ideal conditions" for a tennis tournament when rain has drenched the courts and forced cancellation of matches speaks ironically. Here is a longer example of the same sort of irony:

> The baron, though a small man, had a large soul, and it swelled with satisfaction at the consciousness of being the greatest man in the little world about him. He loved to tell long stories about the dark old warriors whose portraits looked grimly down from the walls around, and he found no listeners equal to those that fed at his expense. He was much given to the marvellous, and a firm believer in all those supernatural tales with which every mountain and valley in Germany abounds. The faith of his guests exceeded even his own; they listened to every tale of wonder with open eyes and mouths, and never failed to be astonished, even though repeated for the hundredth time. Thus lived the Baron Von Landshort, the oracle of his table, the absolute monarch of his little territory, and happy, above all things, in the persuasion that he was the wisest man of the age.
>
> Washington Irving, "The Spectre Bridegroom"

Irving never directly states the baron's shortcomings. Rather, suggestive details such as the swelling of the baron's soul, his belief in the supernatural, and his deception by the sponging guests portray one who, far from being "the wisest man of the age," is pompous, superstitious, and gullible.

Eliminating Flawed Diction

7.4

Avoid using flawed diction in your writing.

"Blah, blah, blah." Wordiness, ambiguity, euphemisms, slang, clichés, mixed metaphors, and sexist language can cause your readers to tune you out. As you revise, search out these common culprits and eliminate them if they are causing trouble.

Wordiness

Watch the Animation on **Reducing Wordiness**

Wordiness has more than one cause. Some writers try to sound more impressive, some pad an assignment, and some simply don't realize they're doing it. Whatever the reason, the results are the same: ponderous papers that lack punch. To inject vigor, cut out every word that doesn't serve a purpose. If five words are doing the work of one, drop four.

The two major forms of wordiness, deadwood and gobbledygook, often occur together. *Deadwood*, which does nothing but take up space and clutter the writing, is bracketed in the following sentence:

> Responsible parents [of today] neither allow their children [to have] absolute freedom [to do as they please] nor severely restrict their children's activities.

Now read the sentence without the deadwood:

> Responsible parents neither allow their children absolute freedom nor severely restrict their children's activities.

Careful revision has increased the clarity and reduced the words from 23 to 14.

Gobbledygook consists of long, abstract, or technical words that help create unnecessarily long and complex sentences. Some people who write it mistakenly believe it "dignifies" their thoughts. Others want to conceal their meanings by clouding their statements. And some naively think that long words are better than short ones. All of these writers use gobbledygook, but none of their readers appreciates it. Following are some samples of gobbledygook followed by revised versions in plain English:

Original Version	**Revised Version**
The fish exhibited a 100 percent mortality response.	All the fish died.
We have been made cognizant of the fact that the experiment will be terminated in the near future.	We have learned that the experiment will end soon.

Ambiguity

"The teacher carefully read *a paper* while drinking coffee." Is the teacher reading a newspaper or a student paper? It is important to choose words that are precise enough that the reader isn't left to guess your intent. Ambiguity just makes readers work too hard and can lead to misunderstanding. If you suggest that "someone killed off his employees," it sounds like the person needs to be arrested for murder, even if you meant that he fired them.

Euphemisms

Euphemisms take the sting out of something unpleasant or add stature to something humble. Familiar expressions include *pass away* for *die*, *preowned* for *used*, and *sanitation engineer* for *garbage collector*.

In most cases, the writer simply intends to cushion reality. But euphemisms also have grisly uses. Mobsters don't *beat up* merchants who refuse *protection* (itself a euphemism); they *lean on* them. Hitler didn't talk about *exterminating the Jews* but about *the final solution to the Jewish problem*. These euphemisms don't just blur reality; they blot out images of horror. Of merchants with broken limbs and bloodied faces. Of cattle cars crammed with men, women, and children en route to death camps. Of barbed wire and gas ovens and starved corpses in the millions.

Any euphemism, however well-intentioned, probably obscures an issue. On occasion you may need one in order to protect the sensitive reader, but usually you will serve readers best by using direct expressions that present reality, not a tidied-up version.

Colloquial Language and Slang

Colloquial originally meant "the language of ordinary conversation between people of a particular region." *Slang*, according to *Webster's Tenth New Collegiate Dictionary*, is "an informal nonstandard vocabulary composed typically of coinages, arbitrarily changed words, and extravagant, forced, or facetious figures of speech." These two categories shade into each other, and even authorities sometimes disagree on whether to label a term *colloquial* or *slang*. The word *bender*, meaning "a drinking spree," seems firmly in the colloquial camp, and *bummer*, a term once used by young people to mean "a bad time," is just as clearly slang. *Break a leg* is theater slang used to wish a performer success. But what about *guy* and *kid*? Once they were slang, but so many people have used them for so long that they have now become colloquial.

Regardless of their labels, colloquial and slang terms are almost never appropriate in formal writing. They sometimes serve a useful purpose in informal writing by creating a special effect or increasing audience appeal. Even so, careful writers use them sparingly. Some readers may not understand some colloquial language, and slang usually becomes dated quickly. The following paragraph uses colloquial and slang expressions successfully:

> . . . When I was just a kid on Eighth Avenue in knee pants [Big Bill] was trying to get himself killed. He was always in some fight with a knife. He was always cutting or trying to cut somebody's throat. He was always getting cut or getting shot. Every Saturday night that he was out there, something happened. If you heard on Sunday morning that somebody had gotten shot or stabbed, you didn't usually ask who did it. You'd ask if Big Bill did it. If he did it, no one paid much attention to it, because he was always doing something like that. They'd say, "Yeah, man. That cat is crazy."
>
> Claude Brown, *Manchild in the Promised Land*

Kid, yeah and *cat* reflect the speech of Brown's characters and thus add authenticity to his account. Despite the informal diction, Brown uses parallelism in the second, third, and fourth sentences; repetition of "he was always" emphasizes the single-minded self-destructiveness of Big Bill's behavior. However, this is the exception to the rule, and colloquial language and slang need to be avoided in most writing.

Clichés and Mixed Metaphors

Clichés   Clichés are expressions that have become stale from overuse. Rather than respond to experience with their own perceptions, writers sometimes resort to oft-repeated words or phrases that stem from patterned thinking. Dullness follows. Daily conversation abounds with stale expressions because talk is unplanned, but writing allows you time to find invigorating and effective language. Your individual response is what draws the reader's interest, and only fresh thinking will produce that response. The following list of clichés barely "scratches the surface:"

acid test	burn the midnight oil	green with envy
almighty dollar	chip off the old block	last but not least
beat a hasty retreat	clear as a bell	nipped in the bud
better late than never	cool as a cucumber	rears its ugly head
black sheep	easier said than done	set the world on fire
blind as a bat	goes without saying	sick as a dog

Mixed Metaphors   Clichéd writing often suffers as well from mixed metaphors—inappropriate combinations that startle or amuse the reader. How would you respond if you came across this example?

> When he opened that can of worms, he bit off more than he could chew.

Can you visualize someone chewing a mouthful of worms? The point is obvious.

Sexist Language

((•— Listen to the
Podcast on
**Avoiding Sexist
Language**

Sexist language can assume several guises. Sometimes it appears as unneeded information that dilutes or even demeans someone's accomplishments. It can occur when the writer uses gender-exclusive pronouns like *he* and *she* inappropriately. And it may attach arbitrary gender labels to persons and groups. All U.S. government agencies, most businesses, and most academic publications prohibit sexist language. Deliberate or accidental, such language has no place in your writing. These guidelines will help you avoid it.

1. Don't unnecessarily mention a person's appearance, spouse, or family.

   Sexist: The cute new loan officer at the Godfather Finance Company is a real hit with customers.

   Sexist: Craig Helmond, husband of nationally known cardiologist Dr. Jennifer Helmond, won election to the Beal City Board of Education.

   Sexist: After eight years of attending college part time, Angelica Denham, a three-time grandmother, was awarded a bachelor of science degree.

   Nonsexist: The efficient new loan officer at the Godfather Finance Company is a real hit with customers.

   Nonsexist: Craig Helmond, an accountant at Oakwood Growth Enterprise, won election to the Beal City Board of Education.

   Nonsexist: After eight years of attending college part time, Angelica Denham was awarded a bachelor of science degree.

Note how, in each case, the sentence has been rewritten to include only relevant information.

2. Use the pronouns *he, him, his,* and *himself* only when referring to antecedents that are clearly masculine and *she, her, hers,* or *herself* only when their antecedents are clearly feminine.

   Sexist: Each tourist must carry his passport with him at all times.

   Sexist: If a collector wishes to find an out-of-print book, she should try http://www.bibliofind.com on the Web.

Correct this type of error by substituting plural antecedents and pronouns for the singular ones or by rewriting the sentence to eliminate the pronouns.

Nonsexist: Tourists must carry their passports with *them* at all times.

Nonsexist: Any collector wishing to find an out-of-print book should try http://www.bibliofind.com on the Web.

3. Don't use occupational labels that imply the positions are held only by one sex.

Sexist	Nonsexist
chairwoman	chair
draftsman	drafter
fireman	fire fighter
policeman	police officer
postman	letter carrier
weatherman	weather reporter

A word of caution here. To avoid sexism, some writers substitute the suffix *-person* for *-man* in many job titles (such as *handyperson* for someone who does odd jobs). Such attempts, however, often create awkward expressions that you should avoid.

The following sentences are flawed by wordiness, ambiguity, euphemisms, slang, clichés, mixed metaphors, and sexist language. When you have identified the faults, revise the sentences.

1. The awesome American eagle will never, in the face of foreign threats, pull in its horns or draw back into its shell.
2. Last summer, I was involved in the repair of automobiles.
3. You're seeming as bright as a button this morning.
4. My mother was called to her heavenly reward last winter.
5. Any student wishing to attend summer school at Burns State College must pay his tuition one week before registration day.
6. My brother is in the process of pursuing a curriculum of industrial chemistry.
7. The ball's in your court, and if you strike out, don't expect me to pick up the pieces.
8. The hot, sultry-voiced clerk quickly finished the order.
9. Winning first prize for her essay was a real feather in Peggy's cap.
10. Our company plans to confer retirement on 200 employees by year's end.

Complete additional exercises and practice in your MyLab

Eliminating Flawed Diction

Based on your topic, readers, purpose, and discourse community select the style that is most appropriate.

- Formal—for serious, professional communication
  - More abstract and multisyllabic words, longer and more structured sentences, though varied.
- Informal—for lighter topics or more familiar communication
  - More conversational with ordinary words, looser sentences, some contractions and even colloquial expressions
- Technical—for specifically technical fields and audiences
  - Uses specialized vocabulary for the field, longer and more complex sentences.

Choose the write words.

- Check words you don't know well in the dictionary
- Use the Thesaurus to find alternate word choices
- Determine if your word choices are the right level of concrete/abstract. Most writers need to change more abstract words to concrete and more general words to specific words.

Eliminate Flawed Diction.

- Cut unnecessary words and tighten wordy phrases
- Test for and eliminate ambiguity
- Re-write euphemisms unless the phrases are needed
- Eliminate slang unless required for a deliberate effect
- Rework clichés and mixed metaphors
- Reword any sexist language

CHAPTER 8

Narration: Relating Events

In this chapter you will learn how to:

8.1 Use narrative as a writing strategy.

8.2 Develop and organize your narrative with action, conflict, and point of view.

8.3 Brainstorm the key events of your narrative.

8.4 Integrate dialogue into your narrative.

8.5 Write so that your narrative is ethical.

8.6 Prewrite, plan, draft, and revise your narrative.

Rubberball/Corbis

Clicking off the evening news and padding toward bed, Heloise suddenly glimpsed, out of the corner of her eye, a shadow stretching across the living room floor from under the drawn curtains.

"Wh—who's there?"

No response.

Edging backward toward the table where she left her cell phone, her eyes riveted on the shadow, she stammered, "I–I don't have any money."

Still no answer.

She reached for her phone and started to call 911. Just then . . .

If you want to know more, the above *narrative* has worked. A narrative relates a series of events, whether real such as histories, biographies, or news stories, or imaginary as in short stories and novels. Everyone responds to narratives and shares stories. We gossip about friends, share odd events that happen to us, or report on a story we heard on the news.

Many classroom and on-the-job writing situations call for narratives.

- Your English instructor might ask you to trace the development of a literary character.
- Your history instructor might have you recap the events leading to a major war.
- Your psychology instructor could ask you to report on society's changing attitudes toward the treatment of depression.
- A police officer may record the events leading to an arrest.
- A nurse will have to report on the deteriorating conditions of a patient.
- A manager might prepare a history of an employee work problem.

Purpose

8.1

Use narrative as a writing strategy.

A narrative, like any other kind of writing, makes a point or has a purpose. The point can either be stated or left unstated, but it always shapes the writing.

Some narratives simply tell what happened or establish an interesting or useful fact. The reporter who writes about a heated city council meeting or a lively congressional committee hearing usually wants only to set facts before the public.

Most narratives, however, go beyond merely reciting events. Writers of history and biography delve into the motives underlying the events and lives they portray, while narratives of personal experience offer lessons and insights. In the following conclusion to a narrative about an encounter with a would-be mugger, the writer offers an observation on self-respect.

I kept my self-respect, even at the cost of dirtying my fists with violence, and I feel that I understand the Irish and the Cypriots, the Israelis and the Palestinians, all those who seem to us to fight senseless wars for senseless reasons, better than before. For what respect does one keep for oneself if one isn't in the last resort ready to fight and say, "You punk!"?

Harry Fairlie, "A Victim Fights Back"

Action

Action plays a central role in any narrative. Other writing often only suggests action, leaving readers to imagine it for themselves:

> A hundred thousand people were killed by the atomic bomb, and these six were among the survivors. They still wonder why they lived when so many others died. Each of them counts many small items of chance or volition—a step taken in time, a decision to go indoors, catching one streetcar instead of the next—that spared him. And now each knows that in the act of survival he lived a dozen lives and saw more death than he ever thought he would see. At the time, none of them knew anything.

John Hersey, *Hiroshima*

8.2

Develop and organize your narrative with action, conflict, and point of view.

This passage suggests a great deal of action—the flash of an exploding bomb, the collapse of buildings, screaming people fleeing the scorching devastation— but *it does not present the action*. Narration, however, recreates action:

> When I pulled the trigger I did not hear the bang or feel the kick—one never does when a shot goes home—but I heard the devilish roar of glee that went up from the crowd. In that instant, in too short a time, one would have thought, even for the bullet to get there, a mysterious, terrible change had come over the elephant. He neither stirred nor fell, but every line of his body had altered. He looked suddenly stricken, shrunken, immensely old, as though the frightful impact of the bullet had paralyzed him without knocking him down. At last, after what seemed a long time—it might have been five seconds, I dare say—he sagged flabbily to his knees. His mouth slobbered. An enormous senility seemed to have settled upon him. One could have imagined him thousands of years old. I fired again into the same spot. At the second shot he did not collapse but climbed with desperate slowness to his feet and stood weakly upright, with legs sagging and head drooping. I fired a third time. That was the shot that did it for him. You could see the agony of it jolt his whole body and knock the last remnant of strength from his legs. But in falling he seemed for a moment to rise, for as his hind legs collapsed beneath him he seemed to tower upward like a huge rock toppling, his trunk reaching skywards like a tree. He trumpeted, for the first and only time. And then down he came, his belly towards me, with a crash that seemed to shake the ground even where I lay.

George Orwell, "Shooting an Elephant"

Orwell's account offers a stark, vivid replay of the slaying, leaving nothing significant for the reader to infer.

A few words of caution are in order here. Action entails not only exotic events such as the theft of mass-destruction weapons, then the ransom demand, the recovery of the weapons and the pursuit of the villains. A wide variety of more normal events also qualify as action: a long, patient wait that comes to nothing, an unexpected kiss after some friendly assistance, a disappointing gift that signals a failed relationship. Furthermore, the narrative action must all relate to the main point—not merely chronicle a series of events.

Conflict

 Watch the Video on **Conflict**

The events in our world are often shaped by conflicts that need to be resolved. It should not be surprising then that conflict and its resolution, if any, are crucial to a narrative since they motivate and often structure the action. Some conflicts pit one individual against another or against a group, such as a union, company, or religious body. In others, the conflict may involve either an individual and nature or two clashing impulses in one person's head.

Read the following student paragraph and note how common sense (highlighted in yellow) and fear (highlighted in blue) struggle within the writer, who has experienced a sharp, stabbing pain in his side:

> Common sense and fear waged war in my mind. The first argued that a pain so intense was nothing to fool with, that it might indicate a serious or even life-threatening condition. Dr. Montz would be able to identify the problem and deal with it before it worsened. But what if it was already serious? What if I needed emergency surgery? I didn't want anyone cutting into me. "Now wait a minute," I said. "It's probably nothing serious. Most aches and pains aren't. I'll see the doctor, maybe get some pills, and the problem will clear up overnight. But what if he finds something major, and I have to spend the night in the hospital getting ready for surgery or recovering from it? I think I'll just ignore the pain."
>
> Luis Rodriguez

Point of View

 Watch the Animation on **Point of View**

Narrative writers may adopt either a first-person or third-person point of view. In first-person narratives, one of the participants tells what happened, whereas with third-person narration the storyteller stays completely out of the tale. Narratives you write about yourself use the first person, as do autobiographies. Biographies and histories use the third person, and fiction embraces both points of view.

In first-person narration, pronouns such as *I, me, mine, we,* and *ours* identify the storyteller. With the third person, the narrator remains unmentioned, and the characters are identified by nouns and such pronouns as *he, she, him,* and *her.* These two paragraphs illustrate the difference, using highlighting to draw your attention to the use of first- or third-person:

First-Person Narration

We would go to the well and wash in the ice-cold, clear water, grease our legs with equally cold stiff Vaseline, then tiptoe into the house. We wiped the dust from our toes and settled down for schoolwork, cornbread, clabbered milk, prayers and bed, always in that order. Momma was famous for pulling the quilts off after we had fallen asleep to examine our feet. If they weren't clean enough for her, she took the switch . . . and woke up the offender with a few aptly placed burning reminders.

Maya Angelou, "Momma's Encounter"

As this example shows, first-person narrators may refer to other characters in the narrative by using nouns and third-person pronouns:

Third-Person Narration

In the depths of the city walk the assorted human creatures who do not suspect the fate that hangs over them. A young woman sweeps happily from store to store, pushing a baby carriage along. Businessmen stride purposefully into their office buildings. A young man sulks down the sidewalks of his tenement, and an old woman tugs her shopping basket across a busy thoroughfare. The old woman is not happy: she has seen better days. Days of parks and fountains, of roses and grass, still stir in her memory. Reaching the other side, she stops and strains her neck upward, past the doorways, past the rows and rows of mirror glass, until her eyes rest on the brilliant blue sky so far away. She looks intently at the sky for a few minutes, noting every cloud that rolls past. And the jet plane. She follows the plane with her deep-socketed eyes and for some unexplainable reason suspects danger. She brings her gaze back to earth and walks away as the jet releases a large cloud of brownish-yellow gas. The gas hangs ominously in the air for a while, as if wanting to give humankind just a few more seconds. Then the cloud slowly descends to the surface, dissipating as it goes. By the time it reaches the glittering megalopolis, it is a colorless, odorless blanket of death.

Richard Latta

EXERCISE

Identify the point of view in each of the following excerpts:

1. The bus screeched to a stop, and Pat stepped out of it and onto the sidewalk. Night enveloped the city, and a slight drizzle fell around her as she made her way to Al's office. Turning the corner, she stepped into the dark entryway.

> The receptionist had gone home, so she proceeded directly to the office. She knocked on the door and entered. Al, standing behind his desk and looking out the window, turned toward her with a startled look on his face.
>
> Jennifer Webber

2. In the darkness before dawn I stood on the precipice of a wilderness. Inches in front of my toes, a lava cliff dropped away into the mammoth bowl of Haleakala, the world's largest dormant volcano. Behind me lay a long green slope where clouds rolled up from the sea, great tumbleweeds of vapor, passing through the pastures and eucalyptus forests of upland Maui to the volcano's crest, then spilling over its edge into the abyss.

   Barbara Kingsolver, *High Tide in Tucson: Essays from Now or Never*

Key Events

8.3

Brainstorm the key events of your narrative.

Any narrative includes many separate events, enough to swamp your narrative boat if you try to pack them all in. Suppose you wish to write about your recent attack of appendicitis in order to make a point about heeding early warnings of an oncoming illness. Your list of events might look like this:

Awakened	Ate lunch	Entered building
Showered	Ate breakfast	Greeted fellow
Experienced acute	Opened garage door	employees
but passing pain	Started car	Began morning's work
in abdomen	Drove to work	Felt nauseated
Dressed	Parked in employee	Met with boss
Took coffee break	lot	Underwent diagnostic
Visited bathroom	Returned to work	tests
Experienced more	Began afternoon's	Had emergency
prolonged pain	work	operation
in abdomen	Collapsed at work	
Walked to cafeteria	Was rushed to hospital	

A narrative that included all, or even most, of these events would be bloated and ineffective. To avoid this outcome, identify and build your narrative around its key events—those that bear directly on your purpose. Include just enough secondary events to keep the narrative flowing smoothly. Here's how you might present the first attack of pain:

> My first sign of trouble came shortly after I stepped out of the shower. I had just finished toweling when a sharp pain in my lower right side sent me staggering into the bedroom, where I collapsed onto an easy chair in the corner. Biting my lip to hide my groans, I sat twisting in agony as the pain gradually ebbed, leaving me gray faced, sweat drenched, and shaken. What, I asked myself, had been the trouble? Was it ulcers? Was it a gallbladder attack? Did I have stomach cancer?

This passage convinces, not just tells, the reader that an attack has occurred. Its details vividly convey the nature of the attack as well as the reactions of the victim. As in any good narrative, the reader shares the experience of the writer, and the two communicate.

Dialogue

Dialogue, or conversation, animates narratives, enlivening the action and drawing the reader into the story. Written conversation, however, doesn't duplicate real talk. In speaking with friends, we repeat ourselves, throw in irrelevant comments, use slang, lose our train of thought, and overuse expressions like *you know, uh,* and *well.* Dialogue that reproduced real talk would weaken any narrative.

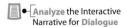

8.4

Integrate dialogue into your narrative.

Good dialogue resembles real conversation without copying it. It features simple words and short sentences while avoiding the over-repetition of phrases like *she said* and *he replied.* If the conversation unfolds smoothly, the speaker's identity will be clear. To heighten the sense of reality, the writer may use an occasional sentence fragment, slang expression, or pause, as in this passage:

Analyze the Interactive Narrative for **Dialogue**

> Mom was waiting for me when I entered the house.
>
> "Your friends. They've been talking to you again. Trying to persuade you to change your mind about not going into baseball. Honey, I wish you'd listen to them. You're a terrific ballplayer. Just look at all the trophies and awards you've . . ." She paused. "Joe's mother called me this morning and asked if you were playing in the game on Saturday. Davey, I wish you would. You haven't played for two weeks. Please. I want you to. For me. It would be so good for you to go and—and do what you've always . . ."
>
> "O.K., Mom, I'll play," I said. "But remember, it's just for you."
>
> Diane Pickett

Note the mother's use of the slang expression "terrific" and of sentence fragments like "your friends" and "for me" as well as the shift in her train of thought and the repetition of "and." These strategies lend an air of realism to the mother's words.

Besides making your dialogue realistic, be sure that you punctuate it correctly. Following are some key guidelines:

- Each shift from one speaker to another requires a new paragraph. ✗
- When an expression like *he said* interrupts a single quoted sentence, set it off with commas.
- When such an expression comes between two complete sentence, put a period after the expression and capitalize the first word of the second sentence. "I know it looks bad," she said. "But I didn't mean to blow up the lab."
- Put commas, periods, and other punctuation marks that come at the end of a direct quote inside of the quotation marks. "What do you want from me?"

Ethical Issues

8.5

Write so that your narrative is ethical.

Think of your response if you were surfing the Internet and came across a narrative about your first date that used your actual name and cast you in an unfavorable light. At the very least you would find it embarrassing. As you mull over any narrative you write, you'll want to think about several ethical issues, especially if you're depicting an actual event.

- Am I providing a truthful account that participants will recognize and accept? Deliberate falsification of someone's behavior that tarnishes that person's reputation is libel and could result in legal action.
- Would the narrative expose any participants to possible danger if it became public? Do I need to change any names to protect people from potential harm? Say your narrative includes someone who cooperates behind the scenes with authorities to help solve a case. You should probably give that person a fictitious name.
- Does the narrative encourage unethical or illegal behavior? For example, extolling the delights of smoking marijuana for a teenage audience is clearly unethical.

These guidelines don't rule out exaggerated, humorous, or painfully truthful narratives. As with any writing, however, narratives can impact the lives of people; as ethical writers we need to consider the possible consequences of our work.

Writing a Narrative

8.6

Prewrite, plan, draft, and revise your narrative.

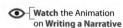 **Watch** the Animation on **Writing a Narrative**

Most of the narratives you write for your composition class will relate a personal experience and therefore use the first person. On occasion, though, you may write about someone else and therefore use the third person. In either case make sure the experience you pick illustrates some point. A paper that indicates only how you violated a friend's confidence may meander along to little purpose. But if that paper is shaped by some point you wish to make—for instance, that you gained insight into the obligations of friendship—the topic can be worthwhile.

Prewriting the Narrative

To get started, do some guided brainstorming, asking yourself these questions:

FINDING YOUR TOPIC
- What experience in my life or that of someone I know interests me?
- Is there an event in my community or history that I would like to relate?
- Who was involved and what parts did they play?
- What main point would you want to make about this event in one or two sentence?

When you have pinpointed a topic, use further brainstorming to generate supporting material. Here are some suggestions:

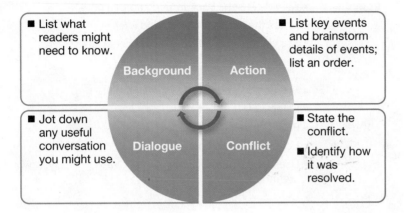

Planning and Drafting the Narrative

Before you start to write, develop a plot outline showing the significant events of your narrative.

For each one, jot down what you saw, heard, or did, and what you thought or felt.

To create a **thesis statement**, ask yourself what was the important lesson from the event. As Brittany Coggin thought about her grandmother, she realized that the most important lesson she taught was the value of the love of the family. The thesis statement, in turn, helps you select the events and details that matter, in Coggin's case, the way the grandmother interacted with her family, even while dying.

Following are suggestions for organizing your narrative:

Introduction
- Sets the stage for what follows.
- Possibly tells when and where the action occurred.
- Provides useful background information.
- Notes the incident that started events.
- States main point here or in the conclusion.

Body
- Moves action forward to turning point.
- Establishes conflict.
- Provides sequence of main events.
- Usually resolves conflict.
- Uses time singals such as "now," "next," "finally," "when I returned" to help reader.
- Uses dialogue.

Conclusion
- Ties up loose ends.
- Gives a sense of completion.
- May include a reflective summary of events, note your reactions, offer a surprise twist, or discuss aftermath.

Revising the Narrative

As you revise, follow the guidelines in Chapter 4. With narratives, it is especially useful to brainstorm details for the events in the narrative or try jotting down additional dialogue. Sometimes it is useful to briefly freewrite about the narrative from someone else's point of view. In addition, ask yourself these questions:

- Have I made the point, stated or unstated, that I intended? What events or wording could strengthen that point?
- What background is missing that the reader might need to better follow the narrative?
- What action does not relate to the main point or could be cut to make the sequence of events stronger?
- How could the order of events or transitions be made clearer?
- What could make the conflict clearer and stronger for the reader?
- What events have been left out that are important to the purpose of the narrative? What details would make the narrative more powerful and interesting? Have time indicators been used where needed, but not excessively?
- Does the point of view work for the reader? Are there any places where it changes and is confusing?

- Where is more dialogue necessary, where does it get in the way, and where does it seem artificial and uninteresting?
- Where could paragraphs be better focused or developed?
- Where could you strengthen the word choice by using concrete verbs and enhance sentence structure?
- What could be done to make the conclusion better provide an interesting resolution to the narration?
- Is the narrative ethical or are there sections that cause misgivings?

STUDENT ESSAY OF **NARRATION**

Joy Through the Tears

Brittany Coggin

1   When I was growing up, there was a plaque in my grandmother's kitchen that read, "Don't get too busy making a living that you forget to make a life." My grandmother certainly followed this precept. Family was the most important thing in the world to her, and my family and I knew that we were loved.

Establishes first person point of view. Uses quote to define main character. States thesis of narrative

2   As a child, I spent most days with my grandmommy while my mother was finishing school. My days were filled with baking cookies, playing games, reading stories, and making our famous mud pies. Grandmommy made time for all of this while working and taking care of all the daily chores around the house. When my mother would arrive to pick me up, it was no surprise for her to walk into the house and see Grandmommy and me prancing through the house banging pans while singing "Jingle Bells," with bright red buckets on our heads. We even called ourselves the "bucket heads."

Establishes context of relationship with grandmother with specific examples to define character

3   My grandmother was a remarkable woman. I have always thought of her as the "center" of my family because she was. Grandmommy held high standards for her children and grandchildren, but she held even higher standards for herself. There was never a time that we did not know where she stood on an issue or where we stood with her. She had a way of holding us accountable while still leaving us in no doubt of her love for us. Although I can recall many times that I disappointed her, there was never a time that my grandmother ever disappointed me. If I thought I was in trouble and might get spanked, I usually was and did. If I thought she would be proud of me, she was. Honesty and integrity were very important to her, and she had both in abundance.

Provides additional context to define relationship and character

Continued on next page

Continued from previous page

Identifies initial conflict

4   Tragedy usually strikes when we least expect it. Nothing could have prepared me for what happened with my grandmother. She was the larger-than-life force who kept our family focused. If ever there was a problem, we took it to Grandmommy, knowing she would be able to point us in the right direction.

Presents event 1 in sequence with detailed accounts

5   The first sign that there was a problem was when she began having excruciating pain in her legs. Her doctor thought it could be neuropathy or nerve damage because she had shingles when she was young. The doctor then sent her to a specialist, who could find nothing wrong. The following months were filled with specialist after specialist who prescribed pain medication after pain medication but could never diagnose the problem. The second clue that there was actually more to the story began when my grandmother complained that every time she ate, it felt as if her chest was on fire, and she would experience a lot of pressure in her chest. Once again, specialist after specialist could find nothing wrong. By this point, my grandmother's weight went from 125 pounds to 85 pounds. Despite the weight loss, our family doctor told her that he could find nothing wrong with her. He told her to take Tylenol and to "go home and live her life."

Presents next major event that intensifies the conflict with the mention of "cancer"

6   Two weeks later, she was so weak that she fell down the porch steps of our family's farmhouse. We rushed her to the hospital in Henderson, Texas. She had broken her ankle, wrist, and both of her hips when she fell. While in the hospital, the doctor ordered a "swallow study" to be completed. My aunt, who is a speech pathologist, knew the speech pathologist doing the study. She asked her to go down lower into the esophagus and to use contrast. That was when we found out that my grandmother's esophagus had completely closed and the opening into the stomach was blocked. Everything she swallowed, including any medication that was prescribed, had gathered at the end of her esophagus. By this time, she was much too weak to have the procedure to open the esophagus. Her doctor sent her to Tyler to have a procedure to remove all of the material in her esophagus and to try alternatives to surgery. During this time, the doctor finally ordered a scan, which revealed that she had lung cancer and that the cancer had metastasized to the bone.

Describes the narrator's first person reaction, how the writer rected to the news

7   This news was shocking to all of us. I had the surreal feeling that I was dreaming and that at any moment, I would wake up and my world would be as it had always been. Instead, the reality was that my world would never be the same again. Grandmommy was devastated but ready to fight. My mom stayed with her the first night in the hospital because she had to

have three rounds of chemotherapy the first night. Mom said that after each round, she and Grandmommy "high-fived." That's my Grandmommy!

8   During this time, amazingly, it was my grandmother who gave us the strength to handle each day. Mom started graduate school that summer, so I would stay with Grandmommy while she was at school. Each day, Grandmommy seemed to lose the use of something. I found that I could handle more than I ever thought possible. I had to learn how to feed her and administer medication through a feeding tube. All I could think about was how I could not possibly do this. It was just too much and too hard. After a while, it became second nature. I can remember putting her false teeth in without thinking twice about it. When she lost all of her hair, we would play with hats and headbands. I would give her a make-over every time she had a doctor's appointment. Even when she began to lose the use of her hands, she cooked dinner for my mother. Grand-mommy was disappointed with how it came out, but my mom said those were the best salmon patties she had ever eaten. That dinner was a labor of love because every step in the process involved immense pain.

Continues sequence of events to reconfirm the positive family centered nature of the grand-mother. Demonstrates transformation of the writer's role

9   While this was a time of loss, it was also a time of happiness. The time I was able to spend with my grandmother drew us closer. Each moment I spent with her seemed suspended in time. Every word, facial expression, and hug became an everlasting memory. Sometimes it seemed that my whole family was in so much pain, and no one could reach out to help each other. My grandmother loved each of us so much, so she reached out to help each family member. Her love enveloped each of us, and it kept us believing that she would get better. I know that love is not tangible, but during this time, Grandmommy could look at me, and I could feel how much she loved me. In the midst of her suffering, she gave me love and comfort. In a sense, she helped prepare me for what was to come.

Develops paragraph 8, showing relationship tied to the main point concerning family love

10   In December 2005, my grandfather was taking Grandmommy to her doc-tor's appointment. After getting in the car, she collapsed and then became unconscious. I rushed to meet my family at the emergency room. When I got there, Grandmommy had regained consciousness but was not getting enough oxygen. My mother explained to her that she had pneumonia, and the doctors wanted to put her on a breathing machine until she got over it. Mom asked her to squeeze her hand if that was okay. Though Grandmommy could not speak, she squeezed my mom's hand to tell her to let the doctors go ahead with the procedure. She then went into a coma that lasted a week.

Event that brings events to crisis point. Confirms the relationship

11   When she awoke, she was terrified. The doctors said that she had a severe staph infection. This scared her because her father died of a

Continued on next page

Continued from previous page

staph infection. Doctors told us she would not be able to live without the breathing machine. Grandmommy had signed an advance directive requesting that she not be allowed to live with such suffering. The days following were miserable. I did not want to lose the one person who truly understood me, but we could not let her suffer. Even without the use of her body, her mind remained alert. We would stand around the bed in her room, and she would look past us with the most beautiful smile on her face. She mouthed that she was tired, and we knew it was time. The following morning, the doctor took her off the breathing machine, and she died with her family around her.

> Culminates sequence of event with death that reconfirms importance of family

12   My grandmother lost her battle with cancer in December 2005. While I still mourn her loss, I feel honored to have known her. Grandmommy's life will always serve as an example of how to live a life that needs no apology. She taught me that love is everlasting and that people are more important than material things. Because of her, I am stronger than I ever thought possible. I am blessed to have had this remarkable woman as my grandmother.

Discussion Questions

1. Identify the point of view of the narrative. Why is that choice of point of view important to this particular narrative?
2. What context did the writer provide before the central conflict of her grandmother's illness? What was the role of this context information?
3. Narratives depend on very specific details. What details best helped develop the character of the writer's grandmother? Why were those details effective?
4. What is the main point of this narrative? What other possible conflicts or themes might the reader have focused on? How would the narrative have to be rewritten to make that point?
5. This narrative uses very little dialogue. Would the narrative have been improved by dialogue? Where could dialogue have been added effectively?

Suggestions for Writing

1. Write a personal narrative about an experience that

   a. altered either your opinion of a friend or acquaintance or your views about some important matter;
   b. taught you a lesson or something about human nature;
   c. acquainted you with some previously unrecognized facet of your character or personality;
   d. brought about a significant change in your way of life.

   Keep in mind all the key narrative elements: purpose, action, conflict, point of view, key events, and dialogue.

2. A *maxim* is a concise statement of a generally recognized truth. Noting the key elements above, write a first-person or third-person narrative that illustrates one of the following maxims or another that your instructor approves:

   a. A little learning is a dangerous thing.

   b. The more things change, the more they stay the same.

   c. Don't judge a book by its cover.

   d. The road to hell is paved with good intentions.

   e. Pride goeth before a fall.

   f. Sometimes too much of a good thing can be wonderful.

   g. Sometimes good intentions have unexpected consequences.

3. Write a third-person narrative based on the following activities:

   a. Interview someone who works in a career area that interests you. Ask them about how they got involved in that area and write a narrative reporting the results.

   b. Find out about the history of a place that you know well and write a narrative about how the place changed.

   c. Interview someone in your class about an important event that made them who they are and write a narrative about that person.

   d. Talk to a small business owner in your area or a leader of a nonprofit group to find out how it got started in your area and write a narrative about that business or group.

STEPPING UP TO **SYNTHESIS**

 Sometimes writers create narratives by weaving together information from different sources. When developing a narrative about some childhood experience, you might supplement your own recollections by asking relatives and friends to supply details that you've forgotten or clear up points that have become hazy. A police officer investigating an accident questions witnesses, examines physical evidence, and uses the findings to draft an accurate report. A historian writing a biography draws upon public documents, newspaper accounts, diaries, notes of other investigators, and—depending on when the subject lived—other material such as newsreels, TV clips, and interviews in order to create a balanced portrait.

Integrating material from several sources into a coherent piece of writing is called *synthesis*. When you synthesize, you reflect on ideas you have found in various sources, establish on your own the connections among those ideas, and then determine how the ideas and connections can advance the purpose of your writing. Thus, synthesis features independent thinking in which *you* evaluate, select, and use the material of others—which, of course, must be properly documented—to further your own purpose. Although synthesis can be challenging and does call for judgment on your part, following an effective procedure can help ensure success.

Prewriting for Your Synthesis   Start by jotting down the main points of information from your sources and identifying where those points agree.

Continued on next page

Continued from previous page

Sometimes accounts of the same event differ. A friend's memory of your childhood experience may differ markedly from your own. A police officer may find that two witnesses disagree about how an accident happened. A historian may discover that public documents and newspapers offer different motives for an action by a biographical subject. When you encounter this type of contradiction, you'll need to weigh each position carefully in order to determine the most believable account.

Critically Evaluating Your Sources Narratives can be one sided or exclude vital information. You should test the narratives of your sources to determine whether they present multiple perspectives on the issue, seem complete enough, or consistent enough with the narratives of other sources. You may wish to deliberately seek out sources representing different perspectives on an event.

Planning and Drafting Your Synthesis As in developing any narrative, arrange your material in a pattern that helps make your point. Let's say, for example, that you're narrating the history of a suburban housing development for low-income families built on land that was formerly owned by a nearby chemical plant and later was found to be contaminated by toxic chemicals. Company officials admit that wastes were buried there but insist that the chemicals were properly contained and posed absolutely no health threat. After stating the company's position, you present the findings of government investigators who analyzed soil samples from the site. These findings revealed that the containers were corroded and leaking and that the wastes included chemicals that attack the nervous system, as well as highly toxic herbicides designed for chemical warfare operations. You conclude that the company is responsible for the serious health problems that now plague the people living in the housing development. Note how the strategy of presenting the company's position early in the narrative lends added force to the point that shapes your writing—company accountability for the health of the housing development's residents.

Getting Started

1. Review a number of articles in your school or local newspaper to develop a sense of journalistic style. Then interview several people about a recent event on campus or at the place you live, and write a narrative that reports the event and draws on the interviews.
2. Read "Momma's Encounter" (in The Reader) and then write a narrative that relates a particular minority experience and incorporates material from any of the three essays.
3. Takes notes from several newspaper accounts of an important or controversial event, and write an account of the event that includes your notes.

Complete additional
exercises and practice
in your MyLab

Writing a Narrative

Prewriting the narrative.

- Identify part of topic if assigned or brainstorm personal experiences or observations for ideas.
- Check to see the topic is ethical and not likely to encourage unethical or harmful behaviors.
- Talk to others to get ideas, more information and for new perspectives.
- Read for information if needed.
- Brainstorm background information, actions, key conflicts and possible dialogue.

Planning the narrative.

- Let main point guide you.
- Identify the key conflict.
- List sequence of events (plot outline).
- Identify point of view: first or third.
- Identify needed context.
- Would the narrative harm any person mentioned if it becomes public?

Drafting the narrative.

- Introduction sets context, provides background, initiates action and may state main point.
- Body develops action in sequence of key event—signals transitions in time.
- Conclusion pulls together narrative and may state main point.
- Is the account being written truthfully and fairly?

Revising the narrative.

- Did you make your main point?
- Does the action fit the main point?
- Are any key events missing?
- Is the point of view appropriate?
- Does the dialogue ring true?

Repeat the process as necessary.

Proofread.

9 Description: Presenting Impressions

In this chapter you will learn how to:

9.1 Use description as a writing strategy.

9.2 Use sensory perceptions to create a dominant impression.

9.3 Determine a vantage point for your description.

9.4 Select and arrange the details of your description.

9.5 Write so that your description is ethical.

9.6 Prewrite, plan, draft, and revise your description.

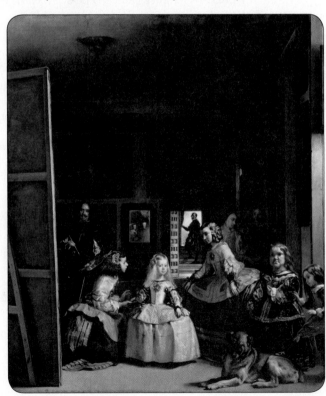

Las Meninas (1656), Diego Rodriguez Velazquez. Oil on canvas, 318 × 276 cm. Museo del Prado, Madrid/Scala/Art Resource , NY

The sound of hot dogs sizzling on a grease-spattered grill gave way to the whirling buzz of a cotton-candy machine. Fascinated, we watched as the white cardboard cone was slowly transformed into a pink, fluffy cloud. Despite their fiberglass appearance, the sticky puffs dissolved on my tongue into a sugar-like sweetness. Soon our faces and hands were gummed with a sticky mess.

You are there. Seeing, hearing, touching, tasting. This is one student writer's *description* of a small segment of a county fair. Effective description creates sharply etched word pictures of objects, persons, scenes, events, or situations. Sensory impressions—reflecting sight, sound, taste, smell, and touch—form the backbone of descriptive writing. Often, they build toward one dominant impression that the writer wants to evoke, impressions that can convey emotions such as shock we experience in response to a description of an abused child.

Many occasions call for description.

- In a lab report for your chemistry class, you might have to describe the odor or appearance of a chemical substance.
- For an art class, you might need to describe a painting.
- For a brochure prepared for your hospitality management class, you might need to describe a banquet room.
- A realtor might write a glowing description of a house for an advertisement.
- A nurse might describe the postoperative status of a surgical incision in her notes on a patient's recovery.

Purpose

Sometimes description stands alone; sometimes it enriches other writing. It appears in histories and biographies, fiction and poetry, journalism and advertising, and even in technical writing. Some descriptions merely create images and mood, as when a writer paints a word picture of a boggy, fog-shrouded moor. But description can also stimulate understanding or lead to action. A historian may juxtapose the splendor of French court life with the wretchedness of a Paris slum to help explain the French Revolution. And everyone knows the persuasive power of advertising's descriptive enticements.

Description will provide effective backup for the writing you do in your composition classes, helping you to drive home your points vividly.

9.1

Use description as a writing strategy.

Sensory Impressions

9.2

Use sensory perceptions to create a dominant impression.

Watch the Animation on **Sensory Details**

Precise sensory impressions begin with close observation. If you can reexamine your subject, do it. If not, recall it; then capture its features with appropriate words. When you can't find the right words, try a comparison. Ask yourself what your subject (or part of it) might be likened to. Does it smell like a rotten egg? A ripe cantaloupe? Burning rubber? Does it sound like a high sigh? A soft rustle? To come across, the comparison must be accurate and familiar. If the reader has never smelled a rotten egg, the point is lost.

Following is a passage marked by particularly vivid sight impressions:

> After our meal we went for a stroll across the plateau. The day was already drawing to a close as we sat down upon a ledge of rock near the lip of the western precipice. From where we sat, as though perched high upon a cloud, we looked out into a gigantic void. Far below, the stream we had crossed that afternoon was a pencil-thin trickle of silver barely visible in the gloaming. Across it, on the other side, the red hills rose one upon another in gentle folds, fading into the distance where the purple thumblike mountains of Adua and Yeha stretched against the sky like a twisting serpent. As we sat, the sun sank fast, and the heavens in the western sky began to glow. It was a coppery fire at first, the orange streaked with aquamarine; but rapidly the firmament expanded into an explosion of red and orange that burst across the sky sending tongues of flame through the feathery clouds to the very limits of the heavens. When the flames had reached their zenith, a great quantity of storks came flying from the south. They circled above us once, their slender bodies sleek and black against the orange sky. Then, gathering together, they flew off into the setting sun, leaving us alone in peace to contemplate. One of the monks who sat with us, hushed by the intensity of the moment, muttered a prayer. The sun died beyond the hills; and the fire withdrew.
>
> Robert Dick-Read, *Sanamu: Adventures in Search of African Art*

At first, the western sky glows with "a coppery fire," which then expands into "an explosion of red and orange" that sends "tongues of flame" heavenward and then withdraws as the sun disappears. Comparisons strengthen the visual impression: the "pencil-thin" stream, the "thumblike" mountains stretching across the sky "like a twisting serpent." The familiar pencil, thumb, and serpent help us to visualize the unfamiliar landscape.

Most descriptions blend several sense impressions rather than focusing on just one. In the following excerpt, Mark Twain, reminiscing about his uncle's farm, includes all five. As you read it, note which impressions are most effective.

> As I have said, I spent some part of every year at the farm until I was twelve or thirteen years old. The life which I led with my cousins there was full of charm, and so is the memory of it yet. I can call back the solemn twilight and mystery of the deep woods, the earthy smells, the faint odors of the wild flowers, the sheen of rain-washed foliage, the rattling clatter of drops when the wind shook the trees, the far-off hammering of woodpeckers and the muffled drumming of wood pheasants in the remoteness of the forest, the snapshot glimpses of disturbed wild creatures scurrying through the grass—I can call it all back and make it as real as it ever was,

and as blessed. I can call back the prairie, and its loneliness and peace, and a vast hawk hanging motionless in the sky, with his wings spread wide and the blue of the vault showing through the fringe of their end feathers. I can see the woods in their autumn dress, the oaks purple, the hickories washed with gold, the maples and the sumachs luminous with crimson fires, and I can hear the rustle made by the fallen leaves as we plowed through them. I can see the blue clusters of wild grapes hanging among the foliage of the saplings, and I remember the taste of them and the smell. I know how the wild blackberries looked, and how they tasted, and the same with the pawpaws, the hazelnuts, and the persimmons; and I can feel the thumping rain, upon my head, of hickory nuts and walnuts when we were out in the frosty dawn to scramble for them with the pigs, and the gusts of wind loosed them and sent them down. I know the stain of blackberries, and how pretty it is, and I know the stain of walnut hulls, and how little it minds soap and water, also what grudged experience it had of either of them. I know the taste of maple sap, and when to gather it, and how to arrange the troughs and the delivery tubes, and how to boil down the juice, and how to hook the sugar after it is made, also how much better hooked sugar tastes than any that is honestly come by, let bigots say what they will.

Mark Twain, Autobiography

EXERCISE

Spend some time in an environment such as one of the following. Concentrate on one sense at a time. Begin by observing what you see; then jot down the precise impressions you receive. Now do the same for impressions of touch, taste, smell and sound.

1. The woods in the early morning
2. A city intersection
3. A restaurant or cafeteria
4. A scenic spot under a full moon
5. A storm
6. A pool or other recreation area
7. A crowded classroom or hallway
8. A construction site
9. A park or playground
10. A holiday gathering

Dominant Impression

Skillful writers select and express sensory perceptions in order to create a *dominant impression*—an overall mood or feeling such as joy, anger, terror, or distaste. This impression may be identified or left unnamed for the reader to deduce. Whatever the choice, a verbal picture of a storm about to strike, for example, might be crafted to evoke feelings of fear by describing sinister masses of clouds, cannon salvos of thunder, blinding lightning flashes, and viciously swirling wind-caught dust.

The following paragraph establishes a sense of security as the dominant impression:

> A marvelous stillness pervaded the world, and the stars together with the serenity of their rays seemed to shed upon the earth the assurance of everlasting security. The young moon recurved, and shining low in the west, was like a slender shaving thrown up from a bar of gold, and the Arabian Sea, smooth and cool to the eye like a sheet of ice, extended its perfect level to the perfect circle of a dark horizon. The

propeller turned without a check, as though its beat had been part of the scheme of a safe universe; and on each side of the *Patna* two folds of water, permanent and sombre on the unwrinkled shimmer, enclosed within their straight and diverging ridges a few white swirls of foam bursting in a low hiss, a few wavelets, a few ripples, a few undulations that, left behind, agitated the surface of the sea for an instant after the passage of the ship, subsided splashing gently, calmed down at last into the circular stillness of water and sky with the black speck of the moving hull remaining everlastingly in its centre.

Joseph Conrad, Lord Jim

EXERCISE

Select one of the following topics and write a paragraph that evokes a dominant impression. Omit details that run counter to your aim.

1. A multi-alarm fire
2. A repair facility (automobile, appliance, and so on)
3. A laboratory
4. Some aspect of summer in a particular place
5. A religious service

6. A doctor's or dentist's office
7. A dark street
8. A parade or other celebration
9. Some landmark on your college campus
10. A municipal night court or small-claims court

Vantage Point

9.3

Determine a vantage point for your description.

You may write a description from either a fixed or a moving vantage point. A fixed observer remains in one place and reports only what can be perceived from there. Here is how Marilyn Kluger describes the Thanksgiving morning sounds she remembers hearing from her bed as a child:

> On the last Thursday in November, I could stay in bed only until the night chill left the house, hearing first the clash of the heavy grates in the huge black iron range, with its flowery scrolls and nickled decorations, as Mother shook down the ashes. Then, in their proper sequence, came the sounds of the fire being made—the rustle of newspaper, the snap of kindling, the rush of smoke up the chimney when Mother opened the damper, slid the regulator wide open, and struck a match to the kerosene-soaked corncobs that started a quick hot fire. I listened for the bang of the cast-iron lid dropping back into place and for the tick of the stovepipes as fierce flames sent up their heat, then the sound of the lid being lifted again as Mother fed more dry wood and lumps of coal to the greedy new fire. The duties of the kitchen on Thanksgiving were a thousand-fold, and I could tell that Mother was bustling about with a quicker step than usual.
>
> Marilyn Kluger, "A Time of Plenty"

A moving observer views things from a number of positions, signaling changes in location with phrases such as "moving through the turnstile" and "as I walked around the corner." Below, H. L. Mencken takes us with him as he observes from a moving express train.

On a Winter day some years ago, coming out of Pittsburgh on one of the expresses of the Pennsylvania Railroad, I rolled eastward for an hour through the coal and steel towns of Westmoreland county. It was familiar ground; boy and man, I had been through it often before. But somehow I had never quite sensed its appalling desolation. Here was the very heart of industrial America, the center of its most lucrative and characteristic activity, the boast and pride of the richest and grandest nation ever seen on earth—and here was a scene so dreadfully hideous, so intolerably bleak and forlorn that it reduced the whole aspiration of man to a macabre and depressing joke. Here was wealth beyond computation, almost beyond imagination—and here were human habitations so abominable that they would have disgraced a race of alley cats.

I am not speaking of mere filth. One expects steel towns to be dirty. What I allude to is the unbroken and agonizing ugliness, the sheer revolting monstrousness, of every house in sight. From East Liberty to Greensburg, a distance of twenty-five miles, there was not one in sight from the train that did not insult and lacerate the eye. Some were so bad, and they were among the most pretentious—churches, stores, warehouses, and the like—that they were downright startling; one blinked before them as one blinks before a man with his face shot away. A few linger in memory, horrible even there: a crazy little church just west of Jeannette, set like a dormer-window on the side of a bare, leprous hill; the headquarters of the Veterans of Foreign Wars at another forlorn town, a steel stadium like a huge rat-trap somewhere further down the line. But most of all I recall the general effect—of hideousness without a break. There was not a single decent house within eye-range from the Pittsburgh suburbs to the Greensburg yards. There was not one that was not misshapen, and there was not one that was not shabby.

H. L. Mencken, "The Libido for the Ugly"

Signals moving observer

Establishes direction

Establishes physical location and its significance

Pinpoints extent of journey

Locates narrator's position and position of the church

Re-establishes extent of journey and description.

Whatever your vantage point, fixed or moving, report only what would be apparent to someone on the scene. If you describe how a distant mountain looks from a balcony, don't suddenly leap to a description of a mountain flower; you couldn't see it from your vantage point.

EXERCISE

1. **Writing as a fixed observer, describe in a paragraph your impressions of one of the following. Be sure to indicate your vantage point.**

   a. A post office lobby two weeks before Christmas
   b. The scene following a traffic accident
   c. A classroom when the bell rings
   d. A campus lounge
   e. An office

2. **Writing as a moving observer, describe in a paragraph or two your impressions as you do one of the following things. Clearly signal your movements to the reader.**

   a. Walk from one class to another
   b. Shop in a supermarket or clothing store

c. Walk from your home to the corner

d. Water-ski

e. Go through a ticket line and enter a theater, auditorium, or sports arena

Selection of Details

9.4

Select and arrange the details of your description.

Effective description depends as much on exclusion as on inclusion. Don't try to pack every possible detail into your paper by providing an inventory of, for example, a room's contents or a natural setting's elements. Such an approach shows only that you can see, not write. Instead, select details that deliberately point toward the mood or feeling you intend to create. Read the following student description:

> At night, a restful stillness falls over the suburbs. . . . Everyone has vanished inside the carefully maintained homes that line the winding streets. The children have gone to bed, leaving the occasional motionless wagon or tricycle in the driveway. A light gleams in some bedroom windows. TV sets silently flicker a tranquil blue in a few living rooms. The street lamps curve protectively over the empty streets and sidewalks. The stillness is only disturbed by the brief, familiar bark of a neighbor's dog, quickly hushed, intensifying in its wake the silence that holds sway with the dark.
>
> Kim Granger

This writer evokes a sense of stillness by noting "the occasional motionless wagon or tricycle," that "TV sets silently flicker a tranquil blue," that "the street lamps curve protectively," that the dog is "quickly hushed." She ignores the car that cruises homeward, stereo booming; the husband and wife screaming at each other; the caterwauling cat fight. Mentioning these things would detract from the desired mood.

Arrangement of Details

Analyze the Interactive Description for **Arrangement**

Description, like any other writing, must have a clear pattern of organization to guide the reader and help you fulfill your purpose. Often some spatial arrangement works nicely. You might, for example, move systematically from top to bottom, left to right, front to back, nearby to far away, or the reverse of these patterns. To describe Saturday afternoon at the football game, you might:

start with crowded parking lot → move into bustling stadium → zoom in on the playing field

For other purposes, you might start with some central feature, then branch out to things around it. To capture the center of a mall, you might:

Sometimes when a writer tries to change, a time sequence makes sense. A writer might portray the changes in a woodland might:

Ethical Issues

Imagine a police description of an auto accident that misstated the length of a car's skid marks or failed to note the icy patches of road at the scene. It might cost a blameless driver a heavy fine and a steep increase in auto insurance premiums. Imagine your disappointment and anger if you booked a weekend at a distant resort only to find it situated on an algae-covered pond instead of the beautiful lake described in the brochure. Imagine your irritation if a going-out-of-business sale described as "fabulous" turned out to offer only 10 percent price reductions. Clearly, inaccurate descriptions can create a wide range of undesirable consequences. Ask and answer these questions about your description.

- Am I making my observations carefully, accurately, and fairly?
- Am I writing so that readers find my writing credible if they were at the scene?
- Am I giving readers adequate clues so that they will recognize any deliberate exaggeration?
- Am I being careful to insure that my description will not deceive readers in a harmful way?

You have an ethical obligation to present a reasonably accurate portrayal of your topic.

9.5

Write so that your description is ethical.

Writing a Description

9.6

Prewrite, plan, draft, and revise your description.

Prewriting the Description

If you're choosing your own topic:

FINDING YOUR TOPIC

👁 ⌐Watch the Animation
   └on **Writing a Description**

- Select something with which you are familiar.
- Review your journal for ideas.
- Talk to friends or post on Facebook to determine what readers may want to know about.
- Look through old photos of trips you have taken, at art, movies, or other points of interest.

To help gather and organize support for your topic,

DEVELOPING YOUR DESCRIPTION

- Determine what you want your description to do: create an impression or persuade a reader to act.
- Identify the interest of your readers—perhaps talk to others.
- Brainstorm additional details.
- Link sensory impressions to details with key words.
- Connect details with the dominant impression you want to make.
- Map the order of your description.

After brainstorming a list of potential details, you might use branching to start accumulating sensory impressions. This illustrates how student writer Kim Swiger used branching to obtain and group the sensory impressions for a paragraph describing the sounds of her kitchen at breakfast time. Note that her grouping provided Swiger with the pattern used to organize her paragraph. Thus, the paragraph begins with stove-related sounds, moves to sounds associated with coffee-making and cooking, and ends with the sounds of mixing orange juice.

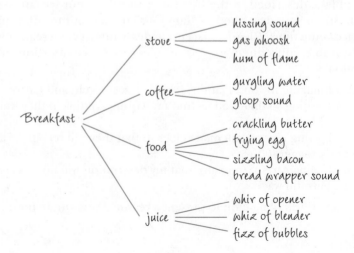

Planning and Drafting the Description

To formulate a **thesis statement**, focus on the dominant impression or what you think the description shows. "Suburban developments, often a joke on TV shows, instead are beautiful parks that can nourish the soul." "In only a few years, a once vibrant community became a visual wasteland." Here is how to organize your paper.

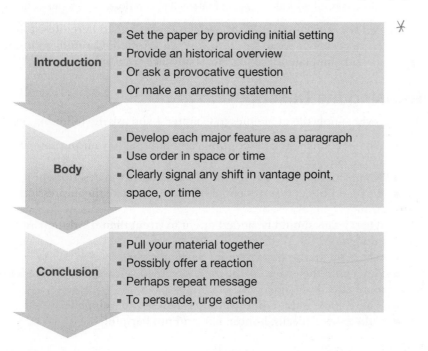

Introduction
- Set the paper by providing initial setting
- Provide an historical overview
- Or ask a provocative question
- Or make an arresting statement

Body
- Develop each major feature as a paragraph
- Use order in space or time
- Clearly signal any shift in vantage point, space, or time

Conclusion
- Pull your material together
- Possibly offer a reaction
- Perhaps repeat message
- To persuade, urge action

As you write, aim for vivid, original language. We've all encountered writers who tell us that raindrops "pitter-patter," clouds are "fleecy white," and the sun is "a ball of fire." Such stale, worn-out language does nothing to sharpen our vision of the rain, the clouds, or the sun. The Swiger paragraph avoids this pitfall.

> Sure signs of a new day are the sounds in the kitchen as breakfast is prepared. The high sigh of the gas just before it whooshes into flame and settles into a whispering hum blends with the gurgling of the water for the morning coffee. Soon the gloop, gloop, gloop of the coffee sets up a perky beat. Then in mingles the crackle of creamy butter on a hot skillet and the shush of an egg added to the pan. Ribbons of bacon start to sizzle in the spitting grease. The soft rustle of plastic as bread is removed from its wrapper contributes to the medley. The can opener whirs, and the orange juice concentrate drops with a splat into the blender, which whizzes together the orange cylinder and splashed-in water. For minutes after the blender stops, bubbles of various sizes fizz.

> Kim Burson Swiger

You are there in the kitchen, hearing the carefully selected and freshly described sounds.

A word of caution about making your writing vivid. Some students are tempted to enhance their descriptions by stringing together a chain of adjectives without considering the effect on a reader. Think how you'd react if told that

A dented, cylindrical, silver-gray, foul-smelling, overloaded trash can sat in the alley.

As you can see, more than the garbage can is overloaded here. Resist the temptation to inject similar sentences into your description. Carefully examine your adjectives and eliminate those that don't advance your purpose.

Revising the Description

As you revise, apply the guidelines in Chapter 4 and ask the following questions:

- What sections of the description can better tie to your purpose and audience?
- Where could additional sensory details add to the description?
- What additional features could be added to make the impression stronger?
- What details should be added or cut to strengthen the dominant impression?
- Where might the vantage point be confusing?
- How could the order for the details be made clearer for the reader or more effectively signaled?
- Where could paragraphs be more focused or developed?
- Is the essay ethically, honest, fair, and not harmful?

SAMPLE

STUDENT ESSAY OF **DESCRIPTION**

My Serenity

Rachel Harvey

1   The building blends in with the landscape, its faint yellow tinsiding disguising it from passersby on the road. As the icicles split-splop from the entryway overhang, one devious droplet sneaks into my shirt to roll down my neck. As I step into the barn, I am bombarded with the musty smell of clay dirt, sawdust, and sweet hay. The air here is more inviting than outside; it beckons me as an old friend would. I know my welcoming committee is in full swing when I hear a faint meow and a

series of whinnies rising up out of the stalls. A large black-and-white barn cat, appropriately named Sylvester for his markings and ability to catch birds, stares at me with his intense yellow eyes. My boots sink into the soft dirt as I wade my way over to the worn, wooden stalls and stoop to pet the oversized feline. I stop at Dynamite Kid's stall to pay him a visit.

Establishes context— moves from outside to inside with writer with details. Includes visual and sound

2   Kid stands a beautiful five feet two inches tall, with his white blond mane and tail and sleek white coat dappled with gray. As I approach him, he starts to dance, or at least a horse's version of dancing. His front legs splayed wide and rocking his weight from side to side, he resembles a flagpole in a gusty storm. I find myself giggling because he thinks I'm going to feed him; he always dances for his food. I slip into his stall and his petal-soft lips scour my hand for his treat. His teeth sound as if they're cutting bolts as he pulverizes the pea-green pellet into bits. I nuzzle up to his soft neck and inhale his aroma. The musk of a horse is unforgettable because it's natural but so unique. This scent brings some of my most treasured memories back. Here I can forget about my ten-page paper that's due Friday and about the fight my significant other and I just had.

Focuses on horse. Continues moving vantage point with writer. Uses multiple senses including sight, sound, feeling, and smell and writer's emotional reaction

3   Everything seeps away from my mind as I snatch a stiff-bristled brush and start grooming him, plumes of dust rising off his back. Here it's only Kid, me, and the rustles and sighs of the other horses in their stalls. Twenty minutes later, once I've lunged and tied him, I head to the tack room to find Kid's equipment. I step into a room full of worn leather, colorful nylon, and jangling metal. I sort out his equipment: a burgundy leather bridle with a jointed bit, matching reins, and chocolate saddle trimmed with burgundy suede. The feel of chafed leather in my hand is a familiar one, both comforting and exciting. I slip the bridle over Kid's head and force the bit between his teeth. He mauls it, trying to get comfortable with the feel and taste of the harsh metal. I heft the heavy woolen saddle blanket and awkward saddle over his back to his withers and cinch it down. After some fine tuning and other adjustments, I'm sitting five foot two taller and making my way out toward the woods.

Focuses on horse. Continues moving vantage point with writer. Uses multiple senses including sight, sound, feeling, and smell and writer's emotional reaction

At the end identifies change of vantage point

4   On top of Kid, I feel as if nothing can touch me. The rich smell of wet, rotting wood and melting snow waft over me as I pick my way through the trees. The dull colors of the landscape contrast with the white snow that is slowly but surely disappearing. The first robins are back: I can't see them, but their fluttering voices reveal their presence. Red squirrels

Starts with clear change of vantage point and writer's emotional reaction

Follows sequence of writer's movements in time and space

Continued on next page

Continued from previous page

are starting to venture out to harvest their stores of nuts, their red fur a sharp distinction from their surroundings. I steer Kid through a small depression. His feet squish into the ground, and I realize a small creek has revived. As I breathe deeply, I inhale the spring breeze picking its way over the fields. Here, spring is a timid but gay being; she will take her time in showing herself, but what she shows is wonderful and can enrapture the most stubborn of souls. I stop and close my eyes.

5   Surrounded by the countryside, I have a sense of peace and tranquility. I try my hardest to stow away this emotion, this feeling of completeness. Nature has always been able to capture my mind and whisk it away from my problems, giving me a temporary relief from the pressures of life. Kid snorts impatiently underneath me. He's eager to continue exploring, but I'm content to just stay here. After a few minutes of serenity, my cell phone blares out an excerpt of a song from George Strait, its noise a searing intrusion, and my head is violently ripped from its retreat. It's my boyfriend. I choose not to answer, trying to prolong my escape, but the spell is broken. I turn Kid back toward the barn and reality.

Marginal notes:

Uses personification, giving inanimate objects the quality of life

Clearly locates setting in countryside and emotional reaction of writer that defines dominant impression of essay

Ends with a contrast of the quiet place and cell phone to end description by a return to the starting place

Discussion Questions

1. Identify details that appeal to each of the senses. Describe the dominant impression these details produce.
2. How is this description organized? Given the purpose of the essay, how effective is this pattern?
3. Where does the writer indicate movement in time and space? Does she keep the reader clearly located?
4. How effectively does the description of the phone call in the conclusion contrast with the rest of the description?

Suggestions for Writing

Choose one of the following topics or another that your instructor approves for a properly focused essay of description. Create a dominant impression by using carefully chosen, well-organized details observed from an appropriate vantage point. Try to write so that the reader actually experiences your description.

1. Holiday shopping
2. A concert of some type
3. An exercise class
4. A crafts class
5. An amusement park, a miniature or full-sized golf course, or some other type of recreational facility

6. A juice bar or coffee shop
7. A pet store or zoo
8. The lobby of a theater
9. A professional wrestling performance
10. A shopping center or minimart
11. A fast-food restaurant
12. Some type of party
13. An outdoor place of special importance to you
14. A Thanksgiving dinner
15. A reunion of some type
16. A NASCAR race
17. A video game arcade
18. An advertisement
19. A scene of environmental damage
20. A historical building or site

STEPPING UP TO **SYNTHESIS**

Most of us know that any two people are likely to see and describe the same object, place or event differently. A motorist whose car broke down in the desert would note the impossible distances, the barrenness, the absence of human life, the blazing sun. A biologist who was well-supplied with food and water would see a rich ecosystem with a wide variety of plant life and an interesting population of insects and animals. Each would produce a different description that served a different purpose. The motorist would emphasize the grueling heat and desolation to establish the danger of the situation. The biologist would provide a detailed description of the plants, insects, and animals to advance scientific understanding of the area.

Prewriting for Your Synthesis As a writer, you may occasionally need to synthesize information supplied by others when creating your own description. Suppose that you're writing a paper about the old growth forests of Oregon. You may read a naturalist's description of the ancient, rare species of trees and how the forest provides a habitat for much unique wildlife. You might also read a lumber industry study indicating that the trees are an important economic resource. You might even uncover an account by an early explorer that captures the emotions aroused by the discovery of the forest.

Critically Evaluating Your Sources Descriptions can be slanted, sometimes in ways that can misrepresent a problem. An account of logging may exclude the new growth in the areas harvested. As you read the descriptions of others, you may want to see how consistent they are with the works of others or your own experience. Where a description seems exaggerated, implausible, or too deliberately slanted to the author's point, you may want to verify it against the work of others.

Continued on next page

Continued from previous page

Planning and Drafting Your Synthesis Armed with these and other descriptions, you could create a composite picture that captures all the different perspectives. You might start by offering the views of the Native American forest dwellers, and then detail the towering majesty of the trees and the abundance of game as reported by early explorers. Next, you might turn to the accounts of early farmers, who regarded the forest as an obstacle to be cleared away, and continue by presenting the view of the forest as a lumber resource, perhaps including a description of a depleted lumbering site. To end the paper, you might note how contemporary conservationists view what remains of the forest. Collectively, this information would offer a stark portrayal of the near-total destruction of a splendid natural resource and by implication argue for preserving what is left. While this kind of writing task seems daunting, you can simplify it if you take up one perspective at a time.

Revising your Synthesis Because different people are likely to see and describe the same object, place or event differently, it's important to look critically at any description you consider for your paper. When you finish reading, ask yourself what features might have been omitted and what another slant on the material might have yielded. To illustrate, in "Once More to the Lake" E. B. White describes early morning fishing as follows: "We went fishing the first morning. I felt the same damp moss covering the worms in the bait can, and saw the dragonfly alight on the tip of my rod as it hovered a few inches from the surface of the water." If White had found fishing repugnant, he could just as easily have described the worms squiggling in the can as if they were afraid of the hook, the slimy feel of his hands after baiting the hook, the swarm of mosquitoes around his face, and the tangle in his line. Clearly, description demands choices. Different impressions and varying emphases can be selected. And like any other writer, you should carefully consider the details and slant of any description you write.

Getting Started

1. Select a famous U.S. landmark, such as the Grand Canyon, and read several writers' descriptions of it. After taking notes, write a description that includes their differing perspectives.
2. Rewrite a different version of "When the Full Moon Shines Its Magic over Monument Valley" (in The Reader) to create a different emphasis.
3. Interview several students to learn their impressions of your campus and weave those impressions into a descriptive essay.

Complete additional exercises and practice in your MyLab

Writing a Description

Prewriting the description.

- Read assignment and select familiar topic.
- Identify your purpose for your description.
- Identify and analyze audience.
- Observe subject of the paper carefully, if possible.
- Make certain your observations are complete and fair.
- Identify the dominant impressions.
- Brainstorm details, possibly using branching.
- Check to be sure your description is ethical and will not harm the reader or others.

Planning the description.

Select an organizational structure:
- Space
- Time
- Importance

Drafting the description.

- Introduction—ease your reader into paper.
- Identify your thesis.
- Develop each major feature in one or more paragraphs.
- Use vivid, detailed language.
- Be sure you ethically represent the scene.

Repeat the process as necessary.

Revising the description.

- Read description critically, collect reader response, re-observe if possible.
- Be consistent with impression.
- Add details as needed.
- Cut details that don't fit.
- Test organization, and make consistent with transitions.
- Review again whether the description is credible.

Proofread.

Process Analysis: Explaining How

In this chapter you will learn how to:

10.1 Use process analysis as a writing strategy.

10.2 Distinguish between processes that readers will or won't perform.

10.3 Write so that your process analysis is ethical.

10.4 Prewrite, plan, draft your process analyses for readers who will perform them.

10.5 Prewrite, plan, draft your process analyses for readers who won't perform them.

10.6 Revise your process analysis.

Paul Mckinnon/Alamy

Drat, you can't get your course software to run at all. After getting out of your browser and trying all over again, you call your school's technical support. The person on the help desk walks you through several steps. She has you check to see if your browser is up to date and compatible with the software. Next, she has you run a diagnostic to determine if you have the appropriate, up-to-date software, including something called Java. You discover that your Java Script is not up to date. The technician then talks you through the steps of going to the web site, indentifying the version appropriate for your computer, downloading the software, and finally eliminating older versions of Java. You try again

As we pursue our affairs, we perform processes almost constantly, ranging from such daily rituals as brewing a pot of coffee to taking a picture, burning a compact disc, preparing for a date, or replacing a light switch. Often we share our special technique for doing something—for example, making chicken cacciatore—by passing it on to a friend.

Many popular publications feature process analyses that help readers to sew zippers in garments, build catamarans, live within their means, and improve their wok technique. Process analysis also frequently helps you meet the writing demands of your courses and future careers.

10.1

Use process analysis as a writing strategy.

- For political science, you may need to explain how your state governor won nomination.
- For biology, you may need to explain how bees find their way back to the hive.
- You may need to explain how to analyze a chemical compound, take fingerprints, or prepare a slide for a lab test.
- As a lab manager, you may have to explain the process of a new technique.
- An IT specialist may need to explain to employees how to use new software.
- A nurse may need to provide home care instructions for diabetes patients.

As these examples show, a process can be technical, nontechnical, historical, scientific, or natural, and it can have audiences with very different levels of expertise.

Kinds of Process Analysis Papers

Process papers fall into two categories: those intended for readers who will perform the process and those intended to explain the process for nonperformers. Papers in either category can range from highly technical and sophisticated to nonspecialized and simple.

10.2

Distinguish between processes that readers will or won't perform.

175

Processes for Readers Who Will Perform Them   The audience for these papers may be technical and professional personnel who need the information to carry out a work-related task or individuals who want to perform the process for themselves.

A how-to-do-it paper must include everything the reader needs to know in order to ensure a successful outcome. Its directions take the form of polite commands, often addressing readers directly as "you." This approach helps involve readers in the explanation and emphasizes that the directions must, not merely should, be followed. Here is an illustration:

> To prepare a bacterial smear for staining, first use an inoculating loop to place a drop of distilled water on a clean glass microscope slide.
>
> Next, pass the loop and the opening of the tube containing the bacterial culture to be examined through a Bunsen burner flame to sterilize them.
>
> From the tube, remove a small bit of culture with the loop and rub the loop in the drop of water on the slide until the water covers an area one and one-half inches long and approximately the width of the slide.
>
> Next, reflame the opening of the culture tube to prevent contamination of the culture, and then plug it shut.
>
> Allow the smear to air dry, and then pass the slide, smear side up, through the flame of the burner until it is warm to the touch. The dried smear should have a cloudy, milky-white appearance.

Darryl Williams

Warning of possible risk.

Feedback on what will be seen with a successful completion.

Watch the Animation on Process Order

Often each separate step is represented as a step in separate paragraphs or a numbered list to make it easier for the reader to see the separate actions that need to be completed. In a process, each step must be signaled by key words that let the reader know a shift took place. The key words are highlighted above in yellow. Also, it is important to provide readers with warnings when there are risks, either from the procedure or in making a mistake, as well as feedback that will let them know if they have been successful, noted above.

Processes for Readers Who Won't Perform Them   These papers may tell how some process is or was performed or how it occurs or occurred. A paper might, for instance, detail the stages of grief, the procedure involved in an operation, the role of speech in the development of children's thinking, or the sequence involved in shutting down a nuclear reactor. These papers serve many purposes—for example, to satisfy popular curiosity; to point out the importance, difficulty, or danger of a process; or to cast a process in a favorable or unfavorable light. Even though the writers of such papers often explain their topic in considerable detail, they do not intend to provide enough information for readers to carry out the process.

Papers of this sort present the needed information without using polite commands. Sometimes a noun, a pronoun like *I, we, he, she,* or *it,* or a noun–pronoun combination identifies the performer(s). At other times, the performer remains unidentified. Three examples follow, using highlight to identify the performer.

Pronouns Identify Performer

Thus, when I now approach a stack of three two-inch cinder blocks to attempt a breaking feat, I do not set myself to "try hard," or to summon up all my strength. Instead I relax, sinking my awareness into my belly and legs, feeling my connection with the ground. I breathe deeply, mentally directing the breath through my torso, legs, and arms. . . . When I make my final approach to the bricks, if I regard them at all they seem light, airy, and friendly; they do not have the insistent inner drive in them that I do.

Don Ethan Miller, "A State of Grace:
Understanding the Martial Arts"

Noun–Pronoun Combination Identifies Performers

Termites are even more extraordinary in the way they seem to accumulate intelligence as they gather together. Two or three termites in a chamber will begin to pick up pellets and move them from place to place, but nothing comes of it; nothing is built. As more join in, they seem to reach a critical mass, a quorum, and the thinking begins. They place pellets atop pellets, then throw up columns and beautiful, curving, symmetrical arches, and the crystalline architecture of vaulted chambers is created.

Lewis Thomas, "Societies as Organisms"

Performer Unidentified

The analyzer was adjusted so the scale read zero and was connected to the short sampling tube, which had previously been inserted into the smokestack. The sample was taken by depressing the bulb the requisite number of times, and the results were then read and recorded. The procedure was repeated, this time using the long sampling tube and sampling through the fire door.

Charles Finnie

EXERCISE

1. Examine your favorite newspaper or magazine for examples of process analysis. Bring them to class for group discussion of which kind each represents and the writer's purpose.
2. Examine science textbooks and professional journals for more complex examples of process analysis. Bring your examples to class and discuss how they differ from simple instructions.

Ethical Issues

10.3

Write so that your process analysis is ethical.

Unclear, misleading, incomplete, or erroneous instructions written for someone to follow can spawn a wide range of unwanted consequences. Often frustration and lost time are the only results. Sometimes, though, the fallout is more serious, as in the case of a lab explosion. And in extreme cases, the outcome can be catastrophic, as when an accident occurs in a nuclear power plant. As writers, we have an ethical obligation to write clear and complete instructions. To help you do this, ask and answer the following questions when you're writing a process that the reader will perform.

- Am I using clear and unambiguous language so that the reader will not encounter unnecessary frustration and inconvenience?
- Am I clearly indicating any requirements such as time needed or additional supplies that will have to be purchased?
- Am I clearly warning readers about any possible harm they could face?

Writing a Process Analysis

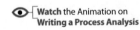
Watch the Animation on
Writing a Process Analysis

As always, when the choice is yours, select a familiar topic. If you're not the outdoor type and prefer a Holiday Inn to the north woods, don't try to explain how to plan a campout. Muddled, inaccurate, and inadequate information will result. On the other hand, if you've pitched many a tent, you might want to share your technique with your readers.

FINDING YOUR TOPIC

- Use the strategies in Chapter 3.
- Select a familiar topic, not something you don't know well.
- List the things you know how to do or have observed.
- Decide why the readers may find the process interesting or useful.
- Decide if you want to provide directions for the reader to follow, explain the process, or explain how others perform it.
- Test to see if it can be explained within the assigned length.

Processes for Readers Who Will Perform Them

Prewriting for the Process Analysis To develop a process for readers to follow:

Prewrite, plan, draft your process analyses for readers who will perform them.

> - Brainstorm the steps and details in the steps.
> - Check to make certain you didn't miss a step.
> - Identify the reasons for each action.
> - Test each action to determine if any warning is necessary to keep readers safe.
> - Build a chart like the one below.
> - Review the chart and add needed material.
> - Group related actions to form steps, the major subdivision of the procedure.

DEVELOPING YOUR PROCESS

Planning and Drafting the Process Analysis When you have your answers, record them in a chart similar to this one:

Action	Reason for Action	Warning
First action	First reason	First warning
Second action	Second reason	Second warning

Sometimes a reason will be so obvious that no mention is necessary, and many actions won't require warnings. When you've completed the chart, review it carefully and supply any missing information. If necessary, make a revised chart.

Once you've listed the actions, group related ones to form steps, or the major subdivisions of the procedure. The following actions constitute the first step—getting the fire going—of a paper explaining how to grill hamburgers:

remove grill rack   light briquets
stack charcoal briquets   spread out briquets

EXERCISE

1. **Develop a complete list of the actions involved in one of the following processes; then arrange them in an appropriate order.**

   a. Registering for class at your college
   b. Assembling or repairing some common household device

   c. Carrying out a process related to sports
   d. Breaking a bad habit
   e. Installing new software from the internet

2. **Examine your favorite newspaper or magazine for examples of process analysis. Bring them to class for group discussion of how they illustrate step-by-step directions.**

The **thesis statement** for a process paper identifies the key process that is being explained and a key point you may want to make about that process. "CPR is easy to perform and can save lives." "Grilling hamburgers outdoors is a simple process." "Geothermal energy is simply a way of using the temperature of the earth to heat or cool a building through very basic techniques."

Introduction
- Identify the process and arouse interest.
- Possibly note importance, usefulness or ease of process.
- Indicate the list of items needed for the work.
- Note any special conditions required for a successful outcome.

The paper explaining how to grill hamburgers might begin as follows:

> Grilling hamburgers on an outdoor charcoal grill is a simple process that almost anyone can master. Before starting, you will need a clean grill, charcoal briquets, charcoal lighter fluid and matches, hamburger meat, a plate, a spatula, and some water to put out any flames caused by fat drippings. The sizzling, tasty patties you will have when you finish are a treat that almost everyone will enjoy.

Discussion Questions

How does the writer try to induce the reader to perform the process?

Use the body of the paper to:

The Body
- Describe the process in detail.
- Present each step in a distinct paragraph clearly and accurately.
- If two steps must be performed simultaneously, tell the reader at the start of the first step.
- In some places, offer feedback to let readers know what to expect if they completed the instructions properly. This lets them know if they are on track.
- Note the reason for each action unless it is obvious.
- Flag with a warning any step that is difficult, dangerous, or in need of special care.
- Check to make certain you included everything readers need.

Let's see how the first step of the hamburger-grilling paper might unfold:

> The first step is to get the fire going. Remove the grill rack and stack about twenty charcoal briquets in a pyramid shape in the center of the grill. Stacking allows the briquets to burn off one another and thus produces a hotter fire.
>
> Next, squirt charcoal lighter fluid over the briquets. Wait about five minutes so that the fluid has time to soak into the charcoal. Then toss in a lighted match. The flame will burn for a few minutes before it goes out. When this happens, allow the briquets to sit for another 15 minutes so that the charcoal can start to burn.
>
> Once the burning starts, do not squirt on any more lighter fluid. A flame could quickly follow the stream back into the can, causing it to explode.
>
> As the briquets begin to turn from pitch black to ash white, spread them out with a stick so that they barely touch one another. Air can then circulate and produce a hot, even fire, the type that makes grilling a success.

Discussion Questions

1. At what points has the writer provided reasons for doing things?
2. Where has the writer included a warning?

Some processes can unfold in *only one order.* When you shoot a free throw in basketball, for example, you step up to the line and receive the ball before lining up the shot, and you line up the shot before releasing the ball. Other processes can be carried out in an *order of choice.* When you grill hamburgers, you can make the patties either before or after you light the charcoal. If you have an option, use the order that has worked best for you.

Conclusion
- Provide a few brief remarks on the process.
- With longer processes, summarize the steps.
- Evaluate the result of the process.

The paper on hamburger grilling notes the results.

> Once the patties are cooked the way you like them, remove them from the grill and place them on buns. Now you are ready to enjoy a mouthwatering treat that you will long remember.

E. M. Pryzblyo

10.5

Prewrite, plan, draft your process analyses for readers who won't perform them.

Processes for Readers Who Won't Perform Them

Prewriting the Process Analysis Like how-to-do-it processes, those intended for nondoers require you to determine the steps—or for natural processes, the stages—that are involved and the function of each before you start to write.

> **DEVELOPING YOUR PROCESS**
>
> - Brainstorm steps, or with natural processes, stages.
> - Since readers won't perform the process, identify your purpose or why readers would be interested.
> - Identify steps that fit that purpose.

Planning and Drafting the Process Analysis If you're trying to persuade readers that the use of rabbits in tests of the effects of cosmetics should be discontinued, the choices you make in developing your steps should reflect that purpose, including some of the painful consequences for the animal.

The thesis statement for a process that won't be performed by the reader often identifies the process and either the main point or the reasons for the reader to know the process. "Children acquire the rules of English in a consistent pattern. Knowing this natural process lets care givers distinguish normal from less common developmental events."

To arouse your reader's interest:

> **Introduction**
> - Offer an historical overview.
> - Or offer a brief summary of the whole process.
> - Or explain its importance.

The following introduction to an essay on the aging of the stars provides a brief historical perspective:

> Peering through their still-crude telescopes, eighteenth-century astronomers discovered a new kind of object in the night sky that appeared neither as the pinprick of light from a distant star nor as the clearly defined disk of a planet but rather as a mottled, cloudy disk. They christened these objects planetary nebulas, or planetary clouds. . . . Modern astronomers recognize planetary nebulas as the fossil wreckage of dying stars ripped apart by powerful winds . . .

Because the reader will not perform the process:

> **Body**
> - The reader will not perform the process, so supply enough details for the understanding that fits your process.
> - Show the function of each stage and how it fits the overall process.
> - Present each stage in a distinct paragraph with clear transitions.

The following excerpt points out the changes that occur as a young star, a red giant, begins the aging process:

> As the bloated star ages, this extended outer atmosphere cools and contracts, then soaks up more energy from the star and again puffs out: with each successive cycle of expansion and contraction the atmosphere puffs out a little farther. Like a massive piston, these pulsations drive the red giant's atmosphere into space in a dense wind that blows with speeds up to 15 miles per second. In as little as 10,000 years some red giants lose an entire sun's worth of matter this way. Eventually this slow wind strips the star down close to its fusion core.

Conclusion
- Provide some perspective.
- Evaluate the results.
- Assess its importance.
- Point out further consequences.

The ending of the essay on star aging illustrates the last option:

> The cloud of unanswered questions surrounding planetaries should not obscure the real insight astronomers have recently gained into the extraordinary death of ordinary stars. In a particularly happy marriage of theory and observation, astronomers have discovered our own sun's fate. With the interacting stellar winds model, they can confidently predict the weather about 5 billion years from now; very hot, with *really* strong gusts from the east.
>
> Adam Frank, "Winds of Change"

Revising the Process Analysis

To revise, follow the guidelines in Chapter 4 and suggestions below:

10.6

Revise your process analysis.

- Have I written consistently for someone who will perform the process or who will merely understand it?
- If my paper is intended for performers, have I included every necessary action, offered reasons where necessary, and provided necessary warnings? Brainstorm briefly to determine additional details that might be necessary.
- Test the process following the instructions to see if they work or help understand the process.
- Are my steps in the appropriate order? Would any other order be more helpful?
- Is my paper ethical?

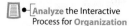
Analyze the Interactive Process for Organization

STUDENT ESSAY OF **PROCESS ANALYSIS**

Basic Songwriting Techniques

Hannah Hill

Tyler Junior College

Faculty Member: Dr. Linda Gary

Establishes reader point of interest. Establishes thesis with main points discussed in paper

1   When listening to a song, one always wonders where the idea of the song comes from. What was the singer thinking, and what provoked him or her to write such a song? Songwriting is a simple technique that anyone can do if they put their hearts into it. Songs are stories put to music through the process of emotion, thought, and rhythm.

Explains parts of how to connect to emotional feelings

Offers concrete practices and clearly marks steps

2   Emotional feelings are important when composing a good song. Start by finding a comfortable place to relax and to think freely. Perhaps a favorite room or an outdoor getaway could rid the mind of distractions. Once settled and comfortable, begin jotting down notes. Focus on feelings and emotions that are current to life or thoughts from the past that weigh heavily on the mind. For example, express how a certain situation feels or affects day-to-day life. Make it either dominantly positive or negative, but avoid mixing the emotions. Allow the mysterious secrets to flow freely. Do not be afraid to let go. Expression of the heart and mind is the most coveted form of music because it is so real. "To take an emotion and make it mean something, take other people into the feeling" is famous country singer/songwriter Kenny Chesney's initial form of songwriting ("Kenny Chesney" 1). He puts his true life on the line to create amazing music for country fans to enjoy. Ultimately, personal experience will always draw the listener in with the passion that comes from loving to write and listen to music.

Offers transition to next step

Foreshadows next step, rhyme, and indicates that the next step should be delayed

Offers sequences for ordering and developing initial idea

3   After putting feelings into words, a clear thought process helps to organize and put these emotions into a clear composition. Don't worry about rhyme scheme yet until all the ideas are put down and arranged. Processing through the jotted notes of life will add organization. This assembling will, in turn, add clarity of understanding for the listener. Add description and detail that brings insight of the writer out to the listener. Although life experience is the best writing utensil, it is not the only one. Add fantasy or exaggeration to liven up and add spice. Be overly emotional in certain and pertinent areas. The most important

Continued on next page

Continued from previous page

situation should show the most drama to the listener. It is common for depressing lyrics to be favored over upbeat ones. For instance, twists and turns are always more interesting than perfectly happy endings. Always remember, less is more. Take out the unnecessary, so there's not an overload of information. Leave mystery to be interpreted by the listener.

4 After modifying thoughts and before moving onto rhyme, put all information in an organized structure. Assembling begins with determining the order of the writing. Pick out the writing and separate it into sections. The first paragraph part becomes the introduction or verse one. Next is the chorus, which will repeat in between each verse. Add the second section, which becomes verse two, and repeat the chorus. If necessary, add a bridge, which is the part that intertwines but differs from the rest of the song. Then repeat the chorus one more time. Organization puts an intellectual tweak on mainstream emotions on which the song is based.

5 Finally, thoughts and feelings are translated into a potential rhythmic pattern. This is where the mainstream thinking turns into a complete thought. The story is then formed into a poetic framework. Manipulate words and sentences to contrast the feelings in the most exciting way. Be sure to avoid clichés, but add interest and uniqueness. Determine a pattern of rhyme as one would in poetry. Rhyming every other line is the most popular style of rhyme, but this is where the exotic twist of the writer can step in. However, avoid overrhyming and nonsense rhyming. Make certain that the rhyme has a reasonable flow. Form the song around individuality. This distinguishing and poetic step perfects the complete thought and finishes the writing step of song formation.

6 Writing songs can be a subtle attempt to make a statement. Songwriting is an emotional release that can be personal to both writer and listener for many different reasons. Writing of any kind should be emotionally sincere and can be very therapeutic for both writer and reader. Honest writing is always the easiest and best procedure. A passionate realization can openly interpret thoughts and feelings in an indescribable way. So get out there, write, and discover the hidden truth.

Work Cited

"Kenny Chesney: Here Comes His Life." *Cincinnati Post* 8 July 2004: T14. Infotrac Newspapers. Web. 20 Sept. 2007.

Margin notes:

Offers transition to next step

Offers concrete actions. Uses verbs at start of sentence to indicate action

Offers transition to next step, rhythm

Offers concrete strategies that might be completed in multiple order

Conclusion summarizes the center of the process—emotional release

Ends by encouraging reader to act

Discussion Questions

1. What is the purpose of this process essay? How does this purpose influence how the process is explained?
2. Identify the key steps the writer recommends for writing a song.
3. Identify places where the writer offers clear warnings.
4. There are many possible ways to write a song, yet the writer only suggests one approach. What are the advantages and disadvantages of this approach?
5. What changes could the writer provide to make this essay even more effective?

Suggestions for Writing

Write a process analysis on one of the topics below or one approved by your instructor. The paper may provide instructions for the reader to follow, tell how a process is performed, or describe how a process develops. Prepare a complete list of steps, arrange them in an appropriate order, and follow them as you write the body of your essay.

1. Observing or researching a natural process, such as erosion
2. Overcoming some particular phobia
3. Explaining the stages in a technical process such as paper production
4. Outlining the stages in a student's adjustment to college
5. Creating a Facebook page
6. Preparing for a romantic picnic in the park, on the beach, or some other place
7. Using a particular computer program
8. Registering for classes online
9. Carrying out a process related to your hobby
10. Placing an item for sale on eBay or bidding on eBay
11. Studying for an examination
12. Performing a process required by your job
13. Performing a process required by one of your classes
14. Breaking a bad habit
15. Performing a weight-training program
16. Throwing a successful party
17. Explaining the stages in some type of storm
18. Describing the stages in a developing friendship
19. Pledging a fraternity or sorority
20. Becoming independent

STEPPING UP TO **SYNTHESIS**

Is there only one way to study effectively, develop a marketing campaign, or cope with a demanding supervisor? No, of course not. As you've already learned, not all processes unfold in a single, predetermined order. The writing process itself illustrates this point.

If you were to think about how you write and talk with other students about their writing processes, you would learn that different writing occasions call for different approaches. When you write a letter to a good friend, you probably spend little or no time on preliminaries but start putting your thoughts on paper as they occur to you. By contrast, other kinds of correspondence, such as inquiry and claim letters, require careful planning, drafting, and perhaps rewriting.

Prewriting for Synthesis Sometimes the same writing occasion may allow for differing procedures so you may need to take notes on multiple kinds of writing people to do. If you're writing an essay for your English class, you might brainstorm for ideas, develop a detailed outline, rough out a bare-bones draft, and add details as you revise. In talking to other students with the same assignment, you might find that they prefer to write a much longer draft and then whittle it down. Still other students might do very little brainstorming or outlining but a great deal of revising, often making major changes in several drafts. Research papers present a more complex challenge, requiring that the student find and read source material, take notes, and document sources properly. Here again variations are possible: One student might prepare the list of works cited before writing the final draft, while another might perform this task last.

Critically Evaluating Your Sources Some important processes have been disputed in print, and if you wanted to investigate them you would need to consult written sources rather than talk to others. Informed disagreements exist about how the human species originated, how language developed, and how children mature. Police officers debate the best way to handle drunks, and management experts determine the best way to motivate employees. When you investigate such controversies, determine which view is supported by the best evidence and seems most reasonable. Then, as a writer, you can present the accounts in an appropriate order and perhaps indicate which one you think merits acceptance.

Planning and Drafting Your Synthesis If you decided to synthesize your findings about student writing practices, you would, of course, need to organize your material in some fashion. Perhaps you might focus on the differences that distinguish one writing occasion from another. You could develop each occasion in a separate section by presenting the practices followed by most students while ignoring variations. A second possibility would be to report different practices used for the same writing occasion, first considering the most common practice and then describing the variations. The result might be likened to a cookbook that gives different recipes for the same dish.

Continued on next page

Continued from previous page

Getting Started

1. Interview several students about the stages they experienced in a developing friendship and write a paper that discusses these stages. Note any discrepancies in the accounts provided by different students.
2. Research the writing process as presented in several first-year composition textbooks; after pointing out how they differ, indicate which process you prefer and why.
3. Research a controversial process, such as the extinction of the dinosaurs. After presenting different theories about the process, explain which one seems most plausible and why.

Complete additional exercises and practice in your MyLab

Writing a Process Analysis

Prewriting the process analysis.

- Select a topic you know well.
- Brainstorm a list of any materials, all steps and any reasons for the steps, any warnings, and any useful feedback.

Planning the process analysis.

- Write out a sequence of steps in their order and double-check them for accuracy.
- Create a table with each step, any reasons, any feedback if available, and any warnings if necessary.

Drafting a process analysis for readers who will perform the action.

- Use the polite implied "you" command.
- Provide an introduction that explains the context for the process.
- Identify the necessary materials.
- Provide steps in sequence with reasons.
- Offer warnings where needed.
- Give periodic feedback so the reader knows if the work is successful.
- Employ clear and unambiguous language.

Drafting a process analysis for readers who will not perform the action.

- Use pronouns, identified performer, or performer unidentified.
- Provide an introduction that engages the reader.
- Provide steps in the process and explain the reasons that they happen.
- Let the reader know the function of each step and stage and how it fits the overall process.

Revising a process analysis.

- Have you rechecked each step, received peer feedback, and revised until satisfactory?
- Have you written consistently for whether the person is performing the action or just understanding it?
- Have you explained all steps, the purpose, and any dangers to insure the safety and success of the reader?
- Are your steps in the appropriate order?

Repeat the process as necessary.

Proofread.

Illustration: Making Yourself Clear

In this chapter you will learn how to:

11.1 Use illustration as a writing strategy.

11.2 Select appropriate examples for your illustration.

11.3 Determine the best number of examples to use.

11.4 Organize the examples of your illustration.

11.5 Write so that your illustration is ethical.

11.6 Prewrite, plan, draft, and revise your illustration.

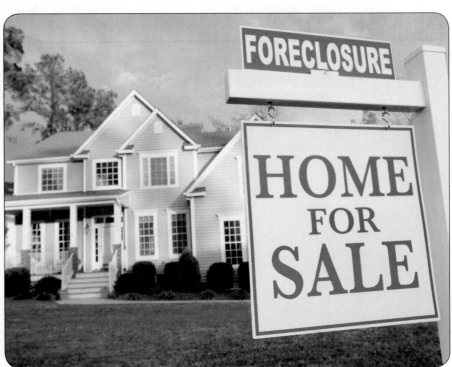

Ariel Skelley/Corbis

"It doesn't pay to fight City Hall. For example, my friend Josie . . ."

"Many intelligent people lack common sense. Take Dr. Brandon . . ."

"Predicting the weather is far from an exact science. Two winters ago, a surprise snowstorm . . ."

People often use examples (*illustrations*) to clarify general statements.

Ordinary conversations teem with "for example, . . ." and "for instance, . . . ," often in response to a puzzled look. A local character, Hank Cassidy, might serve as the perfect example of a "good old boy," or Chicago's Water Tower Place illustrates a vertical shopping mall. But illustration is not limited to concrete items. Teachers, researchers, and writers often present an abstract principle or natural law, then supply concrete examples that bring it down to earth. An economics instructor might illustrate compound interest by an example showing how much $100 that is earning five percent interest would appreciate in 10 years. Examples can also persuade, as when advertisers trot out typical satisfied users of their products to induce us to buy.

11.1
Use illustration as a writing strategy.

Many classroom and job related-writing projects benefit from illustration.

- A paper for a management class can demonstrate effective management techniques by using examples of successful managers.
- A political science paper defining democracy would benefit from examples of several different types of democratic government.
- A literature paper on irony would want to use examples from stories and poems.
- A high school principal writing for a larger counseling staff would use examples of students who needed help and couldn't get it.
- A nurse who advocates for a new method for distributing medication would provide examples of where the current system failed patients.
- A marketing professional arguing for an increased use of social media would use examples of companies that used social media successfully.

Just like you, readers respond to concrete, vivid examples. The concrete is always easier to grasp than the abstract, and examples add flavor and clarity to what might otherwise be flat and vague.

Selecting Appropriate Examples

Make sure that your examples stay on target; that is, that they actually support your general statement and do not veer off into an intriguing side issue. For instance, if you're making the point that the lyrics in a rock group's latest album are not in good taste, don't inject comments on the fast lifestyle of one of its members.

11.2
Select appropriate examples for your illustration.

Watch the Animation on Selecting Examples

Instead, provide examples of lyrics that support your claim, chosen from different songs in the album to head off objections that your examples aren't representative.

Furthermore, see that your examples display all the chief features of whatever you're illustrating. Don't offer a country as an example of a democracy if, despite an election, there is only one party on the ballot and the results are all rigged. Consider the following appropriate student example of someone suffering from depression.

> Carl wasn't just sad. Nothing really bad had happened in his life. But he had lost all interest in his past favorite activities. His skateboard had been discarded in a corner of his room. He no longer bothered to play his video games. Simple things like getting tickets to a rock concert seemed to be too much effort for him. Some days he stayed in bed and missed his classes. Often he irritably snapped at anyone who talked with him. Friends could easily see the difference in him when he shuffled to the dining room, his head down. Without a doubt, Carl was depressed.

This short example meets many of the key characteristics of depression: a lack of interest in normal activities, a sense that ordinary things aren't worth the effort, an inability to attend to ordinary responsibilities, and irritability.

Number of Examples

11.3

Determine the best number of examples to use.

How many examples will you need? One long one, several fairly brief ones, or a large number of very short ones? Look to your topic for the answer.

One Long Example: Topics where traits are combined in a single object

- The qualities of a successful nurse
- The challenges of running a small business
- The excitement of participating in a political campaign.

Several Examples: Historical trends or broader, more general claims

- To show that parents have been raising children more permissively over the last half century, a minimum of three examples are called for: one family from 1955, a second from about 1985, and another from the present.
- To demonstrate the different attitudes of Chinese and American students towards school work, examples would need to include several different children from each culture.

A Large Series of Examples: Very general or very important claims

- To demonstrate that slang arises from many subcultures, examples of many slang words and cultures would be required.
- To demonstrate that individuals abuse Medicare, a writer would need to use many examples to avoid the impression that the practice is not widespread.

EXERCISE

1. **Choose one of the following topic sentences. Select an appropriate example and write the rest of the paragraph.**

   a. Sometimes a minor incident drastically changes a person's life.
   b. _____'s name exactly suits (her/his) personality.
   c. I still get embarrassed when I remember_____.

d. Not all education goes on in the classroom.

e. I learned the value of _____ the hard way.

2. **Explain why you would use one extended illustration, several shorter ones, or a whole series of examples to develop each of the following statements. Suggest appropriate illustrations.**

a. Many parents I know think for their children.

b. The hamburger isn't what it used to be.

c. The ideal pet is small, quiet, and affectionate.

d. Different college students view their responsibilities differently.

e. The hotels in Gotham City run the gamut from sumptuous to seedy.

f. Modern English includes any number of words taken directly from foreign languages.

Organizing the Examples

Your organizational strategy will depend on your topic and the number of examples.

11.4

Organize the examples of your illustration.

A single extended example

- Often follows a narrative, following events in a time sequence such as the busy workday of a small business owner.
- Provides the details spatially or in order of importance, as in an account of the damage that can be done by a tornado.

Multiple examples that try to show degrees of something or change.

- Often in order from least to most or the reverse. Types of sales clerks may go from an example of a hostile clerk, to a pleasant one, to a highly considerate and helpful person.
- Trends offer examples in time. How phones get smarter may go from early rotary dials, to touch phones with Caller ID, to today's smart phones.

A large number of examples

- May be grouped in categories that are arranged in order, such that slang might be organized by words that originate from music, surfing, or teenagers.
- May also be organized by time or by degrees of a quality, as in a paper on the changing ways we work may include multiple examples of different kinds of workers from different time periods.

Sometimes any arrangement will work equally well. Suppose you're showing that Americans are taking various precautions to ward off heart attacks. Although you might move from a person who exercises to one who diets and finally to one who practices relaxation techniques, no special order is preferable.

Large numbers of examples might first be grouped into categories and the categories then arranged in a suitable order. For example, the expressions from the world of gambling could be grouped according to types of gambling: cards, dice, horse racing, and the like. Depending upon the specific categories, one arrangement may or may not be preferable to another.

Ethical Issues

11.5

Write so that your illustration is ethical.

In writing an illustration, we try to show readers something truthful about our understanding of the world. They wouldn't read what we've written if they suspected we were unusually careless in our thinking or knew we were trying to deceive them. Deception may stem from prejudice, which causes people to distort examples. For instance, parents trying to talk their teenager out of a career in acting will probably cite only examples of failed or struggling performers who have miserable lives, and they will fail to mention many successful performers. Such a distortion isn't fair to the acting profession or the teenager. Some distortions can be outright lies. In the past debate about welfare, some commentators wrote about people who lived like millionaires while on welfare. It turned out the examples were falsified, and no real instances of such massive abuse could be found. To avoid ethical pitfalls, ask and answer the following questions:

- Am I giving adequate thought to the point I'll make and the examples I'll use?
- Are the examples supporting my point truthful, or are they slanted to deceive the reader?
- Could my illustrations have harmful consequences? Do they stereotype an individual or group? Do they harm someone's reputation unjustly?
- Will my examples promote desirable or undesirable behavior?

Writing an Illustration

11.6

Prewrite, plan, draft, and revise your illustration.

👁 Watch the Animation on **Writing an Illustration**

Assertions, unfamiliar topics, abstract principles, natural laws—as we've seen, all of these can form the foundation for your paper. If you have a choice, you should experience little difficulty finding something suitable. After all, you've observed and experienced many things—for example, how people can be TV junkies and the ways students manage the stresses of college life. As always, the strategies in Chapter 3 can help generate some possibilities, along with these strategies.

Prewiting for the Illustration

To prewrite for your illustration:

FINDING YOUR TOPIC

- Keep a journal noticing basic patterns or trends you have observed or read about.
- Brainstorm a list of observations you have made about the world.
- Write down some main points you want to make.
- Think about what impact you would want your paper to have on readers.
- Decide if you need one extended example or multiple examples.

Once you have your topic, you can easily develop your illustration.

- Brainstorm a list of examples.
- Brainstorm supporting details for each example.
- Decide which examples and details would be best for your audience.
- Review and add examples and details as necessary.
- Create a chart or use branching as below.

DEVELOPING YOUR ILLUSTRATION

Once you've picked your topic, ask yourself, "What example(s) will work best with my audience?" Then brainstorm each one for supporting details. Use a chart patterned after the one below to help you.

Example 1	Example 2	Example 3
First supporting detail	First supporting detail	First supporting detail
Second supporting detail	Second supporting detail	Second supporting detail

Brainstorming on the difficulty of running a small store.

Drafting the Illustration

A **thesis statement** for an illustration usually states the main point that the rest of the essay demonstrates by example and sometimes adds to the importance the illustration has for readers. The original topic selection will give you a clue for your thesis.

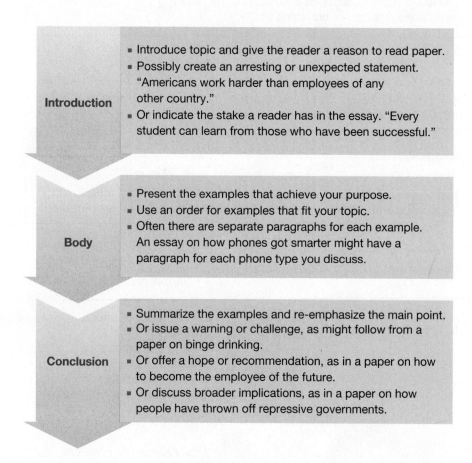

Introduction
- Introduce topic and give the reader a reason to read paper.
- Possibly create an arresting or unexpected statement. "Americans work harder than employees of any other country."
- Or indicate the stake a reader has in the essay. "Every student can learn from those who have been successful."

Body
- Present the examples that achieve your purpose.
- Use an order for examples that fit your topic.
- Often there are separate paragraphs for each example. An essay on how phones got smarter might have a paragraph for each phone type you discuss.

Conclusion
- Summarize the examples and re-emphasize the main point.
- Or issue a warning or challenge, as might follow from a paper on binge drinking.
- Or offer a hope or recommendation, as in a paper on how to become the employee of the future.
- Or discuss broader implications, as in a paper on how people have thrown off repressive governments.

Revising the Illustration

Think about the following suggestions and questions as well as the general guidelines in Chapter 4 as you revise your paper.

- What idea am I trying to present to my reader? Have I chosen the examples that best demonstrate that idea?

- What additional examples or details could make my paper more engaging for my reader?
- What details or choice phrase could make my examples more interesting?
- Do any examples or details fail to fit my main point and distract from the paper and so should be cut?
- How could I organize my paper with transitions or arrange the order of examples that would make my paper easier to read?
- Where could I better focus or develop my paragraphs around key examples?
- Is my paper ethical, with honest examples that are fairly selected?

SAMPLE

STUDENT ESSAY OF **ILLUSTRATION**

If It Is Worth Doing. . . .

Janice Carlton

1   Everyone should keep a slogan in his or her back pocket to pull out at difficult times. Mine may seem a bit ridiculous, but I have found it to be a life saver: "If it is worth doing, it is worth doing badly." This slogan turns my parent's phrase—If it is worth doing, it is worth doing well— completely upside down. To be clear, I am not suggesting that anyone should deliberately do things badly. No one wants to be operated on by a surgeon whose hand shakes. Hopefully, accountants know their subject and offer sound advice. Still, some activities are so worth doing that the fact that we might do them badly is no reason not to take up the task. Far too often we are tempted to give up art because our paintings are bad, avoid writing because our spelling is poor, or avoid helping a friend build a pole barn because we might make mistakes. My slogan reminds me that my possible failure is no reason to avoid a worthwhile project.

2   Consider singing for a moment. Singing can be tremendous fun. A good song can lift the heart. Singing with others can offer a delight-ful sense of sharing. My only problem is that I have a terrible voice. It cracks, soars when it should sink, and rises when it should drop. Usually, I hit the right pitch, but sometimes I have to wiggle into it as though it

Continued on next page

Offers main point of illustration and clarifies that claim. Indicates reason idea is important

Offers a clear thesis in last sentence

Offers first example

Indicates importance of singing to reader

Continued from previous page

were a pair of excessively tight jeans. My more musically gifted friends usually cringe when they hear me sing and mutter something under their breath about "the tone deaf." Should I stop singing just because I do it badly? To me, I sound like a great rock singer, at least when I sing in the shower. Sometimes I sing while I walk from class to class, and I feel, as a result, that I am in an exciting musical. I can even sing with my friends, who only insist that I sing a little more quietly and try, try, try to stay on tune. Probably it would be unfair of me to log in hours at a karaoke bar, and I usually keep from singing around those who tend to stuff their fingers in their ears. But with some reasonable precautions, the fact that I sing badly should not prevent me from enjoying the obvious pleasures of singing.

Ends by tying example to main point

Offers second example

3   Writing poetry is another practice that is worth doing even if we do it badly. What makes poetry worth writing? Writing poetry involves taking time out of the rush of life to reflect on what you're feeling, to perceive more clearly, to hunt for the right word. When it works, you feel like everything in your life has come together.

> As I raced through the forest,
> I stopped to smell a flower,
> a violet, perhaps, a purple pause
> Between home and grandmother's house.
> The flower didn't have any smell,
> But that didn't matter any.
> For a moment, I contemplated
> The breath of a flower,
> And avoided, in the process,
> Meeting any unexpected wolves.

Provides detail to illustrate point

This poem isn't very good, I admit. No one would want to publish it. Most readers may not understand how, feeling like Little Red Riding Hood, I rush from place to place to avoid meeting stray wolves. None of that is the point. When writing the poem, I felt in touch with my life while savoring a creative joy. There is no reason to let anything get in the way of such a delight, not even the poor quality of the resulting poem.

Ends by tying example to main point

Offers a third example that expands the point by extending consequences

4   Of course, it is easy to sing in the shower and write poetry no one ever sees, even if the results, to put it mildly, stink. What about where others are involved? Imagine my predicament when my big brother called and asked me if I would help him put up a pole barn. "Me," I pleaded, "I'm all thumbs." And I meant it, but somehow he needed my help, so despite my complete lack of construction experience,

I chanted my mantra three times and said "yes." For a day I held up beams, sawed boards (sometimes off the measured line), and hammered in nails (bending more than a few). But I did help my brother. He said that he couldn't have done it without me; and while he probably could have built the barn without me, it would have been harder for him. Besides, working side by side for a day, we got to reconnect in ways that I hadn't thought possible. I also learned some construction skills. Without being willing to help badly, I would have missed a tremendous opportunity.

5   There are times when doing something badly is significantly better than doing nothing at all. Our local newspaper featured a story about a hiker who was miles from anywhere on the trail when he came across another hiker who was choking on his lunch. What could he do? He couldn't run for help. He was out of his cell phone region. And he didn't know CPR. What he did know was that the man in front of him was starting to turn blue. He pounded the man on the back, but that didn't work. Finally, in desperation he pushed down underneath the man's rib cage. The pressure popped something out of his windpipe and he started breathing again. The point of the article was the importance of learning CPR, the Heimlich maneuver, and other lifesaving skills. The hiker, of course, knew none of those skills and could have done tremendous damage, perhaps breaking the victim's ribs. Clearly, it would be worthwhile to be expert at lifesaving skills. But what should the hiker have done? If he had just stood there paralyzed by his lack of expertise, the man would have choked to death. Fortunately, he seems to have believed in my slogan and did what was worth doing, saving a life, even if he did it badly.

6   There are lots of pressure in our culture to "leave it to the experts." We can listen to CDs instead of sing ourselves. We can call towing services that are glad to change our flats for us. We can watch soccer instead of play it. With so many skilled people, it is easy to be embarrassed by our own lack of expertise and abandon everything except what we do well. Unfortunately, our lives would be significantly poorer for such a surrender. Instead, we would be better off adapting the adage that "if it is worth doing, it is worth doing badly" and step up to the plate at a softball game, grab a sketch pad and draw what we see, write a poem, sing, cook a meal for a friend. In the end, we have nothing to lose but our false pride.

Margin notes:

Uses narrative organization

Ends by detailing benefit

Offers a fourth example that is the most serious yet in narrative

Ends with important consequence of principle

Conclusion. Reiterates general point

Challenges the reader

Discussion Questions

1. What is the writer trying to illustrate?
2. How is this particular illustration developed?
3. Why did the writer include a poem in her essay?
4. What does the paragraph on the use of CPR add to the essay?
5. In the last paragraph, why does the writer use the pronoun "we"?

Suggestions for Writing

Use one of the following ideas or another that your instructor approves for your illustration essay. Select appropriate examples, determine how many you will use, and decide how you will organize them.

1. "I don't have enough time" is a common complaint of many people today.
2. Many people appear obsessed with exercise (or diet).
3. Incivility has become quite common in public places.
4. New communication technologies help keep friends in close touch.
5. Dedication is the secret of success for many athletes (or use any other field or occupation).
6. Video games can take over people's lives.
7. Sometimes actions can have unintended consequences.
8. Many intelligent people lack common sense.
9. Sleep deprivation is causing problems for many young people.
10. Talk show hosts often leave much to be desired (or stimulate listeners to think).
11. "Doing your own thing" does not always work out for the best.
12. Not to decide is to decide.
13. Today's college student is _____ .
14. Sometimes we need to take risks.
15. Wanting more than we need can be destructive.
16. Many people become obsessed with appearance.

STEPPING UP TO **SYNTHESIS**

When we write an illustration paper, we don't always draw our examples from personal experience. As we reflect on a topic, we may talk with other people and read various source materials to broaden our understanding. We explore differing perspectives and determine the connections between them en route to arriving at our own views and insights.

Prewriting for Synthesis   Take, for instance, the topic of racism in America. "The Scholarship Jacket", "Momma's Encounter", and "I Have a Dream" (in The Reader) offer poignant illustrations of how racism affects people's personal lives. Reading these essays, drawing upon your own observations, and perhaps questioning other students could lead you to an important insight: for example, that racism can have personal effects that are very different from the more widely discussed kinds of institutional discrimination. You might then synthesize others' illustrations and your own to produce a paper that presents this insight.

Critically Evaluating Your Sources   Sometimes illustrations don't reflect reality. An author trying to make the point that many college students are irresponsible might offer examples of students who skip classes, fail to hand in assignments, and party constantly. These examples, however, overlook the many students who hold part-time jobs while taking a full load of classes, participate in professional organizations, and function successfully as spouses, and even parents, while earning good grades. Because published material can paint an inaccurate picture, develop the habit of judging the examples you read in the light of what your knowledge, further investigation, and other sources reveal. Critical thinking is one of the most important skills a writer can cultivate.

Planning and Drafting Your Synthesis   Whether you draw on material from informal resources, conversations, or notes from reading, the process for planning and drafting your synthesis follows a familiar pattern. Determine how many examples you will use to illustrate your point. Check to be sure those points fit. Determine an appropriate order for them and build paragraphs around your key point. For example, if you were trying to illustrate how video games interfere with studying, you might start a paragraph with data from a source followed by your own personal observations. Sometimes in representing conflicting viewpoints, you may want to organize the paper based on those viewpoints leading to the position you support the most. You will need to clearly shift any changes in the point you want to make with effective transitions.

Getting Started

1. Examine the Reader essays on racism cited above. Then, drawing upon examples from the essays and perhaps the observations of minority students you know, write a paper presenting your own conclusions about the personal effects of racism.
2. Read several issues of a magazine such as *Sports Illustrated* or *Working Woman* and determine what the articles suggest about American life. Then write an essay that illustrates your conclusions and incorporates relevant material from the articles.
3. "Pulling Off the Ultimate Career Makeover" illustrates the way people successfully adapted to economic change. Do your own research on how students and others adapt to such change, and write your own essay that supports or disagrees with Douglas Warshaw's account.

Complete additional exercises and practice in your MyLab

Writing an Illustration

Prewriting the illustration.

- Identify and write the key concept or observation to illustrate by reading, talking to others, or jotting down your own observations.
- Identify your purpose.
- Identify your audience.
- Brainstorm examples and supporting details.
- Select the most effective examples.
- Determine if the illustration could have harmful consequences or promote undesirable behavior.

Planning the illustration.

- Decide on the examples to use.
- Decide on an organizational strategy such as order of time, order of climax (least to greatest or the reverse), or by categories.
- Create a rough outline.
- Make certain to give adequate thought to the point you want to make and your examples.

Drafting the illustration.

- Introduction engages the reader and establishes the topic.
- Body provides examples with detail following order.
- Chosen examples are truthful and not slanted.
- Specific, concrete language is used to make the examples vivid.
- Conclusion reestablishes the main point.

Repeat the process as necessary.

Revising the illustration.

- Collect peer responses and reread the illustration critically.
- Check fit to the main point.
- Add examples or details.
- Cut what doesn't work.
- Test organization.
- Test for ethics.

Proofread.

CHAPTER 12

Classification: Grouping into Categories

In this chapter you will learn how to:

12.1 Use classification as a writing strategy.

12.2 Select categories for classification.

12.3 Determine the best number of categories.

12.4 Develop categories with specific details.

12.5 Write so that your classification is ethical.

12.6 Prewrite, plan, draft, and revise your classification.

Elena Schweitzer/Shutterstock

Help Wanted, Situations Wanted, Real Estate, Personal. Do these terms look familiar? They do if you've ever scanned the classified ads of the newspaper. Ads are grouped into categories, and each category is then subdivided. The people who assemble this layout are *classifying.* Figure 12.1 shows the main divisions of a typical classified ad section and provides a further breakdown of one of them.

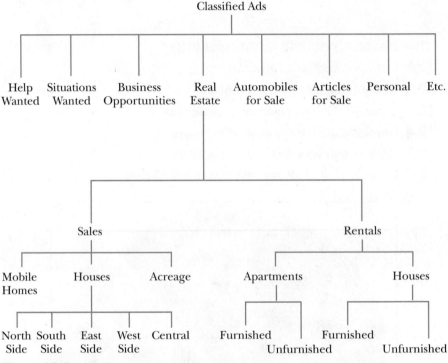

Figure 12.1

As this figure indicates, grouping allows the people who handle ads to divide entries according to a logical scheme and helps readers find what they are looking for. Imagine the difficulty of checking the real estate ads if all the entries were run in the order that the ads were placed.

Our minds naturally sort information into categories. Within a few weeks after their birth, infants can tell the faces of family members from those of outsiders. Toddlers learn to distinguish between cats, dogs, and rabbits. In both cases the classification rests solely on physical differences. As we mature we start classifying in more abstract ways, and by adulthood we are constantly sorting things into categories: dates or mates, eating places, oddballs, friends, investments, jobs, or political views.

Classification also helps writers and readers come to grips with large or complex topics. It breaks a broad topic into categories according to some specific principle, presents the distinctive features of each category, and shows how the features vary among categories. Segmenting the topic simplifies the discussion by presenting the information in small, neatly sorted piles rather than in one jumbled and confusing heap.

Furthermore, classification helps people make choices. Identifying which groups of consumers—students, accountants, small-business owners—are most likely to buy some new product allows the manufacturer to advertise in appropriate media. Knowing the engine size, maneuverability, seating capacity, and gas mileage of typical subcompact, compact, and intermediate-size cars helps customers decide which one to buy. Examining the features of term, whole-life, and endowment insurance enables prospective buyers to select the policy that best suits their needs.

Because classification plays such an important part in our lives, it is a useful writing tool in many situations.

- For an accounting class, you might categorize accounting procedures for retail businesses.
- For a computer class, you may classify computer languages and then specify appropriate applications for each grouping.
- For an industrial hygiene class, you might categorize types of respiratory protective equipment and indicate when each type is used.
- On the job, a state health department employee may prepare a brochure grouping illegal drugs into categories based on their effects.
- A financial advisor might write a customer letter categorizing investments according to their degree of risk.
- An employee at Amazon might list new books under categories that interest readers.

12.1

Use classification as a writing strategy.

Selecting Categories

People classify in different ways for different purposes, which generally reflect their interests. A clothing designer might classify people according to their fashion sense, a representative of the National Organization for Women according to their views on women's rights, and the Secretary of Labor according to their occupations. A college's director of housing might classify students according to their type of residence, the dean of students according to their behavior problems, and the financial aid officer according to their sources of income.

When you write a classification paper, choose a principle of classification that's suited not only to your purpose but also to your audience. To illustrate, if you're writing for students, don't classify instructors according to their manner of dress, body build, or car they drive. These breakdowns probably wouldn't interest most students and certainly wouldn't serve their needs. Instead, develop a more useful principle of classification—perhaps by teaching styles, concern for students, or grading policies.

12.2

Select categories for classification.

👁 Watch the Animation on **Classification and Division**

Sometimes it's helpful or necessary to divide one or more categories into subcategories. If you do, use just one principle of classification for each level. Both levels in Figure 12.2 meet this test because each reflects a single principle: place of origin for the first, number of cylinders for the second.

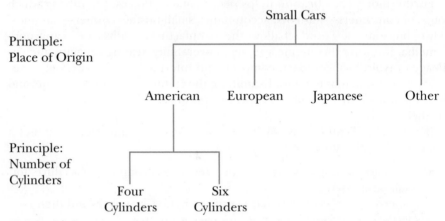

Figure 12.2

Now examine Figure 12.3. This classification is *improper* because it groups cars in two ways—by place of origin and by kind—making it possible for one car to end up in two categories. For example, the German Porsche is both a European car and a sports car. When categories overlap in this way, confusion reigns and nothing is clarified.

Figure 12.3

EXERCISE

1. **How would each of the following people be most likely to classify the families in Anytown, USA?**

   a. The bishop of the Roman Catholic diocese in which the city is located

   b. The state senator who represents the city

   c. A field worker for the NAACP

   d. The director of the local credit bureau

2. **The following lists contain overlapping categories. Identify the inconsistent item in each list and explain why it is faulty.**

Nurses	Pictures	Electorate in Midville
Surgical nurses	Oil paintings	Republicans
Psychiatric nurses	Magazine illustrations	Democrats
Emergency room nurses	Lithographs	Nonvoters
Terminal care nurses	Watercolors	Independents
Night nurses	Etchings	

Number of Categories

12.3
Determine the best number of categories.

Some classification papers discuss every category included in the topic. Others discuss only selected categories. Circumstances and purpose dictate the scope of the discussion. Suppose you work for the commerce department of your state and are asked to write a report that classifies the major nonservice industries in a certain city and assess their strengths and weaknesses. Your investigation shows that food processing, furniture making, and the production of auto parts account for more than 95 percent of nonservice jobs. Two minor industries, printing and toy making, provide the rest of the jobs. Given these circumstances, you'd probably focus on the first three industries, mentioning the others only in passing. But if printing and toy making were significant industries, they too would require detailed discussion.

Developing Categories

12.4
Develop categories with specific details.

Develop every category you include with specific, informative details that provide a clear picture of each one and help the reader grasp the distinctions and relationships among them.

Consider the student example on video games at the end of this chapter. The student does not just identify interactive simulation games as a type of game. She explains how these games are distinctive and provides a detailed example of how the games must be played. "One of the earliest of these games was an arcade game called *Dance Dance Revolution*. It requires players to match on a dance pad the moves they are instructed to do on the screen. . . . The success of this game prompted many others like *Karaoke Revolution* in which players sing popular songs into a microphone for points and *Guitar Hero* and *Donkey Konga* where players play on controllers that emulate a guitar and a set of bongos." By developing the paragraph with different examples of how interactive games are played, she builds a better understanding of that distinctive kind of game.

Ethical Issues

12.5
Write so that your classification is ethical.

Classification can seem quite innocent, and yet it can cause great harm. In India, an entire group numbering millions of people was once classified as "untouchables," and so members of this group were denied the jobs and rights of other citizens. Although political progress has considerably improved the lot of these people, discrimination still hobbles their lives. In this country, many high school students have suffered the sting of being classified as "nerds" or "geeks." Clearly you'll have to evaluate the appropriateness and consequences of your classification scheme. To avoid problems, ask and answer these questions:

- Is my classification called for by the situation? It may be appropriate to classify students in a school environment according to their reading skills, but classifying factory workers in this fashion may well be inappropriate and unfair to the people involved.
- Have I avoided the use of damaging classifications? We resent stereotyping because it unjustly reduces us to some distorted general idea. No one is simply a "hillbilly" or a "jock."
- Have I applied my classification without resorting to overgeneralization? In a paper classifying student drinkers, it would be a mistake, and even harmful, to imply that all college students drink excessively.
- Could my classification promote harmful behavior? When classifying the behavior patterns of young urban dwellers, it would be unethical to present favorably the lifestyle of a group that uses hard drugs and engages in disruptive behavior at sporting events.

We are ethically responsible for the classification systems that we use in our writing. Always examine the one you use for suitability, fairness, and potential harm.

Writing a Classification

12.6

Prewrite, plan, draft, and revise your classification.

Many topics that interest you are potential candidates for classification. If you're selecting your own topic, you might explain different kinds of rock music to novices, take a humorous look at types of teachers, or, in a more serious vein, identify types of discrimination.

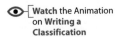

Watch the Animation on **Writing a Classification**

Prewriting for the Classification

FINDING YOUR TOPIC

- Brainstorm areas where you and others make decisions or distinguish between types of things.
- Keep notes on places where people you know make choices.
- Branch from brainstorming why people might be interested in classification of topic.
- Test topic by seeing if you can identify three or more distinct categories.

- List the reasons readers may use classification.
- List real examples of the topic and organize into categories.
- Develop a table like the one below identifying the different categories and the features that distinguish the category.
- Brainstorm examples and details for each category.

DEVELOPING YOUR CLASSIFICATION

Planning and Drafting the Classification

Once you have your details, create an outline or a second map of categories that distinguishes features and details in the order that you want to present them.

Category 1	Category 2	Category 3
First distinguishing feature	First distinguishing feature	First distinguishing feature
Second distinguishing feature	Second distinguishing feature	Second distinguishing feature

A **thesis statement** for classification often, though not always, identifies the reason for the reader to know the classification and the major categories that will be discussed. For example: "The ecofriendly consumer needs to decide between fully electric, hybrid, flex-fuel, and fuel-efficient vehicles, each with their own advantages and challenges." To develop your thesis statement, review your brainstorming on how readers would use your classification and the major categories.

Introduction

- Capture your reader's attention by identifying the reader's interest, as in selecting among a complex range of cell phones.
- Or stress the importance of the topic, as in the types of pollutants affecting our atmosphere.
- Or offer a personal experience that is interesting, as in taking a class with a teacher whose teaching style was wrong for you but right for your friend.
- Provide a thesis that clearly identifies the reason for the paper, the fundamental topic, and major categories.

Body
- Organize the paper by categories in the order that makes sense to you (most common to least common; most fuel efficient to least fuel efficient).
- Clearly signal the shifts from category to category, not with common words like "next" but phrases that show your logic. "Though using traditional fuel rather than electricity, the hybrid".
- Follow a pattern in the paragraphs such as major characteristics of the category.

Conclusion
- Summarize the categories the reader may make with key features, possibly with recommendations.
- Or provide some expectation, like the long-term success of hybrids and flex-fuel vehicles over all electric cars.
- Or offer ways of responding to different categories, such as types of teachers.

Revising the Classification

Revise your paper by following the guidelines in Chapter 4 as well as by employing these questions and strategies:

- How could the purpose and audience for the classification be clearer?
- Where do the categories or how they are presented not fit the audience and purpose and therefore need to be cut or redirected?
- What categories, if any, have been forgotten? Apply the paper yourself to the real world and test to see if it works and then brainstorm.
- Do any of your categories overlap? If so, consider redefining your category or cutting some that don't fit.
- Have you chosen an appropriate number of categories?
- Where could the categories be developed with additional details or examples?
- Are the categories and details arranged in an effective order that will be clear to the reader? Try changing the order in an outline or on computer to see if another order works better.
- Where do paragraphs lack focus or development? Brainstorm to develop or organize paragraphs so there is a clear focus.
- Where could the transitions be made clearer, signaling the actual logic of the order rather than using stock words like "first" or "second."
- Is the project of categorizing or the way the categories are presented ethical?

STUDENT ESSAY FOR **CLASSIFICATION**

Types of Video Games for Children
Kyra Glass

1   Gift-giving for children and grandchildren has been getting increasingly difficult as the number of options increase. Today dolls and toy cars and board games just aren't going to cut it. Many children are used to interactive toys and toys with electronic components. Most children don't think of Monopoly or tag when they hear the word *game;* to them games are played on a television or a computer screen. Indeed, video game consoles in homes with children have become almost as ubiquitous household appliances as televisions. Most parents and grandparents are familiar with demands for *the* hot new game, but buying video games for their loved ones can be overwhelming. Many adults never had video games growing up, or if they did, video games meant *Pac Man*, *Donkey Kong*, or two plumbers named Mario and Luigi. Although these gaming icons are still available, many parents and grandparents are concerned that they are far outnumbered by extremely violent or gruesome video games that they don't want their children playing. Those buying for young gamers may feel that they are stuck, that they will either be unable to buy a game or will end up with a hack-and-slash game that is too violent for younger children. In reality, there is a wide variety of fun and family-friendly games that parents or grandparents can feel good about buying for their young gaming enthusiasts. The easiest way to pick safe games is to check the ratings printed on them; anything that is rated E (for everyone) is safe for children of any age to play; anything rated E 10+ may have some mild cartoon violence but is usually acceptable for most families as well. Games that are rated Teen (T) or Mature (M) are not a good bet for younger children, and parents should research these games before giving them to their children. But checking the ratings is only the first step. There are many different categories of games with options that are appropriate for younger players: interactive simulation games, adventure/role-playing games, party games, and sports games.

2   One of the most common types of games for children or adults is adventure/role-playing games. In these games, players take on the

Continued on next page

Identifies reason for reader's interest

Identifies reader's concern that motivates purpose of essay

States thesis

Transition clearly identifies first category and logic for organization

Identifies distinguishing characteristic

Continued from previous page

persona of a character (or several characters) and work their way through a narrative as that character. Although there are many games of this type that aren't appropriate for younger children, a number of age-appropriate games do fall into this category. The key to finding adventure/role-playing games that are appropriate for younger players is in looking at what story the game tells and who the main characters are. A large number of games in this category are based on characters with which children are already familiar. Some of these are based on both live-action and animated children's movies. *A Series of Unfortunate Events* and *The Incredibles* inspired games of the same name, and a whole series of games based on the popular Harry Potter books and movies have been produced. Many of these games based on movies let the players go through an enhanced version of the plot of the movies or books, letting children interact with their favorite stories. Other games are based on TV cartoons like *Jimmy Neutron*, *Kim Possible*, and *SpongeBob SquarePants*, to name only a few. These games often retain the characters and themes of the shows while inventing a new narrative for players to go through in the game. Many of these games, including *Kingdom Hearts* for Play Station 2 or *Nicktoons Unite!* for GameCube, combine many characters owned by the same company such as Disney or Nickelodeon. However, there are also adventure/role-playing games with well-known and beloved characters from other children's video games. The familiar kid-friendly Mario has a role-playing game called *Paper Mario* and an adventure game called *Super Mario Sunshine*, while older children might enjoy *Sonic the Hedgehog*'s cousin in the adventure game *Shadow the Hedgehog*. When trying to choose an adventure or simulation game for a child, often the best place to start is by picking one of the child's favorite stories or characters from movies, cartoons, and games and seeing if there is a game that features them. It is surprising how often the answer is "yes."

3   In general, the category of sports games is a pretty safe choice when picking games for children. Sports games emulate a version of a sports competition or event for the player's participation. Many different types of games fall into this category: racing games are included here, as are games based on team sports like basketball or football, extreme sports like skateboarding or motorbike racing, and individual sports like skiing or golf. Although there are some sports games that aren't appropriate for children, shoppers can usually find a game rated E for everyone

---

Provides criteria for decision based on reader's interest

Provides examples with details tied to purpose of selecting a game as a gift

Provides criteria for making a choice

Provides transition to next category

Provides distinguishing criteria

in nearly any category of sports. However, although most sports games are appropriate for children, there are also, on every platform, sports games that are made especially for children to play. These games, like the adventure/role-playing games, keep the best aspects of their genre but draw on characters and environments that are familiar to children. Disney's *Extreme Skate Adventure*, on all three platforms, is a skateboarding game that allows children to create their own character or play as a familiar Disney character. They can then skate in environments from *Toy Story 2*, *The Lion King*, and *Tarzan*. Because this game is tailored to children, it allows them to pick objects such as mirrors or frying pans as well as skateboards. This is part of a series of Disney sports games including *Soccer*, *Football*, and *Basketball*, all on GameCube, and *Golf*, on Playstation 2. The ever-present Mario also has his own series of sports games for children, including *Mario Kart* racing games; *Super Mario Strikers*, a racing game; and games based on baseball, tennis, and golf. These sports franchises might be good for younger players because they are often easier to play and use familiar characters, while Madden, Fifa, or NBA sports games from Electronic Arts may be better choices for older children.

4   Interactive simulation games are an excellent choice for families because they are capable of getting children off the couch, something that many parents worry about with TV and video games. Interactive simulation games give players a hands-on experience that is as close as possible to what their character is doing in the game. One of the earliest of these games was an arcade game called *Dance Dance Revolution*. It requires players to match on a dance pad the moves they are instructed to do on the screen. Versions of this game are now available on the three main game consoles: X-Box, Playstation 2, and GameCube. The success of this game prompted many others like *Karaoke Revolution*, in which players sing popular songs into a microphone for points, and *Guitar Hero* and *Donkey Konga*, where players play on controllers that emulate a guitar or set of bongos. Most interactive simulation games require special controllers or accessories to play, and one of these accessories, the Eye Toy for Playstation 2, might change the way children think about "sitting" in front of the TV and playing video games. Eye Toy uses a USB camera so the player's body becomes the controller. Games using Eye Toy respond to the movement of the player's body to interact with the game play on screen. Eye Toy was originally packaged with the game *Play*, which featured 12 mini

Offers examples with detail of the categories

Offers examples with detail of the categories

Identifies how category fits gift giving purpose

Provides transition to next category and value of category to reader

Identifies distinguishing characteristics

Provides examples with details

Continued on next page

Continued from previous page

games that used this body motion for everything from dancing to kung fu. Since then, Eye Toy has come out with a variety of interactive games including *Play 2*, *Operation Spy*, and *AntiGrav*, as well as workout-minded games such as *Eye Toy Groove* and *Kinetic*. Interactive simulation games are the perfect choice for parents and grandparents who want to see their children physically active while having a good time.

5 Along with the concern that children spend too much time in front of the TV or on the couch, another common complaint parents have about video games is that unlike board games, they don't always encourage siblings or families to play together. That is why party games are such a great option for parents who want to be able to play along with their children and are interested in making video game time part of family time. Party games usually involve up to four players in competition and are short enough to play a round in one sitting. Most of them are made up of a series of many mini-games (short and simple games or puzzles) that are easy to learn. Most, although not all, of these party games are styled after board games and are turn-based. A few, like *Monopoly Party*, are exactly like popular board games in video game form. Like adventure games, most party games are based on well-known children's characters. Some of these family-friendly party games are *Disney Party*, *Nickelodeon Party Blast*, *Muppets Party Cruise*, *Shrek*, *Super Party*, and *Wario Ware Inc.* These games range across a variety of console platforms, and all feature well-known characters from movies, television, and children's games. However, perhaps the best-known game in this category is the *Mario Party* series; for Game Cube, there are *Mario Parties 4 through 7*. All these games are different and feature an extensive number of levels and mini-games for families to play together.

6 There are clearly many options for parents and grandparents who want to allow their children to enjoy the same electronic entertainment as their peers while still making sure that they are playing games that are appropriate for them. Buyers can choose from a variety of sports and adventure games that allow children to play as their favorite cartoon characters from movies like Harry Potter to video game icons like Mario or Sonic. Sports games in general are usually good choices for children, but Disney and Mario series can be easier and more fun for younger children. Interactive simulation games get children on their feet dancing, singing, and moving their body to win the game. Party games allow family members to play together in board-game-like formats filled with mini-games. This account of

---

Provides distinguishing reason for selecting category

Transition to category, indicating the value of the category

Identifies distinguish characteristics

Provides examples with details

Re-stresses the value for the category

Reasserts the purpose of the essay for the reader

Recalls some categories with indication of value of choice

Identifies categories not discussed

video games is, of course, not all-inclusive, and there are other categories of games, including puzzle games, arcade games, and strategy games, that can be appropriate for children as well. The most important thing for any parent or grandparent to realize is that not all video games are the same. <u>Becoming active in how children spend their play time and helping them choose the games that are appropriate for their age and their personality can help to make sure that they are playing games that are both fun for them and good for the family.</u>

Offers challenge to reader

Discussion Questions

1. This classification paper is written to help parents or grandparents select video games for children. How do the purpose and audience of the paper influence how it was written?
2. How does the writer organize each classification section? Is this approach effective?
3. Why does the writer point out the advantage of each kind of video game? Is this appropriate for a classification?
4. In the concluding paragraph the writer indicates that there are other kinds of video games that are not discussed in the paper. How does this affect the credibility and overall effectiveness of the paper?
5. Transitions can be a difficult part of any classification. How would you evaluate the effectiveness of this writer's transitions?

Suggestions for Writing

Write a classification paper on one of the topics below or one approved by your instructor. Determine your purpose and audience, select appropriate categories, decide how many you'll discuss, develop them with specific details, and arrange them in an effective order.

1. College teachers (or college pressures)
2. Pet owners (or types of pets)
3. Herbal remedies
4. Kinds of extreme sports
5. Action movies (or romantic comedies)
6. Video games
7. Dancing
8. Reasons for surfing the Internet
9. Talk show hosts
10. Sports announcers (or fans)
11. Television reality shows (or sitcoms)
12. Alternative medicines
13. Bottled water
14. Careers in your field of interest
15. Friends
16. Dates

17. Web pages
18. Advertisements
19. Cheating (or lies)
20. Leaders

STEPPING UP TO **SYNTHESIS**

Classification provides an effective tool for organizing material into categories. But you won't always rely exclusively on your own knowledge or experience to determine or develop categories. At times you'll supplement what you bring to a writing assignment with information gained through outside reading.

Prewriting for Synthesis Suppose that for an introductory business course, you're asked to prepare a paper that explores major types of investments. You realize that some research will be necessary. After consulting a number of books and magazines, you conclude that stocks, bonds, and real estate represent the three main categories of investments and that each category can be divided into several subcategories. Bonds, for example, can be grouped according to issuer: corporate, municipal, and U.S. Treasury securities.

At this point, you recognize that the strategy of classification would work well for this assignment. Reading further, you learn about the financial risks, rewards, and tax consequences associated with ownership. For example, U.S. Treasury securities offer the greatest safety, while corporate and municipal bonds, as well as stocks and real estate, entail varying degrees of risk depending on the financial condition of the issuer and the state of the economy. Similarly, the income from the different categories and subcategories of investments is subject to different kinds and levels of taxation. Thus, income from municipal bonds is generally tax free; income from U.S. Treasury securities is exempt from state and local taxes, and income from other kinds of investments does not enjoy such exemptions.

Watch the Video on **Evaluating Your Sources**

Critically Evaluating Your Sources Before using the material of others in your writing, examine its merits. Do some sources seem more convincing than others? Why? Do any recommendations stem from self-interest? For example, a writer who seems overly enthusiastic about one type of investment may be associated with an organization that markets it. Are any sources overloaded with material irrelevant to your purpose? Which sources offer the most detail? Asking and answering questions such as these will help you write a more informed paper.

Planning and Drafting Your Synthesis After assimilating the information you've gathered, you could synthesize the views expressed in your sources as well as your own ideas about investments. You might organize your categories and subcategories according to probable degree of risk, starting with the least risky investment and ending with the most risky. For your conclusion you might offer purchase recommendations for different groups of investors, such as young workers, wealthy older investors, and retirees.

Getting Started

1. Examine the Reader essays on our relationship to nature and then write a paper that draws upon these sources and classifies their content into different ways to relate to or respond to nature.
2. Read several authors' views on diversity and then write a paper that draws on these sources and classifies their content into different stances toward diversity, using examples from the works for support.
3. Reflect on the Reader essays that you've studied and then write a paper that presents an appropriate classification system for them, perhaps based on the writers' levels of diction, tone, or reliance on authorities.

Complete additional exercises and practice in your MyLab

Writing a Classification

Prewriting the classification.

- Identify subject for classification.
- Establish purpose for classification.
- Identify audience.
- Brainstorm key categories appropriate to purpose.
- Create a table of categories and brainstorm distinguishing features and details.
- If multiple levels of categories, create a category tree.
- Test categories to make certain they are complete and not overlapping.
- Check to see if your classification is fair to the situation.
- Check to see if your classification could encourage harmful behavior.

Planning the classification.

- Select the organizational strategy:
- From most important to least.
- From least to most important.
- By key topic.
- Use the table to organize.
- Ensure that your classifications avoid excessive or distorting generalizations.

Drafting the classification.

- Introduction: engage reader, identify reason for classification, establish topic.
- Body: explain and exemplify each category in order.
- Conclusion: vary.

Revising the classification.

Gather peer feedback; test hard to see if a category is missing; try other categories.
- Make sure the classification fits the purpose.
- Determine if categories overlap.
- Add necessary details or categories.
- Cut categories that don't fit or help.
- Test the organization.
- Test for ethics.

Repeat the process as needed.

Proofread.

CHAPTER 13

Comparison: Showing Relationships

In this chapter you will learn how to:

13.1 Use comparison as a writing strategy.

13.2 Select items for comparison.

13.3 Use details to develop a comparison.

13.4 Use different patterns to organize a comparison.

13.5 Use analogies in your comparison.

13.6 Write so that your comparison is ethical.

13.7 Prewrite, plan, draft, and revise your comparison.

Fly Fernandez/Corbis

Which candidate for senator should get my vote, Ken Conwell or Jerry Mander?

Let me know whether this new shipment of nylon thread meets specs.

Doesn't this song remind you of Faith Hill?

How does high school in Australia stack up against high school in this country?

Everyone makes *comparisons*, not just once in a while but day after day. When we compare, we examine two or more items for likenesses, differences, or both.

13.1

Use comparison as a writing strategy.

Comparison often helps us choose between alternatives. Some issues are trivial: whether to play World of Warcraft or Warhammer, whether to order pizza or a sub sandwich. But comparison also influences our more important decisions. We weigh majoring in chemistry against majoring in physics, buying against renting, or working for Microsoft against working for IBM.

Comparison also acquaints us with unfamiliar things. To help American readers understand the English sport of rugby, a sportswriter might compare its field, team, rules, and scoring system with those for football. To teach students about France's government, a political science textbook might discuss the makeup and election of its parliament and the method of picking its president and premier, using our own government as a backdrop.

Both your classes and your job will call for comparison writing.

- Your humanities instructor may have you compare a short story and its movie adaptation to explain the adaptation process.
- Your psychology instructor may want you to compare two types of psychosis and assess the legal and medical ramifications of each.
- Your health administration instructor may have you compare two different types of elder care facilities to determine the best choice for different individuals.
- An office manager may compare different types of cell phone services to determine which is best for the company's work force.
- A nurse assesses the condition of a patient before and after a new medicine is given.
- An insurance agent points out the features of two insurance policies to highlight the advantages of one.

Selecting Items for Comparison

13.2

Select items for comparison.

Any items you compare must share some common ground. For example, you could compare two golfers on driving ability, putting ability, and sand play, or two cars on appearance, gas mileage, and warranty; however, you can't meaningfully compare a golfer with a car, any more than you could compare guacamole with Guadalajara or chicken with charcoal. There's simply no basis for comparison.

Any valid comparison, on the other hand, presents many possibilities. Suppose you head the music department of a large store and have two excellent salespeople working for you. The manager of the store asks you to prepare a one- or two-page report that compares their qualifications for managing the music department in a new branch store. Assessing their abilities becomes the guiding purpose that motivates and controls the writing. On the spot you can rule out points such as eye color, hair style, and religion, which have no bearing on job performance. Instead, you must decide what managerial traits the job will require and the extent to which each candidate possesses them. Your thinking might result in a list like this:

 *Listen to the Podcast on **Faulty Comparison***

Points of Similarity or Difference	Pat	Mike
1. Ability to deal with customers, sales skills	Excellent	Excellent
2. Effort: regular attendance, hard work on the job	Excellent	Excellent
3. Leadership qualities	Excellent	Good
4. Knowledge of ordering and accounting procedures	Good	Fair
5. Musical knowledge	Excellent	Good

This list tells you which points to emphasize and suggests Pat as the candidate to recommend. You might briefly mention similarities (points 1 and 2) in an introductory paragraph, but the report would focus on differences (points 3, 4, and 5) since you're distinguishing between two employees.

EXERCISE

Say you want to compare two good restaurants in order to recommend one of them. List the points of similarity and difference that you might discuss. Differences should predominate because you will base your decision on them.

Developing a Comparison

Successful comparisons rest upon ample, well-chosen details that show just how the items under consideration are alike and different. Such support helps the reader grasp your meaning. Read the following student paragraphs and note how the concrete details convey the striking differences between south and north 14th Street:

13.3

Use details to develop a comparison.

> On 14th Street running south from P Street are opulent department stores, such as Woodward and Lothrop and Julius Garfinkle, and small but expensive clothing stores with richly dressed mannequins in the windows. Modern skyscraping office buildings harbor banks and travel bureaus on the ground floors and insurance companies and corporation headquarters in the upper stories. Dotting the concretescape are high-priced movie theaters, gourmet restaurants, multilevel parking garages, bookstores, and candy-novelty-gift shops, all catering to the prosperous population of the city. This section of 14th Street is relatively clean: The

city maintenance crews must clean up after only a nine-to-five populace and the Saturday crowds of shoppers. The pervading mood of the area is one of bustling wealth during the day and, in the night, calm.

Crossing P Street toward the north, one notes a gradual but disturbing change in the scenery of 14th Street. Two architectural features assault the eyes and automatically register as tokens of trouble: the floodlights that leave no alley or doorway in shadows and the riot screens that cage in the store windows. The buildings are old, condemned, decaying monoliths, each occupying an entire city block. Liquor stores, drugstores, dusty television repair shops, seedy pornographic bookstores that display photographs of naked bodies with the genital areas blacked out by strips of tape, discount stores smelling perpetually of stale chocolate and cold popcorn, and cluttered pawnshops—businesses such as these occupy the street level. Each is separated from the adjoining stores by a littered entranceway that leads up a decaying wooden stairway to the next two floors. All the buildings are three stories tall; all have most of their windows broken and blocked with boards or newspapers; and all reek of liquor, urine, and unidentifiable rot. And so the general atmosphere of this end of 14th Street is one of poverty and decay.

Vivid details depict with stark clarity the economic differences between the two areas.

Organizing a Comparison

13.4

Use different patterns to organize a comparison.

You can use either of two basic patterns to organize a comparison paper: block or alternating. The paper may deal with similarities, differences, or some combination of them.

The Block Pattern

The block pattern first presents all of the points of comparison for one item and then all of the points of comparison for the other. Following is the comparison of the two salespeople, Pat and Mike, outlined according to the block pattern:

 I. Introduction: mentions similarities in sales skills and effort but recommends Pat for promotion.
 II. Specific points about Mike
   A. Leadership qualities
   B. Knowledge of ordering and accounting procedures
   C. Musical knowledge

III. Specific points about Pat
   A. Leadership qualities
   B. Knowledge of ordering and accounting procedures
   C. Musical knowledge
IV. Conclusion: reasserts that Pat should be promoted.

The block pattern works best with short papers or ones that include only a few points of comparison. The reader can easily remember all the points in the first block while reading the second.

The Alternating Pattern

The alternating pattern presents a point about one item, then follows immediately with a corresponding point about the other. Organized in this way, the Pat-and-Mike paper would look like this:

   I. Introduction: mentions similarities in sales skills and effort but recommends Pat for promotion.
  II. Leadership qualities
   A. Mike's qualities
   B. Pat's qualities
 III. Knowledge of ordering and accounting procedures
   A. Mike's knowledge
   B. Pat's knowledge
 IV. Musical knowledge
   A. Mike's knowledge
   B. Pat's knowledge
  V. Conclusion: reasserts that Pat should be promoted.

For longer papers that include many points of comparison, use the alternating method. Discussing each point in one place highlights similarities and differences; your reader doesn't have to pause and reread in order to grasp them. The alternating plan also works well for short papers.

Once you select your pattern, arrange your points of comparison in an appropriate order. Take up closely related points one after the other. Depending on your purpose, you might work from similarities to differences or the reverse. Often, a good writing strategy is to move from the least significant to the most significant point so that you conclude with punch.

EXERCISE

Using the points of comparison you selected for the exercise on page 221, prepare outlines for a paper organized according to the block pattern and then the alternating pattern.

Using Analogy

An *analogy*, a special type of comparison, calls attention to one or more similarities underlying two kinds of an item that seem to have nothing in common. While some analogies stand alone, most clarify concepts in other kinds

13.5
Use analogies in your comparison.

of writing. Whatever their role, they follow the same organizational pattern as ordinary comparisons.

An analogy often explains something unfamiliar by likening it to something familiar. Following is an example:

> The atmosphere of Earth acts like any window in serving two very important functions. It lets light in, and it permits us to look out. It also serves as a shield to keep out dangerous or uncomfortable things. A normal glazed window lets us keep our houses warm by keeping out cold air, and it prevents rain, dirt, and unwelcome insects and animals from coming in. . . . Earth's atmospheric window also helps to keep our planet at a comfortable temperature by holding back radiated heat and protecting us from dangerous levels of ultraviolet light.
>
> Lester del Ray, *The Mysterious Sky*

Conversely, an analogy sometimes highlights the unfamiliar in order to help illuminate the familiar. The following paragraph discusses the qualities and obligations of an unfamiliar person, the mountain guide, to shed light on a familiar practice—teaching:

> The mountain guide, like the true teacher, has a quiet authority. He or she engenders trust and confidence so that one is willing to join the endeavor. The guide accepts his leadership role, yet recognizes that success (measured by the heights that are scaled) depends upon the close cooperation and active participation of each member of the group. He has crossed the terrain before and is familiar with the landmarks, but each trip is new and generates its own anxiety and excitement. Essential skills must be mastered; if they are lacking, disaster looms. The situation demands keen focus and rapt attention: slackness, misjudgment, or laziness can abort the venture.
>
> Nancy K. Hill, "Scaling the Heights: The Teacher as Mountaineer"

When you develop an analogy, keep these points in mind:

1. Your readers must be well acquainted with the familiar item. If they aren't, the point is lost.
2. The items must have significant similarities. You could develop a meaningful analogy between a kidney and a filter or between cancer and anarchy but not between a fiddle and a flapjack or a laser and limburger cheese.
3. The analogy must truly illuminate. Overly obvious analogies, such as one comparing a battle to an argument, offer few or no revealing insights.
4. Overextended analogies can tax the reader's endurance. A multipage analogy between a heart and a pump would likely overwhelm the reader with all its talk of valves, hoses, pressures, and pumping.

Ethical Issues

13.6

Write so that your comparison is ethical.

Although an old adage declares that "comparisons are odious," most people embrace comparisons except when they are unfair. Unfortunately, this situation occurs all too often. For example, advertisers commonly magnify trivial drawbacks in competitive products while exaggerating the benefits of their own merchandise. Politicians run attack ads that distort their opponents' views and demean the opponents' character. And when scientific theories clash, supporters of one view have been known to alter their findings in order to undermine the other position. Your readers expect any comparison to meet certain ethical standards. Ask and answer these questions to help ensure that those you write measure up.

- Am I avoiding skewing one or both of my items in order to ensure a particular outcome?
- Are the items I'm comparing properly matched? It would be unethical to compare a student essay to a professional one in order to demonstrate the inadequacy of the former.
- If I'm using an analogy, is it appropriate? Comparing immigration officials to Nazi storm troopers is ethically odious: It trivializes the suffering and deaths of millions of Nazi victims and taints the officials with a terrible label.

Writing a Comparison

Don't write merely to fulfill an assignment; if you do, your paper will likely ramble aimlessly and fail to deliver a specific message. Instead, build your paper around a clear sense of purpose. Do you want to show the superiority of one product or method over another? Do you want to show how sitcoms today differ from those twenty years ago? Purpose governs the details you choose and the organization you follow.

13.7

Prewrite, plan, draft, and revise your comparison.

 Watch the Animation on **Writing a Comparison**

Prewriting the Comparison

> - Brainstorm major areas of interest: movies, TV shows, teaching styles.
> - Brainstorm basic areas of comparison, or narrowing: "the representation of fathers on TV in the 1950s and now."
> - Identify your purpose for the comparison, such as to show progress or help consumers make a choice.
> - Identify what audience would be interested in your comparison.

FINDING YOUR TOPIC

> - If possible, re-observe or use items to be compared and take notes of similarities and differences.
> - Brainstorm or create a chart of the major similarities and differences of the items being compared.
> - Branch or chart the details and examples.
> - Decide what points of comparison you will use based on audience and purpose.
> - Create a chart or create an outline that establishes an order for your comparison.

DEVELOPING YOUR COMPARISON

Planning and Drafting the Comparison

When you decide upon an order, copy the points of comparison and the details, arranged in the order you will follow, into a chart like the one below.

Item A	Item B
First point of comparison	First point of comparison
First detail	First detail
Second detail	Second detail
Second point of comparison	Second point of comparison

A **thesis statement** for a comparison often stresses the major point or two of comparison and relates that point to the reader's interests. "While earthquakes in the East may be more infrequent and less severe than those in California, they may be more widely felt because they tend to be shallower and are not dampened by additional faults." To develop your thesis, review your brainstorming to identify the main points of comparisons that will interest your reader and consider why those points are important.

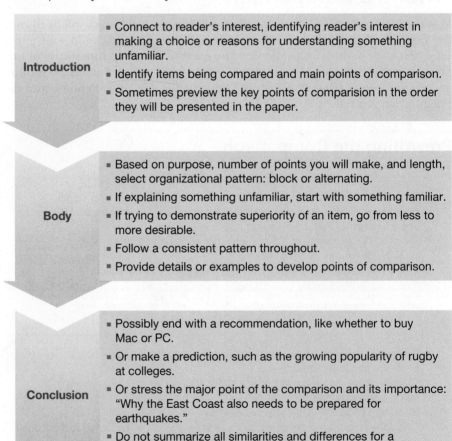

Introduction
- Connect to reader's interest, identifying reader's interest in making a choice or reasons for understanding something unfamiliar.
- Identify items being compared and main points of comparison.
- Sometimes preview the key points of comparision in the order they will be presented in the paper.

Body
- Based on purpose, number of points you will make, and length, select organizational pattern: block or alternating.
- If explaining something unfamiliar, start with something familiar.
- If trying to demonstrate superiority of an item, go from less to more desirable.
- Follow a consistent pattern throughout.
- Provide details or examples to develop points of comparison.

Conclusion
- Possibly end with a recommendation, like whether to buy Mac or PC.
- Or make a prediction, such as the growing popularity of rugby at colleges.
- Or stress the major point of the comparison and its importance: "Why the East Coast also needs to be prepared for earthquakes."
- Do not summarize all similarities and differences for a short paper. You may provide such a summary on a much longer paper.

Revising the Comparison

Revise your paper in light of the general guidelines in Chapter 4 and the questions and suggestions that follow:

- What could help strengthen the achievement of the paper's purpose, whether to choose between alternatives or acquaint the reader with something unfamiliar?
- For something unfamiliar, where could the unfamiliar features be made clearer by a stronger comparison with something familiar?
- Where could the paper be better directed to the audience? Cut or revise material not appropriate to the audience and purpose.
- What additional points of similarity and difference might be included? Brainstorm.
- Where would additional details or examples strengthen the paper? Brainstorm or use branching.
- Does the organization of the paper not fit the purpose and audience? Where doesn't the paper follow a consistent pattern? Experiment with reorganization.
- Where could the transitions be strengthened to better show the shifts in points of comparison?
- Where do paragraphs lose focus or try to deal with too many points of comparison?
- Where, if anywhere, does the paper unfairly distort the comparison unethically?

Watch the Animation on **Comparison Signal Words**

SAMPLE

STUDENT ESSAY OF **COMPARISON**

Differences between Korean and English

Sunho Lee

1   As the world undergoes globalization, English is given a great deal of weight as an official language; as a result, many people have been trying to learn English. The Korean people have also been making efforts to acquire the language; however, learning is troublesome for Korean students because English and Korean have a lot of differences. <u>Three major differences between English and Korean give people from Korea special difficulty in learning English: accent, tense, and articles.</u>

2   <u>Accent is one of the obvious differences that frustrate Korean people who try to become skilled at English.</u> For instance, *impact* can be a noun or a verb, depending on how it is stressed. When people who speak English emphasize the first syllable, *impact* is a noun. If people who use English stress the second syllable, *impact* is a verb. The Korean tongue

Establishes point of topic

Identifies major items to be compared and ordered

Identifies key points of comparison and reasons for the discussion of those points

Identifies first major point of comparison and reason for discussion

Identifies differences with example

Continued on next page

Continued from previous page

does not use accents in this way and spells noun and verb forms completely differently. Thus distinguishing parts of speech by accent is not something familiar to Korean learners.

Identifies second point of difference

Explains difference with example

3   The second difference is tense, especially the present perfect tense. The present perfect tense describes actions or states that begin in the past, continue into the present, and might continue into the future. This kind of tense does not exist in Korean grammar. For example, the meanings of "I worked out" and "I have worked out" are slightly dissimilar. Of course, Korean students can interpret both meanings, yet when people who are used to speaking Korean use the present perfect tense in English, they have trouble because past and present perfect are not distinguished in the Korean language.

Identifies final difference to be discussed

Explains difference with examples

4   The last noticeable difference between Korean and English is the use of articles: definite and indefinite. "Ducks like to swim," "There is a duck in my bathtub," and "The duck quacked all night" are good examples. Each *ducks* or *duck* is different in these examples, but a Korean learner cannot easily see the difference between the usages. One English instructor said, "When I speak English, a bird flies to me and gives me some tips about what article I should use in this situation." This means that even native English speakers cannot define exactly how to use articles. To be sure, English grammar has some rules about how to use articles, but the number of exceptions is more than the regulations. The Korean language does not have articles; in addition, before Korean students learn English, they do not know what an article is exactly. Accordingly, for someone learning English using articles precisely is very complicated.

Explains importance of difference

Reaffirms importance of difference

Challenges Korean readers

5   All languages have differences. Thus for a second language learner, studying English is very hard, and it is challenging to overcome the variations between the two languages. It is especially difficult because of the differences in stress, the present perfect tense, and articles. Although these features of English are not easy to understand and use, if Koreans who struggle to use English fluently study constantly, they can finally conquer English.

Discussion Questions

1. This writer decided to use a point-by-point rather than a block comparison. Was this the right decision? Why?
2. While the writer provides clear examples in English, there are no matching examples in Korean. Is this the right choice for this communication situation? Why or why not?
3. What is the audience and purpose for this essay? Does it achieve its purpose?

4. What are some of the effective organizational strategies of this essay?
5. What are the advantages and disadvantages that would result if the writer had looked at additional differences between English and Korean?

Suggestions for Writing

1. Write a properly focused comparison essay on one of the topics below or another that your instructor approves. Determine the points you will discuss and how you will develop and arrange them. Emphasize similarities, differences, or both.

   a. The representation of women, fathers, teenagers, or some other group in a 1950s or 1960s sitcom and in a similar contemporary sitcom
   b. The physical or mental demands of two jobs
   c. Male and female styles of conversation
   d. Online and brick-and-mortar shopping
   e. The playing styles of two NBA or WNBA superstars
   f. Online and traditional classes
   g. The effectiveness of two pieces of writing
   h. Traditional and extreme sports
   i. Two or more college or business Web pages
   j. Two musical groups or musical styles
   k. Two or more products being considered for purchase
   l. Two or more video games or types of video games

2. Develop an analogy based on one of the following sets of items or another set that your instructor approves. Proceed as you would for any other comparison.

   a. The offerings in a college catalog and a restaurant menu
   b. A heart and a pump or airport hub
   c. Writing and gardening or mountain climbing or spelunking
   d. A teacher and a merchant or coach or prison guard
   e. A brain and a computer or rock concert or busy city
   f. Developing an idea and building a house or exploring new territory
   g. Succeeding at school and winning a military campaign or a sporting event
   h. A workaholic and an alcoholic
   i. A cluttered attic and a disorderly mind
   j. Reading a book and exploring a new place or hunting for treasure

STEPPING UP TO **SYNTHESIS**

Although you rely on your own knowledge or findings to develop many comparisons, in some cases you'll synthesize material from other sources.

Prewriting for Synthesis Let's say that your business management instructor has asked you to prepare a report on the

Continued on next page

Continued from previous page

management styles of two high-profile chief executive officers (CEOs) at Fortune 500 companies that manufacture the same kinds of products. You realize that you'll need to do some reading in business periodicals like *Forbes, Fortune,* and the *Wall Street Journal* in order to complete this assignment. Your sources reveal that the first CEO favors a highly centralized managerial structure with strict limits on what can be done by all employees except top executives. The company has pursued foreign markets by establishing factories overseas and has aggressively attempted to merge with or acquire its domestic competitors. The second CEO has established a decentralized managerial structure that allows managers at various levels of the company to make key decisions. The company has also established a strong foreign presence, but it has done so primarily by entering into joint ventures with foreign firms. Most of its domestic expansion has resulted from the construction of new plants rather than from mergers or takeovers. Both CEOs have borrowed heavily to finance their companies' expansion.

Critically Evaluating Your Sources   After you've read the views expressed by your sources, examine them critically. Does any of the information about the two CEOs seem slanted so that it appears to misrepresent their management styles? For example, do any of the writers seem to exaggerate the positive or negative features of centralized or decentralized management? Do appropriate examples support the writers' contentions? Does any relevant information appear to be missing? Does any source contain material that isn't related to your purpose? Judging the works of others in this fashion will help you write a better report.

Planning and Drafting Your Synthesis   The three differences and one similarity between CEOs are your points of comparison, which you can organize using either the block or alternating pattern. You could make a chart with each of the key points of comparison in order with information from your sources. When you write your rough draft, you will want to decide in advance whether you want an unbiased comparison or whether you will lead to a preference. If the latter, your introduction might focus on the challenges of determining a more effective management style; your paragraphs would compare the styles point by point that lead to an emphasis on the qualities of the one you favor. You might conclude by indicating why you prefer one of the two management styles.

Getting Started

1. Read "Going Nuclear" by Patrick Moore and "Ten Reasons Why New Nuclear was a Mistake—Even before Fukushima" by Alexis Rowell (in the Reader) and then compare the views of these two writers on the feasibility and safety of nuclear power
2. Read several reviews of the same movie and then compare what the critics have written.
3. Write a criticism of a comparison you read recently that you thought was unreasonable.

Writing a Comparison

Prewriting the comparison.

- Identify items for comparison, purpose, and audience.
- Make observations of objects to compare if possible.
- Brainstorm or create a branching tree of details for comparison.
- Check to make certain that the items being compared are properly matched.

Planning the comparison.

- Create a table laying out points of comparison and details.
- Determine pattern: block or point by point.
- Create a rough outline.
- Test to determine whether points are complete, meet the purpose, and are not skewed.

Drafting the comparison.

- Introduction establishes purpose for comparison and main point.
- Body develops each point of comparison with detail using pattern.
- Conclusion may vary but reaffirms the main point.

Revising the comparison.

- Gather peer responses, talk over the topic, and reexamine items being compared.
- Check to make certain everything fits the purpose.
- Add additional similarities or differences as needed.
- Cut points that don't fit.
- Test organization, especially transitions.

Repeat the process as needed.

Proofread.

CHAPTER 14 Cause and Effect: Explaining Why

In this chapter you will learn how to:

14.1 Use cause and effect as a writing strategy.

14.2 Select an organizational pattern for your causal analysis.

14.3 Avoid making reasoning errors about cause and effect.

14.4 Write so that your causal analysis is ethical.

14.5 Prewrite, plan, draft, and revise your causal analysis.

Eleanor Bentall/Corbis

Cause and effect are inseparably linked and together make up *causation*. Cause probes the reasons why actions, events, attitudes, and conditions exist. Effect examines their consequences. Causation is important to us because it can explain historical events, natural happenings, and the actions and attitudes of individuals and groups. It can help us anticipate the consequences of personal actions, natural phenomena, or government policies.

Everyone asks and answers questions of causation. Scott wonders why Sue *really* broke off their relationship, and Jennifer speculates on the consequences of changing her major. People wonder why child abuse and homelessness are on the rise, and millions worry about the effects of corporate cost cutting and violence in our schools.

Inevitably, therefore, you will need to write papers and reports that employ causation.

14.1

Use cause and effect as a writing strategy.

- For a history class, you might write on the causes of the American Revolution.
- For a criminal justice class, you might write about the consequences of white-collar crime.
- For an ornamental horticulture course, you might examine the effects of different fertilizers on plant growth.
- An employer may want a report on why a certain product malfunctions.
- A transportation professional might analyze the consequences if a community redesigns its traffic pattern.
- A public health professional might seek the causes of food poisoning.

Patterns in Causal Analysis

Several organizational patterns are possible for a causal analysis. Sometimes, a single cause produces several effects. For instance, poor language skills prevent some college students from keeping up with required reading, taking adequate notes, writing competent papers, and completing essay exams. To explore such a single cause-multiple effect relationship, construct outlines similar to the following two:

14.2

Select an organizational pattern for your causal analysis.

◉—Watch the Animation on **Patterns in Cause and Effect**

I. Introduction: identifies cause
II. Body
  A. Effect number 1
  B. Effect number 2
  C. Effect number 3
III. Conclusion

I. Poor language skills
II. Body
  A. Can't keep up with required reading
  B. Can't take adequate notes
  C. Can't write competent papers or exams
III. Conclusion

Alternatively, you might discuss the cause after the effects are presented.

On the other hand, several causes may join forces to produce one effect. Zinc production in the United States, for example, decreased because it can be produced more cheaply abroad than it can here, it has been replaced on cars by plastics and lighter metals, and it cannot be recycled. Here's how you might organize a typical multiple cause-single effect paper:

I. Introduction: identifies effect	I. Decrease in U.S. zinc production
II. Body	II. Body
A. Cause number 1	A. Produced more cheaply abroad
B. Cause number 2	B. Replaced on cars by plastics, lighter metals
C. Cause number 3	C. Cannot be recycled
III. Conclusion	III. Conclusion

Sometimes discussion of the effect follows the presentation of causes.

At times a set of events forms a causal chain, with each event the effect of the preceding one and the cause of the following one. For example, a student sleeps late and so misses breakfast and ends up hungry and distracted, which in turn results in a poor performance on an exam. Interrupting the chain at any point halts the sequence. Such chains can be likened to a row of upright dominoes that fall one after the other when the first one is pushed. Belief in a domino theory—which held that if one nation in Southeast Asia fell to the communists all would, one after the other—helped bring about the U.S. entry into the Vietnam War. Causal chains can also help explain how devices function and how some social changes proceed. The following outlines typify the arrangement of a paper explaining a causal chain:

I. Introduction	I. Introduction
II. Body	II. Body
A. Cause	A. Sleep late
B. Effect	B. Miss breakfast
C. Cause	C. Become hungry and distracted
D. Effect	D. Perform poorly on exam
III. Conclusion	III. Conclusion

Papers of this kind resemble process analyses, but process is concerned with *how* the events occur, cause and effect with *why*.

In many situations the sequence of causes and effects is too complex to fit the image of a chain. Suppose you are driving to a movie on a rainy night. You approach an intersection screened by bushes and, because you have the right-of-way, start across. Suddenly a car with unlit headlights looms directly in your path. You hit the brakes but skid on the slippery pavement and crash into the other car, crumpling its left fender and damaging your own bumper. Later, as you think about the episode, you begin to sense its complexities.

Obviously, the *immediate cause* of the accident was the other driver's failure to heed the stop sign. But other causes also played roles: the bushes and unlit headlights that kept you from seeing the other car sooner; the starts and stops, speedups and slowdowns that brought the two cars to the intersection at the same time; the wet pavement you skidded on; and the movie that brought you out in the first place.

You also realize that the effects of the accident go beyond the fender and bumper damage. After the accident, a police officer ticketed the other driver. As a result of the delay, you missed the movie. Further, the accident unnerved you so badly that you couldn't attend classes the next day and therefore missed an important writing assignment. Because of a bad driving record, the other driver lost his license for 60 days. Clearly, the effects of this accident rival the causes in complexity.

Here's how you might organize a multiple cause-multiple effect essay:

Introduction	The accident
Body	Body
I. Causes	I. Causes of the accident
A. Cause number 1	A. Driver ran stop sign
B. Cause number 2	B. Bushes and unlit headlights
C. Cause number 3	impaired vision
II. Effects	C. Wet pavement caused skidding
A. Effect number 1	II. Effects of the accident
B. Effect number 2	A. Missed the movie
C. Effect number 3	B. Unnerved so missed classes next day
Conclusion	C. Other driver lost license
	Conclusion

In some situations, however, you might first present the effects, and then turn to the causes.

EXERCISE

1. **Read the following selection and then arrange the events in a causal chain:**

   Although some folk societies still exist today, similar human groups began the slow process of evolving into more complex societies many millennia ago, through settlement in villages and through advances in technology and organizational structure. This gave rise to the second level of organization: civilized preindustrial, or "feudal," society. Here, there is a surplus of food because of the selective cultivation of grains— and also because of the practice of animal husbandry. The food surplus permits both the specialization of labor and the kind of class structure that can, for instance, provide the leadership and command the manpower to develop and maintain extensive irrigation systems (which, in turn, makes possible further increases in the food supply). . . .

   Gideon Sjöberg, "The Origin and Development of Cities"

2. **Trace the possible effects of the following occurrences:**

   a. You pick out a salad at the cafeteria and sit down to eat. Suddenly you notice a large green worm on one of the lettuce leaves.

   b. As you leave your composition classroom, you trip and break your arm.

   c. Your boss has warned you not to be late to work again. You are driving to work with 10 minutes to spare when you get a flat tire.

Reasoning Errors in Causal Analysis

14.3

Avoid making reasoning errors about cause and effect.

Ignoring Multiple Causes

An effect rarely stems from a single cause. The person who believes that permissive parents have caused the present upsurge of venereal disease or the one who blames television violence for the climbing numbers of emotionally disturbed children oversimplifies the situation. Permissiveness and violence perhaps did contribute to these conditions. Without much doubt, however, numerous other factors also played important parts.

Mistaking Chronology for Causation

Don't assume that just because one event followed another that the first necessarily caused the second. This kind of faulty thinking feeds many popular superstitions. Horace walks under a ladder, later stubs his toe, and thinks that his path caused his pain. Sue breaks a mirror just before Al breaks their engagement; then she blames the cracked mirror. Many people once believed that the election of Herbert Hoover as president in 1928 brought on the Great Depression in 1929. Today, some people believe that the testing of atomic weapons has altered our weather patterns. Don't misunderstand: One event *may* cause the next; but before you go on record with your conclusion, make sure that you're not dealing with mere chronology.

Confusing Causes with Effects

Young children sometimes declare that the moving trees make the wind blow. Similarly, some adults may think that Pam and Paul married because they fell in love, when in reality economic necessity mandated the vows, and love came later. Scan your evidence carefully in order to avoid such faulty assertions.

EXERCISE

1. **Which of the following statements point toward papers that will focus on causes? Which point toward papers that will focus on effects? Explain your answers.**

   a. Most of the problems that plague newly married couples are the direct outgrowth of timidity and pride.

   b. The Marshall Plan was designed to aid the economic recovery of Europe after World War II.

   c. The smoke from burning poison ivy can bring on a skin rash and lung irritation.

   d. Popularity in high school stems largely from good looks, a pleasing personality, participation in school activities, the right friends, and frequent dates.

2. **Identify which of the following paragraphs deals with causes and which with effects. List the causes and effects.**

a. Color filters offer three advantages in black-and-white photography. First, a particular color will be lightened by a filter of the same color. For example, in a photograph of a red rose in a dark blue vase, both will appear almost the same shade of gray if no filter is used. However, when photographed through a red filter, the rose will appear much lighter than the vase; and through a blue filter the vase will appear much lighter than the rose. This effect can be useful in emphasizing or muting certain objects in a photograph. Second, a particular color filter will darken its complementary color in the scene. Consequently, any orange object will appear darker than normal if a blue filter is used. Finally, color filters can reduce or increase atmospheric haze. For example, in a distant aerial shot there will often be so much haze that distant detail is obscured. To eliminate haze almost entirely, the photographer can use a deep red filter. On the other hand, if more haze is desired in order to achieve an artistic effect, varying shades of blue filters can be used.

Timothy Kelly

b. Overeating, which has become a national pastime for millions of Americans, has several roots. For example, parents who are concerned that their children get enough to eat during the growing years overfeed them and thereby establish a lifetime overeating habit. The child who is constantly praised for cleaning up his plate experiences a sort of gratification later on as he cleans up all too many plates. The easy availability of so much food is a constant temptation for many people, especially the types of food served at fast-food restaurants and merchandised in the frozen food departments of supermarkets. Equally tempting are all the snack foods constantly advertised on TV. But many people don't need temptation from the outside; their overeating arises from such psychological factors as nervousness, boredom, loneliness, insecurity, an overall discontent with life, or an aversion to exercise. Thus, overeating can actually be a symptom of psychological surrender to, or withdrawal from, the complexities and competition of modern life.

Kenneth Reichow

Ethical Issues

14.4

Write so that your causal analysis is ethical.

Causation is not immune from abuse, either accidental or deliberate. Imagine the consequences of an article that touts a new herbal remedy but fails to mention several potentially serious side effects that could harm many users. Think about the possible strain on your relationship with a friend if she unjustly suspected you of starting a vicious rumor about her. Writing cause and effect papers creates an ethical responsibility. Asking and answering these questions will help you meet that obligation.

- Am I trying to uncover all of the causes that might result in a particular outcome? A report blaming poor instruction alone for a high student failure rate in a certain town's public schools almost certainly overlooks such factors as oversized classes, inadequate facilities, and poor home environments.
- Have I carefully weighed the importance of the causes I've uncovered? If a few, but not most, of the classes in the problem school system are oversized, then the report should not stress their significance.
- Have I tried to uncover and discuss every important effect, even one that might damage a case I'm trying to make? A report emphasizing the beneficial effects of jogging would be dangerously negligent if it failed to note the potential for injury.
- What would be the consequences if people act on my analysis?

Careful evaluation of causes and effects not only fulfills your writing obligation but also your ethical one.

Writing a Causal Analysis

14.5

Prewrite, plan, draft, and revise your causal analysis.

 Watch the Animation on **Writing a Causal Analysis**

Because you have probably speculated about the causes and effects of several campus, local, state, or national problems, writing this type of paper should pose no great difficulty.

Prewriting the Cause and Effect Essay

FINDING YOUR TOPIC

- Brainstorm events or circumstances in your life that you might explain for an audience or whose effect could be of interest, such as "why I dropped out of high school," or "the effects of counseling on my life."
- Keep notes of social trends or news events that are of interest, such as the rapid growth of the Tea Party movement. You might read or watch the news to get ideas.
- Note topics that may be of interest and broad appeal, such as why people become addicted to video games.

- Identify your audience and purpose for your paper. What do you want to accomplish and why would people be interested?
- Decide whether you would be better off focusing on causes, effects, or both.
- Brainstorm causes and/or effects. Research examples and details.
- For causes, identify how significant each cause is, what role it played in producing the effect, and whether it is part of a chain.
- For effects, identify the importance of the evidence and how the cause produced the effects.

DEVELOPING YOUR CAUSE AND EFFECT

Planning and Drafting a Cause and Effect Essay

Use a chart like the one below or an outline or a cognitive map with detail to organize your paper.

To tabulate causes, use an arrangement like this one:

Cause	Contribution to Effect
First cause	Specific contribution
Second cause	Specific contribution

For effects, use this chart:

Effect	Importance
First effect	Why important
Second effect	Why important

A **thesis statement** for a cause and effect often identifies the event to be explained or the effects to be considered, explains the importance of understanding the causes or effects, and sometimes offers a summary of the major causes or effects. "The debt crisis in Greece which may damage the world economy was not only caused by excessive public spending and the failure of many to pay taxes, but also the factors that produced a non-competitive environment for business." To aid in forming your thesis statement, identify the reasons you think the topic is important and the major causes or effects you need to discuss. Your thesis statement can be a question that the paper answers and often signals whether the paper concerns causes, effects, or both.

To prepare for a focus on causes, you might use the words *cause, reason,* or *stem from,* or you might ask why something has occurred. To signal a paper on effects, you might use *effect, fallout,* or *impact,* or you might ask what has happened since something took place. Read these examples:

Signals causes: Midville's recent decrease in street crime stems primarily from its expanded educational program, growing job opportunities for young people, and the falling rate of drug addiction.

Signals effects: Since my marriage to Rita, how has my social life changed?

Introduction
- Employ an attention getter that ties the topic to a reader's interest. "Your home may be hazardous to your health."
- Identify the topic that will be explored.
- Clearly signal whether the paper will focus on cause or effect.
- In a longer paper, possibly mention the major causes or effects that will be discussed.

Body
- Determine if you are going to discuss all the causes or effects or narrow them.
- Determine the best organizational strategy: main cause followed by causes with a supporting role, or multiple causes discussed in order of importance, or chains leading to an effect.
- Support causes or effects with examples, details, or statistics.
- Paragraph according to key causes or effects, with clear transitions.

Conclusion
- Stress the consequences of not taking such action, as the impact of acid rain on America's lakes.
- Or suggest something will be done or encourage the reader to act.
- Or evaluate the importance of their causes or effects.

As you write, don't restrict yourself to a bare-bones discussion of causes and effects. If, for instance, you're exploring the student parking problem on your campus, you might describe the jammed lots or point out that students often miss class because they have to drive around and look for spots. Similarly, don't simply assert that the administration's insensitivity contributes to the problem. Instead, cite examples of the college's refusal to answer letters about the situation or to discuss it. To provide statistical evidence of the problem's seriousness, you might note the small number of lots, the limited spaces in each, and the approximate number of student cars on campus.

Watch the Animation on **Reading a Cause and Effect Essay**

It's important to remember, however, that you're not just listing causes and effects; you're showing the reader their connection. Let's see how one student handled this connection. After you've read "Why Students Drop Out of College," the student essay that follows, carefully reexamine paragraph 3. Note how the sentence beginning "In many schools" and the two following it show precisely how poor study habits develop. Note further how the sentence beginning "This laxity produces" and the three following it show precisely how such poor habits result in "a flood of low grades and failure." Armed with this information, readers are better able to avoid poor study habits and their consequences.

Revising the Cause and Effect Analysis

Follow the guidelines in Chapter 4 and answer these questions and suggestions as you revise your causal analysis:

- How could the paper better achieve its purpose or reach its audience?
- Does the focus on causes, effects, or both accomplish the goal of the paper?
- Does the paper address the important causes and effects necessary for its purpose? Brainstorm or do additional research.
- Does the paper address the right relationships? Check brainstorming to determine if the paper needs to address a causal chain, an immediate cause with several supporting causes, or multiple causes and effects.
- Are there any mistakes in reasoning? Test to see that other causes aren't neglected, chronology is not mistaken for causation, and causes are not confused with effects?
- Where could the order and relationship between causes and effects be clearer or placed in a better order?
- Where could the discussion be supported with better explanation, details, examples, or statistics?
- Where could the paragraphs be better focused or developed? Too many causes or effects in a paragraph can be confusing.
- Where could the transitions be made clearer?
- Does the paper accurately represent the causes or effects and their relationships without distortion in an ethical manner?

SAMPLE

STUDENT ESSAY OF **CAUSE AND EFFECT**

Why Students Drop Out of College

Diann Fisher

1   Each fall a new crop of first-year college students, wavering between high hopes for the future and intense anxiety about their new status, scan college maps searching for their classrooms. They have been told repeatedly that college is the key to a well-paying job, and they certainly don't want to support themselves by flipping hamburgers or working at some other dead-end job. So, notebooks at the ready, they await what college has in store. Unfortunately many of them—indeed, over 30 percent— will not return after the first year. Why do so many students leave?

Identifies importance of topic and area of concern

Identifies primary question and main causes to be discussed

Continued on next page

Continued from previous page

There are several reasons. Some find the academic program too hard, some lack the proper study habits or motivation, others fall victim to the temptations of the college environment, and a large group leave for personal reasons.

Transition identifies first major cause

Provides detail of related causes producing lack of preparation

2   Not surprisingly, the academic shortcomings of college students have strong links to high school. In the past, a high school student who lacked the ability or desire to take a college-preparatory course could settle for a diploma in general studies and afterward find a job with decent pay. Now that possibility scarcely exists, so many poorly prepared students feel compelled to try college. Getting accepted by some schools isn't difficult. Once in, though, the student who has taken nothing beyond general mathematics, English, and science faces serious trouble when confronted with college algebra, first-year composition, and biological or physical science. Most colleges do offer remedial courses and other assistance that may help some weaker students to survive. In spite of everything, however, many others find themselves facing ever-worsening grade-point averages and either fail or just give up.

Offers qualification, but links major cause with effect

Transition to second cause

Provides details that lead to poor study habits

3   Like academic shortcomings, poor study habits have their roots in high school, where even average students can often breeze through with a minimum of effort. In many schools, outside assignments are rare and so easy that they require little time or thought to complete. To accommodate slower students, teachers frequently repeat material so many times that slightly better students can grasp it without opening their books. And when papers are late, teachers often don't mark them down. This laxity produces students who can't or don't want to study, students totally unprepared for the rigorous demands of college. There, courses may require several hours of study each week in order to be passed with even a C. In many programs, outside assignments are commonplace and demanding. Instructors expect students to grasp material after one explanation, and many won't accept late papers at all. Students who don't quickly develop disciplined study habits face a flood of low grades and failure.

Explains relationship between cause and result

Provides transition to next cause

Details related sequence of events that result in effect

4   Poor student motivation aggravates faulty study habits. Students who thought high school was boring find even less allure in the more challenging college offerings. Lacking any commitment to do well, they shrug off assigned papers, skip classes, and avoid doing required reading. Over time, classes gradually shrink as more and more students stay

away. With final exams upon them, some return in a last-ditch effort to salvage a passing grade, but by then it is too late. Eventually, repetition of this scenario forces the students out.

5   The wide range of freedoms offered by the college environment can overwhelm even well-prepared newcomers. While students are in high school, parents are on hand to make them study, push them off to class, and send them to bed at a reasonable hour. Once away from home and parents, however, far too many students become caught up in a constant round of parties, dates, bull sessions, and other distractions that seem more fascinating than schoolwork. Again, if such behavior persists, poor grades and failure result.

Offers a transition to the next cause

Provides supporting details

Links cause to result under discussion

6   Personal reasons also take a heavy toll on students who might otherwise complete their programs successfully. Often money problems are at fault. For example, a student may lose a scholarship or grant, fail to obtain needed work, or find that the family can no longer afford to help out. Some students succumb to homesickness; some are forced out by an illness, injury, or death in the family; and yet others become ill or injure themselves and leave to recuperate. Finally, a considerable number become disillusioned with their programs or the size, location, or atmosphere of their schools and decide not to return.

Offers transition to final cause discussed

Provides supporting examples

7   What happens to the students who drop out? Some re-enroll in college later, often in less demanding two- and four-year schools that offer a better chance of academic success. Of the remainder, the great bulk find civilian jobs or enlist in the armed forces. Most, whatever their choice, go on to lead productive, useful lives. In the meantime, campus newcomers need to know about the dangers that tripped up so many of their predecessors and make every effort to avoid them.

Identifies effects of item under consideration

Challenges the reader

Discussion Questions

1. Identify the thesis statement in this essay.
2. Trace the causal chain that makes up paragraph 2.
3. What is the function of the first sentence in paragraph 3?
4. In which paragraphs does the writer discuss causes? Effects?

Suggestions for Writing

Use one of the following topics, or another that your instructor approves, to develop a causal analysis. Determine which causes and/or effects to consider. Scrutinize your analysis for errors in reasoning, settle on an organization, and write the essay.

1. Reasons why relationships fail
2. The effect of some friend, acquaintance, public figure, or writer on your life
3. Effects of divorce on children
4. Why you are a _____ major
5. Causes, effects, or both of the popularity of Facebook
6. Causes of school violence
7. Causes, effects, or both of widespread cell phone use
8. Reasons that you have a particular habit or participate in a particular sport
9. Causes or effects of sleep deprivation
10. Effects of some recent Supreme Court decision or change in public policy
11. The effects of environmental concerns on our way of life
12. Causes, effects, or both of our hunger for heroes
13. Causes, effects, or both of drinking on college students
14. Causes of procrastination
15. Reasons that some students drop out of high school

STEPPING UP TO **SYNTHESIS**

Although nearly everyone recognizes the role of causation in human affairs, differences of opinion often surface about the causes and effects of important matters. What lies behind the widespread incivility in the United States today? Why are women more likely than men to leave management jobs? How do video games affect children? What impact does the high divorce rate have on American society? Obviously such questions lack simple answers; as a result investigators, even when they agree on the causes and effects involved, often debate their relative importance.

Prewriting for Synthesis Suppose your women's studies instructor has asked you to investigate the departure of women from managerial positions. A library search reveals several articles on this topic as well as a number of reasons for resigning. Some women leave because they find it harder to advance than men do, and as a result they seldom attain senior positions. Others leave because they receive lower salaries than their male counterparts. Still others leave because of the stifling effects of corporate rigidity, unrealistic expectations, the demands of raising a family, or possibly diminished chances of marriage. Although most articles cite these causes, their relative importance is debatable. One writer, for example, emphasizes family concerns by discussing them last and at greatest length. Another puts the chief blame on obstacles to upward mobility—the existence of a "glass ceiling" that blocks women from upper-level positions along with an "old-boy network" of entrenched executives that parcels out jobs among its members.

Critically Evaluating Your Sources Once you've finished your research, you're ready to synthesize the views of your sources as well as your own views. Before you start to write, though, take some time to consider carefully each cause and effect you've uncovered. Obviously you should ground your paper on well-supported and widely acknowledged causes and effects, but you might also include more speculative ones as long as you clearly indicate their secondary nature. To illustrate, one writer, while mentioning corporate rigidity as a reason that women leave management jobs, clearly labels this explanation as a theory and backs it with a single example. As you examine your material, ask yourself these critical questions as well as any others that occur to you: Does any writer exhibit obvious bias? Do the studies cited include a sufficient number of examples to be meaningful? Do the statistics appear reliable, or are some out of date, irrelevant, or skimpy? Have the writers avoided the reasoning errors discussed on page 236? Whenever you find a flaw, note where the problem lies so that you can discuss it in your writing if you choose. Such discussions often clear up common misconceptions.

Planning and Developing Your Synthesis There are various possibilities for organizing your paper. If your sources substantially agree on the most important cause, you might begin with that one and then take up the others. A second possibility, the order-of-climax arrangement, reverses the procedure by starting with secondary causes and ending with the most significant one. You can use the same options for organizing effects. When no clear consensus exists about the relative importance of the different causes and effects, there is no best arrangement of the material.

Getting Started

1. Read three articles on the causes of a major social problem, such as domestic violence, and incorporate those causes and your own views in a paper.
2. Read two articles that disagree about the effects of a proposed government program, such as oil and gas drilling on public land, and write a paper that incorporates the writers' views and presents your own conclusions.
3. Write an essay that corrects a common misconception about the causes or effects of a matter about which you feel strongly. Possibilities might include the causes of homelessness or the impact of capital punishment on murder rates in different states.

Complete additional exercises and practice in your MyLab

Writing a Causal Analysis

Prewriting the cause and effect analysis.

- Identify key topic based on assignment or personal interest.
- Identify audience and purpose.
- Decide if you are more interested in causes or effects.
- Brainstorm and take notes on causes and effects based on reading, observations, and talking with others.
- Test your causes and effects to make certain that you are not:
  - Missing causes or effects
  - Ignoring multiple causes
  - Mistaking correlation for causation
  - Confusing cause and effect
- Have you carefully uncovered all the appropriate causes and effects and weighed their importance fairly?
- Have you considered the consequence if people act on your analysis?

Planning the cause and effect analysis.

- Identify the most appropriate pattern: effects of a single cause, or a single event, a chain of effects or causes, and effects of an event.
- Create a table that organizes causes or effects and provides the details you will stress.
- Create a rough outline, or plan, of the pattern of causes and effects.

Drafting the cause and effect analysis.

- Introduction introduces topic, reasons for analysis, and focuses on cause or effect.
- Body provides causes or effects with details and reasons, shows connections, and follows pattern.
- Conclusion may specify consequences, warn readers, or evaluate importance of cause or effect.
- Check to determine whether you are discussing every important cause or effect, even if it might damage a case you are trying to make.

Revising the cause and effect analysis.

Repeat process as necessary.

- Does the focus on cause or effect fit the purpose and facts?
- Add missing cause or effect, detail, or evidence.
- Cut parts that don't fit.
- Evaluate accuracy of account and pattern.
- Test organization to make it clear to reader.

Proofread.

CHAPTER 15 Definition: Establishing Boundaries

In this chapter you will learn how to:

15.1 Use definition as a writing strategy.

15.2 Develop synonyms and essential definitions.

15.3 Avoid common pitfalls of definition.

15.4 Employ various writing strategies to create extended definitions.

15.5 Write so that your definition is ethical.

15.6 Prewrite, plan, draft, and revise your extended definition.

Mercury Venus Earth Mars Ceres Jupiter Saturn Uranus Neptune Pluto and Charon 2003 UB$_{313}$

The International Astronomical Union/Martin Kornmesser

That movie was egregious.

Once the bandage is off the wound, swab the proud flesh with the disinfectant.

Speaking on statewide television, Governor Blaine called his opponent a left-winger.

Do you have questions? You're not alone. Many people would question the sentences above: "What does *egregious* mean?" "How can flesh be *proud?*" "What does the governor mean by *left-winger?* What specific policies does the opponent support that warrant this label?" To avoid puzzling and provoking your own readers, you'll often need to explain the meaning of some term. The term may be unfamiliar *(egregious)*, used in an unfamiliar sense *(proud flesh)*, or mean different things to different people *(left-winger)*. Whenever you clarify the meaning of some term, you are *defining*.

Humans are instinctively curious. We start asking about meanings as soon as we can talk, and we continue to seek, as well as supply, definitions all through life.

- In school, instructors expect us to explain all sorts of literary, historical, scientific, technical, and social terms.
- On the job, a member of a company's human resources department might prepare a brochure that explains the meaning of such terms as *corporate responsibility* and *product stewardship* for new employees.
- An accountant might define *statistical sampling inventory* in a report calling for a change in the inventory system.
- A special education teacher might write a memo explaining *learning disabled* to the rest of the staff.

15.1

Use definition as a writing strategy.

When you define, you identify the features that distinguish a term, thereby putting a fence around it, establishing its boundaries, and separating it from all others. Knowing these features enables both you and your reader to use the term appropriately.

Sometimes a word, phrase, or sentence will settle a definition question. To clear up the mystery of "proud flesh," all you'd need to do is insert the parenthetical phrase "(excessively swollen and grainy)" after the word *proud*. But when you're dealing with new terms—*information superhighway* and *virtual reality* are examples—brief definitions won't provide the reader with enough information for proper understanding.

Abstract terms—those standing for things we can't see, touch, or otherwise detect with our five senses—often require extended definitions, too. It's impossible to capture the essence of *democracy* or *hatred* or *bravery* in a single sentence: The terms are too complex, and people have too many differing ideas about what they mean. The same holds true for some concrete terms—those standing for actions and things we can perceive with our five senses. Some people, for instance, limit the term *drug pusher* to full-time sellers of hard drugs like cocaine and heroin. Others, at the opposite extreme, extend the term to full- and part-time sellers of any illegal drug. Writing an argument recommending life sentences for convicted drug pushers would require you to tell just what you mean by the term so that the reader would have solid grounds for judging your position.

Types of Definitions

Three types of definition—synonyms, essential definitions, and extended definitions—serve writers' needs. Although the first two seldom require more than a word or a sentence, an extended definition can run to several pages. The three types, however, are related, and synonyms and essential definitions both furnish starting points for extended definitions.

Synonyms

Synonyms are words with very nearly the same meanings. *Lissome* is synonymous with *lithe* or *nimble,* and *condign* is a synonym of *worthy* and *suitable.* Synonyms let writers clarify meanings of unfamiliar words without using cumbersome explanations. To clarify the term *expostulation* in a quoted passage, all you'd have to do is add the word *objection,* in brackets, after it. Because synonyms are not identical twins, using them puts a slightly different shade of meaning on a message. For example, to "protest" and to "object" are certainly similar in many ways. Yet the claim that we "object" to the establishment of a nuclear waste site in our area fails to capture the active and sustained commitment implied in our willingness to "protest" against such a site.

15.2

Develop synonyms and essential definitions.

Essential Definitions

An essential definition does three things: (1) names the item being defined, (2) places it in a broad category, and (3) distinguishes it from other items in that category. Following are three examples:

Item Being Defined	Broad Category	Distinguishing Features
A howdah	is a covered seat	for riding on the back of an elephant or camel.
A voiceprint	is a graphical record	of a person's voice characteristics.
To parboil	is to boil meat, vegetables, or fruits	until they are partially cooked.

Writing a good essential definition requires careful thought. Suppose your instructor has asked you to write an essential definition of one of the terms listed in an exercise, and you choose vacuum cleaner. Coming up with a broad category presents no problem: A vacuum cleaner is a household appliance. The hard part is pinpointing the distinguishing features. The purpose of a vacuum cleaner is to clean floors, carpets, and upholstery. You soon realize, however, that these features alone do not separate vacuum cleaners from other appliances. After all, carpet sweepers also clean floors, and whisk brooms clean upholstery. What then does distinguish vacuum cleaners? After a little thought, you realize that, unlike the other items, a vacuum cleaner works by suction. You then write the following definition:

> A vacuum cleaner is a household appliance that uses suction to clean floors, carpets, and upholstery.

The same careful attention is necessary to establish the distinguishing features of any essential definition.

Limitations of Essential Definitions   Essential definitions have certain built-in limitations. Because of their brevity, they often can't do full justice to abstract terms such as *cowardice, love, jealousy,* or *power.* Problems also arise with terms that have several settled meanings. To explain *jam* adequately, you'd need at least three essential definitions: (1) a closely packed crowd, (2) preserves, and (3) a difficult situation. But despite these limitations, an essential definition can be useful by itself or as part of a longer definition.

15.3

Avoid common pitfalls of definition.

Pitfalls in Preparing Essential Definitions   When you prepare an essential definition, guard against these flaws:

Circular definition. Don't define a term by repeating it or changing its form slightly. Saying that a psychiatrist is "a physician who practices psychiatry" will only frustrate someone who's never heard of psychiatry. Repress circularity and provide the proper insight by choosing terms the reader can relate to; for example, "A psychiatrist is a physician who diagnoses and treats mental disorders."

Overly broad definition. Shy away from definitions that embrace too much territory. If you define a skunk as "an animal that has a bushy tail and black fur with white markings," your definition is not precise. Many cats and dogs also fit this description. But if you add "and that ejects a foul-smelling secretion when threatened," you will clear the air.

Overly narrow definition. Don't hem in your definition too closely. "A kitchen blender is a bladed electrical appliance used to chop foods" illustrates this error. Blenders perform other operations, too. To correct the error, add the missing information: "A kitchen blender is a bladed electrical appliance used to chop, mix, whip, or otherwise process foods."

Omission of main category. Avoid using "is where" or "is when" instead of naming the main category. Here is an example of this error: "A bistro is where food and wine are served." The reader will not know exactly what sort of thing (a bar? a party?) a *bistro* is. Note the improvement when the broad category is named: "A bistro is a small restaurant where both food and wine are served."

1. **Identify the broad category and the distinguishing traits in each of these essential definitions:**

   a. Gangue is useless rock accompanying valuable minerals in a deposit.
   b. A catbird is a small American songbird with a slate-colored body, a black cap, and a catlike cry.
   c. A soldier is a man or woman serving in an army.
   d. Myelin is a white, fatty substance that forms a sheath around some nerve fibers.
   e. A gargoyle is a waterspout carved in the likeness of a grotesque animal or imaginary creature and projecting from the gutter of a building.
   f. A magnum is a wine bottle that holds about two-fifths of a gallon.

2. **Indicate which of the following statements are acceptable essential definitions. Explain what is wrong with those that are not. Correct them.**

   a. A scalpel is a small knife that has a sharp blade used for surgery and anatomical dissections.
   b. A puritan is a person with puritanical beliefs.
   c. A kraal is where South African tribes keep large domestic animals.
   d. A rifle is a firearm that has a grooved barrel and is used for hunting large game.
   e. A motorcycle is a two-wheeled vehicle used mainly for human transportation.
   f. Fainting is when a person loses consciousness owing to inadequate flow of blood to the brain.

3. **Write an essential definition for each of the following terms:**

   a. groupie   d. jock   f. hard grader
   b. happy hour   e. pushover
   c. hit man

Extended Definitions

Sometimes it's necessary to go beyond an essential definition and write a paragraph or whole paper explaining a term. New technical, social, and economic terms often require extended definitions. To illustrate, a computer scientist might need to define *data integrity* so that computer operators understand the importance of maintaining it. Terms with differing meanings also frequently require extended definitions. To let voters know just what he means by *left-winger*, Governor Blaine might detail the kinds of legislation his opponent favors and opposes.

Extended definitions are not merely academic exercises; they are fundamental to your career and your life. A police officer needs to have a clear understanding of what counts as *reasonable grounds for search and seizure*; an engineer must comprehend the meaning of *stress*; a nuclear medical technologist had better have a solid grasp of *radiation*. And all of us are concerned with the definition of our basic rights as citizens.

Extended definitions are montages of other methods of development—narration, description, process analysis, illustration, classification, comparison, and cause and effect. Often, they also define by negation: explaining what a term *does not* mean. The following paragraphs show how one writer handled an extended definition of *sudden infant death syndrome*. The student began by presenting a case

15.4

Employ various writing strategies to create extended definitions.

Watch the Animation on **Definitions and Examples**

history (illustration), which also incorporated an essential definition and two synonyms.

> Jane and Dick Smith were proud, new parents of an eight-pound, ten-ounce baby girl named Jenny. One summer night, Jane put Jenny to bed at 8:00. When she went to check on her at 3:00 A.M., Jane found Jenny dead. The baby had given no cry of pain, shown no sign of trouble. Even the doctor did not know why she had died, for she was healthy and strong. The autopsy report confirmed the doctor's suspicion—the infant was a victim of "sudden infant death syndrome," also known as SIDS or crib death. SIDS is the sudden and unexplainable death of an apparently healthy, sleeping infant. It is the number-one cause of death in infants after the first week of life and as a result has been the subject of numerous research studies.

Discussion Questions

1. What synonyms does the writer use?
2. Which sentence presents an essential definition?

In the next paragraph, the writer turned to negation, pointing out some of the things that researchers have ruled out about SIDS.

> Although researchers do not know what SIDS is, they do know what it is *not*. They know it cannot be predicted; it strikes like a thief in the night. Crib deaths occur in seconds, with no sound of pain, and they always happen when the child is sleeping. Suffocation is *not* the cause, nor is aspiration or regurgitation. Researchers have found no correlation between the incidence of SIDS and the mother's use of birth control pills or tobacco or the presence of fluoride in water. Since it is not hereditary or contagious, only a slim chance exists that SIDS will strike twice in the same family.

Finally, the student explored several proposed causes of SIDS as well as how parents may react to the loss of their child.

> As might be expected, researchers have offered many theories concerning the cause of crib death. Dr. R. C. Reisinger, a National Cancer Institute scientist, has linked crib deaths to the growth of a common bacterium, *E. coli*, in the intestines of newborn babies. The organisms multiply in the intestines, manufacturing a toxin that is absorbed by the intestinal wall and passes into the bloodstream. Breast milk stops the growth of the organism, whereas cow's milk permits it. Therefore, Dr. Reisinger believes, bottle-fed babies run a higher risk of crib death than other babies. . . .

Trudy Stelter

Ethical Issues

How we define can have devastating consequences. For centuries, the practice of defining Africans as "subhuman" helped justify the slave trade and slavery. During the 1930s and early 1940s, labeling Jews as "vermin" was used to fuel the attempt to exterminate them both in Nazi Germany and much of Western Europe. Even in the absence of malice, definition can have far-reaching effects, both good and bad. For instance, a change in the federal definition of "poverty" can increase or decrease by millions the number of individuals and households eligible for benefits such as Medicaid. Although the consequences of your writing won't approach those of the above examples, you'll nevertheless need to think about possible ethical implications. Addressing the following questions will help you do this.

15.5

Write so that your definition is ethical.

- Have I carefully evaluated all of the features of my definition? In clarifying what constitutes "excessive force" by the police, it would be unfair to include the reasonable means necessary to subdue a highly dangerous suspect.
- Have I slanted my definition to reflect some prejudice? Let's say a writer opposed to casino gambling is defining "gambling addicts." The paper should focus on those who spend an excessive amount of time in casinos, bet and often lose large sums of money, and in so doing neglect family, financial, and personal obligations. It would be unfair to include those who visit casinos occasionally and strictly limit their losses.
- Have I avoided unnecessary connotations that might be harmful? A definition of teenagers that overemphasized their swift changes in mood might be unfair, perhaps even harmful, since it may influence the reactions of readers.

Writing an Extended Definition

If you choose your own topic, pick an abstract term or one that is concrete but unfamiliar to your reader. Why, for instance, define *table* when the discussion would likely bore the reader? On the other hand, a paper explaining *computer virus* might well prove interesting and informative.

15.6

Prewrite, plan, draft, and revise your extended definition.

Prewriting the Extended Definition

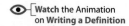
Watch the Animation on **Writing a Definition**

FINDING YOUR TOPIC

- Brainstorm key words or phrases that interest you or you have disputed.
- Write down terms you have read that are points of contention.
- Identify a term you know about or that interests you.
- Determine what purpose would be served by defining the term. Clarify a specialized concept? Persuade the reader to adopt an attitude towards it? Discuss some neglected facet? Show what it means to you.
- Jot down ideas about audiences that would be interested in this term.

DEVELOPING YOUR DEFINITION

- Select clear examples of what you wish to define, such as the United States as an example of democracy.
- Brainstorm major identifying characteristics, such as majority rule, free elections, and separately elected chief executive.
- Test these characteristics against other legitimate examples, such as Britain, which is a democracy but lacks a separately elected chief executive.
- Test your characteristics against clear counterexamples, such as the People's Republic of China, which the definition shouldn't fit.
- Chart the method you will use and brainstorm details.

Planning and Drafting the Extended Definition

Each method has its own set of special strengths, as the following list shows:

Narration. Tracing the history of a new development or the changing meaning of a term: the birth of the Internet

Description. Pointing out interesting or important features of a device, an event, or an individual: a blizzard

Process. Explaining what a device does or how it is used, how a procedure is carried out, or how a natural event takes place: an earthquake

Illustration. Tracing changes in meaning and defining abstract terms by providing examples: tyranny

Classification. Pointing out the different categories into which an item or an event can be grouped: types of romantic comedies

Comparison. Distinguishing between an unfamiliar and a familiar item: terrorist distinguished from soldier

Cause and effect. Explaining the origins and consequences of events, conditions, problems, and attitudes: disease defined by cause

Negation. Placing limitations on conditions and events and correcting popular misconceptions: why liberty isn't anarchy

Don't hesitate to use a method for some purpose not mentioned here.

The example that follows is for a paper using a chart to develop four methods of development.

Narration	Classification	Process	Negation
Beginning American Democracy	Types of democracy	Election process	Not democracies
Forming a constitutional committee	Parliamentary democracy: England	Initial exploration	Single party states: Old Soviet Union
Drafting a constitution	Independent presidency: U.S.	Fund raising	Controlled elections: Egypt

The **thesis statements** for extend definitions often focus on the reason the readers may be interested in a term or concept combined with a major defining characteristic. "Many politicians claim the libertarian mantle, but few really accept the core idea that government and laws should be drastically limited." Look to your major defining characteristic and the reason in your brainstorming on why this term is important for ideas for your thesis.

Definition papers can begin in various ways. In writing the body of the paper, present the methods of development in whatever order seems most appropriate. A paper defining *drag racing* might first describe the hectic scene as the cars line up for a race, then classify the different categories of vehicles, and finally explain the steps in a race. One defining *intellectual* might start by showing the differences between intellectuals and scholars, then name several prominent intellectuals and note how their insights have altered our thinking, and conclude by trying to explain why many Americans hold intellectuals in low regard.

 Analyze the Interactive Definition for **Organization**

Introduction
- If no agreed upon definition (as in "conservatism"), maybe note different views and then your own.
- If the term reflects a new development (as in "the cloud"), possibly mention how it came to be.
- A definition of a colloquial or slang word (chutzpah), but other topics as well, can start with an example that grabs the reader.
- Sometimes a short dictionary definition can be useful, but this can often create a stale beginning.

Body
- Have a clear, logical order for your reader
- Select the strategies you use based on your purpose and audience. Don't use strategies just to use them.
- Develop each part of the definition with examples and details that will make it concrete for your reader.
- Provide clear transitions for your reader.

Conclusion
- If defining some undesirable condition (such as sudden infant death syndrome), maybe express hope for a speedy solution.
- Or if reporting a new development, discuss its impact.
- Or if defining a socially important term (such as "post-racial"), you might call for a certain action.
- Or if the paper is longer, summarize main points.

Revising the Extended Definition

Use the general guidelines in Chapter 4 and these specific questions and suggestions as you revise your extended definition:

- Where could the paper better fit your audience and purpose? If your definition of "drought" is to show the social impact and encourage action, you may need to strengthen your personal examples.
- If an essential definition was used, does it avoid the pitfalls?
- What other defining characteristics may be missing? Look for some additional examples and brainstorm.
- Where are additional examples and details necessary to make the definition clear and vivid for readers? Try brainstorming tied to specific paragraphs.
- What other strategies might have helped clarify the definition? Was any strategy unhelpful? Try writing some additional approaches on a separate page.
- Where could the organization of the paper be made more effective?
- Where could transitions be strengthened to more clearly signal shifts in focus to the reader?
- Where could paragraphs be more specifically focused? It can be helpful to label each paragraph to see what it is intended to contribute to the paper.
- Has the paper avoided being slanted by prejudice or presenting harmful and unnecessary connotations so that the paper is ethical?

SAMPLE

STUDENT ESSAY OF **DEFINITION**

Rediscovering Patriotism

Peter Wing

Uses a telling event to establish significance of the term

1 After the horrifying events of September 11, 2001, when terrorists flew jet planes into the World Trade Center and the Pentagon, killing thousands of Americans, there was a surge of patriotism. America was under attack, and as we frequently do when our nation is threatened, we rallied around the flag. Flags were pasted in the back windows of cars and the front windows of homes. So many Americans bought flags that stores were quickly sold out. It was a rare car that didn't have a United We Stand bumper sticker. Rock groups that had built their image around cynicism gleefully participated in patriotic concerts. In short, it became fashionable once again to be a flag-waving, "Star Spangled Banner"-singing, country-loving patriot.

2   These results were good, but there was also an alarming side to this newfound patriotism. Those who even suggested that American foreign policy might have contributed to the attack were branded *traitor* and were effectively silenced. People, including members of Congress, who criticized the way the war on terrorism was being conducted were lambasted as unpatriotic. In my neighborhood, those who didn't fly flags, who didn't have patriotic bumper stickers, who didn't seethe with righteous anger at America's enemy were labeled un-American. All of this raises an obvious question: What is patriotism?

Indicates possible harmful definitions and reason for definition

3   The obvious answer is that patriotism is love for one's country. But clearly that answer is too broad. Someone could easily love the skyscrapers of Manhattan, the gorgeous vistas of the Grand Canyon, and even the cornfields of Iowa and still sell military secrets to an enemy of America, a far-from-patriotic act. Timothy McVeigh would probably have said that he loved his country, but it would be troubling to consider his attack on the Alfred P. Murrah Federal Building a patriotic act. Certainly patriotism can include an intense love for the land, an appreciation for the people that make up our nation, and a pride in the accomplishments of our country. Part of the heart-swelling quality of patriotism is the recognition of all that is great and good about our nation: the valiant role of our soldiers in World War II; the innovative spirit that forged new technologies, cured diseases, and allowed Americans to journey to the moon. However, that pride would be incomplete without an appreciation for and dedication to the core principles that define this nation.

Indicates obvious definition to dispute

Demonstrates limits to definition without completely rejecting it

4   In the end, what is most essential to America is not our industrial wealth, our military power, or artistic works. America is defined by its initial vision, the commitment to democracy, to basic political equality for all Americans, to liberty, to the rights of the individual. Consider how odd it would be if someone's claim to patriotism were a desire for a military coup that toppled democracy to establish a more powerful military. Surely we would find someone seriously misguided who loved American industry but wanted to discard the Constitution and have only the heads of corporations serve in Congress. While there may be many aspects to patriotism, the core of American patriotism would have to be a solid commitment to the core values of the Constitution.

Provides reason to consider alternative definition

5   What is it, then, to have a love for and commitment to the core values of a nation? It is easy to confuse patriotism with the symbols of

Continued on next page

Continued from previous page

Offers comparison to sharpen definition

patriotism, the flag waving and anthem singing. Just as a husband who gives his wife a love poem and a diamond ring and then rushes out to cheat on her isn't really the best husband, someone who proudly flies a flag but never votes, refuses to serve on juries, and actively discriminates is not the best patriot. Serving in the military is rightly considered one of the most distinguished acts of patriotism, and properly so. Soldiers don't just say they love their country; they risk their lives to protect the people and the principles of their nation, to preserve liberty. Just as love for a spouse isn't simply a matter of gushy greeting cards but rather concerted day-to-day action, including listening patiently to the other's problems, so patriotism lives and breathes through actions. That doesn't have to be military action but can be participation in anything that preserves and strengthens what is best about a nation. Patriotism then means voting in elections, actively participating in campaigns, writing to legislators, serving on juries, volunteering for schools, building homes for the poor, obeying laws, honoring those who serve, and criticizing things that are wrong.

Illustrates through example

Identifies implication of offered definition

6   One of the paradoxes of this notion of patriotism is that it makes it essential to criticize and even protest against government policy. It would be a poor friend who let a buddy slide into alcoholism without comment. It would be a poor patriot who would let America move away from the best it can be without action. To really love one's country is to struggle to help make that country realize its best ideals. Those who protested against segregation in America were patriots, recalling America to the fundamental commitment to equality. Many who marched against the Vietnam War were patriotic since they believed that the war violated America's commitment to justice. So too were those who felt the Vietnam War was necessary to American security, for they only wanted to protect America from a perceived communist threat. Those who objected to the way the war against terrorism was being conducted also, then, could be considered patriotic, for they too, out of a love for their country, were participating in the democratic process, raising their voice so that America would choose the best course of action. Patriotism doesn't reside in being on one side or the other of a political debate; it exists in the honest struggle to realize the best ideals of the country. Given this view, in a democracy, no group has a monopoly on patriotism.

Illustrates through examples

Identifies consequence of definition

7   That is why some of the bitter slogans of supposed patriotism—My Country Right or Wrong or America: Love It or Leave It—are just plain wrong. While it is true that patriotism would suggest that we not disown

our country when it takes what we consider a misguided direction, it would surely not be patriotic to defend and support a direction we thought wrong. Those who are alarmed by the policies of the government or are deeply dissatisfied with some injustice, such as the horrible conditions of many inner-city schools, are not lacking in patriotism and have no obligation to leave. Those who complain, carp, protest, (or) point out shortcomings are acting out of a profound patriotism. Because of their love for their country, they struggle to move the country to realize its best ideals. If there were any bumper sticker I would want to see for patriotism, it would be Our Country: Make It the Best It Can Be.

Defines through comparison

8   It is heartening to see the revival of patriotism. Hopefully, that patriotism will go beyond simple flag waving and dig deeper to the core meaning of patriotism where Americans together struggle to preserve and develop American ideals. Patriotism will really have taken root in America when citizens become involved in the political process, eagerly serve on juries, work to improve the lives of fellow citizens, and, surprisingly enough, raise their voices in criticism when we, as a government and a people, fall short of the very best we can become.

Results in a call to action

Discussion Questions

1. Identify the essay's essential definition.
2. What purpose do the first two paragraphs serve?
3. How does the writer develop his definition?
4. What do the first three sentences of paragraph 6 accomplish?
5. Why might the writer have decided to discuss bumper sticker slogans in the next to the last paragraph?
6. By this definition, would the author consider members of the Tea Party patriots? Why or why not?

Suggestions for Writing

Write a properly focused extended definition using one of the following suggestions or one approved by your instructor. The term you define may be new, misused, or misunderstood or may have a disputed meaning. Develop the essay by any combination of writing strategies.

1. Integrity
2. Green technologies
3. Stress
4. Human genome
5. Extreme sports
6. Alternative rock
7. Breaking as a dance form

8. Campus security
9. Feminist
10. Hate crimes
11. Family values
12. Some term from your field
13. Online class
14. The Christian Right
15. Rap music

STEPPING UP TO **SYNTHESIS**

 Definitions are always social creations. The way various people and communities understand and use any word determines its definition. As a result, writers who use complex words such as *justice, love,* and *charisma* to convey a message may need to consult a number of sources to determine how others have used the words. With their findings of this research in mind, the writers can stake out their own meanings of those words.

Prewriting for Synthesis If you were writing a paper defining *dance* for a humanities class, you would probably find several conflicting meanings of the term. Frank Thiess, writing in *The Dance as an Artwork*, defines dance as the use of the body for expressive gesture. But as you mull over that definition, you realize that it is both too broad and too narrow. While some forms of dance, such as ballet, feature expressive gesture, so does pantomime or even a shaken fist; and neither of these qualifies as dance. A square dance clearly qualifies, but does it represent expressive gesture? Susanne Langer, in *Philosophy in a New Key*, defines dance as "a play of Powers made visible," pointing to the way dancers seem to be moved by forces beyond themselves. You recognize that this definition may apply to religious dance forms, that dancers sometimes appear swept away by the music, and that you yourself have experienced a feeling of power when dancing. Nevertheless, upon reflection you decide that often it's the dancer's skill that attracts us, and rarely do we dance to reveal invisible powers. Finally, you discover that Francis Sparshott, in *The Theory of the Arts*, defines dance as a rhythmical, patterned motion that transforms people's sense of their own existence according to the dance they do. As you evaluate Sparshott's contention, you decide that it has considerable merit, although you aren't convinced that every dance transforms our sense of existence.

Critically Evaluating Your Sources Carrying out this type of project requires you to look critically at the definitions of others. Do they accurately reflect the examples you know about? Do they describe examples that do not fit the definition? Are any parts of the definition questionable? Once you've answered these questions, you can then draw on the appropriate elements of the definitions to formulate your own.

Planning and Drafting Your Synthesis   When you think about the kinds of dance you know and the various definitions you have uncovered, you conclude that each of these writers, like the blind men who felt different parts of an elephant and tried to describe it, is only partly correct. For your humanities paper, you decide to synthesize the different definitions. You might explain that all dance involves a rhythmical, patterned movement of the body for its own sake. Sometimes such movement can transform our sense of existence, as in trance dances or even waltzes. Other dances, such as story ballets, use rhythmical movements as expressive gestures that tell stories or convey emotions. Still other dances may suggest the manifestation of powers beyond the dances themselves. You proceed to explain each of these features with details drawn from both your sources and personal experience.

You might organize such a paper by developing each definition in a separate section, first presenting it in detail and then pointing out its strengths and weaknesses. In the final section, you could offer your own definition and support it with your reasoning and suitable examples.

Getting Started

1. Read the essay "Supermarket Pastoral" (in the Reader) as well as several others on organic food that you find in the library. Reflect on the different definitions of "organic." Then, drawing on your reading, offer your own definition.
2. Read What Thoreau Knew: Walden and the Meaning of Voluntary Simplicity and "I Have a Dream" (in the Reader). Then write your own definition of success, taking into account the views expressed in these essays.
3. Do some reading about an abstract term like *bravery, democracy,* or *hatred* in at least three sources. Use the sources to develop your own definition of the term.

Complete additional exercises **and** practice in your MyLab

Writing an Extended Definition

Prewriting the definition.

- Identify your topic, audience, and purpose.
- Read about the term, talk to others, and observe its use.
- Brainstorm distinguishing characteristics, examples, and characteristic that are excluded.
- Test your defining features against ordinary usage to determine if they are too broad or narrow.
- Evaluate all the features of the definition.

Planning the definition.

- Create a table or chart of your definition with key characteristics, examples, and conclusions.
- Identify useful strategies for the definition: narration, description, process, illustration, cause-effect, negation.
- Create a plan of organization; organization may reflect strategies used or may be arranged by key defining characteristics.
- Check to be sure that the definition isn't being slanted to reflect prejudice.

Drafting the definition.

- Introduction introduces term, reason for definition, and dominant characteristic.
- Body presents distinctive defining characteristics.
- Conclusion may summarize main point, call for action, predict an outcome, or stress importance.
- Check that unnecessary harmful connotations are avoided.

Repeat the process as needed.

Revising the definition.

- Check to see if the definition is too general, too narrow, or uses circular definitions.
- Do defining characteristics fit?
- Add needed traits or examples.
- Cut unneeded elements.
- Test to make certain definition is complete and follows a clear pattern.

Proofread.

CHAPTER 16   Argument: Convincing Others

In this chapter you will learn how to:

16.1 Use argument as a writing strategy.

16.2 Critically evaluate and use different kinds of claims and evidence.

16.3 Construct effective inductive and deductive arguments, and use analogy.

16.4 Use effective emotional appeals to persuade.

16.5 Use effective ethical appeals to persuade.

16.6 Recognize and avoid logical fallacies.

16.7 Write so that your argument is ethical.

16.8 Prewrite, plan, draft, and revise your argument.

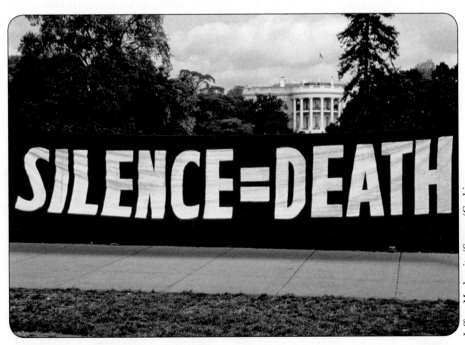

Jeffrey Markowitz/Sygma/Corbis

"What did you think of that movie?"

"Great!"

"What do you mean, *great?* I thought the acting was wooden and the story completely unbelievable."

"That's about what I'd expect from you. You wouldn't know a good movie if it walked up and bit you."

"Oh yeah? What makes you think you're such a great. . . . ?"

Argument or quarrel? Many people would ask, "What's the difference?" To them, the two terms convey the same meaning, both calling to mind two angry people, shouting and trading insults. In writing, however, *argument* stands for something quite different: a paper, grounded on logical, structured evidence, that attempts to convince the reader to accept a claim, take some action, or do both. Argument is also a process during which you explore an issue fully, considering different perspectives, assumptions, reasons, and evidence to reach your own informed position.

16.1

Use argument as a writing strategy.

The ability to argue effectively will help you succeed both in class and on the job.

- A business instructor may ask students to defend a particular management style.
- A political science instructor may want you to support or oppose limiting the number of terms that members of a legislature can serve.
- A special education instructor may have students make a written case for increased funding for exceptional students.
- In the workplace, a computer programmer may argue that the company should change its account-keeping program.
- An automotive service manager may call for new diagnostic equipment.
- A hospital administrator may argue for a better system to track patient care.

Arguments don't always involve disagreements. Some simply support a previously established decision or course of action, as when a department manager sends her boss a memo justifying some new procedure that she implemented. Others try to establish some common ground, just as you might do when you and your date weigh the pros and cons of two films and pick one to see.

When preparing to write an argument, you need to be aware that certain kinds of topics just aren't arguable. There's no point, for instance, in trying to tackle questions of personal preference or taste. (Is red prettier than blue?) Such contests quickly turn into "it is," "it isn't" exchanges that establish nothing. Questions of simple fact (Was Eisenhower first elected president in 1952?) don't qualify either. Bickering will never settle these issues; reference books quickly will. We turn to argument when there is room for disagreement.

When you write an argument, you don't simply sit down and dash off your views as though they came prefabricated. Instead, argument represents an opportunity to think things through, to gradually, and often tentatively, come to some conclusions, and then, in stages, begin to draft your position with the support you have discovered. You should try to keep an open mind as you formulate and then express your views. And remember, you rarely start from scratch. Instead, you join a conversation where ideas and evidence have already been exchanged. As a result, you need to be thoughtful and informed.

The most successful arguments rest on a firm foundation of solid, logical support. In addition, many arguments include emotion because it can play an important part in swaying reader opinion. Furthermore, writers often make ethical appeals by projecting favorable images of themselves since readers form conclusions based on their judgments of the writer.

The Rational Appeal

In society, and certainly in professional circles, you are usually expected to reach your conclusions on the basis of good reasons and appropriate evidence. Reasons are the key points or general ideas you'll use to defend your conclusions. If, for instance, you support the needle-exchange program for intravenous drug users, one reason might be the considerable reduction in AIDS-related deaths that could result. If you oppose the program, one reason may be the drug dependency that will continue.

To convince readers, your reasons must be substantiated by evidence. If you favor needle exchange, you could cite figures that project the number of deaths that will be prevented. If you're against the program, you might quote a respected authority who verifies that dependency will become entrenched.

When you appeal to reason in an argument, then, you present your reasons and evidence in such a way that if your readers are also reasonable they will likely agree with you, or at least see your position as plausible. That assumes, of course, that you and your readers start from some common ground about the principles you share and what you count as evidence. Evidence falls into several categories: established truths, opinions of authorities, primary source information, statistical findings, and personal experience. The strongest arguments usually combine several kinds of evidence.

16.2

Critically evaluate and use different kinds of claims and evidence.

Watch the Animation on **Appeals to Reason**

Established Truths

These are facts that no one can seriously dispute. Following are some examples:

Historical fact:	The First Amendment to the United States Constitution prohibits Congress from abridging freedom of the press.
Scientific fact:	The layer of ozone in the earth's upper atmosphere protects us from the sun's harmful ultraviolet radiation.
Geographical fact:	The western part of the United States has tremendous reserves of coal.

Established truths aren't arguable themselves but do provide strong backup for argumentative propositions. For example, citing the abundant coal supply in the western regions could support an argument that the United States should return to coal to supply its energy needs.

Most such "truths" are often repeated across a number of reputable sources, including standard encyclopedias and textbooks. Some established truths, the result of careful observations and thinking over many years, basically amount to enlightened common sense. The notion that everyone possesses a unique combination of interests, abilities, and personality characteristics illustrates this kind of truth. Few people would seriously question it.

Opinions of Authorities

An authority is a recognized expert in some field. Authoritative opinions play a powerful role in winning readers over to your side. The views of metropolitan police chiefs and criminologists could support your position on ways to control urban crime. Researchers who have investigated the effects of air pollution could help you argue for stricter smog-control laws. Whatever your argument, don't settle for less than heavyweight authorities, and, when possible, indicate their credentials to your reader. This information makes their statements more persuasive. For example, "Ann Marie Forsythe, a certified public accountant and vice-president of North American operations for Touche Ross Accounting, believes that the president's tax cut proposal will actually result in a tax increase for most Americans." You should, of course, also cite the source of your information. Follow your instructor's guidelines.

The following paragraph, from an article arguing that extra-high-voltage electric transmission lines pose a health hazard, illustrates the use of authority:

Identifies professional role that confirms authority

Identifies credible institutions

Documents length of work in the field that makes him an expert

Ties claims to specific research

Robert Becker, a physician and director of the Orthopedic–Biophysics Laboratory at the Syracuse, New York, Veterans Administration Hospital–Upstate Medical Center, has been researching the effects of low-frequency electric fields (60 Hz) for fifteen years. Testifying at health and safety hearings for proposed lines in New York, he said that exposure to the fields can produce physiological and functional changes in humans—anything from increased irritability and fatigue to raised cholesterol levels, hypertension and ulcers. Studies of rats exposed to low-level electric fields showed tumor growths and abnormalities in development. Dr. Becker believes we are performing unauthorized medical experiments by exposing people to the electromagnetic fields surrounding the transmission lines.

Kelly Davis, "Health and High Voltage: 765 KV Lines"

Beware of biased opinions. The agribusiness executive who favors farm price supports or the labor leader who opposes any restrictions on picketing may be writing merely to guard old privileges or garner new ones. Unless the opinion can stand especially close scrutiny, don't put it in your paper; it will just weaken your case with perceptive readers.

Because authorities don't always see eye to eye, their views lack the finality of established truths. Furthermore, their opinions will convince only if the audience accepts the authority *as* authoritative. Although advertisers successfully present football stars as authorities on shaving cream and credit cards, most people would not accept their views on the safety of nuclear energy.

Primary Source Information

You'll need to support certain types of argument with primary source information—documents or other materials produced by individuals directly involved with the issue or conclusions you reached by carrying out an investigation yourself. To argue whether the United States should have dropped the atom bomb on Japan to end World War II, for example, you would want to examine the autobiographies of those involved in making the decision and perhaps even the documents that prompted it. To take a position on the violence mentioned in some gangster rap, you would want to analyze the actual lyrics in a number of songs. To make a claim about the press coverage of the first Persian Gulf War, you would want to read the newspaper and magazine accounts of correspondents who were on the scene. To convince readers to adopt your solution for the homeless problem, you might want to visit a homeless shelter or interview (in a safe place) some homeless people. This type of information can help you reach sound conclusions and build strong support for your position. Most college libraries contain a significant amount of primary source materials. Document the sources you use according to your instructor's guidelines.

Statistical Findings

Statistics—data showing how much, how many, or how often—can also buttress your argument. Most statistics come from books, magazines, newspapers, handbooks, encyclopedias, and reports, but you can use data from your own investigations as well. *Statistical Abstract of the United States* is a good source of authoritative statistics on many topics.

Because statistics are often misused, many people distrust them, so any you offer must be reliable. First, make sure your sample isn't too small. Don't use a one-day traffic count to argue for a traffic light at a certain intersection. City Hall might counter by contending that the results are atypical. To make your case, you'd need to count traffic for perhaps two or three weeks. Take care not to push statistical claims too far. You may know that two-thirds of Tarrytown's factories pollute the air excessively, but don't argue that the same figures probably apply to your town. There's simply no carryover. Keep alert for biased statistics; they can cause as serious a credibility gap as biased opinions. Generally, recent data are better than old data, but either must come from a reliable source. Older information from the *New York Times* would probably be more accurate than current data from some publication that trades on sensationalism. Note how the following writer uses statistics in discussing America's aging population and its impact on the federal budget:

> . . . In 1955 defense spending and veterans benefits accounted for almost 70 percent of federal outlays. By 1995 their share was 19 percent. In the same period social security and Medicare (which didn't exist until 1965) went from 6 percent to 34 percent of the budget. Under present trends, their share would rise to 39 percent by 2005, projects the Congressional Budget Office. . . . Between 2010 and 2020, the older-than-65 population will rise by about a third; in the next decade, it will rise almost another third. Today, about one in eight Americans is older than 65; by 2030, the proportion is projected to be one in five. The older-than-85 population will rise even faster.
>
> Robert J. Samuelson, "Getting Serious"

Again, follow your instructor's guidelines when documenting your sources.

Personal Experience

Sometimes personal experience can deliver an argumentative message more forcefully than any other kind of evidence. Suppose that two years ago a speeder ran into your car and almost killed you. Today you're arguing for stiffer laws against speeding. Chances are you'll rely mainly on expert opinions and on statistics showing the number of people killed and injured each year in speeding accidents. However, describing the crash, the slow, pain-filled weeks in the hospital, and the months spent hobbling around on crutches may well provide the persuasive nudge that wins your reader over.

Often the experiences and observations of others, gathered from books, magazines, or interviews, can support your position. If you argue against chemical waste dumps, the personal stories of people who lived near them and suffered the consequences—filthy ooze in the basement, children with birth defects, family members who developed a rare form of cancer—can sway your reader.

Despite its usefulness, personal experience generally reinforces but does not replace other kinds of evidence. Unless it has other support, readers may reject it as atypical or trivial.

Evaluation of Evidence

Once you have gathered the appropriate type(s) of evidence, certain standards govern the evaluation and use of that evidence. That a piece of information is in some way connected to your topic does not make it good evidence or qualify it for inclusion in your paper. Readers won't be convinced that trains are dangerous merely because you were in a train wreck. You should not reach a conclusion based on such flimsy evidence either. In order to reach a reasonable conclusion and defend a position with suitable evidence, you should apply the following principles.

Evaluation Criteria	Explanation
How credible are the sources of the information? How reliable is the evidence?	Not all sources are created equal. U.S. Census data about population change is more credible than a local newspaper's estimate, though both may be more valid than your own estimate.
How much confirming evidence is there?	With evidence, more is better. One scientific study on the efficacy of high-protein diets would be good, but several would be better. One authority who claims that global warming is a reality becomes more credible when confirmed by several other authorities.
How much contradictory evidence is there?	If several scientific studies or authorities point to the efficacy of high-protein diets and several other studies find such diets harmful, clearly you would need to weigh the evidence more carefully.
How well established is the evidence?	Extremely established evidence, such as the evidence for atoms, becomes the basis for textbooks and is assumed in most other research. This evidence is usually unquestionable, although it also can be overturned.
How well does the evidence actually support or fit the claim?	The fact that most Americans are immigrants or descendents of immigrants has no bearing on whether the country is admitting too many or too few immigrants. To make a case for or against some policy on immigration, the evidence would have to focus on its good or bad results.
What does the evidence actually allow you to conclude?	The evidence shouldn't lead you to reach an exaggerated conclusion. Studies showing that television violence causes children to play more aggressively do not warrant the conclusion that it causes children to kill others.

Sometimes unwarranted conclusions result because a writer fails to take competing claims and evidence into consideration. For example, evidence shows that children in Head Start programs do better than others during the first three years of school. Other evidence, however, shows that in later years these students do not do significantly better. Yet other evidence shows that they are more likely to stay in school and less likely to get into trouble. Clearly, you shouldn't argue that Head Start ensures continuing success at all grade levels. You would need to weigh the credibility, quantity, reliability, and applicability of the available evidence to reach and defend a more limited conclusion.

Reasoning Strategies

An argument, then, consists of a conclusion you want to support, your reasons for that conclusion, and the evidence that supports your reasons. But how are reasons and evidence fitted together? Rational appeals include three reasoning strategies: induction, deduction, and analogy.

16.3

Construct effective inductive and deductive arguments, and use analogy.

Induction

An argument from induction occurs when a general claim is supported by specific evidence, whether direct observations, statistical data, or scientific studies. Most of our conclusions are supported inductively. When we conclude that a movie is worth watching because our friends liked it, when we decide a college program is effective because most students in it get jobs, or even when we support a scientific hypothesis based on formal experimentation, we are basing a conclusion on bits of evidence. We need to be thoughtful in reaching such conclusions. Are our friends like us and trustworthy? Are the jobs that students get good jobs? All the principles for evaluating evidence apply.

Induction makes our conclusions probable but rarely proves them. To prove something by induction, we must check every bit of evidence and often that's just not practical or possible. The greater the number of observations and the larger the populations surveyed, the more strongly the conclusion is supported. Obviously then, just a few observations makes the evidence very weak. If you ask 10 of 15,000 students whether they like the meal plan, you cannot conclude much if eight of the students liked the plan. These students may just be atypical.

All inductive evidence only makes supported conclusions likely. It is important to measure the strength of the supporting evidence.

You have several options for organizing an inductive argument.

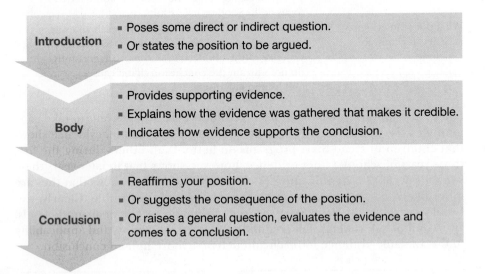

Introduction
- Poses some direct or indirect question.
- Or states the position to be argued.

Body
- Provides supporting evidence.
- Explains how the evidence was gathered that makes it credible.
- Indicates how evidence supports the conclusion.

Conclusion
- Reaffirms your position.
- Or suggests the consequence of the position.
- Or raises a general question, evaluates the evidence and comes to a conclusion.

The following short example illustrates inductive argument.

| States claim to be proven | Systematic phonics, the method of reading instruction that shows children how to sound out letters, is an effective method of teaching word reading in the first three grades. A large study, sponsored by the federal |

government in the 1970s, compared how effective different instructional methods were in helping disadvantaged children. The direct instruction program resulted in children, otherwise expected to fall below the norm, to meet or be close to the national standard for reading (Stebbins, et al., 1977). Another study compared the effect of the whole-language instruction, embedded phonics, and direct code instruction on 285 students in a district with a high risk of reading failure. The university researchers found that the children taught by direct instruction improved in word reading much faster than students in the other groups. In fact, most taught with the whole-language approach had no measurable gains in word reading, even if they did have a more positive attitude towards reading (Stahl et al., 1994). While these studies may not fully demonstrate that systematic phonics is the best method for teaching reading, the fact that in experiments students taught with direct code instruction demonstrated greater gains in word reading than those taught by other methods at least shows that systematic phonics can help students make gains in word reading.

Marjorie Hawkins

> Identifies justification of study

> Provides results of evidence that supports major claim

> Offers a second study to strengthen support

> States results that support claim

> Provides qualification to support credibility

> Connects evidence clearly as support for claim

When writing an induction argument, in addition to presenting the available evidence, there are two other important things you should do. It is helpful to demonstrate the credibility of your evidence. Here the student writer identified that the first study was large and sponsored by the federal government and gave the exact number of subjects in the second study, as well as the information that the researchers were from a university.

Also, if possible, try to show how the evidence fits the conclusion you want to reach. The author, above, made certain her claims were not overstated by being clear about what she was not stating and then directly tied the research studies to her conclusion.

Deduction

Deduction is a process of argumentation that demonstrates how a specific conclusion follows logically from some initial premises about which people might agree. For example, to convince a friend to study harder, you begin with the assumption that a profitable career requires a good education; proceed to argue that for a good education students must study diligently; and conclude that, as a result, your friend should spend more time with the books. Politicians who assert that we all want to act in ways beneficial to future generations, then point out how the policies they favor will ensure that outcome, argue deductively.

As with induction, you have several options when organizing a deductive argument.

Introduction	▪ Starts with the position you intend to prove. ▪ Or a question that will be answered by the argument. ▪ Or by a summary of the argument.

Body	▪ Develops the implications of your assumption. ▪ Explains why one idea follows from the next in a way that shows the logical relation among ideas. ▪ Provides clarifying examples.

Conclusion	▪ Restates your position. ▪ Or suggests the consequence of the position. ▪ Or raises a question that the reader should be able to follow. ▪ Or summarizes the logical links of your argument that yield the conclusion.

Here is a short example of deductive argument:

States the point to be argued

Establishes basic agreed upon assumption

States the chain of logical relationships

Attempts to draw a parallel to lead the reader to the logical conclusion

The recent spot-checks of our rooms by the dorm's head advisor are an unacceptable invasion of privacy. This practice should stop immediately.

The United States Constitution prohibits searches by police officers unless these officers have adequate reason. That is why the police need a search warrant before they can search any home. If they fail to obtain one, a case that ends up in court will likely be thrown out. Our right to privacy, then, can't be violated without due cause.

If the police can't search our homes without good reason, why should our head advisor spot-check our rooms for signs of wrongdoing?

Sammy Borchardt

When arguing from deduction, you need to make clear how your conclusions do actually follow from the agreed-upon premises. Those premises may also be questionable and need support, whether by induction or by demonstrating their deductive relationship to other strongly held ideas.

Reductio ad Absurdum   A common and powerful form of deduction called *reductio ad absurdum* ("to reduce to absurdity") is used to question a position by showing that its consequences are problematic if carried to their logical end. To counter the position that the government should impose no restrictions on the public's right to bear arms, you might point out that, carried to its logical extreme, such a policy would allow individuals to own bazookas, cannons, and nuclear bombs. This absurd result makes it clear that certain restrictions should apply to our right to bear arms. The question then becomes where we should draw the ownership line.

Syllogism   Sometimes a deductive argument is built around a categorical syllogism, a set of three statements that follow a fixed pattern to ensure sound reasoning. The first statement, called the *major premise,* names a category of things and says that all or none of them shares a certain characteristic. The *minor premise* notes that a thing or group of things belongs to that category. The *conclusion* states that the thing or group shares the characteristics of the category. Here are two examples:

Major premise:	All persons are mortal.
Minor premise:	Sue Davis is a person.
Conclusion:	Therefore, Sue Davis is mortal.
Major premise:	No dogs have feathers.
Minor premise:	Spot is a dog.
Conclusion:	Therefore, Spot does not have feathers.

Note that in each case both major and minor premises are true and the conclusion follows logically.

Syllogisms frequently appear in stripped-down form, with one of the premises or the conclusion omitted. The following example omits the major premise: "Because Wilma is a civil engineer, she has a strong background in mathematics." Obviously the missing major premise is as follows: "All civil engineers have strong backgrounds in mathematics."

Syllogistic Argument at Work   A syllogism can occur anywhere in an essay: in the introduction to set the stage for the evidence, at various places in the body, even in the conclusion in order to pull the argument together. Following is an example that uses a syllogism in the introduction:

> In 1966, when the Astrodome was completed in Houston, Texas, the managers concluded that it would be impossible to grow grass indoors. To solve their problem, they decided to install a ruglike synthetic playing surface that was fittingly called Astroturf. In the ensuing years, many other sports facilities have installed synthetic turf. Unfortunately, this development has been accompanied by a sharp rise in the number and severity of injuries suffered by athletes—a rise clearly linked to the surface they play upon. Obviously, anything that poses a threat to player safety is undesirable. Because synthetic turf does this, it is undesirable and should be replaced by grass.
>
> Denny Witham

To support his position, the writer then notes that turf, unlike grass, often becomes excessively hot, tiring players and increasing their chances of injury; that seams can open up between sections of turf and lead to tripping and falling; that players can run faster on artificial turf and thus collide more violently; and that the extreme hardness of the turf leads to torn ligaments and tissues when players slam their toes into it.

Avoiding Misuse of Syllogisms

Two cautions are in order. *First*, make sure any syllogism you use follows the proper logical order. The writer of the following passage has ignored this caution:

> And that's not all. Newton has stated openly that he favors federally funded abortions for the poor. Just the other day, the American Socialist party took this same stand. In my book, Newton's position puts him squarely in the Socialist camp. I strongly urge anyone supporting this man's candidacy to reconsider. . . .

Restated in syllogistic form, the writer's argument goes like this:

> Socialists favor federally funded abortions for the poor.
>
> Newton favors federally funded abortions for the poor.
>
> Therefore, Newton is a Socialist.

The last two statements reverse the proper logical relationship, and as a result the syllogism proves nothing about Newton's politics: he may or may not be "in the Socialist camp."

Second, make sure the major premise of your syllogism is in fact true. Note this example:

> All conservatives are opposed to environmental protection.
>
> Mary is a conservative.
>
> Therefore, Mary is opposed to environmental protection.

But is every conservative an environmental Jack the Ripper? In some communities, political conservatives have led fights against air and water pollution, and most conservatives agree that the environment needs to be protected, within reason. Mary's sympathies, then, may well lie with those who want to heal, rather than hurt, the environment.

EXERCISE

Which of these syllogisms is satisfactory, which have false major premises, and which is faulty because the last two statements reverse the proper order?

1. All singers are happy people.
    Mary Harper is a singer.
    Therefore, Mary Harper is a happy person.

2. All cowards fear danger.
    "Chicken" Cacciatore is a coward.
    Therefore, "Chicken" Cacciatore fears danger.

3. All cats like meat.
Towser likes meat.
Therefore, Towser is a cat.

4. No salesperson would ever misrepresent a product to a customer.
Sabrina is a salesperson.
Therefore, Sabrina would never misrepresent a product to a customer.

Analogy in Argument

An analogy compares two unlike situations or things. Arguers often use analogies to contend that because two items share one or more likenesses, they are also alike in other ways. Familiar analogies assume that humans respond to chemicals as rats do and that success in school predicts success on the job. You have used analogy if you ever pressed your parents for more adult privileges, such as a later curfew, by arguing that you were like an adult in many ways.

Because its conclusions about one thing rest upon observations about some different thing, analogy is the weakest form of rational appeal. Analogies never prove anything. But they often help explain and show probability and therefore are quite persuasive.

For an analogy to be useful, it must feature significant similarities that bear directly on the issue. In addition, it must account for any significant differences between the two items. It is often helpful to test an analogy by listing the similarities and differences. Here's an effective analogy, used to back an argument that a liberal education is the best kind to help us cope successfully with life:

> Suppose it were perfectly certain that the life and fortune of every one of us would, one day or other, depend upon his winning or losing a game of chess. Don't you think that we should all consider it to be a primary duty to learn at least the names and the moves of the pieces; to have a notion of a gambit, and a keen eye for all the means of giving and getting out of check? Do you not think that we should look with a disapprobation amounting to scorn, upon the father who allowed his son, or the state which allowed its members, to grow up without knowing a pawn from a knight?

Establishes basis of analogy

> Yet it is a very plain and elementary truth, that the life, the fortune, and the happiness of every one of us, and, more or less, of those who are connected with us, do depend upon our knowing something of the rules of a game infinitely more difficult and complicated than chess. It is a game which has been played for untold ages, every man and woman of us being one of the two players in a game of his or her own.

Finishes defining analogy by indicating how life is like a game

> The chessboard is the world, the pieces are the phenomena of the universe, the rules of the game are what we call the laws of Nature. The player on the other side is hidden from us. We know that his play is always fair, just, and patient. But also we know, to our cost, that he never overlooks a mistake, or makes the smallest allowance for ignorance. To the man who plays well, the highest stakes are paid, with that sort of overflowing generosity with which the strong shows delight in strength. And one who plays ill is checkmated—without haste, but without remorse. . . .

Details the comparison of life and chess

> Well, what I mean by Education is learning the rules of this mighty game. In other words, education is the instruction of the intellect in the law of Nature, under which name I include not merely things and their forces, but men and their ways;

and the fashioning of the affections and of the will into an earnest and loving desire to move in harmony with those laws. For me, education means neither more nor less than this. Anything which professes to call itself education must be tried by this standard, and if it fails to stand the test, I will not call it education, whatever may be the force of authority, or of numbers, upon the other side.

Thomas Henry Huxley, "A Liberal Education and Where to Find It"

To develop an argument by analogy, brainstorm the two items being compared for significant similarities and prepare a chart that matches them up. The greater the number and closeness of these similarities, the better the argument by analogy.

Completes the argument by demonstrating the rules that need to be learned and how that is an education

The Emotional Appeal

16.4

Use effective emotional appeals to persuade.

👁 **Watch the Animation on Appeals to Emotion**

Although effective argument relies mainly on reason, an emotional appeal can lend powerful reinforcement. Indeed, emotion can win the hearts and the help of people who would otherwise passively accept a logical argument but take no action. Organizations raise funds to fight famine with television ads that feature skeletal, swollen-bellied children. Still other groups use emotion-charged stories and pictures to solicit support for environmental protection, to combat various diseases, and so on. Advertisers use emotion to play upon our hopes, fears, and vanities in order to sell mouthwash, cars, clothes, and other products. Politicians paint themselves as God-fearing, honest toilers for the public good while lambasting their opponents as the uncaring tools of special interests. In evaluating or writing an argument, ask yourself whether the facts warrant the emotion. Is the condition of destitute children truly cause for pity that requires financial action? Is any politician unwaveringly good, any other irredeemably bad?

The following passage, from a student argument favoring assisted suicide for the terminally ill, draws on the strategies of narration and description to create an appropriate use of emotions to demonstrate the painfully debilitating nature of terminal illnesses.

Description indicates dependency and weakness

Contrast shows change in quality of life

Identifies degradation.

Shows narrator's love which makes subsequent argument more credible

When I visited Grandpa for the last time, he seemed imprinted on the hospital bed, a motionless, skeleton-like figure tethered by an array of tubes to the droning, beeping machine at his bedside. The eyes that had once sparkled with delight as he bounced grandchildren on his knee now stared blankly at the ceiling, seemingly ready to burst from their sockets. His mouth, frozen in an open grimace, emitted raspy, irregular noises as he fought to breathe. Spittle leaked from one corner of his mouth and dribbled onto the sheet. A ripe stench from the diaper around his middle hung about the bedside, masking the medicinal sickroom smells. As I stood by the bedside, my mind flashed back to the irrepressible man I once knew, and tears flooded my eyes. Bending forward, I planted a soft kiss on his forehead, whispered "I love you, Gramps," and walked slowly away.

Dylan Brandt Chafin

To develop an effective emotional appeal, identify the stories, scenes, or events of the topic that arouse the strongest emotional response within you. Do some thinking about the types of words that will best convey the emotion you feel. Then write the section so that it builds to the kind of emotional conclusion that will help your argument.

The Ethical Appeal

Before logic can do its work, the audience must be willing to consider the argument. If a writer's tone offends the audience, perhaps by being arrogant or mean-spirited, the reasoning will fail to penetrate. But if the writer comes across as pleasant, fair-minded, and decent, gaining reader support is much easier. The image that the writer projects is called the *ethical appeal.*

16.5

Use effective ethical appeals to persuade.

If you write with a genuine concern for your topic, a commitment to the truth, and a sincere respect for others, you will probably come across reasonably well. When you finish writing, check to see that an occasional snide comment or bitter remark didn't slip unnoticed onto the page. In the following introductory paragraph, from an essay arguing that many universities violate the Constitution by imposing campus rules that restrict freedom of speech, the student establishes an appealing ethical image:

> Most of us would agree that educated people should not indulge in name-calling and stereotyping in their speaking and writing. To do so is an essential mark of irrational prejudice. Nevertheless, such speaking and writing are protected by the United States Constitution, which prohibits anyone from abridging freedom of expression. Today, many colleges and universities, in a well-meaning attempt to shield particular groups from unwelcome or insensitive words, are subverting this prohibition. Former Supreme Court Justice William Brennan, noted for his liberal views, has stated, "If there is a bedrock principle underlying the First Amendment, it is that the government may not prohibit the expression of an idea simply because society finds the idea offensive or disagreeable."

> Linda Kimrey

Concedes how others feel, projecting a fair-minded approach

Suggests a founding support for position other than prejudice

Indicates understanding for the position she opposes

Uses an authority the reader is likely to acknowledge to present her position to show sympathy with the opponents "experts"

The writer opposes on constitutional grounds any attempts to ban the expression of two forms of "irrational prejudice." Nevertheless, she characterizes these attempts as "well-meaning" and acknowledges that they are prompted by worthy motives. As a result, she emerges as fair-minded, decent, sensitive, and concerned, an image she maintains throughout the essay.

Ferreting Out Fallacies

Fallacies are lapses in logic that reflect upon your ability to think clearly, and therefore they weaken your argument. The fallacies described below are among

16.6

Recognize and avoid logical fallacies.

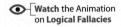
Watch the Animation on **Logical Fallacies**

the most common. Correct any you find in your own arguments, and call attention to those used by the opposition.

Hasty Generalization

Hasty generalization results when someone bases a conclusion on too little evidence. The student who tries to see an instructor during one of her office hours, finds her out, and goes away muttering, "She's never there when she should be" is guilty of hasty generalization. Perhaps the instructor was delayed by another student, attended a special department meeting, or went home ill. Even if she merely went shopping, that's not a good reason for saying she always shirks her responsibility. Several more unsuccessful office visits would be needed to make such a charge stick.

Non Sequitur

From the Latin "It does not follow," the *non sequitur* fallacy draws unwarranted conclusions from seemingly ample evidence. Consider this example: "Bill's been out almost every night for the last two weeks. Who is she?" These evening excursions, however numerous, point to no particular conclusion. Bill may be studying in the library, participating in campus organizations, taking night classes, or walking. Of course, he *could* be charmed by a new date, but that conclusion requires other evidence.

Stereotyping

A person who commits this fallacy attaches one or more supposed characteristics to a group or one of its members. Typical stereotypes include "Latins make better lovers," "Blondes have more fun," and "Teenagers are lousy drivers." Stereotyping racial, religious, ethnic, or nationality groups can destroy an argument. The images are often malicious and always offensive to fair-minded readers.

Card Stacking

In card stacking, the writer presents only part of the available evidence on a topic, deliberately omitting essential information that would alter the picture considerably. For instance: "College students have a very easy life; they attend classes for only twelve to sixteen hours a week." This statement ignores the many hours that students must spend studying, doing homework and/or research, writing papers, and the like.

Either/Or Fallacy

The either/or fallacy asserts that only two choices exist when, in fact, several options are possible. A salesperson who wants you to buy snow tires may claim, "Either buy these tires or plan on getting stuck a lot this winter." But are you really that boxed in? You might drive only on main roads that are plowed immediately after every snowstorm. You could use public transportation when it snows.

You could buy radial tires for year-round use. If very little snow falls, you might not need special tires at all.

Not all either/or statements are fallacies. The instructor who checks a student's record and then issues a warning, "Make at least a *C* on your final or you'll fail the course," is not guilty of a reasoning error. No other alternatives exist. Most situations, however, offer more than two choices.

Begging the Question

A person who begs the question asserts the truth of some unproved statement. Here is an example: "Vitamin A is harmful to your health, and all bottles should carry a warning label. If enough of us write the Food and Drug Administration, we can get the labeling we need." But how do we know vitamin A does harm users? No evidence is offered. People lacking principles often use this fallacy to hit opponents below the belt: "We shouldn't allow a right-wing sympathizer like Mary Dailey to represent us in Congress." Despite a lack of suitable evidence, voters often accept such faulty logic and vote for the other candidate.

Circular Argument

Circular argument, a first cousin to begging the question, supports a position merely by restating it. "Pauline is a good manager because she runs the company effectively" says, in effect, that "something is because something is." Repetition replaces evidence.

Arguing off the Point

The writer who argues off the point, which is sometimes called "ignoring the question" or "a red herring," sidetracks an issue by introducing irrelevant information. To illustrate: "The Ford Thunderbolt is a much better value than the Honda Harmony. Anyway, far too many foreign cars are coming into the country. As a result, thousands of auto workers have lost their jobs and had to take lower-paying jobs. Many Americans strongly oppose this state of affairs." The writer sets out to convince us that the American car is superior in value but then abruptly shifts to the plight of downsized auto workers—a trend that has no bearing on the argument.

The Argument ad Hominem

The Latin term "to the man" designates an argument that attacks an individual rather than that individual's opinions or qualifications. Note this example: "Sam Bernhard doesn't deserve promotion to personnel manager. His divorce was a disgrace, and he's always writing letters to the editor. The company should find someone more suitable." This attack completely skirts the real issue—whether Sam's job performance entitles him to the promotion. Unless his personal conduct has caused his work to suffer, it should not enter into the decision.

Appeal to the Crowd

An appeal of this sort arouses an emotional response by playing on the irrational fears and prejudices of the audience. Terms like *communists, fascists, bleeding hearts, right-winger, welfare chiselers,* and *law and order* are tossed about freely to sway the audience for or against something. Consider:

> The streets of our country are in turmoil. The universities are filled with students rebelling and rioting. Communists are seeking to destroy our country. Russia is threatening us with her might, and the public is in danger. Yes, danger from within and without. We need law and order. Yes, without law and order our nation cannot survive. Elect us, and we shall by law and order be respected among the nations of the world. Without law and order our republic shall fall.

Tapping the emotions of the crowd can sway large groups and win acceptance for positions that rational thinking would reject. Think what Adolf Hitler, the author of the foregoing excerpt, brought about in Germany.

Guilt by Association

This fallacy points out some similarity or connection between one person or group and another. It tags the first with the sins, real or imagined, of the second. The following excerpt from a letter protesting a speaker at a lecture series illustrates this technique:

> The next slated speaker, Dr. Sylvester Crampton, was for years a member of the Economic Information Committee. This foundation has very strong ties with other ultraright-wing groups, some of which have been labeled fascistic. When he speaks next Thursday, whose brand of Americanism will he be selling?

Post Hoc, Ergo Propter Hoc

The Latin meaning, "after this, therefore because of this," refers to the fallacy of assuming that because one event follows another, the first caused the second. Such shoddy thinking underlies many popular superstitions ("If a black cat crosses your path, you'll have bad luck") and many connections that cannot be substantiated ("I always catch cold during spring break"). Sometimes one event does cause another: A sudden thunderclap might startle a person into dropping a dish. At other times, coincidence is the only connection. Careful thinking will usually lay far-fetched causal notions to rest.

Faulty Analogy

This is the error of assuming that two circumstances or things are similar in all important respects, when in fact they are not. Here's an example: Harvey Thompson, high school football coach, tells his players, "Vince Lombardi won two Super Bowls by insisting on perfect execution of plays and enforcing strict disciplinary measures. We're going to win the conference championship by following the same methods." Thompson assumes that because he and Lombardi are coaches, he can duplicate Lombardi's achievements by using Lombardi's methods. Several important differences, however, mark the two situations:

1. Lombardi had very talented players, obtained through the player draft or trades; Thompson can choose only from the students in his high school.
2. Lombardi's players were paid professionals who very likely were motivated, at least in part, by the financial rewards that came from winning the Super Bowl; Thompson's players are amateurs.
3. "Perfect execution of plays" is probably easier to attain on the professional level than in high school because of the players' experience.
4. Despite Lombardi's rigid disciplinary measures, very few of his players quit, perhaps because they were under contract. Could Thompson expect his players, essentially volunteers, to accept the kind of verbal and physical rigors Lombardi was famous for?

EXERCISE

Identify and explain the fallacies in the following examples. Remember that understanding the faulty reasoning is more important than merely naming the fallacy.

1. After slicing a Golden Glow orange, Nancy discovers that it is rotten. "I'll never buy another Golden Glow product," she declares emphatically.
2. A campaigning politician states that unless the federal government appropriates funds to help people living in poverty, they will all starve.
3. A husband and wife see an X-rated movie called *Swinging Wives*. A week later the husband discovers that his wife, while supposedly attending an evening class, has been unfaithful to him. He blames the movie for her infidelity.
4. "Look at those two motorcycle riders trying to pick a fight. All those cycle bums are troublemakers."
5. "Bill really loves to eat. Some day he'll have a serious weight problem."
6. "Because no-fault divorce is responsible for today's skyrocketing divorce rate, it should be abolished."
7. "This is the best-looking picture in the exhibit; it's so much more attractive than the others."
8. "I do not support this school millage proposal. It's sponsored by James McAndrews, who's about the most ill-tempered, quarrelsome person I've ever met. I'd never favor anything he supports."
9. "My position on social and economic issues is easy to state. I am against wooly-brained do-gooders and big-spending, pie-in-the-sky social programs that have brought us to the brink of social disaster. I stand foursquare behind our free-enterprise system, which has given us a standard of living the whole world envies; and if elected, I will defend it with everything at my command."
10. "I am against the proposed ban on smoking in public places. As long as I don't inhale and I limit my habit to 10 cigarettes a day, my health won't suffer."
11. "Life today has become far too frenzied and stressful. It was much better a century ago."

Ethical Issues

16.7

Write so that your argument is ethical.

When writing an argument we attempt to alter attitudes or spark some action. These objectives create an ethical responsibility for both the quality and the possible consequences of our arguments. Suppose a doctor writing a nationally syndicated advice column recommends an over-the-counter herbal product but fails to disclose that it may cause a serious reaction in users who also take a certain prescription drug. Clearly this writer has acted irresponsibly and risks legal action if some readers suffer harm. Asking and answering the following questions will help you avoid any breach of ethics.

- Have I carefully considered the issue I'm arguing and the stance I'm taking? Since you're trying to convince readers to adopt your views, you'll need either to make sure they are credible or make very clear that your position is tentative or dependent on certain conditions.
- Am I fair to other positions on the issue? Careless or deliberate distortion of opposing views is ethically dishonest and could raise questions about your credibility.
- Are my reasons and evidence legitimate? Presenting flawed reasons as if they were credible or falsifying evidence are attempts to deceive the reader.
- Do I use fallacies or other types of faulty thinking to manipulate the reader unfairly?
- What consequences could follow if readers adopt my position? Say a writer strongly opposes genetically modified foods and advocates disrupting installations that help develop them. If some who agree act on the recommendation, innocent people could be injured.

Writing an Argument

16.8

Prewrite, plan, draft, and revise your argument.

Some instructors assign argumentative topics, and some leave the choice of topic to you.

Prewriting the Argument

FINDING YOUR TOPIC
- Take notes on current disputes on television, the radio, and other media.
- Write down the major issues you and others find yourselves discussing or posting about on Facebook.
- Select from class notes issues that are raised and that interest you.

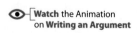
Watch the Animation
on **Writing an Argument**

Focusing Your Question

As you explore your topic you should be prepared to focus your question. You may begin to examine whether you should support or oppose gun control, but you will soon begin to discover there are hundreds of related, narrower questions. Does the right to carry concealed weapons reduce crime? How should the

Second Amendment be interpreted? Should guns be registered? Does the Brady Bill work? Do background checks deter criminals from purchasing guns? Should there be a ban on automatic and semiautomatic weapons? You may discover that one of your related questions is more than enough of a subject.

Exploring Your Topic

You never really start an argument with a blank page. There is almost always an ongoing conversation about the issue. Before you enter a conversation, it helps to be informed. You can do research by reading. If your paper is based on sources, you may want to review information about proper documentation. You may want to talk to others to get their views on the matter. Or you might make your own formal or informal observations.

Watch the Video on **Finding an Argument Topic**

Some students approach an argument with such strong attitudes that they ignore evidence that contradicts their thinking. Don't make this mistake. Instead, maintain an open mind as you research your issue, and then, after careful thought, choose the position you'll take. Often, several possible positions exist. On the question of whether individuals should have the right to carry handguns, the positions might include (1) banning the right to carry handguns by anyone except law enforcement officers and military personnel, (2) allowing anyone who legitimately owns a handgun to carry that weapon without a permit, (3) or allowing citizens to carry concealed weapons but only with a permit granted after training and a background check. Even if you don't shift your position, knowing the opposition's strengths allows you to counter or neutralize it, and thus enhance your argument. Suppose you favor the first position. You need to know that several state constitutions grant citizens the right to carry handguns without those states collapsing into Wild West shoot-outs. Unless you acknowledge and somehow counter this fact, your case will suffer.

Some find it useful to create a table like the following to sort out the different positions.

Ban Concealed Handguns	Right to Carry Handguns by All Owners	Allow Right to Carry Handguns but Registered and for Justified Purposes
■ People have the right to be protected from potential harm from others.	■ Right to self-protection. ■ Broad interpretation of Second Amendment.	■ Commonly register cars and other significant property that people then use according to the law.
■ Handguns result in accidental shootings. ■ Could cause increase in emotional killings. ■ Could create increased risk to public safety.	■ Persons could protect self and others. ■ Could reduce crime. ■ People have a constitutional right.	■ A combination of the reasons from the first two. ■ Gun owners need to be held responsible. ■ Guns should not be carried by unstable or dangerous people.

- Statistics and examples of accidental shootings.
- Statistics on states with right-to-carry laws.
- Examples of emotional uses of hand guns.

- Statistics on overall crime rates.
- Examples of when guns prevented crimes.
- Statistics comparing right-to-carry states with other states.
- Authoritative material on the Second Amendment.

- The evidence on the first two.
- Examples and statistics on handguns used in crimes.
- Examples and statistics on how such restrictions would have had a positive consequence.

- Is the position unconstitutional given the 2010 Supreme Court ruling?

- Who should really get to say who should have handguns?

- Don't criminals carry guns anyway?
- How often are legitimately owned and carried guns misused?

- Aren't there other interpretations of the Second Amendment?
- Why do police groups often oppose this position?

- Can't a registration process be misused?
- Can't criminals or others find illegal ways to get guns and carry them?

Obviously, this table is far from complete, and the writer would need to supply the actual evidence and flesh out the reasons. Still, such a table can be a useful device in sorting out and organizing an argument.

As you investigate the various positions, ask and answer the following questions about each:

- What are the reasons for the various positions?
- What values are at stake, and what conclusions do they imply?
- What shared ideas do we accept, and what can be deduced from those ideas?
- What kinds of evidence support the position?
- If the evidence includes statistics and authoritative opinions, are they reliable or flawed for some reason?
- What are the objections to each position, and how can they be countered?
- If the issue involves taking some action, what might be its consequences?

Another effective technique for developing an argument is to write a dialogue between two or more people that explores the various sides of an issue without trying to arrive at a conclusion. The beginning of such a dialogue on the right to carry handguns might look like the following:

Joe: If people have a right to own a gun for self-protection, as the Supreme Court indicated, they should have a right to carry that gun, not just keep it in the home. How can they use the gun for self-protection if it isn't with them? Besides, allowing them to carry a handgun could act to make criminals think twice. It could surely deter crime.

Doug: It could also lead to public shoot-outs where innocent people could be killed. The United States has the highest murder rate in the industrialized world and the largest number of people owning guns. This is no coincidence. A handgun makes it easy to kill people. Letting people carry a concealed weapon would only make it easier for emotional people to kill each other. Imagine a bar fight with guns.

Leslie: People who legitimately carry concealed weapons don't go around having public shoot-outs. Just owning and carrying a gun doesn't make someone kill. Most legitimate handgun owners who carry a concealed weapon will never use their guns on another human being. Many criminals do, however, kill with illegal weapons, including already banned semiautomatic weapons.

Kyra: Do states where people have a right-to-carry law actually have lower crime rates? I don't think so.

Joe: I didn't say it would always reduce the crime rate. For me the most important issue is that the right-to-carry is the obvious consequence of the Second Amendment.

Writing such a dialogue can help start your mental juices flowing, help you see the issue from many sides, and help you develop effective material for your paper.

> - Research your topic, examining all sides of the issue.
> - Create a table with the major options on your position with the available reasons and evidence.
> - Create a dialogue that tries to represent different sides of the issue to try out your argument.
> - Write down your major reasons and link to evidence and justification for evidence.
> - Identify the purpose and audience for your argument and use that to select reasons, evidence, and approach.
> - Create a draft outline to help see how the reasons and evidence fit together and brainstorm for possible objections, then answer objections.

DEVELOPING YOUR ARGUMENT

Planning and Drafting an Argument

Arguments for Different Purposes   As you contemplate your position and evidence, consider the purpose of your argument and how that might affect the strategies you choose to employ. Arguments are written for several purposes, each requiring a different approach.

Purpose for argument	Strategy
Demonstrating something is a fact—nursing is hard work, dormitories are poor study places, phonics increases word recognition.	■ Depends on the appropriate evidence–examples, statistics, authoritative claims, personal experience. ■ Nursing is demanding: narrate and describe typical nursing day, cite city hospital nursing supervisors on the job, give statistics of turnover because of stress.
Defend or oppose some policy, action, or project—for example, first-year students should be allowed cars or a company should drug-test employees, adding WiFi to the entire campus.	■ Identify need for policy or action, how it can be met, cost or feasibility of recommendation, and the resulting benefit. ■ For WiFi, the need for students with laptops to connect to the Internet between classes and as part of class projects, the available technology for making a campus and cost, the actual usefulness for students in connecting to course material between class and use in classrooms.
Assert the greater or lesser value of someone or something, as a supervisor ranking candidates for promotion.	■ Indicate what your trying to prove, criteria or points for evaluation, reasons along with evidence (details, examples, or statistics). ■ May be deductive showing how conclusions follow from agreed-upon values. ■ Candidate may be shown to have more years of experience, greater skills such as more programming languages, more examples of leadership.

Directing Arguments to Readers   With an argument, as with any essay, purpose and audience are closely linked. For example, imagine that your audience is a group of readers who are neutral or opposed to your position; there's no point in preaching to the converted. Take a little time to analyze these readers so that you can tailor your arguments appropriately. Pose these questions as you proceed:

What are the readers' interests, expectations, and needs concerning this issue?

What evidence is most likely to convince them?

What objections and consequences would probably weigh most heavily with them?

How can I answer the objections?

To convince an audience of farmers that the federal school lunch program needs expanding, you might stress the added income they would gain. For nutritionists, you might note the health benefits that would result, and for school officials, the improved class performance of the students. Even though you are unlikely to convince everyone, it is best to adopt the attitude that most readers are willing to be convinced if your approach is appealing and your evidence is sound.

Rogerian Arguments

If you're arguing an emotionally charged issue such as gun control or federally funded abortions for the poor, you may want to use *Rogerian argument*. Named for psychologist Carl Rogers, this type of argument attempts to reduce the antagonism that people with opposing views might feel toward your position. To succeed, you must show that you understand and respect the opposing position as well as acknowledge its good points. You try to establish some common point of agreement, then show how the conclusion you want really follows from the reader's own values and assumptions without compromising your own. If you want stricter gun-control laws, for example, you might begin by acknowledging that the Constitution grants citizens the right to bear arms and that you believe anyone with legitimate uses for guns—hunters, target shooters, those who feel a need for a gun in their home for protection, and the like—should have access to them.

Moving on, you might point out that gun owners and those who agree with the Second Amendment support the proper, safe use of firearms and are concerned about firearm abuse. You might then possibly agree with the premise that people, rather than guns themselves, kill people, and for that reason, no one wants criminals to have guns. Finally, you might demonstrate that requiring computer background checks before issuing handgun permits would deprive criminals of such weapons while protecting the constitutional right to bear arms.

Watch the Animation on **Rogerian Argument**

Exploratory Argument

You do not always have to write an argument to forcefully convince someone. You can also write to share with your reader how you came to your conclusion. This form of discussion allows you to indicate your doubts about your own position, explain why certain reasons and evidence have weight for you, include personal reasons that influenced you, and address alternative positions and arguments that may tempt you. The goal in such an argument is really to provide the readers with your thinking on the matter; if they are convinced along the way, so much the better. Below is a short excerpt of what a section of an answer to an argument against a ban on semi-automatic weapons might look like.

> While the authors of the Bill of Rights may have intended the Second Amendment to allow all citizens the right to bear arms, the amendment was drafted in a very different period of our history, which would seem to raise some questions about its current application. We had just won a revolutionary war that had depended on a citizen army. Americans faced real threats from the native population and other armed groups and states were protective of their own state militias. Their weapons were different as well. Citizens mostly owned a muzzle-loading musket that was slow and cumbersome to use, as well as inaccurate. It would seem that understanding the intent of these authors would require us to understand the historical period shaping their vision, a period when a well-ordered militia seemed essential. What would they make, then, of our

Tentative question to explore

Note the exploratory and tentative nature of question

current situation where the threat we face is almost always from fellow citizens and the power of today's guns would have been unimaginable?

Exploratory essays do not need to be informal or personal. An academic paper that considers the political influences on television programming may make little use of the personal pronoun and yet still explain tentative ideas and show connections in an exploratory rather than strictly argumentative fashion. Sometimes it can be useful to write out an exploratory essay to find your position before you craft a more focused argument.

Analyze the Interactive Images for **Visual Argument**

Short Arguments with Visuals   This image with its sub-heading makes a quick point about lectures. Photographs, cartoons, or a few pithy phrases can make powerful arguments. A photo of a river clogged with litter makes a strong environmental point. A cartoon showing a rich person picking the pocket of a poor person quickly presents a political argument. A short phrase like "your latte could have fed five children today" concisely appeals to our charity. While these short arguments are rarely appropriate to a college setting where reasons and evidence are more carefully weighed, they are part of how we communicate to persuade. For shorter arguments to be effective, the image needs to be easily understood, directly illustrate the point, and have emotional punch.

Lectures don't always promote learning.

Image Source/Getty Images

Drafting the Argument

When you have a good grasp on your position, reasons, evidence, and the approach you want to take, you're ready to draft your paper. Because arguments can be complex, it can be very useful to start by creating an outline of your main reasons, evidence, possible objections to your position, and an answer to those objections. Or you may wish to more informally write out your reasons in order with supporting evidence, possibly even initially labeling them to insure that the reasons are supported.

Reason 1;
    Evidence:
    Evidence:
Reason 2
    Evidence:
    Objection
Answer to objection

The more detailed the outline, formal or informal, the easier it will be to draft the paper.

The thesis statement for an argument often indicates which position the writer will take, sometimes including the major reasons for that position. It can declare that something is a fact, support a policy, call for a certain action, or assert that something has greater value than something else. Following are examples:

1. Carron College does not provide adequate recreational facilities for its students. *(Declares something is fact.)*
2. Our company's policy of randomly testing employees for drug use has proved effective and should be continued. *(Supports policy.)*
3. Because the present building is overcrowded and unsafe, the people of Midville should vote funds for a new junior high school. *(Calls for action.)*
4. The new Ford Fire-Eater is superior to the Honda Harmony in performance and economy. *(Asserts value.)*

To formulate your thesis, review your main reasons and focus on the claim you may want to make. Avoid making a claim broader than you want to support. If you believe students need to enhance their computer literacy to be employable, you would over reach if you suggested that students need to become computer *experts*.

Any of the techniques in Chapter 5 can launch your paper.

Introduction
- Jolt your reader, for example by describing a teen paralyzed in a car accident to argue against texting and driving.
- Or start with defining an unfamiliar term, "Why oppose oligarchy?"
- In a longer essay, preview main points.
- In a Rogerian argument, affirm the readers' core beliefs or values.
- In an exploratory essay, you might raise the question you will discuss without taking a position.

After the introduction comes the evidence, arranged in whatever order you think will work best. If one of your points is likely to arouse resistance, hold it back and begin by making points your reader can more easily accept. Argument always goes more smoothly if you first establish some common ground of agreement that recognizes the values of your reader. Where strong resistance is not a factor, you could begin or end with your most compelling piece of evidence.

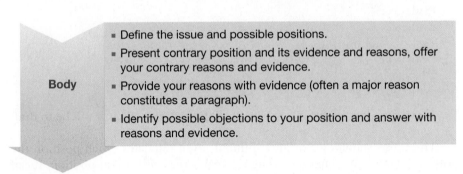

Body
- Define the issue and possible positions.
- Present contrary position and its evidence and reasons, offer your contrary reasons and evidence.
- Provide your reasons with evidence (often a major reason constitutes a paragraph).
- Identify possible objections to your position and answer with reasons and evidence.

The strategies discussed in earlier chapters can help you develop an argument. Some papers incorporate one strategy, while others rely on several. Let's see how you might combine several in an argument against legalized casino gambling.

- You might open with a brief *description* of the frantic way an all-too-typical gambling addict keeps pulling the lever of a slot machine, his eyes riveted on the spinning dials, his palms sweating, as flashing lights and wailing sirens announce winners at other machines.
- Next, you could offer a brief *definition* of gambling fever so that the writer and reader are on common ground, and, to show the dimensions of the problem, *classify* the groups of people who are especially addicted.
- Then, after detailing the negative *effects* of the addiction, you might end by *comparing* gambling addiction with drug addiction, noting that both provide a "high" and both kinds of addict know their habits hurt them.

Whatever strategies you use, make sure that substantiating evidence is embedded in them. To illustrate, in discussing the negative effects of gambling, you might cite statistics that show the extent and nature of the problem. An expert opinion might validate your classification of addicts. Or you might use personal experience to verify gambling's addictive effects.

Besides presenting evidence, use this part of your paper to refute; that is, to point out weaknesses or errors in the opposing position. You might try the following:

- **Point out any evidence that undermines that position.** If one viewpoint holds that drug testing violates cherished privacy rights, you might note that employers already monitor phone calls, check employees' desks, and violate privacy in other ways.
- **Identify faulty assumptions and indicate how they are faulty: they don't lead to the implied conclusion, they lack the effectiveness of an alternative, or they are false or unsupported.** If you oppose drug testing, you could point out problems in the assumption that such tests are necessary to protect the public. Closer supervision of work performance might be a

better protection; after all, fatigue, stress, negligence, and alcohol abuse can all result in serious problems, and they are not detected by drug tests.

- **Identify problems in the logic of the argument.** Are there missing premises, faulty connections between reasons, or conclusions that don't follow from the premises? The argument against drug testing usually proceeds by asserting that privacy is a fundamental right, that drug testing violates privacy, and that therefore drug testing should not be allowed. There is a missing premise, however: that because privacy is a fundamental right it should never be violated. This premise is, in fact, at the heart of the dispute and therefore cannot be accepted as a reason to disallow drug testing.

You can place refutations throughout the body of the paper or group them together just ahead of the conclusion. Whatever you decide, don't adopt a gloating or sarcastic tone that will alienate a fair-minded reader. Resist the urge to engage in *straw man* tactics—calling attention to imaginary or trivial weaknesses of the opposing side so that you can demolish them. Shrewd readers easily spot such ploys. Finally, don't be afraid to concede secondary or insignificant points to the opposition. Arguments have two or more sides; you can't have all the ammunition on your side. (If you discover you must concede major points, however, consider changing your position.) Following is a sample refutation from a student paper:

> Not everyone agrees with workplace drug testing for employees in public transportation companies, electric utilities, nuclear power plants, and other industries involving public safety. Critics assert that such tests invade privacy and therefore violate one of our cherished freedoms. While the examination of one's urine does entail inspection of something private, such a test is a reasonable exception because it helps ensure public safety and calm public fears. Individuals have a right to be protected from the harm that could be caused by an employee who abuses drugs. An airline pilot's right to privacy should not supersede the security of hundreds of people who could be injured or killed in a drug-induced accident. Thus the individual's privacy should be tempered by concern for the community—a concern that benefits all of us.
>
> Annie Louise Griffith

Identifies opponents objection

Concedes basic objection

Answers with an opposing value or right

Conclude in a manner that will sway the reader to your side.

Conclusion

- Possibly restate you main point and summarize main points.
- Or predict the consequences if your position doesn't prevail.
- Or offer a powerful example or story that clinches your position.
- Or make an emotional appeal for action.
- Look at the strategies in Chapter 5.

There can be more than one pattern for an argument. Below are three examples.

Example 1	**Example 2**	**Example 3**
Introduction	Introduction	Introduction
Definition of the issue (optional)	Definition of the issue (optional)	Definition of the issue (optional)
Your reasons and evidence (can be a large number of paragraphs)	Alternative positions and reasons for those positions	Common objections or questions and answers to both
	Objections and contrary evidence and reasons to those positions (can be several paragraphs)	
Objections or questions and answers to both (can be several paragraphs)	Restatement of your position and reasons and evidence for that position. Objections or questions and answers to both	Your reasons and evidence
Conclusion	Conclusion	Conclusion

You are not limited to these patterns. Alternative positions and objections can be discussed and answered within the context of presenting your own reasons. An argument can be built around answering common questions. A Rogerian argument starts by affirming the reader's core values and beliefs and then shows deductively and by supporting evidence how those values and beliefs yield the conclusion you hope to support.

Revising the Argument

Review the guidelines in Chapter 4 and ponder these questions as you revise your argument paper:

- Is my topic controversial? Have I examined all of the main positions? Assessed the evidence supporting each one? Considered the objections to each position and how they can be countered? Weighed the consequences if a position involves taking some action?
- Is the paper aimed at the audience I want to reach? Have I tailored my argument to appeal to that audience?
- Is my evidence sound, adequate, and appropriate to the argument? Are my authorities qualified? Have I established their expertise? Are they biased? Will my audience accept them as authorities? Do my statistics adequately support my position? Have I pushed my statistical claims too far?
- If I've used analogy, are my points of comparison pertinent to the issue? Have I noted any significant differences between the items being compared?
- If I've included an emotional appeal, does it center on those emotions most likely to sway the reader?
- Have I made a conscious effort to present myself in a favorable light?

- Is my proposition clearly evident and of the appropriate type—that is, one of fact, policy, action, or value? If the proposition takes the form of a syllogism, is it sound? If faulty, have I started with a faulty premise? Reversed the last two statements of the syllogism?
- Is my evidence effectively structured? Have I adequately refuted opposing arguments? Developed my position with one or more writing strategies?
- Is my argument free of fallacies?
- Have I considered appropriate ethical issues?

SAMPLE

STUDENT ESSAY OF **ARGUMENT**

Bottled Troubled Water

Scott Lemanski

1   A disease has swept over our nation. It's called consumeritis, and its symptoms, among many others, include sluggishness, chronic apathy, alienation, obesity, and a constant, nagging feeling that there is something missing from our lives. We temporarily relieve these symptoms, or at least distract ourselves from them, by seeing or hearing an advertisement, label, or slogan that convinces us that we absolutely need some useless product, then call a toll-free number to place an order or drive over to the local megamart to buy it, along with a few other superfluous items we feel that we just can't do without. Perhaps the most senseless product with which we've been treating our consumeritis in recent years is that clear, cool, tasteless drink that comes in a plastic container— bottled water. It comes in many attractive shapes and sizes from mountain springs and glaciers all over the world, promising us better health and a convenient way to attain it. The thought of drinking tap water for some people today is simply ridiculous because of the commonly held belief that it's just not pure enough. But do we really know how pure our beloved bottled water is? How often do we think about the impact our obsession with bottled water is having on the world or how much we actually benefit from such a product? The harm done to our environment, the waste of our resources, and the potential health risks caused by bottled water's mass production, distribution, and consumption far outweigh its possible benefits.

2   Our thirst for bottled water has become seemingly unquenchable, and as it grows, so does its impact on our environment. According to Tony Azios

Continued on next page

Identifies a general negative trend and uses emotionally charged terms to influence reader

Ties key topic to negative trend

Anticipates reader's objection

Raises questions that will guide the argument

Thesis identifies main position and key reasons to be examined

Identifies consequence of practice

Continued from previous page

Uses statistics in a logical way to suggest negative impact

in his article "The Battle over Bottled vs. Tap Water," over 25 billion plastic water bottles per year are sold in the United States (3). Since 2002, production has increased an average of 9% per year; and since 2003, water has become the highest-selling commercial drink, second only to soft drinks (Azios 1). In "Bottled Water: Pure Drink or Pure Hype?" the National Resources Defense Council (NRDC) reports that "in 2006, the equivalent of 2 billion half-liter bottles of water were shipped to U.S. ports, creating thousands of tons of global-warming pollution and other air pollution" (par. 7). The transport of bottled water that year from eastern Europe to New York contributed approximately 3,800 tons of global-warming pollution to the atmosphere, while the shipping of 18 million gallons of bottled water from Fiji to California produced about 2,500 tons of such pollution (par. 7).

Identifies next major consequence with logical transition

Uses sources to indicate statistics concerning quantity of waste

3   Given the virtually incomprehensible quantities of bottled water manufactured, transported, bought, and sold, it is no surprise that the waste from it amounts to alarmingly large numbers. In some U.S. states, we are required by law to pay a small deposit when purchasing plastic soda bottles, which works quite well as an incentive to bring them back for recycling. The same is not true for bottled water, although the bottles are recyclable. The NDRC notes that, "only about 13% of the bottles we use get recycled. In 2005, 2 million tons of plastic water bottles ended up clogging up landfills" (par. 7). Oil, however ultimately damaging to the future of our world it may be, is an ever-increasingly precious resource, now perhaps more than ever, and we're wasting that on bottled water, too. Azios points out that in 2006, "more than 17 million barrels of oil (not including fuel for transportation) were used in plastic bottle production" (3). Even water, arguably our most precious resource, is used in copious amounts in the production. Water is necessary to cool machinery in power plants and molds that form plastic parts, so when taking into account the huge volume of plastic water bottles made every year, it's no wonder that "it takes about 3 liters of water to produce 1 liter of bottled water" (3). It's also no wonder, with all the energy and resources wasted, that we end up paying 2,000 times more for a liter of bottled water than we would a liter of tap water (2).

Identifies next possible negative consequence

4   While it's obvious we are willing to pay entirely too much money for it, are we also willing to gamble our health on bottled water? Since so many different brands of bottled water have words on their labels such as *pure* or *natural*, we are led to believe that drinking bottled water is a choice that will be a benefit to our health. It would be prudent, then, to become educated on some of the risks involved. According to Janet Jemmott in "Bottled

Water vs. Tap Water," most of the bottles are made of a plastic called polyethylene tereptholate, or PET, which is suppose to be generally safe, but if heated, the plastic could leach chemicals into the water (3). There are hazards linked to these chemicals, but "the exact health risks are unknown" (3). Consequently, we are taking a chance with our health if we, for example, leave a bottle in a hot car all day long and later return to drink it. Though a consensus hasn't been reached on the risks of PET chemicals, Jemmott notes that some findings may be unsettling.

Provides causal analysis of possible health risk

5   In the meantime, experts have raised a warning flag about a few specific chemicals. Antimony is a potentially toxic material used in making PET. Last year, scientists in Germany found that the longer a bottle of water sits around (in a store, in your home), the more antimony it develops. High concentrations of antimony can cause nausea, vomiting, and diarrhea. In the study, levels found were below those set as safe by the EPA, but it's a topic that needs more research (Jemmott 3).

Second causal argument of health risk

6   Many of us are willing to take our chances with the possible health risks associated with bottled water because, if nothing else, we see it as such a convenient way to obtain the water we need to drink every day. Is it really more convenient to go to the store and spend entirely too much money on a bottle of water than it is to simply fill a glass at home at the faucet? If we want to take it with us while we're out, there are plenty of containers that we can purchase for just such a purpose. Advertisers have cleverly convinced us that somehow it's more convenient to go out of our way to buy what they're selling than it is to take a moment and think about whether we truly need it or not. Do we really need to buy a product such as bottled water?

Identifies reader's objection

Offers alternative to answer objection

7   Many of us cite the most compelling reason to drink bottled water, besides convenience, is the concern over impurities in the water that comes out of our faucets and drinking fountains. It is a legitimate concern but one that doesn't necessarily have to result in the automatic response of reaching for the bottle. In "Water Quality: Bottled Water," the Cornell University Cooperative Extension says that tap water can and often does contain contaminants in varying concentrations, such as microorganisms, including pathogens, and sulfur compounds, including metals and metalloids, such as arsenic, lead and iron, just to name a few. However, the regulation of tap water is somewhat more reliable and transparent:

Identifies next major objection

Acknowledges readers concern and values

> Tap water from municipal drinking water treatment plant is regulated by the U.S. Environmental Protection Agency (EPA) . . . for

Provides comparison to answer objection with authorized data

Continued on next page

Continued from previous page

close to a hundred chemicals and characteristics, [while] bottled water sold across state lines is regulated by the U.S. Food and Drug Administration (FDA). Your supplier must notify the community if there are problems with the water supply. Municipal plants are generally subject to much more frequent testing and inspection and must report test results to the public. (Cornell)

Furthermore, since more than 25% of the bottled water comes from a municipal source (Jemmott 4), there is a sizable chance that the water in the bottles from which we drink is just as contaminated as the water that comes out of the faucet in our kitchen sink.

8   The fluoridation of tap water is another positive health benefit. Most of us have seen enough television toothpaste commercials go uncontested for long enough to be reasonably confident in fluoride's ability to help prevent tooth decay. Tap water is generally fluoridated, while most bottled water is not, and since many children are drinking more bottled water than tap water, this could explain the current rise in tooth decay among children (Jemmott 5).

9   Recently in the *USA Today* article "AP: Drugs Show Up in Americans' Water," it has been reported that quite a few pharmaceuticals, "including antibiotics, anti-convulsants, mood stabilizers and sex hormones have been found in the water supply of at least 41 million Americans" (Donn, Mendoza, and Prichard). Though utilities say their water is safe and that the levels of the drugs found are measured in parts per billion or trillion, "far below the levels of a medical dose . . . [their presence is] heightening worries among scientists of long-term consequences to human health" (Donn, Mendoza, and Pritchard). Though these concerns are certainly valid, they still don't warrant turning to bottled water as the solution to the problem. Going back to the point Cornell University made about water regulation, it follows that it is unlikely that bottled water companies are doing the sort of rigorous testing of their water for substances such as pharmaceuticals that could ease our concerns on this matter; and even if they were, would they report it to the public? Also, if over 25% of bottled water comes from municipal sources, what percentage of that percentage might contain such pharmaceuticals?

10   "In general, toxins in drinking water don't exceed EPA limits" (Jemmott 5). However, there are steps we can take to inform ourselves of and reduce the risks of tap water contamination. A water quality or

---

Marginal annotations:

Offers a contrary reason to objection by identifying benefit of tap water

Provides evidence for position

Further acknowledges concern

Provides evidence and reason to answer objection that bottled water would be better

Offers an additional answer to objection to water problem issue

Offers an alternate reason to objection-testing

consumer confidence report is generally sent out to all customers of local water companies once a year, and it will show if any contaminants have gone over the maximum allowable levels (5). We can also have our water tested by a state-certified lab (5). There are also many varieties of tap-water filters we can buy to purify the water coming out of our taps, but in order to ensure their effectiveness, they should be "approved by NSF, Underwriters Laboratories, or the Water Quality Association" (5). If after taking all this information into account, you still feel it necessary to replace tap water with bottled water, you can at least look for a brand that comes from a local source, so as to at least limit the environmental impact and waste or resources caused by long-distance mass transport. Also, look for brands with "NSF certification or [those that] belong to the IBWA. Check out the lists at NSF.org or bottledwater.org, or look at the bottle itself" for the NSF logo (5).

Offers an alternative to primary position

11   In our consumerist society, where so many things are available to us and convenience often seems to be of the greatest importance, it's easy to forget that everything we do in our personal lives has a direct or indirect effect on the rest of the world and our planet. If we go on ignoring growing environmental threats and the resources we're wasting, the consequences will affect us all. No absolute cure has been found for consumeritis, but we can take steps to minimize its impact by taking a little time out from our overly busy lives and trying to think rationally about the implications of something so seemingly harmless as drinking bottled water. The convenience and minimal, if any, health benefits we receive from drinking bottled water don't come close to justifying the harm it causes the earth and perhaps ourselves.

Returns to primary interest of effect in conclusion

Confirms main point by comparing benefits to harms

Works Cited

Azios, Tony. "The Battle over Bottled vs. Tap Water." *Christian Science Monitor*. 17 Jan. 2008. Web. 17 Mar. 2008.

Cornell University Cooperative Extension. "Water Quality: Bottled Water." *Cornell University Cooperative Extension*. 13 Feb. 2008. Web. 20 Mar. 2008.

Donn, Jeff, Martha Mendoza, and Justin Prichard. "AP: Drugs Show Up in Americans' Water." *USAToday.com* 9 Mar. 2008. Web. 20 Mar. 2008.

Jemmott, Janet Majeski. "Rethink What You Drink : Growing Thirst." *Reader's Digest*. 10 Jan. 2008. Web. 17 Mar. 2008.

"National Resources Defense Council: Bottled Water FAQ." *NRDC: The Earth's Best Defense*. 12 Sept. 2007. Web. 17 Mar. 2008.

Discussion Questions

1. This essay tries to convince many readers to give up a common habit. Often readers can be sensitive about such an approach. How does this writer lessen the possible negative impact of his criticism?
2. How does this author's argument appeal to his readers' concerns and values, assuming that many who drink bottled water are concerned about the environment and are health conscious?
3. What types of evidence does the writer use in his argument?
4. Why does the writer in paragraph 10 offer some suggestions for buying bottled water when the entire paper is dedicated to discouraging the practice?
5. In the introduction and the conclusion the writer links buying bottled water with something he calls "consumeritis." Is this strategy effective? Why or why not?

Suggestions for Writing

Write a properly focused argument on some topic you feel strongly about. Study all sides of the issue so you can argue effectively and appeal to a particular audience. Support your proposition with logical evidence. Here are some possibilities to consider if your instructor gives you a free choice:

1. Compulsory composition classes in college
2. Requiring safety locks on firearm triggers
3. Prohibiting the development of private property to save endangered species
4. Prayer in public schools
5. English as the official language of the United States
6. Filters on Internet stations at public libraries
7. Increasing federal support of developing alternative energy such as solar power
8. Gay marriage
9. Universal health care
10. Bilingual instruction in schools
11. The effectiveness of some kind of alternative medicine (or some particular diet)
12. Allowing or prohibiting guns on college campuses
13. Taxpayer funding for professional athletic facilities
14. Use of animals for research
15. A campus, local, or state issue
16. Immigration reform
17. Providing federal funding to support religious charities
18. Publicly funded private school vouchers
19. Monitoring U.S. citizens' phone conversations to detect potential terrorist threats
20. Virtual universities where all classes are conducted on the Internet

STEPPING UP TO **SYNTHESIS**

 A successful argument, by its very nature, requires critical thinking. This chapter has given you the tools you'll need to test the logic and evaluate the evidence offered in support of argumentative positions. After all, rarely will you generate an idea on your own and then argue for it. Instead, because most important issues have already been debated in print, you'll enter a discussion that's already under way. Sometimes it's on a topic of national interest, such as the desirability of politically correct speech and writing or the need to limit the number of terms elected officials can serve. At other times, the topic may be more localized: Should your state outlaw teacher strikes, your company install new equipment to control air pollution, or your college reduce its sports programs? On any of these issues you begin to form your own view as you read and assess the arguments of other writers.

Prewriting for Synthesis A good way to take stock of conflicting opinions is to make a chart that summarizes key reasons and evidence on each side of the argument. Here is a segment of a chart that presents opposing viewpoints on whether industrial air pollution poses a significant threat of global warming:

Pro-threat side

Industrial emissions of carbon dioxide, methane, and chlorofluorocarbons let sun's rays in but keep heat from escaping.

      Andrew C. Revkin

Atmospheric levels of carbon dioxide are now 25 percent higher than in 1860. Computer models indicate a continuing rise will cause a temperature increase of 3–9°F.

    Revkin

No-threat side

Natural sources account for almost 50 percent of all carbon dioxide production.

      Dixy Lee Ray

The computer models are inaccurate, don't agree with each other, and fail to account for the warming effects of the oceans.

      H. E. Landsberg

Critically Evaluating Your Sources Even though you investigate the reasons and evidence of others, deciding what position to take and how to support it—that is, establishing your place in the debate—is the real work of synthesis. This chapter should have helped you focus on how to evaluate the evidence and arguments others make.

Planning and Drafting the Synthesis Therefore, after evaluating your sources, outline the main points you want to make. You can then incorporate material that supports your argument. Let's say that you're considering

Continued on next page

Continued from previous page

the issue of global warming. After examining the differing viewpoints, you might conclude that although those who believe that global warming is occurring sometimes overstate their case, those who disagree tend to dismiss important scientific evidence. Because global warming is a serious possibility if not a certainty, you decide to argue for immediate environmental action. You might begin your paper by pointing out the dire consequences that will ensue if global warming becomes a reality, then offer evidence supporting this possibility, acknowledge and answer key opposing viewpoints, and finally offer your recommendations for averting a crisis.

Getting Started

1. Read several sources that explore the best solution to the challenges of illegal immigration and then write an argument supporting your own position based on those differing responses.
2. Read several sources that take different positions on how we can meet the energy challenges of the future and write an argument supporting your position on this issue. You may, however, want to focus on specific issues such as the safety or danger of nuclear energy or the feasibility of alternative energy systems.
3. Read several sources that explore the issue of our legal and ethical responsibility for what and how we present ourselves on various social networks and write an argument that takes a position on this issue, drawing on the available sources.

Complete additional exercises and practice in your MyLab

Writing an Argument

Prewriting the argument.

- Identify question or topic you want to explore.
- Read about issue.
- Talk to others.
- Take notes and keep references clear.
- Brainstorm and perhaps create a table of reasons and evidence for and against the position.
- Evaluate the evidence, including the credibility of sources, confirmation of the evidence, contradictory evidence, strength of evidence, and evidence support for the claims.
- Consider the possible consequences if the readers adopted the position.
- Make certain that all sides of the issue are fairly considered.

Planning and drafting the argument.

- Establish your position and draft thesis statement.
- Establish purpose.
- Identify audience—what key beliefs and attitudes do readers have you can build on?
- Determine the approaches you are going to use—rational with key reasons and evidence; reduction ad absurdum, Rogerian, emotional appeal, ethical appeal.
- Create a rough draft or outline of the major argument.
- Write so that the argument is fair to all positions on the issue without misrepresenting the views of thers.
- Make certain the reasons and evidence are legitimate.

Option for organization.

- Definition of issue.
- Other positions and reasons for those positions.
- Objections and contrary evidence for positions.
- Your position.
- Reasons and evidence.
- Objections to your view.
- Answer to objections.

Option for organization.

- Definition of issue.
- Your reasons and evidence.
- Objections or questions and answers.

Option for organization.

- Definition of issue.
- Common objections and questions.
- Answers.
- Your position.
- Your reasons and evidence.

Revising the argument.

Gather reader responses; read critically as if you oppose your own position. Talk it over with others; check to see if there is another position that makes more sense.

- Do arguments fit audience?
- Add any additional reasons or evidence; answer any outstanding objections.
- Cut reasons, evidence that seems invalid or that doesn't work.
- Test reason and evidence to ensure validity.
- Test tone to be sure it seems reasonable.
- Test organization so easy to follow with clear transitions.
- Test to make certain that there are no flaws in argument or informal fallacies.

Repeat the process as necessary.

Proofread.

17 Mixing the Writing Strategies

In this chapter, you will learn how to:

17.1 Combine multiple writing strategies.

17.2 Write a problem/solution report.

17.3 Write an evaluation report.

John Lund/Blend Images/Corbis

Why and How to Mix Strategies

Writing strategies seldom occur in pure form. Writers nearly always mix them in assorted combinations for various purposes, not just in papers of definition and argument, as we've noted in Chapters 15 and 16, but also in papers of narration, description, process analysis, illustration, classification, comparison, and cause and effect. An essay that is primarily narration might contain descriptive passages or note an effect. A comparison might include illustrations or carry an implied argument. The purpose, audience, and occasion of the individual essay dictate the mixture, which can't be predetermined. Your best bet is to familiarize yourself with the individual strategies and use them as needed.

17.1

Combine multiple writing strategies.

👁 Watch the Animation on **Mixing Writing Strategies**

Assignments in other classes and on the job will also require you to mix the writing strategies.

- Your political science professor might ask for a paper that evaluates the advantages of a democratic state over a totalitarian one. You could open with contrasting *definitions* of the two forms of government and then, to make them more concrete, offer XYZ as an *illustration* of a typical democracy, ABC as a typical totalitarian state. After *describing* the key characteristics of each type, you might *compare* their social, economic, and religious effects on their citizens.
- At work, a sales manager might have to write a year-end analysis that *compares* sales trends in the first and second quarters of the year, suggests the *causes* of any areas of weakness, and *classifies* the regions with superior potential in the upcoming year. And almost any employee could be asked to compose a report that *defines* and *illustrates* a problem, examines its *causes*, and *argues* for a particular solution.

When tackling a multi-strategy writing assignment, break the project into separate stages. Determine first what you need to accomplish, then which strategies will serve your purpose, and finally how best to implement and organize them. It also helps to list all the strategies before you start reflecting on which ones to use. After a brief consideration of ethical issues, let's apply these guidelines to the writing of a problem/solution report and then to an evaluation report: two common projects that rely on a mix of writing strategies.

Ethical Issues

As you might guess, when your writing includes several strategies, the ethical issues pertinent to each apply. You may, however, need to consider additional issues with problem/solution and evaluation reports.

Problem/Solution. What consequences might follow if my recommendation is adopted? If a college with a grade inflation problem implements a policy that instructors grant no more than 10 percent As and 20 percent Bs, some students who do excellent work could be denied the grades they deserve.

Evaluation. Are my evaluation criteria fair? When evaluating the job performance of the clerks in a bookstore, it would seem unfair and discriminatory to include their ability to do heavy lifting if a number of them are older employees.

Problem/Solution Report

17.2

Write a problem/solution report.

Analyze the Interactive Problem/Solution Report

Suppose many students have experienced serious delays in getting to use the computers in your college library and you want to report the situation to the administration. Your goal is to eliminate the problem. After a little thought, you realize that you must first demonstrate that a problem exists and that it warrants action.

Before you can write such a report, you need to investigate the extent of the problem (does it really need solving?), look for its causes (possibly hidden causes), and determine the possible effects. Almost always these are your first steps before you decide on any solutions. Often you can find effective solutions by addressing the causes of the problem, but you might also explore new ways of improving the situation. You'll want to consider carefully whether your solution will work. After you review your options, you decide to use illustration and description to demonstrate the problem, and then to examine the effects and their causes.

Here's how you might proceed as you write the report. Your introduction states the problem. Then you portray a typical evening with long lines of students waiting to use the computers, while others mill around, grumble, and sometimes leave in disgust. Next, you take up effects, noting a number of occasions when both you and your friends have turned in late papers due to unavailable computers and received low grades. Turning to causes, you report your findings. Perhaps the library lacks funds to buy more computers. Perhaps it has limited hours, or instructors tend to schedule research projects at the same time.

The solution you recommend will, of course, depend on the cause(s). If extending the library hours would solve the problem, then purchasing more computers would just waste funds. The best solution may consist of several actions: buying a few computers, extending the library hours, and persuading instructors to stagger their research assignments. In some cases, you may have to explain the process of implementing your solution and/or defend (argue) its feasibility by showing that it will not have unacceptable consequences. For instance, in our computer example, you would need to consider the costs of keeping the library open and staffed for longer hours.

Evaluation Report

Imagine that your school has been experimenting with metal whiteboards that use markers instead of chalk. The administration has asked you to assess how effectively these boards serve student and instructor needs and to present your findings in an evaluation report.

17.3

Write an evaluation report.

As you think the project through, you realize that you first need to determine the key criteria for evaluation, which you decide are glare, the quality of the writing left by the markers, and the effectiveness of erasing. Because these boards compete with conventional blackboards, you decide that you need a comparison of the two that includes a description of the whiteboards and illustrations supporting your observations. You also decide that a discussion of the effects the boards have on students would be in order.

Analyze the Interactive Evaluation Report

After drawing your conclusions, you begin your report by indicating why it's being written, providing a definition and description of the whiteboards, and noting the criteria you will use. Following this introduction, you discuss each criterion in turn, describing with illustrative examples how well the whiteboard measures up in comparison to conventional blackboards. You also note the effects of any shortcomings on students. In your conclusion, you argue that the irregular performance of the markers, the glare of the whiteboard surfaces, and the difficulty of erasing the marking frustrate students and make classes more difficult for instructors to conduct. You recommend that the college discontinue using whiteboards except in computer classrooms, where chalk dust damages the units.

EXERCISE

Suggest what combination of writing strategies you might use in each of the following situations.

1. The company you work for, school you attend, or club you belong to has a serious morale problem. You have been asked to evaluate its various dimensions, propose feasible solutions, and then make a recommendation to the appropriate person.
2. Your company, school, or club is about to purchase some specific type of new equipment. You have been asked to write a report examining the available brands and recommending one.
3. Your local newspaper has asked you to write about your college major or occupation and how you regard it. The article will help high school students decide whether this major or occupation would be appropriate for them.
4. Your general science instructor has asked you to study and report on some industrial chemical. The report must answer typical questions a layperson would likely ask about the chemical.

The margin notes on the following essay show the interplay of several writing strategies.

ESSAY **USING SEVERAL WRITING STRATEGIES**

BRUCE FRIEDMAN

Eating Alone in Restaurants

Bruce Jay Friedman (born 1930) is a native of New York City and a 1951 graduate of the University of Missouri, where he majored in journalism. Between 1951 and 1953, he served in the U.S. Air Force and for the next decade was editorial director of a magazine management company. He now freelances. A versatile writer, Friedman has produced novels, plays, short stories, and nonfiction, earning critical acclaim as a humorist. In our selection, taken from The Lonely Guy's Book of Life *(1979), he offers the urban male who must dine out alone witty advice on coping with the situation.*

1   Hunched over, trying to be as inconspicuous as possible, a solitary diner slips into a midtown Manhattan steakhouse. No sooner does he check his coat than the voice of the headwaiter comes booming across the restaurant.

2   "Alone again, eh?"

3   As all eyes are raised, the bartender, with enormous good cheer, chimes in: "That's because they all left him high and dry."

4   And then, just in case there is a customer in the restaurant who isn't yet aware of the situation, a waiter shouts out from the buffet table: "Well, we'll take care of him anyway, won't we fellas!"

5   *Haw, haw, haw,* and a lot of sly winks and pokes in the ribs.

6   Eating alone in a restaurant is one of the most terrifying experiences in America.

7   Sniffed at by headwaiters, an object of scorn and amusement to couples, the solitary diner is the unwanted and unloved child of Restaurant Row. No sooner does he make his appearance than he is whisked out of sight and seated at a thin sliver of a table with barely enough room on it for an hors d'oeuvre. Wedged between busboy stations, a hair's breadth from the men's room, there he sits, feet lodged in a railing as if he were in Pilgrim stocks, wondering where he went wrong in life.

8   Rather than face this grim scenario, most Lonely Guys would prefer to nibble away at a tuna fish sandwich in the relative safety of their high-rise apartments.

9   What can be done to ease the pain of this not only starving but silent minority—to make dining alone in restaurants a rewarding experience? Absolutely nothing. But some small strategies *do* exist for making the experience bearable.

Before You Get There

10   Once the Lonely Guy has decided to dine alone at a restaurant, a sense of terror and foreboding will begin to build throughout the day. All the more reason for him to get there as quickly as possible so that the experience can soon be forgotten and he can resume his normal life. Clothing should be light and loose-fitting, especially around the neck—on the off chance of a fainting attack during the appetizer. It is best to dress modestly, avoiding both

Margin labels:

Illustration in narrative form

Definition

Description

Effect

Step in process

the funeral-director-style suit as well as the bold, eye-arresting costume of the gaucho. A single cocktail should suffice; little sympathy will be given to the Lonely Guy who tumbles in, stewed to the gills. (The fellow who stoops to putting morphine in his toes for courage does not belong in this discussion.) En route to the restaurant, it is best to play down dramatics, such as swinging the arms pluckily and humming the theme from *The Bridge on the River Kwai*.

Once You Arrive

Description

11   The way your entrance comes off is of critical importance. Do not skulk in, slipping along the walls as if you are carrying some dirty little secret. There is no need, on the other hand, to fling your coat arrogantly at the hatcheck girl, slap the headwaiter across the cheeks with your gloves and demand to be seated immediately. Simply walk in with a brisk rubbing of the hands and approach the headwaiter. When asked how many are in your party, avoid cute responses such as "Jes lil ol' me." Tell him you are a party of one; the Lonely Guy who does not trust his voice can simply lift a finger. Do not launch into a story about how tired you are of taking out fashion models, night after night, and what a pleasure it is going to be to dine alone.

Step in process

Comparison

12   It is best to arrive with no reservation. Asked to set aside a table for one, the restaurant owner will suspect either a prank on the part of an ex-waiter, or a terrorist plot, in which case windows will be boarded up and the kitchen bomb-swept. An advantage of the "no reservation" approach is that you will appear to have just stepped off the plane from Des Moines, your first night in years away from Marge and the kids.

13   All eyes will be upon you when you make the promenade to your table. Stay as close as possible to the headwaiter, trying to match him step for step. This will reduce your visibility and fool some diners into thinking you are a member of the staff. If you hear a generalized snickering throughout the restaurant, do not assume automatically that you are being laughed at. The other diners may all have just recalled an amusing moment in a Feydeau farce.

Effect

14   If your table is unsatisfactory, do not demand imperiously that one for eight people be cleared immediately so that you can dine in solitary grandeur. Glance around discreetly and see if there are other possibilities. The ideal table will allow you to keep your back to the wall so that you can see if anyone is laughing at you. Try to get one close to another couple so that if you lean over at a 45-degree angle it will appear that you are a swinging member of their group. Sitting opposite a mirror can be useful; after a drink or two, you will begin to feel that there are a few of you.

15   Once you have been seated, and it becomes clear to the staff that you are alone, there will follow The Single Most Heartbreaking Moment in Dining Out Alone—when the second setting is whisked away and yours is spread out a bit to make the table look busier. This will be done with great ceremony by the waiter—angered in advance at being tipped for only one dinner. At this point, you may be tempted to smack your forehead against the table and curse the fates that brought you to this desolate position in life. A wiser course is to grit your teeth, order a drink and use this opportunity to make contact with other Lonely Guys sprinkled around the room. A menu or a leafy stalk of celery can be used as a shield for peering out at them. Do not expect a hearty greeting or a cry of "huzzah" from these frightened and

Definition

Continued on next page

Continued from previous page

browbeaten people. Too much excitement may cause them to slump over, curtains. Smile gently and be content if you receive a pale wave of the hand in return. It is unfair to imply that you have come to help them throw off their chains.

Effect

16   When the headwaiter arrives to take your order, do not be bullied into ordering the last of the gazelle haunches unless you really want them. Thrilled to be offered anything at all, many Lonely Guys will say "Get them right out here" and wolf them down. Restaurants take unfair advantage of Lonely Guys, using them to get rid of anything from withered liver to old heels of roast beef. Order anything you like, although it is good to keep to the light and simple in case of a sudden attack of violent stomach cramps.

Step in process

Some Proven Strategies

17   Once the meal is under way, a certain pressure will begin to build as couples snuggle together, the women clucking sympathetically in your direction. Warmth and conviviality will pervade the room, none of it encompassing you. At this point, many Lonely Guys will keep their eyes riveted to the restaurant paintings of early Milan or bury themselves in a paperback anthology they have no wish to read.

Effect

Classification

18   Here are some ploys designed to confuse other diners and make them feel less sorry for you:

19   ■ After each bite of food, lift your head, smack your lips thoughtfully, swallow and make a notation in a pad. Diners will assume you are a restaurant critic.

20   ■ Between courses, pull out a walkie-talkie and whisper a message into it. This will lead everyone to believe you are part of a police stake-out team, about to bust the salad man as an international dope dealer.

21   ■ Pretend you are a foreigner. This is done by pointing to items on the menu with an alert smile and saying to the headwaiter: "Is good, no?"

22   ■ When the main course arrives, brush the restaurant silverware off the table and pull some of your own out of a breastpocket. People will think you are a wealthy eccentric.

23   ■ Keep glancing at the door, and make occasional trips to look out at the street, as if you are waiting for a beautiful woman. Half-way through the meal, shrug in a world-weary manner and begin to eat with gusto. The world is full of women! Why tolerate bad manners! Life is too short.

The Right Way

Step in process

Implied Argument

24   One other course is open to the Lonely Guy, an audacious one, full of perils, but all the more satisfying if you can bring it off. That is to take off your dark glasses, sit erectly, smile broadly at anyone who looks in your direction, wave off inferior wines, and begin to eat with heartiness and enormous confidence. As outrageous as the thought may be—enjoy your own company. Suddenly, titters and sly winks will tail off, the headwaiter's disdain will fade, and friction will build among couples who will turn out to be not as tightly cemented as they appear. The heads of other Lonely Guys will lift with hope as you become the attractive center of the room.

25   If that doesn't work, you still have your fainting option.[1]

[1]From *The Lonely Guy's Book of Life* by Bruce Jay Friedman. Copyright © 1979 by McGraw-Hill, Inc. Reproduced with permission.

STEPPING UP TO **SYNTHESIS**

Most writing, including writing that draws on outside sources, uses a mixture of several strategies.

Prewriting for Synthesis Let's say that you're taking an elementary education class and are asked to write a paper evaluating the effectiveness of computers as an educational tool in elementary schools. Obviously, this assignment would require you to synthesize the results of your outside reading and very likely the conclusions drawn from one or more observations of computer use in classrooms. It would, in short, require both secondary (that is, library) research and direct observations, a form of primary research.

Critically Evaluating Your Sources As you determine which strategies will help you present your ideas, you can draw upon the principles of critical thinking that you used with each individual strategy. You can, for example, evaluate the merits of different writers' opinions, look for evidence of bias, weigh the type and amount of support backing each assertion, and select the key points you'll include in your paper.

Planning and Drafting the Synthesis You might begin your paper by describing a typical morning's activities in a computer-equipped classroom, noting particularly the students' responses to computer instruction. Next, you might classify the different uses of computers in the classroom and provide a brief history of the movement toward this type of instruction. You could proceed by citing the positive effects of computers in the classroom, as noted by those who advocate their use, and then evaluate whether these claims are exaggerated or reflect any bias. For example, you might notice some kind of bias in a comparison of classrooms with and without computers and then suggest how to make such a comparison so as to eliminate the bias. Finally, you might also critically examine the objections of those who oppose computer instruction. After you've completed this research and analysis, you could argue for or against the use of computers as an educational tool. Even though this type of assignment may seem overwhelming, you can meet the challenge if you tackle the project one stage at a time.

Getting Started

1. Using a combination of strategies, write a paper that investigates and assesses the placement of students with mental and emotional handicaps in "mainstream" rather than special classes. You might visit classrooms with and without handicapped students.

Continued on next page

Continued from previous page

2. Examine several sources that favor or oppose the use of community tax revenues to modernize an existing sports stadium or construct a new one. Then use a combination of strategies to write a paper that presents and assesses your findings.

3. Investigate using outside sources a current national phenomenon such as the upsurge in sensationalist television programming, the popularity of diet and exercising, or the increase in antismoking sentiment. Then use a combination of strategies to write a paper that presents and assesses these findings.

4. Identify what you consider a problem with some social policy of your college. Discuss this problem with several responsible students and also examine any available printed material that addresses this policy. Then use a combination of strategies to write a paper that identifies the problem and proposes a reasonable solution.

5. Identify what you consider a problem with some local, state, or national law. Perhaps you see it as unjust, unfairly applied, outdated, or the like. Examine several sources that discuss this law and then use a combination of strategies to write a paper that identifies the problem and proposes a reasonable solution.

Complete additional exercises and practice in your MyLab

CHAPTER 18   The Essay Examination

In this chapter, you will learn how to:

18.1   Study for an examination.

18.2   Analyze the types of test questions.

18.3   Prepare to write an exam essay by determining what is expected.

18.4   Write an effective essay for an exam.

Instructors use essay examinations to gauge your grasp of ideas, noting how well you apply, analyze, challenge, compare, or otherwise handle them. Facts and figures, on the other hand, are more often tested by objective examinations. Writing essay answers under pressure and with minimal time to rethink and revise differs from writing at home. Instructors expect reasonably complete and coherent answers that are legible. The skills learned in composition class can help you write successful essay exams. A plan, a thesis, specific support, staying on track, and the pointers presented in this chapter—all are grade boosters.

Studying for the Examination

Following are some pointers for studying:

1. Allow adequate preparation time. For a comprehensive test, start reviewing several days in advance. For one that covers a small segment of the course, a day or two should be enough.

2. Reread the key points you've marked in your class notes and textbook. Use them to develop a set of basic concepts.

3. Make up a set of sample questions related to these concepts and do some freewriting to answer them. Even if none of the questions appears on the test, your efforts will ease pretest jitters and supply insights that apply to other questions.

4. Answer your questions by drawing on your concepts and supplying details from your notes and textbook.

18.1

Study for an examination.

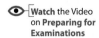

Watch the Video on **Preparing for Examinations**

Types of Test Questions

Analyze the types of test questions.

Some instructors favor narrow, highly focused test questions with detailed answering instructions. Others like broad items, perhaps with simple directions. The sample questions below range from very broad to very narrow. Note how when answering them you can often use the writing strategies discussed in Chapters 5–13.

1. Analyze the *influences* of the industrial revolution on European society.
2. Discuss the most important *causes* of the Spanish–American War.
3. *Compare and contrast* the David statues of Michelangelo and Bernini.
4. Select three different camera shots used in the movie *Titanic*. Identify at least one scene that *illustrates* each shot, then explain how each shot functions by *describing* the relationship between the shot and the action or dialogue.
5. Discuss the stock market plunge of October 27, 1997. Consider the major *factors* involved, such as the liberal lending practices of international banks, the growth in global manufacturing capacity, the severe recessions and monetary turmoil in Pacific Rim countries like Thailand and Malaysia, the concerns of Wall Street, and how these *factors* interacted. Use a thesis statement that signals the points you will discuss.

A highly focused question such as item 5 suggests how to organize and develop the essay. If you know the answer, you can begin writing quickly. In contrast, item 1 forces you to focus and narrow the subject before you respond. Answering this type of item requires careful planning.

Preparing to Write

Prepare to write an exam essay by determining what is expected.

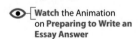
Watch the Animation on **Preparing to Write an Essay Answer**

Effective exam writing requires thoughtful planning. Often students fail to read general directions or to answer what is asked. To avoid penalizing yourself, scan the test items, noting how many must be answered and which ones, if any, are optional. When you have a choice, select the questions you can answer most thoroughly. Pay attention to any suggestions or requirements concerning length (one paragraph, two pages) or relative weight (25 points, 30 minutes, 40 percent), and budget your time accordingly.

The first requirement for most essay tests is to read the question for *key words*. Does the instructor want you to analyze, compare, criticize, defend, describe, discuss, evaluate, illustrate, explain, justify, trace, or summarize? If you are asked to explain how Darwin's theory of evolution affected nineteenth-century thinking, do just that; you won't like your grade if, instead, you summarize the theory. Merely putting ideas on paper, even perceptive ideas, does not substitute for addressing the question.

EXERCISE

Indicate what each of the following questions calls for. What is required? By what methods—arguing, describing, or the like—would you develop the answer?

1. Distinguish between mild depression and severe depression. You might focus on the nature, the symptoms, or the potential treatments of each condition.
2. Support or refute the following statement: Because waste incineration generates stack gases and ash that contain high levels of toxic substances, it is not an acceptable solution to waste-disposal problems.
3. Explain how to pressure test a radiator.
4. Briefly relate the events in the Book of Job and then explain the significance of the tale to questions of divine justice. Could the tale be called symbolic? Why or why not?

When you have the essay question clearly in mind, don't immediately start writing. Instead, take a few moments to plan your answer. Following these steps will help you do this:

1. Jot down specific supporting information from your reading lecture notes.
2. Make a rough outline that sketches the main points you'll cover and an effective order for presenting them.
3. Prepare a thesis statement that responds to the question and will control your answer.

Writing an essay exam, like writing an essay, is a front-end-loaded process. Much of the brain work occurs before you put your answer on paper.

Writing the Examination Answer

Here are some guidelines that will help you write a successful exam:

1. Position your thesis statement at the beginning of your answer. Make sure each paragraph is controlled by a topic sentence tied to the thesis statement.
2. Don't become excessively concerned about your wording. Focus on content and, if time permits, make stylistic changes later.
3. Fight the impulse to jot down everything you know about the general subject. The grader doesn't want to plow through verbiage to arrive at your answer.

The following essay illustrates these guidelines:

18.4

Write an effective essay for an exam.

Question: Discuss the various appeals described by classical rhetoric that an orator can use. Give a brief example of each kind of appeal.

Answer: Classical rhetoric defines three major appeals—

Thesis statement previews logical, emotional, and ethical—that orators may

focus and order of answer	use to win support from their audience.
Topic sentence:	Most rhetoricians agree that any argument must be based on logic; that is, it must appeal to the intellect of the listeners. Unless it does,
Example 1:	the orator will fail to convince them. For example, a speaker who is urging the election of a candidate and presents the candidate's voting record is appealing to logic, asking the audience to understand that the voting record predicts how the candidate will continue to vote if
Example 2:	elected. Likewise, a candidate for public office who describes how a tax cut will stimulate the economy and create new jobs is using a logical appeal.
Topic sentence:	In addition to logic, emotional appeals are a powerful means of swaying people, especially groups. Though emotional appeals work along with logical appeals, they are quite different because they are directed at the listener's hopes,
Example 1:	fears, and sympathies. The presidential candidate who indicates that a vote for an opponent is a vote to increase government spending and risk a financial crisis is making an emotional
Example 2:	appeal. So, too, is the gubernatorial candidate who asserts that her state's industry can be revitalized and serve as a model for all other states.
Topic sentence:	The ethical appeal is more subtle than either of the other two but probably just as important. The orator must strike the audience as a sensible, good person if they are to believe the
Example 1:	message. Sometimes the speaker's logic and also the tone—moderate, sensible, or wise—
Example 2:	will convey sufficient ethical appeal. At other times, a speaker will use statements that are deliberately intended to create ethical appeal. "In developing this program, I will work closely with both houses of the legislature, including the members of both political parties" and "Despite our differences, I believe my opponent to be a decent, honest person" are examples of such statements.
Restatement of thesis:	In any speech, all these appeals—logical, emotional, and ethical—work together to convince an audience.

Student Unknown

In contrast, the next two responses to the same question illustrate common faults of examination essays.

Answer A

1   There are three basic appeals that a speaker can make to captivate an audience. These are the ethical appeal, the logical appeal, and the emotional appeal.

2   The first of these—the ethical appeal—includes all the speaker's efforts to be viewed as rational, wise, good, and generous. Needless to say, the ethical appeal is very important. Without it, no one would pay attention to the speaker's argument.

3   The second appeal—logical—is also extremely important. It carries the burden of the argument from speaker to listener and appeals to the intellect of the audience.

4   Emotional appeal—the third and final one—is made to the passions and feelings of the listeners. The significance of such an appeal is obvious.

5   A speaker often uses all three appeals to win an audience over.

Answer *A* starts with a thesis statement and includes brief definitions of the three appeals; however, it omits any concrete examples and includes no specific details. As a result, the significance of the emotional appeal is not "obvious," as paragraph 4 claims, nor does the answer offer any hints as to why the other appeals are important. This response resembles an outline more than an answer and suggests the student lacked the knowledge to do a good job.

Answer B

1   Orators may make three different kinds of appeals to win favor from an audience: emotional appeal, logical appeal, and ethical appeal.

2   Let's start with emotional appeal because this is the one that is not essential to a speech. Logical and ethical appeals are always included; emotional appeal may be used to help sway an audience, but without logical and ethical appeals no argument is accepted. This simply makes sense: If there is no logic, there is no argument; and if the speaker doesn't come across as an ethical person—someone to be relied upon—then no one will accept the message. But emotional appeal is different. Unemotional arguments may be accepted.

3   Nevertheless, emotional appeal is important. It includes whatever a speaker does to move the feelings of the audience. The speaker asks, "Don't you want to protect your families?" Such an appeal is emotional. A speaker may appeal to the prejudices or biases of listeners. Someone at a Ku Klux Klan rally does that. So does a minister who exhorts people to be "saved." Both speakers address the emotions of the groups they talk to.

4   There is a very fine use of emotional appeal in the "Letter from Birmingham Jail" by Martin Luther King, Jr. At one point King asks his audience of white clergy how they would feel if, like blacks, they had to deny their children treats such as amusement parks and had to fear for the lives of their families, and so on. He also describes the bombings and burnings that blacks are subjected to. All the details move readers emotionally, so that they come to sympathize with blacks who live in fear.

5   Logical appeal, as noted earlier, is crucial. The speaker must seem to have an intelligent plan. The listeners want the plan to meet their needs.

6   The other appeal is the ethical one. It is made when speakers make themselves seem generous, good, and wise.

7   All three appeals can be used in one speech, although the logical and ethical appeals are essential to it.

Although the writer opens with an acceptable thesis statement, this answer shows little evidence of advance planning. Does it make sense to begin in paragraph 2 with an appeal tagged "not essential"? And note how the paragraph drifts from the emotional appeal to the other two types, despite its topic sentence. Paragraphs 3 and 4 do focus on the emotional appeal and ironically, through specific examples, make a good case for its importance. Paragraphs 5 and 6 shortchange logical and ethical appeals by saying next to nothing about them. The essay contradicts itself: If logical and ethical appeals are the essential ones and emotional appeals "not essential," why is more than half of the essay about emotional appeal?

Read the examination questions and answers below. Then respond to the questions that follow the answers.

A. Question

Living organisms are composed of cells. On the basis of structure, biologists categorize cells into two groups: the prokaryotic cells and the eukaryotic cells. What are the major differences between prokaryotic cells and eukaryotic cells, and in which living organisms are these cells found?

Answer

1 Eukaryotic cells have a true nucleus and their genetic material, the DNA-containing chromosomes, is located within this nucleus, which is surrounded by a nuclear membrane. Prokaryotic cells lack a true nucleus, and their genetic material lies free in the cytoplasm of the cell.

2 Eukaryotic cells are also much more complex than prokaryotic cells. Eukaryotic cells commonly contain organelles such as mitochondria, a Golgi complex, lysosomes, an endoplasmic reticulum, and in photosynthetic cells, chloroplasts. These organelles are typically lacking in the simpler prokaryotic cells.

3 Prokaryotic cells make up the structure of all bacteria and the blue-green algae. These are the simplest of all known cellular organisms. All other cellular organisms, including humans, are composed of eukaryotic cells.

Scott Wybolt

a. Does the response answer the question that was asked? Discuss.

B. Question

Analyze the significant relationships between imagination and reality in Coleridge's "This Lime-Tree Bower My Prison." In your answer, you might consider some of the following questions: What is the importance of setting in the poem? Is the speaker's mind a form of setting? How is reality implicitly defined in the poem? How, and through what agencies, can reality be transmitted? What relationship is finally perceived between the spiritual and the concrete? How does friendship or fellow feeling trigger the essential insights revealed in the poem?

Answer

1   Coleridge's "This Lime-Tree Bower My Prison" shows imagination to be a powerful force that can control one's perception of reality and that is, in itself, a kind of reality—perhaps the most important reality. Thus, imagination and reality are more intimately linked and more similar in Coleridge's poem than they are ordinarily thought to be.

2   The relationship between imagination and reality is revealed by the speaker of "Lime-Tree Bower," although he doesn't openly state it. The technique for revelation is dramatic monologue, with the speaker seemingly talking spontaneously as his situation gives rise to a series of thoughts.

3   As the poem begins, the speaker finds himself "trapped" at home in his lime-tree bower, while his friends go on a walk he had hoped to take with them. This situation at first bothers the speaker, causing him to feel imprisoned. As the poem progresses, however, the speaker begins to imagine all the places his friends are visiting on their walk. Though he laments not being with them, he shows excitement as he describes the scenes his friends are viewing: the "roaring dell," the sea, and so on. Thus the speaker recognizes that he is able to participate imaginatively in the walk and, in doing so, to escape his "prison" reality and enter the reality of his friends.

4   The moment of recognition occurs at the beginning of stanza three: "A delight/Comes sudden on my heart, and I am glad/As I myself was there!" Interestingly, however, this point marks a turn in the speaker's thoughts. Once again he realizes where he actually is—the lime-tree bower. But now he appreciates its beauties. The natural beauties he imagined have taught him to appreciate the beauties of nature right before him. He has learned that there is "No plot so narrow, be but Nature there." The lime-tree bower is no longer a prison but a rich and beautiful, if somewhat small, world.

5   Imagination has again shaped the speaker's perceptions of reality. It controls the perception of circumstances—whether one views a place as a prison or a microcosm of a larger world, with beauties and possibilities in its own right. The use of imagination can teach one about reality, as it has Coleridge's speaker. And, if one surrenders to it completely—as the speaker does when he envisions the world of the walkers—imagination is a delightful reality, as valid as the reality of the place in which one sits.

6   Imagination and reality are merged in "This Lime-Tree Bower My Prison," and though this identification is apparently temporary, one may learn through imagination how to cope with and enjoy reality. Thus, imagination is intimately involved in shaping the perception of reality.

Lori McCue

a. Which of the possible approaches suggested in the question does the student select?

b. Which of the other questions does she indirectly answer? Which ones are not addressed?

c. Identify the thesis statement and explain how it controls the answer.

d. Show how the answer demonstrates careful planning.

e. Point out some effective supporting details.

Complete additional exercises and practice in your MyLab

CHAPTER 19 Writing About Literature

In this chapter, you will learn how to:

19.1 Identify the key elements of literature.

19.2 Analyze and write about the way plot works in a piece of literature.

19.3 Analyze and write about the way point of view works in a piece of literature.

19.4 Analyze and write about the way character works in a piece of literature.

19.5 Analyze and write about the way setting works in a piece of literature.

19.6 Analyze and write about the way symbols work in a piece of literature.

19.7 Analyze and write about the way irony works in a piece of literature.

19.8 Analyze and write about the way theme works in a piece of literature.

19.9 Write so that your literary analysis is ethical.

19.10 Prewrite, plan, draft, and revise your literary analysis.

Teachers of literature generally expect you to write about what you've read. Typically they might ask you to

- show how an author handled one element of a short story, play, or poem;
- compare how two different works treat a particular element;
- weigh several elements and then determine the writer's intention;
- air your reactions to some work.

Writing about literature offers several benefits. Weighing and recording your thoughts on the different elements sharpen your critical thinking ability. Literary papers also pay artistic dividends, as careful reading and subsequent writing deepen your appreciation of the writer's craft or themes. Furthermore, you'll feel a sense of accomplishment as you coherently express your perceptions. Finally, writing a literature paper offers yet another opportunity to apply the writing guidelines discussed in Chapters 1–4. Focusing, gathering information, organizing, writing, revising, and editing—the old familiar trail leads to success here too.

The Elements of Literature

Most writing assignments on literature will probably feature one or more of the following elements:

19.1

Identify the key elements of literature.

Plot	Symbols
Point of view	Irony
Character	Theme
Setting	

Depending on the work, some of these will be more important than others. Read the following story by Stephen Crane, "The Bride Comes to Yellow Sky." The discussions that follow it point out the basic features of each element and offer useful writing suggestions.

The Bride Comes to Yellow Sky

Stephen Crane

I

The great Pullman was whirling onward with such dignity of motion that a glance from the window seemed simply to prove that the plains of Texas were pouring eastward. Vast flats of green grass, dull-hued spaces of mesquit and cactus, little groups of frame houses, woods of light and tender trees, all were sweeping into the east, sweeping over the horizon, a precipice.

A newly married pair had boarded this coach at San Antonio. The man's face was reddened from many days in the wind and sun, and a direct result of his new black clothes was that his brick-colored hands were constantly performing in a most conscious fashion. From time to time he looked down respectfully at his attire. He sat with a hand on each knee, like a man waiting in a barber's shop. The glances he devoted to other passengers were furtive and shy.

The bride was not pretty, nor was she very young. She wore a dress of blue cashmere, with small reservations of velvet here and there, and with steel buttons abounding. She continually twisted her head to regard her puff sleeves, very stiff, straight, and high. They embarrassed her. It was quite apparent that she had cooked, and that she expected to cook, dutifully. The blushes caused by the careless scrutiny of some passengers as she had entered the car were strange to see upon this plain, under-class countenance, which was drawn in placid, almost emotionless lines.

They were evidently very happy. "Ever been in a parlor-car before?" he asked, smiling with delight.

"No," she answered; "I never was. It's fine, ain't it?"

"Great! And then after a while we'll go forward to the diner, and get a big layout. Finest meal in the world. Charge a dollar."

"Oh, do they?" cried the bride. "Charge a dollar? Why, that's too much—for us—ain't it, Jack?"

"Not this trip, anyhow," he answered bravely. "We're going to go the whole thing."

Later he explained to her about the trains. "You see, it's a thousand miles from one end of Texas to the other; and this train runs right across it and never stops but four times." He had the pride of an owner. He pointed out to her the dazzling fittings of the coach; and in truth her eyes opened wider as she contemplated the sea-green figured velvet, the shining brass, silver, and glass, the wood that gleamed as darkly brilliant as the surface of a pool of oil. At one end a bronze figure sturdily held a support for a separated chamber, and at convenient places on the ceiling were frescos in olive and silver.

To the minds of the pair, their surroundings reflected the glory of their marriage that morning in San Antonio; this was the environment of their new estate; and the man's face in particular beamed with an elation that made him appear ridiculous to the negro porter. This individual at times surveyed them from afar with an amused and superior grin. On other occasions he bullied them with skill in ways that did not make it exactly plain to them that they were being bullied. He subtly used all the manners of the most unconquerable kind of snobbery. He oppressed them; but of this oppression they had small knowledge, and they speedily forgot that infrequently a number of travelers covered them with stares of derisive enjoyment. Historically there was supposed to be something infinitely humorous in their situation.

"We are due in Yellow Sky at 3:42," he said, looking tenderly into her eyes.

"Oh, are we?" she said, as if she had not been aware of it. To evince surprise at her husband's statement was part of her wifely amiability. She took from a pocket a little silver watch; and as she held it before her, and stared at it with a frown of attention, the new husband's face shone.

"I bought it in San Anton' from a friend of mine," he told her gleefully.

"It's seventeen minutes past twelve," she said, looking up at him with a kind of shy and clumsy coquetry. A passenger, noting this play, grew excessively sardonic, and winked at himself in one of the numerous mirrors.

At last they went to the dining car. Two rows of negro waiters, in glowing white suits, surveyed their entrance with the interest, and also the equanimity, of men who had been forewarned. The pair fell to the lot of a waiter who happened to feel pleasure in steering them through their meal. He viewed them with the manner of a fatherly pilot, his countenance radiant with benevolence. The patronage, entwined with the ordinary deference, was not plain to them. And yet, as they returned to their coach, they showed in their faces a sense of escape.

To the left, miles down a long purple slope, was a little ribbon of mist where moved the keening Rio Grande. The train was approaching it at an angle, and the apex was Yellow Sky. Presently it was apparent that, as the distance from Yellow Sky grew shorter, the husband became commensurately restless. His brick-red hands were more insistent in their prominence. Occasionally he was even rather absent-minded and far-away when the bride leaned forward and addressed him.

As a matter of truth, Jack Potter was beginning to find the shadow of a deed weigh upon him like a leaden slab. He, the town marshal of Yellow Sky, a man known, liked, and feared in his corner, a prominent person, had gone to San Antonio to meet a girl he believed he loved, and there, after the usual prayers, had actually induced her to marry him, without consulting Yellow Sky for any part of the transaction. He was now bringing his bride before an innocent and unsuspecting community.

Of course people in Yellow Sky married as it pleased them, in accordance with a general custom; but such was Potter's thought of his duty to his friends, or of their idea of his duty, or of an unspoken form which does not control men in these matters, that he felt he was heinous. He had committed an extraordinary crime. Face to face with this girl in San Antonio, and spurred by his sharp impulse, he had gone headlong over all the social hedges. At San Antonio he was like a man hidden in the dark. A knife to sever any friendly duty, any form, was easy to his hand in that remote city. But the hour of Yellow Sky—the hour of daylight—was approaching.

He knew full well that his marriage was an important thing to his town. It could only be exceeded by the burning of the new hotel. His friends could not forgive him. Frequently he had reflected on the advisability of telling them by telegraph, but a new cowardice had been upon him. He feared to do it. And now the train was hurrying him toward a scene of amazement, glee, and reproach. He glanced out of the window at the line of haze swinging slowly in toward the train.

Yellow Sky had a kind of brass band, which played painfully, to the delight of the populace. He laughed without heart as he thought of it. If the citizens could dream of his prospective arrival with his bride, they would parade the band at the station and escort them, amid cheers and laughing congratulations, to his adobe home.

He resolved that he would use all the devices of speed and plainscraft in making the journey from the station to his house. Once within that safe citadel, he could issue some sort of vocal bulletin, and then not go among the citizens until they had time to wear off a little of their enthusiasm.

The bride looked anxiously at him. "What's worrying you, Jack?"

He laughed again. "I'm not worrying, girl; I'm only thinking of Yellow Sky."

She flushed in comprehension.

A sense of mutual guilt invaded their minds and developed a finer tenderness. They looked at each other, with eyes softly aglow. But Potter often laughed the same nervous laugh; the flush upon the bride's face seemed quite permanent.

The traitor to the feelings of Yellow Sky narrowly watched the speeding landscape. "We're nearly there," he said.

Presently the porter came and announced the proximity of Potter's home. He held a brush in his hand, and, with all his airy superiority gone, he brushed Potter's new clothes as the latter slowly turned this way and that way. Potter tumbled out a coin and gave it to the porter, as he had seen others do. It was a heavy and muscle-bound business, as that of a man shoeing his first horse.

The porter took their bag, and as the train began to slow they moved forward to the hooded platform of the car. Presently the two engines and their long string of coaches rushed into the station of Yellow Sky.

"They have to take water here," said Potter, from a constricted throat and in mournful cadence, as one announcing death. Before the train stopped his eye had swept the length of the platform, and he was glad and astonished to see there was none upon it but the station-agent, who, with a slightly hurried and anxious air, was walking toward the water-tanks. When the train had halted, the porter alighted first, and placed in position a little temporary step.

"Come on, girl," said Potter, hoarsely. As he helped her down they each laughed on a false note. He took the bag from the negro, and bade his wife cling to his arm. As they slunk rapidly away, his hang-dog glance perceived that they were unloading the two trunks, and also that the station-agent, far ahead near the baggage-car, had turned and was running toward him, making gestures. He laughed, and groaned as he laughed, when he noted the first effect of his marital bliss upon Yellow Sky. He gripped his wife's arm firmly to his side, and they fled. Behind them the porter stood, chuckling fatuously.

II

The California express on the Southern Railway was due at Yellow Sky in twenty-one minutes. There were six men at the bar of the Weary Gentleman saloon. One was a drummer[1] who talked a great deal and rapidly; three were Texans who did not care to talk at that time; and two were Mexican sheepherders, who did not talk as a general practice in the Weary Gentleman saloon. The barkeeper's dog lay on the boardwalk that crossed in front of the door. His head was on his paws, and he glanced drowsily here and there with the constant vigilance of a dog that is kicked on occasion. Across the sandy street were some vivid green grass-plots, so wonderful in appearance, amid the sands that burned near them in a blazing sun, that they caused a doubt in the mind. They exactly resembled the grass mats used to represent lawns on the stage. At the cooler end of the railway station, a man without a coat sat in a tilted chair and smoked his pipe. The fresh-cut bank of the Rio Grande circled near the town, and there could be seen beyond it a great plum-colored plain of mesquit.

Save for the busy drummer and his companions in the saloon, Yellow Sky was dozing. The new-comer leaned gracefully upon the bar, and recited many tales with the confidence of a bard who has come upon a new field.

"—and at the moment that the old man fell downstairs with the bureau in his arms, the old woman was coming up with two scuttles of coal, and of course—"

The drummer's tale was interrupted by a young man who suddenly appeared in the open door. He cried: "Scratchy Wilson's drunk, and has turned loose with both hands." The two Mexicans at once set down their glasses and faded out of the rear entrance of the saloon.

The drummer, innocent and jocular, answered: "All right, old man. S'pose he has? Come in and have a drink, anyhow."

But the information had made such an obvious cleft in every skull in the room that the drummer was obliged to see its importance. All had become instantly solemn. "Say," said he, mystified, "what is this?" His three companions made the introductory gesture of eloquent speech; but the young man at the door forestalled them.

"It means, my friend," he answered, as he came into the saloon, "that for the next two hours this town won't be a health resort."

The barkeeper went to the door, and locked and barred it; reaching out of the window, he pulled in heavy wooden shutters, and barred them. Immediately a solemn, chapel-like gloom was upon the place. The drummer was looking from one to another.

"But say," he cried, "what is this, anyhow? You don't mean there is going to be a gun-fight?"

"Don't know whether there'll be a fight or not," answered one man, grimly; "but there'll be some shootin'—some good shootin'."

The young man who had warned them waved his hand. "Oh, there'll be a fight fast enough, if any one wants it. Anybody can get a fight out there in the street. There's a fight just waiting."

The drummer seemed to be swayed between the interest of a foreigner and a perception of personal danger.

"What did you say his name was?" he asked.

"Scratchy Wilson," they answered in chorus.

"And will he kill anybody? What are you going to do? Does this happen often? Does he rampage around like this once a week or so? Can he break in that door?"

"No; he can't break down that door," replied the barkeeper. "He's tried it three times. But when he comes you'd better lay down on the floor, stranger. He's dead sure to shoot at it, and a bullet may come through."

Thereafter the drummer kept a strict eye upon the door. The time had not yet been called for him to hug the floor, but, as a minor precaution, he sidled near to the wall. "Will he kill anybody?" he said again.

[1]Traveling salesman

The men laughed low and scornfully at the question.

"He's out to shoot, and he's out for trouble. Don't see any good in experimentin' with him."

"But what do you do in a case like this? What do you do?"

A man responded: "Why, he and Jack Potter—"

"But," in chorus the other men interrupted, "Jack Potter's in San Anton'."

"Well, who is he? What's he got to do with it?"

"Oh, he's the town marshal. He goes out and fights Scratchy when he gets on one of these tears."

"Wow!" said the drummer, mopping his brow. "Nice job he's got."

The voices had toned away to mere whisperings. The drummer wished to ask further questions, which were born of an increasing anxiety and bewilderment; but when he attempted them, the men merely looked at him in irritation and motioned him to remain silent. A tense waiting hush was upon them. In the deep shadows of the room their eyes shone as they listened for sounds from the street. One man made three gestures at the barkeeper; and the latter, moving like a ghost, handed him a glass and a bottle. The man poured a full glass of whisky, and set down the bottle noiselessly. He gulped the whisky in a swallow, and turned again toward the door in immovable silence. The drummer saw that the barkeeper, without a sound, had taken a Winchester from beneath the bar. Later he saw this individual beckoning to him, so he tiptoed across the room.

"You better come with me back of the bar."

"No, thanks," said the drummer, perspiring: "I'd rather be where I can make a break for the back door."

Whereupon the man of bottles made a kindly but peremptory gesture. The drummer obeyed it, and, finding himself seated on a box with his head below the level of the bar, balm was laid upon his soul at sight of various zinc and copper fittings that bore a resemblance to armorplate. The barkeeper took a seat comfortably upon an adjacent box.

"You see," he whispered, "this here Scratchy Wilson is a wonder with a gun—a perfect wonder; and when he goes on the wartrail, we hunt our holes—naturally. He's about the last one of the old gang that used to hang out along the river here. He's a terror when he's drunk. When he's sober he's all right—kind of simple—wouldn't hurt a fly—nicest fellow in town. But when he's drunk—whoo!"

There were periods of stillness. "I wish Jack Potter was back from San Anton'," said the barkeeper. "He shot Wilson up once—in the leg—and he would sail in and pull out the kinks in this thing."

Presently they heard from a distance the sound of a shot, followed by three wild yowls. It instantly removed a bond from the men in the darkened saloon. There was a shuffling of feet. They looked at each other. "Here he comes," they said.

III

A man in a maroon-colored flannel shirt, which had been purchased for purposes of decoration, and made principally by some Jewish women on the East Side of New York, rounded a corner and walked into the middle of the main street of Yellow Sky. In either hand the man held a long, heavy, blue-black revolver. Often he yelled, and these cries rang through a semblance of a deserted village, shrilly flying over the roofs in a volume that seemed to have no relation to the ordinary vocal strength of a man. It was as if the surrounding stillness formed the arch of a tomb over him. These cries of ferocious challenge rang against walls of silence. And his boots had red tops with gilded imprints, of the kind beloved in winter by little sledding boys on the hillsides of New England.

The man's face flamed in a rage begot of whisky. His eyes, rolling, and yet keen for ambush, hunted the still doorways and windows. He walked with the creeping movement of the midnight cat. As it occurred to him, he roared menacing information. The long revolvers in his hands were as easy as straws; they were moved with an electric swiftness. The little fingers of each hand played sometimes in a musician's way. Plain from the low collar of the shirt, the cords of his neck straightened and sank, straightened and sank, as passion moved him. The only sounds were his terrible invitations. The calm adobes preserved their demeanor at the passing of this small thing in the middle of the street.

There was no offer of fight—no offer of fight. The man called to the sky. There were no attractions. He bellowed and fumed and swayed his revolvers here and everywhere.

The dog of the barkeeper of the Weary Gentleman saloon had not appreciated the advance of events. He yet lay dozing in front of his master's door. At sight of the dog, the man paused and raised his revolver humorously. At sight of the man, the dog sprang up and walked diagonally away, with a sullen head, and growling. The man yelled, and the dog broke into a gallop. As it was about to enter an alley, there was a loud noise, a whistling, and something spat the ground directly before it. The dog screamed, and, wheeling in terror, galloped headlong in a new direction. Again there was a noise, a whistling, and sand was kicked viciously before it. Fear-stricken, the dog turned and flurried like an animal in a pen. The man stood laughing, his weapons at his hips.

Ultimately the man was attracted by the closed door of the Weary Gentleman saloon. He went to it and, hammering with a revolver, demanded drink.

The door remaining imperturbable, he picked a bit of paper from the walk, and nailed it to the framework with a knife. He then turned his back contemptuously upon this popular resort and, walking to the opposite side of the street and spinning there on his heel quickly and lithely, fired at the bit of paper. He missed it by a half-inch. He swore at himself, and went away. Later he comfortably fusilladed the windows of his most intimate friend. The man was playing with this town: it was a toy for him.

But still there was no offer of fight. The name of Jack Potter, his ancient antagonist, entered his mind, and he concluded that it would be a glad thing if he should go to Potter's house, and by bombardment induce him to come out and fight. He moved in the direction of his desire, chanting Apache scalp-music.

When he arrived at it, Potter's house presented the same still front as had the other adobes. Taking up a strategic position, the man howled a challenge. But this house regarded him as might a great stone god. It gave no sign. After a decent wait, the man howled further challenges, mingling with them wonderful epithets.

Presently there came the spectacle of a man churning himself into deepest rage over the immobility of a house. He fumed at it as the winter wind attacks a prairie cabin in the North. To the distance there should have gone the sound of a tumult like the fighting of two hundred Mexicans. As necessity bade him, he paused for breath or to reload his revolvers.

IV

Potter and his bride walked sheepishly and with speed. Sometimes they laughed together shamefacedly and low.

"Next corner, dear," he said finally.

They put forth the efforts of a pair walking bowed against a strong wind. Potter was about to raise a finger to point the first appearance of the new home when, as they circled the corner, they came face to face with a man in a maroon-colored shirt, who was feverishly pushing cartridges into a large revolver. Upon the instant the man dropped his revolver to the ground and, like lightning, whipped another from its holster. The second weapon was aimed at the bridegroom's chest.

There was a silence. Potter's mouth seemed to be merely a grave for his tongue. He exhibited an instinct to at once loosen his arm from the woman's grip, and he dropped the bag to the sand. As for the bride, her face had gone as yellow as old cloth. She was a slave to hideous rites, gazing at the apparitional snake.

The two men faced each other at a distance of three paces. He of the revolver smiled with a new and quiet ferocity.

"Tried to sneak up on me," he said. "Tried to sneak up on me!" His eyes grew more baleful. As Potter made a slight movement, the man thrust his revolver venomously forward. "No; don't you do it, Jack Potter. Don't you move a finger toward a gun just yet. Don't you move an eyelash. The time has come for me to settle with you, and I'm goin' to do it my own way, and loaf along with no interferin'. So if you don't want a gun bent on you, just mind what I tell you."

Potter looked at his enemy. "I ain't got a gun on me, Scratchy," he said. "Honest, I ain't." He was stiffening and steadying, but yet somewhere at the back of his mind a vision of the Pullman floated: the sea-green figured velvet, the shining brass, silver, and glass, the wood that gleamed as darkly brilliant as the surface of a pool of oil—all the glory of the marriage, the environment of the new estate. "You know I fight when it comes to fighting, Scratchy Wilson; but I ain't got a gun on me. You'll have to do all the shootin' yourself."

His enemy's face went livid. He stepped forward, and lashed his weapon to and fro before Potter's chest. "Don't tell me you ain't got no gun on you, you whelp. Don't tell me no lie like that. There ain't a man in Texas ever seen you without no gun. Don't take me for no kid." His eyes blazed with light, and his throat worked like a pump.

"I ain't takin' you for no kid," answered Potter. His heels had not moved an inch backward. "I'm takin' you for a damn fool. I tell you I ain't got a gun, and I ain't. If you're goin' to shoot me up, you better begin now; you'll never get a chance like this again."

So much enforced reasoning had told on Wilson's rage; he was calmer. "If you ain't got a gun, why ain't you got a gun?" he sneered. "Been to Sunday-school?"

"I ain't got a gun because I've just come from San Anton' with my wife. I'm married," said Potter. "And if I'd thought there was going to be any galoots like you prowling around when I brought my wife home, I'd had a gun, and don't you forget it."

"Married!" said Scratchy, not at all comprehending.

"Yes, married. I'm married." said Potter, distinctly.

"Married?" said Scratchy. Seemingly for the first time, he saw the drooping, drowning woman at the other man's side. "No!" he said. He was like a creature allowed a glimpse of another world. He moved a pace backward, and his arm, with the revolver, dropped to his side. "Is this the lady?" he asked.

"Yes; this is the lady," answered Potter.

There was another period of silence.

"Well," said Wilson at last, slowly, "I s'pose it's all off now."

"It's all off if you say so, Scratchy. You know I didn't make the trouble." Potter lifted his valise.

"Well, I 'low it's off, Jack," said Wilson. He was looking at the ground. "Married!" He was not a student of chivalry; it was merely that in the presence of this foreign condition he was a simple child of the earlier plains. He picked up his starboard revolver, and, placing both weapons in their holsters, he went away. His feet made funnel-shaped tracks in the heavy sand.

Plot

19.2

Analyze and write about the way plot works in a piece of literature.

◉—[Watch the Video on **Plot**

Plot Factors   Plot is the series of events that moves a narrative along. The opening of a story with a conventional plot introduces important characters and sets the stage for what happens. Then one or more conflicts develop, some pitting person against person, others setting characters against society, nature, fate, or themselves. Action gradually builds to a climax, where events take a decisive turn. The ending can do a number of things—clear up unanswered questions, hint at the future, state a theme, or reestablish some sort of relationship between two foes. In "The Bride," Potter experiences two conflicts: one with Scratchy Wilson and the other within himself over his marriage. The climax comes when Potter and Scratchy meet face to face, and Scratchy learns about his old adversary's marriage. As Scratchy walks away, we sense that the two old foes have had their last confrontation, that Potter's marriage has altered forever the relationship between them.

To organize plots, writers use a number of techniques. In foreshadowing, for example, the writer hints at later developments, thus creating interest and building suspense. In H. H. Munro's short story "The Open Window," a visitor to a country house observes that "An undefinable something about the room seemed to suggest masculine habitation." Yet he accepts the story of a young girl that her uncle, the man of the house, had lost his life in a bog three years before. Because he ignores his observation and accepts the girl's story at face value, the visitor is terrified by the sudden appearance of the uncle, who seems to be a ghost. The careful reader, however, senses what's coming and enjoys the trick more for having been in on it.

When using a flashback, another organizational technique, the writer interrupts the flow of events to relate one or more happenings that occurred before the point at which the story opened, then resumes the narrative at or near the point of interruption. Ernest Hemingway's short story "The Short Happy Life of Francis Macomber" provides an illustration. As the story opens, we meet characters who hint that Macomber displayed cowardice by running from, rather than shooting, a charging, wounded lion. A bit later the story flashes back to detail the actual incident. Flashbacks supply essential information and either create or resolve suspense.

Not every plot unfolds in clear stages. Many modern stories lack distinct plot divisions and focus on psychological, not physical, conflicts. In extreme cases, writers may abandon the traditional plot structure and present events in a disorganized sequence that helps accomplish some literary purpose, such as reflecting a character's disturbed state of mind. Joyce Carol Oates's short story "How I Contemplated the World from the Detroit House of Correction and Began My Life Over Again" fits this mold. To dramatize her chief character's mental turmoil, Oates presents the story as a series of notes for an English composition. These notes, labeled "Events," "Characters," "Sioux Drive," "Detroit," and "That Night," are internally disorganized and arranged in a jumbled sequence.

A poem sometimes includes a series of actions and events, as Edwin Arlington Robinson's "The Mill" illustrates:

> The miller's wife had waited long,
>   The tea was cold, the fire was dead;
> And there might yet be nothing wrong
>   In how he went and what he said:
> "There are no millers any more,"
>   Was all that she had heard him say:
> And he had lingered at the door
>   So long that it seemed yesterday.
>
> Sick with a fear that had no form
>   She knew that she was there at last;
> And in the mill there was a warm
>   And mealy fragrance of the past.
> What else there was would only seem
>   To say again what he had meant;
> And what was hanging from a beam
>   Would not have heeded where she went.
>
> And if she thought it followed her,
>   She may have reasoned in the dark
> That one way of the few there were
>   Would hide her and would leave no mark;
> Black water, smooth above the weir
>   Like starry velvet in the night,
> Though ruffled once, would soon appear
>   The same as ever to the sight.

Most poems, however, present a series of images, building statements that make a philosophical point rather than tell a conventionally plotted story.

Writing About Plot   Unless your instructor asks for a plot summary, don't merely repeat what happens in the story. Instead, help your reader understand what's special about the plot and how it functions. Does it build suspense, mirror a character's confusion, shape a conflict, show how different lives can intersect, or help reveal a theme?

Before starting to write, answer the following questions:

What are the key events of the story? Do they unfold in conventional fashion or deviate from it in some way?

Does the writer use foreshadowing or flashback? If so, for what purpose?

Is the plot believable and effective, or does it display weakness of some sort?

Does it include any unique features?

Is it similar to the plot of another story or some type of story?

What plot features could I write about? What examples from the story would support my contentions?

As you prepare your analysis, determine the important events and how they relate to your topic. If the story is disjointed or incoherent, arrange the events so that they make sense and ask yourself why the writer chose that sequence. To mirror the main character's disordered state of mind? To show that life is chaotic and difficult to understand? Similarly, assess the reason for any use of foreshadowing or flashback. Does it build, create, or resolve suspense?

Not all plots are successful. A character's actions may not fit his or her personality or the situation. The plot might be too hard to follow or fail to produce the desired effect, as in a mystery where the clues are too obvious to create suspense. Or a writer might rely on chance or coincidence to resolve a conflict or problem: It's unacceptable to have the cavalry charge in gallantly out of nowhere and rescue the hero.

If there's something unique about the plot—perhaps a surprise event that works well—describe it and tell how it functions in the story, or perhaps you can compare the plot with one in another story in order to show how both develop some key insight.

The organization of a paper on plot is simple: You'll either present a thesis and then support it with examples taken from the text, or you'll write a comparison. Writing about "The Bride Comes to Yellow Sky," you could show how foreshadowing moves the story toward an inevitable showdown. As support, you could cite the deliberate, forward motion of the train, the repeated emphasis on clocks and time, the repeated suggestions of Potter's anxiousness, and Scratchy's ongoing conflict with Potter. As a more ambitious project, you might compare the plot of "The Bride" to that of a conventional western showdown, noting any important differences and what they accomplish. A more critical approach would be to argue that the plot is implausible, citing Potter's unplanned marriage and the coincidence of his return to Yellow Sky precisely when Scratchy Wilson was drunk and shooting up the town.

EXERCISE

In a short story with a strong plot line, identify conflicts and climax and tell what the ending accomplishes. Point out any use of foreshadowing or flashback.

Point of View

19.3

Analyze and write about the way point of view works in a piece of literature.

Watch the Video on **Point of View**

Point-of-View Factors   The point of view is the vantage point from which the writer of a literary work views its events. A writer may adopt either a first-person or a third-person point of view. In *first-person* narration, someone in the work tells what happens and is identified by words like *I, me, mine,* and *my.* A *third-person* narrator stays completely out of the story and is never mentioned in any way. "The Bride Comes to Yellow Sky" illustrates third-person narration.

The most common form of first-person narration features a narrator who takes part in the action. This technique puts the readers directly on the scene and is excellent for tracing the growth or deterioration of a character. Instead of participating in the action, the narrator may view it from the sideline, an approach that preserves on-the-scene directness and allows the narrator to comment on the characters and issues. The narrator, however, cannot enter the mind and reveal the unspoken thoughts of anyone else.

Third-person narrators don't participate in the action but can survey the whole literary landscape and directly report events that first-person narrators would know only by hearsay. Most third-person narrators reveal the thoughts of just one character. Others, with *limited omniscience,* can enter the heads of several characters, while still others display *full omniscience* and know everything in the literary work, including all thoughts and feelings of all characters. Omniscience allows the narrator to contrast two or more sets of thoughts and feelings and draw general conclusions from them. The narrator of Stephen Crane's "The Open Boat" is fully omniscient. The story is about four shipwrecked sailors adrift in a lifeboat, and the narrator, knowing what they all think, traces their developing awareness that nature is completely indifferent to their plight.

Yet another type of third-person narration, *dramatic,* has emerged in contemporary fiction. A dramatic narrator, like a motion-picture camera, moves about recording the characters' actions and words but without revealing anyone's thoughts. Stories with surprise endings often use this technique.

Writing About Point of View   For a paper about point of view, ask and answer these questions:

> What point of view is used? Why is it used?
>
> Is it suitable for the situation? Why or why not?
>
> If the story uses first-person narration, is the narrator reliable? What textual evidence supports my answer?
>
> What focus would produce an effective paper? What textual evidence could support its discussion?

Various reasons might prompt the choice of a particular point of view. For example, an author might use the first person to show a character's mental deterioration. A third-person narrator might enter two minds to contrast opposing attitudes toward some incident or enter no minds at all to heighten the emotional impact of a story's climax.

If a point of view seems unsuitable, say so and suggest why. Suppose a man is planning an elopement that will create a surprising ending. A point of view that revealed the man's thoughts would give away that ending.

First-person narrators are sometimes unreliable; that is, they offer the reader a warped view of things. To gauge reliability, compare the narrator's version of the facts with what the work otherwise reveals. The narrator may come off as stupid, psychologically warped, or too biased to view events fairly. If so, speculate on the reasons. A mentally unreliable narrator may be meant, for example, to heighten the horror of events.

Although organization can vary, papers on point of view basically follow a cause-and-effect format, first identifying the point of view used and then demonstrating, with examples, its effect on the story and reader. In "The Bride," the third-person point of view allows Crane to shift from Potter and his new wife to the men in the saloon to the rampaging Scratchy and then to Potter and

Scratchy as they confront each other. Shifting scenes in this way builds a sense of impending conflict, which would be difficult to produce with a first-person narrator, who could not move about in this fashion.

Read the following two excerpts and answer the questions that follow them:

Max shook his head no at the mugger, his mouth in a regretful pout.

The teenager lunged at Max's chest with the blade. Instinctively, Max moved one step to his right. He didn't shift far enough. The knife sank into him. Max lowered his head and watched as the metal disappeared into his arm and chest. He felt nothing. With the blade all the way in, the teenager's face was only inches from Max's; he stared at the point of entry, stunned, his mouth sagging open. The mugger's eyes were small and frightened. Max didn't like him. He put his hand on the kid's chest and pushed him away. He didn't want to die looking into scared eyes.

The mugger stumbled back, tripped over his feet and fell....Max felt the point of the blade in his armpit. He realized he wasn't cut. The stupid kid had stuck the knife in the space below Max's armpit, the gap between his arm and chest. He had torn Max's polo shirt, but missed everything else. For a moment the knife hung there, caught by the fabric. Max raised his arm and the switchblade fell to the ground.

The teenager jumped to his feet and ran away, heading uptown.

Rafael Yglesias, *Fearless*

"Now!" I cry, aloud or to myself I don't know. Everything has boiled down to this instant. There's nothing in the world except the hand of the gate judge, lowering in slow motion to the catch that contains us. I see each of his fingers clearly, separately, as they fold around the lever, I see the muscles in his forearm harden as he begins to push down.

Wheeling and spinning, tilting and beating, my breath the song, the horse the dance. Time is gone. All the ordinary ways of things, the gettings from here to there, the one and twos, forgot. The crowd is color, the whirl of a spun top. The noises blend into a waving band that flies around us like a ribbon on a string. Beneath me four feet dance, pounding and leaping and turning and stomping. My legs flap like wings. I sail above, first to one side, then the other, remembering more than feeling the slaps of our bodies together. Things happen faster than understanding, faster than ideas. I'm a bird coasting, shot free into the music, spiraling into a place without bones or weight.

Michael Dorris, *A Yellow Boat in Blue Water*

1. In this third-person excerpt, Yglesias depicts the climax of an unsuccessful mugging, entering one character's mind but not the other's. Whose mind does he enter, and how does he convey the other person's mental state?
2. What does Dorris accomplish by using the first-person point of view?

Character

Character Factors   The characters in a literary work function in various ways. Some are centers of physical and mental action. Others furnish humor, act as narrators, provide needed information, act as *foils* who highlight more important characters by contrast, serve as symbols, or simply populate the landscape. In "The Bride," the drummer helps funnel information to the reader. He asks questions, the bartender answers them, and the reader learns all about Scratchy.

Writers present characters in several ways. Some tell the reader point-blank that a person is brave, stupid, self-serving, or the like. But most authors take an indirect approach by indicating how their characters look and act, what they think and say, how they live, and how other characters regard them.

Beware of uncritically accepting Character X's assessment of Character Y. X may be prejudiced, simpleminded, a deliberate liar, or too emotionally involved or disturbed to be objective. To illustrate, Scratchy Wilson, despite the bartender's fearful comments, proves to be something less than a real terror. He makes no real attempt to break down any doors and toys with, rather than shoots, the dog and Potter.

In picturing Potter, Crane first notes his appearance and self-conscious behavior, then delves into his mind to show the turmoil his marriage has stirred. Somewhat later, the bartender adds his brush strokes to Potter's portrait. At the confrontation, we again observe Potter's thoughts and behavior, as well as what he says to Scratchy. From all this, Potter emerges not as a mere one-dimensional lawman but as someone with a recognizably lifelike personality.

Some characters remain static; others mature, gain insight, or deteriorate in some telling way. Potter changes. As the story unfolds he abandons his doubts about the course he's charted and ends up fully committed to "the environment of the new estate." Scratchy, on the other hand, ends just as he started, "a simple child of the earlier plains."

19.4

Analyze and write about the way character works in a piece of literature.

⊙ Watch the Video on Character

Writing About Character   Start the process by asking yourself these questions:

What characters offer the potential for a paper?

What are their most important features, and where in the story are these features revealed?

Do the characters undergo any changes? If so, how and why do the changes occur?

Are the characters believable, true to life? If not, why?

What focus would produce an effective paper?

What textual evidence could support the discussion?

Usually, you'll write about the main character, but at times you might choose the chief adversary or some minor character. For a lesser character, point out how that person interacts with the main one.

Most main characters change; most lesser ones do not. But sometimes a main character remains frozen, allowing the writer to make an important point. To show that a certain social group suffers from paralysis of the will, an author might create a main character who begins and ends weak and ineffectual. Whatever the situation, when you determine what purpose your character serves, tell the reader.

Think hard about your character's credibility. Ask yourself if he or she is true to life. Cruel stepmothers, brilliant but eccentric detectives, mad scientists, masked seekers after justice—these and other stereotyped figures don't square with real-life people, who are complex mixtures of many traits. Inconsistent acts or unexplained and unmotivated personality changes don't ring true: Most people behave the same in similar situations and change only when properly motivated. Not every character needs to be a full-dress creation, but all require enough development to justify their roles.

Start your paper by identifying your character's role or personality; then back your contention with illustrations that support it, possibly following the sequence in which the writer presents them. If a character changes, say so, tell why, and indicate the results of the change, again using supporting examples. Such a paper is usually a cause-and-effect analysis. Papers that evaluate two characters are essentially comparisons.

For an example of a paper analyzing a character, see pages 343–344.

EXERCISE

Write a paragraph describing the personality of the character in the following passage:

The thousand injuries of Fortunato I had borne as I best could, but when he ventured upon insult, I vowed revenge. You, who so well know the nature of my soul, will not suppose, however, that I gave utterance to a threat. *At length* I would be avenged; this was a point definitely settled—but the very definiteness with which it was resolved precluded the idea of risk. I must not only punish, but punish with impunity. A wrong is unredressed when retribution overtakes its redresser. It is equally unredressed when the avenger fails to make himself felt as such to the one who has done the wrong.

Edgar Allan Poe, "The Cask of Amontillado"

Setting

19.5

Analyze and write about the way setting works in a piece of literature.

👁— **Watch the Video on Setting**

Setting Factors   Setting locates characters in a time, place, and culture so they can think, feel, and act against this background. Writers can generate feelings and moods by describing settings. Sunny spring landscapes signal hope or happiness, dark alleys are foreboding, and thunderstorms suggest violent possibilities. Poetry, especially, uses setting to create mood. In "Cannery Town in August," Lorna Dee Cervantes combines images of tired, work-stained employees, a noisy workplace, and dismal streets to evoke an unpleasant setting.

> All night it humps the air.
> Speechless, the steam rises
> from the cannery columns. I hear
> the night bird rave about work
> or lunch, or sing the swing shift

home. I listen, while bodyless
uniforms and spinach specked shoes
drift in monochrome down the dark
moon-possessed streets. Women
who smell of whiskey and tomatoes,
peach fuzz reddening their lips and eyes—
I imagine them not speaking, dumbed
by the can's clamor and drop
to the trucks that wait, grunting
in their headlights below.
They spotlight those who walk
like a dream, with no one
waiting in the shadows
to palm them back to living.

Setting can also help reveal a character's personality. In this excerpt from Amy Tan's novel *The Joy Luck Club,* the size and contents of the wealthy merchant Wu Tsing's house reflect the owner's love of wealthy display:

> As soon as we walked into that big house, I became lost with too many things to see; a curved staircase that wound up and up, a ceiling with faces in every corner, then hallways twisting and turning into one room then another. To my right was a large room, larger than I had ever seen, and it was filled with stiff teakwood furniture: sofas and tables and chairs. And at the other end of this long, long room, I could see doors leading into more rooms, more furniture, then more doors. To my left was a darker room, another sitting room, this one filled with foreign furniture: dark green leather sofas, paintings with hunting dogs, armchairs, and mahogany desks. And as I glanced in these rooms I would see different people. . . .

Settings sometimes function as symbols, reinforcing the workings of the other elements. A broad, slowly flowing river may stand for time or fate, a craggy cliff for strength of character, a blizzard-swept plain for the overwhelming power of nature. The following section, a discussion of symbols, points out some symbolic settings in "The Bride."

At times, setting provides a clue to some observation about life. At one point in Stephen Crane's story "The Open Boat," the men spot a nearby flock of seagulls sitting comfortably on the turbulent waves. Juxtaposing the complacent gulls and the imperiled men suggests the philosophical point of the story: that the universe is indifferent to human aspirations and struggles.

Shifts in setting often trigger shifts in a character's emotional or psychological state. Jack Potter, typically calm and assured in Yellow Sky, displays great awkwardness and embarrassment in the unfamiliar environment of the Pullman car.

Writing About Setting   Begin your search for a topic by identifying the settings in the story and then asking these questions about each one:

What are its key features?

What does it accomplish? Does it create a mood? Reveal a character? Serve as a symbol? Reinforce the story's point? How does it accomplish these things?

In what ways does it support or interfere with the story?

Does the setting seem realistic? If not, why not?

What focus would produce an effective paper? What textual evidence would support it?

Check the impact of setting on mood by seeing how well the two match up for each setting. Sometimes, as in "The Bride," the two bear little or no relationship to each other. In other cases, the two intertwine throughout the work.

Try to establish connections between settings and characters. If an emotionally barren individual always appears against backdrops of gloomy furnished rooms, cheerless restaurants, and decaying slums, you can assume that the writer is using setting to convey character. Look for links between changes in characters and changes in settings. If the setting remains the same, point out any shifts in the way the character views it.

Occasionally, a writer drums home settings so insistently that they overpower the characters and story line. A novel about the super rich may linger so lovingly over their extravagant surroundings that the plot lacks force and the characters seem mere puppets. If the setting hobbles the other elements, identify this flaw in your analysis.

When you write about setting, describe it and discuss its impact on the story's other elements, supporting your claims with specific examples. In writing about "The Bride," you might argue that Crane used as his chief setting a pulp fiction cliché of a western town in order to heighten the atypical nature of the showdown. As support, you could cite such stock features as the train station, saloon, dog, and dusty streets, all of which point toward an actual shootout rather than Scratchy Wilson's backdown.

EXERCISE

What mood does the following description of a room generate? What does it suggest about the situation of the room's inhabitants, two women in an Old Ladies' Home?

Marian stood enclosed by a bed, a washstand, and a chair; the tiny room had altogether too much furniture. Everything smelled wet—even the bare floor. She held onto the back of the chair, which was wicker and felt soft and damp....How dark it was! The window shade was down, and the only door was shut. Marian looked at the ceiling. . . . It was like being caught in a robbers' cave. . . .

Eudora Welty, "A Visit of Charity"

Symbols

19.6

Analyze and write about the way symbols work in a piece of literature.

👁 **Watch** the Video on **Symbols**

Symbol Factors   To strengthen and deepen their messages, writers use symbols: names, persons, objects, places, colors, or actions that have significance beyond their surface meaning. A symbol may be very obvious—as a name like Mr. Grimm, suggesting the person's character—or quite subtle, as an object representing a universal human emotion.

Some symbols are private and others conventional. A private symbol has special significance within a literary work but not outside it. Conventional symbols are deeply rooted in our culture, and almost everyone knows what they represent. We associate crosses with Christianity and limousines with wealth and power. In "The Bride," the plains pouring eastward past the Pullman windows, Scratchy's eastern clothing, and the mirage-like grass plots in front of the saloon are all private symbols that stand for the passing of the Old West. Because people of Crane's time associated Pullman cars with an urbane, eastern lifestyle, the Pullman is a conventional symbol that represents the new order of things. Like the Pullman, a symbol may appear more than once in a literary work.

Whether or not a recurring item is a symbol depends upon its associations. In Ernest Hemingway's novel *A Farewell to Arms,* rain may fairly be said to symbolize doom because it consistently accompanies disasters, and one of the main characters says that she has visions of herself lying dead in the rain. But if rain is randomly associated with a rundown lakeside resort, a spirited business meeting, a cozy weekend, and the twentieth-anniversary celebration of a happy marriage, the writer probably intends no symbolism.

Writing About Symbols   When you examine the symbols in a literary work, think about these questions:

What symbols are used and where do they appear?

Are they private or conventional?

What do they appear to mean?

Do any of them undergo a change in meaning? If so, how and why?

Which symbol(s) could I discuss effectively?

What textual evidence would support my interpretation?

To locate symbols, read the literary work carefully, looking for items that seem to have an extended meaning. You might, for example, discover that the cracked walls of a crumbling mansion symbolize some character's disordered mental state or that a voyage symbolizes the human journey from birth to death. Several symbols often mean the same thing; writers frequently use them in sets. In "Bartleby the Scrivener," for instance, Herman Melville uses windows that look upon walls, a folding screen, and a prison to symbolize Bartleby's alienated condition; that is, his mental separation from those around him.

Sometimes a symbol changes meaning during the course of a work. A woman who regards her lover's large, strong hands as symbols of passion may, following an illness that leaves him a dangerous madman, view them as symbols of danger and brute strength. Note any changes you discover, and suggest what they signify.

A word of caution: Don't let symbol hunting become an obsession. Before you assert that something has a different and deeper meaning than its surface application, make sure the evidence in the work backs your claim.

For each symbol you discuss, state what you think it means and then support your position with appropriate textual evidence. You could argue, for example, that the Pullman car in "The Bride" symbolizes the Eastern civilization that is encroaching on the West, offering as evidence the car's "figured velvet . . . shining brass, silver, and glass" and darkly gleaming wood appointments.

EXERCISE

Read the following poem and answer the questions that follow:

Heritage

Margaret Abbott

We were building there together,
Two children playing blocks,
And I debated whether
To copy your cautious scheme
That would withstand the knocks
Of a careless hand or try
My own impracticable plan
Of block on block until a high
Column, random and unsure, would stand
Memento to my dream.
I looked at you and planned
My tower. Each block fanned
My zeal. The shaft rose higher
And higher, like a spire
To my joy. I knew it could not last at all,
And yet—yet, when I saw it fall,
Some nameless hope came tumbling, too.
I crept, forlornly, close to you
And laid a finger on your solid square
And wished my heart would learn to care
For safety. Then, within that selfsame hour,
My traitor hands began another tower.

1. What does the "high / Column, random and unsure" symbolize? The "solid square"?
2. What is the significance of the final statement?

Irony

19.7

Analyze and write about the way irony works in a piece of literature.

Analyze the Interactive Short Story for Irony

Irony Factors   Irony features some discrepancy, some difference between appearance and reality, expectation and outcome. Sometimes a character says one thing but means something else. The critic who, tongue in cheek, says that a clumsy dancer is "poetry in motion" speaks ironically.

Irony also results when the reader or a character recognizes something as important, but another character does not. In "The Bride" this situation occurs when Potter, not knowing that Scratchy is on a rampage, flees the station agent, who tries to let him know. A character's behavior sometimes offers ironic contrasts, too. There's high irony in the contrast between Potter's unflinching face-off with Scratchy and his fear of telling the townsfolk about his marriage.

At times the ending of a work doesn't square with what the reader expects: the confrontation between Potter and Scratchy ends not in a fusillade of bullets but a flurry of words. To add to the irony, Potter wins because he is armed with a new and unfamiliar weapon—his wife. The emotional impact of an ironic ending depends upon the circumstances of plot and character. As Scratchy walks off, we're likely to view matters with amusement. In other cases, we might register joy, horror, gloom, or almost anything else.

Writing About Irony   Start by answering these questions:

Where does irony occur?

What does it accomplish?

What could my thesis be, and how could I support it?

In probing for irony, check for statements that say one thing and mean something else, situations in which one character knows something that another doesn't, and contrasts between the ways characters should and do behave. Review the plot to see whether the outcome matches the expectations.

To prove that irony is intended, examine the context in which the words are spoken or the events occur. Also, tell the reader what the irony accomplishes. In "The Bride," it is ironic that someone as wild as Scratchy Wilson would be awed by, and retreat from, Potter's wife; yet this irony is central to the idea that the Old West, despite its violence, was no match for the civilizing forces of the East.

EXERCISE

Discuss the irony in this poem:

Yet Do I Marvel

Countee Cullen

I doubt not God is good, well-meaning, kind,
And did He stoop to quibble could tell why
The little buried mole continues blind,
Why flesh that mirrors Him must some day die,
Make plain the reason tortured Tantalus[2]
Is baited by the fickle fruit, declare
If merely brute caprice dooms Sisyphus[3]
To struggle up a never-ending stair.
Inscrutable His ways are, and immune
To catechism by a mind too strewn
With petty cares to slightly understand
What awful brain compels His awful hand.
Yet do I marvel at this curious thing:
To make a poet black, and bid him sing!

---

[2]In Greek mythology, a king confined to hell who is teased by water and fruit trees forever beyond his reach.
[3]In Greek mythology, a king confined to hell who must continually roll a heavy rock up a hill and then see it roll back down.

Theme

19.8

Analyze and write about the way theme works in a piece of literature.

 Watch the Video on **Theme**

Theme Factors   The theme of a literary work is its controlling idea, some observation or insight about life or the conditions and terms of living, such as the prevalence of evil, the foolishness of pride, or the healing power of love. Many literary works suggest several themes: sometimes one primary motif and several related ones, sometimes a number of unrelated motifs. Theme is central to a work of literature; frequently all of the other elements help develop and support it.

On occasion, the writer or a character states the theme directly. Mrs. Alving, the main character in Henrik Ibsen's play *Ghosts*, notes that the dead past plays a powerful and evil role in shaping human lives:

> . . . I am half inclined to think that we are all ghosts, Mr. Manders. It is not only what we have inherited from our fathers and mothers that exists again in us, but all sorts of old dead ideas and all kinds of old dead beliefs and things of that kind. They are not actually alive in us; but there they are dormant, all the same, and we can never be rid of them.

Ordinarily, though, the theme remains unstated and must be deduced by examining the other elements of the literary work.

There is a current trend to analyze thematic like issues related to theories such as feminism or critical race theory. Scholars examine literary works to see how gender is represented or how women are portrayed, examine the value systems in the work, identify how the work constructs the family, how race is addressed or left out, they way ethnic identity is defined, how national identity is presented, how economic class and class conflict are represented and more. Any social issue can be the starting point for critically examining the work of literature. However, it is important to be careful to be accurate to the evidence of the work and the historical period and not simply read in your own position.

Writing About Theme   Before you begin writing, ask and answer these questions:

What are the themes of this work? Which of these should I write about? Are they stated or unstated?

If stated, what elements support them?

If unstated, what elements create them?

What, if any, thematic weaknesses are present?

Check the comments of the characters and the narrator to see whether they state the themes directly. If they don't, assess the interaction of characters, events, settings, symbols, and other elements to determine them.

Let's see how the elements of Nathaniel Hawthorne's short story "Young Goodman Brown" work together to yield the primary theme. The story has four characters—Goodman Brown; his wife, Faith; Deacon Gookin; and Goody Cloyse—whose names symbolically suggest that they are completely good. Another symbol, Faith's pink hair ribbon, at first suggests innocence and later its loss. The story relates Brown's nighttime journey into a forest at the edge of a Puritan village and subsequent attendance at a baptismal ceremony for new converts to the Devil. He proceeds into the forest, suggestive of mystery and lawlessness, during a dark night, suggestive of evil, where he meets his guide, the Devil in the guise of his grandfather. As he proceeds, Brown vacillates between reluctance to join the Devil's party and fascination with it. Innocent and ignorant, he is horrified when he finds that the deacon and Goody Cloyse seem to be in league with the Devil. Brown tries to preserve his pure image of his wife, Faith, but her pink ribbon falls out of a tumultuous sky seemingly filled with demons, and Brown sees her at the baptismal ceremony. He shrieks out to her to "resist the wicked one" and is suddenly alone in the woods, not knowing whether she obeyed. The end of the story finds Brown back in his village, unable to view his wife and neighbors as anything but totally evil.

In light of these happenings, it's probably safe to say that the primary theme of the story is somewhat as follows:

> Human beings are a mixture of good and evil, but some individuals can't accept this fact. Once they realize that "good" people are susceptible to sin, they decide that everyone is evil, and they become embittered for life.

Point out any thematic weakness that you find. Including a completely innocent major character in a story written to show that people are mixtures of good and evil would contradict the writer's intention.

A paper on theme is basically an argument, first presenting your interpretation and then supporting it with textual evidence. You might argue that the primary theme of "The Bride" is the demise of the Old West under the civilizing influence of the East. You could cite the luxurious Pullman car in contrast to the drab town, Potter's uncomfortable submission to the waiter and porter, and Scratchy Wilson's retreat at the story's end. In addition, you could suggest a related theme: People out of their element often founder—sometimes even appear ridiculous. As support, you might point to Potter's behavior on the train, the drummer's subdued attitude when Scratchy's arrival is imminent, and Scratchy's reaction when told about Potter's wife.

EXERCISE

State the controlling idea of this poem by Emily Dickinson:

> 'Twas like a Maelstrom, with a notch,
> That nearer, every Day,
> Kept narrowing its boiling Wheel
> Until the Agony
>
> Toyed coolly with the final inch
> Of your delirious Hem—
> And you dropt, lost,
> When something broke—
> And let you from a Dream—
>
> As if a Goblin with a Gauge—
> Kept measuring the Hours—
> Until you felt your Second
> Weigh, helpless, in his Paws—

And not a Sinew—stirred—could help,
And sense was setting numb—
When God—remembered—and the Fiend
Let go, then, Overcome—

As if your Sentence stood—pronounced—
And you were frozen led
From Dungeon's luxury of Doubt
To Gibbets, and the Dead—

And when the Film had stitched your eyes
A Creature gasped "Reprieve"!
Which Anguish was the utterest—then—
To perish, or to live?

Ethical Issues

19.9

Write so that your literary analysis is ethical.

When you write about literature, you'll need to be aware of certain ethical considerations. Imagine someone reading only part of a short story and then writing a scathing analysis that suggests he has read the entire work. Imagine a thematic analysis of a novel that deliberately ignores large sections of the text in order to develop a twisted interpretation about the evils of capitalism. Imagine citing atypical quotations from the heroine of a play that deliberately create a distorted impression of her character. To help fulfill your ethical responsibility, ask and answer the following questions.

- Have I read the entire work carefully?
- Is my interpretation supported by the preponderance of textual evidence? Does it avoid deliberate distortion? A student who emphasizes a story's passing description of the pleasant feelings that accompany cocaine use while downplaying the drug's progressive effects that destroy a character could send a dangerous message.
- Have I avoided using quotations that are atypical or taken out of context?
- Is my interpretation fair to the text and the author rather than distorting events to promote an agenda?

Writing a Paper on Literature

The Writing Procedure

19.10

Prewrite, plan, draft, and revise your literary analysis.

Focusing, gathering information, organizing, writing, revising, and editing—the same procedure leads to success in a literature paper as in any other type.

First, make sure you *understand the assignment*. Let's assume you have been asked to do the following:

> Write a 750-word essay that analyzes one of the elements in Stephen Crane's "The Bride Comes to Yellow Sky." Take into account all the pertinent factors of whatever element you choose.

For this assignment you could focus on plot, point of view, character, setting, symbols, irony, or theme.

Next, *decide on a suitable topic.* For papers on literature, your best approach is to reread the work carefully and then reflect on it. As you do this for the assignment on "The Bride," you rule out a paper centering on plot, setting, irony, point of view, or theme. Because your class has discussed the first three so thoroughly, you doubt you can offer anything more. The matter of the narrator stumps you; you can understand why Crane uses a third-person narrator who airs Potter's thoughts, but you can't see what's accomplished by the brief looks into other characters' minds. Regarding theme, you doubt you can do justice to the topic in 750 words. As you mentally mine character and symbolism for possible topics, your thoughts turn to the many gunfighters you've watched in the movies and read about in western fiction. Because gunfighters have always fascinated you and Scratchy Wilson seems an intriguing example of the breed, you decide to analyze his character.

To complete the next stage, *gathering information,* reread the story again and as you do, list all pertinent information about Scratchy that might help develop a character analysis. Your efforts might yield these results:

1. Scratchy "a wonder with a gun."
2. "about the last one of the old gang that used to hang out along the river here."
3. "He's a terror when he's drunk," the opposite otherwise.
4. Potter "goes out and fights Scratchy when he gets on one of these tears."
5. Has shot Scratchy once, in the leg.
6. Does nothing to stop "tears" from happening.
7. On street, Scratchy "in a rage begot of whisky." Neck works angrily.
8. Utters "Cries of ferocious challenge."
9. Moves with "the creeping movement of the midnight cat."
10. Guns move "with an electric swiftness."
11. Clothes—maroon shirt, gilded red-topped boots—not adult western garb.
12. Doesn't shoot dog.
13. Doesn't try breaking down doors.
14. Warns Potter not to go for gun rather than shooting him.
15. Says he'll hit Potter with gun, not shoot him, if Potter doesn't "mind what I tell you."
16. Only sneers when Potter calls him "damn fool," and when Potter says, "If you're goin' to shoot me up, you better begin now; you'll never get a chance like this again."
17. Backs down and walks away when confronted with Potter's marriage.

List in hand, you are now ready to *organize your information.* As you examine your items and answer the questions about character on page 331, you start to realize that Scratchy is not merely a one-dimensional gunslinging menace. To reflect your discovery, you prepare a formal topic outline.

I. Bartender's assessment
   A. Evidence that Scratchy is a menace
      1. A wonder with a gun
      2. Former outlaw gang member
      3. A terror when drunk

B. Contradictory evidence
   1. Mild when sober
   2. Only one actual shootout with Potter

II. Scratchy's behavior
  A. Evidence that Scratchy is a menace
     1. Rage
     2. Wary movements
     3. Skillful handling of guns
  B. Contradictory evidence
     1. Mode of dress
     2. Failure to shoot dog
     3. Failure to try breaking down doors
     4. Behavior during confrontation
     5. Final retreat

The next stage, *developing a thesis statement*, presents few difficulties. After examining the outline and thinking about its contents, you draft the following sentence:

> A close look at Scratchy Wilson shows that he has much more depth than his pulp fiction counterparts.

Drawing on your notes and following your outline, you now *write a first draft* of your essay, and then follow up with the necessary revising and editing. In addition, you review the story and verify your interpretation.

As you *prepare your final draft,* follow these guidelines.

Handling Quotations   Like aspirin, quotations should be used when necessary, but not to excess. Cite brief, relevant passages to support key ideas, but fight the urge to quote huge blocks of material. Place short quotations, fewer than five lines, within quotation marks and run them into the text. For longer passages, omit the quotation marks and indent the material ten spaces from the left-hand margin. When quoting poetry, use a slash mark (/) to show the shift from one line to the other in the original: "A honey tongue, a heart of gall, / Is fancy's spring, but sorrow's fall." Refer to a handbook for additional information on handling quotations.

Documentation   Document ideas and quotations from outside sources by following the appropriate guidelines.

If your instructor wants you to document quotations from the work you're writing about, include the information within parentheses following the quotations. For fiction, cite the page number on which the quotation appeared: (83). For poetry, cite the word "line" or "lines" and the appropriate numbers: (lines 23–24). For plays, cite act, scene, and line numbers, separated by periods: (1.3.18–19). When discussing a work of fiction not in your textbook, identify the book you used as your source. Your instructor can then easily check your information. In short papers like the following student essay, internal documentation is often omitted.

Tense   Write your essay in the present rather than the past tense. Say "In *The Sound and the Fury*, William Faulkner uses four narrators, each of whom provides a different perspective on the events that take place," not "...William Faulkner used four narrators, each of whom provided a different perspective on the events that took place."

SAMPLE

STUDENT ESSAY ON **LITERATURE**

Scratchy Wilson: No Cardboard Character

Wendell Stone

1   Stephen Crane's short story "The Bride Comes to Yellow Sky" is artful on several counts. For one thing, the story is rich in irony. It makes use of an elaborate set of symbols to get its point across. It is filled with vivid language, and in Jack Potter and Scratchy Wilson it offers its readers two very unusual characters. Potter's actions and thoughts clearly show that he is a complex person. In fact, his complexity is so conspicuous that it becomes easy to regard Scratchy as nothing more than a one-dimensional badman. But this judgment is mistaken. A close look at Scratchy shows that he, like Potter, has much more depth than his pulp fiction counterparts.

2   Nothing in what the bartender says about Scratchy hints that there is anything unusual about the old outlaw. We learn that Scratchy is "a wonder with a gun," that he is "about the last one of the old gang that used to hang out along the river here," and that "He's a terror when he's drunk" but mild-mannered and pleasant at other times. One thing may strike the careful reader as a little odd, though. Although Potter "goes out and fights Scratchy when he gets on one of these tears," he has wounded Scratchy just once, and then only in the leg. Apparently, Potter has been able to talk the supposed terror out of a shootout each of the other times. Nor has Potter apparently tried doing anything to stop Scratchy's "tears."

3   As he steps onto the main street of Yellow Sky, Scratchy seems every bit as menacing as the bartender has described him. His face flames "in a rage begot of whisky," the cords in his neck throb and bulge with anger, and he hurls "cries of ferocious challenge" at the barricaded buildings. Scratchy is clearly no stranger to either weapons or shootouts. He walks

Continued on next page

Identifies work in question including author and title

Establishes focus on character

Thesis statement

Identifies initial one dimensional account of the character with quotes for support

Uses plot to raise questions about the cliched characterization

Description that seems to confirm cliched characterization

Continued from previous page

with "the creeping movement of the midnight cat," moves his revolvers with "an electric swiftness," and keeps constantly on the alert for an ambush.

Offers contrasting interpretation of the above interpretation

4   Nevertheless, Scratchy comes across as less than totally menacing. For one thing, his maroon shirt and gilded, red-topped boots make him look not like a westerner but like some child's notion of one. When he sees the dog, he deliberately shoots to frighten rather than to kill it. And in spite of all his bluster, he makes no real attempt to break down any doors and get at the people hiding behind them. Scratchy's clothing shows that eastern ways have touched even this "child of the earlier plains." But one could easily argue that eastern gentleness has had some slight softening influence on him, too. Be that as it may, it seems evident that Scratchy, perhaps without quite realizing it himself, is mainly play-acting when he goes on his rampages and that Potter knows this.

Provides details of the final confrontation to confront stereotype

5   During the whole final confrontation, Scratchy seems more of an actor than a gunman wanting revenge against his "ancient antagonist." Instead of shooting when Potter makes a slight movement, Scratchy warns him not to go for a gun and says that he intends to take his time settling accounts, to "loaf along with no interferin'." Significantly, he threatens to hit Potter with a gun, not shoot him, if the marshal does not "mind what I tell you." Even when Potter, recovered from his brief fright, calls Scratchy a "damn fool" and says "If you're goin' to shoot me up, you better begin now: you'll never get a chance like this again," Scratchy does nothing except sneer. This confrontation, like all but one of the others, ends with no shots fired. But one thing is different. Potter's marriage has forced Scratchy to realize that something unstoppable is changing the Old West forever. When he drops his revolver to his side, stands silent for a while, and then says, "I s'pose it's all off now," we sense that he means not just this episode but any future clashes as well.

Reconfirms thesis

Connects characterization with larger theme and imagery

6   Scratchy is not a cardboard creation. His behavior is by no means as easily explainable as it at first seems, and he is capable of some degree of insight. Nonetheless, Scratchy remains very much a creature of the past, something that time has passed by. As he leaves, his feet make "funnel-shaped tracks," reminiscent of hourglasses, in the sand. Soon these tracks, along with Scratchy and his way of life, will disappear.

STEPPING UP TO **SYNTHESIS**

Obviously you are not the first one to write about an established piece of literature. To help deepen your understanding, your instructor may ask you to draw upon various sources that analyze the work you are discussing.

Prewriting the Synthesis The database Jstor is an excellent place to start if you are researching literature. Search for articles on your literary work. As you read these secondary sources, jot down any insights you find helpful. Be sure to record the name of the author and the source so that you can document appropriately and therefore avoid plagiarism. Keep track of where you disagree or have a different insight. Some students keep a reading journal in which they record useful quotes or information about both the piece of literature and the secondary source.

Planning and Drafting the Synthesis When you write the paper, you can synthesize the views of the critics you've read and offer them as additional support for your view. Alternatively, you might summarize the conclusions, or perhaps the conflicting views, of critics and then offer your own observations along with appropriate support. Think of writing in response to others' views as entering a conversation with friends about a good book; they have their opinions, but your insights will add something to the discussion.

Getting Started

With your instructors approval, research some aspect of a work of literature that you find interesting and write a paper that draws on your sources, but do so in a way that you build your own argument and demonstrate your own insights.

EXERCISE

Using the guidelines offered in this chapter, write a short essay comparing and contrasting the two writers' assessments of the women in the following poems. (You might find it helpful to review Chapter 13 on comparison.) Limit your focus and back any general statements you make with appropriate support from the poems.

There Is a Garden in Her Face

Thomas Campion (1617)

There is a garden in her face,
Where roses and white lilies grow;
A heavenly paradise is that place,

Wherein all pleasant fruits do flow.
There cherries grow which none may buy
Till "Cherry ripe" themselves do cry.

Those cherries fairly do inclose
Of orient pearl a double row,
Which when her lovely laughter shows,
They look like rosebuds filled with snow;
Yet them nor peer nor prince can buy,
Till "Cherry ripe" themselves do cry.
Her eyes like angels watch them still;
Her brows like bended bows do stand.
Threat'ning with piercing frowns to kill
All that attempt with eye or hand
Those sacred cherries to come nigh,
Till "Cherry ripe" themselves do cry.

Sonnet 130

William Shakespeare (1609)

My mistress' eyes are nothing like the sun;
Coral is far more red than her lips red;
If snow be white, why then her breasts are dun;
If hairs be wires, black wires grow on her head.
I have seen roses damask'd, red and white,
But no such roses see I in her cheeks;
And in some perfumes there is more delight
Than in the breath that from my mistress reeks.
I love to hear her speak, yet well I know
That music hath a far more pleasing sound;
I grant I never saw a goddess go;
My mistress, when she walks, treads on the ground.
And yet, by heaven, I think my love as rare
As any she belied with false compare.

Complete additional exercises and practice in your MyLab

Research Guide

Much of your college and workplace writing will require some type of research—obtaining information from one or more sources to help achieve your writing purpose. The nature of your writing task and the demands of the situation determine the format you use and the way you document your sources.

This section of the text explores in detail the research tools and procedures you will use to develop various types of papers and reports. Sometimes you'll draw upon books, magazines, newspapers, and other printed sources, as well as electronic sources, in order to prepare a longer library research paper; at other times you'll do the same for shorter papers. Still other situations call for using primary research—the type in which you develop the information you use—to accomplish your purpose. The four chapters in this section will help you to meet these writing demands.

Chapter 20 explains how to choose a suitable library research topic and then focuses on carrying out the necessary steps to write a research paper, and offers guidelines for avoiding plagiarism. The chapter includes a continuing case history that leads to the finished paper in Chapter 21, complete with margin notes that will provide guidance as you prepare your own paper.

Chapters 21 (MLA) and 22 (APA) show how to prepare correct references for your paper's bibliography. They also show the correct formats for references within the body of the paper and explain how to handle quotations.

Chapter 23 explains and illustrates the most common primary research strategies—interviews, questionnaires, and direct observations. In each case, student models, annotated with margin notes, embody the key features of that strategy.

Together, the material in these four chapters should provide all the information you will need to complete writing assignments that require research.

CHAPTER 20   The Research Paper

In this chapter, you will learn how to:

20.1 Identify and use your library's resources.

20.2 Select and narrow a research topic and brainstorm to create a research question.

20.3 Conduct research using an online catalog, databases, internet searches, and other sources.

20.4 Evaluate your sources, take notes using summary and paraphrase, and assemble a working bibliography.

20.5 Organize your notes to create an outline for a research paper.

20.6 Write so that your research paper is ethical.

20.7 Write a draft of your research paper, and include visuals to enhance your paper.

20.8 Avoid plagiarism by integrating your sources with proper internal documentation.

"Janice, I need a report on the Chinese economy and its role in solar energy."

"Wait a minute, that sounds like a research paper, I thought that was something for college."

"I don't care what you call it. I need a clear understanding of their growing role in an industry so related to our company."

There are very few decisions we want to make based on just our personal experience, not when there has been a lot of previous study done on most topics. Whether we are trying to understand how to treat an unusual illness or deciding on the risks of global warming, we turn to the research others have done to formulate our own views. Often when we become knowledgeable about issues and formulate informed conclusions, we share what we have discovered with others.

It is likely that you will be asked to prepare a research paper for your composition class. This assignment calls for you to gather information from a variety of sources and then to focus, organize, and present it in a formal paper that documents your sources. The procedure will familiarize you with the mechanics of documentation, and when you finish you'll have a solid grasp of your topic and pride in your accomplishment. In addition, the experience will help you learn how to meet the research demands of other courses and your job.

Writing a research paper really isn't so formidable. You can acquaint yourself with the various resources that will provide easy access to the information you need. Reading what others have written on a topic will give you a chance to draw your own conclusions. And as a writer you can limit your topic so that it doesn't balloon out of control.

Research writing is common both in the classroom and on the job.

- A history professor might require a long report on the causes of the Vietnam War.
- A business instructor might ask you to trace the history of a company, evaluate an advertising campaign, or review the latest styles of management.
- A building trades instructor might call for a short report that compares the effectiveness of several new insulating materials.
- At work, a marketing analyst might report on the development costs, sales potential, and competition for a product the company is considering introducing.
- An engineer might write a journal article that summarizes recent developments in plastic fabrication.
- A physical therapist might prepare a seminar paper that evaluates different exercise programs to follow arthroscopic surgery.

Whatever the writing project, let your purpose guide your research and determine the information you elect to use. When you write, the conclusions you have reached from thinking about what you have read and your purpose in communicating, not your notes, should dictate what you say.

Learning About Your Library

Before starting a library research paper, take time to familiarize yourself with your library. Many college libraries offer guided tours, and almost all of them display floor plans that show where and how the books are grouped. If your library doesn't have tours, browse through it on your own and scan its contents. As you do, note the following features:

20.1

Identify and use your library's resources.

Computer Catalog: The computer catalog allows you to effectively search for the library's books and often most of its other holdings as well. Pages 356–359 discuss computerized catalogs.

Databases: These databases provide organized ways to find articles in magazines and newspapers, and many even provide the full text of the article. Pages 360–365 discuss databases.

Stacks: These are the bookshelves that hold books and bound periodicals (magazines and newspapers). Stacks are either open or closed. Open stacks allow you to go directly to the books you want, take them off the shelf, and check them out. Closed stacks do not allow you direct access to shelved material. Instead, a staff member brings you what you want.

Periodical Area: Here you'll find some current and recent issues of magazines and newspapers. If your topic calls for articles that have appeared within the last few months, you're likely to find them in this area or as an online article.

Microfilm and Microfiche Files: Microfilm is a filmstrip bearing a series of photographically reduced printed pages. Microfiche is a small card with a set of photographically reduced pages mounted on it. A library's older magazine and newspaper collection is on film.

Circulation Desk: Here's where you check materials in and out, renew books you want to keep longer, and pay overdue fines. If you can't find something you want, the desk clerk will tell you whether it's missing, on reserve, or checked out. If it's out, enter a request on the computer or fill out a hold card, and the library will notify you when it is available.

Reserve Area: This area contains books that instructors have had removed from general circulation so students can use them for particular courses. Ordinarily, you can keep these books for only a few hours or overnight.

Interlibrary Loan: Few libraries are large enough to contain all of the major books, government documents, and periodicals. Most have an arrangement for borrowing works from another library. You may be able to request this loan online or confirm the loan and pick up the work at a specific Interlibrary Loan desk. If you will need a resource through interlibrary loan, leave yourself at least three weeks to get the work.

Reference Area: This area houses the library's collection of encyclopedias, periodical indexes, almanacs, handbooks, dictionaries, and other research tools that you'll use as you investigate your topic. You'll also find one or more reference guides—Eugene P. Sheehy's *Guide to Reference Books* (1996), for example—that direct you to useful reference tools. To ensure that these books are always available, they must be used in the library.

Librarian Help Desk: The greatest assets in any library are the librarians who are experts in finding information. They can help you better define your question, use the research tools effectively, and locate the materials you need. Many colleges provide online librarian help as well.

Choosing a Topic

20.2

Select and narrow a research topic and brainstorm to create a research question.

Instructors take different approaches to assigning library research papers. Some want explanatory papers, others want papers that address a two-sided question, and still others allow students a free choice.

■ An explanatory paper takes no position but provides information that gives the reader a better grasp of the topic. For example, it may explain the key advantages of solar heating, thereby clearing up popular misconceptions.

- An argument paper, on the other hand, attempts to sway the reader toward one point of view—for instance, that solar heat is commercially feasible.

Some instructors specify not only the type of paper but also the topic. Others restrict students to a general subject area, ask them to pick topics from lists, or give them free choice. If you have little to say in the selection, recognize that you can still make the project effective by committing to the topic and search for what interests you.

Whatever the circumstances, it's a good idea to follow a schedule that establishes completion dates for the various stages of your paper. Such a timetable encourages you to plan your work, clarifies both your progress and the work remaining, and provides an overview of the project. You can use the following sample schedule as a guide, modifying the stages or adding other ones as necessary.

Sample Schedule for a Library Research Paper

Activity	Targeted Completion Date		
Topic Selection	_____		
Working Bibliography	_____		
Research Question and Tentative Thesis	_____		
Note Taking	_____		
Working Outline	_____		
First Draft	_____		
Revised Drafts	_____	_____	_____
Date Due	_____		

Topics to Avoid

If you have free rein to pick your topic, how should you proceed? To begin, rule out certain types of topic.

- Those based entirely on personal experience or opinion such as "The Thrills I Have Enjoyed Waterskiing" or "Colorado Has More [or Less] Scenic Beauty than New Mexico." Such topics can't be supported by library research. Don't hesitate, however, to include personal judgments and conclusions that emerge from your reading.
- Those fully explained in a single source. An explanation of a process, such as cardiopulmonary resuscitation, or the description of a place, such as the Gobi Desert, does not require coordination of materials from various sources. Although you may find several articles on such topics, basically they all contain the same information.
- Those that are brand new. Often it's impossible to find sufficient source material about such topics.
- Those that are overly broad. Don't try to tackle such elephant-sized topics as "The Causes of World War II" or "Recent Medical Advances." Instead, slim them down to something like "How Did Germany's Depression Contribute to the Rise of Hitler?" or "Eye Surgery with Lasers."

- Those that have been worked over and over, such as abortion and the legal drinking age. Why bore your reader with information and arguments that are all too familiar already?

Using the advice on topics to avoid, explain why each of the following would or would not be suitable for a library research topic:

1. Genetic counseling
2. The impact of the Tea Party on politics
3. The challenges of cybersecurity
4. What led to the mass murder last week
5. Tweeting as a marketing strategy
6. A Third World hot spot as described on the evening news
7. Reforming the financing of presidential election campaigns

Drawing on Your Interests

((•⊷ Listen to the Podcast on **Finding a Topic**

Let your interests guide your choice. A long-standing interest in basketball might suggest a paper on the pros and cons of expanding the number of teams in the National Basketball Association. An instructor's lecture might spark your interest in a historical event or person, an economic crisis, a scientific development, a sociological trend, a medical milestone, a political scandal, or the influences on an author. An argument with a friend might spur you to investigate latch-key children. A television documentary might arouse your curiosity about a group of primitive people. A recent article or novel might inspire you to explore the occult or some taboo.

Be practical in selecting a topic. Why not get a head start on a particular aspect of your major field by researching it now? Some management, marketing, or advertising strategy; the beginnings of current contract law; medical ethics—all of these topics, and many others, qualify. Think about your audience, the availability of information, and whether you can fit it into the guidelines for your paper.

To develop a focus for your paper, it's often helpful to brainstorm, skim online resources, encyclopedias and other materials, and use the branching or clustering technique. If you're exploring the topic of child abuse, preparing a clustering diagram like the one in Figure 20.1 can help you decide how to narrow your topic as well as provide a rough map of areas to research. The more you brainstorm, the richer your map will be. Brainstorming often results in a series of questions, perhaps based on the writing strategies discussed in Chapters 8–16, that will help guide your research. Often it is helpful to state your main research question, followed by a series of related questions that elaborate on it. From our cluster example, a student wishing to explore the topic of psychological abuse might develop the following set of questions:

What is psychological abuse?
What long-term and short-term effects does it have on a child?

How can a child living at home be helped?

What psychological help is available for an adult who experienced childhood abuse?

What can be done to help victims of psychological abuse?

Are there services to help limit the abuse?

Is family therapy an option?

What is family therapy, and what does it do?

What therapies work best?

What do they do?

How effective are they?

These questions make research easier. After all, the purpose of research is to answer questions. Later, as you examine source material, you will be seeking specific answers, not just randomly searching for information.

A quick search online or other sources may help focus your topic, determine possible directions for your research, or gain a broader context on the subject. Because Wikipedia is edited by users and can have inaccuracies, many faculty members do not want it used as a formal source; however, it can provide you with a quick general background on a number of topics. While they may not be later formal sources, skimming, or quickly reading, a number of the articles, blogs, and even discussions online can help you generate ideas. Often Wikipedia and other articles may have links to other information that can guide your search. If you have a more technical topic or issue, online encyclopedias, such as the Encyclopedia of Life Sciences or International Encyclopedia of Linguistics may help. Sometimes quickly skimming books, even their table of contents, can

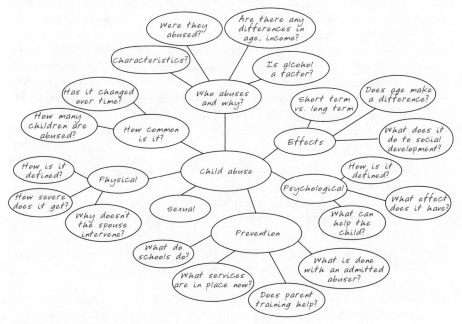

Figure 20.1   Clustering Diagram on Child Abuse.

offer ideas. Keep in mind the purpose of your first search. You are trying to help focus your topic, determine the different issues that you want to address, and gain some sense of the resources available on your topic. You are scouting the terrain. Move fast and cover a lot of initial area. You can always go back to something you found interesting.

More often than not, things won't fall neatly into place as you probe for a topic and then a focus. Don't be discouraged by false starts and blind alleys. Think of yourself as an explorer who will gradually become well-versed in your chosen topic.

FINDING YOUR TOPIC

- Make a list of your major interests that prompt questions.
- Identify issues or questions raised in class or the media.
- Brainstorm questions related to your initial question for focus.
- Do some initial readings around your topic to get an overview to focus your topic.

CASE HISTORY

Keith Jacque was a first-year composition student majoring in criminal justice when he wrote the library research paper at the end of this chapter. The assignment was to write about a recent technological development or an innovative solution to a social problem. Intrigued by the possible solutions to the problem of prison overcrowding, Keith decided to explore several options: building more prisons, developing early release programs for the least dangerous criminals, setting up house-arrest programs verified by electronic monitoring systems, utilizing halfway houses, converting empty military bases into prisons, and reevaluating legal codes to determine which offenses should require incarceration. After a little thought, Keith realized that in order to develop his paper properly he would need to concentrate on only one option. Because he had recently watched a televised report on electronic monitoring and found it interesting, he decided to investigate this alternative.

To establish a focus for his paper, Keith drafted a series of questions suggested by the writing strategies discussed in Chapters 8–16. Here are the questions he developed:

Could I *narrate* a brief history of electronic monitoring?
Could I *describe* how a monitoring system works?
Could I *classify* monitoring systems?
Could I *compare* monitoring systems to anything?
Could I explain the *process* involved in monitoring?
What *causes* led to the development of monitoring?
What *effects* is monitoring likely to have?
What systems best *illustrate* the essence of monitoring?
Is there a widely accepted *definition* of electronic monitoring?
Could I *argue* for or against the expanded use of monitoring?

These writing strategies can often help you narrow a subject down to a manageable topic.

For background reading, Keith consulted two general encyclopedias: the *Encyclopedia Americana* and the *Encyclopaedia Britannica*. After preparing a list of possible entries that included "electronic monitoring," "electronic surveillance," "electronic incarceration," "home incarceration," and "house arrest," he began searching for those entries but found none of them. Next, he decided to look in more specialized publications. Not knowing how to proceed, he asked a reference librarian, who directed him to the latest editions of the *Encyclopedia of Crime and Justice* and the *McGraw-Hill Encyclopedia of Science and Technology*. These sources also contained no useful information.

At this point, drawing on what he had learned from his criminal justice instructor and the television report, Keith brainstormed in order to determine a possible focus for his paper. He came up with the following list:

1. Brief history of electronic monitoring
2. Technical problems in developing systems
3. Types of monitoring systems
4. Benefits of monitoring
5. Problems associated with monitoring

Upon reflection, Keith eliminated the second item because it would require reading highly technical material, which he might not understand. The other items were interesting to him, and he believed that they would also interest his audience—fellow students at the vocationally oriented school he attended.

Next, Keith used branching to expand his list and guide his library search, concentrating on what he knew at this stage.

Benefits of monitoring
- *reduces jail population*
- *less expensive than prison*
- *effective for non-violent offenders*
- *several systems available*

Problems associated with monitoring
- *signal interference problems*
- *legal concerns*

Discovering Your Sources

Once you have a topic, you're ready to see whether the library has the resources you'll need to complete the project. This step requires you to check additional reference tools and compile a working bibliography—a set of notes (electronic

20.3

Conduct research using an online catalog, databases, internet searches, and other sources.

notes or cards) that list promising sources of information. This section discusses these reference tools and how to use them.

Online Catalog

What It Is   An online catalog lists all the books in the library, usually along with other holdings like magazines, newspapers, government documents, and electronic recordings. It may also provide additional information, such as whether a book has been checked out and, if so, the return date. Some catalogs even include the holdings of nearby libraries. Books are usually cataloged using Library of Congress call numbers, although some libraries use the Dewey decimal system.

Online Catalogs vary from institution to institution. If you are not familiar with your system, be sure to ask your librarian. Because such systems work by matching the term or title you offer to its listing, it is very important to be careful of your spelling and try to experiment with lots of different terms. The phrase "Shrinks" will not find you much if you are looking for works on "Psychoanalysis," "Freud," "Freudian Analysis," or "The Unconscious." Computers cannot do the thinking for you.

Most systems let you conduct searches by key terms (those appearing in book titles and descriptions), author, title, and subject (based on the Library of Congress's cataloging system). Most systems let you select the kind of search by a menu or icons as in Figure 20.2. Searching may require you to view a series of screens having increasingly specific instructions, with the final screen providing

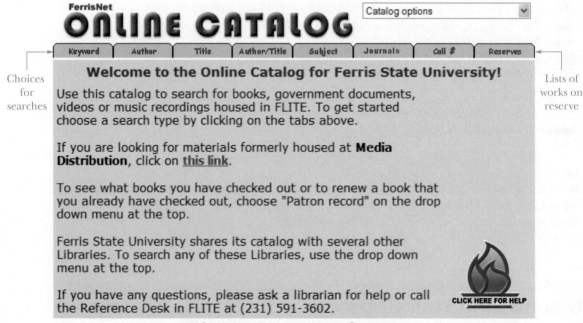

Figure 20.2   The Online Catalog's opening screen allows you to select the type of search.
Software of Innovative Interface, Inc. Screens presented by permission of Innovative Interfaces, Inc.

Figure 20.3 Keyword Search.

information from a single book. Figure 20.3 illustrates a keyword search. Figure 20.4 shows the list of works discovered by the search, including the publication date; Figure 20.5 one specific work, including the call number to locate the book in your library stacks, an indication of the availability of the book, a brief description of the contents, and a list of subjects that could be used in additional searches.

Often, a key term search (see Figure 20.4) can be the most helpful way to approach a topic. In this type of search, the computer checks the titles and descriptions of books for the key terms you enter and lists any that it finds. Different key terms will produce varying strings of publications, so it is a good idea to try different words or phrases for the same topic. For example, if you're searching for material on "electric cars," you might also try "electronic cars," "alternative fuels," and so on. Because such searches are very rapid, you can experiment with different combinations of terms to focus your search. If,

Buttons to move through the search program

Allows you to save selected records

Texts found by search

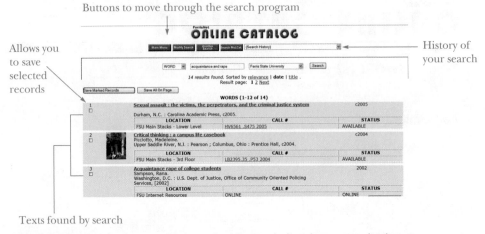

History of your search

Figure 20.4   Results Screen. Click on the blue underlined terms to display more information.

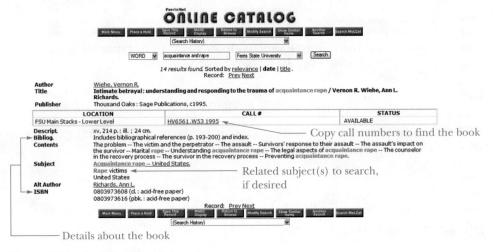

Copy call numbers to find the book

Related subject(s) to search, if desired

Details about the book

Figure 20.5   Detailed Search Results.

for instance, you're asked to write a paper on some aspect of Japanese culture, you might investigate such combinations as "Japanese business," "Japan and education," and "Japanese feminists." Because key term searches allow you to use logical terms like *and, or, but,* and *not,* they are especially useful for narrowing a broad focus.

Obtaining the Books   Most researchers start with a key term search. Following the instructions in the paragraph on page 357, type in one or several terms, using the appropriate logical terms. Advanced search functions will allow you to limit the dates of your search if you are only looking for more recent texts.

When you have found a promising title, make a note of the relevant information. With some systems, this screen indicates whether the book is in the library or checked out and tells you how to proceed if you can't find it on the shelf.

If your terminal has a printer, use it to make a copy of each promising reference. Otherwise, record the following information in your electronic notes or on a note card:

Author(s)

Title

Editor(s) and translator(s), as well as author(s) of any supplementary material

Total number of volumes (if more than one) and the number of the specific volume that you want to use

City of publication

Name of publisher

Date of publication

Also, copy the book's call number into your electronic notes on or in the upper left corner of the card.

Next, scan the books themselves. If your library stacks are closed, give the librarian a list of your call numbers and ask to see the books. If you can enter the stacks, locate the general areas where your books are shelved. Once you find your book, spend a few extra minutes browsing in the general area of each book; you may discover useful sources that you overlooked in the card catalog.

Skim each book's table of contents and any introductory material, such as a preface or introduction, to determine its scope and approach. Also check the index and note the pages with discussions that relate to your topic. Finally, thumb through portions that look promising. If the book won't help you, throw away the note card.

If a book is missing from the shelf and the computer hasn't indicated that someone has checked it out, then it's probably on reserve. Check at the circulation desk; if the book is on reserve, go to that section and examine it there. If someone has checked the book out and the due date is some time away, perhaps a library nearby will have a copy. Check with your librarian.

How to Use It Follow the procedure given on pages 356–359 for computerized card catalogs, making any needed modifications.

EXERCISE

1. **Select five of the following subjects. Go to the online catalog and find one book about or by each. List each book's call number, author, title, publisher, and date of publication. Because subject headings may vary, investigate related categories, if necessary, to find an entry. To illustrate, if you find nothing under "mountaineering," check "mountain climbing" or "backpacking."**

1. AIDS research
2. The American family
3. The American workplace
4. Campaign reform

5. Cancer research
6. Charter schools
7. Children and divorce
8. Hillary Clinton

9.	Diets	20.	Bobby Knight
10.	Electric cars	21.	Taylor Swift
11.	Gloria Estefan	22.	Mountaineering
12.	Bill Gates	23.	Colin Powell
13.	Genetic research	24.	Robots
14.	Global warming	25.	Glenn Beck
15.	HMOs	26.	School vouchers
16.	Home schooling	27.	Drake
17.	The Internet and business	28.	Telecommuting
18.	The Internet and games	29.	Andrew Weil
19.	Stephen King	30.	Oprah Winfrey

2. **Provide your instructor with a list of the books you found that appear useful for developing your paper's topic. For each book, furnish the information specified in Exercise 1, along with a brief note indicating why you think the book will be useful.**

Database Indexes

What They Are   Databases are computerized indexes of material in academic journals, magazines, newspapers and other formats. They allow you to search a wide range of topics by keyword or subject, and many provide access to the full article online. Other times they identify the actual print version you are searching for and where you can locate it. In general it is helpful to explore the available databases and the kind of information they make available. Often librarians offer sessions on the database, have handouts on the available databases and their usage, or can direct you to the database that will best serve your needs.

Perhaps the best place to start a search is with a general periodical database such as *First Search* or *InfoTrac* or *WilsonSelect plus*. These databases provide access to listings of articles, arranged and subdivided by subject and keyword, that have appeared in over a thousand magazines and newspapers, including the entries in various other indexes. There are more specific databases for newspapers, for business, and for many other disciplines. Some databases such as *ERIC* (Educational Resources Information Center) and *Medline* (National Library of Medicine) give you access to citations of articles appearing in professional journals in a specific area. These articles, however, are usually aimed at a specialized audience and may be difficult to comprehend. Your library may have access to a number of different indexes, including ones to regional newspapers. Below are just a very few of the more general indexes.

Index	Uses
Article First	Good broad overview of journal and article publications
Business Newsbank	Access on articles specifically on business-related issues
Facts on File	Provides access to select databases that compile information rather than access articles. The Issues and Controversies Database can be a good place to get an overview of a topic or narrow your topic
General Reference Center Gold	Access to material on a broad range of topics in journals, magazines, and newspapers

Index	Uses
JStor	Provides access to academic articles on academic issues, especially useful for the humanities
Lexis-Nexis Academic Universe	Access to a range of articles in journals and magazines
Lexis-Nexis Newspapers	Access to information in newspapers
Literature Resources from Gale	Specific database directed to literature-related research
Newsbank Retrospective	An index of older newspaper stories from 1970–1991
Readers Guide Retrospective	An index to older journal, magazine, and newspaper articles
Wilson Omnifile	Access to a large range of online articles
Wilson Business	Access to business-related articles in magazines and newspapers

While sometimes you can obtain the full article directly online, sometimes the database entry offers instead an abstract—a brief summary of the articles' main points. *A word of caution: Don't mistake an abstract for the full article; an abstract is a 200–300-word summary of a journal article and should not be used as a source. Always take notes on the full article.* Also, do not restrict your research to just articles available online.

Figure 20.6 is an example of a database screen that allows the user to select a specific subject area, which will make the databases for that area available. Unless you are prepared to use specialty information in an area, start by reviewing General and Multidisciplinary Resources.

Often the next screen offers you a choice of different databases. Many users find FirstSearch and Wilson Select Plus as useful places to start their research, but let your topic be your guide (Figure 20.7).

Keyword Search   Most databases allow you to search for a key term. Just follow the instructions for beginning the search and then enter your key term. If, for example, your topic is "teenage suicide," type "teenagers and suicide" onto the screen that's already showing and press the search or enter key. The

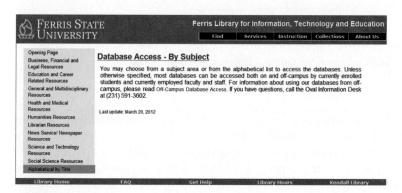

Figure 20.6   Initial Library Screen. From this list of database topics, choose the database that best matches the subject of your research.
Software by Innovative Interface, Inc.

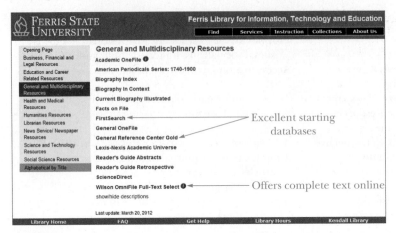

Figure 20.7 Second Library Screen. From this list of databases, you can choose those that are most likely to have resources you can use in your research papers.

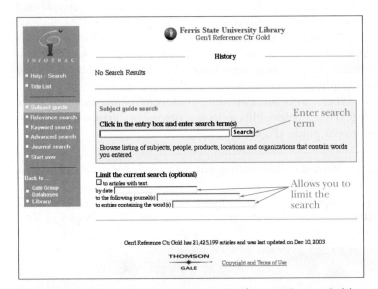

Figure 20.8 Search Screen for General Reference Center Gold.
Screens included by permission of Thomson Gale.

computer will check titles and abstracts for the key terms and provide a list of the corresponding articles. Allow ample time to explore a number of possibilities. If you try several terms related to your topic, you will find a wider variety of articles that serve your purpose. Figure 20.8 is a sample database screen where users can indicate the term or terms they intend to search and, if desired, select limits on the search. You would be well served by not limiting your search initially unless your teacher has placed certain restrictions on the dates of sources.

Subject Search   Because some periodical indexes, like *InfoTrac,* are organized around subject headings, it's a good idea to try a variety of subject terms because each will yield different articles. Often your keyword search results will suggest subject headings. If your entry matches a subject heading or you are referred to a cross-reference, the computer will use a series of screens to direct you to a list of articles.

Along the way, one of the screens may list subdivisions of the request being searched, as in the following example:

Acquaintance Rape, subdivisions of

—analysis	—prevention
—cases	—psychological aspects
—investigation	—research
—laws, regulations, etc.	—social aspects
—media coverage	—statistics
—moral and ethical aspects	—studying and teaching
—personal narratives	—usage

Such a list can uncover facets of your topic that you hadn't considered and that might enrich your final paper. For example, the subdivision "personal narratives" might contain an experience that would provide a powerful opening for the paper. Similarly, articles cataloged under "statistics" could provide information on the scope of the acquaintance rape problem.

Advanced Search   The final result of any search is a list of articles like the following one, obtained through General Reference Center Gold, for the search term "acquaintance rape":

The results for a search might look like the screen shot below. Notice that several of the sources are available directly online by locating your cursor on the text choice and clicking (Figure 20.9).

This list shows that all three magazines are available in the library and that two articles are abstracted in the computer. (If the database provides the full text of an article, the notation "full text available" will appear after the citation.) The coded notation "Mag. Coll." indicates that the magazine is available on microfilm. The first two numbers and the letter in the code identify the number of the microfilm cassette. The remaining numbers indicate the microfilm page on which the article starts. The exact listings of your system may be somewhat different from what's shown here; the same kind of information, however, should be available.

Besides the previously mentioned specialized indexes, many others are available that you could use to supplement your search of general indexes. Here is a brief sampling of them:

Applied Science and Technology Index, 1958–date (indexed by subject)

Education Index, 1929–date (indexed by subject and author)

Humanities Index, 1974–date (indexed by subject and author)

International Index to Periodicals, 1907–1964 (indexed by subject and author; titled *Social Sciences and Humanities Index,* 1965–1974, and then separated into the *Humanities Index* and the *Social Sciences Index*)

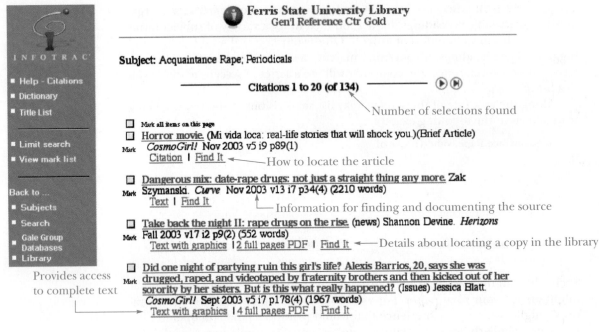

Figure 20.9   List of Results. Click on the blue underscored "Text" to see the complete article.

Social Sciences and Humanities Index, 1965–1974 (indexed by subject and
   author)

Social Sciences Index, 1975–date (indexed by subject and author)

All come in printed form, and most are also available on compact discs and
online.

With periodical indexes, as with the online catalog, don't give up if a subject
heading you're exploring yields few or no entries. Instead, explore related headings. For example, if your topic is teenage marriages, look also under "adoles-
cence," "divorce," "teen pregnancies," and the like. Browse through the system
and try a variety of options. Use this as an opportunity to gain different perspectives on your research project.

Obtaining the Articles   If the article is available online, the database often
allows you to mail the article to yourself or save the article to your computer. For
references without the complete articles, print a copy of each promising reference you find. Otherwise, copy the following information into your notes.

Author(s), if identified

Title of article

Name of periodical

Volume or issue number (for professional and scholarly journals only)

Date of periodical

For newspapers, the edition name (city, metro) if more than one published, and section letter

The page range of the entire article

Obtain printouts of whatever articles you can and check the topic sentences of paragraphs for essential points. Also, scan any accompanying abstracts or summaries. If an article appears useful, check to see whether it has a bibliography, which might include additional useful sources. Keep the notes for articles that seem promising—and any useful articles—and discard the others.

If the database does not indicate whether the library has the article and periodical, check the remaining references, including the ones from encyclopedia bibliographies, against the library's periodical catalog, often part of the online catalog, to see which periodicals are available and where they are located. Libraries frequently keep current issues in a periodical room or some other special section. Back issues of magazines are often kept on microfilm or bound into hardcover volumes and shelved. Most newspapers are on microfilm. Check the articles for which you don't have printouts in the same manner that you checked the others.

Select five of the following subjects and find one magazine article about each. Use at least three periodical indexes to locate the articles. List the author, if given; the title of the article; the name of the magazine; its date; the page range; and the name of the index used. Because subject categories may vary, investigate related categories, if necessary, to find an entry. To illustrate, if you find nothing under "bioengineered foods," check "genetically modified foods" or "bioaltered foods."

1. Animal rights
2. Bandwidth technology
3. Bioengineered foods
4. Black holes
5. Paul Ryan
6. Campaign funds
7. Campus drinking
8. Cellular phones
9. Corporate mergers
10. DNA testing
11. Cyber Warfare
12. Ben Bernanke
13. Hedge funds
14. Laser surgery
15. NASDAQ stock exchange
16. Drones
17. Jon Steward
18. Shaquille O'Neal
19. Oral history
20. Racial profiling
21. John Rocker
22. Crossover Vehicles
23. Telemarketing
24. Televangelism
25. Unemployment Rate
26. Vegan
27. Venus or Serena Williams
28. Wiretapping
29. X-ray astronomy
30. Yale University

Searching the World Wide Web

The Internet includes a stupendous amount of information. As a result, finding just the material you want can be difficult. To solve this problem, several *search engines* have been developed that can connect any search term or terms with potentially millions of sites that include the keywords. While studies have found that most students automatically use Google for searches, Figure 20.10 provides

Watch the Animation on **Conducting Online Searches**

the addresses of several other search engines. Because the various search engines often select differently and produce different results, it's a good idea to use several engines while conducting your search.

Search Engine	Address
Google	www.google.com
Bing	www.bing.com
Yahoo	www.yahoo.com
Ask	www.ask.com

Figure 20.10   Popular Search Engines.

While each search engine works in a slightly different manner, they all provide similar sorts of information. Search engines often provide information that isn't useful. For that reason, you'll often want to narrow your search when you begin. Single terms such as "health," "cancer," or "crime" could give you a million possible sites; instead, you may want to search for "ovarian cancer" or even "ovarian cancer cures." Most search engines also let you add keywords that will further narrow what has already been found. Different words or phrases can produce different results, so try a variety of words for the same topic. It is important to be patient and scroll through several pages of search results. Often you might find a very helpful article only after scrolling through several pages of results.

You can scroll through the list of sites the engine has found. The sites are usually accompanied by a short description that may help you decide whether they are useful. If you select any highlighted words, the search engine will connect you to the selected web page.

Figures 20.11 and 20.12 show the results of searching the subject "robotic advances." Figure 20.11 shows some of the web sites found during the search, and Figure 20.12 shows a web page with potentially useful information.

◉─⌐Watch the Animation
on **Evaluating Online
Sources**

Evaluating Internet Material   Because anyone can post virtually anything on the Internet, it is crucial that you check the accuracy and validity of information you obtain from it. A source that sounds like a research center, for example, the Institute for Social Justice, could be a political or even a cult organization giving out one-sided or false information for its own purposes. While articles for professional journals are reviewed by experts to ensure that the information is reliable, no such safeguard exists on the Internet. Carelessly researched or ethically questionable material can and does appear. Here are some guidelines for checking the validity of an Internet source:

1. Is the source identified as a reputable professional organization, such as the American Cancer Society, a university like MIT, or a government agency like the Department of Justice? Keep in mind that anyone can use a professional-sounding name, so be alert.

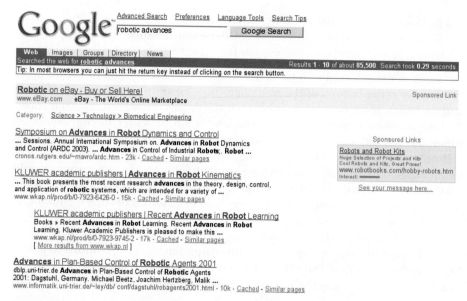

Figure 20.11   Search Screen Showing Results of Search.

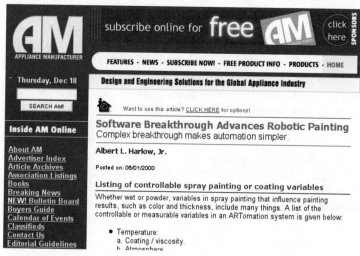

Figure 20.12   Online Article.

2. Is there an identified author whose credentials you can check and who speaks with some authority? If there is no e-mail contact listed or you can't find another way to verify the contents of the web site, don't use it.

3. Is the tone of the site professional? Does it maintain an objective stance and support its position with credible evidence?

4. Is the information consistent with the other material you have found? If the site disagrees with the standard information, does it offer adequate support for its claims?

5. Does the site explain how the data were obtained?

6. Does the site appear to misuse any data? For instance, is the sample too small? Are the claims pushed too far? Are the statistics biased?

Look at the selected web page. The address of this web site in Figure 20.12 is normally at the bottom of the web page (not shown here). This article has an author, which increases the credibility of the report. However, research shows that the author is founder and vice president of a robotics technology company, which though it demonstrates a clear expertise suggests a bias in favor of such technologies. A check of the home page shows that Appliance Manufacturer is an established organization promoting applied technologies. This group would have the professional expertise to make certain the article is credible. However, they might also have a slight bias to stress the effectiveness of such technologies rather than dwell on the negatives.

Sometimes, of course, you may want to check out pages that present the views of individuals or organizations with strong but slanted positions to gain a better understanding of their thinking, but don't consider such pages to be reliable sources. When using the Internet, "Reader beware" is a prudent attitude.

E-Mail You probably have your own e-mail address. You may also have an address provided to you by your university. In some cases, your professor may be using a web-based instructional program that includes e-mail specific to your class. It is a good idea to jot down the e-mail addresses of other students in your class, making certain it is the one they actually are using, so that you can exchange ideas. Your professor, however, may prefer that you use the class or university e-mail.

You can use e-mail to ask knowledgeable people about your research topic and get swift answers to your questions. Use this approach, however, as a last resort since busy people have limited time. If you must contact experts, don't bother them with questions that you could easily answer by reading background material. Reserve e-mail for specific queries that defy answer after extensive research. Most search engines have clearly identified directories that allow you to look up an e-mail address if you know a person's name. Sometimes you can find the name of an expert through the web pages of major universities. If you do get a response to your query, evaluate it carefully; an overburdened expert may dash off a quick response while doing something else.

Newsgroups A newsgroup is a group of people who discuss a common interest by posting their responses to a common address for everyone to read. These discussions can be informal and often are not monitored; as a result, they leave something to be desired as a source for research. Still, your university system will likely give you access to newsgroups, so ask your computer center for an instruction sheet. A word of caution: Many newsgroups are intolerant of uninformed people intruding upon their conversation. Common netiquette (the etiquette of the Internet) calls for you to read what has already been written and to think before you write. Increasingly online news stories or blogs are followed by a number of comments by those interested. While such discussions may offer ideas, remember that almost anyone can post comments without correction, and so the comments may be very inaccurate.

Listservs   A listserv consists of numerous e-mail addresses that make up a mailing list of people interested in a particular topic. Once you sign up, everything posted to that listserv will be sent to your e-mail address. People who subscribe to three or four listservs may receive 30 or 40 e-mail messages every day. If you post a question on a listserv, you may get dozens of responses from professionals interested in the topic, and sorting out the validity of the different responses can be difficult. As with newsgroups, netiquette calls for you to acquire an understanding of your subject and follow the discussions on the listserv for some time before you post a question or a response. Your university computer professionals can probably supply you with instructions on how to find and sign up for a listserv. You can access a subject index of listservs at http://www.liszt.com.

FAQs   Whenever you find a promising web site, newsgroup, or listserv, you will often see a line for FAQs (frequently asked questions). It's a good idea to read the FAQs first since they may well answer your questions.

EXERCISE

1. **Using an appropriate search engine, find information on each of the following topics:**
   a. the Vietnam War
   b. current crime statistics
   c. sexual harassment
   d. current government immigration policy

2. **Enter the name of a major university into a search engine and then search. You should find that university's home page. Try to access the university's library to find what books are available on a topic of your choice. You might try schools like Harvard, Duke, or Notre Dame.**

Creating an Annotated Bibliography

Your instructor may ask you to create an annotated bibliography, which is simply a bibliography following either the MLA (Chapter 21) or APA (Chapter 22) styles with the addition of a brief summary of the article or book. Scholars sometimes produce annotated bibliographies for publication to help other scholars have an overview of the research on a particular topic. Below is a sample entry for an annotated bibliography in MLA style.

Anzaldua, Gloria. "La Conciencia De La Mestiza: Towards a New Consciousness" in *Making Face, Making Soul/Haciendo Caras*, ed. by Gloria Anzaldua, 377–389. San Francisco: Aunt Lute Books, 1990. Print. Gloria Anzaldua explores the concept of the mestiza, a borderlands figure pulled in multiple directions. Anzaldua narrates how this figure is simultaneously present in multiple spaces, having a foot in multiple cultures. The result of this experience, Anzaldua claims, is a tolerance for ambiguity and contradiction. Furthermore, the mestiza is here articulated as a powerful cultural figure, able to embody possibilities for change.

Primary Research Findings

Besides relying on library materials, you may wish to use information obtained by conducting primary research. Chapter 23 provides detailed instructions for interviewing specialists, sending out questionnaires, and making direct observations. Before doing any type of primary research, always get your instructor's permission.

Adjusting Your Topic

After finishing your search for sources, you may need to adjust the scope and emphasis of your topic. If you start with "America's First Nuclear-Powered Submarine" but fail to turn up enough sources, you might expand your emphasis to "America's First Nuclear-Powered Warships." On the other hand, if you're working with "America's First Nuclear-Powered Warships" and find yourself floundering in an ocean of sources, you might zero in on one type of vessel. Gathering evidence helps to develop your judgment about how many sources you need to do the job.

CASE HISTORY Once Keith Jacque had selected a focus for his paper on electronic monitoring, he began compiling his working bibliography. First he turned to the computerized card catalog and began his search for books and government documents by typing in the subject entry "house arrest," but he found nothing. Next he tried "electronic monitoring of prisoners." This entry yielded a cross-reference directing him to the entries "punishment—United States" and "criminal statistics—analysis." These two entries yielded a list of seven books and eleven government documents. Further examination revealed that three of the books and four of the documents appeared promising.

Keith's search for periodical articles took him to the college's *InfoTrac* database. Using this system, he found three useful subject headings: "home detention," "electronic monitoring of prisoners," and "criminal statistics—analysis." A search of these subjects turned up 24 journal articles, all of which were available in the library. Eight looked as if they would be useful. Three newspaper articles seemed suitable, and a search of *NewsBank* revealed another promising newspaper article.

Since his library offered access to the Internet, Keith also searched the world wide web. He used the Google and Bing search engines and entered complete phrases such as "electronic incarceration," "home detention," "electronic monitoring," and "incarceration, electronic." Many of the web sites he found were not relevant to his topic, but he persisted and finally found two that seemed promising. One, from an organization concerned with public policy, discussed the indirect costs of incarceration. The other, from the Probation Division of Georgia's Department of Corrections, discussed alternatives to jail sentences.

After completing his search for library and Internet sources, Keith sought and obtained his instructor's permission to conduct primary research on his topic. Unsure of how to proceed, he talked to his advisor in the criminal justice department. She suggested that he ask the director of Michigan's electronic surveillance program for a personal interview. (See Chapter 23). He was able to obtain the interview, which provided information on the scope, operation, and success rate of the program as well as the savings it has achieved.

Satisfied that ample information was available, Keith carefully evaluated the content of the articles and of pertinent sections of the books and government documents he had located. His instructor had suggested that one good way to approach a topic is to pose a question about it and then draft a *tentative* answer, if possible. Here's how Keith proceeded:

Q. What benefits does electronic monitoring offer jurisdictions that adopt it?

A. Electronic monitoring is less expensive than incarceration, presents no serious problems, and offers a choice among several systems.

This answer provided a *tentative thesis,* an informed opinion that guided Keith's later note taking, giving him a sense of direction and indicating what information would probably prove useful and what was likely to be useless. Tentative theses can be altered slightly or changed completely if necessary. If later reading indicated that electronic monitoring can sometimes be more expensive than incarceration, Keith could alter his thesis accordingly.

Taking Notes

To take notes, read your references carefully and record significant information. You might review or even expand your original research questions (pages 352–353) so that you can read with a better sense of purpose. Notes are the raw materials for your finished product, so develop them accurately.

20.4

Evaluate your sources, take notes using summary and paraphrase, and assemble a working bibliography.

Evaluating Your Sources

Evaluate your sources by considering these factors.

The Expertise of the Author   Judge an author's expertise by examining his or her professional status. Say you're searching for information on some new cancer-treating drug. An article by the director of a national cancer research center would be a better bet than one by a staff writer for a magazine. Similarly, a historian's account of a national figure will probably have more balance and depth than a novelist's popularized account of that person's life. Gauging a writer's credentials is not difficult. Articles in periodicals often note authors' job titles along with their names. Some even supply thumbnail biographies. For a book, check its title page, preface, or introduction, and—if it's been left on—the dust jacket. Finally, notice whether the writer has other publications on this general subject. If your sources include two or more items by one person or if that person's name keeps cropping up as you take notes, you're probably dealing with an expert.

The Credibility of the Publication A book's credibility hinges on its approach and its reception by reviewers. Cast a cautious eye on books that take a popular rather than a scholarly approach. For research papers, scholarly treatments provide more solid fare. Weigh what reviewers said when a book first appeared. Two publications excerpt selected reviews and provide references to others. The *Book Review Digest* (1905–date) deals mainly with nontechnical works, while the *Technical Book Review Index* (1935–date) covers technical and scientific books. Turn first to the volume for the year the book came out. If you don't find any reviews, scan the next year's index. Often books published in the fall are not reviewed until the following year.

Periodical articles can also take a scholarly or popular tack. Editors of specialized journals and of some wide-circulation magazines—for example, *Scientific American* and *The Atlantic Monthly*—publish only in-depth, accurate articles. Most newsstand publications, however, popularize to some extent, and some deliberately strive for sensationalism. Popularizing may result in broad, general statements, skimpy details, and a sensational tone.

Don't automatically reject a source because the writer lacks expertise or offers a popularized treatment. Often, especially when writing about a current topic, you'll need to use material that falls short in some way. Remember, though, that you undertake research to become more knowledgeable than general readers are about a topic. When information in popular periodicals provides less than adequate coverage, candidly acknowledge the shortcomings.

Mechanics of Note Taking

There are many ways people effectively take notes: some use regular notebooks, others take notes with their computers or tablets, and many still use note cards. The goal in all these methods is the same. You need to make certain all your notes remain undividable, linked to their source, and will be easy to organize later. Table 20.1 on page 373 presents some strategies.

Responding to Notes

As you take notes, reflect on your topic and try to come up with new ideas, see connections to other notes, and anticipate future research. Think of yourself as having a conversation with your sources, and jot down your responses on the backs of your note cards or next to or beneath your computer notes in italics or other distinct fonts. Ask yourself these questions: Does this information agree with what I have learned so far? Does it suggest any new avenues to explore?

Table 20.1   Note-Taking Strategies

Medium	Taking Notes	Linking to Source	Organization
Computer or Tablet	Most people end up taking notes from an article on a single page. Separate notes on the page. Some people use a note taking program that makes it easy to connect notes. Avoid cutting and pasting from the source and clearly indicate all quoted material with quotes.	Identify the article's bibliographical information on the top of the page. Next to each note indicate author's name, an abbreviation of the source name, and the information's page number.	Identify the subject of the note directly above the note. Later, it can be helpful to use the find function of your program to find all the related notes and group them together by subject on the same page.
Note Cards (4 × 6 cards)	Take one note per card. Staple two cards with the same note together. Be sure to mark quoted material with quotes.	Use a number linking to a bibliography with all the information. Identify author and abbreviated title on the bottom of the card. Always record page number of information.	Identify subject of the note card at the top for easy arrangement. Sometimes assign a number or color to major topics.
Notebook or Yellow Pad	In many ways similar to computers. Some people do organize their notebooks by topic and take notes accordingly.	Same as computers.	It can be difficult to try out different groupings using a notebook or yellow pad. Some people cut out the notes to rearrange them.

Does it leave me with questions about what's been said? Although it may take a few minutes to record your responses to a note, this type of analysis will help you write a paper that reflects *your* opinions, decisions, and evaluations, not one that smacks of notes merely patched together from different sources.

Types of Notes

A note can be a summary, paraphrase, or quotation. *Whenever you use any kind of note in your paper, give proper credit to your source. Failure to do so results in plagiarism—that is, literary theft—a serious offense even when committed unintentionally.* Pages 386–389 discuss plagiarism, and Chapters 22 and 23 explain proper documentation of sources. *Just as a note can be in these forms, the draft of your paper may also include a summary, paraphrase, or quotation.*

👁 — Watch the Animation on
Writing a Summary

Summary   A summary condenses original material, presenting its core ideas *in your own words*. In order to write an effective summary, you must have a good grasp of the information, and this comprehension ensures that you are ready to use the material in your paper. You may include brief quotations if you enclose them in quotation marks. A properly written summary presents the main points in their original order without distorting their emphasis or meaning, and it omits supporting details and repetition. Summaries, then, serve up the heart of the matter.

Begin the summarizing process by asking yourself, "What points does the author make that have an important bearing on my topic and purpose?" To answer, note especially the topic sentences in the original, which often provide essential information. Copy the points in order; then condense and rewrite them in your own words. Figure 20.13 summarizes the Bertrand Russell passage that follows. We have underscored key points in the original.

Necessity for law

About a century and a half ago, there began a still-existing preference for impulsive actions over deliberate ones. Those responsible for this development believed that people are naturally good but institutions have perverted them. Actually, unfettered human nature breeds violence and brutality, and law is our only protection against anarchy. The law assumes the responsibility for revenge and settles disputes equitably. It frees people from the fear of being victimized by criminals and provides a means of catching them. Without it, civilization could not endure.

Russell, pp. 63–65

Figure 20.13   Summary.

Under the influence of the romantic movement, a process began about a hundred and fifty years ago, which has continued ever since—a process of revaluing the traditional virtues, placing some higher on the scale than before, and others lower. The tendency has been to exalt impulse at the expense of deliberation. The virtues that spring from the heart have come to be thought superior to those that are based upon reflection: a generous man is preferred to a man who is punctual in paying his debts. *Per contra*, deliberate sins are thought worse than impulsive sins: a hypocrite is more harshly condemned than a murderer. The upshot is that we tend to estimate virtues, not by their capacity for providing human happiness, but by their power of inspiring a personal liking for the possessors, and we are not apt to include among the qualities for which we like people, a habit of reflecting before making an important decision.

The men who started this movement were, in the main, gentle sentimentalists who imagined that, when the fetters of custom and law were removed, the heart would be free to display its natural goodness. Human nature, they thought, is good, but institutions have corrupted it; remove the institutions and we shall all become angels. Unfortunately, the matter is not so simple as they thought. Men who follow their impulses establish governments based on pogroms, clamour for war with foreign countries, and murder pacifists and Negroes. Human nature unrestrained by law is violent and cruel. In the London Zoo, the male baboons fought over the females until all the females were torn to pieces; human beings, left to the ungoverned impulse, would be no better. In ages that have had recent experience of anarchy, this has been obvious. All the great writers of the middle ages were passionate in their admiration of the law; it was the Thirty Years' War that led Grotius to become the first advocate of international law. *Law, respected and enforced, is in the long run the only alternative to violent and predatory anarchy*; and it is just as necessary to realize this now as it was in the time of Dante and Grotius.

What is the essence of law? On the one hand, it takes away from private citizens the right of revenge, which it confers upon the government. If a man steals your money, you must not steal it back, or thrash him, or shoot him; you must establish the facts before a neutral tribunal, which inflicts upon him such punishment as has seemed just to the disinterested legislators. On the other hand, *when two men have a dispute, the law provides a machinery for settling it*, again on principles laid down in advance by neutrals. The advantages of law are many. It diminishes the amount of private violence, and settles disagreements in a manner more nearly just than that which would result if the disputants fought it out by private war. *It makes it possible for men to work without being perpetually on the watch against bandits. When a crime has been committed it provides a skilled machine for discovering the criminal.*

Without law, the existence of civilized communities is impossible. In international law, there is as yet no effective law, for lack of an international police force capable of overpowering national armies, and it is daily becoming more evident that this defect must be remedied if civilization is to survive. Within single nations there is a dangerous tendency to think that moral indignation excuses the extra-legal punishment of criminals. In Germany an era of private murder (on the loftiest grounds) preceded and followed the victory of the Nazis. In fact, nine-tenths of what appeared as just indignation was sheer lust for cruelty; and this is equally true in other countries where mobs rob the law of its functions. In any civilized community, toleration of mob rule is the first step towards barbarism.

Bertrand Russell, "Respect for Law," *San Francisco Review,* Winter 1958, 63–65.

EXERCISE

1. **Select two passages that your instructor approves from an essay in the Reader and prepare summaries for them.**
2. **Submit summaries of three pieces of information that you plan to use in writing your paper; also submit complete versions of the original.**

Paraphrase   To paraphrase is to restate material *in your own words* without attempting to condense it. Unlike a summary, a paraphrase allows you to present an essentially complete version of the original material. A note of caution, however: Don't copy the original source nearly verbatim, changing only a word here and there. To do so is to plagiarize. To avoid this offense, follow a read, think, and write-without-looking-at-the-original strategy when you take notes so that you concentrate on recording the information in your own words. Then verify the accuracy of your notes by checking them against the original source. Here is a sample passage; Figure 20.14 is its paraphrase.

Over time, more and more of life has become subject to the controls of knowledge. However, this is never a one-way process. Scientific investigation is continually increasing our knowledge. But if we are to make good use of this knowledge, we must not only rid our minds of old, superseded beliefs and fragments of magic, but also recognize new superstitions for what they are. Both are generated by our wishes, our fears, and our feelings of helplessness in difficult situations.

Margaret Mead, "New Superstitions for Old,"
A Way of Seeing, New York: McCall, 1970. 266.

Combatting Superstitions

As time has passed, knowledge has asserted its sway over larger and larger segments of human life. But the process cuts two ways. Science is forever adding to the storehouse of human knowledge. Before we can take proper advantage of its gifts, however, we must purge our minds of old and outmoded convictions, while recognizing the true nature of modern superstitions. Both stem from our desires, our apprehensions, and our sense of impotence under difficult circumstances.

Mead, p. 266

Figure 20.14 Paraphrase.

Paraphrase a short passage from one of your textbooks, including this one. Submit a complete version of the passage with the assignment.

 Watch the Animation on Using Quotations

Quotation A quotation is a copy of original material. Since your paper should demonstrate that you've mastered your sources, don't rely extensively on quotations. You need practice in expressing yourself. As a general rule, avoid quotations except when

- the original displays special elegance or force
- you really need support from an authority
- you need to back up your interpretation of a passage from a literary work.

Paraphrasing a passage as well-written as the one below would rob it of much of its force.

Man is himself, like the universe he inhabits, like the demoniacal stirring of the ooze from which he sprang, a tale of desolation. He walks in his mind from birth to death the long resounding shores of endless disillusionment. Finally, the commitment to life departs or turns to bitterness. But out of such desolation emerges the awful freedom to choose beyond the narrowly circumscribed circle that delimits the rational being.

Loren Eiseley, *The Unexpected Universe*

Special rules govern the use of quotations. If, for clarity, you need to add an explanation or substitute a proper name for a personal pronoun, enclose the addition in *brackets*.

> The Declaration of Independence asserts that "the history of the present King of Great Britain [George III] is a history of repeated injuries and unsurpations. . . ."

If your keyboard doesn't have brackets, insert them neatly with a dark pen.

Reproduce any grammatical or spelling errors in a source exactly as they appear in the original. To let your reader know that the original author, not you, made the mistake, insert the Latin word *sic* (meaning "thus") within brackets immediately after the error.

> As Wabash notes, "The threat to our enviroment [sic] comes from many directions."

If you're using the MLA documentation system and exclude an unneeded part of a quotation, show the omission with three spaced periods. Indicate omissions *within sentences* as follows:

> Writing in *The Age of Extremes*, Eric Hobsbawm observed, "What struck both the opponents of revolution and the revolutionists was that, after 1945, the primary form of revolutionary struggle . . . seemed to be guerilla warfare."

When an omission comes *at the end of a sentence* and what is actually quoted can also stand as a complete sentence, use an unspaced period followed by an ellipsis.

> In his second inaugural address, Lincoln voiced his hopes for the nation: "With malice toward none, with charity for all, with firmness in the right as God gives us to see the right, let us strive on to finish the work we are in. . . ."

Do the same when you drop *a whole sentence* within a quoted passage.

> According to newspaper columnist Grace Dunn, "Williamson's campaign will undoubtedly focus primarily on the legalized gambling issue because he hopes to capitalize on the strong opposition to it in his district . . . .Nonetheless, commentators all agree he faces an uphill fight in his attempt to unseat the incumbent."

Don't change or distort when you delete. Tampering like the following violates ethical standards:

Original passage: This film is poorly directed, and the acting uninspired; only the cameo appearance by Laurence Olivier makes it truly worth seeing.

Distorted version: This film is . . . truly worth seeing.

If the original passage you are quoting already includes ellipsis, place your own ellipsis in brackets [. . .] to distinguish your ellipsis from the one in the original. Some instructors may require you to enclose all ellipses in brackets. Follow your instructor's directions. *If you're using the APA documentation system, never enclose ellipsis within brackets.*

You can summarize or paraphrase original material but retain a few words or phrases to add vividness or keep a precise shade of meaning. Simply use quotation marks but no ellipsis.

> Presidential spokesperson Paula Plimption notes that because of the "passionate advocacy" of its supporters, the push to roll back property taxes has been gaining momentum across the country.

When you copy a quotation onto a note card, put quotation marks at the beginning and the end so you won't mistake it for a paraphrase or a summary when you write the paper. If the quoted material starts on one page and ends on the next, use a slash mark (/) to show exactly where the shift comes. Then if you use only part of the quotation in your paper, you'll know whether to use one page number or two.

Don't expect to find a bonanza on every page you read. Sometimes one page will yield several notes, another page nothing. If you can't immediately gauge the value of some material, take it down. Useless information can be discarded later. Place a rubber band around your growing stack of note cards. Store them in a large envelope closed with a snap or string and labeled with your name and address. Submit them with your completed paper if your instructor requests.

CASE HISTORY Working bibliography in hand, Keith Jacque prepared his notes. Most of his notes were summaries of the source material, but in a few cases he chose quotations because of the importance of the source or the significance of the material. For example, one quotation cited a former U.S. Attorney General who pointed out the disproportionate number of crimes committed by habitual violent offenders. Another quotation cited a key reason for the growing use of electronic monitoring: the high cost of prisons. Still another detailed various difficulties encountered in transmitting signals.

As Keith took notes, a plan for his paper began to emerge. The introduction would explain the reasons behind the growing use of electronic monitoring. The body would present a brief history of monitoring and then detail the different kinds of systems, examine the problems encountered when using them, and point out their effectiveness.

20.5

Organize your notes to create an outline for a research paper.

Organizing and Outlining

Next comes your formal outline, the blueprint that shows the divisions and subdivisions of your paper, the order of your ideas, and the relationships between ideas and supporting details. An outline is a tool that benefits both writer and reader.

A formal outline follows the pattern shown below:

I.
    A.
    B.
        1.
        2.
            a.
            b.
II.

You can see the significance of an item by its numeral, letter, or number designation and by its distance from the left margin; the farther it's indented, the less important it is. All items with the same designation have roughly the same importance.

> **Watch** the Animation on **Outlining with a Word Processor**

Developing Your Outline

Developing an outline is an excellent way to think through your paper. It involves arranging material from various sources in an appropriate manner. Sorting and re-sorting your notes is a good way to proceed. First, determine the main divisions of your paper by checking the summarized notations at the tops of your notes, and then make one stack of cards for each division or organize a page of related computer notes. Next, review each stack or collection of notes carefully to determine further subdivisions and sort it into smaller stacks sections. Finally, use the stacks or sections to prepare your outline. Your word processing program usually has an outline option that provides an outline format for you.

There are two types of formal outline: *topic* and *sentence*. A topic outline presents all entries as words, short phrases, or short clauses. A sentence outline presents them as complete sentences. To emphasize the relationships among elements, items of equal importance have parallel phrasing. Although neither is *the* preferred form, a sentence outline includes more details and also your attitude toward each idea. Many students first develop a topic outline, do additional research, and then polish and expand this version into a sentence outline. While it's easy to be sloppy in a topic outline, forming a sentence outline requires you to reach the kinds of conclusions that will be the backbone of your paper. The following segments of a topic and a sentence outline for a paper on tranquilizer dependence illustrate the difference between the two:

Topic Outline

    I. The tranquilizer abuse problem
      A. Reasons for the problem
        1. Overpromotion
        2. Overprescription

        3. Patient's misuse
          a. Dosage
          b. Length of usage
    B. Growth of the problem

Sentence Outline

  II. Tranquilizers are widely abused.
    A. Several factors account for the abuse of tranquilizers.
      1. Drug companies overpromote their product.
      2. Doctors often unnecessarily prescribe tranquilizers.
      3. Patients often do not follow their doctors' instructions.
        a. Some patients take more than prescribed doses.
        b. Some continue to use tranquilizers beyond the prescribed time.
    B. The problem of tranquilizer abuse appears to be growing.

Note that the items in the sentence outline are followed by periods, but those in the topic outline are not.

Keying Your Computer Notes or Note Cards to Your Outline

When your outline is finished, key your note cards or computer notes to it by writing at the top of each card or note the letters and numbers—such as IIA or IIIB2—for the appropriate outline category. Now arrange the cards into one stack, following the order shown in the outline, or move your computer notes into a new file in the order of the outline. If you use note cards start with the top card in the stack and number all of them consecutively. If they later fall off the table or slide out of place, you can easily put them in order again. You might have a few stragglers left over when you complete this keying. Some of these may be worked into your paper as you write or revise it. With computer notes, resist the temptation to simply write the paper around your notes, which will produce a choppy effect. Instead, it is helpful to create an entirely new page to write the paper and draw on the notes when it meets your needs.

CASE HISTORY Sorting and resorting was challenging and at times frustrating for Keith. Since some of his material could be arranged in different ways, he found himself experimenting, evaluating, and rearranging as he tried various options. After much thought and some trial and error, the following *initial draft* of his outline emerged:

  I. Reasons why monitoring used
    A. Serious crime problem and number of people in prisons
    B. High cost of prisons
  II. Brief history of electronic monitoring

III. Types of monitoring systems
    A. Programmed-contact systems
    B. Continuous-contact systems
    C. Hybrid systems
IV. Problems with these systems
    A. Practical problems
       1. Offenders' problems
       2. Transmission difficulties
    B. Legal problems
       1. Do the systems violate constitutional rights?
       2. "Net-widening" effect
V. Effectiveness of electronic monitoring
    A. Effectiveness with low-risk offenders
    B. Cost effectiveness
VI. Expanded use of monitoring likely

This version is marked by nonparallel structure and inadequate attention to some points. Despite these weaknesses, it provided an adequate blueprint for the first draft of Keith's paper. You can see the final sentence outline and read the completed research paper starting on page 410 in Chapter 21.

Ethical Issues

When you present the information you've gathered from a variety of sources, you'll want to proceed in an ethically responsible way. Asking and answering the following questions will help you do just that.

20.6

Write so that your research paper is ethical.

- Have I carefully researched my topic so that my conclusions are well-founded? Imagine the consequences if slipshod testing by an auto company led to the erroneous conclusion that the steering mechanism on one of its models met current safety standards.
- Have I adequately acknowledged any evidence that runs counter to the conclusions I draw? A paper that stresses the advantages of charter schools but deliberately avoids mentioning their disadvantages could be a form of deception.
- Have I properly documented my sources? Using someone else's words or ideas without giving proper credit is a form of academic dishonesty.
- Have I honestly represented the authority of my sources? If you read an article touting almond extract as a cure for cancer that was written by a practicing foot doctor, it would be dishonest to suggest that the article was written by a "prominent research scientist." Refer to someone as an "expert" only when that person's credentials warrant the label.
- Could my information have an undesirable effect on readers? If so, how can I address their concerns? A report describing a new antibiotic-resistant strain of tuberculosis might alarm some readers, and therefore the writer could provide appropriate reassurances of the limited risk to most people.

Writing Your Research Paper

20.7

Write a draft of your research paper, and include visuals to enhance your paper.

👁 **Watch** the Animation on **Writing a Research Paper**

Some students think of a library research paper as a series of quotations, paraphrases, and summaries, one following the other throughout the paper. Not so. Without question, you use the material of others, but *you* select and organize it according to *your purpose. You* develop insights, and *you* draw conclusions about what you've read. You can best express your conclusions by setting your notes aside, stepping back to gain some perspective, and then expressing your sense of what you've learned. Many students find it helpful to write two or three pages on which they summarize what they want to say as well as whom they want to reach with their message and why. Like all forms of writing, research papers are written for some purpose and aimed at some audience.

DEVELOPING YOUR RESEARCH PAPER

- Identify audience and purpose.
- Brainstorm related questions.
- Research using available index.
- Narrow or adjust your topic based on initial research and reading.
- Identify key related material and take appropriate notes.
- Label notes by subject.
- Consider writing a quick draft without looking at notes to discover your direction.
- Create an outline.
- Connect notes to outline and organize notes.
- Begin writing based on outline.

Writing the First Draft

Your final research results will be expressed in a thesis. You've already drafted a tentative thesis, and now you'll probably refine or revise it to accommodate any changes in your perspective on the topic. Position the thesis in the introductory part of your paper unless you're analyzing a problem or recommending a solution; then you might hold back the thesis until later in the essay. If you do hold it back, state the problem clearly at the outset. Because of the paper's length, it's a good idea to reveal your organizational plan in your introductory section.

Introduction
- Provide a context for the importance of your topic.
- Employ a strategy from Chapter 5 to engage your reader.
- Clearly state your theory.
- Often offer some indication of the organization of the research paper.

Write the paper section by section, following the divisions of your outline. But keep in mind that you're not locked into its pattern. If you see an opportunity to develop an important idea that you omitted from your outline, try it. If you discover that it might be better to introduce an item earlier than you intended, go ahead. Just be sure to check your organization later. As you write, think of yourself as supporting the conclusions you have reached with the appropriate material in your notes, not just as stringing these notes together. You, your argument, and your language should be in charge, not your sources. Some find that it can be helpful to put the sources aside, write the draft, and then go back to incorporate source material. Either way, you will then incorporate the material on your notes with your own assessments and with transitional elements that clarify your information and orient the reader. As you proceed, here again you'll use the writing strategies presented earlier in the book.

Because of this paper's length, you will probably need to connect its major sections with transitional paragraphs that pull together the material already covered and prepare the reader for what follows. Don't fret if the style bumps along or connections aren't always clear. These problems can be smoothed out when you revise. You will, of course, need to know how to document your sources properly, handle quotations, and avoid plagiarism. Chapters 21 and 22 present guidelines on documentation for MLA and APA styles.

On occasion you may want to include supplementary information that would interrupt the flow of thought if you placed it in the paper. When this happens, use an *explanatory note*.[1] A typical explanatory note might clarify or elaborate on a point, discuss some side issue, or define a term used in a specialized way.

Body
- Organized in major sections that support the main claims.
- Written mostly in your main voice, employing support from notes without excess quotation.
- Follows a clear logic that the reader can follow, usually consistent with your outline.
- Often offers some indication of the organization of the research paper.
- Provides clear transition paragraphs between major sections and transitions between paragraphs

Conclusion
- Many strategies may work, so review special strategies in Chapter 5, but provide the reader with a sense of closure.
- May summarize main point and key evidence or argument.
- Or offer a call to action based on the paper's research.
- Or suggest future research that might be called for in this area.

[1]This is an explanatory note. Position it at the bottom of the page, spaced four lines away from the main text. If more than one note occurs on a page, double-space between them. If the note carries over to the next page, separate it from your text with a solid, full-length line. Put two spaces above the line and two spaces below it.

When you finish writing, let this version sit for a day or two. Then revise it, just as you would with a shorter essay. Keep track of all sources so that preparing the bibliography will go smoothly. Check and recheck your paper to avoid plagiarism.

Using Images, Illustrations, and Graphs

Computer programs make it easy to import photographs, illustrations, and graphs into an essay and report. Visuals can be useful. An essay on different kinds of cats would be enhanced by pictures of cats. The best way to explain the bones in the skull is a labeled drawing. Complicated numbers can be presented best through the appropriate graphs or charts.

General Principles for Using Visuals

- **Use visuals only when they help.** Excess visuals detract from a text; visuals should be used when they are the best way of presenting the information. Clichéd clip art only detracts from important messages.
- **Visuals should fit the text.** Visuals shouldn't be just thrown in. Instead, they should have a connection to nearby text so that the meanings are related.
- **Visuals need to be explained.** Visuals don't always stand on their own. You need to explain to readers why they should look at the visual and direct their attention to what they should notice. With graphs and tables, it is helpful to explain first what to look for in the visual and then, after the visual, identify the major conclusion the readers could reach from the visual.
- **Visuals often need a title.** To direct the reader's attention, label all visuals. The title should tell the story of the visual.
- **Place visuals so they don't break up the text.** You want your page to be attractive but not distracting. Visuals need to be positioned so the page looks good but the flow of the text is not seriously interrupted.
- **Visuals should be honest.** It is important to represent the data fairly and not distort the image or graph to slant the information.

Pictures   The use of a scanner or digital camera makes it easy to import pictures, which can spice up the text. It is very easy to find images on the Internet related to your topic that you can download and incorporate into your paper. If you use pictures, make certain they are clear and simple. Readers shouldn't have to spend time trying to decipher the picture. Always document any image that comes from a source.

Tables   Including tables with columns and rows is an excellent way of comparing information such as the features of different computers, the quantity of sales, or even the quality of different employees. Make certain your table is clearly labeled. See Table 20.2 for an example.

Table 20.2 Use Different Classroom Media for Different Purposes

Features	Blackboard	Overhead	PowerPoint
Class Time Used	Extensive; text written out in class	Minimal; prepared before class	Minimal; prepared before class
Equipment Required	Usually in every classroom	In most classrooms or easily obtained	Limited by limited number of computers and screens
Information Presented	Text and hand-drawn images or low-resolution graphs	Text and images or graphs; variable resolutions	All text and visuals with good resolution
Flexibility in Classroom Environment	Plans can be easily changed; readily accepts new direction and student input	Limited flexibility: order can be varied between overheads; can write on blank overheads	Limited; hard to change order of presentation or enter new input

Pie Charts   Pie charts are an excellent way to present percentages or quantities of a whole. Figure 20.15 is a sample pie chart.

Figure 20.15   How Teachers Use Their Time.

Bar Graphs   Bar graphs can help you present and compare data that isn't a continuous trend, as Figure 20.16 shows.

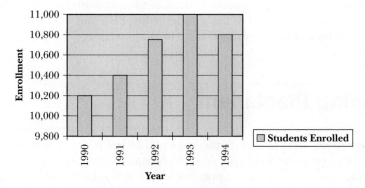

Figure 20.16   Student Enrollment Grows.

Line Graphs   Line graphs are an excellent way to show data that are continuous over time and show trends effectively. See Figure 20.17 for an example.

Figure 20.17   Temperatures at Noon Show Cold Spell.

Headers, Numbered Lists, and Bullets

Information in longer reports is not always presented in an unbroken stream of text. You can use a number of devices to help readers.

- **Bold headings and subheadings can guide the reader to different sections of the text.** When the sections of a longer report, or even a shorter business memo, can be broken into distinct sections, it can be helpful to label those sections with bold words or phrases that will direct the reader's attention. This text uses headings and subheadings, and so do some of the articles in the Reader.
- **Lists can be a useful way to present organized information.** Steps in a process, several recommendations, or the identification of important qualities can all be well represented by an indented list. The discussion questions in this text are all presented as numbered lists.
- **Bullets are used when listed information shouldn't be numbered because there is no implied sequence.** The recommendations for using visuals in this section are presented as a bulleted list. Lists and bullets should use parallelism, the same grammatical form.

Avoiding Plagiarism

20.8

Avoid plagiarism by integrating your sources with proper internal documentation.

Plagiarism occurs when a writer uses another person's material without properly acknowledging the debt. Sometimes plagiarism is deliberate, but often it happens because students simply don't understand what must be acknowledged and documented. Deliberate or not, plagiarism is absolutely unacceptable. *Any summary, paraphrase, or quotation you include in your paper must be documented as must statistics and graphics.* The only types of information escaping this requirement are those listed below:

1. *Common knowledge.* Common knowledge is information that most educated people would know. For instance, there's no need to document a statement that the Disney theme parks in California and Florida attract thousands of visitors each year. However, if you include precise daily, monthly, or yearly figures, then documentation is necessary.

2. *Your own conclusions.* As you write your paper, you'll incorporate your own conclusions at various points. (See the margin notes accompanying Keith Jacque's library research paper, page 419, for examples.) Such comments require no documentation. The same holds true for your own research. If you polled students on a campus issue, simply present the findings as your own.

3. *Facts found in many sources.* Facts such as the year of Shakespeare's death, the size of the 2001 national budget surplus, and the location of the Taj Mahal need not be documented. However, where there may be disputes about the facts in question (such as the size of the 2003 deficit) or where there may be some need to enforce the credibility of your figures, provide the source for your facts. If you are not certain that something is common knowledge, indicate your source.

4. *Standard terms.* Terms widely used in a particular field require no documentation. Examples include such computer terms as *mouse, CD-ROM,* and *download.*

Any piece of information not set off with quotation marks must be in your own words. Otherwise, even though you name your source, you plagiarize by stealing the original phrasing.

The following passages illustrate the improper and proper use of source material.

Original Passage

One might contend, of course, that our country's biological diversity is so great and the land is so developed—so criss-crossed with the works of man—that it will soon be hard to build a dam anywhere without endangering some species. But as we develop a national inventory of endangered species, we certainly can plan our *necessary* development so as to exterminate the smallest number possible.

James L. Buckley, "Three Cheers for the Snail Darter,"
National Review, September 14, 1979: 1144–45. Print.

■ Plagiarism

Our country's biological diversity is so great and the land is so developed that it will soon be hard to build a dam anywhere without

> endangering some species. But as we develop a national inventory of endangered species, we certainly can plan our necessary development so as to exterminate the smallest number possible.

This writer clearly plagiarizes. The absence of Buckley's name and the failure to enclose his words in quotation marks create the impression that this passage is the student's own work.

■ Plagiarism

> Given the extensive diversity of species in America, development such as the construction of dams is likely to endanger some species, whether it is a rare plant, a species of frog, or a rare variety of fish. By creating a database of endangered species, however, we can facilitate a planning process that will place the minimum number of species at risk.

Although this writer uses original language, the absence of documentation suggests that these ideas are the student's without any recognition of Buckley's contribution. Despite the paraphrase, this is still plagiarism.

■ Plagiarism

> Our country's biological diversity is so great and the land so developed that in the near future we may pose a threat to some creature whenever we construct a dam. By developing a national inventory of endangered species, however, we can plan necessary development so as to preserve as many species as possible (Buckley 1144).

This version credits the ideas to Buckley, but the student has plagiarized by failing to put quotation marks around the phrasing (underlined here) that was copied from the original. As a result, readers will think that the passage represents the student's own wording.

■ Proper Use of Original

> America has so many kinds of plants and animals, and it is so built up, that in the near future we may pose a threat to some living thing just by damming some waterway. If, however, we knew which of our nation's plants and animals were threatened, we could use this information to preserve as many species as we can (Buckley 1144).

This student has identified the author and used her own words. As a result, no plagiarism occurs.

Plagiarism is a serious offense because it robs the original writer of recognition. Students caught plagiarizing risk failure in the course or perhaps suspension from school. Whenever you are unsure whether material requires documentation, supply a reference.

Integrating Sources

While the styles for documentation may vary, there are some principles you should follow. You should consistently seek to avoid plagiarism by indicating where you got information from even if you did not quote it. The following observations are related to the MLA format. You can signal the author before the information. For a more detailed account of summarizing and paraphrasing, see the section on note taking on pages 374–378.

Watch the Animation on Integrating Sources

> According to Steven Hawkings,.............. (75)

You may also place the source information after the information you got from the source by placing it in parentheses (Hawkings 75).

If you paraphrased a section, you must be careful you did not directly quote large sections of the sentence. You can document paraphrases similar to other information, but it is important to clearly indicate where the paraphrase ends. Sometimes it is useful to signal that you are paraphrasing.

> To paraphrase Mark Twain,........... (32)

You are likely to have quotations in your paper. Quotes are always documented. Shorter quotes, less than five lines are marked by quotation marks. You may start by signaling the author of the quote. John Mayer argues that: "........."46). Or you may place the identifying information directly after the quote........... (Mayer 46).

Longer quotes are indented (tens spaces for MLA and five for APA) without quotation marks. Again, you should provide the identifying source information. Refer to the appropriate chapter for the style you are using. Below is more detailed information on presenting quotes, using the MLA format for documentation and indentation.

▪ Short Quotation

> Ellen Goodman offers this further observation about writers who peddle formulas for achieving success through selfishness: "They are all Doctor Feelgoods, offering placebo prescriptions instead of strong medicine. They give us a way to live with ourselves, perhaps, but not a way to live with each other" (16).

▪ Quotation within Short Quotation

> The report further stated, "All great writing styles have their wellsprings in the personality of the writer. As Buffon said, 'The style is the man.'" (Duncan 49).

■ Quotation within Longer, Indented Quotation

Barbara Tuchman's *Proud Tower* presents a somewhat different view of the new conservative leaders:

> Besides riches, rank, broad acres, and ancient lineage, the new government also possessed, to the regret of the liberal opposition, and in the words of one of them, "an almost embarrassing wealth of talent and capacity." Secure in authority, resting comfortably on their electoral majority in the House of Commons and on a permanent majority in the House of Lords, of whom four-fifths were conservatives, they were in a position, admitted the same opponent, "of unassailable strength." (4)

Always provide some context for material that you quote. Various options exist. When you quote from a source for the first time, you might provide the author's full name and the source of the quotation, perhaps indicating the author's expertise as well. The passage just above omits the author's expertise; the passage below includes it.

> Writing in *Newsweek* magazine, Riena Gross, chief psychiatric social worker at Illinois Medical Center in Chicago, said, "Kids have no real sense that they belong anywhere or to anyone as they did ten or fifteen years ago. Parents have loosened the reins, and kids are kind of floundering" (74).

Or you might note the event prompting the quotation and then the author's name.

> Addressing a seminar at the University of Toronto, Dr. Joseph Pomeranz speculated that "acupuncture may work by activating a neural pain suppression mechanism in the brain" (324).

On other occasions, you might note only the author's full name and expertise.

> Economist Richard M. Cybert, president of Carnegie Mellon University, offers the following sad prediction about the steel industry's future: "It will never be as large an industry as it has been. There are a lot of plants that will never come back and many laborers that will never be rehired" (43).

After first citing an author's full name, use only the last name for subsequent references.

> In answering the objections of government agencies to the Freedom of Information Act, Wellford commented, "Increased citizen access

should help citizens learn of governmental activities that weaken
our First Amendment freedoms. Some administrative inconvenience
isn't too large a price to pay for that" (137).

When quoting from a source with no author given, introduce the quotation
with the name of the source.

Commenting on the problems that law enforcement personnel have
in coping with computer crime, *Credit and Financial Management*
magazine pointed out, "A computer crime can be committed in three
hundredths of a second, and the criminal can be thousands of miles
from the 'scene,' using a telephone" ("Computer Crime" 43).

*From the article "For Cops, Citizen Videos Bring Increased Scrutiny,"
summarize paragraphs 19–34, and create a paraphrase of paragraph
9. Assume the original source of USA Today online edition. Page A1.
Published 3/14/2011. Viewed 10/16/12.*

   *Indicate if each of the following statements used in a paper that
drew on a reading of "For Cops, Citizen Videos Bring Increased Scrutiny" is plagiarism or not and why.*

1. Almost phone includes a video camera, allowing almost anyone to capture any
   event, including crimes of any kind, including poor conduct by the police.
2. Video has helped to resolve many instances of police misbehavior, but such images
   also can present a more varied account of officer behavior (Johnson A1).
3. A video of a beating that a University Maryland student received from a police
   officer received more than 200,000 hits on YouTube.
4. There are police officers who are concerned that the possibility of being video
   recorded while conducting their duty might cause them to hesitate when they need
   to act (Johnson A1).
5. The police in a few states have tried "to limit such recordings when they believe
   those recordings interfere with police actions" (Johnson A1).
6. According to the training officer for the Sheriff's office in Broward County, "her
   agency knows firsthand the power of video and has learned from it."

CASE HISTORY Using his outline and thesis statement as
a guide, Keith prepared a first draft of his
paper, following the MLA format required by
his instructor. It didn't all come easily. In order to ensure an effective presentation, he checked his notes carefully to determine which material would
provide the strongest support for his conclusions. He was careful to use his

Continued on next page

Continued from previous page

own words except when he was quoting. To achieve smoothness, he tried to connect his major sections with transitions, aware that he could polish these connections when he revised the paper.

When he had completed the first draft, Keith set it aside for two days in order to distance himself from his writing. Then he returned to it and revised it carefully. Reading the paper from the perspective of a slightly skeptical critic, he looked for unsupported claims, questions that readers might have, sections that might be confusing or poorly organized, and weak transitions. Like most writers, Keith found sections that could be improved. Next, he revised his initial topic outline and followed it when drafting the sentence outline that appears on pages 410–411. Keith then prepared the final draft of the paper itself, which is on page 411. Direct your attention to its noteworthy features, which include italicized notations next to the paper indicating where Keith used the writing strategies discussed earlier in the text.

Preparing Your Finished Copy

Follow the revision guidelines in Chapter 4. In addition, verify that you have:

- included all key information
- clearly organized your material
- not overloaded your paper with quotations
- worked in your own observations
- put in-text documentation and source information in proper form.

Prepare your final draft with a word-processing program. Be sure you have access to a laser or inkjet printer that produces dark, readable copy. Double-space throughout, including indented block quotations and the list of works you used to prepare the paper.

Two systems for formatting and documenting library research papers are in common use: the Modern Language Association (MLA) system, favored by many English and humanities instructors, and the American Psychological Association (APA) system, used by many social science and psychology instructors.

Writing Your Research Paper Checklist

Search Checklist

- Brainstorm to focus your topic.
- Get an overview by searching general references such as encyclopedias.

- Search your library for books.
    Use either key term or subject searches using a computer
        catalog.
    Copy or print out the call number that locates the book.
    Scan the books in your located section for unexpected finds.
- Search your periodical indexes and databases.
    Select an index or database that fits your topic.
    InfoTrac and Wilson Select are often useful starting indexes.
    Use either key term or subject searches.
    Use the headings you find to narrow or guide your search.
    Print or copy the title of the articles, the author, the magazine, the
        volume number, the page number, and the date.
    If you use a full text of an online article, be sure to copy the reference
        information.
    Find the hard copy, microfiche, or microfilm version of your article.
- Search the Internet.
    Use an appropriate search engine, such as Google or Yahoo.
    Try several combinations of terms or modify them to narrow
        a search.
    Assess the credibility of all Internet sources based on the source for
        the site, author, quality of the web pages, consistency with other
        credible information.
    Be sure to copy or print the URL, author (if any), and title (if any).

Taking Notes Checklist

- Evaluate your source by author's qualification, publication's credibility,
  and obvious bias.
- Take notes using cards, yellow pad, or computer file.
    Keep track of source and page number for each note.
    You may want to cross-reference notes with bibliography cards.
    Give a title to each note card that identifies the notes topic.
- Respond as you take notes with your own thoughts and observations.
- Consciously decide to summarize, paraphrase, or quote in your notes.
    If you paraphrase, it must be completely in your own words.
    If you quote, be sure to mark your quotes so you don't forget.
- Always consciously work to avoid plagiarism.
    Always carefully record your sources for notes.
    Do not simply change a few words in a paraphrase.
    Do not forget to mark quotes when you quote.
    Ask your teacher or a tutor if you are not sure of the rules.

Drafting Your Paper Checklist

- Take steps to integrate your information.
    Read over your notes.
    Possibly write a brief draft without looking at your notes.

- Write an outline.
  - Determine the main divisions of your paper.
  - Read note cards for subdivisions.
  - Detail either a sentence or topic outline.
- Key your note cards to your outlines.
- Determine if you need to perform additional research.
- Draft your paper in sections.
  - Work to keep the paper in your own voice.
  - Don't get stuck on the introduction. Just write.
  - Use your notes to support your claims but don't just cut and paste.
  - Be sure to document as you write.
  - Avoid plagiarism.
  - Create deliberate transitions between sections.
  - Go back and rework the introduction and conclusion.
  - Carefully document using the material from the next chapter.

Revising Your Draft Checklist

- Do not be afraid to make extensive changes.
- Read and change the paper with an eye to your original purpose.
- Get feedback from other readers.
- Check for material that doesn't fit and needs to be cut.
- Check for holes that may require additional research and do it if needed.
- Check your notes to see that you didn't leave out something important.
- Check to see that the paper is easy to follow.
- Smooth your transitions and add transition paragraphs where needed.
- Make certain the draft is in a consistent voice.

Complete additional exercises and practice in your MyLab

Documenting Sources: MLA Style

In this chapter, you will learn how to:

21.1 Prepare papers using the MLA system.

21.2 Prepare bibliographic references using the MLA style.

21.3 Follow MLA style to cite sources in your essay.

21.4 Integrate and cite quotations using the MLA style.

In order to acknowledge and handle sources, you must know how to (1) prepare proper bibliographical references and (2) document sources within your text.

The kind of information included in bibliographical references depends on the type of source and the documentation system. Two most common systems are the Modern Language Association (MLA) system and the American Psychological Association (APA) system. There are other styles such as the Chicago Manual of Style that are used for other purposes. This chapter presents the MLA style. Chapter 22 presents the APA style. The MLA style is often used for papers in the humanities.

For more information, consult the *MLA Handbook for Writers of Research Papers,* 7th ed., 2009.

MLA System for Preparing Papers

- Number each page in the upper right corner, one-half inch from the top. Precede each page number with your last name.
- Starting one inch from the top of the first page, type your full name, the instructor's name, the course designation, and the date, all flush with the left margin.
- Double-space below the date, and center the title; then double-space before starting the first paragraph.
- Leave one-inch margins on all four sides except at the top of the first page. Indent the first line of each paragraph five spaces or one-half inch.
- The MLA system does not require a title page. If your instructor wants one, however, center (1) the title of the paper about two inches below the top

21.1

Prepare papers using the MLA system.

👁 Watch the Animation on **Formatting an MLA Paper**

of the sheet, (2) your name in the middle of the sheet, and (3) the instructor's name, course designation, and date about two inches from the bottom. Use capital and lowercase letters for everything. Repeat the title, again in capital and lowercase letters, on the first text page, centered about two inches from the top.

- Begin the bibliography on a new page that follows the text of the paper, and give it the heading "Works Cited," without quotation marks. Center the heading on the page.

- List each bibliographic entry alphabetically according to the author's last name or, if no author is given, by the first significant word in the title. For a work with more than one author, alphabetize by the name that comes first. If there's more than one entry for an author, substitute three unspaced hyphens, followed by a period and a double space, for the author's name in the second and subsequent entries.

- Begin the first line of each entry at the left margin and indent subsequent lines five spaces.

Preparing Proper MLA Bibliographic References

Books

21.2

Prepare bibliographic references using the MLA style.

◉ Watch the Animation on **Citing Sources Using the MLA Style**

■ A Book with One Author

Wilk, Max. *Every Day's a Matinée*. New York: Norton, 1975. Print.

■ A Book with Two Authors

Duncan, Dayton, and Ken Burns. *Lewis and Clark*. New York: Knopf, 1997. Print.

■ A Book with More than Three Authors

Alder, Roger William, et al. *Mechanisms in Organic Chemistry*. New York: Wiley, 1971. Print.

The MLA system permits the use of "et al." for four or more authors or editors. (Listing all authors is also permitted.)

■ A Book with a Title That Includes Another Title

Set off the title of the mentioned work with quotation marks.

Tanner, John. *Anxiety in Eden: A Kierkegaardian Reading of "Paradise Lost."* Oxford: Oxford UP, 1992. Print.

■ A Book with Corporate or Association Authorship

United Nations. Public Administration Div. *Local Government Training*. New York:
United Nations, 1968. Print.

■ An Edition Other than the First

Turabian, Kate L. *A Manual for Writers of Term Papers, Theses, and Dissertations.*
6th ed. Chicago: U of Chicago P, 1996. Print.

■ A Book in Two or More Volumes

Bartram, Henry C. *The Cavalcade of America*. 2 vols. New York: Knopf, 1959. Print.

■ A Reprint of an Older Work

Matthiessen, F. O. *American Renaissance: Art and Expression in the Age of
Emerson and Whitman*. 1941. New York: Oxford UP, 1970. Print.

■ A Book with an Editor Rather than an Author

Deetz, James, ed. *Man's Imprint from the Past: Readings in the Methods of Archaeology*. Boston: Little, 1971. Print.

■ A Book with Both an Author and an Editor

Melville, Herman. *The Confidence Man*. Ed. Hershel Parker. New York: Norton,
1971. Print.

■ A Translation

Beauvoir, Simone de. *All Said and Done*. Trans. Patrick O'Brian. New York:
Putnam, 1974. Print.

■ An Essay or Chapter in a Collection of Works by One Author

Woolf, Virginia. "The Lives of the Obscure." *The Common Reader, First Series.*
New York: Harcourt, 1925. 111–18. Print.

■ An Essay or Chapter in an Anthology

Angell, Roger. "On the Ball." *Subject and Strategy*. Ed. Paul Eschholz and Alfred
Rosa. New York: St. Martin's, 1981. 34–41. Print.

2 # REPRESENTATIONS OF THE POST/HUMAN

*Monsters, aliens and others
in popular culture*

1 ELAINE L. GRAHAM

Rutgers University Press **4**
3 New Brunswick, New Jersey

1 Author—last name first
2 Title in italics
3 City of publication followed by a colon
4 Publisher
5 Date of publication
6 Medium

First published in the United States 2002 by
Rutgers University Press, New Brunswick, New Jersey

First published in Great Britain 2002 by
Manchester University Press
Oxford Road, Manchester M13 9NR, UK
www.manchesteruniversitypress.co.uk

ISBN 0-8135-3058-X (cloth)
ISBN 0-8135-3059-8 (paperback)

British Cataloging-in-Publication information is
available from the British Library.

---

1 ——————— **2**
Graham, Elaine L. *Representations of the
Post/Human: Monsters, Aliens and Others
in Popular Culture.* New Brunswick: Rutgers
UP, 2002. Print. **3** **4**
4 **5**
6

---

6   **3**   **4**   **5**
18 SCIENCE FICTION STUDIES, VOLUME 33 (2006)

1 **Robert Harding**

2 **Manuel Castells's Technocultural Epoch in *The Information Age***

Manual Castells writes on economy and society in the age of postmodern capital in his sociological trilogy *The Information Age,* published in 1996-98. Aiming for a "grounded theory" (Kreisler 3)—a hybridized approach that synthesizes contemporary French thought with an American empirical tradition—Castells stresses that his work is based on direct observation rather than merely "playing with words" (Kreisler 3), an approach he associates with those who "deconstruct" and abstractly theorize. As he writes at the beginning of the second volume of the trilogy, *The Power of Identity:* "This is not a book about books" (2).

In this essay, I will trace the development of what Castells calls information society. My approach involves three overlapping tracks. First, I sketch what Castells calls network "flows"—of images, wealth, and power—in global information technology. Second, I evaluate social changes arising out of the network society and how they redefine identity in both global and local contexts. Finally, I read selected science fiction texts with a view to remarking on fictional parallels with Castells's theses on informationalism.

Castells is known for his cross-cultural approach, fusing research into the information-technology revolution in the San Francisco Bay area with quantitative and qualitative data drawn from Europe, Latin America, and the Asian-Pacific Rim. In Volume 1 of *The Information Age, The Rise of Network Society,* Castells demonstrates that an information-based future will materialize in the form of a new kind of urban space: the "new global economy and the emerging informational society have indeed a new spatial form, which develops in a variety of social and geographical contexts: megacities" (*Rise*434). He then outlines how future urban development will assume new levels of power and influence: "mega-cities articulate the global economy, link up the informational networks, and concentrate the world's power" (*Rise*434). Castells projects this mode of development by detailing a Chinese example, the emerging "Hong Kong—Shenzen—Canton—Peral River Delta—Macau—Zhuhai metropolitan regional system" (*Rise*436), which constitutes a massive transformation of the social world for global marketing and informational purposes.

Like sociologist Max Weber, Castells seeks to define the spirit of the age. Where Weber studied the animating force of the industrial age in the Protestant work ethic, Castells sees the ethos of the information age in the *network.* In his essay "The New Weber," Chris Freeman writes that Castells "characterises the 'informational society' as essentially a capitalist system" (156). As Castells himself puts it:

1   Author—last name first
2   Title of article in quotation marks with period inside quotation marks
3   Title of journal in italics
4   Volume number
5   Date of publication
6   First page number
7   Final page number on final page of article
8   Medium

1   **2**
Harding, Robert. "Manuel Castells's Technocultural Epoch in *The
Information Age*." Science Fiction Studies 33 (2006): 18-38 Print.
2   **3**   **4** **5** **6** **7** **8**

What Was Jim Crow?

Jim Crow FERRIS STATE UNIVERSITY
MUSEUM OF RACIST MEMORABILIA

What Was Jim Crow?

Many Blacks resisted the indignities of Jim Crow, and, far too often, they paid for their bravery with their lives.

1

© Dr. David Pilgrim, Professor of Sociology
Ferris State University
Sept., 2000 **4**

[1]Kennedy, Stetson. Jim Crow Guide: The Way It Was. Boca Raton: Florida Atlantic University Press, 1959/1990, pp.216–117.

[2]This list was derived from a larger list composed by the Martin Luther King, Jr., National Historic Site Interpretive Staff

6

http://www.ferris.edu/jimcrow/what.htm

1   Author—last name first
2   Title of article in quotation marks
3   Periodical or source location
4   Date the article was published
5   Page numbers of the article
6   Medium
7   Date it was retrieved

1   **2**   **3**
Pilgrim, David. "What Was Jim Crow?" *Jim Crow Museum
of Racist Memorabilia.* Sept. 2000: 1-8. 20 Mar. 2006.
4 Web. 9.
6   **4**   **5**   **7**

Periodicals

Periodicals include newspapers, popular magazines, and specialized occupational and scholarly journals. The basic information for a periodical article includes the name of the article's author, name of the periodical, title of the article, date of publication, page range of the entire article, and, for scholarly journals, the volume number of the periodical. The MLA system capitalizes periodical titles; however, the MLA style omits an introductory *The* from these titles.

■ An Article in a Scholarly Journal Consecutively Paged through
the Entire Volume

Pfennig, David. "Kinship and Cannibalism." *Bioscience* 47 (1997): 667–75. Print.

■ An Article in a Scholarly Journal That Pages Each Issue Separately

Block, Joel W. "Sodom and Gomorrah: A Volcanic Disaster." *Journal of Geological
Education* 23.5 (1976): 74–77. Print.

■ An Unsigned Article in a Scholarly Journal

"Baby, It's Cold Inside." *Science* 276 (1997): 537–38. Print.

■ A Signed Article in an Occupational or Popular Magazine

Gopnik, Adam. "The Good Soldier." *New Yorker* 24 Nov. 1997: 106–14. Print.

■ An Unsigned Article in an Occupational or Popular Magazine

"Robot Productivity." *Production Engineering* May 1982: 52–55. Print.

■ A Signed Article in a Daily Newspaper

Wade, Nicholas. "Germ Weapons: Deadly but Hard to Use." *New York Times*
26 Nov. 1997, natl. ed.: A13+. Print.

■ An Unsigned Article in a Daily Newspaper

"The Arithmetic of Terrorism." *Washington Post* 14 Nov. 1997: A26. Print.

Encyclopedia Articles

When documenting familiar works, such as the *Encyclopedia Americana*, the basic information for the MLA system includes the name of the article's author if known, the title of the article, the name of the encyclopedia, and the date of the edition.

Sobieszek, Robert A. "Photography." *World Book Encyclopedia*. 1991 ed. Print.

The MLA system requires additional information when less familiar publications are documented.

Fears, J. Rufus. "Emperor's Cult." *Encyclopedia of Religion*. Ed. Mircea Eliade. 16 vols. New York: Macmillan, 1987. Print.

For an anonymous article, references begin with the article's title.

Government Documents

The basic information for a federal, state, or foreign government publication includes the name of the author; title of the publication; name of the government and agency issuing the publication; place of publication; name of the printing group, if known; and date. If no author is named, begin by identifying the government and then cite the government agency as the author.

Carpenter, Russell D. *Defects in Hardened Timber*. United States. Dept. of Agriculture, Forest Service. Washington: GPO, 1989. Print.

United States. Environmental Protection Agency, Consumer Products Safety Commission. *Asbestos in the Home*. Washington: GPO, 1989. Print.

United States. Cong. Office of Technology Assessment. *The Biology of Mental Disorders*. 102nd Cong., 2nd sess. Washington: GPO, 1992. Print.

Other Sources

■ Book Reviews

Koenig, Rhoda. "Billy the Kid." Rev. of *Billy Bathgate*, by E. L. Doctorow. *New York* 20 Feb. 1989: 20–21. Print.

If the review is untitled, follow the above format but omit the missing element.

■ Published Interviews

Noriega, Manuel. "A Talk with Manuel Noriega." By Felipe Hernandez. *News Report* 20 Mar. 1997: 28–30. Print.

■ Personal Interviews

If you conducted the interview yourself, start with the name of the person interviewed and follow it with the kind of interview and the date conducted.

Newman, Paul. Personal interview. 18 May 2001.

■ Audiovisual Media

Frankenstein. Dir. James Whale. Perf. Boris Karloff, John Boles, Colin Clive, and
Mae Clarke. Universal, 1931. Film.

If you are interested in the contribution of a particular person, start with that
person's name. Use the same model for videocassette and DVD recordings, and
add release dates and distributors.

Whale, James, dir. *Frankenstein*. Perf. Boris Karloff, John Boles, Colin Clive, and
Mae Clarke. Universal, 1931. Film.

Whale, James, dir. *Frankenstein*. Perf. Boris Karloff, John Boles, Colin Clive, and
Mae Clarke. 1931. DVD. Universal, 1999. DVD.

■ Television and Radio Programs

Washington Week in Review. Prod. S. Ducat. PBS. WKAR, East Lansing. 6 Jan. 1995.
Television.

Use the following format when additional information is pertinent:

Peril at End House. By Agatha Christie. Adapt. Clive Exton. Dir. Renny Rye. Prod.
Brian Eastman. Perf. David Suchet and Hugh Fraser. Mystery. Introd. Diana
Rigg. PBS. WKAR, East Lansing. 12 Aug. 1993. Television.

■ Music and Sound Recordings

Smith, Bessie. *The World's Greatest Blues Singer*. Columbia, 1948. LP.

Smith, Bessie. "Down Hearted Blues." *The World's Greatest Blues Singer*. Columbia, 1948. LP.

■ CD-ROMs

Norman, J. L. "Barcelona." *Software Toolworks Multimedia Encyclopedia*. Disc 1.
Danbury: Grolier, 1996. CD.

Online Sources

Often data from the Internet are incomplete, perhaps lacking an author, a title,
or page or paragraph number. Include all the available information, but omit
the correct address.

■ Books

The basic information for a book includes the name of the author, if known; title of the book; place and date of original publication, if applicable; electronic site, if named; date of electronic publication if the online version has never been published in print or if it is part of a scholarly project; sponsor of the site; medium by which it was retrieved; and the date the material was retrieved.

Chaney, Walter J., William J. Diehm, and Frank Seeley. *The Second 50 Years: A Reference Manual for Senior Citizens*. Weed: London Circle, 1999. Web. 8 Aug. 2000.

Locke, John. *An Essay concerning Human Understanding*. London, 1690. Inst. of Learning Technologies, 1995. Columbia U. Web. 24 June 2000.

■ Periodicals on the World Wide Web

Periodicals online include specialized occupational and scholarly journals, popular magazines, newspapers, and newsletters. The basic information for a periodical includes the author's name, if known; the title of the article; the title of the periodical; the volume and issue numbers, if applicable; the date the article was published; the article's page numbers (or *n. pag.* if none are given); the medium of the material; the date the material was retrieved; and the online address only when necessary to find the material.

Cervetti, Nancy. "In the Breeches, Petticoats, and Pleasures of Orlando." *Journal of Modern Literature* 20.2 (1996): n. pag. Web. 8 Jan. 1998.

Navarro, Mireya. "Women in Sports Cultivating New Playing Fields." *New York Times on the Web* 13 Feb. 2001. Web. 22 Feb. 2001.

"No Link Found in Violence, Videos." *Boston Globe Online* 8 Aug. 2000. Web. 27 Aug. 2000.

Oakes, Jeannie. "Promotion or Retention: Which One Is Social?" *Harvard Education Letter* Jan.–Feb. 1999: n. pag. Web. 8 Aug. 2000.

■ Periodicals Accessed through an Online Library
  Service or Large Network Provider

Full-text articles are available online at libraries or at home through services such as LexisNexis, ProQuest Direct, and America Online. Cite the author's name, if known; the title of the article; the title of the periodical; the date the article was published; the page numbers for the article (if the service identifies only the initial page of the article, indicate the page followed by a plus sign, 132+; if no page is given, use *n. pag.*); the name of the database or web site in italics; *Web* as the medium of publication; and the date the material was accessed.

Clemetson, Lynette. "A Ticket to Private School." *Newsweek* 27 Mar. 2000: n. pag.

LexisNexis. Web. 5 May 2000.

Mayo Clinic. "Lung Cancer." 21 Feb. 2000. *America Online*. Web. 10 June 2000.

■ Encyclopedia Articles

The basic information for an encyclopedia article accessed through the web includes the author's name, if known; title of the article; name of the encyclopedia; date of the edition; vendor; medium of publication; and date of access.

Daniel, Ralph Thomas. "The History of Western Music." *Britannica Online: Macro-*

paedia. Encyclopaedia Britannica, 1995. Web. 14 June 1995.

■ Government Documents

The basic information for a government document includes the name of the author, if known; the title; the name of the government and agency issuing the document; the place of publication and printing group, if known; the date of publication; the medium of publication; the date the material was retrieved; and the online address only if necessary to find the material. If no author is given, begin by identifying the government and then give the government agency as the author.

Georgia State. Probation Div. of the Georgia Dept. of Corrections. *Alternatives to*

Incarceration. 1 July 1997. Web. 3 Feb. 1998.

■ Personal Home Page

The basic information for a personal home page includes the name of its originator, if known; the title of the site, if any (use *Home page* or other such description if no title is given); the date of the latest update, if given; the medium of publication; and the date the material was retrieved from the site.

Lanthrop, Olin. Home page. Web. 24 June 2000.

■ Newsgroups, Electronic Mailing Lists, and E-Mail

MLA gives guidelines for including newsgroups, electronic mailing lists (sometimes called Listservs), and e-mail within the Works Cited list.

Corelli, Aldo. "Colleges and Diversity." Dept. of English, U of Michigan,

20 Apr. 2003. Web. 25 Apr. 2003.

Nicholson, Brad. "Casino Gambling." Message to Jason Elridge. 2 Feb. 2001.

E-mail.

EXERCISE

1. **Using the MLA system, write a proper reference for each of the unstyled information sets that follow:**

   a. A book titled Gas Conditioning Fact Book. The book was published in 1962 by Dow Chemical Company in Midland, Michigan. No author is named.

   b. An unsigned article titled Booze Plays a Big Role in Car Crashes. The article was published in the November 28, 1997, state edition of the Detroit News. It appears on page 2 of section C.

   c. An essay written by C. Wright Mills and titled The Competitive Personality. The essay appeared in a collection of Mills's writings titled Power, Politics, and People. The collection was published in 1963 by Ballantine Books in New York. The book is edited and introduced by Irving Louis Horowitz. The essay appears on pages 263 through 273.

   d. An unsigned article titled Global Warming Fears on Rise. The article was published in the October 25, 1997, issue of Newswatch magazine. It appears on pages 29 to 31.

   e. A book written by Paul Theroux and titled The Kingdom by the Sea. The book was published in 1983 by the Houghton Mifflin Company in Boston.

   f. A book written by Kate Chopin and titled The Awakening. The book, edited by Margaret Culley, was published in 1976 by W. W. Norton and Company in New York.

   g. An article written by James E. Cooke and titled Alexander Hamilton. The article appears on pages 31 and 32 of the World Book Encyclopedia, Volume 9, published in 1996.

   h. An article written by Sarah McBride and titled Young Deadbeats Pose Problems for Credit-Card Issuers. The article was published in the November 28, 1997, Midwest edition of the Wall Street Journal. It appears on pages 1 and 6 of section B.

   i. A book written by Magdalena Dabrowski and Rudolph Leopold and titled Egon Schiele. The book was published in 1997 by the Yale University Press in New Haven, Connecticut.

   j. A book written by Jean Descola and titled A History of Spain. The book, translated by Elaine P. Halperin, was published in 1962 by Alfred A. Knopf in New York.

   k. An article written by John T. Flanagan and Raymond L. Grimer and titled Mexico in American Fiction to 1850. The article was published in 1940 in a journal called Hispania. It appears on pages 307 through 318. The volume number is 23.

   l. A United States government document titled Marine Fisheries Review. It was published by the National Marine Fisheries Service of the U.S. Department of Commerce in 1993 and is available from the Government Printing Office. No author is given.

   m. A book written by David Kahn and titled The Codebreakers. The second edition of the book was published in 1996 by Scribner's in New York.

   n. A book written by Joseph Blotner and titled Faulkner: A Biography. The book was published in two volumes in 1974 by Random House in New York.

   o. An article written by Calvin Tompkins and titled The Importance of Being Elitist. The article was published in the November 24, 1997, issue of the New Yorker. It appears on pages 58 through 69.

   p. A book written by Thomas Beer and titled Stephen Crane: A Study in American Letters. The book was published in 1923 and reprinted in 1972 by Octagon Books in New York.

q. A review of a book written by Jacques Barzun and titled The Culture We Deserve. The review, by Beth Winona, appeared in the March 1989 issue of American Issues magazine and was titled Barzun and Culture. It appeared on pages 46 through 50.

r. An interview of playwright Neil Simon. The interview was titled Neil Simon on the New York Theater and appeared in the September 3, 1997, issue of the Long Island News, on pages C4 and C5. The interviewer was Pearl Barnes.

s. A film titled Casablanca. The film was directed by Michael Curtiz and starred Humphrey Bogart, Ingrid Bergman, Claude Rains, and Paul Henreid. It was released in 1942 by Warner Brothers.

t. A television program titled Grizzly. It appeared on WNTR, New York, on February 3, 1997. The station is part of the CBS network.

u. An online article with no author titled Robert Frost: A Reader Response Perspective. The article appears on the online journal Off the Wall and had a location of http://www.offthewall.com/articles/backdated_bin_RobertFrost_ archive.html>. The article is listed with the date May 8, 2003, but you found it on January 4, 2004.

v. An article written by May Gottchalk and titled Reconsidering Dyslexia that you accessed through a database. The article was published in the May 24, 2002, issue of Education Matters, and you retrieved the article using Wilson Select on November 22, 2003, on the Ferris State University Library Web Database Access with the address http://library.ferris.edu/databaseframes.html.

w. A personal page by Randy Cordial titled My Best Science Fiction Movies Ever. You found the web page on May 4, 2004, at http://www.cordial.com/bestscifi.htm.

2. **Prepare a proper MLA reference for each of the works you plan to use in writing your paper.**

3. **Prepare an annotated bibliography, explained on page 369, using MLA style for each of the works you have reviewed for your paper.**

Handling In-Text Citations

The MLA system uses notations that appear within the text and are set off by parentheses. The citation consists of the last name of the author and the page number of the publication in which the material originally appeared.

21.3

Follow MLA style to cite sources in your essay.

Basic Citation Form

■ Bibliographic Reference

Rothenberg, Randall. "Life in Cyburbia." *Esquire* Feb. 1996: 56–63. Print.

■ Passage and Citation

A mania for the Internet has invaded . . . our poorest children have a stake in the Internet (Rothenberg 59).

Rothenberg states that a mania for the Internet . . . have a stake in the Internet (59).

■ Bibliographic Reference

Weider, Benjamin, and David Hapgood. *The Murder of Napoleon*. New York:
    Congdon, 1982. Print.

■ Passage and Citation

Four different autopsy reports were filed. . . . Nevertheless, cancer has become
accepted as the cause (Weider and Hapgood 72).

If a source has more than three authors use "et al.," meaning "and others," for all
but the first-named one.

■ Bibliographic Reference

Baugh, Albert C., et al. *A Literary History of England*. New York: Appleton, 1948. Print.

■ Passage and Citation

Although no one knows . . . writing plays together (Baugh et al. 573).

Authors with the Same Last Name

If your citations include authors with the same last name, use the initials of their
first names to distinguish them.

■ Bibliographic Reference

Adler, Jerry. "Search for an Orange Thread." *Newsweek* 16 June 1980: 32–34. Print.

Adler, William L. "The Agent Orange Controversy." *Detroit Free Press* 18 Dec. 1979,
    state ed.: B2. Print.

■ Passage and Citation

As early as 1966, government . . . miscarriages, liver abscesses, and nerve damage
(J. Adler 32).

Separate Works by the Same Author

If your references include two or more works by the same author, add shortened
forms of the titles to your in-text citation. Put shortened book titles in italics, and
use quotation marks around article and essay titles.

■ Bibliographic Reference

Mullin, Dennis. "After U.S. Troops Pull Out of Grenada." *US News & World Report*
    14 Nov. 1983: 22–25. Print.

- - -. "Why the Surprise Move in Grenada—and What Next." *US News & World
Report* 7 Nov. 1983: 31–34. Print.

■ Passage and Citation

As the rangers evacuated students,...and free the governor (Mullin, "Why the
Surprise" 33).

Two Sources for the Same Citations

If two sources provide essentially the same information and you wish to mention
both in one parenthetical citation, alphabetize them according to their authors'
last names, list them with a semicolon between them, and position the citation
as you would any other citation. Citations in MLA style do not need to be listed
alphabetically.

■ Bibliographic Reference

Bryce, Bonnie. "The Controversy over Funding Community Colleges." *Detroit Free
Press* 13 Nov. 1988, state ed.: A4. Print.

Warshow, Harry. "Community College Funding Hits a Snag." *Grand Rapids Press*
15 Nov. 1988, city ed.: A2. Print.

■ Passage and Citation

In contending that a 3% reduction in state funding,...enrollment was expected to
jump by 15% during the next year (Warshow A2; Bryce A4).

Unsigned References

When you use a source for which no author is given, the in-text citation consists
of all or part of the title, and the appropriate page numbers.

■ Bibliographic Reference

"Money and Classes." *Progressive* Oct. 1997: 10. Print.

■ Passage and Citation

According to the General Accounting Office, repairing...many billions more
("Money and Classes" 10).

21.4

Integrate and cite quotations using the MLA style.

👁 Watch the Video in **Citing Quotations**

Citing Quotations

Set off quotations fewer than five lines long with quotation marks and run them into the text of the paper. For longer quotes, omit the quotation marks and indent the material ten spaces from the left margin. Double-space the typing. If you quote part or all of one paragraph, don't further indent the first line. If you quote two or more consecutive paragraphs, indent each one's first line three additional spaces. Use single quotation marks for a quotation within a shorter quotation and double marks for a quotation within a longer, indented quotation. There are more detailed examples in Chapter 20. When the quotation is run into the text, position the citation as shown in the following examples.

■ Bibliographic Reference

Schapiro, Mark. "Children of a Lesser God." *Harper's Bazaar* Apr. 1996: 205+. Print.

■ Passage and Citation

UN investigators who have studied the extent of child labor in Third World countries estimate that "as many as 200 million children go to work rather than to school . . . making everything from clothing and shoes to handbags and carpets" (Schapiro 205).

With longer, indented quotations, skip one space after the end punctuation and type the reference in parentheses.

■ Bibliographic Reference

Newhouse, John. "The Diplomatic Round: A Freemasonry of Terrorism."
　　New Yorker 8 July 1985: 46–63. Print.

■ Passage and Citation

One commentator offers this assessment of why foreign terrorist groups don't operate in this country:

> The reason that America has been spared so far, apparently, is that it is less vulnerable than Europe, especially to Middle Eastern extremists. Moving in and out of most European countries isn't difficult for non-Europeans; border controls are negligible. But American customs and immigration authorities, being hyper-alert to drug traffic, tend to pay attention to even marginally doubtful people, and a would-be terrorist . . . could come under surveillance for the wrong reason. (Newhouse 63)

Indirect Citations

In MLA style, if you use a quotation from person A that you obtained from a book or article written by person B, or you paraphrase such a quotation, put "qtd. in" before the name of the publication's author in the parenthetical reference.

■ Bibliographic Reference

Klein, Joe. "Ready for Rudy." *New York* 6 Mar. 1989: 30–37. Print.

■ Passage and Citation

Rudolph Giuliani favors the death penalty for "the murder of a law-enforcement officer, mass murder, a particularly heinous killing" but would impose it only "when there is certainty of guilt well beyond a reasonable doubt" (qtd. in Klein 37).

Authors Identified in Text

Sometimes you'll want to introduce a paraphrase, summary, or quotation with the name of its author. In this case, the page number may be positioned immediately after the name or follow the material cited.

■ Bibliographic Reference

Jacoby, Susan. "Waiting for the End: On Nursing Homes." *New York Times Magazine* 31 Mar. 1974, city ed.: 80+. Print.

■ Passage and Citation

Susan Jacoby (80) sums up the grim outlook of patients in bad nursing homes by noting that they are merely waiting to die.

Susan Jacoby sums up the grim outlook of patients in bad nursing homes by noting that they are merely waiting to die (80).

EXERCISE

1. *Using the MLA system, write a proper in-text citation for exercise 1 on pages 404–405. The type of information (info only or quote) and page number in the original source are provided: a (info p. 222), and c (a quote p. 271), and g (info p. 31), i (info only p. 221), o (a partial quote on page 60, also use same author published a different year).*
   Assume that you have not used the author's name to introduce the material you cite. Where there are multiple pages in the reference, you can select the page or pages appropriate to your citation.
2. Using the MLA system, write a proper in-text citation for each of the bibliographic references you prepared for part 2 on page 405. Assume that you have not used the author's name to introduce the material you cite. Where there are multiple pages in the reference, you can select the page or pages appropriate to your citation.

SAMPLE

MLA STUDENT RESEARCH PAPER

Sentence Outline

Thesis statement: House arrest offers a choice of several monitoring systems, presents no insurmountable problems, proves effective in controlling low-risk offenders, and costs less than incarceration.

Sentence outline: Note use of complete sentences throughout, use of periods following section and subsection markers, and the indentation arrangement.

I. The use of house arrest stems from the country's serious crime problem.
   A. Violent crimes are committed by a small number of repeat offenders.
   B. These crimes have led to tougher crime-control legislation.
   C. This legislation has increased the country's prison population and the cost of incarceration.
   D. As a result, many jurisdictions have adopted house-arrest programs for low-risk offenders.

II. Electronic monitoring has a short history.
   A. The idea first appeared in the comic *Spiderman*.
   B. A New Mexico judge asked computer companies to develop an electronic bracelet.
   C. Monitoring was first used in 1984 to control offenders, and the concept quickly spread across the country.

III. Electronic monitoring devices fall into three categories.
   A. A programmed-contact system calls the offender's home during curfew periods and reports absences.
      1. A computer may simply record the offender's voice.
      2. A computer may compare the voice heard over the phone to a recording of the offender's voice.
      3. The offender may wear an encoded bracelet and insert it into a special telephone transmitter.
      4. A camera may transmit photos of the offender over telephone lines.
   B. A continuous-signal system requires the offender to wear a transmitter that sends uninterrupted electronic signals.

C. A hybrid system combines programmed-contact and continuous-signal techniques.

    1. The programmed-contact component usually includes voice- and photo-transmission units.

    2. Jurisdictions can tailor systems to their needs.

IV. Electronic systems have created practical and legal problems.

A. Practical problems include both difficulties experienced by offenders and transmission difficulties.

    1. Encoded bracelets can cause offenders discomfort and embarrassment.

    2. Telephone lines and objects in the offender's home can interfere with signal pickup.

B. Legal problems include possible constitutional infringements and the net-widening effect.

    1. Charging surveillance fees and limiting surveillance to the least dangerous persons may infringe on offenders' equal-protection rights.

    2. Monitoring may violate the right to privacy of others in offenders' homes.

    3. Net-widening can result in an excessive number of individuals under house arrest.

V. Electronic monitoring has proved effective with low-risk offenders.

A. The great majority of offenders successfully complete monitoring programs.

B. Monitoring costs less than incarceration.

VI. The advantages of house arrest should increase its use.

MLA

1"

1/2"

Jacque 1

Keith Jacque

Professor Reinking

English 250

May 4, 2001

House Arrest: An Attractive Alternative to Incarceration

Few of us would deny that crime is a serious national problem. Almost daily, newspapers and television screens offer accounts of "white-collar crimes" such as embezzlement and tax evasion and violent crimes such as aggravated assault, rape, and murder. Unlike nonviolent crimes, most violent ones are committed by chronic offenders. As former U.S. Attorney General William Barr notes, "Study after study shows that there is a tiny fraction of the population who...commit a disproportionate amount—a vast amount—of predatory violence in our society."

These violent crimes have hardened society's attitude toward criminals and brought about a demand for "get-tough" policies in dealing with all kinds of offenses. The result has been federal legislation like the Crime Control Act of 1984 and the Anti-Drug Abuse Act of 1986. The first of these makes incarceration mandatory for certain habitual offenders; the second does the same for persons convicted of specified drug offenses (U.S., Senate 12). The introduction of mandatory sentencing guidelines, now common on the state as well as the federal level, provides consistent punishment for similar crimes. It has led, however, to an explosion in the number of prison inmates, which by mid-1999 totaled over 1.8 million, including a 4.4 percent increase between mid-1997 and mid-1998 (Gearan). Between 1980 and 1995, the nation's prison population grew 242 percent ("Inmate Populations" 10). Many of these inmates are guilty of nonviolent offenses. In 1997, three-fourths of all prisoners fell into the nonviolent category (Richey).

It is likely that the prison population will continue to grow. The National Council on Crime and Delinquency has estimated

1"

1"

1"

that the total number of prisoners might reach 1.4 million by the year 2000, a jump of 24 percent over the 1995 level ("Inmate Populations" 10). The Bureau of Prisons has projected construction costs of some four billion dollars for new federal prisons scheduled to open in the 1996–2006 decade and between ten billion and fourteen billion dollars for the new state prisons required to house the anticipated increase in prisoners (10).

No author, so abbreviated title and page number

Offers credible source with additional support on cost. Same source as previous, so only page number

Even these figures don't tell the whole story. Director of the Federal Bureau of Prisons J. Michael Quinlan comments that over the lifetime of a prison, "construction costs are only 5–7 percent of the total expense. This means that from 15–20 times the construction costs will have to be budgeted over the life of each prison now being built" (114). Underestimating operating costs can result in unused facilities as in Florida, where in 1992, two newly constructed 900-person prisons and a 336-person death-row facility remained empty because the state lacked the money to operate them (Katel).

Introduces source of quotation first and employs quote for credibility and impact

Provides paraphrase and source

Overcrowding and the high costs of prisons have seriously undermined state spending on public services and created a number of hidden expenses. In Michigan, for example, corrections spending increased over 300 percent between 1979 and 1989, as compared to a 98 percent increase in social services spending and a 40 percent increase in education spending (Baird 122). And these figures do not include hidden costs such as welfare payments to the families of imprisoned offenders and the loss of tax revenues from prisoners removed from the job market (Lynch).

Identifies transition to next main point of paper

Employs data from source and documents with last name and page

Adds additional implications. Documented without a page since web source that is without page numbers

Faced with the social and educational consequences of current policy, many state legislators have recommended using prison space only for violent offenders and developing, for non-violent ones, low-cost alternatives that provide adequate public protection. At times, results have been mixed. In the early 1980s, for example, the state of Georgia attempted to relieve severe prison overcrowding by greatly expanding the use of closely supervised probation. While significant cost savings were realized, tremendous work overloads on the probation staff resulted, according to the Georgia Probation Division.

Clearly signals transition to next major section

Offers qualification, indicating practice that was mixed in its success

MLA

House arrest—a strategy that confines nonviolent offenders to their homes and monitors their compliance with electronic devices—avoids the drawbacks of other approaches. It offers a choice of several monitoring systems, presents no insurmountable problems, is effective in controlling low-risk offenders, and costs less than incarceration.

Electronic monitoring (sometimes called electronic tethering, electronic surveillance, electronic house arrest, or electronic incarceration) has curious roots—the comic *Spider-Man*. The idea first occurred in 1979 to New Mexico Judge Jack Love, who observed that Kingpin, Spider-Man's nemesis, used an electronic bracelet to control his crime-fighter enemy. Love asked computer companies to develop a similar device (Scaglione, "Jails" 32; Sullivan). The first house-arrest program using electronic monitoring was implemented in 1984, and five years later, programs had been established in over a hundred jurisdictions across more than thirty states (Peck 26; Scaglione, "You're Under Arrest" 26). By 1993, the number of offenders being electronically monitored totaled 65,650 nationwide (Carey and McLean).

The U.S. Department of Justice classifies electronic monitoring systems according to their signaling characteristics (1). Types include programmed contact, continuous signal, and hybrid systems—a combination of the first two.

With a programmed-contact system, a computer calls an offender's residence on a random basis during established curfew periods and reports any unauthorized absence to correctional authorities. Various levels of sophistication are possible, depending on how much certainty is desired. In the simplest system, the computer merely records the offender's voice. Correctional authorities then review the taped responses the next day to determine any curfew violations. A variant approach uses a prerecording of the offender's voice, which the computer compares to the voice heard during random calls. If the two do not match, the computer can immediately notify authorities of a violation. Voice systems are comparatively inexpensive as no special equipment needs to be installed in the offender's home or worn by the individual (Hofer and Meierhoefer 36–37).

Jacque 4

A more sophisticated means of checking on offenders makes use of an encoded bracelet worn by the offender. Again, a computer calls randomly during curfew. Instead of answering in the usual manner, however, the offender responds by inserting the bracelet into a special transmitter attached to the telephone. The bracelets can be made in such a way that unauthorized attempts to remove them will damage their transmitting ability (Hofer and Meierhoefer 36–37).

Visual verification probably offers the best assurance against curfew violation. A special camera that can transmit photographs over telephone lines is installed in the offender's home. During calls, the computer can request the monitored individual to provide a variety of poses to the camera. These photographs can then be stored in the computer for later review or compared immediately to a reference key for the individual (Hofer and Meierhoefer 37).

Continuous-signal systems, unlike programmed-contact systems, require the offender to wear a transmitter that sends a continuous sequence of electronic signals, often several times a minute, to his or her home telephone. If a break in transmission occurs during a detention period, the monitoring computer notifies authorities. The transmitters are relatively small and generally worn on a tamper-resistant strap around the ankle. Attempts to remove the strap could cause the unit to stop sending signals or could be detected during periodic inspections. These systems provide a greater degree of supervision than programmed-contact systems, which check on offenders only intermittently (Hofer and Meierhoefer 38–39).

Hybrid systems combine programmed-contact and continuous-signal techniques in order to realize the advantages of each (U.S. Dept. of Justice 1). Typically, the programmed-contact component includes both voice and video units. This component can function as a backup for continuous-signal monitoring or as a supplement to it. In the first case, the computer is programmed to call for voice-video identification whenever the offender's transmitter fails to send a continuous signal. In the second case, the computer randomly calls for voice-video verification as well as receives transmitter signals (Scaglione, "Jails" 36).

MLA

Transition

Defines by explaining process

Offers comparison to first mentioned strategy

Transition and brief comparison claim

Defines by process

MLA

Offers transition to
discuss options

Jurisdictions can develop hybrid systems tailored to their individual needs. For example, a house-arrest program for drunk drivers could employ a continuous-signal transmitter supplemented by random telephone verification. Home monitoring equipment could even include a Breathalyzer to determine and transmit to the computer the offender's blood-alcohol level during telephone verification calls (Scaglione, "Jails" 36). A variation of this type of system is used in Annapolis, Maryland, where video cameras have been installed in the homes of some convicted drunk drivers. The offenders are called periodically and required to give themselves a blood-alcohol test in front of the camera (Peck 28).

Transition to next
major section

Identifies problem as
effects and answers
each problem

Not surprisingly, electronic monitoring has resulted in some practical problems and legal concerns. Most problems arise with those who wear encoded verification bracelets or transmitters. These offenders complain that the devices cause physical discomfort or embarrassment. Correction officials can adjust the fit of the device or suggest that offenders wear a cut-off tube sock, tennis-type wrist band, or other type of padding under the strap. Wearers, however, must find their own ways of coping with embarrassment. In studying the electronic monitoring of federal parolees, Beck, Klein-Saffran, and Wooten found that offenders could be quite innovative in explaining why they were wearing units. When questioned by strangers, "the majority told the truth, while other parolees stated that [the unit] was a heart monitor, pager, battery charger for a video camera, or a fish caller" (29).

Transition

Transmitting difficulties have created other practical problems. In some areas, existing telephone lines may be inadequate or incompatible with the transmitting characteristics of certain monitoring systems. In other cases, the offender's home may cause difficulties. Ford and Schmidt, who conducted research for the National Institute of Justice, point out that

Longer quote, so
indented 10 spaces
with first line indented
3 spaces, consistent
with MLA

> The typical room has dead space in which the receiver cannot pick up the transmitter's signal. In particular, metal tends to limit the range of the transmitter; kitchens are therefore an especially difficult environment.

Jacque 6

Transmission breaks have also been attributed to metal furniture, faulty wiring, other electronic devices, bathroom fixtures, waterbeds, and even certain sleeping positions. Mobile homes constitute a problem for offenders trying to do yard chores: The range outside the building is as little as ten feet, as compared to as much as 200 feet from a mainframe building. (3)

Other researchers have noted similar interference problems. In one situation, authorities suspected noncompliance when they discovered breaks in an offender's continuous signal transmissions. These breaks always occurred during the same time period and only on Sundays. Investigation revealed that a large rock and metal coffee table was blocking the signal from the transmitter on the offender's ankle while he was watching football on television (Beck, Klein-Saffran, and Wooten 27).

Most practical problems associated with electronic monitoring pose no serious challenge. Troublesome bracelets and transmitters can be adjusted or padded. Offenders often develop ingenious explanations for the units they wear. Difficulties in signal transmission can often be overcome by having trained technicians install equipment or by having offenders slightly modify their routine. Legal problems, on the other hand, pose a greater challenge.

Electronic surveillance programs necessarily involve some type of entry into offenders' homes. Therefore, they need careful examination to ensure that they don't violate the equal protection and right to privacy provisions of the Constitution. The American Civil Liberties Union is concerned that two common practices—charging a fee to cover surveillance costs and restricting surveillance to classes of offenders least likely to violate house arrest—may infringe on the equal protection clause of the Constitution. The first practice, the ACLU notes, can discriminate against young and indigent offenders by imprisoning them because they cannot pay their fees. The second, by singling out persons guilty only of property crimes and without serious criminal

Uses additional research to confirm claims

Offers solution to above problem

Transition to next major section

Describes next major problem

MLA

Provides answers to objections above

NOTE, though only part of the sentence is quoted, quotation marks still are used

Transition to next objection. Note unique phrase used by literature is placed in quotations

Significant phrase not commonly used by author but the source is quoted

Offers illustration, examples, to answer problem

records or histories of drug abuse, may target disproportionately high numbers of white-collar offenders (Petersilia 3).

These concerns can be answered. Because electronic monitoring programs are always voluntary, participants essentially waive their right to privacy. By agreeing to a program in lieu of prison, they have indicated their willingness to undergo surveillance. Still, as the Bureau of Justice Assistance notes, court rulings may uphold a convicted person's right to privacy if electronic surveillance "cannot be justified in terms of an articulated security interest, ability to deter future criminal conduct or ability to reduce the risk of flight" (U.S., Dept. of Justice 5). Furthermore, electronic monitoring can invade the privacy of others in the offender's home. Family members who have not committed an offense and have not waived their right to privacy can accidentally be photographed or recorded. To prevent such intrusions, Kentucky, Nevada, and West Virginia have banned the use of equipment that might accidentally record extraneous sights and sounds. And because North Carolina prohibits photographing juveniles, visual verification cannot be used in that state (Scaglione, "Jails" 34).

Besides protecting an offender's constitutional rights, correction officials must try to avoid a "net-widening" effect when electronic monitoring is used. This effect occurs when a judge approves surveillance for offenders who would formerly have received probation but denies it to anyone who would formerly have gone to prison. The result is a "widening of the net of social control" to encompass more individuals. When such abuses take place, the system does not provide an option for those who would otherwise have gone to prison, and it serves as a new form of punishment for those who would otherwise have been placed on probation. Prison overcrowding is not reduced, and the costs of punishment actually rise because of the excess number of individuals under surveillance (Morris and Tonry 225). The net-widening effect has been avoided in some jurisdictions by establishing strict rules for the selection of participants. New Jersey, for instance, restricts alternative punishment programs to offenders who have already been sentenced to prison (Hofer and Meierhoefer 22).

Richard N. Irrer, who supervises the Michigan Department of Corrections electronic monitoring program, has provided convincing evidence that monitoring works well in supervising low-risk prisoners. Monitoring began experimentally in 1986, and the following year, the program was expanded to include the entire state. Offenders monitored by the department include circuit-court probationers, prison parolees, and prisoners released from halfway houses. By mid-2000, some twenty-nine hundred offenders were being monitored.

The department uses the continuous-signal monitoring system exclusively. Before being fitted with bracelets, offenders are fully briefed on the operation of the system and must read and sign a set of rules and regulations that includes a list of possible penalties for violations. These preliminaries and the fact that the program includes only carefully screened offenders with minimum-security status have undoubtedly helped the program achieve its high success rate. For 2000, according to Irrer, only 2.2 percent of the offenders were arrested for new felonies, and just 6.7 percent disappeared. The penalty for program violators depends on the status of the violator and the nature of the crime. For example, parolees and probationers who commit serious violations may go to prison, while prisoners on furlough from halfway houses may be returned there. Minor violations could result in extended curfew hours.

The Michigan program has also been a financial success. Imprisoning offenders costs the state an average of $65 a day. In contrast, Irrer notes, electronic monitoring costs just $7.30 a day, and financially able offenders must reimburse the state. Those who can't pay must perform community service. Earlier findings reported by Hofer and Meierhoefer also reveal wide spreads between the costs of imprisoning and monitoring offenders (54–55). Clearly, electronic monitoring can significantly reduce the country's enormous prison costs.

Electronic monitoring is not a cure-all for prison overcrowding. But it does offer a number of advantages that deserve serious consideration: Several systems are available,

Transition tied to source

Explains process

Provides evidence of success of the program

Transition within the major section to next success

Includes supporting data

Conclusion offers a qualification but summarizes major arguments presented in the paper and ends with a prediction

MLA

no insurmountable problems are evident, low-risk offenders are effectively controlled, and the costs are less than those for incarceration. As we move on into the twenty-first century, authorities in increasing numbers can be expected to establish house-arrest programs that monitor compliance with electronic devices.

Works Cited

Baird, Christopher. "Building More Prisons Will Not Solve Prison Overcrowding." *America's Prisons: Opposing Viewpoints.* Ed. David Bender, Bruno Leone, and Stacey Tipp. San Diego: Greenhaven, 1991. 118–24. Print.

Barr, William. "Corraling the Hard-Core Criminal." *Detroit News and Free Press* 18 Oct. 1992, state ed.: B3. Print.

Beck, James L., Jody Klein-Saffran, and Harold B. Wooten. "Home Confinement and the Use of Electronic Monitoring with Federal Parolees." *Federal Probation* Dec. 1990: 22–31. Print.

Carey, Anne R., and Elys A. McLean. "Electronic Prison Bars." *USA Today* 30 Sept. 1993: A1. Print.

Ford, Daniel, and Annesley K. Schmidt. *Electronically Monitored Home Confinement.* United States. Natl. Inst. of Justice, Dept. of Justice. Washington: GPO, 1989. Print.

Gearan, Anne. "1.8M in U.S. Prisons, the Most Ever." *USA Today* 15 Mar. 1999: A1. Print.

Georgia State. Georgia Dept. of Corrections. Probation Div. *Alternatives to Incarceration.* 1 July 1997. Web. 3 Feb. 1998.

Hofer, Paul J., and Barbara S. Meierhoefer. *Home Confinement: An Evolving Sanction in the Federal Criminal Justice System.* Washington: Federal Judicial Center, 1987. Print.

"Inmate Populations, Costs and Projection Models." *Corrections Compendium* Jan. 1997: 10–11. Print.

Irrer, Richard N. Personal interview. 20 Feb. 2001.

Katel, Peter. "New Walls, No Inmates." *Newsweek* 18 May 1992: 63. Print.

Provides bibliographic information following MLA style

Alphabetical using hanging indent

State used for government document as author

Title of article used alphabetically since no author

Personal interview also documented in MLA style

MLA

Jacque 10

Lynch, Allen. *Cost Effectiveness of Incarceration.* 1994. Web. 1
July 1997.

Morris, Norval, and Michael Tonry. *Between Prison and Probation: Intermediate Punishments in a Rational Sentencing
System.* New York: Oxford UP, 1990. Print.

Peck, Keenan. "High-Tech House Arrest." *Progressive* July 1988:
26–28. Print.

Petersilia, Joan. *House Arrest.* United States. Natl. Inst. of Justice,
Dept. of Justice. Washington: GPO, 1988. Print.

Quinlan, J. Michael. "Building More Prisons Will Solve Prison
Overcrowding." *America's Prisons: Opposing Viewpoints.*
Ed. David Bender, Bruno Leone, and Stacey Tipp. San Diego:
Greenhaven, 1991. 112–16. Print.

Richey, Warren. "Bulging Cells Renew Debate over Prisons as
Tools to Fight Crime." *Christian Science Monitor* 22 Jan. 1997:
3. Print.

Scaglione, Fred. "Jails without Walls." *American City and
County* Jan. 1989: 32–40. Print.

- - -. "You're Under Arrest—at Home." *USA Today Magazine* Nov.
1988: 26–28. Print.

Sullivan, Robert E. "Reach Out and Guard Someone: Using
Phones and Bracelets to Reduce Prison Overcrowding."
Rolling Stone 29 Nov. 1990: 51. Print.

United States. Dept. of Justice. Bureau of Justice Assistance.
Office of Justice Programs. *Electronic Monitoring in Intensive Probation and Parole Programs.* Washington: GPO,
1989. Print.

United States. Senate. Subcommittee on Federal Spending,
Budget, and Accounting of the Committee on Governmental
Affairs. 100th Cong., 1st sess. *Prison Projections: Can the
United States Keep Pace?* Washington: GPO, 1987. Print.

Same author for next
article so replaced by
dash

Complete additional
exercises and
practice in your
MyLab

22 Documenting Sources: APA Style

In this chapter, you will learn how to:

22.1 Prepare papers using the APA system.

22.2 Prepare bibliographic references using the APA style.

22.3 Follow APA style to cite sources in your essay.

22.4 Integrate and cite quotations using the APA style.

The American Psychological Association (APA) system is used by many social sciences, psychology, and many other academic disciplines. The APA is currently in its 6th edition.

To better meet the challenges of online publications, APA style now recommends that the unique work you are referencing in print and electronic form be identified by the digital object identifier (DOI), a unique identification sequence assigned by the International DOI Foundation. The DOI can often be found near the copyright notices of electronic journal articles or in some cases at the top of the first page of the article. When the DOI is used, there is no need to indicate the URL of the reference.

■ Sample

Mesmer-Magnus, J. R., & DeChurch, L. A. (2009). Information sharing and team performance: A meta-analysis. *Journal of Applied Psychology, 94*(2), 535–546. doi:10.1037/a0013773

Consult with your faculty member on whether they wish you to employ the DOI with print and online sources when it is available.

APA System for Preparing Papers

Prepare papers using the APA system.

- The APA system includes a brief abstract on the first main page of the article which summarizes the main argument concisely.
- The APA system requires a title page. Center (1) the title of the paper about four inches from the top and (2) your name, two spaces below the

title. About three-fourths of the way from the top, provide the course designation, the name of your instructor, and the date, typed double-spaced
and flush with the right margin. Two inches from the top of the page,
type the words "Running Head," without quotation marks, flush with the
left margin; then type a colon and a word or phrase that identifies the paper's topic. Type the running head in capital letters; type everything else
in capital and lowercase letters.

- Repeat the title of the paper on the first text page, centered about one-
  and-a-half inches from the top and typed in capital and lowercase letters.
- Number every page of the text in the upper right corner, starting with
  the title page. Put the running head (an abbreviated version of the
  paper's title) in the upper left corner, in all capital letters.
- Leave one-inch margins at the bottom and at both sides of each page.
  Indent the first line of each paragraph five spaces.
- Begin the bibliography on a new page that follows the text of the paper,
  and give it the heading "References," without quotation marks. Center
  this heading on the page. Follow the alphabetizing and positioning
  guidelines for the MLA system except that if the listing includes more
  than one entry for an author, repeat the author's name.
- Begin the first line of each entry at the left margin and indent subsequent lines five spaces. In most word-processing programs, you can select
  "hanging indent" as a format option, under Format/Paragraph in *Word*,
  which will automatically provide the proper indentation for each entry.
  Double-space all entries.

Watch the Animation on Formatting an APA Paper

APA

Preparing Proper APA Bibliographic References

Books

The APA system uses initials rather than first and middle names for authors,
editors, and translators.

22.2

Prepare bibliographic references using the APA style.

■ A Book with One Author

Wilk, M. (1975). *Every day's a matinée*. New York: Norton.

Watch the Animation on Citing Sources Using the APA Style

■ A Book with Two Authors

Duncan, D., & Burns, K. (1997). *Lewis and Clark*. New York: Knopf.

■ A Book with More than Three Authors

Alder, R. W., Finn, T., Bradley, M. A., & Li, A. W. (1971). *Mechanisms in organic
chemistry*. New York: Wiley.

The APA system gives up to and including six author or editor names in the
reference list. Substitute "et al." for the seventh or more.

■ A Book with a Title That Includes Another Title

Words that would be italicized on their own should be set roman as part of an italicized title.

Tanner, J. (1992). *Anxiety in Eden: A Kierkegaardian reading of* Paradise Lost. Oxford, England: Oxford University Press.

■ A Book with Corporate or Association Authorship

United Nations, Public Administration Division. (1968). *Local government training.* New York: Author.

When the author of the work is also the publisher, the APA system uses the word "Author" following the place of publication. If the work is published by another organization, its name replaces "Author."

■ An Edition Other than the First

Turabian, K. L. (1996). *A manual for writers of term papers, theses, and dissertations* (6th ed.). Chicago: University of Chicago Press.

■ A Book in Two or More Volumes

Bartram, H. C. (1959). *The cavalcade of America* (Vols. 1–2). New York: Knopf.

■ A Reprint of an Older Work

Matthiessen, F. O. (1970). *American renaissance: Art and expression in the age of Emerson and Whitman.* New York: Oxford University Press. (Original work published 1941)

■ A Book with an Editor Rather than an Author

Deetz, J. (Ed.). (1971). *Man's imprint from the past: Readings in the methods of archaeology.* Boston: Little, Brown.

■ A Book with Both an Author and an Editor

Melville, H. (1971). *The confidence man* (H. Parker, Ed.). New York: Norton. (Original work published 1857)

■ A Translation

Beauvoir, S. de. (1974). *All said and done* (P. O'Brian, Trans.). New York: Putnam. (Original work published 1972)

■ An Essay or Chapter in a Collection of Works by One Author

Woolf, V. (1925). The lives of the obscure. In *The common reader, first series* (pp. 111–118). New York: Harcourt Brace.

■ An Essay or Chapter in an Anthology

Angell, R. (1981). On the ball. In P. Eschholz & A. Rosa (Eds.), *Subject and strategy*
(pp. 34–41). New York: St. Martin's Press.

Periodicals

Periodicals include newspapers, popular magazines, and specialized occupational and scholarly journals. The basic information for a periodical article includes the name of the article's author, the date of publication, the title of the article, the name of the periodical, the page range of the entire article, and, for scholarly journals, the volume number of the periodical.

■ An Article in a Scholarly Journal Consecutively Paged through
the Entire Volume

Pfennig, D. (1997). Kinship and cannibalism. *Bioscience, 47,* 667–675.

■ An Article in a Scholarly Journal That Pages Each Issue Separately

Block, J. W. (1976). Sodom and Gomorrah: A volcanic disaster. *Journal of
Geological Education, 23*(5), 74–77.

■ An Unsigned Article in a Scholarly Journal

Baby, it's cold inside. (1997). *Science, 276,* 537–538.

■ A Signed Article in an Occupational or Popular Magazine

Gopnik, A. (1997, November 24). The good soldier. *The New Yorker, 73,* 106–114.

■ An Unsigned Article in an Occupational or Popular Magazine

Robot productivity. (1982, May). *Production Engineering, 29,* 52–55.

■ A Signed Article in a Daily Newspaper

Wade, N. (1997, November 26). Germ weapons: Deadly but hard to use. *The New
York Times,* pp. A13, A15.

■ An Unsigned Article in a Daily Newspaper

The arithmetic of terrorism. (1997, November 14). *The Washington Post,* p. A26.

Encyclopedia Articles

The APA system requires publication information for all encyclopedia citations when documenting familiar works, such as the *Encyclopedia Americana.*

Fears, J. R. (1987). Emperor's cult. In *The encyclopedia of religion*
(Vol. 5, pp. 101–102). New York: Macmillan.

For an anonymous article, references for the APA system begin with the article's title. Position the publication date, within parentheses, after this title. The remaining format is identical to citations with an author.

Government Documents

The APA system includes the name of the author, the date of publication, and the place of publication and adds a cataloging code where one exists.

Carpenter, R. D. (1989). *Defects in hardened timber* (UCLC Publication No. 20504424). U.S. Department of Agriculture, Forest Service. Washington, DC: Government Printing Office.

U.S. Environmental Protection Agency, Consumer Products Safety Commission. (1989). *Asbestos in the home* (SUDOCS Report No. Y3.C76/3:2/A51/989). Washington, DC: Government Printing Office.

U.S. Congress, Office of Technology Assessment. (1992). *The biology of mental disorders* (SUDOCS Report No. Y3.T22/2:2/B57/10). Washington, DC: Government Printing Office.

Other Sources

■ Book Reviews

Koenig, R. (1989, February 20). Billy the Kid [Review of the book *Billy Bathgate*]. *New York, 21*, 20–21.

If the review is untitled, follow the above format but omit the missing element.

■ Published Interviews

Hernandez, F. (1997, March 20). A talk with Manuel Noriega. *News Report, 15*, 28–30.

If the interview is untitled, follow the example above, omitting mention of a title.

■ Personal Interviews

For the APA system, a personal interview is considered personal correspondence and is not included in the References list. Instead, use an in-text parenthetical citation. Include the name of the person interviewed, the notation "personal communication," and the date: (Newman, personal communication, May 18, 2001).

■ Audiovisual Media

In the APA format, the citation begins with an individual's name and his or her contribution to the *motion picture* (use this term, not *film*). The country of origin (where it was made and released) is now required.

Whale, J. (Director). (1931). *Frankenstein* [Motion picture]. United States: Universal.

■ Television and Radio Programs

Ducat, S. (Producer). (1995, January 6). *Washington week in review* [Television broadcast]. Washington, DC: Public Broadcasting Service.

Use the following format when additional information is pertinent:

Exton, C. (Writer), & Rye, R. (Director). (1993). Peril at End House [Television series episode]. In B. Eastman (Producer), *Mystery*. Washington, DC: Public Broadcasting Service.

With the APA system, the name of the scriptwriter appears in the author's position, followed by the director. Any in-text references begin with the first name in the bibliographical reference (for example, Exton, 1993).

■ Music and Sound Recordings

The APA format requires identification of all formats, including a CD.

Smith, B. (1997). *The essential Bessie Smith* [CD]. New York: Columbia Records.

Smith, B. (1948). Down hearted blues. On *The world's greatest blues singer* [CD]. New York: Columbia Records. (Original recording February 17, 1923)

Recording dates, if different from the copyright year, follow the entry, enclosed in parentheses, with no final period.

■ Computer Software

Data Desk (Version 6.0) [Computer software]. (1997). Ithaca, NY: Data Description.

In the APA system, only specialized software or computer programs are listed in the References. Standard commercial software and languages should be cited by their proper name and version in the text itself.

■ CD-ROMs and Other Databases

Norman, J. L. (1996). Barcelona. In *Software toolworks multimedia encyclopedia* [CD-ROM]. Boston: Grolier.

The APA *Manual* (6th ed.) takes the view that all aggregated databases are the same type of source, regardless of the format or manner of access (CD-ROM, library or university server, or online Web supplier). Follow the model above when you need to cite an entire CD-ROM (not a document from it). In a reference to information taken from a database (even a CD-ROM), give a "retrieval statement" containing the date you retrieved the document, article, or piece of data, as well as the full, correct name of the database. When you retrieve information from an online database, end the entry with a correct and complete URL for the specific document or version. In this case, the name of the database is omitted, unless this information will help in retrieval from a large or complex site. (See online models in the next section.)

APA

Online Sources

The most recent edition of the *Publication Manual of the American Psychological Association* provides the APA's newest guidelines for documenting online sources. You can also consult the association's web site for its most up-to-date information about citing electronic sources:

http://www.apastyle.org/elecref.html

Be sure to ask your instructor which format to follow and then use that format consistently. Often data from the Internet are incomplete, perhaps lacking an author, a title, or page or paragraph numbers. Include all the available information. The recommendation from the APA is that you cite document locations rather than home pages and that the referenced address actually works for that file. Remember, your goal is to allow your reader to find the source. Note the use of the DOI explained at the beginning of the section on APA References.

■ Books

Follow the general guidelines for a printed book, and conclude with appropriate electronic source information, as modeled here, or use the DOI, if known.

Locke, J. (1995). *An essay concerning human understanding.* New York: Columbia University. Retrieved from http://www.ilt.columbia.edu/projects/ digitexts/locke/understanding/title.html (Original work published 1690)

When some of the basic information is not provided, use whatever is available.

Chaney, W. J., Diehm, W. J., & Seeley, F. (1999). *The second 50 years: A reference manual for senior citizens.* Weed, CA: London Circle. Retrieved from http:// www.londoncircle.com/2d50.html

To cite part of an electronic book, place the part's title after the date of publication. The APA also cites a chapter or section identifier following the title of the complete document.

Trochim, W. M. K. (2001). Language of research. In *The research methods knowledge base* (Foundations sec.). Cincinnati, OH: Atomic Dog. Retrieved from http://www.trochim.human.cornell.edu/kb/language.html

■ Periodicals on the World Wide Web

The APA recommends using the models for print periodicals when documenting online articles that do not vary from their printed versions. In such cases, add [Electronic version] after the title and before the period to complete the citation. When the electronic format alters the printed version (e.g., no pagination, added data or links), then cite as an online document, using a retrieval statement and the name of the database and/or the URL. APA guidelines ask for the identification of the server or the web site in a retrieval statement only when it would be helpful in finding the source; for example, it is not necessary to state "Retrieved from the World Wide Web" since it is the most common access point to the Internet. If the DOI is available, that should be used instead of retrieval data.

Cervetti, N. (1996). In the breeches, petticoats, and pleasures of Orlando. *Journal of Modern Literature, 20*(2). Retrieved from http://www.indiana.edu/~iupress/journals/mod-art2.html

Navarro, M. (2001, February 13). Women in sports cultivating new playing fields. *The New York Times on the Web.* Retrieved from http://www.nytimes.com

No link found in violence, videos. (2000, August 8). *Boston Globe Online,* p. A14. Retrieved from http://www.boston.com/dailyglobe2/no_li_nk_found_in_violence_videos+.shtml

Oakes, J. (1999, January/February). Promotion or retention: Which one is social? *Harvard Education Letter.* Retrieved from http://www.edletter.org/past/issues/1999-jf/promotion.shtml

■ Periodicals Accessed through an Online Library Service or Large Network Provider

Increasingly, full-text articles are available online at libraries or at home through services such as LexisNexis, ProQuest Direct, and America Online. These services may or may not provide an online address for accessed material. In the APA documentation system, cite the author's name, if known; the date the article was published; the title of the article; the title of the periodical; and the page numbers for the article, if available. Do not include the name of the database.

Clemetson, L. (2000, March 27). A ticket to private school. *Newsweek.* Retrieved from http://www.newsweek/com.icl/83469

APA style prefers that the URL that leads directly to the document file be provided, following the word *from.*

■ Encyclopedia Articles

The basic information for an encyclopedia article accessed through the World Wide Web includes the author's name, if known; the date of the edition; the title of the article; the name of the encyclopedia; and the online address.

Daniel, R. T. (1995). The history of Western music. In *Britannica online: Macropaedia.* Retrieved from http://www.eb.com:180/cgi-bin/g:DocF=macro/5004/45/0.html

■ Government Documents

The basic information for a government document includes the name of the author, if known; the date of publication; the title; a cataloging code if one is available; and the online address. If no author is given, begin by identifying the government agency as the author.

APA

Probation Division of the Georgia Department of Corrections. (1997, July 1). *Alter-*

natives to incarceration (CSP Document No. 239875). Retrieved from http://

www.harvard.edu/~innovat/aiga87.html

■ Personal Home Page

The APA *Manual* offers no specific guidelines for personal home pages. We suggest that you use the following pattern, which conforms to general APA practice.
Note that the APA system includes the date of the latest Web page revision, if
known, in parentheses.

Lanthrop, O. (2000, May 28). Home page. Retrieved from http://www.cognivis.com/

olin/photos.htm

■ Newsgroups, Electronic Mailing Lists, and E-Mail

The APA format treats e-mail as personal communications, which are cited in
parentheses in the text only. Newsgroups, online forums, discussion groups, and
electronic mailing lists that maintain archives can be cited in the References.
With these electronic forms, indicate the author's full last name and initials
(screen name if the name is not available), the exact posting date, the name of
the thread or blog, a label in brackets describing the type of message, "Retrieved
from" followed by the name of list if not in the URL; and the address for the
archived message. Categories include Online forum comment (messages posted
to newsgroups, online forums, or discussion group), Electronic mailing list
message (a message on an electronic mailing List or Listserv), Web log message
(for a blog post), and Video file (Video blog post).

Trehub, A. (2002, January 28). Re: The conscious access hypothesis [Online

forum comment]. Retrieved from University of Houston Psyche

Discussion Forum: http://listserv.uh.edu/cig-bin/wa?A2=psyche-

b&F=&S=&P=2334

1. **Using the information on the sources provided on pages 404–405,
   prepare an APA bibliographical reference for each source.**
2. **Prepare a proper APA reference for each of the works you plan
   to use in writing your paper.**
3. **Prepare an annotated bibliography, explained on page 369,
   using APA style for each of the works you have reviewed for
   your paper.**

Handling In-Text Citations

22.3

Follow APA style to cite
sources in your essay.

The APA system uses notations that appear within the text and are set off by parentheses. The system identifies the last name of the author or authors and the
year of publication. A page number is provided in APA both with quotations and
when the information is so specific that it is important to reference the specific
page. The system is illustrated by the following examples.

Basic Citation Form

■ Bibliographic Reference

Rothenberg, R. (1996, February). Life in cyburbia. *Esquire*, 56–63.

■ Passage and Citation

A mania for the Internet has invaded . . . our poorest children have a stake in the Internet (Rothenberg, 1996).

Rothenberg (1996) states that a mania for the Internet . . . have a stake in the Internet.

■ Bibliographic Reference

Weider, B., & Hapgood, D. (1982) *The murder of Napoleon*. New York: Congdon.

■ Passage and Citation

Four different autopsy reports were filed....Nevertheless, cancer has become accepted as the cause (Weider & Hapgood, 1982).

If a source has more than five authors, use "et al.," meaning "and others," for all but the first-named one.

■ Bibliographic Reference

Baugh, Albert C., et al. (1948). *A literary history of England*. New York: Appleton.

■ Passage and Citation

Although no one knows . . . . writing plays together (Baugh et al., 1948).

Authors with the Same Last Name

If your citations include authors with the same last name, use the initials of their first names to distinguish them.

■ Bibliographic Reference

Adler, J. (1980, June 16). Search for an orange thread. *Newsweek*, 32–34.

Adler, W. L. (1979, December, 18). The agent orange controversy. *Detroit Free Press*, state ed., p. B2.

■ Passage and Citation

As early as 1966, government . . . miscarriages, liver abscesses, and nerve damage (J. Adler, 1980).

Separate Works by the Same Author

For the APA system, use the conventional name–date–page number format. (Note: Page numbers are not always needed.)

APA

■ Bibliographic Reference

Mullin, D. (1983a, November 14). After U.S. troops pull out of Grenada. *US News & World Report*, 22–25.

Mullin, D. (1983b, November 7). Why the surprise move in Grenada—and what next. *US News & World Report*, 31–34.

■ Passage and Citation

As the rangers evacuated students, . . . and free the governor (Mullin, 1983b).

If the two works appeared in the same year, put an "a" or a "b," without quotes, after the date to identify whether you are referring to the first or second entry for that author in the bibliography, arranged alphabetically by title.

Two Sources for the Same Citations

If two sources provide essentially the same information and you wish to mention both in one parenthetical citation, alphabetize them according to their authors' last names, list them with a semicolon between them, and position the citation as you would any other citation.

■ Bibliographic Reference

Bryce, B. (1988, November 13). The controversy over funding community colleges. *Detroit Free Press*, state ed., p. A4.

Warshow, H. (1988, November 15). Community college funding hits a snag. *Grand Rapids Press*, city ed., p. A2.

■ Passage and Citation

In contending that a 3% reduction in stat funding...enrollment was expected to jump by 15% during the next year (Bryce, 1988; Warshow, 1988).

Unsigned References

When you use a source for which no author is given, the in-text citation consists of all or part of the title, the appropriate page numbers, and the date.

■ Bibliographic Reference

Money and Classes. (1997, October). *Progressive*, 10.

■ Passage and Citation

According to the General Accounting Office, repairing . . . many billions more ("Money and Classes," 1997).

Citing Quotations

Set off quotations fewer than forty words long with quotation marks and run them into the text of the paper. For longer quotes, omit the quotation marks and indent the material five spaces. Double-space the typing. If you quote part or all of one paragraph, don't further indent the first line. If you quote two or more consecutive paragraphs, indent each one's first line five additional spaces–except for the first paragraph in the quote which should not be additionally indented. Use single quotation marks for a quotation within a shorter quotation and double marks for a quotation within a longer, indented quotation. There are more detailed examples in Chapter 20, following MLA style.

When the quotation is run into the text, position the citation as shown in the following examples.

22.4

Integrate and cite quotations using the APA style.

👁 Watch the Animation on **Citing Quotations**

APA

■ Bibliographic Reference

Schapiro, M. (1996, April). Children of a lesser god. *Harper's Bazaar*, 205+.

■ Passage and Citation

UN investigators who have studied the extent of child labor in Third World countries estimate that "as many as 200 million children go to work rather than to school . . . making everything from clothing and shoes to handbags and carpets" (Schapiro, 1996, p. 205).

With longer, indented quotations, skip one space after the end punctuation and type the reference in parentheses.

■ Bibliographic Reference

Newhouse, J. (1985, July 8). The diplomatic round: A freemasonry of terrorism. *New Yorker*, 46–63.

■ Passage and Citation

One commentator offers this assessment of why foreign terrorist groups don't operate in this country:

> The reason that America has been spared so far, apparently, is that it is less vulnerable than Europe, especially to Middle Eastern extremists. Moving in and out of most European countries isn't difficult for non-Europeans; border controls are negligible. But American customs and immigration authorities, being hyper-alert to drug traffic, tend to pay attention to even marginally doubtful people, and a would-be terrorist. . . could come under surveillance for the wrong reason. (Newhouse, 1985, p. 63)

Indirect Citations

In APA style, name the original work in the text and then give the secondary source in parentheses preceded by "as cited in."

■ Bibliographic Reference

Klein, J. (1989, March 6). Ready for Rudy. *New York*, 30–37.

■ Passage and Citation

Rudolph Giuliani favors the death penalty for "the murder of a law-enforcement officer, mass murder, a particularly heinous killing" but would impose it only "when there is certainty of guilt well beyond a reasonable doubt" (as cited in Klein, 1989, p. 37).

Authors Identified in Text

Sometimes you'll want to introduce a paraphrase, summary, or quotation with the name of its author. In this case, the page number may be positioned immediately after the name or follow the material cited.

■ Bibliographic Reference

Jacoby, S. (1974, March 31). Waiting for the end: On nursing homes. *New York Times Magazine*, city ed., 80+.

■ Passage and Citation

Susan Jacoby (1974, p. 80) sums up the grim outlook of patients in bad nursing homes by noting that they are merely waiting to die.

Susan Jacoby (1974) sums up the grim outlook of patients in bad nursing homes by noting that they are merely waiting to die (p. 80).

EXERCISE

1. *Using the APA system, write a proper in-text citation for exercise 1 on page 430. The type of information (info only or quote) and page number in the original source are provided: a (info p. 222), and c (a quote p. 271), and g (info p. 31), i (info only p. 221), o (a partial quote on page 60, also use same author published a different year).*

    Assume that you have not used the author's name to introduce the material you cite. Where there are multiple pages in the reference, you can select the page or pages appropriate to your citation.

2. *Using the APA system, write a proper in-text citation for each of the bibliographic references you prepared for part 2 on page 430. Assume that you have not used the author's name to introduce the material you cite. Where there are multiple pages in the reference, you can select the page or pages appropriate to your citation.*

APA STUDENT RESEARCH PAPER

Running head: INSTANT COMMUNICATION   1

Instant Communication Does Not Ensure Good Communication
Bruce Gilchrist
Ferris State University

> Running head in all caps is used on the top of pages
>
> Authors name
>
> Affiliation, which could be your course and instructor name

Abstract Page

> A separate page for abstract

INSTANT COMMUNICATION   2
Abstract
This review of the literature finds that increased rates of communication from voice mail, cellular phones, e-mail, and other sources results in increased levels of stress and decreased productivity. Technostress includes interruptions and the perceived demand for immediate response to the stress. Studies have found that the interruption negatively affects productivity and even IQ. Defense mechanisms for instant communication need to be adopted as coping strategies.

Keywords: instant communication, e-mail, text messaging, technostress, productivity.

> Running head
>
> Abstract, a brief objective summary of the paper's main argument
>
> Keywords. Words that would help reader find the article if they were searching on a database

INSTANT COMMUNICATION   3

Instant Communication Does Not Ensure Good Communication

The technological revolution ushered many new communications technologies and devices into the modern office over the past 25 years. "Every day brings yet another new communication device, software program, or piece of computer hardware that workers have to know, need to use, or must have to do their job" (Weil & Rosen, 1999, p. 56). The popularity of these devices at the office and declining costs eventually led to their acceptance for personal use outside the office. After all, who wouldn't want to take advantage of the benefits they offer? The fax machine reduces dependence

> Start of body, repeats running head
>
> Title at top of page
>
> Establishes broad context
>
> Support with short quote, so documented authors last names, date of publication, and page

on the postal system for moving paper documents. Voice mail, pagers, and cell phones make it possible to communicate with others even when they are away from their home or office telephones. Newer technologies such as e-mail and electronic text messaging allow individuals to remain connected with business associates, family, and friends on an almost perpetual basis.

Each new electronic communications gadget is hyped by its creator as yet another labor-and time-saving device. Marketing efforts and corporate management describe these devices almost as if they possess magical powers. Simply by using these devices, one is suddenly able to do more with less. Less time, less manual labor, lower costs, and so on. But are the users of these communications technologies really reaping the benefits that they were promised? Or have the negative aspects of these technologies been masked by clever marketing campaigns and corporate policies? Whether used professionally, personally, or both, many end users of these technologies are unaware of the negative effects to which they are subjecting themselves. Excessive or uncontrolled use of fax machines, voice mail, pagers, cellular phones, e-mail, and text messaging can lead to increased stress levels and decreased productivity.

Speaking in general terms, the first problem presented by instant communication technologies is that they contribute to a specialized form of stress known as technostress. The term was first defined in 1983 by clinical psychologist Craig Brod as "a modern disease of adaptation caused by an inability to cope with the new computer technologies in a healthy manner" (as cited in Genco, 2000, p. 1). Brod's original definition was primarily addressing the personal computer revolution and has since been modified to be more inclusive of newer forms of technology. In 1997, clinical psychologists Michelle Weil and Larry Rosen enhanced the definition of technostress to include "'any negative impact on attitudes, thoughts, behaviors, or body psychology caused directly or indirectly by technology'" (p. 1). Weil further explains technostress as "our reaction to technology and how we are changing due to its influence" (p. 1). Using these expanded definitions it is not difficult to conclude that instant communication technologies can indeed be a source of technostress.

The simplest form of technostress produced by instant communication technologies is the stream of constant interruptions they ultimately produce. As an information technology support specialist, I often find myself working on complex technical problems that require my full attention and mental concentration. Interruptions from pagers, cell phones, and text messaging

---

States common knowledge rationale for new technologies

Uses questions to hook reader and offer transition to main point

Introduces unexpected thesis statement

Transition, offers topic for first section. Definition is offered in this paragraph using a narrative history of the term

Supporting quote provides background. Note even part of a sentence is quoted and documented

Develops history in narrative. Introduces quote by authors and so only page number in parenthesis

Short quote documented

Draws conclusion from definition

Transition sentence that is topic for next section, which identifies cause

Draws on personal evidence, with clarification of credentials to make claims credible

INSTANT COMMUNICATION   5

are distracting, as they force me to break away from the task at hand to deal
with the incoming communication. Not only do these distractions lengthen
the time necessary to complete a task, but they can also introduce errors, as
my attention is not fully focused on a single task.

Adding to this stress is the prevailing attitude that because these technologies provide for instant communication, one should receive an instant
response to any messages they send. For me, having to interrupt the task at
hand and respond to these incoming messages is indeed disruptive and can
lower my productivity when the volume of messages becomes excessive.
Personal interviews revealed that my views are shared by others as well.
One interviewee stated his biggest complaint is that the constant stream of
interruptions brought on by pagers, cell phones, and e-mail make it difficult
for him to prioritize or sometimes even complete tasks (L. Murphy, personal
communication, March 25, 2005). He further added that not only does everyone think their message is a top priority, they are also unaware of how many
other messages the recipient already has waiting for a response. Another
respondent criticizes overzealous management for adding to the problem.
In a crisis situation, management frequently requests status updates via
some form of instant communication. What they fail to realize is that every
message they send requires the recipient to divert their focus away from the
crisis situation and only lengthens the time it takes to resolve the problem
(J. Tice, personal communication, March 25, 2005).

Newly published research supports these individuals' claims that the
constant interruptions resulting from instant communications technologies
are not only disruptive but detrimental to productivity. In one study, more
than 1,000 individuals were subjected to persistent interruptions either
through e-mail or text messaging. Monitoring and testing of the subjects
allowed researchers to determine that such interruptions produce a temporary but measurable drop in intelligence (Burnett & Ortiz, 2005). *The Houston
Chronicle* summarized the study by reporting, "Constant e-mailing and text
messaging reduces mental ability by 10 IQ points, a more severe effect than
smoking cannabis, by distracting the brain from other tasks" (Moore, 2005).
By comparison, a sleepless night will produce the same effect while smoking marijuana only causes a 4 point reduction (Moore, 2005).

Even more troubling is that the disruptions produced by instant communications technologies extend outside the professional and laboratory
environments as well. Because pagers and cell phones with text messaging

Transition to next identified cause of stress

Introduces support from
interview and uses docu-
mentation strategy devel-
oped in class

Introduces additional
support from interview

Documents using class
established strategy

Transition and topic. Identifies effect of technology.

Provides summary of
research as support

Documents study source
with author and publica-
tion, not page

Locates quote source,
introduces a short quote,
and documents

Offers a comparison.
Documents claim

Transition and topic to
additional effect

are portable devices and most employees have Internet access to their corporate e-mail from home, their reach is extended far outside the office.
These devices have invaded the home and are eating away at our personal
time. Research indicates somewhere between one-half and three-quarters of
office professionals use business-related communication technologies outside the office for up to 2 hours per day (Weil & Rosen, 1999). A recent article
in *Today's Parent* discusses how time spent working outside of office hours
is taken away from other activities such as time parents should be spending
with their families (Lopez-Pacheco, 2003).

Psychologists concur that all this electronic communication is contributing to a wide array of undesirable psychological changes and increasing
personal stress levels. People are becoming more isolated as they choose
to use electronic means of communicating over traditional interpersonal
methods (Rizzo, 1999). It is becoming increasingly more difficult for people
to define their personal space boundaries and separate their personal and
professional lives. According to Terrie Hienrich Rizzo (1999), "This boundary
breakdown leads to a feeling of never being able to get away and contributes to an inability to relax" (p. 1). That anyone may be watching TV or reading a good book when a pager or cell phone beckons with a work-related
problem clearly demonstrates this lack of separation and its consequences.

I do not argue that instant communication technologies can offer
benefits to the busy professional. However, the growing body of research
supports my belief that these devices can elevate stress levels and reduce productivity when used inappropriately. I know from personal experience that I was a victim of the negative effects that these technologies
can manifest. The experts call it technostress, multitasking mania, or
information overload, but for me, the end result was career burnout regardless of what term is used to define how or why it happened. In fact, I
am probably one of the statistics cited in an *Information Week* report stating that information technology professionals are burning out in ever-
increasing numbers (Lally, 1997).

The reality is that not only are these electronic communication technologies a current problem we must deal with, but if left unchecked, the
problem will only grow worse in the future. The number one recommendation of experts to reduce the stress manifested by instant communication devices and technologies is to limit their use. While this seems like
an obvious solution, few people fail to put it into practice. Implementing
some basic defense strategies to manage the interruptions of instant

Summarizes supporting
research information with
documentation of authors
and publication date

Second source from sup-
port with documentation

Transition to new effect

Summarized support
documented with author
name and publication

Introduces supporting
quote with author name
and publication, short
quote followed by page
number

Generalizes the prob-
lem in the student's own
words

Offers qualification and
restates student writer's
main point

Uses personal experi-
ence as support

Supports student
example with summary
of authority support
documented with author's
name and publication
date

Transition to a conclusion
that makes prediction

Offers possible solution

Identifies source author-
ity recommendation,
documented

INSTANT COMMUNICATION   7

messages can go a long way toward reducing the stress they can produce (Rizzo, 1999). One is to disable notification of new voice mail and
e-mail so that users can check it on their own schedule rather than when it
demands their attention. Another is for users to take regular time-out periods where they inform others that they will not be reachable via a pager or
cell phone. This will ensure that today's professionals have some time available to redefine personal space boundaries, spend (time) with their family,
or just read a good book (Rizzo, 1999).

INSTANT COMMUNICATION   8

References

Burnett, J. H., & Ortiz, V. (2005, April 23). Does more IM = a lower IQ?
     Milwaukee Journal Sentinel, p. A3.

Genco, P. (2000, September/October). Technostress in our schools and lives.
     Book Report, pp. 42–43. Retrieved from WilsonSelectPlus database.

Lally, R. (1997, October 6). Managing techno-stress. *Getting Results—for the
     Hands-On Manager, 6*, 5–6. Retrieved from WilsonSelectPlus database.

Lopez-Pacheco, A. (2003, February). Baby, baby, don't get hooked on me.
     Today's Parent, 110–112.

Moore, K. J. (2005, April 23). Constant e-mail harms intellect [Electronic
     version]. *The Houston Chronicle*, p. B3.

Rizzo, T. H. (1999, November/December). Taming technostress. *IDEA Health &
     Fitness*. Retrieved from InfoTrac Onefile database.

Weil, M., & Rosen, L. (1999). Don't let technology enslave you. *Workforce*,
     78(2), 56–60.

Summarizes main
recommendations

States authority effect of
enacting recommenda-
tions with documentation

Introduces reference
page

Two authors, newspaper
article

Electronic based source

Electronic journal

Electronic version of a
newspaper article

Single author article in
online journal retrieved
from a database

Two author print journal
with volume and number

 Complete additional
exercises and practice
in your MyLab

CHAPTER 23

Additional Research Strategies: Interviews, Questionnaires, Direct Observations

In this chapter, you will learn how to:

23.1 Identify the value of primary research.

23.2 Apply the general principles for primary research.

23.3 Conduct primary research ethically.

23.4 Prepare for and conduct interviews, and write a report based on interviews.

23.5 Develop and administer questionnaires, and write a report based on the data.

23.6 Conduct direct observations and write a report based on the observations.

The library isn't the only source of information for research writing. Investigators also gather information through *primary research*, which includes such activities as consulting public records in local, state, and federal archives, performing experiments, conducting interviews, sending out questionnaires, and making direct observations of various kinds.

This chapter focuses on the latter three types, the most common primary research strategies.

The Value of Primary Research

23.1

Identify the value of primary research.

What makes primary research so valuable? First, it allows individuals and organizations to collect recent information, often unavailable elsewhere, that precisely suits their needs. A company that has developed a new product can't turn to published data to estimate its sales prospects; such information simply doesn't exist. But polling test users with a well-crafted questionnaire could suggest some answers and perhaps also some tips for improving the product. Similarly, someone wanting to gauge the success of an ongoing clothing drive by a local charitable organization might interview its director.

Even when published material exists, it may not contain desired information. Although numerous articles discuss student attitudes about required courses, you probably wouldn't find a report that explores student reaction to a new general-education requirement at your school. You could, however, assemble this information by distributing a questionnaire. The findings might even contradict, and therefore cause you to question, the conclusions of others.

Primary research can also yield unexpected and significant material. Suppose you're investigating adult illiteracy, and you interview a professor with a specialty in this area of study. She explains the reasons why people who can't read resist help and supplies several relevant examples. Such information might not appear anywhere in print. Certainly the resulting report would carry more weight and elicit more interest than one without such insights.

You can integrate primary research into a report that consists largely of *secondary research*, the kind that depends on library materials. The student who wrote the research paper on electronic monitoring (see pages 410–421) incorporated the results of a personal interview with the director of Michigan's electronic monitoring program. This interview provided information on the scope, operation, success rate, and cost advantage of the program. Often, however, writers detail the findings of primary research in separate reports. This would be the case if, for example, your employer asked you to interview users of a new computer system in order to determine their degree of satisfaction with it.

General Principles for Primary Research

23.2

Apply the general principles for primary research.

Primary research, like all research, requires well-formulated questions. Such questions must be specifically focused, contain clearly defined terms, and be answerable by the actual research. A vague, general question such as "What attitudes do Americans have about their government?" lacks the necessary precision and therefore can't be resolved. What kind(s) of attitudes? What level or branch of government? Which Americans? How would you gather their opinions? A more realistic question might be "According to the Mason College faculty, how adequate is the new congressional proposal for funding academic research in this country?" You could easily develop and distribute to faculty members a questionnaire addressing the different provisions of the proposal. In addition, you can't resolve ethical or philosophical questions through primary research. While you could use a questionnaire to determine student attitudes about the police using sobriety check lanes, such information won't decide the ethical issue of whether the police should use such check lanes.

For valid results, conduct your primary research in an impartial manner. Always aim to determine facts rather than to justify some belief you hold. This means, first of all, that you must develop questions that have no built-in bias. If you poll other students and ask them to tell you "how core-course teachers on this campus marked their papers unreasonably hard," those responding might falsify their answers to give you what you want. Instead, use neutral phrasing such as "Do you believe core-course teachers on this campus mark your papers fairly or unfairly? Explain." Second, don't rely on atypical sources and situations for your data. If you investigate the adequacy of parking space on campus, don't deliberately observe the parking lots on a day when some special event has flooded the campus with visitors. Careful readers will see what you have done and reject your findings.

Just as you avoid bias when gathering information, so also do you report your results fairly. For one thing, don't use inaccurate interpretations of your findings to make them agree with the conclusions you're after. If you believe peer editing produces questionable results, don't claim that the students in a class you observed spent their time sneering at one another's work when in fact they offered constructive criticism. While such criticism can sometimes be straightforward, certainly most people wouldn't consider it sneering. Similarly, don't report conclusions that are unsupported by your actual research. If you observe a large number of violent acts while watching Saturday cartoons, don't leap to the conclusion that the violence in the cartoons causes violent behavior in children. You simply don't have the evidence to support that assertion. Finally, don't cover up results that you don't like. If your survey of teachers' marking practices shows that most of your respondents believe core-course instructors mark fairly, don't hide the fact because it doesn't match what you expected to discover. Instead, report your findings accurately and rethink your original position. The following section further explores ethical matters.

Ethical Issues

23.3

Conduct primary research ethically.

Today most people chuckle at an advertisement for a product recommended by "nine out of ten doctors." We recognize that the doctors were hand picked and don't represent an objective sample of adequate size. As a result, little harm occurs. With primary research, however, distorted investigating and reporting are sometimes hard to detect and can have significant consequences.

Say the officials of Anytown, USA, alarmed at a sharp rise in auto accidents caused by distracted drivers, schedule a special meeting attempting to ban cell phone calls by those driving within city limits. It would be unethical for a reporter opposed to the ban to write a supposedly objective feature article on the issue but include interviews only with people who share his views. Now suppose a presumably neutral group in the city of Lost Wages distributes a questionnaire to residents to gauge their reaction to a proposed gambling casino. It would be unethical to include a biased question such as "Should the city deprive its citizens of the revenue that a casino can provide?" Finally, imagine that a city manager, concerned by reports of motorists running the red light at a major intersection, gets the Department of Public Safety to investigate. A department employee conducts a 20-minute observation, then writes a report concluding that surveillance cameras are not needed there. Clearly, the employee has acted unethically in drawing a conclusion after such a limited observation. To help ensure that your primary research reports are ethically responsible, ask and answer the following questions.

- Have I attempted to avoid bias in gathering and evaluating information?
- Are my data based on an adequate sample size? If not, have the limitations of the sample been clearly indicated?

- Is my information presented objectively and completely with no intentional effort to omit findings that run counter to my position?
- Are the people involved, whether I'm preparing an interview, questionnaire, or direct observation report, aware that they are part of a study and how the information will be used? Are they protected from harm that might result from their inclusion?
- Do I have permission to name in my report persons interviewed or observed?
- In an interview report, would the interviewee recognize and accept statements attributed to him or her?
- Have I noted any apparent bias in the interviewee?
- In a questionnaire report, have I avoided any biased questions?

Ethical Review of Primary Research

Many universities have ethical review panels that oversee all research that uses human and animal subjects to make certain that they are not harmed by the research. In some cases, some schools require studies that involve focus groups or interviews to be reviewed by the panel. If you are going to use primary research such as an interview or a survey, be sure to check with your teacher so that your study is consistent with your university's policies on research review.

Interviews

During an interview, questions are asked and answered. Some interviews amount to little more than brief, informal chats. Others, like those discussed here, may feature extended conversations, involve a series of questions, and require careful preparation. Interviewing an informed person provides you with firsthand answers to your queries, lets you ask follow-up questions, and gives you access to the most up-to-date thinking.

If you major in a business program, an instructor may require you to question a personnel manager about the company's employee relations program. If your field is social work, you might have to interview a case worker as part of your study of some kind of family problem. On the job, you might have to talk with prospective employees and then assess their suitability for a position in the company. Police officers routinely interview witnesses to accidents and crimes, and journalists do the same in pursuit of stories.

Choosing the Interviewee

Professional and technical personnel are a rich source of interview candidates. The faculty of any university can provide insights into a wide range of subjects. Doctors, pharmacists, and other health professionals can draw upon their expertise to help you, as can lawyers, engineers, researchers, corporation managers, and employees at every level of government—federal, state, and local.

23.4

Prepare for and conduct interviews, and write a report based on interviews.

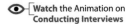

Watch the Animation on **Conducting Interviews**

Whom you interview depends, of course, on what you wish to know. For information on the safe disposal of high-level nuclear waste, you might consult a physics professor. If you want an expert view on the causes of homelessness, contact an authority such as a sociologist, who could provide objective information. If, however, you want to gain a sense of what it's like to be homeless, you might interview the manager of a shelter or (in a safe place) one or more homeless people. Interviews can be face to face, but you may also consider using a phone interview, employing Skype, using Chat, or even interacting via e-mail.

Preparing for the Interview

If you don't relish the thought of phoning to request an interview, keep in mind that most interviewees are eager to discuss their areas of expertise and are often flattered by the opportunity. The worst that can happen is a turndown, and in that event you can always find someone else in the same field.

Before you phone or use other media, review your own upcoming commitments and try to determine which ones you could reschedule if necessary. You may need to make an adjustment to accommodate the schedule of a busy person. When you call, indicate who you are, that you are requesting an interview, the subject of the interview, and how much time you'd like.

If the person agrees to meet with you, then ask when it would be convenient. Carefully record the time, day, and place of the interview, and if for any reason you need to cancel be sure to call well in advance. If you are using a phone interview or other medium, be sure to equally agree on the medium, contact information, and time in advance.

Before the interview, do as much background reading as possible. This reading will help you develop a list of key questions and avoid those with obvious and readily available answers. Write out your questions to help ensure that the interview will proceed smoothly.

Good questions permit elaboration and don't call for simple "yes" or "no" answers. To illustrate:

Poor: Is it difficult to work with adult illiterates? (The obvious answer is "yes.")

Better: What have you found most challenging about working with adult illiterates?

On the other hand, don't ask overly broad questions that can't be answered in a relatively brief interview.

Poor: What's wrong with primary-school education?

Better: Why do you think so many children have trouble learning to read?

Avoid questions that are biased and may insult the interviewee.

Poor: Why do you bother to work with adult illiterates?

Better: Why did you decide to work with adult illiterates?

Likewise, avoid questions that restrict the interviewee's options for answering.

Poor: What do you think accounts for the poor academic performance of so many American secondary-school students—too much TV watching or overly large classes?

Better: People often blame the poor academic performance of so many American students on too much TV watching or overly large classes. What importance do you attach to these factors? Do you think other factors contribute to the problem?

The number of questions you prepare depends on the length of the interview. It's a good idea to draft more questions than you think you'll have time to ask, then arrange them from most to least important. If the interviewee keeps to the schedule, you'll obtain your desired information. If the interviewee grants you extra time, your written follow-up will have even more substance.

Conducting the Interview

Naturally you'll want to arrive on time and to bring a notepad and a pen. Sometimes you can tape-record an interview but only if you ask permission first. Because most people warm up slowly, you might start with one or two brief, general questions that provide you with useful background. Possibilities include "What is the nature of your specialty?" and "How long have you been employed in this field?"

Proceed by asking your most important questions first. If you believe that a question hasn't been answered or that an answer is incomplete, don't hesitate to ask follow-up questions.

As the interview unfolds, take notes but don't attempt to copy everything that's said. Instead, jot down key phrases and ideas that will serve as memory prompts. If you want to capture an essential explanation or some other important material in the interviewee's own words, ask the person to go slowly while you copy them down. When the interview is over, thank the person for talking to you. You may also offer to supply a copy of the finished report. Write a personal note thanking the person for his or her time. With the answers to your questions fresh in your mind, expand on your notes by filling in details, supplying necessary connections between points that were made, and noting your reactions.

Writing About the Interview

The project you're working on determines how to handle your interview information. If you're preparing a library research paper, include the material, suitably presented, at the appropriate spot and document it according to whatever system, MLA or APA, you're using.

Often, however, you'll be asked to prepare a separate report of the interview. Then, as with any other report, you'll need to organize and present the material in an effective order. Your topic, purpose, and audience will determine the arrangement you select. In any event, remember to establish the context for the report, identify the interviewee and his or her position, and present the information accurately.

SAMPLE

STUDENT INTERVIEW REPORT

Budget Cuts Affect State Police: An Interview Report with Officer Robert Timmons

Holly Swain

> Paragraph 1: establishes context for interview

Confronted with a billion-dollar budget deficit, the state legislature and the governor have been forced to make sharp budget cuts. One of these cuts is the allocation to the state police. This decision has threatened the loss of some police jobs and aroused considerable controversy. How, many ask, will the police, who were already on a tight budget, be able to provide the public with adequate protection when they have even less money and fewer personnel?

> Sentence 1, paragraph 2: identifies interviewee and his position

When Trooper Robert Timmons, a state police officer based in Marywood County, first heard that the governor might call for police cutbacks, he didn't believe they would become a reality. Timmons thought the governor was just making "political noise." Actually, the state police head did at first propose cutting 350 jobs, Timmons's among them, to help meet a $19 million cutback. This proposal was rejected in favor of one that combined demotions, pay cuts, and the elimination of special programs. In addition, the amounts allotted for other purposes were also cut.

> Remainder of report: presents information provided by interviewee

All of these actions, Timmons says, have had an unfortunate effect on the operations of the state police. As an example, he mentions a sergeant who was demoted to "accident reconstructionist," a job requiring him to review severe accidents and reconstruct what happened for the court. This demotion, Timmons says, has taken an excellent police officer out of the field, where he's most needed, and put him behind a desk.

Timmons notes several bad effects of cuts in the allocation for gasoline. Because of these cuts, troopers are expected to drive just ninety miles a night. Timmons thinks this limitation has a "direct effect on the public." A motorist stranded on a freeway might not be spotted and aided by a trooper who is unable to make another run through that territory. Late-night accidents might go undiscovered, with serious or fatal consequences for those involved. Many more speeders and drunk drivers will escape being caught.

As of now, Timmons says, there are only 3,000 state police, about 400 fewer than needed. Each year, 100 to 200 officers retire. These vacancies need to be filled, but according to Timmons, the state academy has been closed for over a year. The personnel shortages that already exist and the cutbacks resulting from the state's budget troubles are making it harder and harder for the state police to do an adequate job of protecting the public.

Officer Timmons understands that the state government needs to control its spending. However, he believes that the present budget cutbacks for a department that is already understaffed are very unwise. "I feel the governor should have given the matter more thought," he says.

Questionnaires

A questionnaire consists essentially of a series of statements or questions to which recipients are asked to respond. Questionnaires help individuals and organizations determine what select groups of people think about particular products, services, issues, and personal matters. You yourself have probably completed a variety of questionnaires, including teacher evaluations and market surveys.

Questionnaires are used extensively both on campus and in the workplace. A social science instructor might ask you to prepare a survey that explores community reaction to a recently implemented curfew for teenagers. A business instructor might want you to survey a test-market group to determine its response to some new product. In fact, some marketing classes focus on survey techniques. But even if marketing isn't your specialty, learning how to construct questionnaires can serve you well in your career. If you work in the hotel, restaurant, or health service field, you could use a questionnaire to gauge customer satisfaction. The same holds true if you manage or own a small repair service. As a landscape specialist, you might survey the people in your community to learn what planting and maintenance services they desire. There are a number of survey tools available online, including Survey Monkey, that allow you to send people an electronic survey that is automatically tallied.

23.5

Develop and administer questionnaires, and write a report based on the data.

Developing the Questionnaire

 Watch the Animation on Writing Surveys

When you develop a questionnaire, you need to target precisely what you want to know and what group you intend to survey. You could survey restaurant customers to determine their attitudes about the service and the quality of the food or to assess the types of food they prefer. Zero in on only one area of interest and then explore it with appropriate questions.

Begin the questionnaire with a clear explanation of what you intend to accomplish, and supply brief but clear instructions on how to respond to each part. Keep the questionnaire as short as possible, preferably no longer than a page or two. The longer the survey, the less likely that people will answer all the questions.

As you draw up your questions, take care to avoid these common errors:

1. Don't ask two questions in the same sentence. Their answers may be different.

   Unacceptable: Do you find that this year's Ford Taurus has better acceleration and fuel economy than last year's model?

   To correct this fault, use separate sentences.

   Better: Do you find that this year's Ford Taurus has better acceleration than last year's model?

   Better: Do you find that this year's Ford Taurus has better fuel economy than last year's model?

2. Don't include vague or ambiguous questions. Since people won't understand your intent, their answers may not reflect their beliefs.

   Unacceptable: Is assisted suicide a good idea?

   Better: Should assisted suicide be permitted for terminally ill patients?

3. Avoid biased questions. They might antagonize those who don't share your views and cause them not to complete the questionnaire.

   Unacceptable: Should Century City taxpayers continue to waste money on renovating the North Park Bridge?

   Better: Should Century City taxpayers spend an additional $100,000 to complete the North Park Bridge renovation?

Most questionnaire items fall into the categories that follow. The information you want determines which you choose. Often you'll need to include several or all of the categories in your questionnaire.

Two-Choice Items   Some items have two possible responses: yes/no, true/false, male/female.

Example: Do you plan to repaint your house during the summer months?

☐ yes
☐ no

Multiple-Choice Items   Often there are several possible responses to a questionnaire item. When you prepare this type of item, make sure that you include all significant choices and that the choices share some common ground. Don't ask if someone's primary vehicle is a subcompact, compact, full-size, or foreign car as size and place of manufacture are unrelated. To determine whether the vehicle is domestic or foreign, use a separate item.

Example: Check the income group that describes your combined family income.

☐ less than $9,999 a year
☐ $10,000–$19,999 a year

☐ $20,000–$29,999 a year
☐ $30,000–$39,999 a year
☐ $40,000–$50,000 a year
☐ over $50,000 a year

Checklists Checklists allow respondents to mark more than one option. They can help you determine the range of factors that led to a decision.

Example: Please check any of the following factors that help explain why you decided not to re-enroll your child in Good Growth Private School:

☐ can no longer afford tuition
☐ moved
☐ dissatisfaction with child's progress
☐ disagree with school's educational approach
☐ conflict with teacher
☐ conflict with other staff
☐ child unhappy with school
☐ child had conflict with other children

Ranking Lists Sometimes you may need to ask people to rank their preferences. This information will help you select the most suitable option from among several possibilities.

Example: Designating your first choice as "1," please rank your preferences in music from 1 through 5.

☐ classical
☐ country and western
☐ jazz
☐ rock and roll
☐ heavy metal
☐ rap

Using the responses to this item, the manager of a local radio station could broadcast the type of music that listeners clearly prefer.

Scale Items When you are trying to determine the extent to which members of a group support or oppose some issue, using a scale can be helpful. Be sure to have people respond to a statement, *not* a question.

Example: Please circle the response that best reflects your feelings about the statement below.

SA = strongly agree, A = agree, N = no opinion, D = disagree, SD = strongly disagree

Women should be allowed to fly combat aircraft in time of war.

SA   A   N   D   SD

Open-Ended Items   When you want to gather ideas from other people, you might turn to open-ended items—those that don't limit the reader's response. If you do, keep such items narrow enough to be manageable. You should know, however, that readers are less likely to complete open-ended items and that they are difficult to sort and tally.

Example: Please list the three improvements that you would most like to see in Lowden's high school curriculum.

_____

_____

_____

_____

_____

_____

SAMPLE

STUDENT QUESTIONNAIRE

Survey on Public Smoking

Please take a few minutes to fill out this questionnaire. Your responses will help Bartram College ensure that its smoking policies are sensitive to the smoking habits and attitudes toward public smoking of Bartram College male smokers.

1. Do you smoke cigarettes? (check one) yes/no item

   _____ yes (If you checked yes, please go on to the next question.)

   _____ no (If you checked *no*, please go on to question 4.)

Multiple-choice item

2. If you smoke, indicate how many cigarettes each day. (check one)

   _____ less than half a pack

   _____ between a half and a whole pack

   _____ between one and two packs

   _____ more than two packs

3. If you smoke, what are you likely to do upon entering a public place with no posted smoking restrictions? (check one)

   _____ smoke freely

   _____ check to see whether your smoking is bothering others

   _____ ask others whether they would be bothered if you smoke

   _____ not smoke

4. Check the statements you believe are true.

_____ My health is at risk only if I am a smoker.

_____ Secondhand smoke contains the same ingredients as directly inhaled smoke.

_____ Secondhand smoke poses no health risk to nonsmokers.

_____ Secondhand smoke poses a health risk to nonsmokers.

_____ Secondhand smoke poses less of a health risk than directly inhaled smoke.

Checklist

5. Please rate each of the statements below, using the following scale: SA = strongly agree, A = agree, N = no opinion, D = disagree, SD = strongly disagree.

_____ There should be no restrictions on public smoking.

_____ Smoking should be prohibited in stores, banks, offices, and workshops.

_____ Smoking and nonsmoking sections in restaurants should be separated by a barrier that smoke cannot penetrate.

_____ Smokers and nonsmokers should have separate workplace lounges.

_____ All public smoking should be prohibited.

Scale items

6. Please add one or two comments you might have regarding public smoking.

_____

_____

_____

_____

Open-ended item

Testing and Administering the Questionnaire

When you have finished creating the questionnaire, ask several people to respond to the items and gauge their effectiveness. Are any items vague, ambiguous, biased, or otherwise faulty? If so, rewrite and retest them.

To ensure that you obtain an accurate assessment, make certain that you select an appropriate cross section of recipients. To illustrate, assume that you and many of your campus friends dislike early morning classes. You decide to draw up a questionnaire to sample the attitudes of other students. You suspect that many students share your dislike, and you plan to submit your findings to the college president for possible action. To obtain meaningful results, you'll have to sample a sizable group of students. Furthermore, this group will need to include representative numbers of first-year students, sophomores, juniors, and seniors because these classes may not share a uniform view. Failure to sample properly can call your results into question and cause the administration to disregard them. Proper sampling, on the other hand, pinpoints where dissatisfaction is greatest and suggests a possible response. Thus, if first-year students and sophomores register the most objections, the administration might decide to reduce the number of 100- and 200-level classes meeting at 8 A.M. Some sampling strategies, such as the use of Facebook as a tool to get results, can make it more difficult to get an adequate sample. When you are aware of weaknesses in your sampling, you can still use the data, but you must use it more carefully, clearly state the limitations of your sampling, and make certain you do not make claims that go beyond your sample population.

Totaling the Responses

When the recipients have finished marking the questionnaire, you will need to total the responses. Even without computer scoring, this job is easier than you might think. Simply prepare a table that lists the questionnaire items and the possible responses to each; then go through the questionnaire and add up the number of times each response is marked.

When you finish, turn your numbers into percentages, which provide an easier-to-understand comparison of the responses. Simply divide the number of times each possible response is checked by the total number of questionnaires and then multiply the result by 100.

Writing the Questionnaire Report

When you write your report, don't merely fill it with numbers and responses to the questionnaire items. Instead, look for patterns in the responses and try to draw conclusions from them. Follow the logical order of the conclusions you want to stress.

Typically, a report consists of two or three sections. The first, "Purpose and Scope," explains why the survey was performed, how many questionnaires were distributed and returned, and how the recipients were contacted. The second section, "Results," reports the conclusions that were drawn. Finally, if appropriate, a "Recommendations" section offers responses that seem warranted based on the survey findings.

SAMPLE

STUDENT QUESTIONNAIRE REPORT

Findings from Smoking Questionnaire Distributed to Bartram College Students

Kelly Reetz

Purpose and Scope of Survey

This survey was carried out to determine the smoking habits and attitudes toward public smoking of Bartram College's male students. The

Provides background details on project, profile of respondents assignment was one of my requirements for completing Public Health 201. Each of the 240 male students in Crandall Hall received a copy of the questionnaire in his mailbox, and 72 completed questionnaires were returned. This latter number equals 10 percent of the college's male student population and therefore can be considered a representative sample. Of those responding, 37, or 51 percent, were cigarette smokers. Thirty-five, or 49 percent, were nonsmokers. Of the smokers, all but 11 percent smoked over a pack of cigarettes a day.

Results of Survey

Smokers seemed fairly considerate of nonsmokers in public places. Only 16 percent said they would smoke freely. In fact, 51 percent said they wouldn't smoke at all. The remaining 33 percent indicated they would either look around to see whether they were bothering others or ask others whether they objected to cigarette smoke.

Discusses responses to questionnaire item 3

In general, respondents seemed aware that secondhand smoke poses a health risk. Seventy-six percent believe that such smoke contains the same ingredients as directly inhaled smoke, and an amazing 96 percent believe that anyone exposed to secondhand smoke may be at risk. Only 3 percent think no health risk is involved.

Discusses responses to questionnaire item 4

Opinions were strongly divided on the matter of banning all public smoking, with 79 percent strongly opposed and 21 percent strongly in favor. As might be expected, all of the smokers fell in the first group, but a surprising 51 percent of the nonsmokers did too. A sharp division was equally apparent between supporters and opponents of restaurant barriers, with 81 percent for or strongly for them and 19 percent against or strongly against them. In contrast to the findings on a smoking ban, all of the smokers favored barriers. Respondents overwhelmingly endorsed, 90 percent to 10 percent, prohibiting smoking in stores and banks and providing separate workplace lounges. Nobody registered a "no opinion" vote on any of the statements under item 5.

Discusses responses to questionnaire item 5

Responses to items 3 through 5 reveal an awareness among smokers of the dangers posed by secondhand cigarette smoke, a concern for the well-being of nonsmokers, and a willingness to accept restrictions, though not an outright ban, on public smoking. This attitude was consistent for both light and heavy smokers. For their part, about half the nonsmokers showed a tolerant attitude by supporting smoking restrictions but rejecting an outright ban.

Discusses patterns in responses to items 3–5

Continued on next page

Continued from previous page

Discusses responses
to item 6

No smokers, but 71 percent of the nonsmokers, responded to the request to provide one or two additional comments. All of these comments dealt with how the respondents would act if bothered by someone else's smoke. Two-thirds said they would move to another spot, half of the remainder said they would ask the smoker to stop, and the other half said they would remain silent rather than risk an argument.

Recommendations

As noted previously, this survey included only male students. To determine how its results compare with those for females, the same questionnaire should be administered to a similar group of female students.

Direct Observations

23.6

Conduct direct observations and write a report based on the observations.

Often direct observation is the most effective means of answering research questions. If you want to know the extent and nature of violence in children's TV cartoons, watching a number of shows will tell you. Similarly, a researcher who seeks information about living conditions in an inner-city area of some metropolis can obtain it by visiting that locale. Such observations furnish firsthand answers to our questions. Notice that the material for observation can be very broad. Primary sources for study could include a review of the response of fans on a fansite, the letters of nineteenth-century women on Iowa farms, or the illustrations on cereal boxes.

In college and on the job, you may need to report your own observations. If you're majoring in business, an instructor might require a report on the work habits of employees at a small local company. If your field is biology, you might need to assess and report on the environmental health of a marsh, riverbank, or other ecological area. On the job, a factory superintendent might observe and then discuss in writing the particulars of some problem-plagued operation. Police officers routinely investigate and report on accidents, and waste-management specialists inspect and report on potential disposal sites.

The following suggestions will help you make your observations, record them, and then write your report.

Watch the Animation on **Conducting Direct Observations**

Preparing to Make the Observations

First, determine the purpose of your observations and keep the purpose firmly in mind as you proceed. Otherwise, you'll overlook important details and record less-than-helpful information. Obviously, observing a classroom to assess the interaction of students calls for a different set of notes than if you were observing the teacher's instructional style or the students' note-taking habits.

Next, establish the site or sites that will best supply you with the information you need. If you're trying to determine how college students interact in the classroom, then the time of day, kind of class, and types of students will all make a difference. You might have to visit more than one class in order to observe the different types of behavior.

If your observations will take place on private property or will involve an organized group such as a class or a legislative body, you'll need to obtain permission and to make an appointment. Also, you might want to supplement your observations with an interview. Ordinarily, the interview will take place after you make your observations so that you can ask about what you've seen. If technical information is needed in advance, the interview should precede the observations. However, you should have done research first so that you do not waste the expert's time and goodwill by asking about information that is reasonably available.

Because you'll probably be making a great many individual observations, try to develop a chart and a code for recording them. Suppose you're comparing the extent to which students interact with one another and with the instructor in remedial and nonremedial composition courses. After much thought, you might develop a chart like the one following:

Class Designation: Composition 100				
Minutes into observation when interaction occurred	Classroom location of interacting students	Number and sex of students	Subject of interaction	Length of interaction

With certain kinds of observations, using a chart will not be possible. In developing your code, you would undoubtedly use M = male and F = female to distinguish the sexes. To show the location of the interacting students, FC = front of class, MC = middle of class, and BC = back of class would probably work quite well. Coding the kinds of interaction presents a more difficult task. Here, after considering several possibilities, you might decide upon these symbols: CR = class related, SR = school related, SP = sports, D = dating, O = other matters. To save writing time, you'd probably want to use "min." for "minutes" and "sec." for "seconds" when recording the lengths of the interactions.

Making the Observations

If your visit involves a scheduled appointment, be sure to arrive on time and be ready to take notes. Select a location where you can observe without interfering. If you are observing people or animals, remember that they need to adjust to you before they will behave naturally.

Before you begin taking notes, record any pertinent general information. If you're observing a class, you might note the time it is meeting, its size, the name of the instructor, and whether he or she is present when you arrive. If you're observing an apartment, pertinent information would include the location and condition of the building, the time of the visit, and the general nature of the environment. Note also whether the landlord as well as the tenant knew you were coming: It is amazing how much cleanup landlords can carry out when they know an observer will soon arrive.

Don't feel as though you must take extensive notes. Do, however, record enough details to ensure that you won't forget any events, activities, or features that are important. If you have a chart and coding system, rely on it as much as possible when recording information. Refer to the chart at the bottom of this page for how the coded notes for part of a classroom visit might look.

If you haven't developed a chart, take enough notes so that you can produce a thorough report. Try to follow some note-taking pattern. When observing the condition of an apartment, you could proceed from room to room, jotting down observations such as "Front hallway, entranceway: paint peeling in large strips from wall, paint chips on floor. Hallway dark, bulb burned out. Linoleum curling up along sides. Cockroaches running along lower molding." Remain as objective as possible as you take notes. Record what you see, hear, and smell, and avoid loaded language. If you must record a subjective impression, identify it as such.

Ask questions if necessary, but rely primarily on what you observe, not what you're told. If the landlord of a run-down apartment you're visiting tells you that he's repainting the building but you see no signs that this is happening, ignore what he says or report it along with an appropriate cautionary comment. When you finish, thank the person(s) who made your observations possible or helped you in other ways.

When you leave the observation site, expand your notes by adding more details. Supply any needed connections and record your overall impressions. To illustrate, suppose you are expanding your notes on student interactions in a composition class. You might note that the greatest number of interactions occurred before and immediately after the instructor arrived, that all student–student interactions involved individuals seated together, that student–instructor interactions included students in all parts of the room, and that all the latter interactions were about subject-related matters. This information might stimulate interesting speculation concerning the student–student and student–teacher relationships in the class, causing you to conclude that the students were hesitant about having exchanges with the instructor. As you proceed, record only what you actually observed, not what you wanted or expected to observe.

Class Designation: Composition 100				
Minutes into observation when interaction occurred	Classroom location of interacting students	Number and sex of students	Subject of interaction	Length of interaction
0	FC	M-M	SP	1 min. 30 sec.
3	MC	F-F	D	Instructor arrived
5	FC, MC, BC	M-M-M-F-F	CR	3 min. 45 sec.
20	FC, MC	M-F-M	CR	1 min.

If upon reviewing your notes you find that you require more information, you may need to arrange a second or even a third visit to the observation site.

Writing the Report

Once your notes are in final form, you can start writing your report. On the job your employer may specify a certain form to follow. As a general rule, all such reports reflect their purposes, focus on relevant information, and remain objective.

Usually you begin by explaining the reason for the investigation, noting any preliminary arrangements that were made, and if appropriate, providing an overview of the observation site. Depending on the nature of the report, the primary means of organization may be as follows:

1. *Narration.* A report on the changing conduct of a child over a three-hour period in a day-care center would probably be organized by narration.
2. *Description.* A report assessing the tornado damage in a large urban area could present its details in spatial order.
3. *Classification.* A visit to a toxic-waste dump suspected of violating state regulations might produce a report classifying the types of waste improperly stored there.
4. *Point-by-point comparison.* If you're comparing two possible sites for a baseball stadium, shopping mall, or other structure, a point-by-point comparison will probably best suit your purpose.
5. *Cause and effect.* This pattern works well for reporting events whose effects are of special concern, such as the testing of a new siren intended to scare birds from an airport runway.
6. *Process.* This arrangement is indicated when readers will want to know step-by-step how some process—for example, a new test for determining the mineral content of water—is carried out.

Conclude the report by discussing the significance of the findings and making any other comments that seem justified.

SAMPLE

STUDENT OBSERVATION REPORT

Observations of an Inner-City Apartment Building
Caleb Thomas

To fulfill part of the requirements for Social Service 321, I observed the housing conditions in an inner-city residential area. The building I selected is located in the city of Grand Mound, at the corner of Division Avenue and Hall Street, an area where most of the residents hold minimum-wage jobs or receive some form of public assistance.

Gives reason for visit, location of site

Continued on next page

Continued from previous page

Notes preliminary
arrangements,
provides overview of
site location

I met the building supervisor, who had agreed to this visit, at 9:30 A.M. on Friday, April 13, 2001. The brick sides of the three-story apartment building appeared to be in good repair, but one second-story window was broken out and boarded up. Most windows had standard window shades, but a few were blocked with sheets or black plastic bags. Two had no coverings of any kind. Overall, the building's appearance was similar to that of several nearby apartment buildings.

Continues overview of
site location

Heavy traffic clogged Division Avenue at the time of my visit. Next to the apartment building stood three single-story wooden buildings housing an adult video store, a bar, and a novelty shop, all with boarded windows and peeling paint. Across the street, a single-story Goodwill store occupied the entire block. In front of it, three women in short skirts walked slowly back and forth, eyeing the cars that passed. Two men sat on crates, their backs to the building, drinking something out of paper bags.

Describes building's
hallway

The supervisor opened the unlocked metal door of the apartment building, and we went in. The hallway was lighted by a single dim bulb located on the wall toward the rear. Other bulbs along the wall and in two light fixtures hanging from the ceiling appeared burned out. Scraps of newspaper and chips of paint that had peeled from the ceiling and walls littered the floor. A strong urine-like smell pervaded the air.

Describes apartment
hallway

Stating that he couldn't show me an occupied apartment because he "respected the privacy of the tenants," the supervisor took me to an unoccupied apartment on the first floor. He had trouble unlocking the wooden door; the key appeared to stick in the lock. The inside of the door had two bolt locks, one a few inches above the door handle and the other one near the floor. The door opened into a short hall with rooms off either side. Here, as in the building entrance, paint chips from the peeling walls and ceiling littered the floor. A battered socket on the wall held a single bulb, but when I flicked its switch, the bulb did not light. On the hall floor, linoleum curled at the edges. When I bent down to examine it more closely, several cockroaches scurried under the curl.

Describes apartment
living room

The first door on the right-hand side of the hall led into a 10-by-12-foot room that the supervisor identified as the living room. Here the walls had been recently painted—by a former tenant, the supervisor said—and a strong paint smell was still apparent. However, nothing else had been done to the rest of the room. The radiator was unshielded, several nail heads protruded from the stained and uncovered wooden floor, and the sagging ceiling had several long cracks. Plaster chips dotted the floor.

A small kitchen was situated behind the living room. Again, linoleum floor covering curled from the baseboard, and cockroaches scurried for cover. The kitchen was furnished with a battered-looking gas stove, but there was no refrigerator (the supervisor said one was on order). The surface of the sink was chipped and had many brownish stains. When I turned on the faucet, a rusty brown stream of water spurted out. I asked for a sample to be tested for lead content, but the supervisor refused.

| Describes apartment kitchen |

The bathroom, located at the end of the hall, had no radiator. Its floor tiles, broken in a number of places, exposed a foot-long section of rotted wood. The toilet, with seat missing, would not flush when I tried it but simply made a hissing noise. A brown stain spread over the bottom of the bathtub and a large portion of its sides. The wall tiles around the tub bulged outward and appeared ready to collapse into the tub. The supervisor offered the observation that there had been "some trouble with the plumbing."

| Describes apartment bathroom |

Two small bedrooms opened off the left side of the hall. Like the living room, both had unprotected radiators, uncovered wooden floors, and cracked ceilings. Walls were papered rather than painted, but long strips of the wallpaper were missing. In one bedroom, a piece of plasterboard hung on the wall as if covering a hole. The windows in both bedrooms were covered with sheets tacked to the wall.

| Describes apartment bedrooms |

When I had finished looking at the bedrooms, the supervisor quickly escorted me from the apartment and the building, declaring that he was too busy to show me any other vacant apartments. He also said he had no time to answer any questions.

Clearly, the building I visited fails to meet city housing code: The living conditions are not what most people would consider acceptable. A careful investigation, including a test of the water and of the paint for lead content, seems called for to determine whether this apartment constitutes a health risk.

| Discusses significance of findings |

Complete additional exercises and practice in your MyLab

Reader

NARRATION ▪ ▪ ▪ ▪ ▪ ▪ ▪ ▪ ▪ ▪

Reading Strategies

1. Read the narrative rapidly to get a feel for the story and identify the main point.

2. Identify the main conflict that moves the story forward. Identify the major characters and what they may represent.

3. Read the narrative more slowly with the main point in mind. Keep an eye on how the narrative supports the main point.

Reading Critically

1. Consider if the narrative would seem different if told from another person's point of view. Consider that point of view.

2. Ask whether the narrative really supports the author's main point. Consider what other narratives could be told about the issue and determine whether they might undermine the writer's claims.

Reading As a Writer

1. Determine the setting, conflict, characters, and development of the narrative. You might want to outline the plot to determine how it was organized.

2. Notice any particularly effective movements in the plot. If you find a useful strategy, jot it down.

3. Observe how the writer used dialogue. Make a note of any especially effective uses.

JAMES ALEXANDER THOM

The Perfect Picture[1]

James Alexander Thom (born 1933) is a native of Gosport, Indiana, where his parents were physicians, and a graduate of Butler University. Before becoming a freelance writer in 1973, he worked as an editor for the Indianapolis Star *and the* Saturday Evening Post *and as a lecturer at Indiana University. He has authored one volume of essays and several historical novels, one of which,* Panther in the Sky, *earned the Best Novel Award from the Western Writers of America. His latest novel,* The Red Heart, *appeared in 1998. He is a contributor to many magazines. "The Perfect Picture" depicts an incident and an ethical dilemma that Thom experienced as a cub reporter.*

Introduction: notes time, locale, and cause of action; first-person point of view	1 It was early in the spring about 15 years ago—a day of pale sunlight and trees just beginning to bud. I was a young police reporter, driving to a scene I didn't want to see. A man, the police-dispatcher's broadcast said, had accidentally backed his pickup truck over his baby granddaughter in the driveway of the family home. It was a fatality.

2   As I parked among police cars and TV-news cruisers, I saw a stocky white-haired man in cotton work clothes standing near a pickup. Cameras were trained on him, and reporters were sticking microphones in his face. Looking totally bewildered, he was trying to answer their questions. Mostly he was only moving his lips, blinking and choking up.

Body: paragraphs 2–12; action begins

3   After a while the reporters gave up on him and followed the police into the small white house. I can still see in my mind's eye that devastated old man looking down at the place in the driveway where the child had been. Beside the house was a freshly spaded flower bed, and nearby a pile of dark, rich earth.

Time signal
Key event

4   "I was just backing up there to spread that good dirt," he said to me, though I had not asked him anything. "I didn't even know she was outdoors." He stretched his hand toward the flower bed, then let it flop to his side. He lapsed back into his thoughts, and I, like a good reporter, went into the house to find someone who could provide a recent photo of the toddler.

Dialogue

5   A few minutes later, with all the details in my notebook and a three-by-five studio portrait of the cherubic child tucked in my jacket pocket, I went toward the kitchen where the police had said the body was.

Time signal
Secondary event

6   I had brought a camera in with me—the big, bulky Speed Graphic which used to be the newspaper reporter's trademark. Everybody had drifted back out of the house together—family, police, reporters and photographers. Entering the kitchen, I came upon this scene:

7   On a Formica-topped table, backlighted by a frilly curtained window, lay the tiny body, wrapped in a clean white sheet. Somehow the grandfather had managed to stay away from the crowd. He was sitting on a chair beside the table, in profile to me and unaware of my presence, looking uncomprehendingly at the swaddled corpse.

Key event

8   The house was very quiet. A clock ticked. As I watched, the grandfather slowly leaned forward, curved his arms like parentheses around the head and feet of the little form, then pressed his face to the shroud and remained motionless.

Time signal

9   In that hushed moment I recognized the makings of a prize-winning news photograph. I appraised the light, adjusted the lens setting and distance, locked a bulb in the flashgun, raised the camera and composed the scene in the viewfinder.

10   Every element of the picture was perfect: the grandfather in his plain work clothes, his white hair backlighted by sunshine, the child's form wrapped in the sheet, the atmosphere of the simple home suggested by black iron trivets and World's Fair souvenir plates on the walls flanking the window. Outside, the police could be seen inspecting the fatal rear wheel of the pickup while the child's mother and father leaned in each other's arms.

11   I don't know how many seconds I stood there, unable to snap that shutter. I was keenly aware of the powerful story-telling value that photo would have, and my professional conscience told me to take it. Yet I couldn't make my hand fire that flashbulb and intrude on the poor man's island of grief.

Conflict

12   At length I lowered the camera and crept away, shaken with doubt about my suitability for the journalistic profession. Of course I never told the city editor or any fellow reporters about that missed opportunity for a perfect news picture.

Time signal
Action ends

13   Every day on the newscasts and in the papers, we see pictures of people in extreme conditions of grief and despair. Human suffering has become a spectator sport. And sometimes, as I'm watching news film, I remember that day.

Conclusion: paragraphs 13 and 14; indirectly states point; notes writer's reaction

14   I still feel right about what I did.

Discussion Questions

1. Thom notes in his opening paragraph that he is "driving to a scene I didn't want to see." How does this statement help explain what happens later?
2. These details, while providing the makings of a perfect picture, also highlight the horror of what has happened and through their impact on his sensitivity help influence his decision.
3. Do you think that Thom made the right decision? Why or why not?

Toward Key Insights

How have the media affected our sense of privacy?

Is their influence good or bad?

To answer these questions, consider the role of the newspaper photographer in "The Perfect Picture," TV crews at disasters, and talk shows built around very personal revelations.

Suggestion for Writing

Write a personal narrative that features a conflict over a choice between an advantageous and a morally satisfying decision. State your point directly or indirectly, and use time signals and dialogue as necessary.

DAN GREENBURG

Sound and Fury

Dan Greenburg is a native of Chicago who holds a bachelor of fine arts from the University of Illinois and a master of fine arts from UCLA. A prolific writer, he has authored over 40 books, including such best sellers as How to Be a Jewish Mother, How to Make Yourself Miserable, How to Avoid Love and Marriage, *and a series of more than 24 children's books,* The Zack Files. *His articles have appeared in a wide and diverse range of popular magazines and been reprinted in many anthologies of humor and satire. He has been a guest on* The Today Show, Larry King Live, Late Night with David Letterman, *and other major TV talk shows. In this selection, Greenburg relates a situation in which soft words defused a potentially explosive situation.*

1   We carry around a lot of free-floating anger. What we do with it is what fascinates me.

2   My friend Lee Frank is a stand-up comedian who works regularly in New York comedy clubs. Not long ago I accompanied him to one of these places, where he was to be the late-night emcee and where I myself had once done a stand-up act in a gentler era.

3   The crowd that night was a typical weekend bunch—enthusiastic, hostile and drunk. A large contingent of inebriated young men from Long Island had decided that a comedian named Rusty who was currently on stage was the

greatest thing since pop-top cans and began chanting his name after almost everything he said: "Rus-TEE! Rus-TEE!"

4   My friend Lee knew he had a tough act to follow.

5   Indeed, the moment Lee walked on stage, the inebriated young men from Long Island began chanting "Rus-TEE! Rus-TEE!" and didn't give him a chance. Poor Lee, the flop sweat running into his eyes, tried every trick he knew to win them over, and finally gave up.

6   When he left the stage I joined him at the bar in the back of the club to commiserate.

7   "You did the best you could," I told him.

8   "I don't know," he said, "I could have handled it better."

9   "How?"

10   "I don't know," he said.

11   As we spoke, the young men who'd given him such a tough time trickled into the bar area. One of them spotted Lee and observed to a companion that Lee might want to do something about their heckling.

12   Lee thought he heard the companion reply, "I'm down," a casual acknowledgment that he was willing to have a fistfight. Lee repeated their remarks to me and indicated that he, too, was "down."

13   Though slight of frame, Lee is a black belt in Tae Kwon Do, has had skirmishes with three-card monte con men in Times Square, and once even captured a robber-rapist. I am also slight of frame but have had no training in martial arts. I did have one fistfight in my adult life (with a movie producer), but as Lee's best friend, I assumed that I was "down" as well.

14   Considering that there were more than a dozen of them and only two of us, the period of time that might elapse between our being "down" and our being down seemed exceedingly brief.

15   The young man who'd made the remark drifted toward Lee.

16   The eyes of everyone in the bar shifted slightly and locked onto the two men like heat-seeking missiles. Fight-or-flight adrenaline and testosterone spurted into dozens of male cardiovascular systems. Safeties snapped off figurative weapons. Red warning lights lit up dozens of DEFCON systems; warheads were armed and aimed. In a moment this bar area might very well resemble a saloon in a B grade western.

17   "How ya doing?" said Lee, his voice flat as unleavened bread, trying to make up his mind whether to be friendly or hostile.

18   "Okay," said the guy, a pleasant-looking, clean-cut kid in his mid-20s.

19   I was fascinated by what was going on between the two of them, each feeling the other out in a neutral, unemotional, slightly bemused manner. I saw no hostility here, no xenophobic loathing, just two young males jockeying for position, going through the motions, doing the dance, willing to engage at the slightest provocation. I had seen my cat do this many times when a stranger strayed onto his turf.

20   And then I had a sudden flash of clarity: These guys could either rip each other's heads off now or they could share a beer, and both options would be equally acceptable to them.

21   I'd felt close to critical mass on many occasions myself. But here, feeling outside the action, I could see clearly that it had to do with the enormous reservoir of rage that we men carry around with us, rage that seethes just under the surface and is ready to be tapped in an instant, with or without just provocation.

22   "What're you in town for?" asked Lee casually.

23   The guy was watching Lee carefully, making minuscule adjustments on his sensing and triggering equipment.

24   "It's my birthday," said the guy.

25   Lee mulled over this information for a moment, still considering all his options. Then he made his decision.

26   "Happy birthday," said Lee finally, sticking out his hand.

27   The guy studied Lee's hand a moment. Then, deciding the gesture was sincere, he took the hand and shook it.

28   "Thanks," he said, and walked back to his buddies.

29   All over the room you could hear safeties snapping on, warheads being unarmed. The incident was over, and in a moment it was as if it had never happened.

30   I felt I had just witnessed in microcosm the mechanism that triggers most acts of aggression, from gang fights to international conflagrations. It was so simple: a minor act of provocation. A decision on how to interpret it. Whether or not to escalate. And, in this particular case, a peaceful outcome. What struck me was how absolutely arbitrarily it had all been decided.

Discussion Questions

1. Discuss the appropriateness of Greenburg's title.
2. Does this essay have a stated or an unstated point? If it is stated, indicate where. If it is unstated, express it in your own words.
3. The expression "our being down" occurs twice in paragraph 14. Explain what it means in each instance.
4. Discuss the effectiveness of the figurative language in paragraph 16.
5. In paragraph 21 Greenburg credits "feeling outside the action" for helping him understand the rage involved in this situation as well as in others. Explain what he means.
6. How often do you think that the "equally acceptable" options mentioned in paragraph 20 occur in confrontations?

Toward Key Insights

What reasons can you give for the "free-floating anger" that Greenburg mentions at the outset of the essay?

How frequently and in what ways is this anger manifested?

What are some effective strategies for coping with this anger?

Suggestion for Writing

Write a narrative about a small incident that turned into a serious confrontation. Possible incidents might include an improper or reckless action of another driver, a minor disagreement with a friend or spouse, or a retaliation for an action at a sporting event. The outcome can be peaceful or otherwise.

MAYA ANGELOU

Momma's Encounter[1]

Maya Angelou has earned a reputation as one of this country's foremost black writers. Born (1928) Marguerite Johnson in St. Louis, Missouri, she spent much of her childhood in Stamps, Arkansas, the locale of our selection, where her grandmother ran a general store. Angelou has written plays, poems, and a six-part autobiography that includes I Know Why the Caged Bird Sings *(1970), from which our selection is taken. She has acted in numerous plays and has served as a television narrator, interviewer, and poet. At the January 1993 inauguration of President William Clinton, she recited a poem, "On the Pulse of Morning," that she had written especially for the occasion. In our selection, Angelou tells about an encounter in which her grandmother, whom she calls Momma, triumphs over a pack of taunting neighborhood children.*

1   "Thou shall not be dirty" and "Thou shall not be impudent" were the two commandments of Grandmother Henderson upon which hung our total salvation.

2   Each night in the bitterest winter we were forced to wash faces, arms, necks, legs and feet before going to bed. She used to add, with a smirk that unprofane people can't control when venturing into profanity, "and wash as far as possible, then wash possible."

3   We would go to the well and wash in the ice-cold, clear water, grease our legs with the equally cold stiff Vaseline, then tiptoe into the house. We wiped the dust from our toes and settled down for schoolwork, cornbread, clabbered milk, prayers and bed, always in that order. Momma was famous for pulling the quilts off after we had fallen asleep to examine our feet. If they weren't clean enough for her, she took the switch (she kept one behind the bedroom door for emergencies) and woke up the offender with a few aptly placed burning reminders.

4   The area around the well at night was dark and slick, and boys told about how snakes love water, so that anyone who had to draw water at night and then stand there alone and wash knew that moccasins and rattlers, puff adders and boa constrictors were winding their way to the well and would arrive just as the person washing got soap in her eyes. But Momma convinced us that not only was cleanliness next to Godliness, dirtiness was the inventor of misery.

5   The impudent child was detested by God and a shame to its parents and could bring destruction to its house and line. All adults had to be addressed as Mister, Missus, Miss, Auntie, Cousin, Unk, Uncle, Buhbah, Sister, Brother and a thousand other appellations indicating familial relationship and the lowliness of the addressor.

6   Everyone I knew respected these customary laws, except for the powhite-trash children.

7   Some families of powhitetrash lived on Momma's farm land behind the school. Sometimes a gaggle of them came to the Store, filling the whole room, chasing out the air and even changing the well-known scents. The children crawled over the shelves and into the potato and onion bins, twanging all the time in their sharp voices like cigarbox guitars. They took liberties in my Store

[1]Editors' title.

that I would never dare. Since Momma told us that the less you say to whitefolks (or even powhitetrash) the better, Bailey and I would stand, solemn, quiet, in the displaced air. But if one of the playful apparitions got close to us, I pinched it. Partly out of angry frustration and partly because I didn't believe in its flesh reality.

8   They called my uncle by his first name and ordered him around the Store. He, to my crying shame, obeyed them in his limping dip-straight-dip fashion.

9   My grandmother, too followed their orders, except that she didn't seem to be servile because she anticipated their needs.

10   "Here's sugar, Miz Potter, and here's baking powder. You didn't buy soda last month, you'll probably be needing some."

11   Momma always directed her statements to the adults, but sometimes, Oh painful sometimes, the grimy, snotty-nosed girls would answer her.

12   "Naw, Annie . . . "—to Momma? Who owned the land they lived on? Who forgot more than they would ever learn? If there was any justice in the world, God should strike them dumb at once!—"Just give us some extry sody crackers, and some more mackerel."

13   At least they never looked in her face, or I never caught them doing so. Nobody with a smidgen of training, not even the worst roustabout, would look right in a grown person's face. It meant the person was trying to take the words out before they were formed. The dirty little children didn't do that, but they threw their orders around the Store like lashes from a cat-o'-nine tails.

14   When I was around ten years old, those scruffy children caused me the most painful and confusing experience I had ever had with my grandmother.

15   One summer morning, after I had swept the dirt yard of leaves, spearmint-gum wrappers and Vienna-sausage labels, I raked the yellow-red dirt, and made half-moons carefully, so that the design stood out clearly and mask-like. I put the rake behind the Store and came through the back of the house to find Grandmother on the front porch in her big, wide white apron. The apron was so stiff by virtue of the starch that it could have stood alone. Momma was admiring the yard, so I joined her. It truly looked like a flat redhead that had been raked with a big-toothed comb. Momma didn't say anything but I knew she liked it. She looked over toward the school principal's house and to the right at Mr. McElroy's. She was hoping one of those community pillars would see the design before the day's business wiped it out. Then she looked upward to the school. My head had swung with hers, so at just about the same time we saw a troop of the powhitetrash kids marching over the hill and down by the side of the school.

16   I looked to Momma for direction. She did an excellent job of sagging from her waist down, but from the waist up she seemed to be pulling for the top of the oak tree across the road. Then she began to moan a hymn. Maybe not to moan, but the tune was so slow and the meter so strange that she could have been moaning. She didn't look at me again. When the children reached halfway down the hill, halfway to the Store, she said without turning, "Sister, go on inside."

17   I wanted to beg her, "Momma, don't wait for them. Come on inside with me. If they come in the Store, you go to the bedroom and let me wait on them. They only frighten me if you're around. Alone I know how to handle them." But of course I couldn't say anything, so I went in and stood behind the screen door.

18   Before the girls got to the porch I heard their laughter crackling and popping like pine logs in a cooking stove. I suppose my lifelong paranoia was born in those cold, molasses-slow minutes. They came finally to stand on the

ground in front of Momma. At first they pretended seriousness. Then one of them wrapped her right arm in the crook of her left, pushed out her mouth and started to hum. I realized that she was aping my grandmother. Another said, "Naw, Helen, you ain't standing like her. This here's it." Then she lifted her chest, folded her arms and mocked that strange carriage that was Annie Henderson. Another laughed, "Naw, you can't do it. You mouth ain't pooched out enough. It's like this."

19   I thought about the rifle behind the door, but I knew I'd never be able to hold it straight, and the .410, our sawed-off shotgun, which stayed loaded and was fired every New Year's night, was locked in the trunk and Uncle Willie had the key on his chain. Through the fly-specked screen-door, I could see that the arms of Momma's apron jiggled from the vibrations of her humming. But her knees seemed to have locked as if they would never bend again.

20   She sang on. No louder than before, but no softer either. No slower or faster.

21   The dirt of the girls' cotton dresses continued on their legs, feet, arms and faces to make them all of a piece. Their greasy uncolored hair hung down, uncombed, with a grim finality. I knelt to see them better, to remember them for all time. The tears that had slipped down my dress left unsurprising dark spots, and made the front yard blurry and even more unreal. The world had taken a deep breath and was having doubts about continuing to revolve.

22   The girls had tired of mocking Momma and turned to other means of agitation. One crossed her eyes, stuck her thumbs in both sides of her mouth and said, "Look here, Annie." Grandmother hummed on and the apron strings trembled. I wanted to throw a handful of black pepper in their faces, to throw lye on them, to scream that they were dirty, scummy peckerwoods, but I knew I was as clearly imprisoned behind the scene as the actors outside were confined to their roles.

23   One of the smaller girls did a kind of puppet dance while her fellow clowns laughed at her. But the tall one, who was almost a woman, said something very quietly, which I couldn't hear. They all moved backward from the porch, still watching Momma. For an awful second I thought they were going to throw a rock at Momma, who seemed (except for the apron strings) to have turned into stone herself. But the big girl turned her back, bent down and put her hands flat on the ground—she didn't pick up anything. She simply shifted her weight and did a hand stand.

24   Her dirty bare feet and long legs went straight for the sky. Her dress fell down around her shoulders, and she had on no drawers. The slick pubic hair made a brown triangle where her legs came together. She hung in the vacuum of that lifeless morning for only a few seconds, then wavered and tumbled. The other girls clapped her on the back and slapped their hands.

25   Momma changed her song to "Bread of Heaven, bread of Heaven, feed me till I want no more."

26   I found that I was praying too. How long could Momma hold out? What new indignity would they think of to subject her to? Would I be able to stay out of it? What would Momma really like me to do?

27   Then they were moving out of the yard, on their way to town. They bobbed their heads and shook their slack behinds and turned, one at a time:

28   "'Bye, Annie."

29   "'Bye, Annie."

30   "'Bye, Annie."

31   Momma never turned her head or unfolded her arms, but she stopped singing and said, "'Bye, Miz Helen, 'bye, Miz Ruth, 'bye, Miz Eloise."

32   I burst. A firecracker July-the-Fourth burst. How could Momma call them Miz? The mean nasty things. Why couldn't she have come inside the sweet, cool store when we saw them breasting the hill? What did she prove? And then if they were dirty, mean and impudent, why did Momma have to call them Miz?

33   She stood another whole song through and then opened the screen door to look down on me crying in rage. She looked until I looked up. Her face was a brown moon that shone on me. She was beautiful. Something had happened out there, which I couldn't completely understand, but I could see that she was happy. Then she bent down and touched me as mothers of the church "lay hands on the sick and afflicted" and I quieted.

34   "Go wash your face, Sister." And she went behind the candy counter and hummed, "Glory, glory, hallelujah, when I lay my burden down."

35   I threw the well water on my face and used the weekday handkerchief to blow my nose. Whatever the contest had been out front, I knew Momma had won.

36   I took the rake back to the front yard. The smudged footprints were easy to erase. I worked for a long time on my new design and laid the rake behind the wash pot. When I came back in the Store, I took Momma's hand and we both walked outside to look at the pattern.

37   It was a large heart with lots of hearts growing smaller inside, and piercing from the outside rim to the smallest heart was an arrow. Momma said, "Sister, that's right pretty." Then she turned back to the Store and resumed, "Glory, glory, hallelujah, when I lay my burden down."

Discussion Questions

1. Does this narrative have a stated or an unstated point? If it is stated, indicate where. If it is unstated, express it in your own words.
2. Point out the contrast between Angelou's upbringing and that of the "powhite-trash" children. How does this contrast prepare the reader for the events that follow?
3. Explain what Angelou means in paragraph 22 when she says " . . . but I knew I was as clearly imprisoned behind the scene as the actors outside were confined to their roles."
4. Discuss the significance of the dialogue in paragraphs 28–31.
5. Suggest the significance of the pattern of hearts that Angelou draws in the front yard. Of Momma singing "Glory, glory, hallelujah, when I lay my burden down."
6. Angelou recalls that she was "around ten years old" when the encounter took place. Explain why her age was significant. How would her perception have differed had she been, say, 18?
7. Angelou uses the first-person point of view. Explain why third-person narration would have been inappropriate for this narrative.

Toward Key Insights

Was Momma's strategy for enduring the children's taunts the most effective approach? Why or why not?

What else could she have done?

Has she really won?

Some argue that racism should always be actively confronted since passive endurance only perpetuates it. Do you agree? If not, when and how should racism be
confronted and when should it be endured?

Suggestion for Writing

*Write a narrative that illustrates how a friend, an acquaintance, or a family member achieved
a personal triumph through turning the other cheek.*

MARTA SALINAS

The Scholarship Jacket

Marta Salinas has published stories in the Los Angeles Herald *and in* California Living. *She is also an environmental activist.*

1   The small Texas school that I attended carried out a tradition every year
during the eighth grade graduation; a beautiful gold and green jacket, the
school colors, was awarded to the class valedictorian, the student who had maintained the highest grades for eight years. The scholarship jacket had a big gold
S on the left front side and the winner's name was written in gold letters on the
pocket.

2   My oldest sister Rosie had won the jacket a few years back and I fully expected to win also. I was fourteen and in the eighth grade. I had been a straight
A student since the first grade, and the last year I had looked forward to owning
the jacket. My father was a farm laborer who couldn't earn enough money to
feed eight children, so when I was six I was given to my grandparents to raise.
We couldn't participate in sports at school because there were registration fees,
uniform costs, and trips out of town; so even though we were quite agile and
athletic, there would never be a sports school jacket for us. This one, the scholarship jacket, was our only chance.

3   In May, close to graduation, spring fever struck, and no one paid any attention in class; instead we stared out the windows and at each other, wanting
to speed up the last few weeks of school. I despaired every time I looked in the
mirror. Pencil thin, not a curve anywhere, I was called "Beanpole" and "String
Bean" and I knew that's what I looked like. A flat chest, no hips, and a brain,
that's what I had. That really isn't much for a fourteen-year-old to work with,
I thought, as I absentmindedly wandered from my history class to the gym. Another hour of sweating in basketball and displaying my toothpick legs was coming up. Then I remembered my P.E. shorts were still in a bag under my desk
where I'd forgotten them. I had to walk all the way back and get them. Coach
Thompson was a real bear if anyone wasn't dressed for P.E. She had said I was a
good forward and once she even tried to talk Grandma into letting me join the
team. Grandma, of course, said no.

4   I was almost back at my classroom's door when I heard angry voices and arguing. I stopped. I didn't mean to eavesdrop; I just hesitated, not knowing what to

do. I needed those shorts and I was going to be late, but I didn't want to interrupt an argument between my teachers. I recognized the voices: Mr. Schmidt, my history teacher, and Mr. Boone, my math teacher. They seemed to be arguing about me. I couldn't believe it. I still remember the shock that rooted me flat against the wall as if I were trying to blend in with the graffiti written there.

5   "I refuse to do it! I don't care who her father is, her grades don't even begin to compare to Martha's. I won't lie or falsify records. Martha has a straight A plus average and you know it." That was Mr. Schmidt and he sounded very angry. Mr. Boone's voice sounded calm and quiet.

6   "Look, Joann's father is not only on the Board, he owns the only store in town; we could say it was a close tie and—"

7   The pounding in my ears drowned out the rest of the words, only a word here and there filtered through. " . . . Martha is Mexican . . . resign . . . won't do it . . ." Mr. Schmidt came rushing out, and luckily for me went down the opposite way toward the auditorium, so he didn't see me. Shaking, I waited a few minutes and then went in and grabbed my bag and fled from the room. Mr. Boone looked up when I came in but didn't say anything. To this day I don't remember if I got in trouble in P.E. for being late or how I made it through the rest of the afternoon. I went home very sad and cried into my pillow that night so Grandmother wouldn't hear me. It seemed a cruel coincidence that I had overheard that conversation.

8   The next day when the principal called me into his office, I knew what it would be about. He looked uncomfortable and unhappy. I decided I wasn't going to make it any easier for him so I looked him straight in the eye. He looked away and fidgeted with the papers on his desk.

9   "Martha," he said, "there's been a change in policy this year regarding the scholarship jacket. As you know, it has always been free." He cleared his throat and continued. "This year the Board decided to charge fifteen dollars—which still won't cover the complete cost of the jacket."

10   I stared at him in shock and a small sound of dismay escaped my throat. I hadn't expected this. He still avoided looking in my eyes.

11   "So if you are unable to pay the fifteen dollars for the jacket, it will be given to the next one in line."

12   Standing with all the dignity I could muster, I said, "I'll speak to my grandfather about it, sir, and let you know tomorrow." I cried on the walk home from the bus stop. The dirt road was a quarter of a mile from the highway, so by the time I got home, my eyes were red and puffy.

13   "Where's Grandpa?" I asked Grandma, looking down at the floor so she wouldn't ask me why I'd been crying. She was sewing on a quilt and didn't look up.

14   "I think he's out back working in the bean field."

15   I went outside and looked out at the fields. There he was. I could see him walking between the rows, his body bent over the little plants, hoe in hand. I walked slowly out to him, trying to think how I could best ask him for the money. There was a cool breeze blowing and a sweet smell of mesquite in the air, but I didn't appreciate it. I kicked at a dirt clod. I wanted that jacket so much. It was more than just being a valedictorian and giving a little thank you speech for the jacket on graduation night. It represented eight years of hard work and expectation. I knew I had to be honest with Grandpa; it was my only chance. He saw me and looked up.

16   He waited for me to speak. I cleared my throat nervously and clasped my hands behind my back so he wouldn't see them shaking. "Grandpa, I have a big

favor to ask you," I said in Spanish, the only language he knew. He still waited silently. I tried again. "Grandpa, this year the principal said the scholarship jacket is not going to be free. It's going to cost fifteen dollars and I have to take the money in tomorrow, otherwise it'll be given to someone else." The last words came out in an eager rush. Grandpa straightened up tiredly and leaned his chin on the hoe handle. He looked out over the field that was filled with the tiny green bean plants. I waited, desperately hoping he'd say I could have the money.

17   He turned to me and asked quietly, "What does a scholarship jacket mean?"

18   I answered quickly; maybe there was a chance. "It means you've earned it by having the highest grades for eight years and that's why they're giving it to you." Too late I realized the significance of my words. Grandpa knew that I understood it was not a matter of money. It wasn't that. He went back to hoeing the weeds that sprang up between the delicate little bean plants. It was a time consuming job; sometimes the small shoots were right next to each other. Finally he spoke again.

19   "Then if you pay for it, Marta, it's not a scholarship jacket, is it? Tell your principal I will not pay the fifteen dollars."

20   I walked back to the house and locked myself in the bathroom for a long time. I was angry with Grandfather even though I knew he was right, and I was angry with the Board, whoever they were. Why did they have to change the rules just when it was my turn to win the jacket?

21   It was a very sad and withdrawn girl who dragged into the principal's office the next day. This time he did look me in the eyes.

22   "What did your grandfather say?"

23   I sat very straight in my chair.

24   "He said to tell you he won't pay the fifteen dollars."

25   The principal muttered something I couldn't understand under his breath, and walked over to the window. He stood looking out at something outside. He looked bigger than usual when he stood up; he was a tall gaunt man with gray hair, and I watched the back of his head while I waited for him to speak.

26   "Why?" he finally asked. "Your grandfather has the money. Doesn't he own a small bean farm?"

27   I looked at him, forcing my eyes to stay dry. "He said if I had to pay for it, then it wouldn't be a scholarship jacket," I said and stood up to leave. "I guess you'll just have to give it to Joann." I hadn't meant to say that; it had just slipped out. I was almost to the door when he stopped me.

28   "Martha—wait."

29   I turned and looked at him, waiting. What did he want now? I could feel my heart pounding. Something bitter and vile tasting was coming up in my mouth; I was afraid I was going to be sick. I didn't need any sympathy speeches. He sighed loudly and went back to his big desk. He looked at me, biting his lip, as if thinking.

30   "Okay, damn it. We'll make an exception in your case. I'll tell the Board, you'll get your jacket."

31   I could hardly believe it. I spoke in a trembling rush. "Oh, thank you, sir!" Suddenly I felt great. I didn't know about adrenaline in those days, but I knew something was pumping through me, making me feel as tall as the sky. I wanted to yell, jump, run the mile, do something. I ran out so I could cry in the hall where there was no one to see me. At the end of the day, Mr. Schmidt winked at me and said, "I hear you're getting a scholarship jacket this year."

32   His face looked as happy and innocent as a baby's, but I knew better. Without answering I gave him a quick hug and ran to the bus. I cried on the walk

home again, but this time because I was so happy. I couldn't wait to tell Grandpa and ran straight to the field. I joined him in the row where he was working and without saying anything I crouched down and started pulling up the weeds with my hands. Grandpa worked alongside me for a few minutes, but he didn't ask what had happened. After I had a little pile of weeds between the rows, I stood up and faced him.

33   "The principal said he's making an exception for me, Grandpa, and I'm getting the jacket after all. That's after I told him what you said."

34   Grandpa didn't say anything, he just gave me a pat on the shoulder and a smile. He pulled out the crumpled red handkerchief that he always carried in his back pocket and wiped the sweat off his forehead.

35   "Better go see if your grandmother needs any help with supper."

36   I gave him a big grin. He didn't fool me. I skipped and ran back to the house whistling some silly tune.

Discussion Questions

1. Why is the scholarship jacket so important to Marta?
2. What are some of the key conflicts that are essential to the plot?
3. What is the importance of the overheard conversation in the development of the plot? How effective is it as a technique in this context?
4. Why did the school charge fifteen dollars for the scholarship jacket? How is this important to the developing theme of the narrative?
5. What is the significance of the grandfather's refusal to pay the fifteen dollars for the scholarship jacket?
6. How does the writer use very short pieces of dialogue to reveal the essential values of the characters and how they meet the situation?
7. Why doesn't the story end with the principal's statement that he will make an exception and she will get the jacket? What do the additional scenes with Mr. Schmidt and Martha's grandfather add to the narrative?
8. What is the significance of the fact that the principal calls the narrator "Martha" while her grandfather calls her "Marta"?

Toward Key Insights

Instead of simply giving the jacket to Joann in an outright act of discrimination, the school developed a policy that was likely to have the same result but seem reasonable. What policies or procedures have you observed that may seem reasonable on the surface but could simply serve to perpetuate an injustice?

The main character of this narrative is Mexican American. Is the suggestion that the scholarship jacket go to someone else based on race? Are there other social injustices that may be credited to race but have other causes?

Suggestion for Writing

Write a narrative about an injustice you experienced so that those involved in the situation could better understand what the event meant to you.

DESCRIPTION ▪ ▪ ▪ ▪ ▪ ▪ ▪ ▪

Reading Strategies

   1. Identify a thesis statement (possibly first or last paragraph) and/or a statement of purpose. Read the essay with an anticipation of what the description is intended to accomplish.

   2. Don't get lost in the details. Note, possibly writing in the margins, the overall impression or mood the description is evoking.

   3. Decide how much of the description you need to remember. If the description is intended to create a mood, you may read quickly. If you are reading a description of rock formations for a geology class, you might want to take notes that organize the key features you need to remember under the appropriate headings.

   4. Note if there is a pattern to the organization of the description. Recognizing the organizational pattern can make even dense writing easier to read.

Reading Critically

   1. Identify the point of view of the description. The scene described might look very different from a different vantage point.

   2. Look for how the details were selected. An emphasis on different details might have painted a very different picture.

   3. Check to see if the conclusion of the essay really follows from the description. Just because a wilderness can be described as pristine doesn't mean that careful logging should be entirely banned.

Reading As a Writer

   1. Identify and note down the organizational pattern if it is effective.

   2. Jot down any phrases or sections that you find especially effective.

   3. Examine the essay for word choice. Notice how the writer obtained the effects he or she did.

JOHN V. YOUNG

When the Full Moon Shines Its Magic over Monument Valley

John V. Young (1909–1999) was born in Oakland, California. After attending San Jose State Teachers College, he spent 12 years as a reporter and editor for several rural California newspapers, then held a series of personnel and public relations positions. In 1966, he became a full-time freelance writer, specializing in western travel pieces. His books include The Grand Canyon *(1969),* Ghost Towns of the Santa Cruz Mountains *(1979, 1984),* Hot Type and Pony Wire *(1980),* State Parks of New Mexico *(1984),* State Parks of Arizona *(1986), and* State Parks of Utah *(1989). His articles have appeared in* The New York Times *as well as in numerous travel publications. In the article that follows, he focuses on the sensations generated first by his surroundings and then by the moonrise.*

1   We were camped here in early spring, by one of those open-faced shelters that the Navajos have provided for tourists in this part of their vast tribal park

> Title identifies
> dominant impression:
> magic

> Introduction:
> paragraphs 1 and 2;
> identifies when, where,
> who, why
> Touch impression

on the Arizona–Utah border, 25 miles north of Kayenta. It was cool but pleasant, and we were alone, three men in a truck.

2   We were here for a purpose; to see the full moon rise over this most mysterious and lonely of scenic wonders, where fantastically eroded red and yellow sandstone shapes soar to the sky like a giant's chess pieces and where people—especially white strangers—come quickly to feel like pretty small change indeed.

3   Because all Navajo dwellings face east, our camp faced east—toward the rising sun and the rising moon and across a limitless expanse of tawny desert, that ancient sea, framed by the towering nearby twin pinnacles called The Mittens. We began to feel the magic even before the sun was fully down. It occurred when a diminutive wraith of a Navajo girl wearing a long, dark, velvet dress gleaming with silver ornaments drifted silently by, herding a flock of ghostly sheep to a waterhole somewhere. A bell on one of the rams tinkled faintly, and then its music was lost in the soft rustle of the night wind, leaving us with an impression that perhaps we had really seen nothing at all.

4   Just then, a large woolly dog appeared out of the gloom, seeming to materialize on the spot. It sat quietly on the edge of the glow from our campfire, its eyes shining like mirrors. It made no sound but when we offered food, it accepted the gift gravely and with much dignity. The dog then vanished again, probably to join the girl and her flock. We were not certain it was not part of the illusion.

5   As the sun disappeared entirely, the evening afterglow brush tipped all the spires and cliffs with magenta, deepening to purple, and the sand ripples stood out like miniature ocean waves in darkening shades of orange. Off to the east on the edge of the desert, a pale saffron glow told us the moon was about to rise behind a thin layer of clouds, slashed by the white contrail of an invisible jet airplane miles away.

6   We had our cameras on tripods and were fussing with light meters, making casual bets as to the exact place where the moon would first appear, when it happened—instant enchantment. Precisely between the twin spires of The Mittens, the enormous globe loomed suddenly, seeming as big as the sun itself, behind a coppery curtain on the rim of creation.

7   We were as totally unprepared for the great size of the moon as we were for its flaming color, nor could we have prepared ourselves for the improbable setting. We felt like the wizards of Stonehenge, commanding the planets to send their light through the magic orifices in line at the equinox. Had the Navajo medicine men contrived this for our benefit?

8   The massive disk of the moon seemed to rise very fast at first, an optical effect magnified by the crystalline air and the flatness of the landscape between us and the distant, ragged skyline. Then it seemed to pause for a moment, as if it were pinioned on one of the pinnacles or impaled on a sharply upthrusting rocky point. Its blazing light made inky shadows all around us, split by the brilliant wedge of the moon's path between the spires. The wind had stopped. There was not a sound anywhere, nor even a whisper. If a drum had sounded just then, it would not have been out of place, I suppose, but it would have frightened us half to death.

9   Before the moon had cleared the tops of The Mittens, the show was over and the magic was gone. A thin veil of clouds spread over the sky, ending the spell as suddenly as it had come upon us. It was as if the gods had decided that we had seen enough for mere mortals on one spring night, and I must confess

it was something of a relief to find ourselves back on mundane earth again, with sand in our shoes and a chill in the air.

Touch impression

Discussion Questions

1. How does the last sentence in paragraph 7 ("Had the Navajo medicine men contrived this for our benefit?") relate to the purpose of the essay?
2. This description takes the form of a narrative. Where does the climax occur, and how does it affect the viewers?

Toward Key Insights

What makes certain experiences seem magical?

How important are such magical experiences, and how might they shape our perceptions of the everyday world?

Suggestion for Writing

Select a place you know well and describe it by conveying some dominant impression that emerges during daylight hours. Settle on an appropriate vantage point and either identify the impression or allow readers to determine it for themselves.

KESSLER BURNETT

Seaside Safari

Kessler Burnett is the editor of Chesapeake Life Magazine *and* Jewish Times of Baltimore. *Kessler is also responsible for the blog post* "Girls' Guide to the Eastern Shore." *This essay comes from the June 2009 Virginia Life.*

1   Only a maniacal mind could have built this dock. The odd-sized planks erratically rise, fall, twist and wobble, reducing me to a high-wire act with each shaky step. The "net" below is but a soupy tidal flat, where an inattentive audience of fiddler crabs chaotically flit in and out of their dens, assuring me of a creepy landing place if my third-grade balance-beam skills fail to keep me dry. But the anticipation of finally entering the oyster watch house at dock's end commands my attention, and soon I am striding like an old salt toward my home away from home for the next 24 hours.

2   Like an arthritic spider, the nearly 100-year-old watch house rises above the marshlands of Smith Island, the second southernmost in Virginia's chain of 17 barrier islands that skirt the Atlantic seaboard. Propped on slanting stilts and covered in flaking asphalt shingles, the 400-square-foot structure is quaint from a distance. But to overnight guests such as I who haven't exercised their wilderness muscles in ages, the promise of a day (and night) without electricity or

plumbing is admittedly a bit unnerving. While photographer Michael Bowles and I have come here for an authentic ecotourism experience, the original purpose of these shacks was purely business—Eastern Shore-style.

3   Common sights in this region during the 19th century, these wooden structures were constructed by watermen near their oyster beds, where they'd hole up for weeks on end, well-armed, guarding their harvests from poachers. With the invention of the outboard motor in the early 1900s, watermen could travel to and from the mainland at all hours with ease, thus ending the need for these overnight camps. Out of the estimated 100 watch houses that once dotted this expanse, today fewer than a dozen remain.

4   This particular watch house is the inspiration behind the overnight kayak excursions hosted by Southeast Expeditions, a Cape Charles-based eco-tour company owned by Dave Burden, our guide for the trip. The watch house weekends have become a popular venue for everything from bachelor parties to girlfriends' getaways to second honeymoons. Itineraries can be as rugged or as gentle as clients crave, with activities that range from shell hunting on the islands to tours of an aquaculture farm to dock-side Reiki administered by shipped-in masseuses to chef-prepared sunset suppers. "People who book this trip are looking for something unique," explains Dave, his shaggy, blond hair falling into his face as he lugs a cooler down the pier. "These are people who want an adventure but don't want the same adventure that everybody else has. They want to feel like they've left their world behind for a completely different one."

5   And oh, what a different world this is. Pushing back the front door, scaly with peeling paint and rigged with a coat hanger as the knob, I enter an honest-to-goodness man cave. Cluttered with tools of an outdoorsman's trade—Deep Woods Off, lighter fluid, fishing books, kerosene lanterns, toilet paper rolls—it's an advanced study in testosterone. All four corners of the interior have dedicated themes (living room, dining room, kitchen, bedroom) that spill into one another. The prima donna in me is grateful for the few amenities: the clean, white bed on the lower bunk and the "bathroom," a closet-sized space with a plastic accordion shower door and a portable head, operated by a series of mysterious knobs and levers that I never fully master. While my idea of roughing it is using paper napkins at dinner, Michael is completely at home in these conditions. Raised in Zimbabwe, he has experienced countless safaris, paddled the hippo-laden Zambezi River and hunted crocodiles. Unwilling to be outdone by a man, I face my bathroom breaks with the same unfazed attitude as he and save my cringing for behind the accordion door.

6   While Michael and I map out our day with Southeast Expeditions' Bill Burnham, a guide and certified Virginia Master Naturalist, Dave cranks up the propane stove and prepares a wonderfully civilized lunch of grilled chicken atop mixed field greens and pine nuts. He promises that dinner, to be a surprise, will be equally elegant. In an instant, all concerns I've harbored about surviving this trip vanish. Sometimes the assurance of a good dinner is all the encouragement a girl needs to get through the day.

7   After a quick "kitchen" clean-up, Bill and I climb into a pair of kayaks tethered to the end of the dock and head for the white-sand beaches of Cobb's Island. Michael and Dave opt for the speed of the powerboat, and once their wake has rolled past, we are left to glide amid the wild, gentle rhythm of the salt marsh. Our paddles create a soft splash and gurgle as they cut into the still, murky water, but that is hardly the only sound: There is the buzz of crickets in the background, along with the sporadic chatter from clapper rails nesting deep

within the spiky grasses. A pair of skimmers in flight paces our boats, their fire engine-red mandibles grazing the surface to scoop up to-go meals of shrimp and minnows.

8   Bill encourages me to keep an eye out for diamondback terrapins poking their heads above the grasses as well as for tiny marsh periwinkles that spend their days traveling up and down the cord grass blades, running to and from the tides. Taking a mental inventory, I realize that I've completely surrendered to my surroundings, grateful for the chance to float eye-level with a world that is too easily forgotten amid the clutter of worries that are eight delicious miles away on the mainland.

9   Although the turtles have chosen to remain hidden, the shells on Cobb's Island are a dime a dozen. As the four of us walk the scallop-hemmed shoreline, our heads bowed in shell-seeking mode, Dave explains how, due to waves, weather and tides, these islands live in a constant state of change, shifting shape by degrees every year. The billowy sand sinks like zoysia grass under my feet as we approach a handful of sandpipers erratically darting about. At the water's edge, we stand in silence, listening to the breaking waves toss shells against one another, producing a soulful, muted chime with each buffered collision. "That's one of my favorite sounds," says Dave with soft enthusiasm.

10   The peaceful moment is soon shattered with my inevitable inquiry regarding the island's dark side: sharks. Dave assures me that while nurse, sand and even small great white sharks have been sighted off the coast, they're rare. I take him at his word but inch a tad closer to his defensive tackle-sized frame as we head back to the boats.

11   Pushed homeward by the rush of the incoming tide, the effortless paddle back is a gentle luge ride through the curvy cuts. In no time, the drift delivers us back to the watch house, where our surprise, chef and local caterer Amy Brandt, has been ferried out to prepare dinner. While she whips up an entrée of Chesapeake Bay stew, a brothy concoction of red drum, scallops, clams and basmati rice, Michael and I move the dining room table out to the dock for an al fresco supper, complete with linens, a vase of lavender, candles and wine from Chatham Vineyards in nearby Machipongo. Dave mans the pot of steaming Cherrystone clams, which he serves with a plastic cup of Chardonnay for dipping, an unexpected twist that gives the bite-size bivalves a buttery flavor.

12   As the sun slides below the horizon, the lights from the Chesapeake Bay Bridge-Tunnel flicker in the distance, and the evening's ceiling is a glow-in-the-dark mosaic of planets and stars. After lingering over wine and a few hands of poker, we turn in, I on the bottom bunk, Amy in a cot, and Michael on the air mattress on the floor. As for Dave, he opts to sleep under the stars on the dock.

13   Dawn in the summertime marsh is like a newborn's shrill cry. Once it erupts, everyone in the house is up. The early light is intense and impatient, quickly illuminating every square inch of horizon as it reflects off the water's flat, calm surface. I wake to the sound of Michael climbing on the roof to grab a shot of the sunrise. He shouts an order to me to jump into a kayak for a photo op before the soft light loses it charm. Opening my eyes, my first thought is of Dave, who I fear has rolled off the dock and floated halfway to Bermuda by now. I peer out the window to see him safely asleep, wrapped in a dew-logged Mexican blanket like a human chimichanga.

14   After a short paddle, we pack up our belongings, load the kayaks into the boat, and make the 20-minute cruise back to the mainland. We share the waterway with cownose rays and pass old WWII submarine watchtowers and derelict

hunting lodges on Mockhorn Island, where, in the 20th century, city swells came to shoot sage hens, ducks and geese. Staring at the clouds that dot the blue sky like pillowy snowball hydrangea, my thoughts begin the slow turn back toward reality, where deadlines, lawn care and my anemic 401K steal the spotlight from small wonders like periwinkles, the call of the curlew and the earthen hues of the marsh. I make all those requisite promises to myself that returning travelers conjure, about keeping the memories and holding on to the calm and all the revelations of self-growth. But this time, I will.

Discussion Questions

1. What strategies does the writer use to organize this essay? Why are these strategies used for the audience and purpose of the writing?
2. This is written explicitly as a work of travel writing. What details relate specifically to the travel interest of the piece? Who is its audience? If the writer were writing to botanists and ecologists interested in salt marshes, how would that change her description?
3. What impression is the writer trying to establish in the first paragraph? What descriptive details does the writer use to create that impression?
4. In paragraph 5, what details does the writer use to emphasize the impression of a "man cave?" Is it successful? Why or why not?
5. In paragraph 11, why does the writer spend so little space describing the trip back? Was that an appropriate decision for the essay?
6. In the conclusion, paragraph 14, how does the writer use description to sum up her final point?

Toward Key Insights

In what ways does the way we encounter our place influence our experience and subsequent description. The writer approaches this environment as a brief visitor. How would the experience and description be different, if she were moving in to live for a few years or if she were a waterman who made her living from the water.

Suggestion for Writing

Write an essay of a place you recently visited for a regional travel magazine. If you have the time, you might even take a weekend trip, taking notes in the process, to write your essay.

MICHEL FOUCAULT

Las Menias

Michel Foucault was born in 1926 and died in 1984. He was a French philosopher and historian of ideas whose work is still very influential in scholarship in the humanities. He wrote a number of works examining the evolution of social institutions and concepts including Madness and Civilization, Discipline and Punish, *and three volumes of* The History of Sexuality. *This selection is taken from* The Order of Things, *published in 1966.*

1   The painter is standing a little back from his canvas. He is glancing at his model; perhaps he is considering whether to add some finishing touch, though it is also possible that the first stroke has not yet been made. The arm holding the brush is bent to the left, towards the palette; it is motionless, for an instant, between canvas and paints. The skilled hand is suspended in mid-air, arrested in rapt attention on the painter's gaze; and the gaze, in return, waits upon the arrested gesture. Between the fine point of the brush and the steely gaze, the scene is about to yield up its volume.

2   But not without a subtle system of feints. By standing back a little, the painter has placed himself to one side of the painting on which he is working. That is, for the spectator at present observing him he is to the right of his canvas, while the latter, the canvas, takes up the whole of the extreme left. And the canvas has its back turned to that spectator; he can see nothing of it but the reverse side, together with the huge frame on which it is stretched. The painter, on the other hand, is perfectly visible in his full height; or at any rate, he is not masked by the tall canvas which may soon absorb him, when, taking a step towards it again, he returns to his task; he has no doubt just appeared, at this very instant, before the eyes of the spectator, emerging from what is virtually a sort of vast cage projected backwards by the surface he is painting. Now he can be seen, caught in a moment of stillness, at the neutral center of this oscillation. His dark torso and bright face are half-way between the visible and the invisible: emerging from the canvas beyond our view, he moves into our gaze; but when, in a moment, he makes a step to the right, removing himself from our gaze, he will be standing exactly in front of the canvas he is painting; he will enter that region where his painting, neglected for an instant, will for him, become visible once more, free of shadow and free of reticence. As though the painter could not at the same time be seen on the picture where he is represented and also see that upon which he is representing something. He rules at the threshold of those two incompatible visibilities.

3   The painter is looking, his face turned slightly and his head leaning towards one shoulder. He is staring at a point to which, even though it is invisible, we, the spectators, can easily assign an object, since it is we, ourselves, who are that point: our bodies, our faces, our eyes. The spectacle he is observing is thus doubly invisible: first, because it is not represented within the space of the painting, and, second, because it is situated precisely in that blind spot, in that essential hiding-place into which our gaze disappears from ourselves at the moment of our actual looking. And yet, how could we fail to see that invisibility, there in front of our eyes, since it has its own perceptible equivalent, its sealed-in figure, in the painting itself? We could, in effect, guess what it is the painter is looking at if it were possible for us to glance for a moment at the cavas he is working on; but all we can see of that canvas is its texture, the horizontal and vertical bars of the stretcher, and the obliquely rising foot of the easel. The tall, monotonous rectangle occupying the whole left portion of the real picture, and representing the back of the canvas within the picture, reconstitutes in the form of the surface of the invisibility in depth of what the artist is observing: that space in which we are, and which we are. From the eyes of the painter to what he is observing there runs a compelling line that we, the onlookers, have no power of evading:

it runs through the real picture and emerges from its surface to join the place from which we see the painter observing us; this dotted line reaches out to us ineluctably, and links us to the representation of the picture.

4   In appearance, this locus is a simple one; a matter of pure reciprocity: we are looking at a picture in which the painter is in turn looking out at us. A mere confrontation, eyes catching one another's glance, direct looks superimposing themselves upon one another as they cross. And yet, this slender line of reciprocal visibility embraces a whole complex network of uncertainties, exchanges, and feints. The picture is turning his eyes towards us only in so far as we happen to occupy the same position as his subject. We, the spectators, are an additional factor. Though greeted by that gaze, we are only dismissed by it, replaced by that which was always there before we were: the model itself. But inversely, the painter's gaze, addressed to the void confronting him outside the picture, accepts as many models as there are spectators; in this precise but neutral place, the observer and the observed take part in a ceaseless exchange. No gaze is stable, or rather, in the neutral furrow of the gaze piercing at a right angle through the canvas, subject and object, the spectator and the model, reverse their roles to infinity. And here the great canvas with its back to us on the extreme left of the picture exercises its second function: stubbornly invisible, it prevents the relation of these gazes from ever being discoverable or definitely established. The opaque fixity that is established on one side renders forever unstable the play of metamorphoses established in the center between spectator and model. Because we can see only the reverse side, we do not know who we are, or what we are doing. Seen or seeing? The painter is observing a place which, from moment to moment, never ceases to change its content, its form, its face, its identity. But the attentive immobility of his eyes refers us back to another direction which they have often followed already, and which soon, there can be no doubt, they will take again: that of the motionless canvas upon which is being traced, has already been traced perhaps, for a long time and forever, a portrait that will never again be erased. So that the painter's sovereign gaze commands a virtual triangle whose outline defines this picture of a picture: at the top—the only visible corner—the painter's eyes; at one of the base angles, the invisible place occupied by the model; at the other base angle, the figure probably sketched out on the invisible surface of the canvas.

5   As soon as they place the spectator in the field of their gaze, the painter's eyes seize hold of him, force him to enter the picture, assign him a place at once privileged and inescapable, levy their luminous and visible tribute before him, and project it upon the inaccessible surface of the canvas within the picture. He sees his invisibility made visible to the painter and transposed into an image forever invisible to himself. A shock that is augmented and made more inevitable still by a marginal trap. At the extreme right, the picture is lit by a window represented in a very sharp perspective; so sharp that we can see scarcely more than the embrasure; so that the flood of light streaming through it bathes at the same time, and with equal generosity, two neighboring spaces, overlapping but irreducible: the surface of the painting, together with the volume it represents (which is to say, the painter's studio, or the salon in which his easel is now set up), and, in front of that surface, the real volume occupied by the spectator (or again, the unreal site of the model). And as it passes through the room from right to left, this vast flood of golden light carries both the spectator towards the painter and the model towards the canvas; it is this

light too, which, washing over the painter, makes him visible to the spectator and turns into golden lines, in the model's eyes, the frame of that enigmatic canvas on which his image, once transported there, is to be imprisoned. This extreme, partial, scarcely indicated window frees a whole flow of daylight which serves as the common locus of the representation. It balances the invisible canvas on the other side of the picture; just as that canvas, by turning its back to the spectators, folds itself in against the picture representing it, and forms, by the superimposition of its reverse and visible side upon the surface of the picture depicting it, the ground inaccessible to us, on which there shimmers the Image *par excellence*, so does the window, a pure aperture, establish a space as manifest as the other is hidden; as much the common ground of painter, figures, models, and spectators, as the other is solitary (for none is looking at it, not even the painter). From the right, there streams in through an invisible window the pure volume of light that renders all representation visible; to the left extends the surface that conceals, on the other side of its all too visible woven texture, the representation it bears. The light, by flooding the scene (I mean the room as well as the canvas, the room represented on the canvas, and the room in which the canvas stands), envelops the figures and the spectators and carries them with it, under the painter's gaze towards the place where his brush will represent them. But that place is concealed from us. We are observing ourselves being observed by the painter, and made visible to his eyes by the same light that enables us to see him. And just as we are about to apprehend ourselves, transcribed by his hand as though in a mirror, we find that we can in fact apprehend nothing of that mirror but its lustreless back. The other side of a psyche.

6   Now, as it happens, exactly opposite the spectators—ourselves—on the wall forming the far end of the room. Velázquez has represented a series of pictures; and we see that among all those hanging canvases there is one that shines with particular brightness. Its frame is wider and darker than those of the others; yet there is a fine white line around its inner edge diffusing over its whole surface a light whose source is not easy to determine; for it comes from nowhere, unless it be from a space within itself. In this strange light, two silhouettes are apparent, while above them, and a little behind them, is a heavy purple curtain. The other pictures reveal little more than a few paler patches buried in a darkness without depth. This particular one, on the other hand, opens on to a perspective of space in which recognizable forms recede from us in a light that belongs only to itself. Among all these elements intended to provide representation, while impeding them, hiding them, concealing them because of their position or their distance from us, this is the only one that fulfils its function in all honesty and enables us to see what it is supposed to show. Despite its distance from us, despite the shadows all around it. But it isn't a picture; it is a mirror. It offers us at last that enchantment of the double that until now has been denied us, not only by the distant paintings but also by the light in the foreground and its ironic canvas.

7   Of all the representations represented in the picture this is the only one visible; but no one is looking at it. Upright beside his canvas, his attention is entirely taken up by his model, the painter is unable to see this looking-glass shining so softly behind him. The other figures in the picture are also, for the most part, turned to face what must be taking place in front—toward the bright invisibility bordering the canvas, toward that balcony of light where their eyes can gaze at those who are gazing back at them, and not towards that dark recess

which marks the far end of the room in which they are represented. There are, it is true, some heads turned away from us in profile; but not one of them is turned far enough to see, at the back of the room, that solitary mirror, that shiny glowing rectangle which is nothing other than visibility, yet without any gaze able to grasp it, to render it actual, and to enjoy the suddenly ripe fruit of the spectacle it offers.

8   It must be admitted that this indifference is equaled only by the mirror's own. It is reflecting nothing, in fact, of all that is there in the same space as itself: neither the painter with his back to it, nor the figures in the centre of the room. It is not the visible it reflects, in those bright depths. In Dutch painting it was traditional for mirrors to play a duplicating role: they repeated the original contents of the picture, only inside an unreal, modified, contracted, concave space. One saw in them the same things as one saw in the first instance in the painting, but decomposed and recomposed according to a different law. Here the mirror is saying nothing that has already been said before. Yet its position is more or less completely central: its upper edge is exactly on an imaginary line running half-way between the top and the bottom of the painting, it hangs right in the middle of the far wall (or at least in the middle of the portion we can see); it ought, therefore, to be governed by the same lines of perspective as the picture itself; we might well expect the same studio, the same painter, the same canvas to be arranged within it according to an identical space; it could be the perfect duplication.

9   In fact, it shows us nothing of what is represented in the picture itself. Its motionless gaze extends out in front of the picture, into that necessarily invisible region which forms its exterior face, to apprehend the figures arranged in that space. Instead of surrounding visible objects, this mirror cuts straight through the whole field of the representation, ignoring all it might apprehend within that field, and restores visibility to that which resides outside all view. But the invisibility that it overcomes in this way is not the invisibility of what is hidden: it does not make its way around any obstacle, it is not distorting any perspective, it is addressing itself to what is invisible both because of the picture's structure and because of its existence as painting. What it is reflecting is that which all the figures within the painting are looking at so fixedly, or at least those who are looking straight ahead; it is therefore what the spectator would be able to see if the painting extended further forward, if its bottom edge were brought lower until it included the figures the painter is using as models. But it is also, since the picture does stop there, displaying only the painter and his studio, what is exterior to the picture, in so far as it is a picture—in other words, a rectangular fragment of lines and colors intended to represent something to the eyes of any possible spectator. At the far end of the room, ignored by all, the unexpected mirror holds in its glow the figures that the painter is looking at (the painter in his represented, objective reality, of the painter at his work); but also the figures that are looking at the painter (in the material reality which the lines and the colors have laid out upon the canvas). These two groups of figures are both equally inaccessible, but in different ways: the first because of an effect of composition peculiar to the painting; the second because of the law that presides over the very existence of all pictures in general. Here, the action of representation consists in bring one of these two forms of invisibility into the place of the other, in an unstable superimposition—and in rendering them both, at the same moment, at the other extremity of the picture—at the pole which is the very height of its representation: that of a reflected depth in the far recess of the painting's depth. The mirror provides

a metathesis of visibility that affects both the space represented in the picture and its nature as representation; it allows us to see, in the center of the canvas, what in the painting is doubly invisible.

10   A strangely literal, though inverted, application of the advice given, so it is said, to his pupil by the old Pachero when the former was working in his studio in Seville: 'The image should stand out from the frame.'

Discussion Questions

1. Much of this essay is a description of a painting. However, a lot of the discussion in the essay is what is not visible in the painting, the subjects that are implied as being in front of the painting. What features of the painting does Foucault identify to make the claims about what is not present in the painting itself.

2. In the beginning of paragraph 5, the author talks about how the viewer is going to respond. Often discussions of art and other works make claims about the responses of the audience, often without much evidence to back it up. How credible are the author's claims here? What makes them credible or less credible? Does it matter that we can test his claims ourselves by looking at the art work.

3. In paragraph 2 and other paragraphs, the writer uses active verbs to describe the still scene of the painting? Why rhetorically might the writer use such an approach? How does it affect the essay?

4. Foucault is writing for serious scholars in a number of fields. How did the professional nature of his possible audiences influence the text he produced.

5. Foucault ends with a bit of a pun, "The image should stand out from the frame." In what ways is this claim true of the painting? What is the effect on the reader of this ending?

Toward Key Insights

Movies, television, art, and literature and even essays often include who is looking or pointing where, and often they "define" in some way the reader or viewer. In rhetoric, some scholars talk about the way the text or essay constructs an implied reader or an ideal reader. This text hopes to address you as a willing partner in your own growth as a writer, for example. You should examine the texts around you and see what ways they seem to imply certain readers. You might also consider who your writing asks your reader to be: a friend, a thoughtful critic, a person trying to get a task done.

Suggestions for Writing

1. Take an art work, an interesting section of a movie, or television, and carefully describe the work to make a point about how the work creates its space.

2. Describe any art work in a way that helps your reader see the story in the painting.

3. Describe scenes in everyday life and how those scenes show the ways we look at and notice one another. For example, often at a mall we can see someone watching other people who don't see that person. The irony is you are a person watching the person watching without being noticed.

PROCESS ANALYSIS ■ ■ ■ ■ ■ ■ ■

Reading Strategies

1. Determine the reason you are reading the process essay. If it is to follow instructions you will need to read in one way; if it is to understand a process, you will need to proceed differently.

2. If you are going to follow the instructions, read over the process first to get an understanding of the whole. Look for specific warnings or feedback you should consider. Get an idea of what the end result should look like. Gather any equipment you will need. Then follow the process step by step, checking after each step to make certain the results you are obtaining match those described in the process.

3. If you hope to understand the process, read first quickly to get an overview of the process. As you read through more slowly, it can be very helpful to take notes outlining the major steps of the process.

Reading Critically

1. Check to see if the process could be completed differently or more effectively. Are there any cautions that are not included in the essay that might be reasonable to observe?

2. If the writer is explaining a process, is there evidence that his account is correct? Check to see that there is good reason to believe the given account. Research could show that there are competing accounts.

Reading As a Writer

1. Observe how the writer uses verbs to indicate actions.

2. Notice how the writer gets from step to step in the process. If there is a strategy you could use, make note of it.

PERFECT HOME HVAC DESIGN.COM

Ground-Source-Heat-Pumps: Mother Earth Will Wrap You in Warmth

This selection is a web page posted by the company Perfect Home HVAC Design. Common to many web pages, there is no clear author. Dana Morley is the owner and chief designer for the company and has been a licensed HVAC contractor in Utah with 36 years of experience in HVAC. Since the web page has no clear author, its credibility depends on the professionalism of the site and company and the degree to which it is consistent with other web sites.

Ground-Source Heat Pumps

1   If you are interested in installing an environmentally responsible heating, air conditioning and water heating system in your home, you have come to the right page.

First paragraph let's reader know the relevance of website

Image provides a clear visual overview of how technology works

2   Ground source heat pump systems are still rare mostly due to cost, but seem to be on the upswing each year due to increasing utility bills.

3   The Environmental Protection Agency (EPA) and the Department of Energy (DOE) have both listed the ground source heat pump systems as amongst the highest energy efficient and environmentally responsible home comfort and water heating systems available today.

4   The EPA has stated that geothermal technologies represent a major opportunity for reducing national energy use and pollution, while delivering comfort, reliability and savings to the homeowner.

Identifies importance of technology

5   The greatest heat storage facility available on Earth is the Earth itself. Temperatures below the surface of our planet remain virtually constant, whether it be winter, summer, spring, or fall. Ground source heat pumps tap into this stored energy to provide hot water, cooling and heating for homes. Residential applications are the subject here, but are certainly not the only viable options for use of a ground source heat pump system. Commercial or industrial structures can benefit from these types of systems as well.

Provides fundamental principles behind the process

Closed Loop GSHP System

6   A closed loop system can be installed horizontally under a lawn or garden area, driveway, or even under the home itself, anywhere that the required piping can be installed. The piping can also be installed vertically in shafts drilled for the piping. Your geothermal specialist will determine, after inspecting your site, which approach suits your application best. Factors he will be looking for are soil conditions, available space, installation economy, and the type of rock in the area.

Defines conditions for the process.

Provides broader and more general steps of the process including materials and larger system.

7   Closed loop systems utilize water or an antifreeze solution circulating through plastic or copper piping installed beneath the earth's surface. During the heating season, the fluid is pumped through the loops, collecting heat from the ground and delivers the heat into the heat pump inside the building. During the summer, for cooling, the process is reversed. Heat is pulled from the residence and pumped out through the system loops to store the heat in the ground. Cool fluid returns to cool the residence.

Provides detailed account of key parts and the general process for the heat pump

8   Inside, the heat pump is a package unit, which has a refrigerant loop, a water loop, a compressor, a reversing valve, and a heat exchanger. The transfer of heat actually takes place at the heat exchanger, which transfers the heat from the water into the refrigerant, or vice-versa, depending upon heating or cooling cycle.

Provides more detailed example of heat pump

9   In heating cycle, the water from outside passes past a refrigerant-filled heat exchanger. Heat transfers into the refigerant and boils to become a vapor. The vapor is then compressed, causing it to become even hotter. Then the hot gas passes through the coil, where air is forced through the coil, picking up the heat and distributing it to the living space.

Offers an account of alternative

10   Once again, this process is reversed for cooling.

11   Not to confuse the issue, but some systems actually use the refrigerant to make a direct heat transfer outside with the ground. The process inside the heat pump is very similar to a split system air conditioner's process.

Indicates alternative use in the process

12   This process can also provide free hot water during the summer months, by passing the hot water collected during cooling mode through a water-to-water heat exchanger. A heat transfer takes place and the potable hot water is stored in a tank for use. This same process can deliver substantial hot water savings during the winter also.

Identifies conditions of establishment

13   A ground source heat pump system can be fitted to any residential project, new construction or retrofit, single-family or multi-family. For a retro-fit application, the existing ductwork from your former furnace or air handler can usually be used as the distribution system with minimal alterations.

14   Many geothermal companies work closely with a conventional heating and air conditioning company to provide the full package.

Open Loop Water Source Heat Pump Systems

Provides an account of alternate conditions

15   Some residences have access to a pond or lake on their property. This is another good source for heat transfer from the piping system. An open loop water system can provide similar benefits of the closed loop system.

Provides an account of the general process for the alternative

16   The operation is identical other than the loop piping system is placed directly on the bottom of the pond. The system pumps pull in water for the heating and cooling of the residence and then discharge the water directly back into the pond, into a return well, or into a leech field.

Provides clear warning step for the conditions

17   Installation of this type of system may require the approval of your local authorities. Due to the fact that open dispersal of the water back into the environment will mix with ground water, the authorities may wish to verify its source and cleanliness. It's easier to get approved beforehand than to backpedal for approvals.

Provides general statement of benefits

18   Installation of geothermal, a ground source heat pump, or a water source heat pump is certainly not the most economical route to go for heating and cooling your home, on initial installation. But, the benefits abound. Manufacturers

are offering rebates and special financing. Many utility companies offer rebates to help with installation. Both the homeowner and the builder should check into these programs when considering this type of system.

Benefits of a Ground Source Heat Pump

- Realize up to 50 percent savings on energy used to heat hot water.
- It can both heat and cool your home, and provide all of your hot water needs.
- Equipment size is very similar to a traditional forced air heating and air conditioning system.
- Energy consumption can be cut by 20 to 50 percent.
- Maintenance costs may be reduced.
- Underground piping carries a 50-year warranty.
- Systems are very quiet, both inside and out. No noisy compressors outside.
- No dangerous and unsightly outside fuel storage tanks are needed.
- Air inside the home is distributed more evenly. Hot and cold spots are gone.

> Provides a list as an easy way for the reader to see the benefits of this approach

A ground source heat pump does provide savings.

- Save money in operating and maintenance costs.
- Over time, the energy savings will exceed the installation costs. Make money on the deal! For the right system, your investment dollar may be recouped in only a few years.
- Rebates are available in most areas from local utility companies. Federal tax credits may also be available to help offset the initial installation costs.
- Heating efficiencies are as much as 70 percent higher than conventional. Cooling efficiencies are as much as 40 percent higher than conventional systems.

If that isn't enough to convince you to consider this type of system, think about our environment.

- There is no external venting into our atmosphere of harmful waste byproducts.
- Ground source heat pump systems that do use refrigerants are factory sealed, and seldom need recharging. Possibility of freon released to the atmosphere and damaging our ozone layer almost non-existent.
- Our natural resources are conserved.
- Fossil fuels are not burned.

Discussion Questions

1. What is the purpose of this process description? How does that purpose shape the way the web page is designed and the process is described?
2. Instead of simply providing a step-by-step presentation of the process, this website first describes the more general process and then provides more detailed steps for the process. Why did they do this? Is it effective?
3. Why is the illustration used to help account for this process? How helpful is it?
4. Why doesn't the website detail the process for cooling?
5. At the end of the website, it directly states the advantages of a geothermal system. Does this help or hinder the process account? Why or why not?

Toward Key Insights

How much do we know about the processes that strongly shape our life? Why don't many of us pay attention to such processes? What could be some advantages of our understanding these processes?

Many complete a college education without knowing how their car works, their homes are heated, or their wireless system functions. What if anything should an education teach people about their technological world? What should we be able to learn on our own? What does it take to learn about such processes?

Suggestions for Writing

1. Research a process that influences your life and the lives of others and design a possible website for that process, including the text and images that explain the process.
2. Take a very technical process that you understand and rewrite or revise that process so that it is available to a more general reader.

Beth Wald

Let's Get Vertical!

Beth Wald (born 1960) first felt the attraction of the mountains when, at age 16, she took a backpacking trip to Canada. A native of Minnesota, she studied botany and Russian at the University of Minnesota and then, in the mid-1980s, began a dual career as a freelance writer and photographer. Her career and her love of climbing have taken her around the world. Her articles have appeared in a variety of climbing and outdoor magazines, as have her photographs, which include environmental and cultural subjects as well as sports and travel. From 1988 to 1992, she was a contributing editor for Climbing Magazine. *In our selection, Wald acquaints potential recruits with the sport of rock climbing.*

1   Here I am, 400 feet up on the steep west face of Devil's Tower,[1] a tiny figure in a sea of petrified rock. I can't find enough footholds and handholds to keep climbing. My climbing partner anxiously looks up at me from his narrow ledge. I can see the silver sparkle of the climbing devices I've jammed into the crack every eight feet or so.

2   I study the last device I've placed, a half-inch aluminum wedge 12 feet below me. If I slip, it'll catch me, but only after a 24-foot fall, a real "screamer." It's too difficult to go back; I have to find a way up before my fingers get too tired. I must act quickly.

3   Finding a tiny opening in the crack, I jam two fingertips in, crimp them, pull hard, and kick my right foot onto a sloping knob, hoping it won't skid off. At the same time, I slap my right hand up to what looks like a good hold. To my horror, it's round and slippery.

---

[1]A large, flat-topped rock formation, 876 feet high, in northeastern Wyoming.

4   My fingers start to slide. Panic rivets me for a second, but then a surge of adrenalin snaps me back into action. I scramble my feet higher, lunge with my left hand, and catch a wider crack. I manage to get a better grip just as my right hand pops off its slick hold. My feet find edges, and I regain my balance. Whipping a chock (wedge) off my harness, I slip it into the crack and clip my rope through a carabiner (oblong metal snaplink). After catching my breath, I start moving again, and the rest of the climb flows upward like a vertical dance.

5   **The Challenges and Rewards** I've tried many sports, but I haven't found any to match the excitement of rock climbing. It's a unique world, with its own language, communities, controversies, heroes, villains, and devoted followers. I've lived in vans, tepees, tents, and caves; worked three jobs to save money for expenses; driven 24 hours to spend a weekend at a good rock; and lived on beans and rice for months at a time—all of this to be able to climb. What is it about scrambling up rocks that inspires such a passion? The answer is, no other sport offers so many challenges and so many rewards.

6   The physical challenges are obvious. You need flexibility, balance, and strength. But climbing is also a psychological game of defeating your fear, and it demands creative thinking. It's a bit like improvising a gymnastic routine 200 feet in the air while playing a game of chess.

7   Climbers visit some of the most spectacular places on earth and see them from a unique perspective—the top! Because the sport is so intense, friendships between climbers tend to be strong and enduring.

8   **Anyone Can Climb** Kids playing in trees or on monkey bars know that climbing is a natural activity, but older people often have to relearn to trust their instincts. This isn't too hard, though. The ability to maintain self-control in difficult situations is the most important trait for a beginning climber to have. Panic is almost automatic when you run out of handholds 100 feet off the ground. The typical reaction is to freeze solid until you fall off. But with a little discipline, rational thinking, and/or distraction tactics such as babbling to yourself, humming, or even screaming, fear can change to elation as you climb out of a tough spot.

9   Contrary to popular belief, you don't have to be superhumanly strong to climb. Self-confidence, agility, a good sense of balance, and determination will get you farther up the rock than bulging biceps. Once you've learned the basics, climbing itself will gradually make you stronger, though many dedicated climbers speed up the process by training at home or in the gym.

10   Nonclimbers often ask, "How do the ropes get up there?" It's quite simple; the climbers bring them up as they climb. Most rock climbers today are "free climbers." In free climbing, the rope is used only for safety in case of a fall, *not* to help pull you up. (Climbing without a rope, called "free soloing," is a *very* dangerous activity practiced only by extremely experienced—and crazy—climbers.)

11   First, two climbers tie into opposite ends of a 150-foot-long nylon rope. Then one of them, the belayer, anchors himself or herself to a rock or tree. The other, the leader, starts to climb, occasionally stopping to jam a variety of aluminum wedges or other special gadgets, generically referred to as protection, into cracks in the rock. To each of these, he or she attaches a snaplink, called a carabiner, and clips the rope through. As the leader climbs, the belayer feeds out the rope, and it runs through the carabiners. If the leader falls,

12 When the leader reaches the end of a section of rock—called the pitch—and sets an anchor, he or she becomes the belayer. This person pulls up the slack of the rope as the other partner climbs and removes the protection. Once together again, they can either continue in the same manner or switch leaders. These worldwide techniques work on rock formations, cliffs, peaks, even buildings.

the belayer holds the rope, and the highest piece of protection catches the leader. The belayer uses special techniques and equipment to make it easy to stop falls.

13 **Rocks, Rocks Everywhere** Some of the best climbing cliffs in the country are in the Shawangunk Mountains, only two hours from New York City. Seneca Rocks in West Virginia draws climbers from Washington, D.C., and Pittsburgh, Pennsylvania. Chattanooga, Tennessee, has a fine cliff within the city limits. Most states in the U.S. and provinces in Canada offer at least one or two good climbing opportunities.

14 Even if there are no large cliffs or rock formations nearby, you can climb smaller rocks to practice techniques and get stronger. This is called bouldering. Many climbers who live in cities and towns have created climbing areas out of old stone walls and buildings. Ask someone at your local outdoor shop where you can go to start climbing.

15 **Get a Helping Hand** There's no substitute for an expert teacher when it comes to learning basic techniques and safety procedures. One of the best (and least expensive) ways to learn climbing is to convince a veteran climber in your area to teach you. You can usually meet these types at the local crag or climbing shop.

16 As another option, many universities and colleges, some high schools, and some YMCAs have climbing clubs. Their main purpose is to introduce people to climbing and to teach the basics. Other clubs, such as the Appalachian Mountain Club in the eastern U.S. and the Mountaineers on the West Coast, also provide instruction. Ask at your outdoor shop for the names of clubs in your area.

17 If you live in a place completely lacking rocks and climbers, you can attend one of the fine climbing schools at the major climbing area closest to you. Magazines like *Climbing, Rock & Ice,* and *Outside* publish lists of these schools. Once you learn the basics, you're ready to get vertical.

18 In rock climbing, you can both lose yourself and find yourself. Life and all its troubles are reduced to figuring out the puzzle of the next section of cliff or forgotten in the challenge and delight of moving through vertical space. And learning how to control anxiety, how to piece together a difficult sequence of moves, and how to communicate with a partner are all skills that prove incredibly useful back on the ground!

Discussion Questions

1. Discuss the effectiveness of Wald's title.
2. At the beginning of the essay, Wald notes that she is 400 feet up one side of Devil's Tower and positioned above her climbing partner. What do you think these statements accomplish?
3. In which paragraphs does Wald detail the actual process of climbing? What do the remaining paragraphs in the body of the essay accomplish?

4. Point out two places in the first four paragraphs where Wald cites reasons for her actions.
5. What attributes does Wald believe a rock climber must have? Refer to the essay when answering.
6. After reading this essay, are you ready to begin rock climbing? Does your answer stem from Wald's content, the manner of presentation, or both? Discuss.

Toward Key Insights

What challenging activities appeal to you?
What level of risk are you willing to accept in an activity?
How do you account for your attitude about taking risks?

Suggestion for Writing

Write a process paper in which you explain the attributes required and the steps involved in one of your recreational activities.

Shari Caudron

Can Generation Xers Be Trained?

Shari Caudron earned a B.A. in journalism and a master's degree in human communication. She is currently pursuing an MFA in creative nonfiction. She has been a full-time freelance journalist since 1989. In this selection she presents the procedures that many businesses have found effective in training members of "Generation X."

1   If you want to know how to reach Generation Xers, eavesdrop on a training seminar conducted by Pencom International, a Denver-based company that provides training products to such restaurant chains as Denny's and Pizza Hut. You won't hear the trainers referring to restaurant patrons as "prospective customers." Instead, they're "hot targets." The trainers don't encourage new employees to "recognize and serve customers quickly." They're told to "lock on and fire." The language isn't what you'd typically find at a corporate training seminar. But, then, Generation Xers (a term they detest) aren't typical employees.

2   "These people grew up with Sonic the Hedgehog and Atari, so training has to be attention-grabbing," says Christopher O'Donnell, vice president of Pencom. "Or as Beavis would say, 'The training can't suck.'"

3   Suck indeed. Members of Generation X, those 40 million or so Americans age 20 to 33, are forcing companies to rethink and reengineer their training programs drastically. Gen Xers' values, communication styles, and life experiences are so different from those of baby boomers that traditional training doesn't stand a chance. To connect with these young employees, forget *Father Knows Best;* bring on MTV.

4   Now, before you grumble about catering to a fringe element, here's an incentive: Training geared to the needs of Generation Xers may actually be better for training all workers.

5   "This generation is spearheading change," says O'Donnell. "They're teaching us a lot about how to manage and train everyone in the workforce."

6   Granted, not all companies experience generational differences. At Dallas-based Texas Instruments, for example, employees are hired based on certain values and characteristics. That keeps TI's corporate culture harmonious and minimizes any discrepancies between workers of different generations.

7   "We don't see generational learning differences," says Ray Gumpert, manager of training and organizational effectiveness for TI's Semiconductor Group. "We recruit a certain kind of individual, so there is great consistency among TIers."

8   In *Twentysomething: Managing and Motivating Today's New Workforce* (Master Media, 1992), Claire Raines writes that companies such as Texas Instruments are the exception, not the rule. "(Though) all generations have things in common," she says, "research on Generation Xers shows that this group typically learns very differently from those that came before them."

Who Are These People Anyway?

9   To understand why and how Xers' learning styles are so different, you have to understand the characteristics that set them apart from older workers.

10   To begin with, they are the first generation to grow up with many of their parents both working. As "latchkey kids," many learned to become self-reliant. Consequently, they tend to be independent problem solvers, who are remarkably good at getting a job done on their own.

11   Many, if not most, grew up with computers at home, in school, and at arcades on weekends, so they are amazingly technoliterate. From the Internet to CD-ROMs, familiarity with new technology is just a mouse-click away.

12   In addition, Xers have been conditioned by the American culture to expect immediate gratification. Such things as automatic teller machines, pagers, and microwave ovens have taught them that they can have what they want, when they want it. In the workplace, that can mean that they expect answers and feedback now.

13   Xers came of age in an era that began with the Watergate scandal and ended with massive corporate layoffs, so they tend to distrust institutions. They don't have to be taught that there is no such thing as lifetime employment; they never expected it. Such distrust, combined with an inherent self-reliance, means that they're more likely to regard companies as places to grow, not places to grow old.

14   So, what do all of those characteristics mean for HRD professionals? Bruce Tulgan—founder of Rainmaker, a firm in New Haven, Connecticut, that helps companies recruit, motivate, and retain Generation X workers—reminds us that in the old days, the corporate approach to training was paternalistic.

15   "It used to be 'welcome to the family,'" says Tulgan. "Companies would tell employees, 'Here is your training agenda, this is the training we'll provide, and this is what you need to know.'" That approach just doesn't work with Xers. They want to know why they must learn something, before they will take the time to learn how.

16   Says Tulgan, "I'm not saying you must change the learning objectives; you must change the process." He recommends focusing on outcomes more

than techniques and on what Xers are going to be able to do, not what they need to know.

17   For example, at the Orlando-based Olive Garden restaurants, training for servers had them memorize the menu and ingredients of the dishes. Now, training director Marty Fisher says that training emphasizes what servers are supposed to do with that information.

18   "We tell servers we want them to be tour guides for the menu," says Fisher. Through role play, servers can practice telling customers about each dish in appealing terms. That way, employees not only know why they are learning the ingredients, but they also know how to put the information to work.

19   At Chicago-based Anderson Consulting, trainers spend a lot of time upfront getting trainees' buy-in. According to Joe Kotey, a manager in the consulting education department, young employees have to see value in the training, or they aren't motivated to learn new skills. "Training results vary greatly, depending on how motivated a group is to learn new skills," says Kotey. "By focusing on outcomes, we show up-front why [employees] need this information."

Pushing the Right Buttons

20   Once you have the attention of Generation Xers, keep it by making training experiences meaningful, memorable, and fun. Xers are used to being entertained, having been weaned on portable CD players and Game Boy™. "We can't just pour knowledge into their heads," says Fisher. "We need to combine education with entertainment."

21   One way to keep their attention is to make training experiential. As much as possible, use all six senses, role play, and simulation learning—similar to the approaches used by NASA. Astronauts aren't expected to pilot a space shuttle without having practiced. Don't expect Xers to perform without practice.

22   For example, Andersen Consulting uses CD-ROMs during training to simulate client meetings. Using audio and video clips stored on disc, trainees can interview clients, receive phone calls, obtain advice from senior consultants, and review internal memos.

23   At the end of the computerized course, trainees have an opportunity to deliver a presentation with the findings and recommendations usually delivered to a client. "We want employees to see and feel what a client call is really like," says Roberta Menconi, training manager.

24   Classroom learning can also be made experiential. Pencom's O'Donnell remembers a training session he conducted for young employees of a Denver restaurant.

25   "I was trying to communicate the importance of seating [customers] right away, but getting nowhere. When I asked employees how long [customers] could wait comfortably before being seated, their responses ranged from three minutes to several more."

26   Frustrated, O'Donnell asked the group to time him for one minute. "I acted fidgety for a full 60 seconds while they watched. That minute went on forever and drove home the point that [customers] need to be seated immediately."

27   For a generation that grew up with more remote controls than rattles, the need to control learning is important. Xers need buttons to push. They are independent, and they're used to managing their own time. Because they're accustomed to calling the shots, they tend to resent and resist efforts to

force-feed them training. To give Xers a sense of control over their learning, it's wise to provide as many options as possible where and when they can participate. That means a choice of locations and times.

28   "Because this generation is stubborn, we can't be," says O'Donnell.

29   It's even better to let Xers decide how they can learn. Tulgan tells the story of a Big Six accounting firm with a series of outstanding training courses. But they were so popular that no one could get into them.

30   Says Tulgan, "I suggested that the firm put course content on videotapes, audiotapes, and interactive CDs, and in self-paced manuals and workbooks. That puts the information into employees' hands right away and makes them accountable for learning. Generation Xers like that kind of structured self-study." Given Gen Xers' penchant for technology, computers are a natural choice for delivering training. But their ability to control has to be built into the technological solutions.

31   Menconi says that Andersen tested its first CD-ROM courses with younger employees to gauge their responses. "We discovered that they click around a lot. They want control over the paths they take. They want to stop and start at will."

32   To accommodate those needs, Andersen built sophisticated navigation systems into all of its CD-ROM–based courses.

33   Gen Xers' propensity to jump around—unlike older workers who tend to go step by step—doesn't necessarily signify a lack of attention. It's more an ability to assimilate information quickly and to focus on multiple ideas at once—called, "parallel thinking."

34   "Look at MTV or commercials," says Raines, "and you'll see four or five things going on at the same time. That drives me crazy, but these kids are used to it."

35   Companies can appeal to younger workers by developing training materials that provide multiple sources of information at once. *USA Today* and *Wired* are good examples of how to present information to Xers. Those publications combine charts, photos, text, graphics, and cartoons on a single page.

36   When making your materials more eye-catching, make sure you also keep the information simple. Don't make Gen Xers have to guess what you're trying to say. Raines recommends highlighting key points to make the information highly scannable.

37   A note of caution: Don't go overboard and be too trendy. A few years back, the Wendy's restaurant chain created a training video, "Grill Skills," that featured a rap singer in gold lamé reviewing food-grilling techniques. The video won awards. But, after a year, it lost its effectiveness; employees saw it as outdated.

Prime Targets

38   Generation Xers—more than other employee groups—tend to make job decisions based on whether training is available. So, it may be more important that you provide them with training than how you provide it.

39   Says Tulgan, "Training departments are the ace in the hole for retaining and motivating today's workforce." That's because young employees don't envision long-term relationships with their employers, he says. They know that they must keep growing in order to stay marketable. If they don't receive training, they tend to start looking around at other jobs in other companies.

40   "In today's job market, you want to train employees to leave at any time," says Tulgan. "They won't, because they'll see working for your company as an incredible opportunity to grow and develop."

41   Terri Wolfe, director of HR at Patagonia—a Ventura, California–based clothing retailer—agrees that the biggest emerging trend among younger workers is their desire for continuous education. "We have an extensive continuing education program that a majority of our younger workers take advantage of. They're taking classes not only to advance their careers, but also because they are inherently curious."

What Generation Gap

42   What is perhaps most remarkable about training Generation Xers is that the training approaches that work well with them make sense for almost everyone, regardless of age. Here are some tips for training workers of all ages.

43   **Focus** Training should emphasize end results and place learners in control. Such training helps prepare employees for challenges on the job. After all, isn't the goal of empowerment for employees to focus on business objectives and make the necessary and appropriate decisions to achieve them? Fewer managers means that all employees have to take more responsibility for their work; learner-directed training is a great way to get them used to that.

44   **Be flexible** Large-scale corporate cutbacks mean that more people are overworked and are juggling multiple demands. A flexible training schedule and choice of training resources (such as CD-ROMS, videos, and so forth) help employees fit training into their work schedules.

45   **Emphasize visuals** Create eye-catching, highly scannable training materials. Most people don't have time to read through pages of materials. Like it or not, most of us have been conditioned by the media to expect a point to be made quickly.

46   **Provide continuous education** Though younger workers have never counted on cradle-to-grave employment, older employees are also getting the message that they must prepare for unexpected events. The companies that provide continuous education are in a better position to retain productive employees.

47   "If you want to see the future of work, look into the eyes of a Generation Xer," says Tulgan. "We were shaped by the same forces that have shaped the (current) workplace and economy. We're comfortable with the new workplace because we never got accustomed to the old management style."

48   But whatever you do, don't call them "Generation Xers."

Discussion Questions

1. This process essay starts by defining Generation Xers and identifying their place in the workplace. Why is this important to the purposes of the essay?
2. Instead of offering simple concrete steps in a process, how does this essay present the process of training Generation Xers? Why is this approach most likely used?
3. Identify the key elements of the process recommended by the author. Discuss whether this approach would or would not be appealing to you.
4. What is the purpose of the writer using many different businesses as examples?
5. In the end, the author identifies some specific key principles for training Generation Xers. What are the advantages of this approach?

Toward Key Insights

To what extent are different training methods appropriate to different populations? Explore what kind of job training has been most effective for you. What were the features of that training?

Suggestion for Writing

Write a paper explaining to new employees the process of the job training they might receive at one of the places you have worked.

Select some activity you're familiar with—perhaps planning a party, programming a computer, or dieting successfully—and describe the steps involved, using appropriate comparisons and figurative language.

ILLUSTRATION

Reading Strategies

1. Read the introductory and concluding paragraphs quickly to determine the thesis for the illustration. Then read the essay quickly to get the main point of the essay. Jot down the key points of the illustration.

2. Determine, based on your own purpose for reading and the level of the essay, if it is necessary to read the essay more carefully.

3. If a more careful reading is warranted, read slowly, noticing and jotting down any key details of the illustration that make a more general point.

Reading Critically

1. Test whether the illustration really demonstrates the main point.

2. Determine whether the illustrations are typical or atypical.

3. Test the point by seeing if there are illustrations that would illuminate a different position.

Reading As a Writer

1. Identify and evaluate the kinds of examples used in the illustration.

2. Notice the strategies used to link the illustrations to a main point.

3. Identify and evaluate how the illustrations were organized (as short narratives, as descriptions) and jot down any strategies you found useful.

SABRINA RUBIN ERDELY

Binge Drinking, A Campus Killer

Sabrina Rubin Erdely is an award-winning investigative journalist based in Philadelphia. She is a Senior Writer at Philadelphia *magazine, where she has been on staff since 1995, and has contributed to a wide array of other magazines. Erdely's feature writing*

Illustration **499**

has earned her a number of awards, including a prestigious National Magazine Award nomination. Our selection focuses on a serious and growing problem at American colleges and universities.

1   Pregame tailgating parties, post-exam celebrations and Friday happy hours—not to mention fraternity and sorority mixers—have long been a cornerstone of the collegiate experience. But on campuses across America, these indulgences have a more alarming side. For some of today's college students, binge drinking has become the norm.

2   This past February I headed to the University of Wisconsin–Madison, rated the No. 2 party school in the nation by the college guide *Princeton Review,* to see the party scene for myself. On Thursday night the weekend was already getting started. At a raucous off-campus gathering, 20-year-old Tracey Middler struggled to down her beer as fist-pumping onlookers yelled, "Chug! Chug! Chug!"

3   In the kitchen, sophomore Jeremy Budda drained his tenth beer. "I get real wasted on weekends," he explained. Nearby, a 19-year-old estimated, "I'll end up having 17, 18 beers."

4   Swept up in the revelry, these partyers aren't thinking about the alcohol-related tragedies that have been in the news. All they're thinking about now is the next party. The keg is just about empty.

5   As the 19-year-old announces loudly, these college students have just one objective: "to get drunk!"

6   The challenge to drink to the very limits of one's endurance has become a celebrated staple of college life. In one of the most extensive reports on college drinking thus far, a 1997 Harvard School of Public Health study found that 43 percent of college students admitted binge drinking in the preceding two weeks. (Defined as four drinks in a sitting for a woman and five for a man, a drinking binge is when one drinks enough to risk health and well-being.)

7   "That's about five million students," says Henry Wechsler, who co-authored the study. "And it's certainly a cause for concern. Most of these students don't realize they're engaging in risky behavior." University of Kansas Chancellor Robert Hemenway adds, "Every year we see students harmed because of their involvement with alcohol."

8   Indeed, when binge drinking came to the forefront last year with a rash of alcohol-related college deaths, the nation was stunned by the loss. There was Scott Krueger, the 18-year-old fraternity pledge at the Massachusetts Institute of Technology, who died of alcohol poisoning after downing the equivalent of 15 shots in an hour. There was Leslie Baltz, a University of Virginia senior, who died after she drank too much and fell down a flight of stairs. Lorraine Hanna, a freshman at Indiana University of Pennsylvania, was left alone to sleep off her night of New Year's Eve partying. Later that day her twin sister found her dead—with a blood-alcohol content (BAC) of 0.429 percent. (Driving with a BAC of 0.1 percent and above is illegal in all states.)

9   Experts estimate that excessive drinking is involved in thousands of student deaths a year. And the Harvard researchers found that there has been a dramatic change in why students drink: 39 percent drank "to get drunk" in 1993, but 52 percent had the same objective in 1997.

10   "What has changed is the across-the-board *acceptability* of intoxication," says Felix Savino, a psychologist at UW–Madison. "Many college students today see not just drinking but being *drunk* as their primary way of socializing."

Introduction: identifies serious problem, point to be illustrated

Body: paragraphs 2–39

End of paragraph 2, paragraphs 3 and 5; first examples support main point, as do all examples

Brief examples feature different students, as do all examples, providing more evidence supporting paper's point

11   The reasons for the shift are complex and not fully understood. But researchers surmise that it may have something to do with today's instant-gratification life-style—and young people tend to take it to the extreme.

12   In total, it is estimated that America's 12 million undergraduates drink the equivalent of six million gallons of beer a week. When that's combined with teenagers' need to drink secretly, it's no wonder many have a dangerous relationship with alcohol.

13   The biggest predictor of bingeing is fraternity or sorority membership. Sixty-five percent of members qualified as binge-drinkers, according to the Harvard study.

Extended example:
paragraphs 14–21

14   August 25, 1997, was meant to be a night the new Sigma Alpha Epsilon pledges at Louisiana State University in Baton Rouge would never forget, and by 8 P.M. it was certainly shaping up that way. The revelry had begun earlier with a keg party. Then they went to a bar near campus, where pledges consumed massive quantities of alcohol.

15   Among the pledges were Donald Hunt, Jr., a 21-year-old freshman and Army veteran, and his roommate, Benjamin Wynne, a 20-year-old sophomore. Friends since high school, the two gamely drank the alcoholic concoctions offered to them and everyone else.

16   Before long, many in the group began vomiting into trash cans. (Donald Hunt would later allege in a lawsuit that these "vomiting stations" were set up for that very purpose, something the defendants adamantly deny.) About 9:30, incapacitated pledges were taken back to sleep it off at the frat house.

17   The 911 call came around midnight. Paramedics were stunned at what they found: more than a dozen young men sprawled on the floor, on chairs, on couches, reeking of alcohol. The paramedics burst into action, shaking the pledges and shouting, "Hey! Can you hear me?" Four couldn't be roused, and of those, one had no vital signs: Benjamin Wynne was in cardiac arrest.

18   Checking to see that nothing was blocking Wynne's airway, the paramedics began CPR. Within minutes they'd inserted an oxygen tube into his lungs, hooked up an I.V., attached a cardiac monitor and begun shocking him with defibrillation paddles, trying to restart his heart.

19   Still not responding, Wynne was rushed by ambulance to Baton Rouge General Hospital. Lab work revealed that his blood-alcohol content was an astonishing 0.588 percent, nearly six times the legal driving limit for adults—the equivalent of taking about 21 shots in an hour.

20   Meanwhile, three other fraternity pledges were undergoing similar revival efforts. One was Donald Hunt. He would suffer severe alcohol poisoning and nearly die.

21   After working furiously on Wynne, the hospital team admitted defeat. He was pronounced dead of acute alcohol poisoning.

22   One simple fact people tend to lose sight of is that alcohol is a poison—often pleasurable, but a toxin nonetheless. And for a person with little experience processing this toxin, it can come as something of a physical shock.

23   In general, a bottle of beer has about the same alcohol content as a glass of wine or shot of liquor. And the body can remove only the equivalent of less than one drink hourly from the bloodstream.

24   Many students are not just experimenting once or twice. In the Harvard study, half of binge drinkers were "frequent binge drinkers," meaning they had binged three or more times in the previous two weeks.

Illustration **501**

25   It also is assumed by some that bingeing is a "guy thing," an activity that, like cigar smoking and watching televised sports, belongs in the realm of male bonding. Statistics, however, show that the number of heavy-drinking young women is significant. Henry Wechsler's Harvard study found that a hefty 48 percent of college men were binge drinkers, and women were right behind them at 39 percent.

26   Howard Somers had always been afraid of heights. Perhaps his fear was some sort of an omen. On an August day in 1997 he helped his 18-year-old daughter, Mindy, move into her dorm at Virginia Tech. As they unloaded her things in the eighth-floor room, Somers noted with unease the position of the window. It opened inward like an oven door, its lip about level with her bed. He mentioned it, but Mindy dismissed his concern with a smile.

    Extended example: paragraphs 26–32

27   "I have gone through more guilt than you can imagine," Somers says now quietly. "Things I wish I had said or done. But I never thought this would happen. Who would?"

28   Mindy Somers knew the dangers of alcohol and tried to stay aware of her limits. She'd planned not to overdo it that Friday night, since her mother was coming in that weekend to celebrate Mindy's 19th birthday on Sunday. But it was Halloween, the campus was alive with activity, and Mindy decided to stop in at several off-campus parties.

29   When she returned to her room at 3 A.M., she was wiped out enough to fall into bed fully clothed. Mindy's bed was pushed lengthwise against the long, low window. Her roommate and two other girls, who were on the floor, all slept too soundly to notice that sometime after 4 A.M. Mindy's bed was empty.

30   When the paperboy found her facedown on the grass at 6:45 A.M., he at first thought it was a Halloween prank. Police and EMTs swarmed to the scene in minutes. Somers was pronounced dead of massive chest and abdominal injuries. She had a blood-alcohol content of 0.21 percent, equal to her having drunk about five beers in one hour.

31   Police surmised that Mindy had tried to get out of bed during the night but, disoriented, had slipped out the window, falling 75 feet to her death. "It was a strange, tragic accident," Virginia Tech Police Chief Michael Jones says.

32   A terrible irony was that the week prior to Mindy's death had been Virginia Tech's annual Alcohol Awareness Week.

33   While binge drinking isn't always lethal, it does have other, wide-ranging effects. Academics is one realm where it takes a heavy toll.

34   During my trip to Wisconsin most students told me they didn't plan on attending classes the following day. "Nah, I almost never go to class on Friday. It's no big deal," answered Greg, a sophomore. According to a survey of university administrators, 38 percent of academic problems are alcohol-related, as are 29 percent of dropouts.

35   Perhaps because alcohol increases aggression and impairs judgment, it is also related to 25 percent of violent crimes and roughly 60 percent of vandalism on campus. According to one survey, 79 percent of students who had experienced unwanted sexual intercourse in the previous year said that they were under the influence of alcohol or other drugs at the time. "Some people believe that alcohol can provide an excuse for inappropriate behavior, including sexual aggression," says Jeanette Norris, a University of Washington researcher. Later on, those people can claim, "It wasn't me—it was the booze."

36   Faced with the many potential dangers, college campuses are scrambling for ways to reduce binge drinking. Many offer seminars on alcohol during freshman

orientation. Over 50 schools provide alcohol-free living environments. At the University of Michigan's main campus in Ann Arbor, for instance, nearly 30 percent of undergrads living in university housing now choose to live in alcohol-free rooms. Nationwide several fraternities have announced that by the year 2000 their chapter houses will be alcohol-free.

37   After the University of Rhode Island topped the *Princeton Review* party list two years in a row, administrators banned alcohol at all student events on campus; this year URI didn't even crack the top ten. Some campuses respond even more severely, unleashing campus raids and encouraging police busts.

38   Researchers debate, however, if such "zero-tolerance" policies are helpful or if they might actually result in more secret, off-campus drinking. Other academics wonder if dropping the drinking age to 18 would take away the illicit thrill of alcohol and lower the number of kids drinking wildly. Others feel this would just create more drinking-related fatalities.

39   Whatever it takes, changing student behavior won't be easy. "What you've got here are people who think they are having fun," Harvard's Henry Wechsler explains. "You can't change their behavior by preaching at them or by telling them they'll get hurt."

| Conclusion: paragraphs 4–41; returns to opening example |

40   Around 2 A.M. at UW–Madison a hundred kids congregate at a downtown intersection in a nightly ritual. One girl is trying to pull her roommate up off the ground. "I'm not that drunk," the one on the ground insists. "I just can't stand up."

41   Two fights break out. A police car cruises by and the crowd thins, some heading to after-hours parties. Then maybe at 3 or 4 A.M. they'll go home to get some sleep, so they will be rested for when they start to drink again. Tomorrow night.

Discussion Questions

1. Discuss the effectiveness of Rubin Erdely's title.
2. What does Rubin Erdely accomplish in paragraphs 6–7 and in paragraphs 9–13, 22–25, and 33–38?
3. How do you account for the slang expressions found in this essay: "Chug! Chug! Chug!" in paragraph 2 and "wasted" in paragraph 3?
4. Comment on the effectiveness of the two-word sentence fragment that ends the essay.

Toward Key Insights

Why would "many college students today see not just drinking but being *drunk* as their primary way of socializing"?
What can be done to counter this mind-set?

Suggestion for Writing

Write an essay illustrating some type of benefit available on campus—perhaps academic counseling, the campus ministry, or some ethnic or racial organization. Develop your essay with several short examples or one extended one.

Illustration **503**

DOUGLAS ALDEN WARSHAW

Pulling Off the Ultimate Career Makeover

Douglas Alan Warshaw was born in 1959. He started his career at 17 as an editorial assistant at Sports Magazine. *He received a AB from Princeton. He went on to win four Emmys working for a variety of networks including ESPN, ABC Sports, ABC News, and NBC sports. He has worked in a variety of businesses and is the creator of a media and consulting firm. He also writes for* Fortune *magazine,* The New York Times *and* GQ Magazine. *This selection is a shorter version of an article that appeared in* Fortune, *July 4, 2011.*

1   If you lived in Birmingham, Ala., and wanted to rent a movie on a Friday night back in 2002, the odds were pretty good you'd be paying David Kahn for the privilege. Back then, Kahn, 49, was the effervescent owner of 45 Blockbuster franchises in Alabama and Mississippi; by his estimate, his group of stores made up the seventh-largest video-rental chain in America, and was worth more than $15 million.

2   Then a little company named Netflix came up with a new and disruptive business model for renting videos, and soon it would harness the technology behind delivering movies over the web. Kahn was about to be Blockbusted. He was in jeopardy of losing his financial security, his self-respect, his professional life. He would have to reinvent himself—or the world would do it for him.

3   Feel a chill of recognition while reading this story? Thought so. In this "Age of Disruption," Kahn's story is hardly unique. If you haven't actually been Blockbusted yet, you've doubtless lost sleep over what you'll do when it finally happens.

4   We live and work in a time when technology has made it easier for new companies to be born. That's the good news. The bad news is that increase in productivity has fueled multiple rounds of job cutting. Add to that the lingering wreckage of the financial crisis and the fits-and-starts recovery, and it's clear that job change is the only constant.

5   Job creation is at its lowest point since 1980, while job destruction continues to rise. A full 12.6% of the workforce lost their jobs in the past recession, according to the Bureau of Labor Statistics' Displaced Worker Survey. That's the highest rate since at least 1981.

6   What all these data points make crystal clear is that the very nature of jobs in America has changed. Pensions? An ancient relic. Steady progression up the corporate ladder? Yeah, right. We're living in a project-based economy, one moving from full-time employment with benefits to part-time employment with project-based assignments.

7   Here's proof: By the end of 2010, the number of people working part-time because they couldn't find full-time work has nearly quadrupled since the 1950's, to 2.38 million people. "It's a spot auction market," says Robert Reich, former secretary of labor under Clinton and the chancellor's professor of public policy at the University of California at Berkeley. "What you're paid is what you're worth at that particular time."

8   That means you will change your professional identity frequently—maybe even as often as you spruce up the look of your living room. The youngest baby boomers (those born from 1957 to 1964) held an average of 11 jobs from ages

18 to 44, according to the Bureau of Labor Statistics. The Denali Group, a procurement-services company, predicts that Generation Y will have 15–25 jobs in their lifetime. "This can be a very exciting world," Reich says. "In many ways, it's much better than the old world that was more seniority-based, where you tended to work on the same thing for many years."

9   Exciting if you're in your early twenties. But not so much, Reich adds, if you're an expert in your field, if college tuition is looming, if you aren't as able to relocate as you once were. There's just one way to achieve true job security: stand ready to reinvent yourself—no matter what your age, your education, your skill set, or the color of your collar—sometimes more than once.

10   But how?

11   To find out, we scoured the country to find people who have been disrupted but have managed to create a new career story. Those profiled here have successfully reinvented themselves—not because they wanted to, but because they *had* to. They are not 25-year-old techies; they are established professionals who were happy doing what they were doing—until they weren't doing it anymore.

12   The reason some people have become successful reinventors is more about attitude than experience: One thing they all have in common is that they love learning by doing. They have come to embrace the future, using new technologies, particularly social media, to help them leverage their own professional skills. And they are not victims. At a time when many people react passively to career bumps, our reinventors took control. Read on for five inspiring stories. {three of the five presented here}

Case Study 1: Once Blockbusted, Now Yougurt King

13   Until David Kahn's business model cracked like a defective DVD, he'd been doing just fine as one of Blockbuster's biggest franchisees. "I had a huge mansion with five plasma TVs; I was driving around in a Hummer," Kahn, now 49, recalls. "I was getting my picture taken with President Bush."

14   There was just one problem: His business was doomed. Blockbuster's model, Kahn realized, hinged on the notion that it often didn't have your first choice, though it might have your second or third. Netflix, by contrast, gave you exactly what you wanted. In the spring of 2006, Kahn decided he had to get out. His bank let him do a workout, so he didn't go bust. But this career was over.

15   With no idea what came next, Kahn announced a family austerity plan. Goodbye went the mansion, the club, and the Hummer. Kahn converted credit card points into California Pizza Kitchen gift cards, just so he could treat the family to an occasional dinner out. But he refused to obsess over the loss of social status. "You don't say, 'This is where I'll always be.' You say, 'This is where I am now.'"

16   Next Kahn looked hard at his skills, deciding that his expertise was in franchises, not videos. He bought six Subway franchises in mid-2007 and did a stint at the company's training school. "A few months earlier, I had 500 employees," he says. "Now, you've got mustard on your shirt and you smell like bread. But I was fine with that; I was reinventing myself."

17   It would be the last time. Six months later, Subway rolled out its "$5 Foot-long," smashing Kahn's profit assumptions. He sold the franchises for a small profit, but it was back to square one. What Kahn had going for him was a financial cushion, a supportive family, and a deep belief that he would figure it out.

Illustration   **505**

So he cashed in more miles and told his wife, "I'm going to fly to Los Angeles, and I don't know when I'll be back. All the trendy things start in L.A."

18   In L.A. he drove the streets to see what young people were eating. He was awed by Yogurtland, where people created their own desserts, and filled out a franchise application on the spot. But Yogurtland never called back. So Kahn decided to go it alone. Unfortunately, it was 2008; nine banks turned him down for a loan. Unfazed, he put his house—actually owned by his wife—up for collateral for a $300,000 government loan. "I always told him he could do it," says Carol, "But just in case, I hid $10,000."

19   The Age of Disruption taketh away, but it giveth too. Kahn was able to conduct research, source his product, and find distributors, all online for free. His marketing budget was a $100 "Now Open" banner—and a Facebook page manned by his teenagers.

20   Yogurt Mountain opened on Sept. 10, 2009. By that weekend there were lines out the door, and a second store soon opened. In March 2010, Kahn sold 40% of his business to a private equity group for $3 million, a line of credit, and help opening new stores (there are now 35). He tinkers with yogurt flavors, but he has just one reinvention recipe: "You've got to go into survivor mode, and you've got to reprogram yourself. What's your alternative?"

Case Study 2: Self-Made Social-Media Master

21   Mike Merrill seemed made for the corporate ladder. He spent years moving up the sales chain at Intel and, later, Dell. Merrill, now 41, loved his career. He also loved the trappings of success. "I had this perception that I was going to continue to make more and more money, and get more and more stock," he said. In 2008, Merrill decided it would be a no-brainer to jump from Dell to data-storage company NetApp. It also seemed a no-brainer one February morning in 2009— when he received a companywide e-mail announcing an 8% layoff—that he'd be among the 92% of employees to weather the storm. But one hour later, Merrill found himself out in the pouring rain of the recession without an umbrella.

22   Some people, when they're laid off, feel shame. They take weeks to tell their loved ones. Others head straight to a bar. But Merrill headed straight for LinkedIn, a sight he had used to hunt for sales leads, and posted the following question to his entire network: "Hey, guys, I'm a free agent. Who wants me?" Within 24 hours he heard from the University of Oklahoma's campus computer store, which wanted to boost sales. "It was the first eye-opener for me that, Hey, there's a lot of people reading these updates," Merrill says. He signed on, and using social media managed to double the store's web traffic and triple its sales—with no traditional ads.

23   The experience helped Merrill see how social media was reinventing sales and marketing. He decided it could do the same for his career. He devoured every blog and YouTube video about social media, then posted the items he found most interesting, adding his own thoughts about the topic. "I was faking it until I made it," he adds with a laugh. "I created the perception that I was an expert because I shared content in that space."

24   No longer evangelizing NetApp's products, Merrill started evangelizing himself, leading career talks at his church and speaking to any group that would have him. Always he met professionals curious about Facebook and Twitter but who didn't know where to begin. Merrill encouraged newbies to dive in and not get hung up on being perfect.

25   Nine months after being laid off, Merrill had gained traction as a social-media maven. But bills for his family of four were piling up. "This is a beating," he told friends. Merrill couldn't turn back. He believed in social media, saw how disruptive it was, and had gained real expertise. He'd reinvented himself; he just needed someone willing to pay the new him.

26   Then in the spring of 2010, an employee of ReachLocal, a Dallas-based Internet marketing firm, attended a presentation he gave. By June, Merrill was hired as director of marketing, overseeing ReachLocal's social-media initiates. "I love the job," he says. "I love giving people feedback, knowing that they're learning something from me." Merrill's new career pays less than his last one, but it gives him more security, because he is allowed to continue his speaking and self-branding. Should he ever need another reinvention, he'll be ready.

. . . .

Case Study 5: Once Writer, Now e-Do-It-Yourselfer

27   Paul Levine is 63 years old, but that didn't stop him from reinventing himself—for the second time. In the 1980's he was a successful trial lawyer. Then Levine began writing mystery novels, publishing 13 of them, and selling 400,000 copies of a single title.

28   It worked great until a single button disrupted Levine's life: the "Buy Used" tab on Amazon. The link, which launched in February 2010, is a killer app for finding used books. But it kills authors, because they don't make a dime from it. An author with dwindling royalties in a fast-changing industry, Levine realized he'd better be proactive—or else.

29   While researching the industry, Levine noticed many authors publishing e-books for as little as 99 cents. Levine had an epiphany. To survive, he need to reinvent himself as a digital publisher, distributor, marketer, and even PR machine—not an easy transition for a solitary writer. "I didn't have a grand plan," he says. "I was fueled by fear and desperation." He had to embrace digital media, but he was all about dead trees. "I didn't have a clue," he says. "Not a clue."

30   Not having a clue is a feeling many reinventors face. The key for Levine was not being intimidated. "You just learn from scratch," he says. "I love learning by doing." Happily, much of that learning was free online. After studying Amazon's "Direct Publishing" page, Levine bought the rights to his backlist, which authors are able to do with out-of-print books. Yet covers belong to the artists, so to create new artwork, he did what any reinventor with a dwindling bank account would do: He got his teenaged neighbor to make new covers on his Mac.

31   Levine may have the same career, but his job has radically changed. Whereas, Levine used to spend 95% of his work life writing and 5% selling, he now spends 50% writing and 50% marketing, all online. Every morning he first checks his book sales, then posts thoughts on books and culture on book forums and Facebook and looks at what his 4,859 friends have been doing. To get reviews, he offers free copies of his books to other authors. "We're not competitors seeking to carve up a limited pie," he says. "We're trying to bake a bigger pie."

32   Levine released his first e-book on June 14, 2010. Since then he's put up one backlisted book a month, making around $2 per book. He's projecting an increase of 30% to 40% by Christmas. And he's happy. The upshot? Reinvention

Illustration **507**

isn't easy—it's often terrifying, requiring that you admit what you don't know—and figure it out. It requires believing in yourself at a challenging time. But as the stories here make clear, it *can* be done.

Discussion Questions

1. Though this is an essay in *Fortune*, a magazine for very successful, professional readers, it uses a number of informal writing strategies. What are some examples of these strategies? How did these strategies impact on the effect of the essay?
2. What strategy does the writer use for his introduction? How effective is it? Why?
3. In paragraphs 4–9, the writer explains the state of the economy rather than remaining focused on how people reinvent themselves. What purpose does this discussion serve? Does it achieve the writer's purposes?
4. The cases tend to follow the same pattern. What is that pattern? Is the use of such a pattern effective? Why or why not?
5. The authors choose five case studies (and we reproduced only three for length). Why did they use so many case studies given their purpose?
6. The primary audience for this essay is successful professionals. As a result, the case studies are of successful individuals. Do these examples work as well with other readers? What kinds of examples would you choose if this were being prepared for college students?

Toward Key Insights

Sharing stories of how people face adversity often provides us with a model for how we can respond. Yet, it can also inflate expectations when we are not able to accomplish the same things we have heard in the story. Obviously some people fail when trying to invent themselves. Knowing stories of failure can help us see we are not alone when things don't work out. Do you think we are better off focusing on stories of success or do you see a need for some stories of only moderate success or even failure?

We all need mentors and examples of how we can meet challenging situations. We can use them to inspire us and provide a model for actions. These stories provide a hint of the struggles the people endured. Is this adequate? How much detail about the actual experience is necessary to make such narratives useful to readers?

Writing Suggestions

1. This essay is written to professionals who have careers. Students also have to adapt as they discover that their majors are not the best ones for them. Talk to students who have had to change majors and who have then been successful and then write an essay illustrating how students can adapt.
2. This essay is specifically about careers. However, we all need to adapt in many ways, in our relationship, our life routines, in our eating. Write an essay illustrating with several examples how we can adapt to live a better life or meet adversity.

JUDITH NEWMAN

If You're Happy and You Know It, Must I Know, Too?

Judith Newman is a freelance writer who has appeared in Mademoiselle, The Wall Street Journal, National Geographic, Vogue, Vanity Fair, *and other publications. She is contributing editor for* Allure. *Recently she published* You Make Me Feel Like an Unnatural Woman: Diary of New Old Mother. *This selection occurs in the October 21, 2011, online version of* The New York Times.

1   Mary Lou DiNardo checked three times to make sure: was that a smiley face at the end of the latest e-mail from her most dour client?

2   A West Coast real estate executive, he had an M.B.A. from a prestigious university and was "a very intellectual, serious man," said Ms. DiNardo, president of TK/PR, a public relations firm. "I've been dealing with him for seven years. All of a sudden, while we're discussing problems with a vendor, he's signing off with these smiling or winking faces. I mean, this is a guy who I don't think I've seen with a smile on his *actual* face."

3   Ms. DiNardo joins the ranks of professionals who have found themselves on the receiving end of smileys, winks and LOL's, as the emoticon has rather suddenly migrated from the e-mails and texts of teenagers (and perhaps the more frothy adults) to the correspondence of business people who pride themselves on their gravitas.

4   "Oh, no question, I've been sending and receiving them more often," said Martha Heller, president of Heller Search Associates, a search firm for technology executives for Fortune 500 companies. "Generally I'll use a smiley or a wink when I'm indicating that my previous comment was meant to be a joke. Like, I hired a guy who's head of sales and marketing to launch my company into the wonderful world of social media, and I sent him a note—'I hear there's this thing called Twitter'—and I added the smiley so he knew I wasn't that clueless."

Illustration   **509**

5   Lisa M. Bates, an assistant professor of epidemiology at Columbia, has lately embraced the smiley—as have her academic colleagues, albeit "sparingly and strategically," she said. "Basically, I'm often sarcastic and in a hurry, and a well-planted smiley face can take the edge off and avoid misunderstanding," Dr. Bates wrote in an e-mail. "I figure they have saved me some grief from misconstrued tone many times."

6   Emoticons can produce another layer of confusion, however: they don't always read the same way across different technical interfaces. "In the text function of my BlackBerry there is a sidebar menu of emoticons (how ridiculous is that?) that shows the yellow smiley faces, except they are also crying and raging, and winking and blowing kisses, etc.," Dr. Bates wrote. "I sent a fairly new acquaintance a 'big hug' emoticon—which, for the record, was ironic. But anyway, on his iPhone it came up with the symbols, not the smiley face, which don't look anything like a big hug. From his perspective they look like a view of, er, splayed lady parts: ({}).'"He then ran around his lab showing colleagues excitedly what I had just sent him. Half (mostly men) concurred with his interpretation, and the others (mostly women) didn't and probably thought he was kind of a desperate perv."

7   These little misinterpretations aside, recent adoptees like Dr. Bates and Ms. Heller said that emoticons not only signal intention in a medium where it's notoriously hard to read tone, they also denote a special congenial relationship between sender and recipient. "I see it as a relationship-building exercise," Ms. Heller said.

8   Students of digital communication see the emerging acceptance of whimsical signifiers as inevitable, if not always desirable. "They're part of the degradation of writing skills—grammar, syntax, sentence structure, even penmanship—that come with digital technology," said Bill Lancaster, a lecturer in communications at Northeastern University in Boston. "Certainly I understand the need for clarity. But language, used properly, is clear on its own."

9   Perhaps it's no surprise, then, that writers and teachers of writing are among the last emoticon holdouts. "I am deeply offended by them," said Maria McErlane, a British journalist, actress and radio personality on BBC Radio 2. "If anybody on Facebook sends me a message with a little smiley-frowny face or a little sunshine with glasses on them, I will de-friend them. I also de-friend for OMG and LOL. They get no second chance. I find it lazy. Are your words not enough? To use a little picture with sunglasses on it to let you know how you're feeling is beyond ridiculous."

10   Another harsh critic is Michele Farinet, a parent coordinator in an elementary school in Manhattan who spends much of her days answering and responding to e-mails of the (largely professional) body of parents. The whole subject touches a raw nerve.

12   "To me, it's like bad moviemaking, where as soon as Dad grabs the puppy, the shot immediately goes to Junior's teary face—like the director does not trust the audience to have an appropriately developed emotion by itself," Ms. Farinet wrote in an e-mail. "That's what emoticons do. PLEASE don't 'show' me that I should be happy-faced or sad-faced or that you are sad-faced or happy-faced."

13   "Can you imagine," wrote Ms. Farinet, "reading the end of 'The Great Gatsby' like that?: So we beat on, boats against the current, borne back ceaselessly into the past :-("

Discussion Questions

1. What would you identify as the thesis statement in this essay? What if anything in the essay doesn't fit this thesis statement?
2. How do paragraphs 8–13 fit or not fit the thrust of the essay? Why do you think the writer included these paragraphs? Is this approach effective to her main point?
3. One strategy in a conclusion is to end with some slight humor that makes your point. What point do you think the writer was making with the conclusion on paragraph 13? Is it effective?
4. Instead of using one more detailed example, the author used several shorter examples? Why was it important to use shorter examples? Were they effective?
5. What do you see as the level of diction or language style of this essay? Why did the author select that level of diction?

Toward Key Insights

With text messaging and twitter, people are actually writing more than they did when depending on the phone as a principle means of communication. In what ways are new media changing how we communicate with each other? What are the advantages and challenges of these changes?

Often as people change the way they communicate, there are different attitudes that develop about the available tools and styles of communication. What are the different ways people are responding to some of the social networking styles of communication?

Suggestions for Writing

1. Collect writing samples from social media communication such as texting or Facebook and write a paper illustrating how language is used in such communication.
2. There are always differing reactions to any new technology or style of communication. Interview several different people about social media as a form of communication and write a paper illustrating how people adapt to changing media for communication.

CLASSIFICATION ▬ ▬ ▬ ▬ ▬ ▬ ▬ ▬

Reading Strategies

1. Identify your purpose for reading the essay and the writer's purpose for the classification. This will determine how carefully you will need to read the selection.

2. Do not lose the big picture. Identify what is being classified—types of cars, kinds of dates—and why it is being classified.

3. Notice each of the major categories and the distinctive characteristics of each category. When this material is important to you, it can be very useful to make a table that

identifies each major classification and identifies the distinctive features of each category. When carefully organized, such a table can be very helpful.

Reading Critically

1. Determine if there is reasonable evidence for the classification system or if the system is arbitrary.
2. Try to come up with an alternative classification system.
3. Check to see if the categories of the classification are clear or overlap.
4. Determine whether the defining features are distinct enough to clearly apply the system.
5. Try applying the system. Does it work?

Reading As a Writer

1. Identify how the essay establishes the characteristics of the classification system.
2. Often the transition sentences in a classification essay are awkward. Examine the transition sentences and evaluate the effectiveness of the transitions.

MARION WINIK

What Are Friends For?

Marion Winik (born 1958) is a graduate of Brown University and of Brooklyn College, where she earned a master of fine arts degree in creative writing. Since graduation, she has pursued a career in education, writing, and marketing. Her writings include poems, short stories, essays, and books, and the shorter pieces have appeared in a variety of major newspapers and popular magazines. Her book, The Lunch-Box Chronicles: Notes from the Parenting Underground *(1998), discusses her experiences in raising her sons after her husband's death. In this selection, Winik takes a humorous look at the different categories of friends and the benefits derived from each one.*

1   I was thinking about how everybody can't be everything to each other, but some people can be something to each other, thank God, from the ones whose shoulder you cry on to the ones whose half-slips you borrow to the nameless ones you chat with in the grocery line.

> Introduction: indicates value of friends

2   Buddies, for example, are the workhorses of the friendship world, the people out there on the front lines, defending you from loneliness and boredom. They call you up, they listen to your complaints, they celebrate your successes and curse your misfortunes, and you do the same for them in return. They hold out through innumerable crises before concluding that the person you're dating is no good, and even then understand if you ignore their good counsel. They accompany you to a movie with subtitles or to see the diving pig at Aquarena Springs. They feed your cat when you are out of town and pick you up from the airport when you get back. They come over to help you decide what to wear on a date. Even if it is with that creep.

> Body: paragraphs 2–14
>
> First category

3   What about family members? Most of them are people you just got stuck with, and though you love them, you may not have very much in common. But there is that rare exception, the Relative Friend. It is your cousin, your brother, maybe

> Second category; paragraphs 3–4

even your aunt. The two of you share the same views of the other family members. Meg never should have divorced Martin. He was the best thing that ever happened to her. You can confirm each other's memories of things that happened a long time ago. Don't you remember when Uncle Hank and Daddy had that awful fight in the middle of Thanksgiving dinner? Grandma always hated Grandpa's stamp collection; she probably left the window open during the hurricane on purpose.

4   While so many family relationships are tinged with guilt and obligation, a relationship with a Relative Friend is relatively worry-free. You don't even have to hide your vices from this delightful person. When you slip out Aunt Joan's back door for a cigarette, she is already there.

Third category; paragraphs 5–6

5   Then there is that special guy at work. Like all the other people at the job site, at first he's just part of the scenery. But gradually he starts to stand out from the crowd. Your friendship is cemented by jokes about co-workers and thoughtful favors around the office. Did you see Ryan's hair? Want half my bagel? Soon you know the names of his turtles, what he did last Friday night, exactly which model CD player he wants for his birthday. His handwriting is as familiar to you as your own.

6   Though you invite each other to parties, you somehow don't quite fit into each other's outside lives. For this reason, the friendship may not survive a job change. Company gossip, once an infallible source of entertainment, soon awkwardly accentuates the distance between you. But wait. Like School Friends, Work Friends share certain memories which acquire a nostalgic glow after about a decade.

Fourth category; paragraphs 7–9

7   A Faraway Friend is someone you grew up with or went to school with or lived in the same town as until one of you moved away. Without a Faraway Friend, you would never get any mail addressed in handwriting. A Faraway Friend calls late at night, invites you to her wedding, always says she is coming to visit but rarely shows up. An actual visit from a Faraway Friend is a cause for celebration and binges of all kinds. Cigarettes, Chips Ahoy, bottles of tequila.

8   Faraway Friends go through phases of intense communication, then may be out of touch for many months. Either way, the connection is always there. A conversation with your Faraway Friend always helps to put your life in perspective: when you feel you've hit a dead end, come to a confusing fork in the road, or gotten lost in some crackerbox subdivision of your life, the advice of the Faraway Friend—who has the big picture, who is so well acquainted with the route that brought you to this place—is indispensable.

9   Another useful function of the Faraway Friend is to help you remember things from a long time ago, like the name of your seventh-grade history teacher, what was in that really good stir-fry, or exactly what happened that night on the boat with the guys from Florida.

Fifth category

10   Ah, the Former Friend. A sad thing. At best a wistful memory, at worst a dangerous enemy who is in possession of many of your deepest secrets. But what was it that drove you apart? A misunderstanding, a betrayed confidence, an unrepaid loan, an ill-conceived flirtation. A poor choice of spouse can do in a friendship just like that. Going into business together can be a serious mistake. Time, money, distance, cult religions: all noted friendship killers. . .

Sixth category; paragraphs 11–12

11   And lest we forget, there are the Friends You Love to Hate. They call at inopportune times. They say stupid things. They butt in, they boss you around, they embarrass you in public. They invite themselves over. They take advantage. You've done the best you can, but they need professional help. On top of all this, they love you to death and are convinced they're your best friend on the planet.

12   So why do you continue to be involved with these people? Why do you tolerate them? On the contrary, the real question is, What would you do without

them? Without Friends You Love to Hate, there would be nothing to talk about with your other friends. Their problems and their irritating stunts provide a reliable source of conversation for everyone they know. What's more, Friends You Love to Hate make you feel good about yourself, since you are obviously in so much better shape than they are. No matter what these people do, you will never get rid of them. As much as they need you, you need them too.

13   At the other end of the spectrum are Hero Friends. These people are better than the rest of us, that's all there is to it. Their career is something you wanted to be when you grew up—painter, forest ranger, tireless doer of good. They have beautiful homes filled with special handmade things presented to them by villagers in the remote areas they have visited in their extensive travels. Yet they are modest. They never gossip. They are always helping others, especially those who have suffered a death in the family or an illness. You would think people like this would just make you sick, but somehow they don't.

Seventh category

14   A New Friend is a tonic unlike any other. Say you meet her at a party. In your bowling league. At a Japanese conversation class, perhaps. Wherever, whenever, there's that spark of recognition. The first time you talk, you can't believe how much you have in common. Suddenly, your life story is interesting again, your insights fresh, your opinion valued. Your various short-comings are as yet completely invisible.

Eighth category

Conclusion; memorable observation meshes stylistically with the rest of essay

15   It's almost like falling in love.

Discussion Questions

1. Comment on the effectiveness of Winik's title.
2. Characterize the level of diction that Winik uses in her essay.
3. What elements of Winik's essay interest you the most? What elements interest you the least?

Toward Key Insights

What traits characterize the various types of friends that you have?
In what ways are these friendships mutually beneficial?

Suggestion for Writing

Write an essay classifying the various types of people that you consider undesirable. Choose an appropriate number of categories and support them with appropriate specific details.

SCOTT RUSSELL SANDERS

The Men We Carry in Our Minds

Scott Russell Sanders was born (1945) in Memphis, Tennessee. After earning a B.A. degree from Brown University in 1967 and a Ph.D. from Cambridge University in 1971, he joined the English faculty at Indiana University, where he is a full professor. Sanders is the author of numerous books of fiction and nonfiction. These books span a wide range of genres, including science fiction, historical novels, children's stories, folk tales, biographies, and personal essays. He has contributed to several essay anthologies, and his articles have appeared in literary journals and popular magazines. He has won several awards for his writing. In this essay, Sanders, in light of what he knows about the lives of working men, examines the view that power is rooted in gender.

1   The first men, besides my father, I remember seeing were black convicts and white guards, in the cottonfield across the road from our farm on the outskirts of Memphis. I must have been three or four. The prisoners wore dingy gray-and-black zebra suits, heavy as canvas, sodden with sweat. Hatless, stooped, they chopped weeds in the fierce heat, row after row, breathing the acrid dust of boll-weevil poison. The overseers wore dazzling white shirts and broad shadowy hats. The oiled barrels of their shotguns flashed in the sunlight. Their faces in memory are utterly blank. Of course those men, white and black, have become for me an emblem of racial hatred. But they have also come to stand for the twin poles of my early vision of manhood—the brute toiling animal and the boss.

2   When I was a boy, the men I knew labored with their bodies. They were marginal farmers, just scraping by, or welders, steel workers, carpenters; they swept floors, dug ditches, mined coal, or drove trucks, their forearms ropy with muscle; they trained horses, stoked furnaces, built tires, stood on assembly lines wrestling parts onto cars and refrigerators. They got up before light, worked all day long whatever the weather, and when they came home at night they looked as though somebody had been whipping them. In the evenings and on weekends they worked on their own places, tilling gardens that were lumpy with clay, fixing broken-down cars, hammering on houses that were always too drafty, too leaky, too small.

3   The bodies of the men I knew were twisted and maimed in ways visible and invisible. The nails of their hands were black and split, the hands tattooed with scars. Some had lost fingers. Heavy lifting had given many of them finicky backs and guts weak from hernias. Racing against conveyor belts had given them ulcers. Their ankles and knees ached from years of standing on concrete. Anyone who had worked for long around machines was hard of hearing. They squinted, and the skin of their faces was creased like the leather of old work gloves. There were times, studying them, when I dreaded growing up. Most of them coughed, from dust or cigarettes, and most of them drank cheap wine or whiskey, so their eyes looked bloodshot and bruised. The fathers of my friends always seemed older than the mothers. Men wore out sooner. Only women lived into old age.

4   As a boy I also knew another sort of men, who did not sweat and break down like mules. They were soldiers, and so far as I could tell they scarcely worked at all. During my early school years we lived on a military base, an arsenal in Ohio, and every day I saw GIs in the guardshacks, on the stoops of barracks, at the wheels of olive drab Chevrolets. The chief fact of their lives was boredom. Long after I left the Arsenal I came to recognize the sour smell the soldiers gave off as that of souls in limbo. They were all waiting—for wars, for transfers, for leaves, for promotions, for the end of their hitch—like so many braves waiting for the hunt to begin. Unlike the warriors of older tribes, however, they would have no say about when the battle would start or how it would be waged. Their waiting was broken only when they practiced for war. They fired guns at targets, drove

tanks across the churned-up fields of the military reservation, set off bombs in the wrecks of old fighter planes. I knew this was all play. But I also felt certain that when the hour for killing arrived, they would kill. When the real shooting started, many of them would die. This was what soldiers were *for*, just as a hammer was for driving nails.

5   Warriors and toilers: those seemed, in my boyhood vision, to be the chief destinies for men. They weren't the only destinies, as I learned from having a few male teachers, from reading books, and from watching television. But the men on television—the politicians, the astronauts, the generals, the savvy lawyers, the philosophical doctors, the bosses who gave orders to both soldiers and laborers—seemed as remote and unreal to me as the figures in tapestries. I could no more imagine growing up to become one of these cool, potent creatures than I could imagine becoming a prince.

6   A nearer and more hopeful example was that of my father, who had escaped from a red-dirt farm to a tire factory, and from the assembly line to the front office. Eventually he dressed in a white shirt and tie. He carried himself as if he had been born to work with his mind. But his body, remembering the earlier years of slogging work, began to give out on him in his fifties, and it quit on him entirely before he turned sixty-five. Even such a partial escape from man's fate as he had accomplished did not seem possible for most of the boys I knew. They joined the Army, stood in line for jobs in the smoky plants, helped build highways. They were bound to work as their fathers had worked, killing themselves or preparing to kill others.

7   A scholarship enabled me not only to attend college, a rare enough feat in my circle, but even to study in a university meant for the children of the rich. Here I met for the first time young men who had assumed from birth that they would lead lives of comfort and power. And for the first time I met women who told me that men were guilty of having kept all the joys and privileges of the earth for themselves. I was baffled. What privileges? What joys? I thought about the maimed, dismal lives of most of the men back home. What had they stolen from their wives and daughters? The right to go five days a week, twelve months a year, for thirty or forty years to a steel mill or a coal mine? The right to drop bombs and die in war? The right to feel every leak in the roof, every gap in the fence, every cough in the engine, as a wound they must mend? The right to feel, when the layoff comes or the plant shuts down, not only afraid but ashamed?

8   I was slow to understand the deep grievances of women. This was because, as a boy, I had envied them. Before college, the only people I had ever known who were interested in art or music or literature, the only ones who read books, the only ones who ever seemed to enjoy a sense of ease and grace were the mothers and daughters. Like the menfolk, they fretted about money, they scrimped and made-do. But, when the pay stopped coming in, they were not the ones who had failed. Nor did they have to go to war, and that seemed to me a blessed fact. By comparison with the narrow, ironclad days of fathers, there was an expansiveness, I thought, in the days of mothers. They went to see neighbors, to shop in town, to run errands at school, at the library, at church. No doubt, had I looked harder at their lives, I would have envied them less. It was not my fate to become a woman, so it was easier for me to see the graces. Few of them held jobs outside the home, and those who did filled thankless roles as clerks and waitresses. I didn't see, then, what a prison a house could be, since houses seemed to me brighter, handsomer places than any factory. I did not realize—because such things were never spoken of—how often women suffered from men's bullying.

I did learn about the wretchedness of abandoned wives, single mothers, widows; but I also learned about the wretchedness of lone men. Even then I could see how exhausting it was for a mother to cater all day to the needs of young children. But if I had been asked, as a boy, to choose between tending a baby and tending a machine, I think I would have chosen the baby. (Having now tended both, I know I would choose the baby.)

9   So I was baffled when the women at college accused me and my sex of having cornered the world's pleasures. I think something like my bafflement has been felt by other boys (and by girls as well) who grew up in dirt-poor farm country, in mining country, in black ghettos, in Hispanic barrios, in the shadows of factories, in Third World nations—any place where the fate of men is as grim and bleak as the fate of women. Toilers and warriors. I realize now how ancient these identities are, how deep the tug they exert on men, the undertow of a thousand generations. The miseries I saw, as a boy, in the lives of nearly all men I continue to see in the lives of many—the body-breaking toil, the tedium, the call to be tough, the humiliating powerlessness, the battle for a living and for territory.

10   When the women I met at college thought about the joys and privileges of men, they did not carry in their minds the sort of men I had known in my childhood. They thought of their fathers, who were bankers, physicians, architects, stockbrokers, the big wheels of the big cities. These fathers rode the train to work or drove cars that cost more than any of my childhood houses. They were attended from morning to night by female helpers, wives and nurses and secretaries. They were never laid off, never short of cash at month's end, never lined up for welfare. These fathers made decisions that mattered. They ran the world.

11   The daughters of such men wanted to share in this power, this glory. So did I. They yearned for a say over their future, for jobs worthy of their abilities, for the right to live at peace, unmolested, whole. Yes, I thought, yes yes. The difference between me and these daughters was that they saw me, because of my sex, as destined from birth to become like their fathers, and therefore as an enemy to their desires. But I knew better. I wasn't an enemy, in fact or in feeling. I was an ally. If I had known, then, how to tell them so, would they have believed me? Would they now?

Discussion Questions

1. Why is the essay titled "The Men *We* Carry in *Our Minds*" rather than "The Men *I* Carry in *My Mind*"?
2. Other than starting the essay, what does paragraph 1 accomplish?
3. What primary categories of men does Sanders discuss? What principle of classification does he use?
4. Sanders uses a number of comparisons, such as "zebra suits, heavy as canvas" in paragraph 1, to enhance his writing. Point out other comparisons and comment on their effectiveness.
5. The last sentence of paragraph 10 and the second, sixth, and eighth sentences of paragraph 11 are short statements. What do you think Sanders accomplishes with these statements?
6. Judging by what Sanders writes in the essay, how do you think he would answer the questions he poses in the final two sentences of paragraph 11?

Toward Key Insights

To what extent do you believe that the views expressed in the essay by the college
women and Sanders reflect the views of today's college women and men?
How do you account for any changes you might note?

Suggestion for Writing

*Write an essay classifying the different grade school or high school teachers that you carry in
your mind. Develop your categories with specific, informative details.*

BERNICE MCCARTHY

A Tale of Four Learners

*Bernice McCarthy, Ph.D., earned her doctorate in education and learning theory from North-
western University. She founded About Learning, Inc., a consulting firm on educational theory and research. She has published a number of articles and presented workshops at major
institutions. In this essay, she classifies learners based on THE 4MAT System® she created.*

1   A young man at a midwestern middle school said of his social studies
teacher, "She doesn't label us, and she helps us do all kinds of things." That
student expressed very simply my evolving understanding of style since I created
the 4MAT System in 1979. The way one perceives reality and reacts to it forms a
pattern over time. This pattern comes to dominate the way one integrates ideas,
skills, and information about people and the way one adapts knowledge and
forms meaning.

2   But to learn successfully, a student also needs expertise in other learning
styles; together these styles form a natural cycle of learning. That middle school
teacher apparently honored the unique style that each student brought to her
classroom, while helping each one do some stretching and master all the ways of
learning.

3   Following are true stories about four types of learners. They illustrate how
students with different learning styles experience school and why we must create
opportunities for diverse learning experiences for every child.

4   Linda was in 6th grade when she hit the wall in math. She had loved school
up until then. Her teachers and classmates agreed that her poetry was quite
good, and her poems often appeared in local publications. But math was a problem. She couldn't connect it to anything—she simply could not see the patterns.
Her teachers were not pleased with her and she longed to please them.

5   Linda went on to college, and when she was a junior, a new professor arrived on campus. The day before Linda's statistics class began, she met him in
the hallway. He said, "Oh, you're Linda; I've been reading your poetry. You are
going to do very well in statistics."

6   She looked at him in amazement. "How can you say that? I have such difficulty in all my math classes."

7   He smiled and answered, "I can tell from your poetry that you understand
symmetry. Statistics is about symmetry. As a matter of fact, statistics is the poetry

of math." Linda went on to earn an A in that class. Her professor had connected statistics to her life and showed her the patterns (McCarthy 1996).

8   Linda is a Type 1 learner—the highly imaginative student who favors feeling and reflecting. These learners

9   ■ are at home with their feelings, people-oriented, outstanding observers of people, great listeners and nurturers, and committed to making the world a better place.

10   ■ prefer to learn by talking about experiences; listening and watching quietly, then responding to others and discussing ideas; asking questions; brainstorming; and examining relationships. They work well in groups or teams but also enjoy reading quietly.

11   ■ experience difficulty with long verbal explanations, with giving oral presentations, and with memorizing large chunks of abstract information. They dislike confusion or conflict, environments where mistakes are openly criticized, or where they cannot discuss their perceptions.

12   ■ have a cognitive style that puts perception before judgment, subjective knowledge before objective facts, and reflection before action. They prefer to make decisions based on feeling, are visual/auditory/kinesthetic, and experiential before conceptual.

13   As a Type 1 learner, Linda needed to connect math to her real life, to know why it was useful as a way of thinking and a way of formulating problems and solutions. She also needed her teachers to believe in her and to spend time with and nurture her.

14   Marcus was in 1st grade, and he loved school. Everything he longed for was present there—the teacher's loving interest, the thrill of deciphering the symbols that meant things, the things he could touch and feel, the addition problems that the teacher wrote on the chalkboard. He could always see the answers. His excitement was like that of the basketball player who knows that if he can just get his hands on the ball, he can sink it. Each question became an exciting foray into even more questions. And as his reading improved rapidly, he could not get enough of books. He welcomed the words and ideas of each new writer. He felt confident; he knew he belonged (McCarthy 1996).

15   Marcus is a Type 2 learner—the analytic student who favors reflecting and thinking. These learners

16   ■ have a knowledge-oriented style; are outstanding at conceptualizing material; analyze and classify their experiences and organize ideas; are highly organized and at home with details and data; are good at step-by-step tasks; are fascinated with structure; believe in their ability to understand; and are committed to making the world more lucid.

17   ■ prefer to learn through lectures and objective explanations, by working independently and systematically, and by reading and exchanging ideas.

18   ■ experience difficulty in noisy, high-activity environments, ambiguous situations, and working in groups. They also have trouble with open-ended assignments, as well as with presentations, role-playing, and nonsequential instructions. They have difficulty talking about feelings as well.

19   ■ have a cognitive style that is objective thinking, reflection before action, impersonal, auditory/visual/kinesthetic, conceptual over experiential. They tend to make judgments first, then support them with their perceptions.

20   As a Type 2 learner, Marcus found school an absolute joy. Testing, so frightening to Linda, was a tonic for him, a chance to prove he could do it. Because

he was naturally verbal and school is mostly a verbal challenge, he was—and continues to be—successful.

21   When Jimmy was in 2nd grade he did not like to read, and that made school difficult. He did enjoy having others read to him, and his younger brother, a 1st grader, read him stories every night. Jimmy did excel in math and art. He loved to work alone on projects and never wanted help. When he was asked to illustrate a story or build something to depict a math concept, he approached the task excitedly. He was happiest when he could solve a problem by creating a three-dimensional solution.

22   Unfortunately, Jimmy had a rigid teacher whose timing was always different from his own. Jimmy either finished too fast or took too long when he got really interested in a project. Once his teacher said in exasperation, "I didn't say you had to do your best work, Jimmy, just get it done!" When Jimmy's family bought a new VCR, they read the directions aloud to figure out how it worked. Jimmy stepped up and simply made it work. His reading problem continued into 3rd grade when he caught up with the others, but he never let it get him down—he was simply too busy doing other kinds of things (McCarthy 1996).

23   Jimmy is a Type 3 learner—the common-sense learner who favors thinking and doing. These learners

24   ■ are great problem solvers and are drawn to how things work. They are at home with tasks and deadlines, are productive and committed to making the world work better, and they believe in their ability to get the job done. They are also active and need opportunities to move around.

25   ■ prefer to learn through active problem solving; step-by-step procedures; touching, manipulating, and constructing; demonstrations; experimentation and tinkering; and competition.

26   ■ experience difficulty when reading is the primary means of learning and whenever they cannot physically test what they are told. They have trouble with verbal complexity, paradoxes or unclear choices, subtle relationships, and open-ended academic tasks. They also have difficulty expressing feelings.

27   ■ have a cognitive style that features objective thinking and facts over ideas, action before reflection, and judgment before perception. Their style is impersonal and kinesthetic/auditory/visual.

28   As a Type 3 learner, Jimmy needed to work things out in his own way, to create unique solutions to problems, and, most of all, to show what he learned by doing something concrete with it. His verbal skills did not kick in until well into the 3rd grade. Although this is not unusual with highly spatial learners, teachers treated it as an aberration. School was simply too regimented and too verbal for Jimmy. What saved him was his focus on his own learning.

29   When Leah was a high school freshman, she liked her new friends and some of her teachers. But she had a fierce need to learn, and school was not nearly exciting enough for her. She found so much of it deadening—memorizing endless facts that were totally irrelevant to her life. Leah had a wonderful spontaneity, and when it took hold of her, she focused so intensely that time became meaningless. Her teachers came to regard this spontaneity as a liability that was taking her away from the things she needed to know.

30   At first Leah persevered. Instead of preparing a juvenile justice report based on her social studies text, she asked to be allowed to go to juvenile court and see for herself, and then present her findings in a skit. Her teachers seldom agreed to her proposals, and after a while Leah stopped trying. She had natural leadership talent, which she expressed through her extra-curricular activities—the one

part of school she came to love. She graduated, but has believed ever since then that real learning does not happen in school (McCarthy 1996).

31   Leah is a Type 4 learner—the dynamic learner who favors creating and acting. These learners

32   ■ are proud of their subjectivity, at home with ambiguity and change, and great risk takers and entrepreneurs. They act to extend and enrich their experiences and to challenge the boundaries of their worlds for the sake of growth and renewal, and they believe in their ability to influence what happens. They initiate learning by looking for unique aspects of the information to learn and they sustain learning through trial and error.

33   ■ prefer to learn by self-discovery, talking, convincing others, looking for creative solutions to problems, and engaging in free flights of ideas. They also like to work independently and tackle open-ended academic tasks with lots of options, paradox, or subtle relationships. Their interpersonal skills are good.

34   ■ experience difficulty with rigid routines when they are not allowed to question. They also have trouble with visual complexity, methodical tasks, time management, and absolutes.

35   ■ have a cognitive style that is perception first with slight attention to judgment, subjective, relational, action-oriented, kinesthetic/auditory/visual, and experiential over conceptual.

36   Leah found learning for school's sake incomprehensible. As in Jimmy's case, doing was crucial to her approach. She preferred interviewing over reading, going to court to see for herself, exploring instead of hearing how others see things.

37   In any classroom, Linda, Marcus, Jimmy, Leah, and their many shades and varieties sit before the teacher—challenging and waiting to be challenged. The frustrating question is: why are some learners honored in our schools and others ignored, discouraged, or even frowned upon? Why did Marcus fare so well, while Linda, Jimmy, and Leah struggled to be accepted?

38   In my definition of learning, the learner makes meaning by moving through a natural cycle—a movement from feeling to reflecting to thinking and, finally, to acting. This cycle results from the interplay of two separate dimensions—perceiving and processing (Kolb 1984).

39   In perceiving, we take in what happens to us by (1) feeling, as we grasp our experience, and then by (2) thinking, as we begin to separate ourselves from the experience and name and classify it. The resulting concepts become our way of interpreting our world (Kegan 1982).

40   We also process experiences in two ways: by (1) reflecting on them, and then by (2) acting on those reflections. We also try things; we tinker.

41   The places in this cycle that we find most comfortable—where we function with natural ease and grace—are our learning preferences or styles, the "spins" we put on learning.

42   Unfortunately, schools tend to honor only one aspect of perceiving—thinking. This is very tough on kids whose approach to learning is predominately feeling. Linda and Leah, like many other Type 1 and 4 learners—both male and female—are naturals on the feeling end of experience. Jimmy and Marcus, the Type 2 and 3 learners, favor the thinking end.

43   As with feeling and thinking, reflecting and acting need to be in balance. But our schools favor reflecting. Marcus excelled at that, while both Jimmy and Leah needed to act. The lack of hands-on learning created difficulties for both of them.

44   Even as I define styles in my work, I caution that we must be wary of labels. Over time, and with experience, practice, and encouragement, students become

comfortable with learning styles that aren't naturally their own. Successful learners, in fact, develop multiple styles.

45   The 4MAT framework is designed to help students gain expertise in every learning style. We design lesson units as cycles built around core concepts, each of which incorporates experiencing (Type 1), conceptualizing (Type 2), applying (Type 3), and creating (Type 4). The styles answer the questions:

46
- Why do I need to know this? (the personal meaning of Type 1).
- What exactly is this content or skill? (the conceptual understanding of Type 2).
- How will I use this in my life? (the real-life skills of Type 3).
- If I do use this, what possibilities will it create? (the unique adaptations of Type 4).

47   Had the teachers of Linda, Marcus, Jimmy, and Leah used the entire cycle of learning styles, including those areas in which each student needed to stretch, all four students would have acquired expertise in all facets of the cycle. They would have made personal connections to the learning, examined expert knowledge, used what they were learning to solve problems, and come up with new ways to apply the learning—both personally and in the world at large. (As it happened, the students learned to do these things on their own.)

48   In addressing the various learning styles, the 4MAT System also incorporates elements of brain research—in particular, the different ways that the right and left hemispheres of the cerebral cortex process information (Benson 1985, McCarthy 1981 and 1987, Sylvester 1995, Wittrock 1985). I call these contrasting mental operations the Left and Right Modes.

49   The Left Mode is analytical and knows those things we can describe with precision. It examines cause and effect, breaks things down into parts and categorizes them, seeks and uses language and symbols, abstracts experience for comprehension, generates theory, and creates models. It is sequential and works in time.

50   The Right Mode knows more than it can tell, filling in gaps and imagining. It is intuitive. It senses feelings; forms images and mental combinations; and seeks and uses patterns, relationships, and connections. It manipulates form, distance, and space.

51   Excellence and higher-order thinking demand that we honor both sides of the brain, teaching interactively with hands-on, real-life, messy problem solving. Learners speak in words, signs, symbols, movement, and through music. The more voices students master, the more new learning they will do. Unfortunately, however, teachers persist in lecturing and using logical, sequential problem solving most of the time.

52   In assessing student performance, traditional methods work fairly well for Type 2 learners, who like to prove themselves, and Type 3 learners, who do well on tests in general. Traditional testing doesn't work as well for Types 1 and 4, however. Type 1 learners have difficulty in formal testing situations, especially when tests are timed and call for precise answers. Type 4 learners have trouble doing things by the book and with absolutes and rigid routines when they are not allowed to ask questions.

53   Further, students change roles as they move through the learning cycle. Tests that require students to recall facts obviously do not reflect the subtlety of these changes.

54   We need assessment tools that help us understand the whole person. We must assess the students' ability to picture the concept, to experiment with the idea, to combine skills in order to solve complex problems, to edit and refine their work, and to adapt and integrate learning. We need to know how students are connecting information to their own experiences, how they are blending

expert knowledge with their own, and how creative they are. We also need some way of measuring how students reflect on material, conceptualize, and represent what they have learned through various kinds of performances.

55   Successful learning is a continuous, cyclical, lifelong process of differentiating and integrating these personal modes of adaptation. Teachers do not need to label learners according to their style; they need to help them work for balance and wholeness. Leah needs to learn the ways of Marcus; Jimmy needs Linda's ways. And all learners need encouragement to grow.

56   Learning is both reflective and active, verbal and nonverbal, concrete and abstract, head and heart. The teacher must use many instructional methods that are personally meaningful to each student. The more students can travel the cycle, the better they can move to higher-order thinking.

57   As a final note, what became of the students I described earlier? Linda directs the management division of a major human resources consulting firm. Marcus, a former professor of statistics at a prestigious university, is now president of a research firm. Jimmy will be a senior in high school this fall. He scored 100 percent on the Illinois State Math Achievement Test and achieved cum laude in the International Latin Exam. He also had his art portfolio favorably reviewed by the Art Institute of Chicago. And Leah? Leah is a pseudonym for the author of this article.

■ References

Benson, D. F. "Language in the Left Hemisphere." *The Dual Brain: Hemispheric Specialization in Humans*. Ed. D. F. Benson and E. Zaidel. New York: Guilford, 1985.

Kegan, R. *The Evolving Self: Problems and Process in Human Development*. Cambridge, MA: Harvard UP, 1982.

Kolb, D. A. *Experiential Learning: Experience as the Source of Learning and Development*. Englewood Cliffs, NJ: Prentice-Hall, 1984.

McCarthy, B. *The 4MAT System: Teaching to Learning Styles with Right/Left Mode Techniques*. Barrington, IL: Excel, Inc., 1981, 1987.

McCarthy, B. *About Learning*. Barrington, IL: Excel, Inc., 1996.

Sylvester, R. *A Celebration of Neurons: An Educator's Guide to the Human Brain*. Alexandria, VA: ASCD, 1995.

Wittrock, M. C. "Education and Recent Neuropsychological and Cognitive Research." *The Dual Brain: Hemispheric Specialization in Humans*. Ed. D. F. Benson and E. Zaidel. New York: Guilford, 1985.

Discussion Questions

1. The author starts with an example of praise for a teacher who did not "label" her students but then goes on to classify learning styles. Is this a contradiction?
2. With each type of learning style, the author follows the same pattern. What is the pattern that she uses and is it effective?
3. In paragraphs 4, 22, and 30, the author identifies the problems three out of the four sample students had in school. Why does she do this? Is it effective?

4. After discussing the four learning styles, the author discusses in paragraphs 38–48 what she identifies as the learning cycle. What is the connection between this learning cycle, and how is this important in relation to the classification system?

5. It could be easy to imagine someone who had qualities of more than one learning style. Is this a problem for the writer's classification of learning styles?

6. In the conclusion the author informs us of the successes of her four example students. How is this conclusion important to the essay?

Toward Key Insights

Try to match yourself to the four learning styles. Does one learning style seem most like you? What does this say about the classification system?

What learning styles seem to dominate in most of your classes? What effects does this seem to have on the learning success of students? Do people who have different learning styles have difficulty adjusting to the dominant learning style of educational institutions?

Suggestion for Writing

Write an essay classifying teaching styles, including the different kinds of activities involved in the classroom and the different kinds of assessment.

COMPARISON

Reading Strategies

1. Identify your purpose for reading the comparison and the author's purpose for the comparison. Determine how carefully you need to read the comparison.

2. Identify the items that are being compared.

3. Identify the pattern of organization (point by point or block) that is used in the comparison.

4. Read carefully to establish the points of similarities and differences. When the information might be necessary for future purposes, it can be helpful to create a table that matches similarities and differences.

Reading Critically

1. Test to see if there are any biases guiding the comparison. Does the writer show any preference or prejudice?

2. Determine if the accounts of similarities and differences are accurate or whether they are exaggerated.

3. Test to see if there are other similarities or differences that can be established. Are the items more alike or more different than the author tries to suggest?

Reading As a Writer

1. Examine how the author organized the essay. Was the organization effective in guiding the reader through the essay? Note what organizational pattern was most effective.

2. Notice the sentences that the writer uses for transitions. Jot down any useful techniques.

3. Observe how much detail was used to substantiate the comparison.

BRUCE CATTON

Title sets up differences

Grant and Lee: A Study in Contrasts

Bruce Catton (1899–1978) was a nationally recognized expert on the Civil War. Born in Petoskey, Michigan, he attended Oberlin College, then worked as a reporter for several large newspapers. Between 1942 and 1948, he held several positions in the U.S. government and then became an editor of American Heritage *magazine. His first book on the Civil War,* Mr. Lincoln's Army, *appeared in 1951 and was followed by* Glory Road *(1952) and* A Stillness at Appomattox *(1953). This last book won the Pulitzer Prize and the National Book Award and established Catton's reputation as a Civil War historian. In the years that followed, Catton continued to write books on the Civil War. In 1972 he published the autobiographical* Waiting for the Morning Train *and in 1974* Michigan: A Bicentennial History. *In our selection, Catton points out differences as well as similarities in the two foremost adversaries of the Civil War.*

Introduction: paragraphs 1–3; background; significance of following contrasts

1   When Ulysses S. Grant and Robert E. Lee met in the parlor of a modest house at Appomattox Court House, Virginia, on April 9, 1865, to work out the terms for the surrender of Lee's Army of Northern Virginia, a great chapter in American life came to a close, and a great new chapter began.

2   These men were bringing the Civil War to its virtual finish. To be sure, other armies had yet to surrender, and for a few days the fugitive Confederate government would struggle desperately and vainly, trying to find some way to go on living now that its chief support was gone. But in effect it was all over when Grant and Lee signed the papers. And the little room where they wrote out the terms was the scene of one of the poignant, dramatic contrasts in American history.

3   They were two strong men, these oddly different generals, and they represented the strengths of two conflicting currents that, through them, had come into final collision.

Body: paragraph 4 to first part, paragraph 16; alternating pattern throughout

4   Back of Robert E. Lee was the notion that the old aristocratic concept might somehow survive and be dominant in American life.

First difference paragraphs 4–6; Lee's background, character

5   Lee was tidewater Virginia, and in his background were family, culture, and tradition . . . the age of chivalry transplanted to a New World which was making its own legends and its own myths. He embodied a way of life that had come down through the age of knighthood and the English country squire. America was a land that was beginning all over again, dedicated to nothing much more complicated than the rather hazy belief that all men had equal rights and should have an equal chance in the world. In such a land Lee stood for the feeling that it was somehow of advantage to human society to have a pronounced inequality in the social structure. There should be a leisure class, backed by ownership of land; in turn, society itself should be keyed to the land as the chief source of wealth and influence. It would bring forth (according to this ideal) a class of men with a strong sense of obligation to the community; men who lived not to gain advantage for themselves, but to meet the solemn obligations which had been laid on them by the very fact that they were privileged. From them the country would get its leadership; to them it could look for the higher values—of thought, of conduct, or personal deportment—to give it strength and virtue.

6   Lee embodied the noblest elements of this aristocratic ideal. Through him, the landed nobility justified itself. For four years, the Southern states had fought a desperate war to uphold the ideals for which Lee stood. In the end, it almost

seemed as if the Confederacy fought for Lee; as if he himself was the Confederacy . . . the best thing that the way of life for which the Confederacy stood could ever have to offer. He had passed into legend before Appomattox. Thousands of tired, underfed, poorly clothed Confederate soldiers, long since past the simple enthusiasm of the early days of the struggle, somehow considered Lee the symbol of everything for which they had been willing to die. But they could not quite put this feeling into words. If the Lost Cause, sanctified by so much heroism and so many deaths, had a living justification, its justification was General Lee.

7   Grant, the son of a tanner on the Western frontier, was everything Lee was not. He had come up the hard way and embodied nothing in particular except the eternal toughness and sinewy fiber of the men who grew up beyond the mountains. He was one of a body of men who owed reverence and obeisance to no one, who were self-reliant to a fault, who cared hardly anything for the past but who had a sharp eye for the future.

8   These frontier men were the precise opposites of the tidewater aristocrats. Back of them, in the great surge that had taken people over the Alleghenies and into the opening Western country, there was a deep, implicit dissatisfaction with a past that had settled into grooves. They stood for democracy not from any reasoned conclusion about the proper ordering of human society, but simply because they had grown up in the middle of democracy and knew how it worked. Their society might have privileges, but they would be privileges each man had won for himself. Forms and patterns meant nothing. No man was born to anything, except perhaps to a chance to show how far he could rise. Life was competition.

9   Yet along with this feeling had come a deep sense of belonging to a national community. The Westerner who developed a farm, opened a shop, or set up in business as a trader could hope to prosper only as his own community prospered— and his community ran from the Atlantic to the Pacific and from Canada down to Mexico. If the land was settled, with towns and highways and accessible markets, he could better himself. He saw his fate in terms of the nation's own destiny. As its horizons expanded, so did his. He had, in other words, an acute dollars-and-cents stake in the continued growth and development of his country.

10   And that, perhaps, is where the contrast between Grant and Lee becomes most striking. The Virginia aristocrat, inevitably, saw himself in relation to his own region. He lived in a static society which could endure almost anything except change. Instinctively, first loyalty would go to the locality in which that society existed. He would fight to the limit of endurance to defend it, because in defending it he was defending everything that gave his own life its deepest meaning.

11   The Westerner, on the other hand, would fight with an equal tenacity for the broader concept of society. He fought so because everything he lived by was tied to growth, expansion, and a constantly widening horizon. What he lived by would survive or fall with the nation itself. He could not possibly stand by unmoved in the face of an attempt to destroy the Union. He would combat it with everything he had, because he could only see it as an effort to cut the ground out from under his feet.

12   So Grant and Lee were in complete contrast, representing two diametrically opposed elements in American life. Grant was the modern man emerging; beyond him, ready to come on the stage, was the great age of steel and machinery, of crowded cities and a restless burgeoning vitality. Lee might have ridden down from the old age of chivalry, lance in hand, silken banner fluttering over his head. Each man was the perfect champion of his cause, drawing both his strengths and his weaknesses from the people he led.

Paragraphs 7–9: Grant's background, character

Second difference: Lee's loyalty

Grant's loyalty

Summary of significant differences

Transition paragraph
signals switch to
similarities

13   Yet it was not all contrast, after all. Different as they were—in background, in personality, in underlying aspiration—these two great soldiers had much in common. Under everything else, they were marvelous fighters. Furthermore, their fighting qualities were really very much alike.

First similarity

14   Each man had, to begin with, the great virtue of utter tenacity and fidelity. Grant fought his way down the Mississippi Valley in spite of acute personal discouragement and profound military handicaps. Lee hung on in the trenches at Petersburg after hope itself had died. In each man there was an indomitable quality . . . the born fighter's refusal to give up as long as he can still remain on his feet and lift his two fists.

Second similarity

15   Daring and resourcefulness they had, too; the ability to think faster and move faster than the enemy. These were the qualities which gave Lee the dazzling campaigns of Second Manassas and Chancellorsville and won Vicksburg for Grant.

Third similarity; notes
order of climax

Conclusion:
significance of the
meeting

16   Lastly, and perhaps greatest of all, there was the ability, at the end, to turn quickly from war to peace once the fighting was over. Out of the way these two men behaved at Appomattox came the possibility of a peace of reconciliation. It was a possibility not wholly realized, in the years to come, but which did, in the end, help the two sections to become one nation again . . . after a war whose bitterness might have seemed to make such a reunion wholly impossible. No part of either man's life became him more than the part he played in this brief meeting in the McLean house at Appomattox. Their behavior there put all succeeding generations of Americans in their debt. Two great Americans, Grant and Lee—very different, yet under everything very much alike. Their encounter at Appomattox was one of the great moments of American history.

Discussion Questions

1. Where is Catton's thesis statement?
2. Summarize the way of life that Lee stood for, and then do the same for Grant.
3. Why do the differences between Grant and Lee receive more extended treatment than the similarities? Why are the similarities discussed last?
4. How would you characterize Catton's attitude toward the two men? Refer to specific parts of the essay when answering.

Toward Key Insights

To what extent does modern society reflect the values embodied by Grant and Lee? How would you characterize the upper class in the United States today? Does it consist of leisured individuals who own extensive property, as Lee did, or does it have other characteristics? Are its values the same as Lee's? If not, how are they different? If Grant was typical of the "self-reliant" non-aristocrat, how is his contemporary counterpart similar to and different from him?

Suggestion for Writing

Write an essay comparing two past or present political or military figures—perhaps Abraham Lincoln and Jefferson Davis or Dwight Eisenhower and Erwin Rommel. Try for a balanced treatment and select an appropriate organization.

CHRIS LEE

Invasion of the Bodybuilders

Chris Lee is currently the senior entertainment writer for Newsweek. *Earlier he was Entertainment and culture reporter for the* Los Angeles Times. *He has extensive articles to his credit in a number of publications and has a regular tweet. This selection appeared in* Newsweek *in 2011.*

1   Macho men are back with a vengeance—and they're making the U.S.A. feel good again.

2   It's easy to mistake this summer's behemoth leading men for overactive gym rats. Actor-model Jason Momoa packed on 30 pounds to his runway-ready frame to revive Conan the Barbarian. Chris Evans endured months of nausea-inducing workouts to bulk up for Captain America: The First Avenger. Even Ryan Reynolds got into the game, undergoing a radical pectoral transformation for The Green Lantern.

3   They're hardly alone in favoring bench presses over Brechtian technique for their close-ups. The multiplex exploded in April with the arrival of Fast Five, a shoot-'em-up heist film that showcases the musculature of Vin Diesel and Dwayne "The Rock" Johnson during their rampage across Rio de Janeiro. The following week, the comic-book adaptation Thor featured Chris Hemsworth as the Asgardian god of thunder with biceps the size of canned hams.

4   But even while guys chugging Muscle Milk seem to have the cultural zeitgeist in a headlock, a war is brewing between the he-men and action moviedom's 98-pound weaklings. A new crop of machismo-challenged heroes—call them the "emo" super-dudes—is headed for screens next year. Spider-Man's franchise reboot rests on the shoulders of waifish actor Andrew Garfield, best known as a nerd in The Social Network. Brooding British thespian Henry Cavill (famous to Showtime fans of The Tudors) is on tap as the new Superman. And Hollywood's reigning Sensitive Male, Mark Ruffalo, will portray none other than the Incredible Hulk in Marvel's The Avengers. What could his Hulk possibly smash?

5   Every generation gets the idol it deserves, as the conventional wisdom goes, with marquee actors often standing in as avatars for the collective imagination. Thanks to his Charles Atlas physique and Brylcreemed hair, Adventures of Superman star George Reeves became the television embodiment of Cold War-era American idealism. At the other end of the spectrum, surging with steroids and excess testosterone, Arnold Schwarzenegger and Sylvester Stallone became touchstones of excess in the '80s. (The Governator recently became a symbol of excess again for reasons unrelated to the size of his quads.)

6   It wasn't long ago that superheroes were swathed in Prada suits in sizes much smaller than XXXL. Tobey Maguire and Robert Downey Jr. weren't initially known as action stars, and still managed to translate their brooding shtick into box-office gold.

7   But in 2011, at a time of global economic uncertainty and with the U.S. embroiled in three wars, the pendulum has swung the other way. Today's alpha males are signaling a cultural shift: a "might equals right" moment. "There is a huge vogue for these heroes at the moment," says movie historian David Thomson, author of The New Biographical Dictionary of Film. "The country is very insecure about an awful lot of things. And wanting to watch guys with buffed-up egos and bodies, the toughest guys in the world—it could be a response to that."

8   As Captain America screenwriter Stephen McFeely sees it, "There's little tolerance for guys in fake-muscle suits—people know the difference. We want to know our actors might be able to kick our asses."

9   Movie studios didn't magically decide that size matters. To hear it from Fast Five producer Neal Moritz, the current crop of musclebound stars surfaced only after the number of actors who could actually act while, say, firing a machine gun and running through a jungle had dwindled dramatically. "Hollywood has always looked for macho guys to be in big action films," said Moritz. "The problem is they aren't the ones who spend time studying drama and becoming great actors. But now we do have actors like Vin Diesel and The Rock, guys who have incredible charisma and can run and jump and fight—and as an audience, we're going to believe the things they're doing."

10   Acclaimed Irish actor Michael Fassbender can speak to both sides of the divide. He bulked up to portray a Spartan warrior in the 2007 action epic 300—a seminal work in the macho-cinema canon—and slimmed down to play Magneto, a super-mutant whose mind is his real weapon, in this summer's X-Men: First Class.

11   Fassbender explained that onscreen assets are never flaunted without merit. "It's whatever goes for the character," he said. "In 300, these guys are carrying copper shields and doing battle for, like, eight hours. Magneto's thing is manipulating metal. He doesn't need those muscles."

12   Still, other heroes bank on their chiseled masculinity. Director Kenneth Branagh saw hundreds of potential Thors before hiring Hemsworth, who packed on so much mass for the role that he initially couldn't fit into his costume. Discussing what he looked for in his leading man, Branagh could be describing the trend that has given macho men a temporary leg up on emo boys.

13   "We wanted an old-fashioned leading man," the director said. "A good-looking lad you're happy to watch think. An oak-tree presence. Someone who really occupies the space."

Discussion Questions

1. This essay clearly uses an informal style of writing. What are some examples of the informal style of the essay? Why did the author use this style? Is the style effective? Why or why not?
2. This article does not follow a traditional structure of a comparison essay. What are the major comparisons in the essay? Why doesn't the author follow a straightforward organizational pattern for a comparison? Does the comparison work? Why or why not?
3. What is the thesis of this paper? Where in the article does the author directly state this thesis?
4. The author uses a number of quotes from people in the movie business. How do the quotes affect the article? Could the article be as effective without those quotes? Why or why not?

Toward Key Insights

The author states that "Every generation gets the idol it deserves, as the conventional wisdom goes, with marquee actors often standing in as avatars for the collective imagination." To what extent is or isn't it true that we get the idols we deserve that reflect the "collective imagination?" Why might this occur? What are some examples of this?

The author also suggests that different historical periods face different kinds of concerns, and that in some ways our heroes may be the response to that. In what ways might or might not different historical periods call for different kinds of heroes?

Suggestions for Writing

1. This article does not offer a complete point-by-point comparison. Examine carefully the heroes evoked by the author and then write a more complete comparison between muscular macho heroes and "emo super-dudes." You might want to focus specifically between a hero like Spiderman and a hero like Thor, both adaptations to the movies from comics.

2. Identify a point of comparison in movies or television—it could be how fathers are represented in two historical periods or different types of leading women—and then explore several examples and write a comparison on the topic to make your point.

RICHARD RODRIGUEZ

Private Language, Public Language

Richard Rodriguez (born 1944) is a native of San Francisco who is of Mexican ancestry. After learning English in the elementary grades, he went on to earn a baccalaureate degree in English at Stanford University (1967) and graduate degrees at Columbia University (1969) and the University of California at Berkeley (1975). Rejecting job offers from several major universities, he spent the next six years writing Hunger of Memory: The Education of Richard Rodriguez *(1982), a book that traces his educational odyssey.* Days of Obligation *was published in 1992, and* Brown: The Last Discovery of America *was published in 2003. His articles have appeared in a variety of scholarly magazines. In the following essay, Rodriguez explores his contrasting childhood perceptions concerning English and his native Spanish.*

1   I remember to start with that day in Sacramento—a California now nearly thirty years past—when I first entered a classroom, able to understand some fifty stray English words.

2   The third of four children, I had been preceded to a neighborhood Roman Catholic school by an older brother and sister. But neither of them had revealed very much about their classroom experiences. Each afternoon they returned, as they left in the morning, always together, speaking in Spanish as they climbed the five steps of the porch. And their mysterious books, wrapped in shopping-bag paper, remained on the table next to the door, closed firmly behind them.

3   An accident of geography sent me to a school where all my classmates were white, many the children of doctors and lawyers and business executives. All my classmates certainly must have been uneasy on that first day of school—as most children are uneasy—to find themselves apart from their families in the first institution of their lives. But I was astonished.

4   The nun said, in a friendly but oddly impersonal voice, "Boys and girls, this is Richard Rodriguez." (I heard her sound out: *Rich-heard Road-ree-guess*.) It was the first time I had heard anyone name me in English. "Richard," the nun repeated more slowly, writing my name down in her black leather book. Quickly I turned to see my mother's face dissolve in a watery blur behind the pebbled glass door.

5   Many years later there is something called bilingual education—a scheme proposed in the late 1960s by Hispanic-American social activists, later endorsed by a congressional vote. It is a program that seeks to permit non-English-speaking children, many from lower-class homes, to use their family language as the language of school. (Such is the goal its supporters announce.) I hear them and am forced to say no: It is not possible for a child—any child—ever to use his family's language in school. Not to understand this is to misunderstand the public uses of schooling and to trivialize the nature of intimate life—a family's "language."

6   Memory teaches me what I know of these matters; the boy reminds the adult. I was a bilingual child, a certain kind—socially disadvantaged—the son of working-class parents, both Mexican immigrants.

7   In the early years of my boyhood, my parents coped very well in America. My father had steady work. My mother managed at home. They were nobody's victims. Optimism and ambition led them to a house (our home) many blocks from the Mexican south side of town. We lived among *gringos* and only a block from the biggest, whitest houses. It never occurred to my parents that they couldn't live wherever they chose. Nor was the Sacramento of the fifties bent on teaching them a contrary lesson. My mother and father were more annoyed than intimidated by those two or three neighbors who tried initially to make us unwelcome. ("Keep your brats away from my sidewalk!") But despite all they achieved, perhaps because they had so much to achieve, any deep feeling of ease, the confidence of "belonging" in public was withheld from them both. They regarded the people at work, the faces in crowds, as very distant from us. They were the others, *los gringos*. That term was interchangeable in their speech with another, even more telling, *los americanos*.

8   I grew up in a house where the only regular guests were my relations. For one day, enormous families of relatives would visit and there would be so many people that the noise and the bodies would spill out to the backyard and front porch. Then, for weeks, no one came by. (It was usually a salesman who rang the doorbell.) Our house stood apart. A gaudy yellow in a row of white bungalows. We were the people with the noisy dog. The people who raised pigeons and chickens. We were the foreigners on the block. A few neighbors smiled and waved. We waved back. But no one in the family knew the names of the old couple who lived next door; until I was seven years old, I did not know the names of the kids who lived across the street.

9   In public, my father and mother spoke a hesitant, accented, not always grammatical English. And they would have to strain—their bodies tense—to catch the sense of what was rapidly said by *los gringos*. At home they spoke Spanish. The language of their Mexican past sounded in counterpoint to the English of public society. The words would come quickly, with ease. Conveyed through those sounds was the pleasing, soothing, consoling reminder of being at home.

10   During those years when I was first conscious of hearing, my mother and father addressed me only in Spanish; in Spanish I learned to reply. By contrast, English *(inglés)*, rarely heard in the house, was the language I came to associate with *gringos*. I learned my first words of English overhearing my parents speak to

strangers. At five years of age, I knew just enough English for my mother to trust me on errands to stores one block away. No more.

11   I was a listening child, careful to hear the very different sounds of Spanish and English. Wide-eyed with hearing, I'd listen to sounds more than words. First, there were English *(gringo)* sounds. So many words were still unknown that when the butcher or the lady at the drugstore said something to me, exotic polysyllabic sounds would bloom in the midst of their sentences. Often the speech of people in public seemed to me very loud, booming with confidence. The man behind the counter would literally ask, "What can I do for you?" But by being so firm and so clear, the sound of his voice said that he was a *gringo;* he belonged in public society.

12   I would also hear then the high nasal notes of middle-class American speech. The air stirred with sound. Sometimes, even now, when I have been traveling abroad for several weeks, I will hear what I heard as a boy. In hotel lobbies or airports, in Turkey or Brazil, some Americans will pass, and suddenly I will hear it again—the high sound of American voices. For a few seconds I will hear it with pleasure, for it is now the sound of *my* society—a reminder of home. But inevitably—already on the flight headed for home—the sound fades with repetition. I will be unable to hear it anymore.

13   When I was a boy, things were different. The accent of *los gringos* was never pleasing nor was it hard to hear. Crowds at Safeway or at bus stops would be noisy with sound. And I would be forced to edge away from the chirping chatter above me.

14   I was unable to hear my own sounds, but I knew very well that I spoke English poorly. My words would not stretch far enough to form complete thoughts. And the words I did speak I didn't know well enough to make into distinct sounds. (Listeners would usually lower their heads, better to hear what I was trying to say.) But it was one thing for *me* to speak English with difficulty. It was more troubling for me to hear my parents speak in public: their high-whining vowels and guttural consonants; their sentences that got stuck with "eh" and "ah" sounds; the confused syntax; the hesitant rhythm of sounds so different from the way *gringos* spoke. I'd notice, moreover, that my parents' voices were softer than those of *gringos* we'd meet.

15   I am tempted now to say that none of this mattered. In adulthood I am embarrassed by childhood fears. And, in a way, it didn't matter very much that my parents could not speak English with ease. Their linguistic difficulties had no serious consequences. My mother and father made themselves understood at the county hospital clinic and at government offices. And yet, in another way, it mattered very much—it was unsettling to hear my parents struggle with English. Hearing them, I'd grow nervous, my clutching trust in their protection and power weakened.

16   There were many times like the night at a brightly lit gasoline station (a blaring white memory) when I stood uneasily, hearing my father. He was talking to a teenaged attendant. I do not recall what they were saying, but I cannot forget the sounds my father made as he spoke. At one point his words slid together to form one word—sounds as confused as the threads of blue and green oil in the puddle next to my shoes. His voice rushed through what he had left to say. And, toward the end, reached falsetto notes, appealing to his listener's understanding. I looked away to the lights of passing automobiles. I tried not to hear anymore. But I heard only too well the calm, easy tones in the attendant's reply. Shortly afterward, walking toward home with my father, I shivered when he put his hand on my shoulder. The very first chance that I got, I evaded his grasp and ran on ahead into the dark, skipping with feigned boyish exuberance.

17   But then there was Spanish. *Español:* my family's language. *Español:* the language that seemed to me a private language. I'd hear strangers on the radio and in the Mexican Catholic church across town speaking in Spanish, but I couldn't really believe that Spanish was a public language, like English. Spanish speakers, rather, seemed related to me, for I sensed that we shared—through our language—the experience of feeling apart from *los gringos.* It was thus a ghetto Spanish that I heard and I spoke. Like those whose lives are bound by a barrio, I was reminded by Spanish of my separateness from *los otros, los gringos* in power. But more intensely than for most barrio children—because I did not live in a barrio—Spanish seemed to me the language of home. (Most days it was only at home that I'd hear it.) It became the language of joyful return.

18   A family member would say something to me and I would feel myself specially recognized. My parents would say something to me and I would feel embraced by the sounds of their words. Those sounds said: *I am speaking with ease in Spanish. I am addressing you in words I never use with* los gringos. *I recognize you as someone special, close, like no one outside. You belong with us. In the family.*

19   *(Ricardo.)*

20   At the age of five, six, well past the time when most other children no longer easily notice the difference between sounds uttered at home and words spoken in public, I had a different experience. I lived in a world magically compounded of sounds. I remained a child longer than most; I lingered too long, poised at the edge of language—often frightened by the sounds of *los gringos,* delighted by the sounds of Spanish at home. I shared with my family a language that was startlingly different from that used in the great city around us.

21   For me there were none of the gradations between public and private society so normal to a maturing child. Outside the house was public society; inside the house was private. Just opening or closing the screen door behind me was an important experience. I'd rarely leave home all alone or without reluctance. Walking down the sidewalk, under the canopy of tall trees, I'd warily notice the—suddenly—silent neighborhood kids who stood warily watching me. Nervously, I'd arrive at the grocery store to hear there the sounds of the *gringo*—foreign to me—reminding me that in this world so big, I was a foreigner. But then I'd return. Walking back toward our house, climbing the steps from the sidewalk, when the front door was open in summer, I'd hear voices beyond the screen door talking in Spanish. For a second or two, I'd stay, linger there, listening. Smiling, I'd hear my mother call out, saying in Spanish (words): "Is that you, Richard?" All the while her sounds would assure me: *You are home now; come closer; inside. With us.*

22   "*Sí,*'I'd reply.

23   Once more inside the house I would resume (assume) my place in the family. The sounds would dim, grow harder to hear. Once more at home, I would grow less aware of that fact. It required, however, no more than the blurt of the doorbell to alert me to listen to sounds all over again. The house would turn instantly still while my mother went to the door. I'd hear her hard English sounds. I'd wait to hear her voice return to soft-sounding Spanish, which assured me, as surely as did the clicking tongue of the lock on the door, that the stranger was gone.

24   Plainly, it is not healthy to hear such sounds so often. It is not healthy to distinguish public words from private words so easily. I remained cloistered by sounds, timid and shy in public, too dependent on voices at home. And yet it needs to be emphasized: I was an extremely happy child at home. I remember many nights when my father would come back from work, and I'd hear him call out to my mother in Spanish, sounding relieved. In Spanish, he'd sound light

and free notes he never could manage in English. Some nights I'd jump up just at hearing his voice. With *mis hermanos* I would come running into the room where he was with my mother. Our laughing (so deep was the pleasure!) became screaming. Like others who know the pain of public alienation, we transformed the knowledge of our public separateness and made it consoling—the reminder of intimacy. Excited, we joined our voices in a celebration of sounds. *We are speaking now the way we never speak out in public. We are alone—together,* voices sounded, surrounded to tell me. Some nights, no one seemed willing to loosen the hold sounds had on us. At dinner, we invented new words. (Ours sounded Spanish, but made sense only to us.) We pieced together new words by taking, say, an English verb and giving it Spanish endings. My mother's instructions at bedtime would be lacquered with mock-urgent tones. Or a word like *sí* would become, in several notes, able to convey added measures of feeling. Tongues explored the edges of words, especially the fat vowels. And we happily sounded that military drum roll, the twirling roar of the Spanish *r*. Family language: my family's sounds. The voices of my parents and sisters and brother. Their voices insisting: *You belong here. We are family members. Related. Special to one another. Listen!* Voices singing and sighing, rising, straining, then surging, teeming with pleasure that burst syllables into fragments of laughter. At times it seemed there was steady quiet only when, from another room, the rustling whispers of my parents faded and I moved closer to sleep.

Discussion Questions

1. What does Rodriguez accomplish in his first four paragraphs? What connection do you see between these paragraphs and later parts of the essay?
2. What is Rodriguez's main point? Where is it stated?
3. Discuss the significance of paragraphs 7–9.
4. Why did his parents' difficulties with English cause Rodriguez such concern?
5. In paragraph 16 Rodriguez tells us that he "looked away to the lights of passing automobiles" and that he "ran on ahead into the dark . . ." Explain these actions.
6. Rodriguez does not begin to develop his discussion of Spanish—the private language—until paragraph 17. Why do you think this discussion didn't occur earlier in the essay?
7. Explain why the concluding paragraph is effective.

Toward Key Insights

In what ways other than those noted by Rodriguez do children and their families create or inhabit private worlds that are separate from their public worlds? What are some of the benefits and problems that result from this dichotomy? How important is language to a person's identity and social world?

Suggestion for Writing

Write a comparison essay discussing some noteworthy difference between you, or some group you belong to, and the larger public. The difference may be one of race, ethnic background, religion, or lifestyle. Demonstrate clearly how the difference affects your relationship with that public.

HENRY JENKINS

Art Form for the Digital Age

Henry Jenkins is the John E. Burchard Professor of Humanities and Director of the Comparative Media Studies graduate program at MIT. His column "The Digital Renaissance," from which this selection was taken, is featured in the journal Technology Review *monthly.*

Video games shape our culture. It's time we took them seriously.

1   Last year, Americans bought over 215 million computer and video games. That's more than two games per household. The video game industry made almost as much money from gross domestic income as Hollywood.

2   So are video games a massive drain on our income, time and energy? A new form of "cultural pollution," as one U.S. senator described them? The "nightmare before Christmas," in the words of another? Are games teaching our children to kill, as countless op-ed pieces have warned?

No. Computer games are art—a popular art, an emerging art, a largely unrecognized art, but art nevertheless.

3   Over the past 25 years, games have progressed from the primitive two-paddles-and-a-ball Pong to the sophistication of Final Fantasy, a participatory story with cinema-quality graphics that unfolds over nearly 100 hours of play. The computer game has been a killer app for the home PC, increasing consumer demand for vivid graphics, rapid processing, greater memory and better sound. The release this fall of the Sony Playstation 2, coupled with the announcement of next-generation consoles by Nintendo and Microsoft, signals a dramatic increase in the resources available to game designers.

4   Games increasingly influence contemporary cinema, helping to define the frenetic pace and model the multi-directional plotting of Run Lola Run, providing the role-playing metaphor for Being John Malkovich and encouraging a fascination with the slippery line between reality and digital illusion in The Matrix. At high schools and colleges across the country, students discuss games with the same passions with which earlier generations debated the merits of the New American Cinema. Media studies programs report a growing number of their students want to be game designers rather than filmmakers.

5   The time has come to take games seriously as an important new popular art shaping the aesthetic sensibility of the 21st century. I will admit that discussing the art of video games conjures up comic images: tuxedo-clad and jewel-bedecked patrons admiring the latest Streetfighter, middle-aged academics pontificating on the impact of Cubism on Tetris, bleeps and zaps disrupting our silent contemplation at the Guggenheim. Such images tell us more about our contemporary notion of art—as arid and stuffy, as the property of an educated and economic elite, as cut off from everyday experience—than they tell us about games.

6   New York's Whitney Museum found itself at the center of controversy about digital art when it recently included Web artists in its prestigious biannual show. Critics didn't believe the computer could adequately express the human spirit. But they're misguided. The computer is simply a tool, one that offers artists new resources and opportunities for reaching the public; it is human creativity that makes art. Still, one can only imagine how the critics would have responded to

the idea that something as playful, unpretentious and widely popular as a computer game might be considered art.

7   In 1925, leading literary and arts critic Gilbert Seldes took a radical approach to the aesthetics of popular culture in a treatise title *The Seven Lively Arts*. Adopting what was then a controversial position, Seldes argued that America's primary contributions to artistic expression had come through emerging forms of popular culture such as jazz, the Broadway musical, the Hollywood cinema and the comic strip. While these arts have gained cultural respectability over the past 75 years, each was disreputable when Seldes staked out his position.

8   Readers then were skeptical of Seldes' claims about cinema in particular for many of the same reasons that contemporary critics dismiss games—they were suspicious of cinema's commercial motivations and technological origins, concerned about Hollywood's appeals to violence and eroticism, and insistent that cinema had not yet produced works of lasting value. Seldes, on the other hand, argued that cinema's popularity demanded that we reassess its aesthetic qualities.

9   Cinema and other popular arts were to be celebrated, Seldes said, because they were so deeply imbedded in everyday life, because they were democratic arts embraced by average citizens. Through streamlined styling and syncopated rhythms, they captured the vitality of contemporary urban experience. They took the very machinery of the industrial age, which many felt dehumanizing, and found within it the resources for expressing individual visions, for reasserting basic human needs, desires and fantasies. And these new forms were still open to experimentation and discovery. They were, in Seldes' words, "lively arts."

10   Games represent a new lively art, one as appropriate for the digital age as those earlier media were for the machine age. They open up new aesthetic experiences and transform the computer screen into a realm of experimentation and innovation that is broadly accessible. And games have been embraced by a public that has otherwise been unimpressed by much of what passes for digital art. Much as the salon arts of the 1920s seemed sterile alongside the vitality and inventiveness of popular culture, contemporary efforts to create interactive narrative through modernist hypertext or avant-garde installation art seem lifeless and pretentious alongside the creativity that game designers bring to their craft.

11   Much of what Seldes told us about the silent cinema seems remarkably apt for thinking about games. Silent cinema, he argued, was an art of expressive movement. He valued the speed and dynamism of D. W. Griffith's last-minute races to the rescue, the physical grace of Chaplin's pratfalls and the ingenuity of Buster Keaton's engineering feats. Games also depend upon an art of expressive movement, with characters defined through their distinctive ways of propelling themselves through space, and successful products structured around a succession of spectacular stunts and predicaments. Will future generations look back on Lara Croft doing battle with a pack of snarling wolves as the 21st-century equivalent of Lillian Gish making her way across the ice floes in *Way Down East*? The art of silent cinema was also an art of atmospheric design. To watch a silent masterpiece like Fritz Lang's *Metropolis* is to be drawn into a world where meaning is carried by the placement of shadows, the movement of machinery and the organization of space. If anything, game designers have pushed beyond cinema in terms of developing expressive and fantastic environments that convey a powerful sense of mood, provoke our curiosity and amusement, and motivate us to explore.

12   Seldes wrote at a moment when cinema was maturing as an expressive medium and filmmakers were striving to enhance the emotional experience of going to the movies—making a move from mere spectacle towards character and consequence. It remains to be seen whether games can make a similar transition. Contemporary games can pump us full of adrenaline, they can make us laugh, but they have not yet provoked us to tears. And many have argued that, since games don't have characters of human complexity or stories that stress the consequences of our actions, they cannot achieve the status of true art. Here, we must be careful not to confuse the current transitional state of an emerging medium with its full potential. As I visit game companies, I see some of the industry's best minds struggling with this question and see strong evidence that the games released over the next few years will bring us closer and closer to the quality of characterization we have come to expect from other forms of popular narrative.

13   In the March 6 issue *of Newsweek,* senior editor Jack Kroll argued that audiences will probably never be able to care as deeply about pixels on the computer screen as they care about characters in films: "Moviemakers don't have to simulate human beings; they are right there, to be recorded and orchestrated. . . . The top-heavy titillation of Tomb Raider's Lara Croft falls flat next to the face of Sharon Stone. . . . Any player who's moved to tumescence by digibimbo Lara is in big trouble." Yet countless viewers cry when Bambi's mother dies, and World War II veterans can tell you they felt real lust for *Esquire's* Vargas girls. We have learned to care as much about creatures of pigment as we care about images of real people. Why should pixels be different?

14   In the end, games may not take the same path as cinema. Game designers will almost certainly develop their own aesthetic principles as they confront the challenge of balancing our competing desires for storytelling and interactivity. It remains to be seen whether games can provide players the freedom they want and still provide an emotionally satisfying and thematically meaningful shape to the experience. Some of the best games—Tetris comes to mind—have nothing to do with storytelling. For all we know, the future art of games may look more like architecture or dance than cinema.

15   Such questions warrant close and passionate engagement not only within the game industry or academia, but also by the press and around the dinner table. Even Kroll's grumpy dismissal of games has sparked heated discussion and forced designers to refine their own grasp of the medium's distinctive features. Imagine what a more robust form of criticism could contribute. We need critics who know games the way Pauline Kael knew movies and who write about them with an equal degree of wit and wisdom.

16   When *The Seven Lively Arts* was published, silent cinema was still an experimental form, each work stretching the medium in new directions. Early film critics played vital functions in documenting innovations and speculating about their potential. Computer games are in a similar phase. We have not had time to codify what experienced game designers know, and we have certainly not yet established a canon of great works that might serve as exemplars. There have been real creative accomplishments in games, but we haven't really sorted out what they are and why they matter.

17   But games do matter, because they spark the imaginations of our children, taking them on epic quests to strange new worlds. Games matter because our children no longer have access to real-world play spaces at a time when we've paved over the vacant lots to make room for more condos and the streets make

parents nervous. If children are going to have opportunities for exploratory play, play that encourages cognitive development and fosters problem-solving skills, they will do so in the virtual environments of games. Multi-player games create opportunities for leadership, competition, teamwork and collaboration—for nerdy kids, not just for high school football players. Games matter because they form the digital equivalent of the Head Start program, getting kids excited about what computers can do.

18   The problem with most contemporary games isn't that they are violent but that they are banal, formulaic and predictable. Thoughtful criticism can marshal support for innovation and experimentation in the industry, much as good film criticism helps focus attention on neglected independent films. Thoughtful criticism could even contribute to our debates about game violence. So far, the censors and culture warriors have gotten more or less a free ride because we almost take for granted that games are culturally worthless. We should instead look at games as an emerging art form—one that does not simply simulate violence but increasingly offers new ways to understand violence—and talk about how to strike a balance between this form of expression and social responsibility. Moreover, game criticism may provide a means of holding the game industry more accountable for its choices. In the wake of the Columbine shootings, game designers are struggling with their ethical responsibilities as never before, searching for ways of appealing to empowerment fantasies that don't require exploding heads and gushing organs. A serious public discussion of this medium might constructively influence these debates, helping identify and evaluate alternatives as they emerge.

19   As the art of games matures, progress will be driven by the most creative and forward-thinking minds in the industry, those who know that games can be more than they have been, those who recognize the potential of reaching a broader public, of having a greater cultural impact, of generating more diverse and ethically responsible content and of creating richer and more emotionally engaging stories. But without the support of an informed public and the perspective of thoughtful critics, game developers may never realize that potential.

Discussion Questions

1. What seems to be the author's main purpose in comparing video games with cinema?
2. What points of comparison does the essay make between video games and cinema? Do those points of comparison seem valid?
3. What was the rhetorical advantage of referring to Gilbert Seldes' 1925 essay in paragraph 7 and 8?
4. How is paragraph 11 organized, and why is this paragraph important to the overall comparison?
5. What differences does the author point out between cinema and video games? Do these differences undercut or support his main purpose?
6. In paragraph 2, the author asks whether games teach our children to kill. Does his essay answer the question, and if it does not, does this weaken his comparison-based argument?
7. The author does not mention a lot of specific games. Why might he have made that rhetorical choice? Does it weaken his comparison?

Toward Key Insights

Often comparisons can be used to see something familiar in a new way. In this case, the author is attempting to get us to see the ways video games might be an art form. How might our idea of everyday things change if we look at advertisements as art, everyday objects as sculpture, or short messages as poetry? Are such startling comparisons appropriate or useful?

The author stresses a number of similarities between video games and cinema. That can shape our perceptions. A critical response to comparisons requires us to look for points of disagreements. In what ways may video games be significantly and forever different from cinema?

Suggestions for Writing

Write about how some other popular culture events or objects might be like art. For example, basketball could be like dance; comic books could be like visual art; extreme sports could be like ballet.

Video games such as Lara Croft have been made into movies, and movies such as the Matrix have been made into video games. Compare a specific video game with its movie counterpart.

CAUSE AND EFFECT

Reading Strategies

1. Identify the main event that is trying to be explained or the event whose effects are being studied.

2. Determine whether the writer is identifying a chain of causes that yield a result or is considering multiple causes for the same event.

3. Be careful. In more sophisticated academic writing, authors often look at several causes that they try to show are not the real explanation. Only after ruling out some key explanations do they offer the explanation that they think is most plausible.

4. It can be helpful to make a diagram showing the connection between the causes and the effects.

Reading Critically

1. Evaluate the evidence the writer gives for the relationship between cause and effect. How does he or she prove that the cause(s) have the effect(s) in question?

2. Try to determine if there could be other causes or effects that the writer hasn't mentioned.

3. Writers often confuse "correlation" for causation. Just because something happens before or around another event doesn't mean that it is the cause of the event. Just because George W. Bush was president when the terrorists attacked the World Trade Centers does not mean that his presidency was in any way a cause of the attack. Does the writer confuse correlation and causation?

Reading As a Writer

1. Note how the writer organizes the causes and effects to keep them clear and distinct.

2. Observe what devices the writer uses to demonstrate the connection between the causes and the effects.

3. Examine how the writer pulls his or her ideas together in the conclusion.

KEVIN JOHNSON

For Cops, Citizen Videos Bring Increased Scrutiny. Are Incidents Caught on Tape Hindering Officers?

Kevin Johnson is a reporter for USA Today *where he covers justice and national law enforcement issues. This selection came from the October 14, 2010, print edition of* USA Today.

1 TALLAHASSEE—Diop Kamau's home in a leafy, gated community just north of town is not easy to find—for good reason. For more than two decades, the 52-year-old former Hawthorne, Calif., police officer has made a living embarrassing cops with a video camera.

2 Stung by the rough treatment of his father during a 1987 traffic stop by another California department, Kamau turned to a second career recording police across the country in compromising—often abusive—encounters with the public.

> Narrative introduction to engage readers in topic

3 Some of the controversial videos made using hidden microphones and cameras found their way to network and cable television, exposing police to deserved criticism. Mostly, the videos helped launch a new generation of public accountability for local law enforcement. One of Kamau's most effective weapons is a battered 1968 Chevrolet Impala, wired with microphones and cameras, that Kamau, who is black, drives to test the racial profiling tendencies of local police on behalf of paying clients.

4 "Frankly, there are a lot of people with badges and guns who don't like me very much," Kamau says, motioning to the network of surveillance cameras that protect his home from unwanted visitors. "I step on a lot of toes."

5 Starting with the grainy images first broadcast by Kamau and other pioneer citizen watchdogs—notably the 1991 beating of Rodney King in Los Angeles, shot by a nearby resident—the public surveillance of cops has exploded to potentially include anyone with a cellphone.

6 The videos are so ubiquitous that analysts and police debate whether they are serving the public interest—or undermining public trust in law enforcement and even putting officers' lives in jeopardy. The videos are subjecting officers' actions in public places to new scrutiny and changing the way accusations against cops play out in court. In some communities, police are fighting back by enforcing laws that limit such recordings. Other departments are seeking new training for officers to prepare for the ever-present surveillance on the street.

> States thesis

7 Just about every day, it seems, there is fresh video of cops engaged in controversial actions: Police slamming an unarmed man to the street in Denver. A college student thrashed by officers with batons during a University Maryland basketball victory celebration. An Oakland transit officer fatally shooting an unarmed man on a train platform.

> Example of videos

"There is no city not at risk of a video showing an officer doing something wrong," says San Jose Police Chief Rob Davis, president of the Major Cities Chiefs Association, a coalition representing the 56 largest cities in the USA. "The question, when one of these videos do surface, is what we do about it."

> Raises questions

8 In Illinois, Maryland and Massachusetts, some police have responded by trying to limit such recordings when they believe those recordings interfere with police actions.

> Identifies effect 1

9   In Maryland, motorcyclist Anthony Graber was charged with felony violations of Maryland's wiretapping law for recording a March 5 encounter with a gun-brandishing state trooper during a traffic stop. The law requires both parties to consent to the recording of a private conversation. Graber faced a maximum 16-year prison sentence if convicted until Harford County Circuit Court Judge Emory Pitt threw out the case Sept. 27, saying, "Those of us who are public officials and are entrusted with the power of the state are ultimately accountable to the public."

Details effect 1 with example

10   Some departments have sought training for officers to prepare them for increased surveillance of police activity.

Effect 2

11   "All of our people should be conducting themselves like they are being recorded all the time," says Lt. Robin Larson, who oversees training for the 3,200-officer Broward County, Fla., Sheriff's Office, which once hired Kamau to help prepare new cadets by making them aware their actions could be taped and transmitted.

Effect 2 detailed example

12   Some police believe videotaping officers poses broad risks that reach beyond Internet embarrassments: It could cause officers to hesitate in life-threatening situations.

Effect 3

13   "The proliferation of cheap video equipment is presenting a whole new dynamic for law enforcement," says Jim Pasco, executive director of the Fraternal Order of Police, the nation's largest police union. "It has had a chilling effect on some officers who are now afraid to act for fear of retribution by video. This has become a serious safety issue. I'm afraid something terrible will happen."

Effect 3 detailed

14   Kamau and others argue terrible things already have occurred to victims of officer abuse, and video has brought some of the most brutal cases to the public's attention. Video also has helped narrow the "credibility gap" between police and their accusers, civil rights lawyer John Burris says.

Transition Effect 4

Effect 5

15   "It used to be that the police officer always got the benefit of the doubt," says Burris, who represented Rodney King in a civil lawsuit against the city of Los Angeles related to his videotaped beating by white Los Angeles police officers. Television broadcasts of the infamous tape, one of the first to show the power of citizen videos of police actions, prompted widespread public outrage.

Effect 4 Detailed example

16   "The camera, increasingly, is offering a shock to the consciousness," Burris says.

17   To ignore the effect of video on police credibility, Kamau says, is "like disregarding the influence of the Internet on political campaigns."

18   "Things are changing dramatically," he says, "and police are not prepared for it."

Video Helps Explain Officer's Actions

19   Video has helped to resolve many cases of police misconduct, but such images also can present a more complex account of officer behavior.

Transition Effect 5

20   Former Oakland transit cop Johannes Mehserle is in jail awaiting sentencing on Nov. 5 in connection with the fatal shooting of Oscar Grant largely because the incident was captured on video.

Effect 5 detailed example explaining effect in step-by-step chain

21   Yet video also is the reason, defense attorney Michael Rains says, that Mehserle was convicted July 8 of the lesser offense of involuntary manslaughter after he was charged with murdering the unarmed, 22-year-old train passenger.

22   The criminal allegations followed transit officers' response to reports of fighting aboard a Bay Area Rapid Transit (BART) train in the early morning hours of New Year's Day 2009.

23   Grant was among a group pulled off the train at a local stop, according to court documents. Mehserle and another officer had detained the group, the documents state, when Mehserle shot the unarmed Grant while the man's hands were cuffed behind his back in a scene captured by bystanders on cellphone and

video cameras. The images of the shooting involving a white officer and a black victim quickly hit the Internet, where they prompted violent protests in Oakland and instant comparisons to the Rodney King case.

24   "The King video went viral pretty quickly for back then," says Burris, who also represents the Grant family. "But this went as fast as anything could go. The outrage came much quicker."

25   State prosecutors charged Mehserle with murder, and the case—because of its notoriety and local unrest—was moved to Los Angeles.

26   Defense attorney Rains concedes the raw video initially had a "shocking effect" on jurors.

27   "I tried to prepare them for it," he says. "I guess you don't get oblivious to seeing something like that."

28   What did help Mehserle's case, Rains says, is that more than one video showed what happened that morning; six were introduced at trial. Taken together, Rains argued, the videos captured several angles and supported his client's claim that he meant to draw a stun gun but mistakenly pulled his .40-caliber handgun.

Detailed explanation of evidence for effect 5

29   Rains says his client's hand movements recorded on some of the videos were consistent with attempts to open the snap of the holster of his stun gun.

30   "His body was doing things as if to draw and fire the Taser, not the gun," Rains says.

31   More video, Rains says, shows Mehserle's "compelling" reaction after the shooting.

32   "The video shows him throwing his hands to his head in shock," Rains says. "It was a terrible thing to happen. It was a tragedy it did." But the attorney says he was "very, very happy to have this video."

Continued explanation of evidence for effect 5

33   Although Burris does not agree with the jury's apparent interpretation of the videos (jurors have not spoken publicly about their decision), he also is happy they exist.

34   "Without the videos, there would have been no prosecution," he says. "It meant everything."

A 'Profound Effect' on Officers' Actions

35   David Allred, a former Justice Department official who prosecuted police misconduct cases for more than 30 years, says the proliferation of video in police cases is likely to have "a profound effect" on the long-term behavior of officers.

Transition to next effect

36   "If you're prosecuting a case and you can find video to support it, it's just terrific," Allred says. "But often it's terrific for the police, as well, because it can just as easily exonerate officers."

Repeats earlier effects as part of transition

37   "The real impact, I think, is on what officers will do if they think they are being photographed."

Statement of new effect 6

38   One of the most-viewed incidents—more than 200,000 views on YouTube—is a March encounter between a University of Maryland student and Prince George's County, Md., police officers during a celebration of a Maryland basketball victory.

Causal sequence to effect 6 ; Initial event

39   A video shows senior Jack McKenna approaching officers, who began pummeling him with batons. A police report alleged that McKenna had provoked the encounter by striking mounted officers and their horses, contrary to what is shown in the video.

Reaction to event

40   Three officers have been suspended and the case remains under investigation by Prince George's County and the Justice Department.

Effect based on event

41   In August, the city of Denver's public safety manager resigned and two officers were reassigned after questions surfaced about police conduct in at least

New incident as an
example and its effect

two incidents captured on video. The incidents, which remain under investigation by Denver police, include an April 2009 encounter between police and two pedestrians, one of whom is shown being violently wrestled to the street.

Effect 6; broad effect of
being video taped

42   The encounter was recorded by a security camera mounted on a light pole and later landed the alleged victims on network morning news programs.

43   "At this point, officers need to be constantly reminded that the potential for them to be on video or to be photographed is extraordinarily high," Pasco says.

'It Embarrassed Us'

44   Larson, the Broward County Sheriff's Office training officer, says her agency knows firsthand the power of video and has learned from it.

New example

45   The lesson was delivered about three years ago by Kamau. While working for his private investigative firm policeabuse.com and a client, the former cop walked into one of the agency's reception areas with a hidden camera and found immediate problems with the way officers and employees dealt with the public. Kamau says police routinely provided incorrect information to people or couldn't answer basic questions about department policy, such as how to file a complaint against police.

Effect from above
example

46   "It embarrassed us," Larson says, adding the video found its way to local television.

How example resulted
in effect 6

47   Larson says the incident "sparked a lot of activity" within the agency, leading to changes in public reception area staffing, including retraining. Police officials also invited Kamau to help train new cadets.

48   "Even though he could be viewed as the enemy, we were open to learning from the experience," she says. "If we screwed up, give us your thoughts on how we can make it better."

49   Kamau, who helps clients resolve their grievances with police, says he counsels many of them to arm themselves with cameras to support their cases.

Broad statement of
overall effect

50   "Video is making victims more credible," Kamau says. "If Rodney King would have tried to tell his story without video, nobody would have believed it."

Discussion Questions

1. What are the major effects the writer suggests the videoing of police officers is having? Given the number of effects discussed, how does the writer organize the essay? Why is or isn't this organizational structure effective?
2. In the beginning of the essay, the writer focuses on the experience of one person who engages in videotaping police. Why does the writer start with this one individual? How does it effect the overall essay?
3. The writer uses different examples for the different effects and uses quotes. Why does the writer use this approach? How effective is the approach for the reader?
4. Because this essay is a newspaper article from *USA Today*, it uses a number of shorter paragraphs. Why is this style common in newspapers? How does it affect the reading of the essay?
5. Overall, do you think the writer believes the increased videoing of police is socially beneficial or not? Should the writer have been completely balanced between harmful and beneficial consequences or presented the effects that seem most common? What counts as fairness in writing in this context?

Toward Key Insights

Even simple technological changes can have profound effects. While often we may overlook those effects, careful observations can begin to identify the impact of a technology on our lives. What technologies do you think have been introduced in your lifetime that has had an effect? What do you think are the effects of that technology?

Often we oversimplify the world and look at new technologies or practices as either good or bad. This essay makes clear that even when a technology has mostly beneficial effects, it can have negative effects as well. Where do you see technologies or social practices that many tend to see as good or ill that actually have a complex range of positive and negative consequences?

Writing Suggestions

1. Identify a technology or social practice that has been introduced in your lifetime and identify the effects of that technology or practice on our lives.
2. Interview several teachers on the impact of new technologies and software, such as YouTube, on teaching, positive and negative. Write a paper to new teachers helping them understand the consequences of the technology. You might focus on a single technology or practice, such as Facebook, or you may broaden your focus to include something general like social media.

CAROLINE KNAPP

Why We Keep Stuff: If You Want to Understand People, Take a Look at What They Hang On To

Caroline Knapp, a humane and thoughtful writer, died at the age of 42 in 2002. She worked for the Phoenix newspapers as staff writer, editor, and contributing columnist. This essay is taken from The Merry Recluse: A Life in Essay—*a collection of some of the best of Knapp's writing.*

1   Stuff, stuff, I am surrounded by stuff. Stuff I don't need, stuff I don't use, but stuff I feel compelled to keep. Here in my office, as I write this, I am drowning in a sea of stuff.

2   There is the stuff of procrastination—piles of letters I should answer, manuscripts I should return, memos I should file away.

3   There is the stuff of daily business—interoffice communications in one heap here, this form and that form in that heap there, bills in yet another.

4   But mostly, there is the more generalized stuff, the stuff we all hold on to for inexplicable reasons—the stuff, in other words, of which stuff is made. Old catalogs of stuff I *might* want to order someday. Old magazines I *might* want to read, or reread. Unsolicited freelance articles I *might* want to publish. And even more useless stuff, stuff with no discernible purpose or future value.

5   On one corner of a shelf hangs a bunch of ribbons, saved over the years from various packages. On another, a pile of old letters from readers that I'll no doubt never open again and never answer. On my desk, a Rolodex crammed with numbers I'll never call (the National Association of Theater Operators? The Detroit office of the National Transportation Union? *Huh?*). In one corner, I even have a pile of envelopes containing transaction slips from the automatic teller machine that date all the way back to February 1988. That's more than three years of bank slips—stuff, pure and simple.

6   Yet in an odd way, a lot of the stuff has meaning. Granted, the significance of a pile of old ribbons may be minimal, but I think the things that people choose to hang on to, and the ways they hang on to them, are quite telling—small testimonies to the ways people organize their lives on both external and internal levels. Want to understand people a little more clearly? Look through their stuff.

. . .

7   Several years ago, as I was preparing to move out of an apartment I'd lived in for four years, I undertook my first major purge of stuff, which provided an excellent lesson in the nature of the beast. Historically, I've been a relentless pack rat, the sort of person who keeps vast numbers of relics and mementos in vast numbers of boxes around the house—ticket stubs to concerts and movies; store receipts for goods and clothing I'd long ago stopped thinking about returning; letters from people I'd long ago lost track of; even old shoes. But moving out of that particular apartment was a big step—I was leaving a place where I'd lived alone (with plenty of room for stuff) and into a new apartment—and presumably, a new life—with a man (who had much less room for stuff).

8   Accordingly, the purge was more than a logistical necessity; it also had a certain psychological value. Sure, it made sense to get rid of a lot of it: I didn't really need to hang on to that broken toaster-oven, or that tattered coat I'd stopped wearing years before. I didn't need to save the letter of acceptance from the graduate school I'd long ago decided not to attend. I didn't need the three boxes of back issues of *Gourmet* magazine. But divesting myself of all that stuff meant much more than whittling down my possessions to a manageable degree.

9   At one point, I remember going through a dresser in which I kept several pairs of jeans that I'd worn during a long and protracted struggle with anorexia. They were tiny jeans in tiny, skeletal sizes, jean with bad associations, jeans with no place in the life of someone who was trying to launch into a healthier way of living. But I'd held on to them for years and, in doing so, had held on to a set of possibilities: that I might one day need those tiny, cigarette-legged jeans again; that I might one day fit into them; and accordingly, that what I felt to be my "recovery" from anorexia might be tenuous at best, false at worst.

10   The message hidden away in that dresser drawer had to do with fear, and, needless to say, throwing out the clothes from that earlier time was an enormously healthy move: it was part of an effort to say good-bye to a person I used to be.

11   And so it is with most of our stuff: the things we keep stored away in our closets and shelves often mirror the things we hold on to inside: fears, memories, dreams, false perceptions. A good deal of that stuff in my office, for example, speaks to an abiding terror of screwing up, a fear that I might actually *need* one of those articles from one of those old magazines, or one of those old phone numbers from the Rolodex, or one of those memos or letters or whatever.

12   Lurking behind the automatic-teller-machine slips? My relentless fear of finance, and the accompanying conviction that as soon as I toss them all out, the bank will call and inform me that some huge deposit I could once verify has

disappeared. Even the pile of ribbons on the shelf reflects some vague anxiety, a (comparatively minor and obsessive) worry—that one of these days, I'll have a present to wrap and (gasp) there'll be no ribbon at hand to tie it up. My mother keeps a huge basket at home filled with nothing but rubber bands, and I'm sure she holds on to it for the same reasons: it speaks to an absolute certainty on her part that the moment she throws them away, she'll find herself in desperate need of an elastic.

13   We might need it. We might miss it. It might come back in style and we might want to wear it again. If getting rid of stuff is hard, it's because it feels like cutting off options. Or sides of ourselves. Or pieces of our history. And, the actual value of holding on to stuff notwithstanding, those things can be unsettling to give up. The movie and ticket stubs I'd kept stored away for years in my old apartment, for example, reflected good times, happy moments in relationships that I didn't want to forget; the ragged coat was a piece of clothing I'd felt pretty in, a feeling I didn't want to lose; the *Gourmet* magazines held out hopes for my (then sorely lacking) kitchen skills. Even the broken toaster-oven contained a memory—I'd bought it almost a decade earlier, with a man I'd been involved with, during a very happy year we'd lived together.

14   The trick, I suppose, is to learn to manage stuff, the same way you learn to manage fears and feelings. To throw a little logic into the heaps of stuff. To think a little rationally. Would the world really come crashing down if I tossed out some crucial phone number? Would my personal history really get tossed into the trash along with my mementos? Would I die, or even suffer a mite, without all those ribbons?

15   No, probably not. But I think I'll keep holding on to those bank slips . . . just in case.

BOSTON PHOENIX

JUNE 1991

Discussion Questions

1. What is the value of a personal reflective essay such as this one for writer and reader?
2. What is the real thesis of this essay and where is it located?
3. What role do the several paragraphs detailing the kinds of clutter the author has failed to discard play in the full essay? Why did she spend so much time describing her stuff?
4. What does the author see as the dominant cause for why people fail to discard things? How does the more general cause relate to many other more specific causes?
5. In what ways does this writer sustain a personal and even intimate tone with her readers? Is this effective?
6. How do the final two paragraphs fit the essay?

Toward Key Insights

This essay provides an excellent example of a personal reflective essay. As a result, the author's discussion of why we keep certain things is not scientific. What might be the advantages of this kind of essay over a psychological study of why people retain certain items? What are some weaknesses of this kind of writing?

In the personal reflective essay, writers share with their readers more personal elements of their thoughts and lives, such as Caroline Knapp's discussion of her past struggle with anorexia. How do such intimate revelations affect readers and their relationship with the text?

Suggestion for Writing

Write a personal reflective essay to explain what you think cause some personal behaviors or emotional states, such as procrastination or impulse shopping, for readers who may share those behaviors.

CHRIS MOONEY

The Science of Why We Don't Believe Science

How our brains fool us on climate, creationism, and the vaccine-autism link.

Chris Mooney was born in 1977, grew up in New Orleans, Louisiana, and got his B.A. from Yale. He is the senior correspondent for The American Prospect *and contributing editor for* Science Progress. *He is the author of four books, including* Unscientific America, *co-written with Sheri Kirshenbaum. He maintains a weblog with Kirshenbaum that is currently hosted at http://blogs.discoverymagazine.com/intersection. This selection is from a 2011 online version of* Mother Jones.

1   "A man with a conviction is a hard man to change. Tell him you disagree and he turns away. Show him facts or figures and he questions your sources. Appeal to logic and he fails to see your point." So wrote the celebrated Stanford University psychologist Leon Festinger, in a passage that might have been referring to climate change denial—the persistent rejection, on the part of so many Americans today, of what we know about global warming and its human causes. But it was too early for that—this was the 1950s—and Festinger was actually describing a famous case study in psychology.

2   Festinger and several of his colleagues had infiltrated the Seekers, a small Chicago-area cult whose members thought they were communicating with aliens—including one, "Sananda," who they believed was the astral incarnation of Jesus Christ. The group was led by Dorothy Martin, a Dianetics devotee who transcribed the interstellar messages through automatic writing. Through her, the aliens had given the precise date of an Earth-rending cataclysm: December 21, 1954. Some of Martin's followers quit their jobs and sold their property, expecting to be rescued by a flying saucer when the continent split asunder and a new sea swallowed much of the United States. The disciples even went so far as to remove brassieres and rip zippers out of their trousers—the metal, they believed, would pose a danger on the spacecraft.

3   Festinger and his team were with the cult when the prophecy failed. First, the "boys upstairs" (as the aliens were sometimes called) did not show up and rescue the Seekers. Then December 21 arrived without incident. It was the moment Festinger had been waiting for: How would people so emotionally invested in a belief system react, now that it had been soundly refuted?

4   At first, the group struggled for an explanation. But then rationalization set in. A new message arrived, announcing that they'd all been spared at the last minute. Festinger summarized the extraterrestrials' new pronouncement: "The little group, sitting all night long, had spread so much light that God had saved the world from destruction." Their willingness to believe in the prophecy had saved Earth from the prophecy! From that day forward, the Seekers, previously shy of the press and indifferent toward evangelizing, began to proselytize. "Their sense of urgency was enormous," wrote Festinger. The devastation of all they had believed had made them even more certain of their beliefs.

5   In the annals of denial, it doesn't get much more extreme than the Seekers. They lost their jobs, the press mocked them, and there were efforts to keep them away from impressionable young minds. But while Martin's space cult might lie at on the far end of the spectrum of human self-delusion, there's plenty to go around. And since Festinger's day, an array of new discoveries in psychology and neuroscience has further demonstrated how our preexisting beliefs, far more than any new facts, can skew our thoughts and even color what we consider our most dispassionate and logical conclusions. This tendency toward so-called "motivated reasoning" helps explain why we find groups so polarized over matters where the evidence is so unequivocal: climate change, vaccines, "death panels," the birthplace and religion of the president, and much else. It would seem that expecting people to be convinced by the facts flies in the face of, you know, the facts.

6   The theory of motivated reasoning builds on a key insight of modern neuroscience: Reasoning is actually suffused with emotion (or what researchers often call "affect"). Not only are the two inseparable, but our positive or negative feelings about people, things, and ideas arise much more rapidly than our conscious thoughts, in a matter of milliseconds—fast enough to detect with an EEG device, but long before we're aware of it. That shouldn't be surprising: Evolution required us to react very quickly to stimuli in our environment. It's a "basic human survival skill," explains political scientist Arthur Lupia of the University of Michigan. We push threatening information away; we pull friendly information close. We apply fight-or-flight reflexes not only to predators, but to data itself.

7   We're not driven only by emotions, of course—we also reason, deliberate. But reasoning comes later, works slower—and even then, it doesn't take place in an emotional vacuum. Rather, our quick-fire emotions can set us on a course of thinking that's highly biased, especially on topics we care a great deal about.

8   Consider a person who has heard about a scientific discovery that deeply challenges her belief in divine creation—a new hominid, say, that confirms our evolutionary origins. What happens next, explains political scientist Charles Taber of Stony Brook University, is a subconscious negative response to the new information—and that response, in turn, guides the type of memories and associations formed in the conscious mind. "They retrieve thoughts that are consistent with their previous beliefs," says Taber, "and that will lead them to build an argument and challenge what they're hearing."

9   In other words, when we think we're reasoning, we may instead be rationalizing. Or to use an analogy offered by University of Virginia psychologist Jonathan Haidt: We may think we're being scientists, but we're actually being lawyers. Our "reasoning" is a means to a predetermined end—winning our "case"—and is shot through with biases. They include "confirmation bias," in which we give greater heed to evidence and arguments that bolster our beliefs,

and "disconfirmation bias," in which we expend disproportionate energy trying to debunk or refute views and arguments that we find uncongenial.

10   That's a lot of jargon, but we all understand these mechanisms when it comes to interpersonal relationships. If I don't want to believe that my spouse is being unfaithful, or that my child is a bully, I can go to great lengths to explain away behavior that seems obvious to everybody else—everybody who isn't too emotionally invested to accept it, anyway. That's not to suggest that we aren't also motivated to perceive the world accurately—we are. Or that we never change our minds—we do. It's just that we have other important goals besides accuracy—including identity affirmation and protecting one's sense of self—and often those make us highly resistant to changing our beliefs when the facts say we should.

11   Modern science originated from an attempt to weed out such subjective lapses—what that great 17th century theorist of the scientific method, Francis Bacon, dubbed the "idols of the mind." Even if individual researchers are prone to falling in love with their own theories, the broader processes of peer review and institutionalized skepticism are designed to ensure that, eventually, the best ideas prevail.

12   Our individual responses to the conclusions that science reaches, however, are quite another matter. Ironically, in part because researchers employ so much nuance and strive to disclose all remaining sources of uncertainty, scientific evidence is highly susceptible to selective reading and misinterpretation. Giving ideologues or partisans scientific data that's relevant to their beliefs is like unleashing them in the motivated-reasoning equivalent of a candy store.

13   Sure enough, a large number of psychological studies have shown that people respond to scientific or technical evidence in ways that justify their preexisting beliefs. In a classic 1979 experiment, pro- and anti-death penalty advocates were exposed to descriptions of two fake scientific studies: one supporting and one undermining the notion that capital punishment deters violent crime and, in particular, murder. They were also shown detailed methodological critiques of the fake studies—and in a scientific sense, neither study was stronger than the other. Yet in each case, advocates more heavily criticized the study whose conclusions disagreed with their own, while describing the study that was more ideologically congenial as more "convincing."

14   Since then, similar results have been found for how people respond to "evidence" about affirmative action, gun control, the accuracy of gay stereotypes, and much else. Even when study subjects are explicitly instructed to be unbiased and even-handed about the evidence, they often fail.

15   And it's not just that people twist or selectively read scientific evidence to support their preexisting views. According to research by Yale Law School professor Dan Kahan and his colleagues, people's deep-seated views about morality, and about the way society should be ordered, strongly predict whom they consider to be a legitimate scientific expert in the first place—and thus where they consider "scientific consensus" to lie on contested issues.

16   In Kahan's research, individuals are classified, based on their cultural values, as either "individualists" or "communitarians," and as either "hierarchical" or "egalitarian" in outlook. (Somewhat oversimplifying, you can think of hierarchical individualists as akin to conservative Republicans, and egalitarian communitarians as liberal Democrats.) In one study, subjects in the different groups were asked to help a close friend determine the risks associated with climate change, sequestering nuclear waste, or concealed carry laws: "The friend tells you that he or she is planning to read a book about the issue but would like to get your opinion on whether the author seems like a knowledgeable and

trustworthy expert." A subject was then presented with the résumé of a fake expert "depicted as a member of the National Academy of Sciences who had earned a Ph.D. in a pertinent field from one elite university and who was now on the faculty of another." The subject was then shown a book excerpt by that "expert," in which the risk of the issue at hand was portrayed as high or low, well-founded or speculative. The results were stark: When the scientist's position stated that global warming is real and human-caused, for instance, only 23 percent of hierarchical individualists agreed the person was a "trustworthy and knowledgeable expert." Yet 88 percent of egalitarian communitarians accepted the same scientist's expertise. Similar divides were observed on whether nuclear waste can be safely stored underground and whether letting people carry guns deters crime. (The alliances did not always hold. In another study, hierarchs and communitarians were in favor of laws that would compel the mentally ill to accept treatment, whereas individualists and egalitarians were opposed.)

17   In other words, people rejected the validity of a scientific source because its conclusion contradicted their deeply held views—and thus the relative risks inherent in each scenario. A hierarchal individualist finds it difficult to believe that the things he prizes (commerce, industry, a man's freedom to possess a gun to defend his family) could lead to outcomes deleterious to society. Whereas egalitarian communitarians tend to think that the free market causes harm, that patriarchal families mess up kids, and that people can't handle their guns. The study subjects weren't "anti-science"—not in their own minds, anyway. It's just that "science" was whatever they wanted it to be. "We've come to a misadventure, a bad situation where diverse citizens, who rely on diverse systems of cultural certification, are in conflict," says Kahan.

18   And that undercuts the standard notion that the way to persuade people is via evidence and argument. In fact, head-on attempts to persuade can sometimes trigger a backfire effect, where people not only fail to change their minds when confronted with the facts—they may hold their wrong views more tenaciously than ever.

19   Take, for instance, the question of whether Saddam Hussein possessed hidden weapons of mass destruction just before the U.S. invasion of Iraq in 2003. When political scientists Brendan Nyhan and Jason Reifler showed subjects fake newspaper articles in which this was first suggested (in a 2004 quote from President Bush) and then refuted (with the findings of the Bush-commissioned Iraq Survey Group report, which found no evidence of active WMD programs in preinvasion Iraq), they found that conservatives were more likely than before to believe the claim. (The researchers also tested how liberals responded when shown that Bush did not actually "ban" embryonic stem-cell research. Liberals weren't particularly amenable to persuasion, either, but no backfire effect was observed.)

20   Another study gives some inkling of what may be going through people's minds when they resist persuasion. Northwestern University sociologist Monica Prasad and her colleagues wanted to test whether they could dislodge the notion that Saddam Hussein and Al Qaeda were secretly collaborating among those most likely to believe it—Republican partisans from highly GOP-friendly counties. So the researchers set up a study in which they discussed the topic with some of these Republicans in person. They would cite the findings of the 9/11 Commission, as well as a statement in which George W. Bush himself denied his administration had "said the 9/11 attacks were orchestrated between Saddam and Al Qaeda."

21   As it turned out, not even Bush's own words could change the minds of these Bush voters—just 1 of the 49 partisans who originally believed the Iraq-Al

Qaeda claim changed his or her mind. Far more common was resisting the correction in a variety of ways, either by coming up with counterarguments or by simply being unmovable:

Interviewer: [T]he September 11 Commission found no link between Saddam and 9/11, and this is what President Bush said. Do you have any comments on either of those?

Respondent: Well, I bet they say that the Commission didn't have any proof of it but I guess we still can have our opinions and feel that way even though they say that.

The same types of responses are already being documented on divisive topics facing the current administration. Take the "Ground Zero mosque." Using information from the political myth-busting site FactCheck.org, a team at Ohio State presented subjects with a detailed rebuttal to the claim that "Feisal Abdul Rauf, the Imam backing the proposed Islamic cultural center and mosque, is a terrorist-sympathizer." Yet among those who were aware of the rumor and believed it, fewer than a third changed their minds.

22   A key question—and one that's difficult to answer—is how "irrational" all this is. On the one hand, it doesn't make sense to discard an entire belief system, built up over a lifetime, because of some new snippet of information. "It is quite possible to say, 'I reached this pro-capital-punishment decision based on real information that I arrived at over my life,'" explains Stanford social psychologist Jon Krosnick. Indeed, there's a sense in which science denial could be considered keenly "rational." In certain conservative communities, explains Yale's Kahan, "People who say, 'I think there's something to climate change,' that's going to mark them out as a certain kind of person, and their life is going to go less well."

23   This may help explain a curious pattern Nyhan and his colleagues found when they tried to test the fallacy that President Obama is a Muslim. When a nonwhite researcher was administering their study, research subjects were amenable to changing their minds about the president's religion and updating incorrect views. But when only white researchers were present, GOP survey subjects in particular were more likely to believe the Obama Muslim myth than before. The subjects were using "social desirabililty" to tailor their beliefs (or stated beliefs, anyway) to whoever was listening.

24   Which leads us to the media. When people grow polarized over a body of evidence, or a resolvable matter of fact, the cause may be some form of biased reasoning, but they could also be receiving skewed information to begin with—or a complicated combination of both. In the Ground Zero mosque case, for instance, a follow-up study showed that survey respondents who watched Fox News were more likely to believe the Rauf rumor and three related ones—and they believed them more strongly than non-Fox watchers.

25   Okay, so people gravitate toward information that confirms what they believe, and they select sources that deliver it. Same as it ever was, right? Maybe, but the problem is arguably growing more acute, given the way we now consume information—through the Facebook links of friends, or tweets that lack nuance or context, or "narrowcast" and often highly ideological media that have relatively small, like-minded audiences. Those basic human survival skills of ours, says Michigan's Arthur Lupia, are "not well-adapted to our information age."

26   If you wanted to show how and why fact is ditched in favor of motivated reasoning, you could find no better test case than climate change. After all, it's an issue where you have highly technical information on one hand and very strong

beliefs on the other. And sure enough, one key predictor of whether you accept the science of global warming is whether you're a Republican or a Democrat. The two groups have been growing more divided in their views about the topic, even as the science becomes more unequivocal.

27   So perhaps it should come as no surprise that more education doesn't budge Republican views. On the contrary: In a 2008 Pew survey, for instance, only 19 percent of college-educated Republicans agreed that the planet is warming due to human actions, versus 31 percent of non-college educated Republicans. In other words, a higher education correlated with an increased likelihood of denying the science on the issue. Meanwhile, among Democrats and independents, more education correlated with greater acceptance of the science.

28   Other studies have shown a similar effect: Republicans who think they understand the global warming issue best are least concerned about it; and among Republicans and those with higher levels of distrust of science in general, learning more about the issue doesn't increase one's concern about it. What's going on here? Well, according to Charles Taber and Milton Lodge of Stony Brook, one insidious aspect of motivated reasoning is that political sophisticates are prone to be more biased than those who know less about the issues. "People who have a dislike of some policy—for example, abortion—if they're unsophisticated they can just reject it out of hand," says Lodge. "But if they're sophisticated, they can go one step further and start coming up with counterarguments." These individuals are just as emotionally driven and biased as the rest of us, but they're able to generate more and better reasons to explain why they're right—and so their minds become harder to change.

29   That may be why the selectively quoted emails of Climategate were so quickly and easily seized upon by partisans as evidence of scandal. Cherry-picking is precisely the sort of behavior you would expect motivated reasoners to engage in to bolster their views—and whatever you may think about Climategate, the emails were a rich trove of new information upon which to impose one's ideology.

30   Climategate had a substantial impact on public opinion, according to Anthony Leiserowitz, director of the Yale Project on Climate Change Communication. It contributed to an overall drop in public concern about climate change and a significant loss of trust in scientists. But—as we should expect by now—these declines were concentrated among particular groups of Americans: Republicans, conservatives, and those with "individualistic" values. Liberals and those with "egalitarian" values didn't lose much trust in climate science or scientists at all. "In some ways, Climategate was like a Rorschach test," Leiserowitz says, "with different groups interpreting ambiguous facts in very different ways."

31   So is there a case study of science denial that largely occupies the political left? Yes: the claim that childhood vaccines are causing an epidemic of autism. Its most famous proponents are an environmentalist (Robert F. Kennedy Jr.) and numerous Hollywood celebrities (most notably Jenny McCarthy and Jim Carrey). The *Huffington Post* gives a very large megaphone to denialists. And Seth Mnookin, author of the new book *The Panic Virus*, notes that if you want to find vaccine deniers, all you need to do is go hang out at Whole Foods.

32   Vaccine denial has all the hallmarks of a belief system that's not amenable to refutation. Over the past decade, the assertion that childhood vaccines are driving autism rates has been undermined by multiple epidemiological studies—as well as the simple fact that autism rates continue to rise, even though the alleged offending agent in vaccines (a mercury-based preservative called thimerosal) has long since been removed.

33   Yet the true believers persist—critiquing each new study that challenges their views, and even rallying to the defense of vaccine-autism researcher Andrew Wakefield, after his 1998 *Lancet* paper—which originated the current vaccine scare—was retracted and he subsequently lost his license to practice medicine. But then, why should we be surprised? Vaccine deniers created their own partisan media, such as the website Age of Autism, that instantly blast out critiques and counterarguments whenever any new development casts further doubt on anti-vaccine views.

34   It all raises the question: Do left and right differ in any meaningful way when it comes to biases in processing information, or are we all equally susceptible?

35   There are some clear differences. Science denial today is considerably more prominent on the political right—once you survey climate and related environmental issues, anti-evolutionism, attacks on reproductive health science by the Christian right, and stem-cell and biomedical matters. More tellingly, anti-vaccine positions are virtually nonexistent among Democratic officeholders today—whereas anti-climate-science views are becoming monolithic among Republican elected officials.

36   Some researchers have suggested that there are psychological differences between the left and the right that might impact responses to new information—that conservatives are more rigid and authoritarian, and liberals more tolerant of ambiguity. Psychologist John Jost of New York University has further argued that conservatives are "system justifiers": They engage in motivated reasoning to defend the status quo.

37   This is a contested area, however, because as soon as one tries to psychoanalyze inherent political differences, a battery of counterarguments emerges: What about dogmatic and militant communists? What about how the parties have differed through history? After all, the most canonical case of ideologically driven science denial is probably the rejection of genetics in the Soviet Union, where researchers disagreeing with the anti-Mendelian scientist (and Stalin stooge) Trofim Lysenko were executed, and genetics itself was denounced as a "bourgeois" science and officially banned.

38   The upshot: All we can currently bank on is the fact that we all have blinders in some situations. The question then becomes: What can be done to counteract human nature itself?

39   Given the power of our prior beliefs to skew how we respond to new information, one thing is becoming clear: If you want someone to accept new evidence, make sure to present it to them in a context that doesn't trigger a defensive, emotional reaction.

40   This theory is gaining traction in part because of Kahan's work at Yale. In one study, he and his colleagues packaged the basic science of climate change into fake newspaper articles bearing two very different headlines—"Scientific Panel Recommends Anti-Pollution Solution to Global Warming" and "Scientific Panel Recommends Nuclear Solution to Global Warming"—and then tested how citizens with different values responded. Sure enough, the latter framing made hierarchical individualists much more open to accepting the fact that humans are causing global warming. Kahan infers that the effect occurred because the science had been written into an alternative narrative that appealed to their pro-industry worldview.

41   You can follow the logic to its conclusion: Conservatives are more likely to embrace climate science if it comes to them via a business or religious leader, who can set the issue in the context of different values than those from which environmentalists or scientists often argue. Doing so is, effectively, to signal a détente in what Kahan has called a "culture war of fact." In other words, paradoxically, you don't lead with the facts in order to convince. You lead with the values—so as to give the facts a fighting chance.

Discussion Questions

1. Based on the text, identify what you observe to be the main reasons the article identifies for this common response to scientific claims. Are there others that you think the reader overlooks?
2. In addition to identifying the reasons people reject scientific conclusions, the writer provides the experiments that supports this conclusion. Why does the writer use this evidence and does it help or hinder him in making his point?
3. This is a fairly sophisticated issue that draws on experimental data but uses a more informal style. Identify some of the specific strategies the writer uses to create a more informal style. What affect does this style have on the availability and credibility of the essay?
4. At the end of the essay, the writer discusses political differences in processing such information. Why does the writer address this issue? Does he take sides or seem more neutral? Does this help or hinder the effectiveness of the writing?

Toward Key Insights

What does this suggest to you as a writer about the difficulties of getting your position across and what strategies might be necessary to do so?
In what ways do you see these processes shaping your own response to new information or new ideas.

Suggestions for Writing

1. This essay discusses the causes for not believing science. Write a paper exploring the effects that some of these causes may have on our daily lives or on our political discussions.
2. What are some reasons science might not communicate effectively to lay persons. Examine some of the causes that may make people less likely to follow or believe science based on how science is studied and reported.

BELINDA LUSCOMBE AND KATE STINCHFIELD

Why We Flirt

Often writers work together to create an article, especially in journalism but also in academic settings. Belinda Luscombe has been a Senior Editor for Time *magazine since April 1999. She started in journalism at* The Daily Telegraph *in Sidney, Australia. She joined* Time *in 1995. Her work also appears in* Sports Illustrated, Fortune, Mademoiselle, Vogue, The New York Times *and many other publications.*

Kate Stinchfield is a productive freelance writer who often writes for Time. *Other articles by her include "Early Bird or Night Owl? Brain Scans Show the Difference." and "The Science of Risk Taking."*

This article was published in Time *in January 2008.*

1   That smile! That glance! That rapt attention! We flirt even when we don't need to. And that can be good.

2   Contrary to widespread belief, only two very specific types of people flirt: those who are single and those who are married. Single people flirt because, well, they're single and therefore nobody is really contractually obliged to talk to them, sleep with them or scratch that difficult-to-reach part of the back. But married people, they're a tougher puzzle. They've found themselves a suitable—maybe even superior—mate, had a bit of productive fun with the old gametes and ensured that at least some of their genes are carried into the next generation. They've done their duty, evolutionarily speaking. Their genome will survive. Yay them. So for Pete's sake, why do they persist with the game?

3   And before you claim, whether single or married, that you never flirt, bear in mind that it's not just talk we're dealing with here. It's gestures, stance, eye movement. Notice how you lean forward to the person you're talking to and tip up your heels? Notice the quick little eyebrow raise you make, the sidelong glance coupled with the weak smile you give, the slightly sustained gaze you offer? If you're a woman, do you feel your head tilting to the side a bit, exposing either your soft, sensuous neck or, looking at it another way, your jugular? If you're a guy, are you keeping your body in an open, come-on-attack-me position, arms positioned to draw the eye to your impressive lower abdomen?

4   Scientists call all these little acts "contact-readiness" cues, because they indicate, nonverbally, that you're prepared for physical engagement. (More general body language is known as "nonverbal leakage." Deep in their souls, all scientists are poets.) These cues are a crucial part of what's known in human-ethology circles as the "heterosexual relationship initiation process" and elsewhere, often on the selfsame college campuses, as "coming on to someone." In primal terms, they're physical signals that you don't intend to dominate, nor do you intend to flee—both useful messages potential mates need to send before they can proceed to that awkward talking phase. They're the opening line, so to speak, for the opening line.

5   One of the reasons we flirt in this way is that we can't help it. We're programmed to do it, whether by biology or culture. The biology part has been investigated by any number of researchers. Ethologist Irenaus Eibl Eibesfeldt, then of the Max Planck Institute in Germany, filmed African tribes in the 1960s and found that the women there did the exact same prolonged stare followed by a head tilt away with a little smile that he saw in America. (The technical name for the head movement is a "cant." Except in this case it's more like "can.")

6   Evolutionary biologists would suggest that those individuals who executed flirting maneuvers most adeptly were more successful in swiftly finding a mate and reproducing and that the behavior therefore became widespread in all humans. "A lot of people feel flirting is part of the universal language of how we communicate, especially nonverbally," says Jeffry Simpson, director of the social psychology program at the University of Minnesota.

7   Simpson is currently studying the roles that attraction and flirting play during different times of a woman's ovulation cycle. His research suggests that women who are ovulating are more attracted to flirty men. "The guys they find appealing tend to have characteristics that are attractive in the short term, which include some flirtatious behaviors," he says. He's not sure why women behave this way, but it follows that men who bed ovulating women have a greater chance of procreating and passing on those flirty genes, which means those babies will have more babies, and so on. Of course, none of this is a conscious choice, just as flirting is not always intentional. "With a lot of it, especially the nonverbal stuff, people may not be fully aware that they're doing it," says Simpson. "You

don't see what you look like. People may emit flirtatious cues and not be fully aware of how powerful they are."

Flirting with Intent

8 Well, some people anyway. But then there are the rest of you. You know who you are. You're the gentleman who delivered my groceries the other day and said we had a problem because I had to be 21 to receive alcohol. You're me when I told that same man that I liked a guy who knew his way around a dolly. (Lame, I know. I was caught off guard.) You're the fifty something guy behind me on the plane before Christmas telling his forty something seatmate how sensual her eyes were—actually, I hope you're not, because if so, you're really skeevy. My point is, once you move into the verbal phase of flirtation, it's pretty much all intentional.

9 And there are some schools of thought that teach there's nothing wrong with that. Flirtation is a game we play, a dance for which everyone knows the moves. "People can flirt outrageously without intending anything," says independent sex researcher Timothy Perper, who has been researching flirting for 30 years. "Flirting captures the interest of the other person and says 'Would you like to play?'" And one of the most exhilarating things about the game is that the normal rules of social interaction are rubberized. Clarity is not the point. "Flirting opens a window of potential. Not yes, not no," says Perper. "So we engage ourselves in this complex game of maybe." The game is not new. The first published guide for how to flirt was written about 2,000 years ago, Perper points out, by a bloke named Ovid. As dating books go, *The Art of Love* leaves more recent publications like *The Layguide: How to Seduce Women More Beautiful Than You Ever Dreamed Possible No Matter What You Look Like or How Much You Make* in its dust. And yes, that's a real book.

10 Once we've learned the game of maybe, it becomes second nature to us. Long after we need to play it, we're still in there swinging (so to speak) because we're better at it than at other games. Flirting sometimes becomes a social fallback position. "We all learn rules for how to behave in certain situations, and this makes it easier for people to know how to act, even when nervous," says Antonia Abbey, a psychology professor at Wayne State University. Just as we learn a kind of script for how to behave in a restaurant or at a business meeting, she suggests, we learn a script for talking to the opposite sex. "We often enact these scripts without even thinking," she says. "For some women and men, the script may be so well learned that flirting is a comfortable strategy for interacting with others." In other words, when in doubt, we flirt.

11 The thing that propels many already committed people to ply the art of woo, however, is often not doubt. It's curiosity. Flirting "is a way of testing one's mate-value and the possibility of alternatives—actually trying to see if someone might be available as an alternative," says Arthur Aron, professor of psychology at the State University of New York at Stony Brook. To evolutionary biologists, the advantages of this are clear: mates die, offspring die. Flirting is a little like taking out mating insurance.

12 If worst comes to worst and you don't still have it (and yes, I'm sure you do), the very act of flirting with someone else may bring about renewed attention from your mate, which has advantages all its own. So it's a win-win.

13 Flirting is also emotional capital to be expended in return for something else. Not usually for money, but for the intangibles—a better table, a juicier cut of meat, the ability to return an unwanted purchase without too many questions. It's

a handy social lubricant, reducing the friction of everyday transactions, and closer to a strategically timed tip than a romantic overture. Have you ever met a male hairdresser who wasn't a flirt? Women go to him to look better. So the better they feel when they walk out of his salon, the happier they'll be to go back for a frequent blowout. Flirting's almost mandatory. And if the hairdresser is gay, so much the better, since the attention is much less likely to be taken as an untoward advance.

It's Dangerous Out There

14 But outside the hairdresser's chair, things are not so simple. Flirt the wrong way with the wrong person, and you run the risk of everything from a slap to a sexual-harassment lawsuit. And of course, the American virtue of plainspokenness is not an asset in an activity that is ambiguous by design. Wayne State's Abbey, whose research has focused on the dark side of flirting—when it transmogrifies into harassment, stalking or acquaintance rape—warns that flirting can be treacherous. "Most of the time flirtation desists when one partner doesn't respond positively," she says. "But some people just don't get the message that is being sent, and some ignore it because it isn't what they want to hear."

15 One of the most fascinating flirting laboratories is the digital world. Here's a venue that is all words and no body language; whether online or in text messages, nuance is almost impossible. And since text and e-mail flirting can be done without having to look people in the eye, and is often done with speed, it is bolder, racier and unimpeded by moments of reflection on whether the message could be misconstrued or is wise to send at all. "Flirt texting is a topic everyone finds fascinating, although not much research is out there yet," says Abbey. But one thing is clear: "People are often more willing to disclose intimate details via the Internet, so the process may escalate more quickly."

16 That's certainly the case on sites like Yahoo!'s Married and Flirting e-mail group, as well as on Marriedbutplaying.com and Married-but-flirting.com. "Flirting" in this sense appears to be a euphemism for talking dirty. A University of Florida study of 86 participants in a chat room published in *Psychology Today* in 2003 found that while nearly all those surveyed felt they were initially simply flirting with a computer, not a real person, almost a third of them eventually had a face-to-face meeting with someone they chatted with. And all but two of the couples who met went on to have an affair. Whether the people who eventually cheated went to the site with the intention of doing so or got drawn in by the fantasy of it all is unclear. Whichever, the sites sure seem like a profitable place for people like the guy behind me on the pre-Christmas flight to hang out.

17 Most people who flirt—off-line at least—are not looking for an affair. But one of the things that sets married flirting apart from single flirting is that it has a much greater degree of danger and fantasy to it. The stakes are higher and the risk is greater, even if the likelihood of anything happening is slim. But the cocktail is in some cases much headier. It is most commonly the case with affairs, therapists say, that people who cheat are not so much dissatisfied with their spouse as with themselves and the way their lives have turned out. There is little that feels more affirming and revitalizing than having someone fall in love with you. (It follows, then, that there's little that feels less affirming than being cheated on.) Flirting is a decaf affair, a way of feeling more alive, more vital, more desirable without actually endangering the happiness of anyone you love—or the balance of your bank account. So go ahead and flirt, if you can do it responsibly. You might even try it with your spouse.

A Field Guide to Flirting

Humans observed in a natural mating habitat—here, the Cock and Bull Pub in Los Angeles and Helm's Bakery in neighboring Culver City—exhibit nearly all the major flirting behaviors, whether or not they're flirting at all.

1. **Open Body Position** This come-and-get-me stance suggests the man is neither about to flee nor fight.
2. **Raised Eyebrows** Upon first seeing a potential mate, both men and women often briefly raise their eyebrows.
3. **Head Cant** Women frequently tilt their head to one side, exposing their neck, and sometimes flick their hair at the same time.
4. **Sustained Eye Contact** Men and women both hold the gaze of someone they're interested in for longer than feels quite comfortable.
5. **Leaning Forward** Both genders tend to lean in toward people they're attracted to. Sometimes they'll unconsciously point to them too, even if they're across the room.
6. **Leading Questions** A man will often ask a woman questions that allow her to show off her most attractive features.
7. **Sideways Glances** Often followed by a glance away or down and a shy smile, these coy looks are a classic flirting behavior for both sexes.

Discussion Questions

1. What are the different causes the writers identify for flirting behavior? Are those causes multiple different causes, a chain of causes, or a combination?
2. This essay was written initially for *Time*, a popular news magazine. How did that affect the style of the essay, what are some examples of this style, and how does that impact on the essay?
3. The article relies heavily on the use of experts. Based on some examples from the text, why have the writers adopted this approach? What effect does it have on the credibility of the essay?
4. Why do the writers take the time in paragraph 3 to describe physical nonverbal forms of flirting?
5. In the conclusion, the writers take a stance on flirting as a behavior. Does this conclusion follow appropriately from the rest of the essay?

Toward Key Insights

This essay assumes that there are key biological and social explanations for simple human behaviors. Does this model seem to suggest that all human behaviors can be explained? Is that good or bad?

What kinds of effects might reading such an explanation of a behavior have on readers?

Suggestion for Writing

Take a common behavior such as "small talk" or "fantasy role-playing" and either with or without research write a behavior and offer an explanation for the behavior.

DEFINITION ▪ ▪ ▪ ▪ ▪ ▪ ▪ ▪ ▪ ▪

Reading Strategies

1. Clearly identify the term being defined.

2. Mark as you read the characteristics that are part of the defining characteristic of the concept. It can help to make a list of these defining characteristics.

3. Note specifically what the term being defined is *not* supposed to mean.

4. Observe any analogies, similes, or metaphors, noting specifically what the concept is suppose to be like.

5. Try to see if you can apply the concept.

Reading Critically

1. Check to see if the definition matches your intuition.

2. Determine if the definition is too narrow. If a person defines literature as works of fiction, the definition could leave out poetry.

3. Determine by applying the definition if it is too broad. If a person defines literature as works of writing, the definition would include phone books—a clearly unintended consequence of the definition.

4. Test if there are other available or possible definitions.

Reading As a Writer

1. Notice how the writer uses the introduction to explain the importance of the concept and the definition.

2. Identify the key strategies the writer uses to construct a definition—stating the defining characteristics, providing examples, indicating that to which the term does not apply.

3. Observe how the writer limits the definition so that it is not overapplied.

4. If the writer employs analogy, simile, or metaphor, determine how the device works in the context of the definition.

JAMES BUCKY CARTER

Going Graphic

James Bucky Carter is an Assistant Professor of English Education at the University of Texas in El Paso. He is the author of a number of articles on the graphic novel and is editor of Building Literary Connections with Graphic Novels: Page by Page, Panel by Panel. *He received his M.A. in English from the University of Tennessee and his Ph.D. in English Education from the University of Virginia. This article was published in* Educational Leadership, *March, 2009.*

Author establishes credibility

Identifies the purpose of the writing

1   As a *graphic novel* specialist and teacher educator, I travel across the United States sharing information on how teachers can use this media in their classrooms to expand student literacy skills. The questions, comments, and occasional resistance I've encountered have led me to conclude that some misinformation concerning the pedagogical potential of *graphic novels* is circulating among teachers. Some believe that *graphic novels* are too risky to bring into the curriculum, others resist any form of new literacy altogether, and many think that sequential

art narratives are only useful for remedial or reluctant readers. To clear up these misconceptions, I'd like to share a few facts about the form and a few practical suggestions for teachers considering integrating *graphic novels* into their classes.

As Old as Cave Paintings

2   Sequential art narratives—broadly defined as images placed in sequence to tell a story—have been steadily gaining attention over the last couple of decades as teachers, literacy experts, and librarians have sought new means to engage reluctant readers and inspire more motivated ones. Practitioners and researchers have found these texts, usually published as *graphic novels* or comic books, to be of great use in increasing library circulation, creating new readers, helping English language learners, motivating male readers, and even assisting gifted and talented students. In many ways, it seems that the *graphic novel* as accepted pedagogical text has "arrived."

3   Actually, comics are not a new phenomenon, nor are the attempts to connect them to education. Some would argue that sequential art narratives date back to the earliest cave paintings. Comic books, which grew out of the newspaper comic strips that gained popularity in the 1880s and 1890s, have existed in the United States since the 1920s. Superhero comics debuted in 1938 with Action Comics #1, the first appearance of Superman. Not even the recently popular Japanese import comics, Manga, are 21st century inventions.

4   There is a long history of the form being used for teaching, including hieroglyphics, tapestries, and stained glass windows (McCloud, 1999). M. Thomas Inge's Comics as Culture (1990), Bradford Wright's Comic Book Nation (2001), and Steven Krashen's The Power of Reading (2004) all cite studies from education and sociological journals that date back at least to the late 1930s. The term *graphic novel* has been in use in the United States since around 1964 and gained widespread recognition in 1978 when Will Eisner prominently placed the term on the cover of the paperback edition of A Contract with God and Other Tenement Stories. Although teachers have paid more attention to sequential art narration of late, comics and *graphic novels* are better considered as "new to you" rather than literally new.

An Art Form, Not a Genre

5   Another misconception is that *graphic novels* and comics are a genre of literature (Carter, 2008). Westerns, romances, science fiction, and fantasy are genres. All-American Western, All True Romance, Star Trek, and Sandman are comics that feature each of these genres, respectively. This distinction is important because teachers may be more willing to use sequential art narratives to supplement existing curriculums by looking for genre connections rather than teaching comics in isolation. In fact, I believe that integrating comics into existing thematic units can be more effective than studying the form in isolation.

6   Studying how a *graphic* novelist frames a story benefits students' developing sense of craft and composition. Comparing how Art Spiegelman uses words and art to tell about his family's experiences during the Holocaust in Maus to the conventions that Elie Wiesel or Lois Lowry or Anne Frank (or all of them) use when writing about the same topic is even better. Teachers should weigh their decision to teach comics through study units focusing solely on the form with the possibly more expansive and connection-building method of using this material to supplement existing curriculums.

Provides an overview of what the essay will do

Provides a new broad category for the discussion, offers a short definition, and indicates the value of the form

Identifies reason for readers' interest

Establishes history of comics

Establishes the teaching use as part of a history of defining the term

Provides the history of the words being defined

Defines by showing the difference from common misconception

Compares graphic novel and literature

Not Just for Reluctant Readers

7   Much recent attention to *graphic novels* results from the admirable efforts of librarians who noticed drastic increases in circulation once *graphic novels* were added to their libraries. Articles from their professional literature often proclaim that young people who never saw themselves as readers suddenly devoured books once they were exposed to *graphic novels*. On the basis of these claims, educators began using *graphic novels* to engage low-level or reluctant readers.

There is evidence that certain populations (boys, for example) prefer visual texts over those without visual elements (Smith & Wilhelm, 2002) and that allowing students to read comics may engage students who are otherwise less interested or less proficient in English (Cary, 2004). Research has also shown that comic book readers have a tendency to read more varied texts and that comic book reading often acts as a gateway to both more reading and more varied reading (Krashen, 2004).

8   Comics do have potential to motivate reluctant readers, but the study of sequential art can also benefit students who are already motivated readers. For example, Mitchell and George (1996) used superhero comics to examine morality and ethical issues with gifted students, and I have observed teachers using *graphic novels* as literature with honors-level seniors. I have used sequential art texts with students of various reading levels with an age range that extends from 6th grade to graduate school.

Identifies with examples of how comics are not for reluctant readers, answering common misconception

Not Necessarily "Kid Stuff"

9   Another assumption that may prevent teachers from sharing worthwhile comics with older and more motivated students or that may lead teachers to make unwise decisions about appropriateness in the classroom is that comics are written for a young audience. The notion that comic books are for children is long-standing, and surely young people have always been drawn to them.

10   But, countering these assumptions, exemplary *graphic novels* of the past 30 years have dealt with such mature topics as date rape, teen pregnancy, the Iraq war, Hurricane Katrina, genocide, and gang violence, as well as all of the major issues that adolescents face; coming of age, identity formation, friendship, and change. Even superhero comics have explored such weighty issues as drug addiction, mental illness, HIV infection, and land mine safety.

Defines by topics of graphic novels, examples

11   Teachers can make mistakes easily when they assume that all comic book-style productions are for children. At a recent talk in Normal, Illinois, a teacher told me that a local 4th grade teacher was having her students read Persepolis, a wonderful coming-of-age story about a young woman dealing with the Iranian revolution of the 1970s and 1980s. Although there are parts of the *novel* where the narrator is at the equivalent age of a U.S. 4th grader, there are also explicit visual depictions of violence. I'm a proponent of the form and an advocate of this particular text, but even I think this *graphic novel* may be too much, too fast for elementary students. Teachers who assume that cartoony images or simplified drawings like those in Persepolis signify age- or grade-level appropriateness tread on dangerous ground.

12   I strongly urge teachers to use appropriate procedures for integrating *graphic* texts into the classroom, just as they would for more traditional texts. Writing rationales for texts that someone is likely to challenge is a smart way for teachers to help protect their students, themselves, their parents, and their school leaders, and this is especially true for *graphic novels*. After all, they are *graphic* in that they have a pictorial element. Consider what Steven Cary (2004) calls the naked buns effect, a term he uses to describe the likely difference in

reaction to the words "naked buns" in a letter-based text versus the reaction to an image of naked buns.

Contrasts image and text as part of the definition

13   To effectively and responsibly use *graphic novels* in their classes, teachers must not simply trust the often excellent reviews in the ALAN Review or Voices of Youth Advocate. They must read every page and every panel of a *graphic novel* or comic, weigh it against their understanding of community standards, then decide whether to bring the material into the classroom.

14   Consider the recent case of Connecticut English teacher Nate Fisher, who asked a 14-year-old female student to read a copy of comics pioneer Daniel Clowes's Eightball, which includes a sequence featuring a blue rabbit walking the streets of his town asking for sexual favors. Fisher may have forgotten about this section, or he may have misread his community's standards, but the resultant complaints from the girl's parents ended up with him being fired. Things might have been different if Fisher had paper-clipped to the text a rationale or note seeking a parent signature.

15   I do not share this story to discourage teachers from using *graphic novels* in their classes. I simply urge teachers to act responsibly. Writing rationales that support the book, that discuss any controversial material and how it is handled in the text and will be addressed in class, and that offer parents and students a chance to preview and discuss the reading choice before signing off on it can provide a measure of comfort and protection to all.

16   This gets to another issue of use: Teachers needn't use a *graphic novel* in full to feel the medium's power. For example, another of Clowes's excellent *graphic novels*, Ghost World, details the life of two recent high school graduates and best friends who are now pondering their futures. Although there are sexually explicit scenes that may disqualify the text from whole-class reading, there are also several sequences of panels in which the two friends discuss growing apart that are appropriate for sharing with almost every student. Although a teacher may not care to share the entirety of Gareth Hinds's excellent *graphic novel* of Beowulf, sharing a few pages of the artist's visualization of Grendel or the dragon can help bring the characters and the story alive. Even one powerful panel can help establish or reinforce a major theme and be a jumping-off point for discussion and further literacy-related activities.

Defines with illustrating examples

Creating Comics

17   Another concept that often goes unconsidered is that comics and *graphic novels* needn't only be integrated into the curriculum as additional reading material. Accepting them as books is a nice start, but writing and drawing *graphic novels* is an authentic composing activity. By acknowledging that there is a process behind the production of comics and asking students to consider the process and even engage in it, teachers help students build crafting, composing, viewing, and visualizing skills.

Adds a new feature of graphic novels, that they are composed

18   I have noted teachers using Comic Life software to create their own photo-comic stories. Michael Bitz (2004), founder of the Comic Book Project, teamed with Dark Horse Comics to get paper-based comic page templates into the hands of students across the eastern United States. Bitz found that when students learn the composing techniques associated with the comics form, they tell compelling stories that often connect to students' lived experiences and actual social worlds, rather than to capes and tights.

19   Recently, teacher Diana Weidenbacker and students from Winnacunnet High School in New Hampshire presented me with an anthology of sequential art short stories entitled Scars. Each story revolves around the theme of impression: "Scars, we all have them. Some are small cuts that we got falling off our

bikes, others. . . . Others are deeper and recede from the surface only to reappear at moments when we least expect them." Weidenbacker and her 15 students used simple templates from Comic Book Creator and Microsoft Word, as well as pencils, markers, crayons, and basic photocopying and binding techniques to produce an authentic and heartfelt exploration of the hard times in their lives.

20   I have used a lesson approved by the National Council of Teachers of English and the International Reading Association titled the Comic Book Show and Tell (Carter, 2006, 2007) to teach students the conventions of comic book scripting. Students create a script based on a generic prompt and pass their scripts to partners across the room who must draw panels guided by nothing more than the authors' written words. When students receive their scripts back with the artists' interpretation, the students have a visual record of how detailed and descriptive their script was, and I help them to revise their products accordingly. I have used this activity with 6th graders, high schoolers, and even preservice teachers. Educators have also asked students to produce "how-to" comics and *graphic novel* biographies of famous people, works that can be collected and shared with other students.

A Well-Rounded Literacy

21   The National Council of Teachers of English and the International Reading Association (1996) define the English language arts as reading, writing, speaking, listening, visualizing, and visually representing. Their standards require that students be capable of recognizing and studying a variety of genres and forms and suggest a broad definition of text, reading, and literacy.

22   Reading specialists and scholars speak again and again to the need for authentic reading and writing experiences, textual investigations that help bridge the gap between the school world and the lived world, between narrow notions of what it means to be literate and broad notions of what it means to actually succeed as an intelligent adult in contemporary society. The effective use of *graphic novels* and other forms of sequential art can help teachers accomplish all of these goals. When paired with other forms, old and new, this ancient type of text can be a valuable bridge between student and text, student and teacher, and the centuries themselves.

■ References

Bitz, M. (2004). The comic book project: Forging alternative pathways to literacy. Journal of Adolescent and Adult Literacy, 47, 574–586.

Carter, J. B. (2006). The comic book show and tell. Newark, DE: International Reading Association. Available: www.readwritethink.org/lessons/lesson_view.asp?id=921

Carter, J. B. (2007). Ultimate Spider-Man and student-generated classics: Using *graphic novels* and comics to produce authentic voice and detailed, authentic texts. In J. B. Carter (Ed.), Building literacy connections with *graphic novels*: Page by page, panel by panel (pp. 145–155). Urbana, IL: National Council of Teachers of English.

Carter, J. B. (2008). Die a *graphic* death: Revisiting the death of genre with *graphic novels*, or "Why won't you just die already?" The ALAN Review, 36(1), 15–25.

Cary, S. (2004). Going *graphic*: Comics at work in the multilingual classroom. Portsmouth, NH: Heinemann.

Inge, M. T. (1990). Comics as culture. Jackson: University Press of Mississippi.

Krashen, S. D. (2004). The power of reading: Insights from the research (2nd ed.). Westport, CT: Libraries Unlimited.

McCloud, S. (1999). Understanding comics. New York: DC Comics.

Mitchell, J. P., & George, J. D. (1996). What do Superman, Captain America, and Spiderman have in common? The case for comic books. Gifted Education International, 11, 91–94.

National Council of Teachers of English & International Reading Association. (1996). Standards for the English language arts. Urbana, IL: National Council of Teachers of English.

Smith, M. W., & Wilhelm, J. D. (2002). Reading don't fix no Chevys. Portsmouth, NH: Heinemann.

Wright, B. (2001). Comic book nation. Baltimore, MD: Johns Hopkins Press.

Discussion Questions

1. What specific ways has the purpose and audience shaped this definition? Provide specific examples.
2. The author refers to the works as *comics, graphic novels, and sequential art.* What is the effect of the use of these three different terms in the essay? In what ways does or doesn't this strategy contribute to the author's strategy?
3. Why might some teachers be uncomfortable about using graphic novels in the classroom? To what extent do you think this article effectively answers those concerns?
4. In paragraphs 5 and 6, what strategies does he use to answer the assumption that graphic novels are a genre? Why did the author find such a distinction important?
5. Examine the conclusion, paragraph 21. What strategy does the author use for the conclusion? In what ways is or isn't this strategy effective?

Toward Key Insights

In what ways did the writer revise our understanding of graphic novels?

What terms or categories does your definitions possibly shape your perceptions or expectations?

How are disputes over the words used or the meaning of words influence the decisions we make?

Suggestions for Writing

1. Identify something you think is undervalued because of how it is perceived and write to an audience that is likely to undervalue it to help them reconceive the object or activity. For example, you might redefine items like "hip-hop," "roller derby," or "big time wrestling."
2. Take a popular art form or activity that you think should be taught as part of a college class and write a definition paper to professors to encourage them to let a course be taught in that area. For example, one could argue for a course in "bluegrass" by defining its relation as a folk music tradition with historical and cultural importance.

MARC ZWELLING

The Blended Economy

Marc Zwelling graduated with a BS degree in journalism from Northwestern University in 1968. After graduating, he worked for Canadian Press, the Toronto Telegram, *and as public relations official for the United Steelworkers of America. He is currently president of Vector Research and Development, Inc., and conducts opinion surveys and completes feasibility studies. He has facilitated numerous workshops and written extensively about future trends. In our selection, he examines the changing nature of the business marketplace.*

1   The traditional way to innovate is to carve a specialized niche. Some building contractors specialize in renovating nineteenth-century homes. Lawyers practice trade law, criminal law, family law, labor law, immigration, copyright, or libel. Doctors can be ear-nose-throat specialists, gerontologists, or pediatricians. Specialization is efficient; specialists do their jobs faster because they know them better than non-specialists. And a niche is usually more profitable than the mass market from which someone sliced it. The trouble with a niche is that when competitors recognize it's profitable they rush in.

2   Blending is the opposite of specialization. Instead of burrowing deeper into a field or product to specialize, blending creates a new market category. The secret in the technique is to unite different, not similar, ideas, products, or services. Minivans and sport-utility vehicles, for example, grew from blending cars and trucks, creating whole new categories of consumer vehicles.

3   Companies can continually generate new ideas by blending. Most new products today are simply extrapolations of successful products, such as a faster microprocessor, a cheaper airline ticket, a smaller camera, and so on. These innovations eventually run out of possibilities. Blending different ideas instead produces limitless new directions for innovative products.

4   A food company searching for a new product for kids might think of blending different items from a list of opposites like "frozen or unfrozen," "milk or cola," "peanut butter or peanuts," "salad or soup." Perhaps kids who love peanuts would savor them in a soup. And perhaps a cola could be frozen so it would stay cold longer, requiring no ice. The ideas may prove impractical, nonsensical, or just plain awful, but the point is to generate more ideas because they can lead to practical products.

5   Blending also operates within social and economic trends. For instance, barriers are falling between work and leisure, devastating some retail clothing chains and department stores as employees don the same outfits at home and the office.

6   In the job market, there is vast potential to create opportunities by combining apparently unrelated occupations. Consider the number of specialists you must work with to buy or sell a house: There is a real estate agent, the loan officer, the building inspector, an insurance agent, and the mover. One specialist hands you off to another. The blending opportunity here is for, perhaps, a "home transitions" professional who can manage all these different steps.

Some employees may have over-specialized. Specialization narrows a worker's opportunities in a slowly growing economy and causes bottlenecks in a booming economy. Blending avoids these problems.

7   *The New York Times* recently reported unprecedented growth in the new profession of legal nurse consultant. From none a decade ago, there are more than 4,000 in America today. Blending the skills of nurses and lawyers, legal nurse consultants help lawyers in medical-related lawsuits. Blending professions is not the same as stacking one university degree on another. The legal nurse consultant is still a nurse, not a lawyer. Nurses learn enough law in training institutes to become legal nurse consultants.

8   Another example of a blended career opportunity might be an ergonomic architect—a designer and engineer with special training in child development to make safer houses for families with small children.

9   Try mixing and matching completely dissimilar occupations, such as carpenter, receptionist, software writer, investment adviser, security guard, dentist, chemical engineer, lifeguard, teacher, embalmer, chef, hairstylist, pharmacist, actor.

10   A list like this may yield few blended jobs in the literal sense, but it triggers thinking about ways to add value to products and services and differentiate businesses in super-competitive markets. For instance, a funeral home could offer caskets carved by its own carpenters. A supermarket could build customer loyalty if its meat cutters demonstrate cooking techniques. A chef with pharmaceutical training or a pharmacist with cooking skills could help customers create healthier meals using herbs and other natural supplements.

11   Career blending is most likely to develop among entrepreneurs, as attempts to blend work in traditional settings have historically met with resistance: Unions protest that management wants to make one employee do two jobs for one worker's pay. Management says unions obstruct change and efficiency.

12   Indeed, most fields resist merging and consolidating because of tradition. But since nobody can predict what the market will bear, the greater the number of innovations you can generate in products, services, and careers, the greater your chance of success.

Discussion Questions

1. In the first two paragraphs, the author contrasts blending with specialization. What might be his reason for such an approach?
2. What techniques does the writer use to define blends? How effective are those approaches?
3. What examples of blends were most effective, which least effective, and why?

Toward Key Insights

Often we are trapped in our thinking by established categories. How can blending help break us out of those established categories?

Suggestion for Writing

Create a blend of your own, perhaps even creating a new word for the blend just as brunch is a blend of breakfast and lunch. Write a short paper defining your blend.

Marti Bercaw

Krumping

Marti Bercaw is a writer and video journalist at Social, *an online journal from which this article was taken. She loves dance and frequently writes about that topic. Other articles include "Celebrate Michael Jackson's Life and Music at University City Walk!" and "The Jabbawockeez: America's 1st Best Dance Crew."*

1   On the 3rd Saturday of every month Tommy the Clown and Debbie Allen have a "Battle" that hundreds of L.A. kids join. It is a Clowning Krumping dance war of the creative kind, organized by 2 dedicated adults who love dance, love kids and understand the power of expression through dance.

2   The location is the Debbie Allen Dance Academy in Culver City and the stage is a quasi-boxing ring set up in a huge studio. 500 chairs and standing-room-only space is filled to capacity by the time the show starts . . . and what a show it is!

3   Tommy the Clown serves as the Master of Ceremonies and referee with a whistle. Larry the Clown is the DJ who supplies a powerful mix of music. Ani Dizon, Tommy's manager, coordinates the whole event and process. Lil Tommy, Tommy's brother, is there to help when he is not traveling the world performing Clown and Krump Dance with his crew, and he teaches Clowning classes at D.A.D.A., too.

4   On stage, two girl to girl or boy to boy dancers challenge each other in a series of rounds. One opponent sits while the other performs.

5   Individual dancers "call each other out" as well as the members of a crew but it's always one performer at a time. Dancers have been as young as 4 with no limit on the high end. Everyone, even Grandparents, are welcome to battle onstage but teenagers are in the majority.

6   The audience is made up of kids, parents, grandparents and friends. The challenging dance crew changes every month, unless there is a rematch, and goes up against the current winning crew who holds onto the gold embellished championship belt until it passes to the next winner. There are cash prizes as well. The audience votes by applause at the end of each battle. Battle scores are tallied to determine the winning crew.

7   Sometimes it's clear who has won and sometimes they have to rely on an applause meter to determine the winner. It's a tough call because all the dancers are brilliant at freestyle . . . that's what it's all about.

About Krump

8   "Clowning" is movement invented by Tommy the Clown who developed the strange, stilted, goofy and erratic motion to entertain audiences as a clown at parties and local events around Los Angeles from as far back as 1992. Needless to say, it caught on in a big way.

9   Street dance has an evolutionary life of its own and its very nature demands constant adaptation and change. What was once "Clowning" evolved to "Krump Dance" or Krumping. As Tommy put it, "Krumping is the dark side of Clowning." In homage to the clown, some dancers paint designs on half their face.

10   The first time I saw "Clowning/Krumping" was five years ago. Over time, it has spread to other cities in the U.S., Europe and Asia. "Rize," a documentary

by David Lachappelle, permanently writes "Clowning" and "Krumping" into the pop history record. It will read that this dance was born in South Central Los Angeles beginning in the last decade of the century and was performed by inner city kids who, as the third generation who's offered hip hop, were hungry for something new. They made it happen.

Krump Described

11   Krumping incorporates extreme, almost impossible freestyle body motion, coordination and rhythm. Basics include chest popping, a Charlie Chaplin-esque, comic, stumbling, staccato stride and toe dance, feet that turn out, feet that turn in, arms that go wide in a ranting wave, the body jerking up and down, prancing, the torso bent from the waist that circles around the hips 360 degrees, raised arms that wrap over and around the body, the neck and head jutting forward, the mouth chattering as if in a real or silent monologue. The dance is frenzied and rapid, displaying a set of attitudes running the gamut from hostile to aggressive to seductive to comical and back again. Girls can be as good as the guys but there are fewer who compete. Their attitude can include more sexual, bump and grind elements with a flamboyant, exaggerated edge or they can have an attitude that is hard and aggressive, just like their male counterparts.

12   Krumping is not hip hop, though it uses the music and springs from the same mold. For now, it seems to stand alone as a pure urban expression.

13   It isn't pretty and it offers no apology because it tells a vivid story about being young in a hostile and dangerous world run amok. The dancer can shift from malevolent character to clown in a flash like what comes at you as you surf channels on a TV. Click, click. Life turns on a dime at the push of a button in today's world. We see the reflection in Krumping.

14   Debbie Allen and Tommy the Clown do Los Angeles a great service by providing and supporting the monthly "Battles." It is true that kids who would otherwise be involved with gangs or get into other trouble are given a creative alternative. But it is also true that these kids are already gifted, articulate about their medium and highly motivated to achieve excellence.

15   In exchange for the chance to perform, the "Clowns and Krumpers" offer everyone who cares about dance or the creation of dance form or the poetry of rap, or the embodied voice of our American culture a chance to witness art in the making.

Discussion Questions

1. What is the writer's overall purpose in writing this essay? Where is that purpose most evident?
2. Why does the author start the essay with a brief account of a specific competition?
3. What are some distinguishing features that help define Krumping?
4. The original online article had links to video clips of a Krumping competition. Where, if at all, would such video clips be helpful and why? Where would they not be needed and why?
5. In the end, the author identifies some positive features of Krumping. What impact do paragraphs 15 and 16 have on the reader?

Toward Key Insights

Increasingly, texts are being placed online where they can be supplemented by pictures as well as video and audio clips. To what extent does textual content like a definition need to stand on its own and to what extent can it depend on Web-based support material? You might want to consider the above essay as an example.

Cultural phenomenon like music and dance are especially hard to define. What are some of the challenges of defining things like Hip-Hop, Krumping, Breaking, and other similar phenomenon?

Suggestion for Writing

Take a contemporary movement such as Hip-Hop and, following the example of Marti Bercaw, write a definition paper explaining the movement.

JOHN SHEPLER

What Thoreau Knew: Walden and the Meaning of Voluntary Simplicity

John Shepler is an independent writer and online publisher whose work appears at JohnShepler.com from which this essay was selected.

1   On his personal day of independence, July 4, 1845, Henry David Thoreau moved into his one-room cabin, a home away from home that he had built for himself on the shores of Walden Pond in Concord, Massachusetts. He stayed there a little over two years, living a life of voluntary simplicity and writing the books "A Week on the Concord and Merrimack Rivers" and "Walden." When he left, he had done what he declared he was going to do . . . to live deliberately.

2   "I went to the woods because I wished to live deliberately, to front only the essential facts of life, and see if I could not learn what it had to teach, and not, when I came to die, discover that I had not lived."

3   Thoreau did not die a wealthy man, although he could have. He was a Harvard graduate. Had he so chosen, he could have "fit in" with the prevailing cultures of business, politics or higher education. He could have hitched his wagon to the star of a traditional career and let it pull him comfortably through life. Today that would be called "living the American dream." But is it living deliberately?

4   More and more people today are beginning to wonder what they've gotten themselves into. The cornucopia that is the second half of the twentieth century offers us more and more and more, if only we'll reach in and take it. Yet that horn of plenty is seldom the horn of freedom. If you want more, you can have more, but there is a price to be paid.

5   The price is a faster and faster existence to pay for and use the riches that we've grabbed. Two working partners pursuing promising careers with the ever so near carrots of greater responsibilities and greater rewards may find themselves gasping for breath at the end of the day. Even those on a bit slower track may find themselves asking aloud "What am I doing with all this stuff, and why am I working harder and harder to get more and more of it? I'm not sure what I'm doing with half of it now."

6   So there is a movement afoot. It flies in the face of consumerism, yuppyism and success as we've come to worship it. It's a bumper sticker that goes on top of the one that says "he who dies with the most toys, wins." It's something more along the lines of "he or she who lives, wins."

7   It's called the simplicity movement, voluntary simplicity or living simply. The practitioners might be called simplists. There have always been some around. They are the ones who refuse to live above their means. They avoid debt like a disease and could care less what the Jones' think of them. They're not about to keep up with anyone, because they're not focused on what others have or are doing. They are pursuing something that is driving them from inside.

8   The last time we really heard a lot about "alternative" lifestyles was in the 1960's, when the hippie movement was the prevailing counterculture, and flower-power was in full bloom. Since the end of the Vietnam War, though, flower power has wilted and long since blown away. The last couple of decades have been about superachievement, overspending and upward mobility. Is this simplicity movement just the predictable reverse swing of the pendulum?

9   What seems different this time is that the people involved, many in their twenties and thirties, are not driven by political dissent, a romance with shirking off all responsibilities or a flirtation with drugs. They are simply saying "I have quite enough, thank you. Someone else please take a turn."

10   We've been raised to believe that you must go as far as you possibly can in life, and that distance is measured by how busy you are, how hard you work and how much you've accumulated. This is still a compelling dream for many who are happy to buy in and do what it takes to maintain the upgradeable lifestyle. But now there is also a new alternative lifestyle emerging that neither rejects the affordable luxuries of life nor yearns for more. It is a satisfaction with less, in the sense that less of one thing, pressure, intensity, busyness or affluence means a trade for something else, such as self-determination, personal satisfaction, spiritual fulfillment or other things not valued so highly on the trading floor.

11   Thoreau wasn't abandoning his neighbors when he moved into the cabin at Walden Pond. He went there to grieve the untimely death of his brother, John Jr., who contracted lockjaw from a dirty razor. Henry David's first book was meant to be his tribute to their lives together. He valued that time of solitude and the process of working through his thoughts on life more than what else he could have been doing. He stayed to explain it all in his second book, "Walden."

12   There are choices available in life to each of us. They come time and time again. Picking one path does not mean staying that path forever, or that one way is necessarily better than another. For some it is the power life. For others the acceptance of simplicity as a virtuous way of living comes as a welcome relief.

Discussion Questions

1.   The author could have defined the simplicity movement or simplicity by simply drawing on contemporary examples. Why might he have chosen to use Thoreau as the basis for his essay? What effect does the use of Thoreau have on the essay as a whole?

2.   What are specific features of the definition of "simplicity" offered by the author? How does he define the term?

3.   In paragraph 6 he ties his discussion to bumper sticker phrases. Why might he have done so? Is it effective?

4. In paragraph 8, why does he compare today's movement with the movements in the 60's. How does that affect the reader's understanding of his essay?

5. What are his strategies in concluding the essay? Why do you think that he ends the way he does?

Toward Key Insights

Often we think we need things because they are advertised or others tell us that we need them. Consider what you value most. What do you really need in your life to be happy? How much time would you sacrifice and how much stress would you endure for a more affluent lifestyle? Why?

There are several key American writers who constantly fuel the American imagination and value system. Writers like Thoreau, Martin Luther King, Mark Twain, and others seem to have an ongoing impact on us. What writers, thinkers, or moviemakers have strongly influenced you? Why do these kinds of figures have such an influence on our imagination?

Suggestions for Writing

1. Take a filmmaker, writer, poet, or songwriter or other artist who has defined an important concept or experience for you. Drawing on and expanding on that person's work, write a definition essay that explores the concept or experience in question.

2. Consider some of the important terms in our society such as success, a good life, freedom, simplicity, or others. Write a paper that defines the term in relation to how people live today in relation to that term.

ARGUMENT

Reading Strategies

1. Identify the background of the author if possible. Does the author bring any expertise or experience that helps make the argument more credible?

2. Read the introduction and conclusion to gain a sense of the thesis and main points of the argument.

3. Read the argument quickly to gain an overall sense of the major points of the essay and an understanding of the organizational pattern.

4. Look for the organizational pattern of the essay and keep an eye out for transition sentences. Often an author argues by first presenting the viewpoint of several other authors, then pointing out limitations of those views, then presenting his or her own position and offering support, and finally admitting possible limitations and problems with the author's position (possibly answering these objections). This pattern often confuses readers.

5. Read carefully to identify the major claims of the argument, the reasons for the author's position, and any evidence presented for any of the claims. It can be very helpful to outline an argument, making a special note of the major reasons and evidence for the claim. Note the author's approach. Is the argument mostly deductive or inductive? Does the author try to show the negative consequences of opposing views? Does the author base the argument on authority?

Reading Critically

1. Check to see if the author demonstrates any overt bias.
2. Test to determine if the reasons given really support the author's thesis.
3. Test to see if the evidence is adequate. Does the evidence support the claims? Is the source of the evidence trustworthy and unbiased? Is the evidence extensive or scanty? Could contrary evidence be offered?
4. Check the essay for informal fallacies.
5. Try to offer objections to the author's claims. Write objections in the margins or on a separate piece of paper.
6. See if you can formulate alternative conclusions to those proposed by the author.
7. Try to formulate reasons and concerns that the author may have neglected.
8. Read essays that present other viewpoints and compare.

Reading As a Writer

1. Note the organizational pattern of the argument. Identify how you might use the pattern in your arguments.
2. Examine how the writer connects the reasons with the major thesis.
3. Identify how the evidence is presented and connected as support.
4. Notice any effective word choice that helps cement the emotional argument.
5. Evaluate how the author establishes tone and ethos.
6. Examine how the author answers possible objections.

PATRICK MOORE

Going Nuclear

Patrick Moore was born in 1947, received a Ph.D. in ecology from the university of British Columbia and served as an environmental activist with GreenPeace from 1971–1986. Since then, he has taken very different views from GreenPeace, suggesting that global warming may not be man made and that nuclear power is an important environmental solution. He is co-founder and chief scientist for the consulting firm of Greenspirit Strategies. He is also a paid lobbyist for the Nuclear Energy Institute. One question readers need to consider is whether his history and current affiliations should influence how his article is evaluated. "Going Nuclear" appeared as an opinion piece in the Sunday edition of the Washington Post, *April 16, 2006.*

1   In the early 1970s when I helped found Greenpeace, I believed that nuclear energy was synonymous with nuclear holocaust, as did most of my compatriots. That's the conviction that inspired Greenpeace's first voyage up the spectacular rocky northwest coast to protest the testing of U.S. hydrogen bombs in Alaska's Aleutian Islands. Thirty years on, my views have changed, and the rest of the environmental movement needs to update its views, too, because nuclear energy may just be the energy source that can save our planet from another possible disaster: catastrophic climate change.

Establishes credibility for audience

Defines audience for argument

States thesis.

2   Look at it this way: More than 600 coal-fired electric plants in the United States produce 36 percent of U.S. emissions—or nearly 10 percent of global emissions—of CO_2, the primary greenhouse gas responsible for climate change. Nuclear energy is the only large-scale, cost-effective energy source that can

Identifies problem with evidence

reduce these emissions while continuing to satisfy a growing demand for power. And these days it can do so safely.

3   I say that guardedly, of course, just days after Iranian President Mahmoud Ahmadinejad announced that his country had enriched uranium. "The nuclear technology is only for the purpose of peace and nothing else," he said. But there is widespread speculation that, even though the process is ostensibly dedicated to producing electricity, it is in fact a cover for building nuclear weapons.

4   And although I don't want to underestimate the very real dangers of nuclear technology in the hands of rogue states, we cannot simply ban every technology that is dangerous. That was the all-or-nothing mentality at the height of the Cold War, when anything nuclear seemed to spell doom for humanity and the environment. In 1979, Jane Fonda and Jack Lemmon produced a frisson of fear with their starring roles in "The China Syndrome," a fictional evocation of nuclear disaster in which a reactor meltdown threatens a city's survival. Less than two weeks after the blockbuster film opened, a reactor core meltdown at Pennsylvania's Three Mile Island nuclear power plant sent shivers of very real anguish throughout the country.

5   What nobody noticed at the time, though, was that Three Mile Island was in fact a success story: The concrete containment structure did just what it was designed to do—prevent radiation from escaping into the environment. And although the reactor itself was crippled, there was no injury or death among nuclear workers or nearby residents. Three Mile Island was the only serious accident in the history of nuclear energy generation in the United States, but it was enough to scare us away from further developing the technology: There hasn't been a nuclear plant ordered up since then.

6   Today, there are 103 nuclear reactors quietly delivering just 20 percent of America's electricity. Eighty percent of the people living within 10 miles of these plants approve of them (that's not including the nuclear workers). Although I don't live near a nuclear plant, I am now squarely in their camp.

7   And I am not alone among seasoned environmental activists in changing my mind on this subject. British atmospheric scientist James Lovelock, father of the Gaia theory, believes that nuclear energy is the only way to avoid catastrophic climate change. Stewart Brand, founder of the "Whole Earth Catalog," says the environmental movement must embrace nuclear energy to wean ourselves from fossil fuels. On occasion, such opinions have been met with excommunication from the anti-nuclear priesthood: The late British Bishop Hugh Montefiore, founder and director of Friends of the Earth, was forced to resign from the group's board after he wrote a pro-nuclear article in a church newsletter.

8   There are signs of a new willingness to listen, though, even among the staunchest anti-nuclear campaigners. When I attended the Kyoto climate meeting in Montreal last December, I spoke to a packed house on the question of a sustainable energy future. I argued that the only way to reduce fossil fuel emissions from electrical production is through an aggressive program of renewable energy sources (hydroelectric, geothermal heat pumps, wind, etc.) plus nuclear. The Greenpeace spokesperson was first at the mike for the question period, and I expected a tongue-lashing. Instead, he began by saying he agreed with much of what I said—not the nuclear bit, of course, but there was a clear feeling that all options must be explored.

9   Here's why: Wind and solar power have their place, but because they are intermittent and unpredictable they simply can't replace big baseload plants such as coal, nuclear and hydroelectric. Natural gas, a fossil fuel, is too expensive already, and its price is too volatile to risk building big baseload plants. Given that hydroelectric resources are built pretty much to capacity, nuclear is, by elimination, the only viable substitute for coal. It's that simple.

Marginal annotations:

Offers answer to problem

Acknowledges cricism

Identifies second major criticism

Answers objection with claim that can be tested by reader.

Offers evidence of public support

Sites an authority recognizable by possible readers.

Demonstrates limitations with alternatives.

10   That's not to say that there aren't real problems—as well as various myths—associated with nuclear energy. Each concern deserves careful consideration:

11   *Nuclear energy is expensive.* It is in fact one of the least expensive energy sources. In 2004, the average cost of producing nuclear energy in the United States was less than two cents per kilowatt-hour, comparable with coal and hydroelectric. Advances in technology will bring the cost down further in the future.

12   *Nuclear plants are not safe.* Although Three Mile Island was a success story, the accident at Chernobyl, 20 years ago this month, was not. But Chernobyl was an accident waiting to happen. This early model of Soviet reactor had no containment vessel, was an inherently bad design and its operators literally blew it up. The multi-agency U.N. Chernobyl Forum reported last year that 56 deaths could be directly attributed to the accident, most of those from radiation or burns suffered while fighting the fire. Tragic as those deaths were, they pale in comparison to the more than 5,000 coal-mining deaths that occur worldwide every year. No one has died of a radiation-related accident in the history of the U.S. civilian nuclear reactor program. (And although hundreds of uranium mine workers did die from radiation exposure underground in the early years of that industry, that problem was long ago corrected.)

13   *Nuclear waste will be dangerous for thousands of years.* Within 40 years, used fuel has less than one-thousandth of the radioactivity it had when it was removed from the reactor. And it is incorrect to call it waste, because 95 percent of the potential energy is still contained in the used fuel after the first cycle. Now that the United States has removed the ban on recycling used fuel, it will be possible to use that energy and to greatly reduce the amount of waste that needs treatment and disposal. Last month, Japan joined France, Britain and Russia in the nuclear-fuel-recycling business. The United States will not be far behind.

14   *Nuclear reactors are vulnerable to terrorist attack.* The six-feet-thick reinforced concrete containment vessel protects the contents from the outside as well as the inside. And even if a jumbo jet did crash into a reactor and breach the containment, the reactor would not explode. There are many types of facilities that are far more vulnerable, including liquid natural gas plants, chemical plants and numerous political targets.

15   *Nuclear fuel can be diverted to make nuclear weapons.* This is the most serious issue associated with nuclear energy and the most difficult to address, as the example of Iran shows. But just because nuclear technology can be put to evil purposes is not an argument to ban its use.

16   Over the past 20 years, one of the simplest tools—the machete—has been used to kill more than a million people in Africa, far more than were killed in the Hiroshima and Nagasaki nuclear bombings combined. What are car bombs made of? Diesel oil, fertilizer and cars. If we banned everything that can be used to kill people, we would never have harnessed fire.

17   The only practical approach to the issue of nuclear weapons proliferation is to put it higher on the international agenda and to use diplomacy and, where necessary, force to prevent countries or terrorists from using nuclear materials for destructive ends. And new technologies such as the reprocessing system recently introduced in Japan (in which the plutonium is never separated from the uranium) can make it much more difficult for terrorists or rogue states to use civilian materials to manufacture weapons.

18   The 600-plus coal-fired plants emit nearly 2 billion tons of CO_2 annually—the equivalent of the exhaust from about 300 million automobiles. In addition, the Clean Air Council reports that coal plants are responsible for 64 percent of

Structures essays to answer objections

States objection.

Provides evidence to counter objection.

Identifies objections

Uses evidence to place risk in perspective.

States serious objection.

Partially answers objection by providing factual evidence and suggesting the possible solution to the problem.

Objection

Offers a factual answer to the objection.

Objection

Uses reductio absurdum approach to show that banning a dangerous substance is not practical.

Offers an alternative to solve the problem

sulfur dioxide emissions, 26 percent of nitrous oxides and 33 percent of mercury emissions. These pollutants are eroding the health of our environment, producing acid rain, smog, respiratory illness and mercury contamination.

19   Meanwhile, the 103 nuclear plants operating in the United States effectively avoid the release of 700 million tons of CO_2 emissions annually—the equivalent of the exhaust from more than 100 million automobiles. Imagine if the ratio of coal to nuclear were reversed so that only 20 percent of our electricity was generated from coal and 60 percent from nuclear. This would go a long way toward cleaning the air and reducing greenhouse gas emissions. Every responsible environmentalist should support a move in that direction.

Discussion Questions

1. In paragraph 1, the introduction, the author identifies his role in Greenpeace and his initial opposition to nuclear power before he states his current support for nuclear power. Why does the author start in this way, and is it effective?
2. Should the fact that the author is clearly paid to support nuclear power by the nuclear industry have any bearing on how readers evaluate his argument.
3. Who is the target audience for this argument? Why did the writer choose this target audience? What particular parts of the argument are used specifically for that audience?
4. The author attempts to answer common "myths" about nuclear power. Why does he employ this strategy? Why is or isn't his approach effective with his readers?
5. His argument is that nuclear power is the best answer to global warming, What could he do to strengthen this argument?

Toward Key Insights

Often we face not the best possible answer but rather the least undesirable option. Consider the ways that in this and other situations we may face such unfortunate choices.

The discussion of nuclear power often comes down to an assessment of risk. How much risk is there? How can risk be evaluated in determining whether we should expand the number of nuclear power plants?

Suggestions for Writing

1. Focusing on the core point of this essay, do additional research and write and argument either supporting or opposing the use of nuclear power as a solution to global warming.
2. Take one of the myths he discusses, do additional research, and write a paper arguing for or against that point, such as whether or not nuclear power is expensive.
3. If you oppose nuclear power, write to environmentalists countering this author's argument that nuclear power is the answer to environmental problems.
4. If you support nuclear power, do additional research and write an article specifically to an audience opposed to nuclear power because of the risks involved and who are not strong environmentalists otherwise.

ALEXIS ROWELL

Ten Reasons Why New Nuclear Was a Mistake—Even Before Fukushima

Alexis Rowell was born in 1965. He was for a time a BBC Journalist. He was the founder of the consulting group cuttingthecarbon *and was elected member of Camden Council in 2006. He has been appointed to be Camden Eco Champion and is Chair of the council's All-party Sustainability Task Force. He is author of* Communities, Councils & a Low Carbon Future. *The article below was posted on March 15, 2011, on the website* Transition Culture: an Evolving Exploration into the Head, Heart, and Hands of Energy Descent.

1   It's hardly a surprise that building nuclear power stations on seismic fault lines, as Japan has done, turns out to be a foolish thing. In the pause for reflection about the safety of nuclear power that the Fukushima disaster is bound to create, here are ten reasons why it's a mistake to build a new round of nuclear power stations in the UK.

Nuclear Power Is Too Expensive

2   Nuclear has always been an expensive white elephant. UK taxpayers currently subsidise nuclear directly to the tune of more than £1bn per year.[1] But the indirect subsidies such as decommissioning and insurance are far greater.

3   The cost of decommissioning old nuclear in the UK is now estimated to be at least £73bn.[2] Surely anyone wishing to provide new nuclear should have to put that sort of sum into an up-front clean-up fund. But of course they won't. They can't possibly afford to.

4   If there's a nuclear accident in the UK, then who will pay? An insurance company? Not a hope. Existing UK reactors are insured to the tune of £140m each, which the government is talking about increasing to £1.2bn, but that's still nothing like enough to cover a serious accident like Fukushima or Three Mile Island or Chernobyl.[3]

5   Nuclear power is uninsurable. It's too risky and the potential payouts are too big. The government, meaning the UK taxpayer, will have to pay as we did to bail out the banks. The free market will never bear the true costs of nuclear.

6   A report published by the US Union of Concerned Scientists last month said nuclear power had never operated in the United States without public subsidies.[4] The existence of an Office of Nuclear Development at the Department of Energy and Climate Change (DECC) makes a mockery of Chris Huhne's claim that no public money will be spent on new nuclear.[5]

7   Only two atomic power stations are under construction in Western Europe: one in France and one in Finland. The Finnish reactor, which was supposed to be the first of a new generation of "safe" and "affordable" units, has been subsidised by the French nuclear industry (and therefore the French state) as a loss

[1]www.psiru.org/reports/2008-03-E-nuclearsubsidies.doc
[2]http://news.bbc.co.uk/1/hi/business/4859980.stm; http://www.guardian.co.uk/environment/2008/jan/30/nuclearpower.energy
[3]http://www.decc.gov.uk/en/content/cms/news/pn11_007/pn11_007.aspx
[4]Koplow, D. (2011). http://www.ucsusa.org/assets/documents/nuclear_power/nuclear_subsidies_report.pdf
[5]www.decc.gov.uk/en/content/cms/what_we_do/uk_supply/energy_mix/nuclear/new/office/office.aspx

leader in the hope that it will spark a new nuclear building boom. When the decision was announced Standard & Poor instantly downgraded to "negative" the stock of the Finnish utility commissioning the reactor. The project has been plagued with cost overruns and delays (it was due to open in 2009), is under investigation by the Finnish nuclear safety regulator STUK and is probably the single best reason why new nuclear is a mistake.[6]

New Nuclear Power Stations Won't Be Ready in Time

8   According to the 2007 Energy White Paper the earliest the first new nuclear power station could possibly be ready is 2020.[7] Chris Huhne occasionally says it might be possible by 2018 but most observers disagree. However we need to re-place 40% of our energy generation by 2015 because old nuclear and coal-fired plants are set to close. New nuclear will come too late.

Nuclear Does Not and Will Not Safeguard Our Energy Security

9   Nuclear power currently provides 18% of our electricity but only about 1% of our total energy needs.[8] Three quarters of the UK's primary energy demand comes from gas and oil.[9] Gas is used for most of our space heating and hot water. Oil is used for virtually all forms of transport. Indeed the vast majority of our oil and gas consumption is for purposes other than producing electricity. Nuclear power cannot replace that energy, while gas and oil deliveries are threatened by tightening supply (peak oil) and political instability. A 2008 Sussex University study concluded: "we are not convinced that there is a strong security case for new nuclear, especially if the costs and risks of strategies that include new nuclear are considered alongside those of strategies that do not."[10]

Nuclear Power Is Not Green

10   Mining uranium requires fossils fuels. So does building a nuclear power station. And so does trying to dispose of radioactive waste. Over its lifecycle a nuclear power station produces as much carbon dioxide as a gas-fired power station.[11] Better than oil or coal but not carbon-free. And it will get worse. In the not too distant future uranium will become so hard to mine that it will require more fossil fuels to extract it than the energy that will be produced from it.[12]

Nuclear Power Will Do Little to Reduce Our Carbon Emissions

11   Even if Britain built ten new reactors, nuclear power would only deliver a 4% cut in carbon emissions some time after 2025.[13] But that's too late. We need the carbon reductions now. We'd do better to ban standby buttons on electrical appliances than to develop new nuclear power.

[6]Thomas, S. (2010). "The Economics of Nuclear Power: An Update." http://boell.org/downloads/Thomas_UK_-_web.pdf

[7]http://www.decc.gov.uk/en/content/cms/legislation/white_papers/white_paper_07/white_paper_07.aspx

[8]http://www.decc.gov.uk/en/content/cms/what_we_do/uk_supply/energy_mix; http://www.decc.gov.uk/assets/decc/Statistics/publications/dukes/348-dukes-2010-printed.pdf

[9]http://www.oilandgasuk.co.uk/economics.cfm

[10]Watson, J. & Scott, A. "New Nuclear Power in the UK: A Strategy for Energy Security?" http://www.sussex.ac.uk/Users/prpp4/Supergen_Nuclear_and_Security.pdf

[11]Van Leeuwen, J. & Smith, P. (2008). "Nuclear power the energy balance." http://www.stormsmith.nl/

[12]http://en.wikipedia.org/wiki/Peak_uranium

[13]http://www.greenpeace.org.uk/climate/nuclear-power

Nuclear Power Stations Are Inefficient

12   We really need to stop producing electricity in huge power stations hundreds of miles away which waste 60% of the energy they produce as heat through cooling towers and another 7–9% in transmission losses across the national grid. If we produce energy locally and use Combined Heat and Power (CHP), then we can reach efficiencies of 80–90%.[14] Nuclear cannot and never has been made to work with CHP because to distribute the heat you need residents or businesses to be close by. But how many people want to live near a nuclear power station?

Plane Crashes Are a Risk to Nuclear Power Stations

13   In February 2011 a Loughborough University aviation expert suggested the chance of a plane crashing into a UK reactor was 20% higher than official estimates and The Guardian reported that a Health & Safety Executive internal report had admitted that a crash could trigger "significant radiological releases".[15] Finally, if you can fly a plane into the Twin Towers, then you can certainly fly one into a nuclear power station.

Nuclear Power Kills

14   Miscarriage rates by women living near the Sellafield nuclear reprocessing facility are higher than would be expected.[16] Billions of fish are killed every year when they get trapped in the cooling water intake pipes of nuclear reactors.[17]

It's a Myth that Renewables Cannot Provide Baseload

15   There has never been a day on record when the wind has not blown somewhere in the UK. The point about baseload is that what you need is enough people in enough places producing electricity. The more you decentralise electricity generation the more secure the baseload becomes. The same principle holds for investing in shares—it's much more risky to invest everything in a couple of big companies than it is to invest in a basket of shares that reflect all aspects of the market. The real reason why proponents of nuclear are obliged to talk about baseload is that it's uneconomic to do much with atomic reactors other than run them continuously, whether or not the energy is needed. And in the UK that has usually meant prioritising nuclear over available wind energy.

Global Expansion Could Lead to New Nuclear Security Risks

16   In February 2011 the Royal Society launched an inquiry into nuclear nonproliferation saying that a global expansion of nuclear power "could lead to the wider proliferation of nuclear weapons, as well as creating new nuclear security risks," which could "impact on international progress towards nuclear disarmament."[18] Look at the problems the international community is having with the Iranian nuclear power programme. Many observers believe the US and Israel recently collaborated on a cyber sabotage project to slow the Iranian development up and prevent it from developing atomic weapons.[19]

[14]http://en.wikipedia.org/wiki/Cogeneration
[15]http://www.guardian.co.uk/environment/2011/feb/21/nuclear-risk-plane-crashes
[16]Jones, K. & Wheater, A. (1989). "Obstetric outcomes in West Cumberland Hospital: is there a risk from Sellafield?" http://www.ncbi.nlm.nih.gov/pmc/articles/PMC1292295/
[17]Speight, M. & Henderson, P. (2010). *Marine Ecology—Concepts and Applications.* p. 186
[18]http://royalsociety.org/nonproliferation/
[19]http://www.reuters.com/article/2011/02/07/us-nuclear-iran-idUSTRE71622Z20110207

And We Still Have No Idea What to Do with Nuclear Waste

17   All those arguments against new nuclear and not one of them was about nuclear waste. The 2003 Energy White Paper said one of the reasons why the then government wasn't proposing new nuclear was because there were "important issues of nuclear waste to be resolved." Have they been? No.

18   There are perfectly good non-nuclear solutions but they all require a lot more government intervention than the coalition government seems prepared to contemplate. They are:

1) Energy Efficiency

19   As it stands, the government's Green Deal—under which householders can borrow funds for energy efficiency measures to be repaid out of energy bill savings—is set to be a completely inadequate sticking plaster solution. It feels like the government has decided that existing buildings are too difficult to deal with seriously which is why they're so gung-ho about new nuclear—to fuel electric radiators the energy from which will then be wasted through leaky windows, walls, roofs and floors. The only way to create genuinely low energy buildings is by using Passivhaus design.[20] Asking the UK's building sector to refurbish buildings using a proper engineering standard will be a challenge, but it is at least a coherent approach. Unlike new nuclear and the Green Deal.

2) Renewables (and possibly combined heat & power in urban areas if we can find enough non-fossil fuels to run it)

20   Nuclear has taken up a huge amount of civil servant time over the last few years. That's time that could have been spent on renewables. Britain has by far the most potential for wind and tidal power in Europe because of our geography. 40% of Europe's wind passes through these isles.[21] Yet in 2010 we produced just 3.2% of our electricity from wind. Germany obtained 9.4% of its electricity from wind in 2010, Spain generated 14.4% and Denmark managed a whopping 24%.[22]

21   The reason the Danes are so far ahead on wind is because they learnt the right lessons from the oil shocks of the 1970s and started planning for a renewably-powered future back then. The UK, by contrast, was blinded by the discovery of North Sea Oil.

3) Tradable Energy Quotas (TEQs)

22   Tradable Energy Quotas (TEQs) are a way of using the market to reduce fossil fuel energy consumption.[23] Every adult is given an equal free entitlement of TEQs units each week. Other energy users (government, industry etc.) bid for their units at a weekly auction. If you use less than your entitlement, you can sell your surplus. If you need more, you can buy them. All trading takes place at a single national price, which will rise and fall in line with demand. When you buy energy, such as petrol for your car or electricity for your household, units corresponding to the amount of energy you have bought are deducted from your TEQs account, in addition to your money payment. The total number of units available in the country is set out in the TEQs Budget, which goes down each year.

23   *There are greener, cheaper, more secure, quicker to install, safer alternatives to new nuclear so don't let yourself be persuaded that it's the only solution. It's not.*

---

[20]http://www.cuttingthecarbon.co.uk/home/passivhaus-standard
[21]http://www.energysavingtrust.org.uk/Generate-your-own-energy/Wind-Turbines
[22]http://ewea.org/fileadmin/ewea_documents/documents/statistics/EWEA_Annual_Statistics_2010.pdf
[23]http://www.teqs.net

Discussion Questions

1. The writer offers 10 reasons against nuclear power and organizes them with bold headers. What might be his rhetorical reason for organizing them in this way? Is it effective?
2. The writer spends the most time arguing that nuclear power is too expensive rather than unsafe. Why might he have chosen to focus on that concern? Is that rhetorically appropriate if his goal is to persuade his readers to oppose nuclear power?
3. In paragraph 12, the writer makes a very technical point about efficiency. What did you understand might be the writer's point here? How could this paragraph be rewritten to be more effective for less knowledgeable readers?
4. In rejecting nuclear power, is it important for the writer to suggest other alternatives? Is his argument for alternatives effective? How effective is his evidence in paragraph 20 for the potential of wind industry?
5. The article documents its sources and presents them in a works cited section. To what extent, if at all, does this strengthen or weaken the argument of the article? Why?

Toward Key Insights

Increasingly arguments are carried out through blogs rather than newspaper opinion pages. This article was a blog. How might writing for a blog differ from writing for a print media, and in what ways is it the same?

The article is written about England's nuclear program to an English audience. England faces different challenges from the United States; for example, it is much more populated and does not have any extremely remote areas. England's economy is also different from that of the United States. To what extent are or aren't the arguments applicable to other countries such as the United States that may face different situations?

Suggestions for Writing

1. Identify one key issue raised by the article, such as whether nuclear power is too expensive or whether nuclear power is too inefficient, and then research the topic and write an argument about it.
2. Research the safety of nuclear power and write an argument on whether nuclear power is or is not safe.
3. Having read both articles in the Reader, do additional research and write an argument to concerned American readers on whether or not America should support the construction of new nuclear power plants to meet our energy needs.

MARESSA BROWN

Teacher Natalie Munroe Has a Right to Call Kids Lazy and Rude

Maressa Brown is a 20 something blogger who was Born in a Chicago suburb in 1983. She graduated with a B.S. in Print & Multimedia Journalism from Emerson College. She is staff writer for the Stir on CafeMom.com, writer *and as writer and occasional editor has published in* Better Home & Gardens, Woman's World, *AOL, and other publications. She actively blogs and tweets. This selection is a from* The Stir on CafeMom.com, *posted February 16, 2011.*

1   Natalie Munroe, a 30-year-old Pennsylvania high school teacher, was suspended without pay for writing an anonymous blog about her job, including statements referring to her students such as, "A complete and utter jerk in all ways," ". . . although academically okay your child has no other redeeming qualities," "I hear the trash company is hiring," and "There's no other way to say this, I hate your kid."

2   Local parents and the administration are clearly infuriated. *So what?* That's not a good enough reason for Munroe to have been dismissed.

3   They may be government employees, but public school teachers have the same rights as any other U.S. citizen. It doesn't matter that they're standing in front of a classroom, teaching your children math, science, social studies, or English. They're still entitled to their freedom of speech and self-expression.

4   In fact, some may say venting outside of the classroom—even if it is online (*anonymously!*)—is a MUCH healthier way to express anger and frustration than inside the classroom. Would the administration prefer she take out her frustrations by lashing out at her students in class? Perhaps they'd rather she squawked about it in the teachers' lounge—even though that could lead to some serious staff drama. (I've heard there's quite a bit of gossip and he said/she said behavior that goes on among teachers.)

5   No, actually, I'm sure the school would simply prefer Munroe keep her mouth shut altogether.

6   A friend of mine is an Atheist activist and a public school math teacher. He's even written a book, and he maintains a blog about Atheism. He doesn't write about his students on the Atheist blog. (Although he does tweet and post *totally* benign and funny commentary on how moronic or funny, brilliant or ridiculous his students are. Which I also believe is no big deal.) His online work has absolutely nothing to do with his ability to be a stellar math teacher, so why are some parents in the Illinois community where he works up in arms about the fact that he writes his ideas and opinions online? Because they'd rather he just shut up and teach. It's as if some people expect teachers to just be machines without emotions, without any rights to be individuals outside of the classroom.

7   Granted, this is a different situation from my friend's in that Munroe actually was writing about her students, but again, it was completely anonymous.

8   Plus, if you really take a step back and think about it . . . consider that in one posting, she called her students "out of control" and "rude, lazy, disengaged whiners," can you blame the woman? I can't. I've heard from so many of my friends and relatives who are high school teachers that teens are getting worse—more spoiled, more ill-mannered, rude, etc. There's only so much they can do and only so many ways they can cope in the classroom. They're only human.

9   In response to all the brouhaha, Munroe said:

> I was writing it not about anyone specific, they were caricatures of students that I've had over the years . . . it was meant tongue and cheek for myself and my friends, it was not for mass consumption . . . I'm sorry that it was taken out of context but I stand by what I said.

10   This is certainly not the first time a teacher has written about their life, used it as a jumping off point for thinly veiled fiction. And it shouldn't be the last.

No kids were individually harmed in the making of Munroe's blog. So, why is everyone so worried? The parents and school board should really just shut up themselves, be grateful they have someone teaching their kids who has the ability to think for herself, and allow the teacher to take her annoying job back!

Discussion Questions

1. What are the two basic reasons the writer gives for not dismissing the teacher? In both cases, she seems to assume the principles in question. Is she justified in making these assumptions? If not, how could she strengthen these reasons?
2. How much difference is there in a teacher writing generally about students or students talking generally about teachers rather than writing specifically about named students or teachers? Why do you think or not think this is an important difference?
3. The conclusion is very confrontational. Why might the writer have adopted this tone? In what ways is it effective or ineffective?
4. What techniques does this writer use to create an informal tone? Why might she have adopted such a tone? Is it effective or ineffective?
5. This argument was written as a blog available for a general audience on the Internet. It what ways might its place on the Internet affect how it was written?
6. To what extent should or shouldn't employers be able to reprimand or fire individuals for speech outside of the workplace? Is or isn't this covered by the concept of free speech?

Toward Key Insights

The strategies for writing need to adapt to the context. Editorials in a newspaper or a blog have very different expectations than an article for an important journal. But do these expectations built around holding the attention of readers undercut what should be provided to create an effective argument? Are such public discourses influencing our sense of what counts as a valid argument? How so?

The evocation of general principles like freedom or free speech are very common; yet, the terms are often not as clear as the use of them might suggest. Free speech is a constitutional right that limits the government, not an employer. As writers, then, we need to consider to what extent we may extend the application of these general principles. Should we be very careful and restrict the usage of the principles to their original intent or should we build on the spirit of the concepts and extend them more broadly?

Writing Suggestions

1. Focusing on the case discussed in this blog, do additional research and then write to the school board arguing either for the suspension and possible dismissal of this teacher or re-instating the teacher into the classroom without punishment.
2. How much should or shouldn't employers be able to restrict the speech of employees outside of work? Write an argument to persuade employers wavering on this issue of your view on the matter. You might wish to conduct additional research for examples and reasons that support your view.

JONATHAN ZIMMERMAN

When Teachers Talk out of School

Jonathan Zimmerman is Professor of History and Education as well as Department Chair at New York University. He received his M.A. and Ph.D. from John Hopkins University. He was also a Peace Core volunteer and a high school teacher. He is the author of Small Wonder: The Little Red Schoolhouse in History and Memory *as well as other books and articles. This selection is from June 3, 2011,* The New York Times.

1   In 1927, a schoolteacher in Secaucus, N.J., named Helen Clark lost her teaching license. The reason? Somebody had seen her smoking cigarettes after school hours. In communities across the United States, that was a ground for dismissal. So was card-playing, dancing and failure to attend church. Even after Prohibition ended, teachers could be dismissed for drinking or frequenting a place where liquor was served.

2   Today, teachers can be suspended, and even fired, for what they write on Facebook.

3   Just ask Christine Rubino, the New York City math teacher who may soon be dismissed for posting angry messages about her students. Last June, just before summer vacation began, a Harlem schoolgirl drowned during a field trip to a beach. Ms. Rubino had nothing to do with that incident, but the following afternoon, she typed a quick note on Facebook about a particularly rowdy group of Brooklyn fifth graders in her charge.

4   "After today, I'm thinking the beach is a good trip for my class," she wrote. "I hate their guts."

5   One of Ms. Rubino's Facebook friends then asked, "Wouldn't you throw a life jacket to little Kwami?"

6   "No, I wouldn't for a million dollars," Ms. Rubino replied. She was pulled from the classroom in February and faced termination hearings; the case is now with an arbitrator.

7   Ms. Rubino's online outburst was only the latest example of its kind. In April, a first-grade teacher in Paterson, N.J., was suspended for writing on her Facebook page that she felt like a "warden" overseeing "future criminals." In February, a high school English teacher in suburban Philadelphia was suspended for a blog entry calling her students "rude, disengaged, lazy whiners;" in another post, she imagined writing "frightfully dim" or "dresses like a streetwalker" on their report cards.

8   Such teachers have become minor Internet celebrities, lauded by their fans for exposing students' insolent manners and desultory work habits. Their backers also say that teachers' freedom of speech is imperiled when we penalize their out-of-school remarks.

9   But these defenders have it backward. The truly scary restrictions on teacher speech lie inside the schoolhouse walls, not beyond them. And by supporting teachers' right to rant against students online, we devalue their status as professionals and actually make it harder to protect real academic freedom in the classroom.

10   Last October, a federal appeals court upheld the dismissal of an Ohio high-school teacher who had asked students to report about books that had been banned from schools and libraries. The exercise wasn't in the official

curriculum, and parents had complained about their children reading some of the banned books.

11   Three years before that, the courts allowed an Indiana school board to fire a teacher who told her students that she had honked her car horn in support of a rally against the war in Iraq. The reason was the same: she had deviated from the "approved" curriculum.

12   Meanwhile, in Wisconsin and elsewhere, state legislatures are moving to restrict or eliminate teachers' collective bargaining rights. That means unions will have a more difficult time defending teachers' freedom of speech.

13   So the rest of us need to make a fresh case for why teachers should have this freedom. And the answer starts, paradoxically, with the limits they should impose on themselves.

14   All professionals restrict their own speech, after all, reflecting the special purposes and responsibilities of their occupations. A psychologist should not discuss his patients' darkest secrets on a crowded train, which would violate the trust and confidence they have placed in him. A lawyer should not disparage her clients publicly, because her job is to represent them to the best of her ability.

15   And a teacher should not lob gratuitous barbs at her students, which contradicts her own professional duty: to teach the skills and habits of democracy. Yes, teachers have a responsibility to transmit the topics and principles of the prescribed curriculum. But they also need to teach democratic capacities—including reason, debate and tolerance—so our children learn to think on their own.

16   Teachers won't be able to model those skills if our schools and courts continue to muzzle them. But the same democratic imperative also demands that teachers responsibly restrict what they say, just as other professionals do.

17   A similar sense of restraint is needed in class as well: although I would fully support a teacher's right to voice an anti-war view, I would not want her to tell the class that it is the only appropriate view. That's indoctrination, not education, and it inhibits the critical thinking skills that democracy demands.

18   Outside school, meanwhile, teachers must also avoid public language that mocks, demeans or disparages the children they instruct. Cruel blog posts about lazy or disobedient students echo the snarky smackdown culture of cable TV talk shows. And they're anathema to a truly democratic dialogue.

Discussion Questions

1. This is an argument about values. What are the reasons the author offers for his position? Are those reasons effective or not?

2. Much of the discussion on this issue revolves around questions of value. What kinds of evidence, if any, might readers use to strengthen their claim?

3. What is the purpose of paragraphs 10, 11, and 12 in relation to the writer's main argument? What audiences might it address? Is this approach effective?

4. In the conclusion, the author associates negative comments through social media with a "snarky smackdown culture." Why does he make this comparison in the conclusion? Is it effective?

5. This essay was originally an opinion piece in the *The New York Times*? How do you anticipate different audiences would respond to the article: teachers, parents, school administrators, other professionals?

Toward Key Insights

Little on the web is really private, whether on Facebook, e-mail, or a semi-private blog. In a flash, any posting can be very public. How then should we balance our free speech rights and the possible consequences of our comments on such a media? There have been cases of cyberbullying and online slander that harms a person's reputation. How would you balance free speech with a person's responsibility for what they claim?

Employers increasingly have a concern about a person's out of work behavior. Some companies do not allow employees to smoke off the job, test for it, and fire employees who do not comply. Employees who maintain blogs that express views that the company feels may reflect negatively on the employee and the company may be fired. How much say should any employer, including public employers such as public schools, have over an individual's life?

Writing Suggestions

1. Write to your school board arguing either for or against a policy that would suspend any teacher who makes negative comments about students generally or specifically or about the school itself in any medium that becomes public.
2. Write to your school board arguing either for or against a policy that would suspend any student who made very negative and untrue comments about either teachers or other students in any medium that becomes public.
3. More generally, further research this issue, and write an argument for or against the restriction of the private speech of individuals by their employer or by their professional organization.

BYRON YORK

A Carefully Crafted Immigration Law in Arizona

Byron York works as the chief political correspondent for the Washington Examiner. *He also writes for* The Atlantic, The Wall Street Journal, The Weekly Standard, *and other publications. Born in 1958, he received his B.A. from the University of Alabama and his M.A. from the University of Chicago. This selection was taken from the April 26, 2010, edition of the* Washington Examiner.

1   The chattering class is aghast at Arizona's new immigration law. "Harkens back to apartheid," says the Atlanta Journal-Constitution's Cynthia Tucker. "Shameful," says the Washington Post's E. J. Dionne. "Terrible . . . an invitation to abuse," says *The New York Times*' David Brooks.

2   For his part, President Obama calls the law "misguided" and says it "threaten[s] to undermine basic notions of fairness that we cherish as Americans." Obama has ordered the Justice Department to "closely monitor the situation and examine the civil rights and other implications of this legislation."

3   Has anyone actually read the law? Contrary to the talk, it is a reasonable, limited, carefully-crafted measure designed to help law enforcement deal with a

serious problem in Arizona. Its authors anticipated criticism and went to great lengths to make sure it is constitutional and will hold up in court. It is the criticism of the law that is over the top, not the law itself.

4   The law requires police to check with federal authorities on a person's immigration status, if officers have stopped that person for some legitimate reason and come to suspect that he or she might be in the U.S. illegally. The heart of the law is this provision: "For any lawful contact made by a law enforcement official or a law enforcement agency . . . where reasonable suspicion exists that the person is an alien who is unlawfully present in the United States, a reasonable attempt shall be made, when practicable, to determine the immigration status of the person . . ."

5   Critics have focused on the term "reasonable suspicion" to suggest that the law would give police the power to pick anyone out of a crowd for any reason and force them to prove they are in the U.S. legally. Some foresee mass civil rights violations targeting Hispanics.

6   What fewer people have noticed is the phrase "lawful contact," which defines what must be going on before police even think about checking immigration status. "That means the officer is already engaged in some detention of an individual because he's violated some other law," says Kris Kobach, a University of Missouri Kansas City Law School professor who helped draft the measure. "The most likely context where this law would come into play is a traffic stop."

7   As far as "reasonable suspicion" is concerned, there is a great deal of case law dealing with the idea, but in immigration matters, it means a combination of circumstances that, taken together, cause the officer to suspect lawbreaking. It's not race—Arizona's new law specifically says race and ethnicity cannot be the sole factors in determining a reasonable suspicion.

8   For example: "Arizona already has a state law on human smuggling," says Kobach. "An officer stops a group of people in a car that is speeding. The car is overloaded. Nobody had identification. The driver acts evasively. They are on a known smuggling corridor." That is a not uncommon occurrence in Arizona, and any officer would reasonably suspect that the people in the car were illegal. Under the new law, the officer would get in touch with U.S. Immigration and Customs Enforcement to check on their status.

9   But what if the driver of the car had shown the officer his driver's license? The law clearly says that if someone produces a valid Arizona driver's license, or other state-issued identification, they are presumed to be here legally. There's no reasonable suspicion.

10   Is having to produce a driver's license too burdensome? These days, natural-born U.S. citizens, and everybody else, too, are required to show a driver's license to get on an airplane, to check into a hotel, even to purchase some over-the-counter allergy medicines. If it's a burden, it's a burden on everyone.

11   Still, critics worry the law would force some people to carry their papers, just like in an old movie. The fact is, since the 1940s, federal law has required non-citizens in this country to carry, on their person, the documentation proving they are here legally—green card, work visa, etc. That hasn't changed.

12   Kobach, a Republican who is now running for Kansas Secretary of State, was the chief adviser to Attorney General John Ashcroft on immigration issues from 2001 to 2003. He has successfully defended Arizona immigration laws in the past. "The bill was drafted in expectation that the open-borders crowd would almost certainly bring a lawsuit," he says. "It's drafted to withstand judicial scrutiny."

13   The bottom line is, it's a good law, sensibly written and rigorously focused—no matter what the critics say.

Discussion Questions

1. In several places the author attacks the critics of the law. Where do you see him using such an attack? How does that influence his possible readers?
2. What are the author's main arguments in defense of Arizona's immigration law? Are those arguments persuasive?
3. The author does not address the common objection that immigration laws, like Arizona's, will cause the Hispanic community to be less likely to report a crime, serve as witnesses, or assist the police for fear of harassment. Does the author's choice not to support this concern decrease the effectiveness of his argument?
4. What strategy does he use in his conclusion, paragraph 13? Why does he choose this strategy, and is it effective?

Toward Key Insights

Much of current political discussion seems to center around attacking one's opponent, including denigrating comments. What kind of tone and approach to disagreement would you like to participate in and find most useful for fruitful discussions?

What roles does documentation play in our lives? Is it or isn't such an expectation consistent with what you see as American values?

Writing Suggestions

1. Research current political debate in print and on television. Write a paper for or against the current style of political discussion.
2. Research the Arizona and Alabama law and write a paper for your state legislature arguing for or against the adoption of such a law.

CONOR FRIEDERSDORF

Immigration Policy Gone Loco

Conor Friedersdorf grew up in Orange County, California, and attended Pomona College as an undergraduate and New York University as a graduate student in journalism. He writes for The Atlantic *and* The Daily Beast *and blogs at* True/Slant *and* The American Scene. *This article comes from the April 17, 2010, edition of* The Daily Beast.

1   The Arizona legislature has passed a law that makes it a misdemeanor to be in the United States without proper paperwork, and requires local police to determine the immigration status of anyone they reasonably suspect of being here unlawfully.

2   Arizona Governor Jan Brewer, a Republican, is expected to sign the bill, several area news sources report, and GOP legislators are celebrating its passage. "Illegal immigration brings crime, kidnapping, drugs—drains our government services," Rep. John Kavanagh, a Republican, told the Los Angeles Times. "Nobody can stand on the sidelines and not take part in this battle."

3   Arizona must instead find a way to address aspects of its illegal-immigration problem without subjecting a subset of its citizens to de facto ethnicity-based harassment.

4   Elected officials in Arizona are right to worry about illegal immigration. Its costs are disproportionately born by the state's poorest citizens, who also benefit least from the cheaper services provided by immigrant labor. Area schools suffer when an unpredictable number of students with language barriers enroll each semester. And increasingly violent drug cartels in Mexico and a California border heavily fortified against illegal entrants mean that folks along the Grand Canyon State's 389 mile southern border are particularly vulnerable to international lawlessness.

5   It is nevertheless imprudent to fight illegal immigration with laws targeting otherwise law-abiding residents with arrest. The conventional objection is that doing so discourages people in immigrant neighborhoods from working with police: Undocumented residents won't act as witnesses or good Samaritans or report being victimized by crime if calling 911 might well result in their deportation.

6   These are sound objections.

7   As important is the effect this law is bound to have on the 1.5 million-plus Hispanics in Arizona who are American citizens or legal aliens. Put simply, these people are going to be routinely asked by police for proof of citizenship, especially in a state where racial profiling is already a problem. Witness Maricopa County, Arizona, where the odious Sheriff Joe Arapaio presides over a police force sued multiple times for targeting Hispanics, many of them American born—and where police have already been sanctioned by a judge for destroying evidence related to a profiling lawsuit. The Mexican consulate in Phoenix is already reminding its constituents of their rights if they are harassed.

8   My personal preference is for an increase in the number of people legally allowed into the United States, so that more residents in places like Arizona operate within the legal system, an increased law-enforcement presence along parts of the border unprotected by an effective fence, and sanctions against employers who hire undocumented workers. Of course, these are federal prerogatives, and one can sympathize with states like Arizona that suffer disproportionate costs associated with illegal immigration, yet are unable to address its root causes through legislation or voter initiatives.

9   A state law that can only result in the mistreatment of Hispanic Americans is nevertheless an unjustifiable response. Arizona must instead find a way to address aspects of its illegal immigration problem without subjecting a subset of its citizens to de facto ethnicity-based harassment (it is implausible to think that municipal police forces can be trusted with the discretion to do immigration checks in an ethnically mixed region—it's a recipe for misconduct, corruption, and racial tension).

10   The best solution I can think of is a policy of checking the immigration status of everyone convicted of a crime in Arizona. On serving their sentence, citizens would be released into the United States, and non-citizens would be deported.

11   This policy has the benefit of being race neutral in the inconvenience it imposes on those being investigated—every criminal, black, white, Hispanic or Asian, would be checked. Deportations would be automatically targeted at lawbreakers, as opposed to illegal immigrants who merely seek a place where they can work hard to support their families. And asking jailers to determine

immigration status instead of police officers means that the latter could continue interacting with illegal immigrants while fighting criminals, gathering evidence, and policing neighborhoods.

12   Hispanic advocacy organizations may object even to my compromise policy, but they shouldn't: If these illegal immigrant convicts return to their country of origin rather than their ZIP Code of residence, law-abiding illegal immigrants will benefit as much as anyone.

Discussion Questions

1. What is the role of paragraph 4? How does it serve to rhetorically help the author's argument?
2. What is the author's fundamental objection to the law? Is his objection adequately defended or not?
3. What assumption does the author make in paragraph 9? Will his assumption seem reasonable to most audiences or not?
4. In paragraph 10 and 11, he offers a compromise? How reasonable is or isn't his compromise? How does it affect the ethos of his argument?
5. In the conclusion, the author directly addresses Hispanic readers? Why might he have chosen this strategy? How does this affect the credibility of his argument?

Toward Key Insights

To what extent should we or shouldn't we, in a discussion of public issues, concede what may be right in the point of view of those with whom we ultimately disagree?

The law may or may not in the end result in discrimination. To what extent should or shouldn't we risk the possible harm to some civil rights for a greater good?

Suggestions for Writing

1. Do additional research on police conduct and argue for or against the suggestion that the author made that this law will result in abuses.
2. Will the law harm the relationship of the police and the Hispanic community? Research the issue and write a paper either for or against whether or not the law would have this negative consequence.
3. Research the topic and write a paper on whether or not a state should be able to have a law on immigration, which is usually a federal issue.

MARTIN LUTHER KING, JR.

I Have a Dream

Martin Luther King, Jr. (1929–1968) has earned lasting fame for his part in the civil rights struggles of the 1950s and 1960s. Born in Atlanta, Georgia, he was ordained a Baptist minister in his father's church in 1947. A year later, he graduated from Morehouse

College, then went on to take a Bachelor of Divinity degree at Crozier Theological Seminary (1951) and a Ph.D. in philosophy at Boston University (1954), after which he accepted a pastorate in Montgomery, Alabama. King's involvement with civil rights grew when he organized and led a boycott that succeeded in desegregating Montgomery's bus system. In 1957, he founded and became the first president of the Southern Christian Leadership Conference and assumed a leading role in the civil rights movement. King advocated a policy of nonviolent protest based on the beliefs of Thoreau and Gandhi and never veered from it despite many acts of violence directed at him. The success of King's crusade helped bring about the passage of the Civil Rights Act of 1964 and the Voting Rights Act of 1965 and won him the Nobel Peace Prize in 1964. King was assassinated on April 4, 1968, in Memphis. Since then, his birthday, January 15, has been made a national holiday. The speech "I Have a Dream" was delivered August 28, 1963, at the Lincoln Memorial in Washington, D.C., before a crowd of 200,000 people who had gathered to commemorate the centennial of the Emancipation Proclamation and to demonstrate for pending civil rights legislation. It stands as one of the most eloquent pleas ever made for racial justice.

1   I am happy to join with you today in what will go down in history as the greatest demonstration for freedom in the history of our nation.

2   Five score years ago, a great American, in whose symbolic shadow we stand today, signed the Emancipation Proclamation. This momentous decree came as a great beacon light of hope to millions of Negro slaves who had been seared in the flames of withering injustice. It came as a joyous daybreak to end the long night of their captivity.

3   But one hundred years later, the Negro still is not free; one hundred years later, the life of the Negro is still sadly crippled by the manacles of segregation and the chains of discrimination; one hundred years later, the Negro lives on a lonely island of poverty in the midst of a vast ocean of material prosperity; one hundred years later, the Negro is still languishing in the corners of American society and finds himself in exile in his own land.

4   So we've come here today to dramatize a shameful condition. In a sense we've come to our nation's capital to cash a check. When the architects of our republic wrote the magnificent words of the Constitution and the Declaration of Independence, they were signing a promissory note to which every American was to fall heir. This note was the promise that all men, yes, black men as well as white men, would be guaranteed the unalienable rights of life, liberty, and the pursuit of happiness.

5   It is obvious today that America has defaulted on this promissory note in so far as her citizens of color are concerned. Instead of honoring this sacred obligation, America has given the Negro people a bad check; a check which has come back marked "insufficient funds." But we refuse to believe that the bank of justice is bankrupt. We refuse to believe that there are insufficient funds in the great vaults of opportunity of this nation. And so we've come to cash this check, a check that will give us upon demand the riches of freedom and the security of justice.

6   We have also come to this hallowed spot to remind America of the fierce urgency of now. This is no time to engage in the luxury of cooling off or to take the tranquilizing drug of gradualism. Now is the time to make real the promises of democracy; now is the time to rise from the dark and desolate valley of segregation to the sunlit path of racial justice; now is the time to lift our nation from the quicksands of racial injustice to the solid rock of brotherhood; now is the

time to make justice a reality for all of God's children. It would be fatal for the nation to overlook the urgency of the moment. This sweltering summer of the Negro's legitimate discontent will not pass until there is an invigorating autumn of freedom and equality.

7   Nineteen sixty-three is not an end, but a beginning. And those who hope that the Negro needed to blow off steam and will now be content will have a rude awakening if the nation returns to business as usual. There will be neither rest nor tranquility in America until the Negro is granted his citizenship rights. The whirlwinds of revolt will continue to shake the foundations of our nation until the bright day of justice emerges.

8   But there is something that I must say to my people, who stand on the worn threshold which leads into the palace of justice. In the process of gaining our rightful place, we must not be guilty of wrongful deeds. Let us not seek to satisfy our thirst for freedom by drinking from the cup of bitterness and hatred. We must forever conduct our struggle on the high plain of dignity and discipline. We must not allow our creative protests to degenerate into physical violence. Again and again we must rise to the majestic heights of meeting physical force with soul force. The marvelous new militancy, which has engulfed the Negro community, must not lead us to a distrust of all white people. For many of our white brothers, as evidenced by their presence here today, have come to realize that their destiny is tied up with our destiny. And they have come to realize that their freedom is inextricably bound to our freedom. We cannot walk alone. And as we walk, we must make the pledge that we shall always march ahead. We cannot turn back.

9   There are those who are asking the devotees of Civil Rights, "When will you be satisfied?" We can never be satisfied as long as the Negro is the victim of the unspeakable horrors of police brutality; we can never be satisfied as long as our bodies, heavy with the fatigue of travel, cannot gain lodging in the motels of the highways and the hotels of the cities; we cannot be satisfied as long as the Negro's basic mobility is from a smaller ghetto to a larger one; we can never be satisfied as long as our children are stripped of their selfhood and robbed of their dignity by signs stating "For White Only"; we cannot be satisfied as long as the Negro in Mississippi cannot vote and a Negro in New York believes he has nothing for which to vote. No! No, we are not satisfied, and we will not be satisfied until "justice rolls down like waters and righteousness like a mighty stream."

10   I am not unmindful that some of you have come here out of great trials and tribulations. Some of you have come fresh from narrow jail cells. Some of you have come from areas where your quest for freedom left you battered by the storms of persecution and staggered by the winds of police brutality. You have been the veterans of creative suffering. Continue to work with the faith that unearned suffering is redemptive. Go back to Mississippi. Go back to Alabama. Go back to South Carolina. Go back to Georgia. Go back to Louisiana. Go back to the slums and ghettos of our Northern cities, knowing that somehow this situation can and will be changed. Let us not wallow in the valley of despair.

11   I say to you today, my friends, that even though we face the difficulties of today and tomorrow, I still have a dream. It is a dream deeply rooted in the American dream. I have a dream that one day this nation will rise up and live out the true meaning of its creed, "We hold these truths to be self-evident, that all men are created equal." I have a dream that one day on the red hills of Georgia, sons of former slaves and the sons of former slave owners will be able to sit down together at the table of brotherhood. I have a dream that one day even the state of Mississippi, a state sweltering with the heat of injustice, sweltering with the heat

of oppression, will be transformed into an oasis of freedom and justice. I have a dream that my four little children will one day live in a nation where they will not be judged by the color of their skin, but by the content of their character.

12   I HAVE A DREAM TODAY!

13   I have a dream that one day down in Alabama—with its vicious racists, with its Governor having his lips dripping with the words of interposition and nullification—one day right there in Alabama, little black boys and black girls will be able to join hands with little white boys and white girls as sisters and brothers.

14   I HAVE A DREAM TODAY!

15   I have a dream that one day every valley shall be exalted, every hill and mountain shall be made low. The rough places will be plain and the crooked places will be made straight, "and the glory of the Lord shall be revealed, and all flesh shall see it together."

16   This is our hope. This is the faith that I go back to the South with. With this faith we will be able to hew out of the mountain of despair, a stone of hope. With this faith we will be able to transform the jangling discords of our nation into a beautiful symphony of brotherhood. With this faith we will be able to work together, to pray together, to struggle together, to go to jail together, to stand up for freedom together, knowing that we will be free one day. And this will be the day. This will be the day when all of God's children will be able to sing with new meaning, "My country 'tis of thee, sweet land of liberty, of thee I sing. Land where my fathers died, land of the pilgrim's pride, from every mountain side, let freedom ring." And if America is to be a great nation, this must become true.

17   So let freedom ring from the prodigious hilltops of New Hampshire; let freedom ring from the mighty mountains of New York; let freedom ring from the heightening Alleghenies of Pennsylvania; let freedom ring from the snowcapped Rockies of Colorado; let freedom ring from the curvaceous slopes of California. But not only that. Let freedom ring from Stone Mountain of Georgia; let freedom ring from Lookout Mountain of Tennessee; let freedom ring from every hill and mole hill of Mississippi. "From every mountainside, let freedom ring."

18   And when this happens, and when we allow freedom to ring, when we let it ring from every village and every hamlet, from every state and every city, we will be able to speed up that day when all of God's children, black men and white men, Jews and Gentiles, Protestants and Catholics, will be able to join hands and sing in the words of the old Negro spiritual: "Free at last. Free at last. Thank God Almighty, we are free at last."

Discussion Questions

1. Why do you think King begins with a reference to Lincoln?
2. Does this speech have a stated or an implied proposition? What is the proposition?
3. What does King hope to accomplish by the speech? How does he go about achieving his aim(s)?
4. What is the audience for the speech?
5. How does King organize his speech? How does this organization advance his purpose?
6. Which type(s) of argumentative appeal does King use? Cite appropriate parts of the speech.
7. What kinds of stylistic devices does King use? Where do they occur? How do they increase the effectiveness of the speech?

Toward Key Insights

To what extent do people of all races relate to King's message today? Explain your answer.

Suggestion for Writing

Write an essay calling for some major social or political change. For example, you might recommend that the country enact national health insurance, institute a peacetime draft, ban smoking in all public places, amend the Constitution to ban or legalize abortions, establish federally funded day-care centers for working parents, or offer all workers a 30-day leave of absence without pay.

MIXING THE WRITING STRATEGIES

Reading Strategies

1. When skimming, identify the main point the author is attempting to make.
2. To orient your reading, note in the margins the strategy the reader is using.
3. Focus on how the points fit together to develop the author's thesis.

Reading Critically

1. Test whether the claims throughout the text really support the thesis.
2. Evaluate the claims based on the critical reading strategy appropriate to the technique being used.
3. Judge whether the writer's strategies are appropriate to the point he or she is making.

Reading As a Writer

1. Identify how the writer effectively changes from strategy to strategy.
2. Look to determine how the writer connects each strategy to the main thesis.
3. Read the conclusion carefully to determine how the writer pulls a complex essay back together to make his or her main point.

Most essays mix various writing strategies for assorted purposes. This section features three examples. The discussion questions following the essays direct your attention to the strategies these writers use as well as other relevant aspects of the essays.

MICHAEL POLLAN

Supermarket Pastoral

Michael Pollan received an M.A. in English from Columbia University. He has been a contributing writer to The New York Times Magazine *since 1987. His writing has won a number of awards, including the Global Award for Environmental Journalism. He has published many articles and several books. This selection is from his 2006 book* The Omnivore's Dilemma: A Natural History of Four Meals *published by Penguin Press.*

1   I enjoy shopping at Whole Foods nearly as much as I enjoy browsing a good bookstore, which, come to think of it, is probably no accident. Shopping at Whole Foods is a literary experience, too. That's not to take anything away from the food, which is generally of high quality, much of it "certified organic" or "humanely raised" or "free range." But right there, that's the point. It's the evocative prose as much as anything else that makes this food really special, elevating an egg or chicken breast or a bag of arugula from the realm of ordinary protein and carbohydrates into a much headier experience, one with complex aesthetic, emotional, and even political dimensions. Take the "range-fed" sirloin steak I recently eyed in the meat case. According to the brochure on the counter, it was formerly part of a steer that spent its days "living in beautiful places" ranging from "plant-diverse, high-mountain meadows to thick aspen groves and miles of sagebrush-filled flats." Now a steak like that has got to taste better than one from Safeway, where the only accompanying information comes in the form of a number: the price I mean, which you can bet will be considerably less. But I'm evidently not the only shopper willing to pay more for a good story.

2   With the growth of organics and mounting concerns about the wholesomeness of industrial food, storied food is showing up in supermarkets everywhere these days, but it is Whole Foods that consistently offers the most cutting-edge grocery lit. On a recent visit I filled my shopping cart with eggs "from cage-free vegetarian hens," milk from cows that live "free from unnecessary fear and distress," wild salmon caught by Native Americans in Yakutat, Alaska (population 833), and heirloom tomatoes from Capay Farm ($4.99 a pound), "one of the early pioneers of the organic movement." The organic broiler I picked up even had a name: Rosie, who turned out to be a "sustainably farmed" "free-range chicken" from Petaluma Poultry, a company whose "farming methods strive to create harmonious relationships in nature, sustaining the health of all creatures and the natural world." Okay, not the most mellifluous or even meaningful sentence, but at least their heart's in the right place.

3   In several corners of the store I was actually forced to choose between subtly competing stories. For example, some of the organic milk in the milk case was "ultrapasteurized," an extra processing step that was presented as a boon to the consumer, since it extends shelf life. But then another, more local dairy boasted about the fact they had said no to ultrapasteurization, implying that their product was fresher, less processed, and therefore more organic. This was the dairy that talked about cows living free from distress, something I was beginning to feel a bit of myself by this point.

4   This particular dairy's label had a lot to say about the bovine lifestyle: Its Holsteins are provided with "an appropriate environment, including shelter and a comfortable resting area, . . . sufficient space, proper facilities and the company of their own kind." All this sounded pretty great, until I read the story of another dairy selling raw milk—completely unprocessed—whose "cows graze green pastures all year long." Which made me wonder whether the first dairy's idea of an appropriate environment for a cow included, as I had simply presumed, a pasture. All of a sudden the absence from their story of that word seemed weirdly conspicuous. As the literary critics would say, the writer seemed to be eliding the whole notion of cows and grass. Indeed, the longer I shopped

Marginal annotations:

Narrative to establish context

Illustration of claim

Comparison

Illustration

Illustration

Effect

Illustration

"Eliding" is a
literary critic's term
for cutting out or
avoiding a word

Cause

Comparison

Illustration

Effect

Comparison

Illustration

Effect

Cause

Effect

Definition

Cause

Cause

Definition

5

in Whole Foods, the more I thought that this is a place where the skills of a literary critic might come in handy—those, and perhaps also a journalist's.

Wordy labels, point-of-purchase brochures, and certification schemes are supposed to make an obscure and complicated food chain more legible to the consumer. In the industrial food economy, virtually the only information that travels along the food chain linking producer and consumer is price. Just look at the typical newspaper ad for a supermarket. The sole quality on display here is actually a quantity: tomatoes $0.69 a pound; ground chuck $1.09 a pound; eggs $0.99 a dozen—special this week. Is there any other category of product sold on such a reductive basis? The bare-bones information travels in both directions, of course, and farmers who get the message that consumers care only about price will themselves care only about yield. This is how a cheap food economy reinforces itself.

6

One of the key innovations of organic food was to allow some more information to pass along the food chain between the producer and the consumer—an implicit snatch of narrative along with the number. A certified organic label tells a little story about how a particular food was produced, giving the consumer a way to send a message back to the farmer that she values tomatoes produced without harmful pesticides or prefers to feed her children milk from cows that haven't been injected with growth hormones. The word "organic" has proved to be one of the most powerful words in the supermarket: Without any help from government, farmers and consumers working together in this way have built an $11 billion industry that is now the fastest growing sector of the food economy.

7

Yet the organic label itself—like every other such label in the supermarket—is really just an imperfect substitute for direct observation of how a food is produced, a concession to the reality that most people in an industrial society haven't the time or the inclination to follow their food back to the farm, a farm which today is apt to be, on average, fifteen hundred miles away. So to bridge that space we rely on certifiers and label writers and, to a considerable extent, our imagination of what the farms that are producing our food really look like. The organic label may conjure an image of simpler agriculture, but its very existence is an industrial artifact. The question is, what about the farms themselves? How well do they match the stories told about them?

8

Taken as a whole, the story on offer in Whole Foods is a pastoral narrative in which farm animals live much as they did in the books we read as children, and our fruits and vegetables grow in well-composted soils on small farms much like Joel Salatin's. "Organic" on the label conjures up a rich narrative, even if it is the consumer who fills in most of the details, supplying the hero (American Family Farmer), the villain (Agribusinessman), and the literary genre, which I've come to think of as Supermarket Pastoral. By now we may know better than to believe this too simple story, but not much better, and the grocery store poets do everything they can to encourage us in our willing suspension of disbelief.

9

Supermarket Pastoral is a most seductive literary form, beguiling enough to survive in the face of a great many discomfiting facts. I suspect that's because it gratifies some of our deepest, oldest longings, not merely for safe food, but for a connection to the earth and to the handful of domesticated creatures we've long depended on. Whole Foods understands all this better than we do. One of the company's marketing consultants explained to me that the Whole Foods shopper feels that by buying organic he is "engaging in authentic experiences" and imaginatively enacting a "return to a utopian past with the positive aspects of modernity intact." This sounds a lot like Virgilian pastoral, which also tried to have it both ways. In *The Machine in the Garden* Leo Marx writes that Virgil's shepherd Tityrus, no primitive, "Enjoys the best of both worlds—the sophisticated order of art and the simple spontaneity of nature." In keeping with the pastoral tradition, Whole Foods offers what Marx terms "a landscape of reconciliation" between the realms of nature and culture, a place where, as the marketing consultant put it, "people will come together through organic foods to get back to the origin of things"—perhaps by sitting down to enjoy one of the microwaveable organic TV dinners (four words I never expected to see conjoined) stacked in the frozen food case. How's that for having it both ways?

Illustration

10   Of course the trickiest contradiction Whole Foods attempts to reconcile is the one between the industrialization of the organic food industry of which it is a part and the pastoral ideals on which that industry has been built. The organic movement, as it was once called, has come a remarkably long way in the last thirty years, to the point where it now looks considerably less like a movement than a big business. Lining the walls above the sumptuously stocked produce section in my Whole Foods are full-color photographs of local organic farmers accompanied by text blocks setting forth their farming philosophies. A handful of these farms—Capay is one example—still sell their produce to Whole Foods, but most are long gone from the produce bins, if not yet the walls. That's because Whole Foods in recent years has adopted the grocery industry's standard regional distribution system, which makes supporting small farms impractical. Tremendous warehouses buy produce for dozens of stores at a time, which forces them to deal exclusively with tremendous farms. So while the posters still depict family farmers and their philosophers, the produce on sale below them come primarily from the two big corporate organic growers in California, Earthbound Farm and Grimmway Farms, which together dominate the market for organic fresh produce in America. (Earthbound alone grows 80% of the organic lettuce sold in America.)

Effect

Description

Effect

Cause

11   As I tossed a plastic box of Earthbound prewashed spring mix salad into my Whole Foods cart, I realized that I was venturing deep into the belly of the industrial beast Joel Salatin had called "the organic empire." (Speaking of my salad mix, another small, beyond organic farmer, a friend of Joel's, had told me he "wouldn't use the stuff to make compost"—the organic purist's stock insult.) But I'm not prepared to accept the premise that industrial organic is necessarily a bad thing, not if the goal is to reform a half-trillion-dollar food system based on chain supermarkets and the consumer's expectations that food be convenient and cheap.

Comparison

Narrative

Argument-Reason

12   And yet to the extent that the organic movement was conceived as a critique of industrial values, surely there comes a point when the process of industrialization will cost organic its soul (to use a word still uttered by organic types without irony), when Supermarket Pastoral becomes more fiction than fact: another lie told by marketers.

Argument-Reason

13   The question is, has that point been reached, as Joel Salatin suggests? Just how well does Supermarket Pastoral hold up under close reading and journalistic scrutiny?

Discussion Questions

1. This section of a book uses several strategies. What strategy is dominant? How does this strategy match the main point of this essay?
2. What is the effect of the author starting and returning to a narrative of his own shopping trip at Whole Foods?

3. In several places the author specifically talks about words and phrases. What are some of the words and phrases the writer discusses? Why is it important for him to talk about this language usage?

4. In paragraph 4 the author deliberately uses a sentence fragment. Is this use of a fragment effective? Why or why not?

5. This section ends in paragraph 13 with questions. Of course, the author goes on to answer these questions in the material that follows this selection. Out of context, is this conclusion effective? What do you think based on the earlier content of this text will be the answer to his questions? What evidence leads you to that conclusion?

Toward Key Insights

A large number of essays and a fair amount of college classes spend time discussing the language people use. Based on this essay, why is this discussion of language important?

In this text, the author discusses the importance of using the skills of the literary critic. Why does he think such skills are important to understanding a supermarket? Where else might the skills of the literary critic be useful?

This essay lays out the Supermarket Pastoral as one narrative used to sell food. What other narratives can you identify that are used to sell products?

Suggestions for Writing

Visit a supermarket, a toy store, a car dealership or observe several advertisements, then write an essay explaining the narrative used to sell the products.

Identify an area of life where the talk about the experience and the experience don't match and write a paper that compares the language and the reality, offering an explanation for the language and an account of the effect that the language has on those who hear or read it.

JOHN PHILLIP SANTOS

Back to the Future

John Phillips Santos was born and raised in San Antonio, Texas. He received a B.A. from the University of Notre Dame and an M.A. in English from St. Catherine's College at Oxford. He was the first Mexican-American Rhodes Scholar. He has written articles for The Los Angeles Times, The New York Times, *and* The San Antonio Express-News. *He is also author of* Places Left Unfinished at the Time of Creation. *This article appeared in the* Texas Monthly, *November of 2010.*

1   Dawn near San Agustin Plaza, in downtown Laredo, my mother's birthplace, and the sun is beginning to singe the tips of the lanky cane along the Rio Grande. Already, an unshaded queue of Mexicanos, crossing over for day work or shopping, stretches well beyond the span of International Bridge #1, the city's oldest, also known as the Gateway to the Americas. And these are just the folks with visas. Uncounted others will have crossed the river surreptitiously under the

protective cover of night. Still others could be waiting to cross, arduously hidden away under false truck beds or packed like cargo into crates, hoping luck is with their coyotes as they warily approach the checkpoint. Who knows?

2   Anything involving Mexico is bound to lead to mystery eventually, so it's not surprising that the question of the border and immigration is no exception. But the mystery here doesn't so much involve the border as it does the story of migration itself. The deep subconscious of Mexican culture is full of mythic stories of ancestral migrations, captured in the ubiquitous images of footstep trails that appear in many of the earliest codices that have been preserved. The most important of these myths is the ancient story of the pilgrimage of the tribes who would become the Aztecs. Exhorted by their god Huitzilopochtli to leave their homeland of Aztlán in search of a new home, they uprooted and wandered for years before encountering the promised sign, an eagle standing on a cactus, devouring a serpent. There they founded Tenochtitlén, which later became Mexico City. Since then, it seems that every generation of Mexicanos, indigenous and mestizo, has been searching for a new homeland of great blessings, even if it should require a long journey to find it. It's an Exodus like theme that you can trace from the oldest pictographic records of the indigenous world to the modern accounts of the undocumented people captured by the Border Patrol.

3   An hour passes, and the line barely moves, as the heat of the sun grows more unforgiving, minute by minute. I watch this scene from the balcony of an air-conditioned room in the Hotel La Posada, thinking how every one of those bobbing heads I see could be me. As with many other native Texans, immigration across this increasingly fractious border is a family legacy for me, and a personal issue. My mother's ancestors first came to the northern hinterlands of Nueva España that would eventually become north Mexico and South Texas sometime in the early 1600's, and later they were among the families who founded a constellation of villages along the river, including Laredo, in 1755. The U.S. Mexico border appeared well into their saga, like a haunting wraith of separation laid across lands already long settled by people of an emerging nation.

4   As an inheritor of this legacy, I can't count the times I've crossed the border—back and forth from Eagle Pass into Coahuila, from Laredo into Nuevo Laredo, from McAllen into Reynosa, from Brownsville to Matamoros, from Presidio to Ojinaga. On my father's side, my great-uncle Francisco Garcia crossed out of Coahuila at Piedras Negras, fleeing the turmoil of the revolution, sometime around 1914. He later recalled it as a quiet passing across a steel bridge that cost him a nickel, with no customs or border officers asking for papers. Now traffic is perpetually stalled at the bridges as agents scrutinize papers. Innumerable Border Patrol SUVs crisscross the high ways and back roads of the region, often as helicopters hover overhead. Drones patrol the skies, seeking crossers who've avoided the patchwork cordons of agents, walls, and fences. Soon, we are promised, National Guard troops will arrive to establish forward operating bases to surveil the land, just as in Afghanistan.

5   Today's border is a landscape of ghosts, a geography populated with a host of specters from a long, fraught history, all the upheavals of the past five hundred years in our Texan patch of the New World. For decades, immigration policy has found it hard enough trying to close the border to the living. But it is truly powerless to detain the ghosts of the past. They continue to pass freely, some heading north, some heading south. No policing stratagem will ever capture them, nor can we ever fully know the magnetic force they exert upon us.

6 But what difference might it make if our immigration policy were shaped in full recognition of our complex past? The current debate has emerged from an extremely narrow spectrum of historical awareness. In a recent radio interview, Homeland Security Secretary and former Arizona governor Janet Napolitano observed that "the border is a big and complicated place." By contrast, in the current tumult over immigration, the matter is often presented in the media as a simple choice between law and anarchy, between protecting American values and identity and abandoning them to a wave of immigrants from the south. Fueled by a spiraling whorl of fear and mistrust, the debate has reached the point that many hot-button issues come to, where they detach from reality and history and begin to create a new, self-justifying mythology.

7 I had come to the balcony at La Posada in Laredo to try and reattach to reality. In late summer, as the radios and televisions buzzed with discussions of racial profiling and birthright citizenship and amnesty, I set out from my home in San Antonio on a journey through South Texas, where the ghosts of history are as much a presence as the visions of the future. I went in search of those ghosts and in search of the living too, those who are telling another sort of story about migration that makes a full reckoning of the deep history of our contested, shared borderlands.

8 My first stop was the Kenedy Ranch Museum of South Texas, in Sarita, twenty miles south of Kingsville down U.S. 77. Encompassing 400,000 acres of former Spanish and Mexican land grant territories, the ranch has a uniquely South Texas mestizo legacy that began in the middle of the nineteenth century, when the founder, Mifflin Kenedy, an immigrant from Pennsylvania, married Petra Vela de Vidal, the daughter of one of the oldest Tejano families from that region. Along with the King Ranch, it's among the most legendary spreads of South Texas. But it's also home to one of my favorite museums. Installed in the Spanish Revival-style building in Sarita that once housed the ranch's business office, the Kenedy Ranch Museum's rooms are filled with artifacts and decked with bright historical murals, accompanied by a rigorous audio tour depicting the good, bad, and ugly of the past four centuries.

9 The director of this little-known gem of South Texas historical lore is border polymath Homero S. Vera. I first sought him out when I started inquiring into my family's place in the history of Nuevo Santander, the region of New Spain that included much of the Rio Grande Valley and the northern Mexican state of Tamaulipas. Formerly these lands were known only as las tierras bárbaras de los infieles, "the barbarous lands of the infidels."

10 Homero was raised on a ranch in Duval County in the 1950's, but it might as well have been the 1850's. Spanish was the family language. The Veras' rattlesnake-country rancho was the focus of family life. He hunted and trapped with uncles. The family made monthly trips into town for groceries and provisions. A committed ranchero by age five, Homero hated moving into Premont when his dad got a job as a mechanic in town.

11 Growing up this way gave Homero a powerful desire to help bring the early history of the region to a larger public. But his first chance didn't come until he was 44 years old, in 1997. After being laid off from a longtime job in a nearby Celanese chemical plant, he used his severance benefits to launch a monthly newsletter of South Texas history called El Mesteño, or "the Mustang," a reference to the wild horses that once roamed the coastal plains. During the seven years of its run, El Mesteño developed a loyal following, myself included. For anyone interested in the history of this region, it was a treasure

trove. A typical issue might include features on the history of specific Hispano surnames of the region; analyses of founders' lives and early architectural styles; accounts of tequila-running routes to San Diego during the Prohibition era; recipes using local plants and herbs; traditional dichos, or "sayings," in the Valley; perhaps even aprofile of a visiting conjunto band—from Japan. The piquant rigor of these historical briefs quickly earned him the respect of such eminent Tejano historians as Andres Tijerina, Emilio Zamora, and Frank de la Teja and boosted circulation as high as two thousand before the journal quit publishing, in 2004.

12   I met Homero in his office at the museum. He was dressed in the denim shirt, jeans, and dusty work boots of avaquero. A sofa was piled high with children's drawings of American Indian symbols from a recent school field trip. The walls were hung with a framed satellite photograph of the vast Kenedy Ranch and photos of local wildlife, including one of a white-throated caracara, a bird often called the Mexican eagle. Homero is a born corrector, and this photo occasioned his first correction of the afternoon.

13   "They say the caracara was actually the bird the Aztecs saw consuming the serpent over the cactus in the Valley of Mexico," he told me. "Somehow way back there, somebody switched the golden eagle in its place."

14   Homero is tall, husky, white-haired, fair-skinned, and hazel-eyed. He speaks quietly in a classic Valley manner, a gentle Texas drawl that still carries the hint of a Spanish accent. Explaining El Mesteño, he said, "I wanted to tell the story as it is, tell the facts as they are, so I began to focus on the stories of the ranches from the original Spanish land grants, beginning with the first surveys of the lands that were later settled, from Laredo to Corpus Christi. In schools, we were taught about the Mayflower and the pilgrims, but we were never taught about that."

15   The short version comes down to this, as Homero explained: The lands we now know as South Texas have always been a crossroads of undocumented immigrants, beginning with the indigenous peoples, then settlers from Spain, England and Ireland, Mexico and the United States, among many others. The museum's murals, painted in 2002 by Mexican-born Houston artist Daniel Lechón, reveal the story of how the intertwining destinies of all those nations played out in the hard-scrabble Rio Grande Valley.

16   We left the office and bumped down a long ranch road, through pastures where oaks mingled with sotol plants, to the house on the La Parra division, where Homero lives with his Mexican-born wife, Leticia, a schoolteacher. In the sitting room, with a ceiling fan keeping time and a repast of nilgai jerky and frosty Dos Equis before us, Homero reflected on the profound transformations in his beloved borderlands.

17   "The last five, ten years, the border has changed a lot, for the worse," he said. "And I don't know if it's going to get any better." He described how the experience of undocumented immigration has changed in his lifetime, from its origins in agricultural labor on the ranches of the region to an interval in the more and more complicated labor flows of globalization.

18   "The migration of the indocumentados is a business now," he said. "When I was growing up, they would come on their own, mostly rural people who would work on the ranches, gather one thousand dollars, two thousand dollars, and then it was 'Nos vemos el otro año' ['See you next year']. It's very rare now to see one individual by himself; it's always a pack of people in the back of a truck or in the brush, a group of people led by a coyote, heading for North Carolina, Chicago, Houston."

19   He paused, his face suddenly looking resigned and wary. "Of course, we need some kind of legislation to allow these people to come here legally and live here and work here, but I don't know if that's gonna stop the violence, the trafficking. We need to eliminate the coyote, because the majority want to come and work the correct way." He grew quiet, with a worried look. "The drugs are a different story." He told me how his wife had recently seen suspicious-looking black-uniformed individuals somewhere on the road between Riviera and Falfurrias, possibly narcos. The surging war among rival Mexican drug cartels just across the Rio Grande has introduced yet another confounding factor into the long history of migration in the borderlands. Homero never addressed this in El Mesteño, and he now wonders whether it isn't time to start up the journal again, to inform this new and disturbing chapter.

20   Night fell and we stepped out into the warm Sarita air. The sky was so limpid that the Milky Way glimmered like a band of pearly embers stretched across the sky. A shooting star tracked a path over us, an augur always regarded in my family as a greeting from the ancestors.

21   The next morning I set out for Laredo. All along the highways and farm-to-market roads—through Raymondville, La Gloria, Rio Grande City, and San Ygnacio—there were signs of the old agricultural way of life, verdant fields crowded with tall sugarcane stalks, others strewn with cantaloupes discarded during harvest. Abundant rain had left the land green, and flowers bloomed in every direction. Near Zapata, in the aftermath of the early-July flooding, the Rio Grande looked like a broad and tranquil inland sea.

22   But it was impossible to overlook the changes. I lost count of the number of Border Patrol SUVs I saw along those byways. Searching in San Isidro for the ruins of a Spanish stone noria, a well and aqueduct system, I drove through town and at one intersection saw a man on his knees, his hands cuffed behind his back, his head bowed, while two Border Patrol officers appeared to be finalizing papers for his detention.

23   The noria was Homero's idea. The previous night, before we turned in, we'd spent a few hours looking at artifacts from his private collection. First, a faded tricolor flag, dating from the 1820's, the era of a newly independent Mexican Republic. The insignia showed a Mexican eagle (not a golden eagle) with outstretched wings in the middle, clutching a snake in its beak, only this eagle also wore an imperial crown. The lettering read "Pva. De Texas, San Antonio de Bexar, Primera Brigada de Lanceros a Caballo." Next, a heraldic banner from an earlier era-red crossed staffs sewed onto a beige silk background, with an ornate rosy brocade border all around. Homero guessed it had probably hung from a standard carried in the vanguard of some eighteenth-century colonial regiment in Nueva España. Finally, he showed me several still-older documents. I looked closely at one, a printed mandate from the king of Spain issued on "24 de Junio, 1757" as an edict on the authority of Viceroy El Marques de las Amarillas, ordering the immediate and preemptive expulsion of all foreigners from the dominions of Nueva Espana, a hoary reminder of just how long the issue of illegal immigration has haunted these lands.

24   After this plunge into the continuum of deep South Texas time, I'd wondered aloud where it was still possible to see physical evidence of the Spanish colonial settlement in the borderlands. Farther north, in San Antonio, the missions have been restored and some have even been designated national park sites. But in South Texas, monuments from the past are harder to spot, hidden down dirt roads in small, forgotten towns. Homero had sent me to go looking for the noria.

25   I poked around San Isidro, trying to follow his directions, thinking about the past. Much of the current ardor over the border appears to assume that it has always existed. But rather than a divinely inscribed geographic demarcation that descended from the heavens all at once, the current border evolved slowly after its creation in the Treaty of Guadalupe Hidalgo, following the U.S.-Mexican War, in 1848. First came a series of binational commissions made up of American and Mexican surveyors, astronomers, engineers, and cartographers, who didn't complete their work until 1857. Slowly the sometimes straight, sometimes crooked line of the border emerged out of these expeditions and negotiations, based partly on geodetic surveys, partly on stargazing, and partly on the dodgy cartographic testimony of a palimpsest of maps, which were often at odds with one another.

26   More than a century and a half later, the boundary still stands. In a time when the borders of "Old Europe" are being erased, the line along the Rio Grande has proved to be among the world's more stalwart partitions, taking its place on a recent BBC Mundo list of "Los muros que no han caído" ("The walls that have not fallen"). It's a doleful roll call, including Cyprus, Uzbekistan-Kyrgyzstan, the two Koreas, Botswana-Zimbabwe, and Israel-Palestine, among several others. By comparison with these, the Berlin Wall was an amateur act, a tenuous attempt to bifurcate a kindred nation on ideological terms. Last November I followed the celebrations for the twentieth anniversary of the fall of the Berlin Wall, and I wondered how Americans could feel such an upwelling of compassion for the reunification of a distant land without pausing to think about the wall being erected on their own southern border.

27   National security is a real concern, but in this history there's no denying the underlying cultural dynamic, with its generally unspoken assumptions about Texan and American identity. For instance, with Mexican Americans and other Latinos constituting 38 percent of all Texans, how much different would the reaction have been to the governor's openly talking about secession if his name were not Rick Perry but Ricardo Perez?

28   Things weren't always this way. After its official mapping was completed, the Texas-Mexico border remained porous, just as my Uncle Francisco found it, crossing from Piedras Negras to Eagle Pass in 1914, and indeed, the Border Patrol, created in 1915, didn't become a serious enforcement service until the Prohibition era. Moreover, tightened border security in response to undocumented immigration began in earnest only in the eighties. So, while rooted in a distant past that someone like Homero Verahas illuminated, immigration policy is really an issue of our times, our era of globalization.

29   Finally, after a long hunt, I found the noria. But the wide, deep well with a series of stone canals radiating out from the center had been left to go to seed. The sandstone and mortar construction was breaking down, and tires, old televisions, and other trash were piled up at the bottom of the stone cistern. This noble structure was being used as a dump.

30   Later that afternoon I arrived in Laredo and went straight to another museum. Nestled in the historic center, on the south side of San Agustin Plaza, the Museum of the Republic of the Rio Grande stands as yet another reminder of the complex history of the border region. In 1840, after the Texas Revolution, with borders still in dispute and disgruntled north Mexicans rejecting the centralist government in Mexico City, an insurgent movement led by General Antonio Canales created a new, independent republic encompassing north Mexico, present-day New Mexico, and the lands south of the Nueces River. The ill-starred

Republic of the Rio Grande lasted only 293 days before it was brutally suppressed by the Mexican army, but the movement that sparked it smoldered for decades, inspiring periodic uprisings for independence in the Mexicano community of South Texas into the early twentieth century.

31   Housed in a sun-bleached sandstone hacienda that was the headquarters of the short-lived republic, the museum commemorates that period in a series of rooms arranged with historic home furnishings and vitrines exhibiting weaponry, everyday objects, and documents from the movement. Standing before an array of maps that capture all the shifting borders of those times, Rick Villa-real, the former director of the museum, bemoaned how the story has been excluded from American history textbooks, dismissed as a Mexican intrigue. He quickly rehearsed the history of the movement and its links to the U.S.-Mexican War that soon followed, a war that, he noted, remains meaningful for Mexicanos.

32   "Mexican citizens always seem to have this idea that these lands were stolen by the United States," he said. "So they should have the right to come over, especially in the Southwest. They feel these lands were originally a part of Mexico, so 'Why should we recognize these Johnny-come-lately borders?' It all stems from that war, the U.S.-Mexican War. We're still feeling the repercussions."

33   If that sounds like 162-year-old sour grapes, consider that even Ulysses S. Grant, a veteran of the U.S.-Mexican War, recognized its injustice. The eighteenth president mused in his memoirs that the American Civil War, which erupted two decades later, could be seen as divine retribution for America's role in the war with Mexico. Grant wrote, "Nations, like individuals, are punished for their transgressions. We got our punishment in the most sanguinary and expensive war of modern times."

34   I thought about Grant's theory as I wandered around Laredo the next day. Are nations punished for their transgressions? How should we understand the current sanguinary episode unfolding across the river, the war among Mexican drug cartels vying for territory in the northern states? The day I arrived, there was a shoot-out in a barrio of Nuevo Laredo, with eight reported killed. But any such news is difficult to confirm. With newspaper and television journalists in Mexico unwilling to risk reporting such events, word spreads virally through Facebook, Twitter, and old-fashioned word of mouth. In the long saga of border conflicts affecting the experience of immigration, this one may be the gravest ever, the latest vexation laid over a tragedy, rooted in an enigma.

35   "I think the word is 'incertidumbre,' right?" asked Maria Eugenia Guerra, an old friend and the founder and publisher of LareDos, an independent monthly news journal. I'd stopped into her busy downtown offices to hear the latest. "The uncertainty of it—we're in that." Guerra's ancestors (some of whom are mine as well) date back to the early 1600's in New Spain, and her family continues to own land in and near San Ygnacio, from the original porciones, as the Spanish land grants from the 1700's are widely known throughout South Texas. But for Guerra, along with so many other Laredoans, the widening impact of the narco war has changed everything.

36   "How will we end the violence?" she asked me. "We're so far away from what's really going to happen, and that's unknown to us, of course, but it has all the markings of a horrible era to come." She told me she had been considering something previously unimaginable—leaving Laredo, continuing the migration her ancestors began three hundred years ago.

37   "After centuries, I think—and I've never, ever thought this—but maybe my family should move north," she said. "Maybe this is the next northern migration."

38   Nearing twilight in Laredo, I returned to the museum for a few more snap-shots. A small group of men were bringing in a load of crates, aluminum cases, and electrical cables, setting up light stands and arrays of what appeared to be scopes of some sort. I thought they were engineers or contractors working on a restoration project in the old building, but they turned out to be the seven members of the Laredo Paranormal Research Society (formerly, and more fore-bodingly, known as the Paranormal Entity Research Investigation League, or P.E.R.I.L.), a cohort of ghost hunters, all of them law enforcement professionals by day. In other sites around Laredo, the society's hunters have caught "energy anomalies" in photographs of abandoned buildings, fleeting glimpses of a face in the dark doorway of an old hospital, and faint voices in cemeteries speaking English and Spanish.

39   They told me that there have been numerous reports of anomalous phe-nomena in the historic hacienda museum building. Mysterious orbs appear in tourist photographs, audio tour narrations spontaneously begin playing, and, spookiest of all, a crib made of heavy pecan wood was discovered rocking on its own. The night I found them, the investigators were setting up for a 72-hour surveillance, hoping to capture one of the local spirits in an infrared camera or a digital audio recording. I asked if they could discern the immigration status of their etheric quarry—and they replied only with skeptical looks.

40   I'm serious, I told them. We have this in common: We're all looking for ghosts.

Discussion Questions

   1. The writer approaches much of this work as a narrative about his own personal investigation. How did this approach affect the impact of the essay?
   2. What are the strategies the writer uses? How do those different strategies help the writer make his point?
   3. In paragraph 26 the writer compares the Mexican/American border to the fall of the Berlin wall. Why does he make this comparison? Is it effective rhetorically?
   4. Throughout, the author compares the historical border with the current bor-der? What are some of the comparisons the writer makes? What point does he seem to be making? Does he do so effectively?
   5. In the conclusion, paragraph 40, he talks about "looking for ghosts." What ghosts was he looking for in the essay? What does he see as the importance of hunting ghosts?

Toward Key Insights

Often we discuss issues such as immigration without an understanding of history or how different parties to the discussion may see the situation. It can be use-ful when addressing an issue to step back and identify how the issues devel-oped and changed. How does knowing the history change the perspective on issues?

Often it can be rhetorically advantageous to use a narrative to involve the reader in a narrative of exploration where you share your own search for understanding. What are issues that might benefit from this approach?

Writing Suggestions

1. Explore your own encounter with the history of boundaries that are important to you, whether religious boundaries, economic boundaries, language boundaries, social boundaries, or geographic boundaries.

2. Visit a museum or historical site and write a mixed strategy paper that explores how this visit changes or confirms your expectations.

3. Do the research on the history of an issue that you find contentious and then write a history of the issue as an exploration that helps us understand how we got to our current conflict.

Somini Sengupta

Rushdie Runs Afoul of Web's Real-Name Police

Somini Sengupta was born in Calcutta, India, and raised in California, graduating from the University of California at Berkeley with a major in English and Development Studies. She works as a writer for The New York Times, *where she also served as the Times Bureau Chief in New Delhi from 2005–2009. She won the George Polk award for international reporting in 2004. This article appeared in the November 14, 2011, online edition of* The New York Times.

1   The writer Salman Rushdie hit Twitter on Monday morning with a flurry of exasperated posts. Facebook, he wrote, had deactivated his account, demanded proof of identity and then turned him into Ahmed Rushdie, which is how he is identified on his passport. He had never used his first name, Ahmed, he pointed out; the world knows him as Salman. Would Facebook, he scoffed, have turned J. Edgar Hoover into John Hoover?

2   "Where are you hiding, Mark?" he demanded of Mark Zuckerberg, Facebook's chief executive, in one post. "Come out here and give me back my name!"

3   The Twitterverse took up his cause. Within two hours, Mr. Rushdie gleefully declared victory: "Facebook has buckled! I'm Salman Rushdie again. I feel SO much better. An identity crisis at my age is no fun."

4   Mr. Rushdie's predicament points to one of the trickiest notions about life in the digital age: Are you who you say you are online? Whose business is it—and why?

5   As the Internet becomes the place for all kinds of transactions, from buying shoes to overthrowing despots, an increasingly vital debate is emerging over how people represent and reveal themselves on the Web sites they visit. One side envisions a system in which you use a sort of digital passport, bearing your real name and issued by a company like Facebook, to travel across the Internet. Another side believes in the right to don different hats—and sometimes masks—so you can consume and express what you want, without fear of offline repercussions.

6   The argument over pseudonyms—known online as the "nym wars"—goes to the heart of how the Internet might be organized in the future. Major Internet companies like Google, Facebook and Twitter have a valuable stake in this debate—and, in some cases, vastly different corporate philosophies on the issue that signal their own ambitions.

7   Facebook insists on what it calls authentic identity, or real names. And it is becoming a de facto passport vendor of sorts, allowing its users to sign into seven million other sites and applications with their Facebook user names and passwords.

        Google's social network, Google+, which opened up to all comers in September, likewise wants the real names its users are known by offline, and it has frozen the accounts of some perceived offenders.

8   But Google has indicated more recently that it will eventually allow some use of aliases. Vic Gundotra, the Google executive responsible for the social network, said at a conference last month that he wanted to make sure its "atmosphere" remained comfortable even with people using fake names. "It's complicated to get this right," he said.

9   Twitter, by sharp contrast, follows a laissez-faire approach, allowing the use of pseudonyms by WikiLeaks supporters and a prankster using the name @FakeSarahPalin, among many others. It does consider deceitful impersonation to be grounds for suspension.

10   The debate over identity has material consequences. Data that is tied to real people is valuable for businesses and government authorities alike. Forrester Research recently estimated that companies spent $2 billion a year for personal data, as Internet users leave what the company calls "an exponentially growing digital footprint."

11   And then there are the political consequences. Activists across the Arab world and in Britain have learned this year that social media sites can be effective in mobilizing uprisings, but using a real name on those sites can lead authorities right to an activist's door.

12   "The real risk to the world is if information technology pivots to a completely authentic identity for everyone," said Joichi Ito, head of the Media Lab at the Massachusetts Institute of Technology. "In the U.S., maybe you don't mind. If every kid in Syria, every time they used the Internet, their identity was visible, they would be dead."

13   Of course, people have always used pseudonyms. Some, like Mark Twain, are better known by their fake names. Some use online pseudonyms to protect themselves, like victims of abuse. Still others use fake names to harass people.

14   Facebook has consistently argued for real identity on the grounds that it promotes more civil conversations.

15   "Facebook has always been based on a real-name culture," said Elliot Schrage, vice president of public policy at Facebook. "We fundamentally believe this leads to greater accountability and a safer and more trusted environment for people who use the service."

16   Real identity is also good for Facebook's business, particularly as it moves into brokering transactions for things like airline tickets on its site.

17   Company executives are aware of the difficulties of policing a site with 800 million active users. Plenty of people get away with using fanciful names. And enforcing the real-name policy can present real-life complications. Wael Ghonim, the celebrated Egyptian blogger, used a fake name to set up a popular anti-Mubarak Facebook page. That led Facebook to briefly shut its Arabic version in the middle of the Tahrir Square demonstrations, until a woman in the United States agreed to take it over.

18   Twitter, on the other hand, has vigorously defended the use of pseudonyms, bucking demands most recently from British government officials who pressed for a real-names policy in the aftermath of the civil unrest across Britain.

19   "Other services may be declaring you have to use your real name because they think they can monetize that better," said Twitter's chief executive, Dick Costolo. "We are more interested in serving our users first."

20   At the same time, Twitter is vying with Google and Facebook to be something of a passport authority on the Web. Facebook has the widest reach, offering easy access to sites that deliver things like instant messaging and news. Spotify and MOG, two music sites, require new users to log in with their Facebook identities. This allows those sites to show users what their Facebook friends are listening to.

21   For consumers, this approach can be a mixed blessing. It means not having to keep track of different passwords for different sites. It also means sharing data about what they are doing online with these emerging "identity intermediaries," as Chris Hoofnagle, a law professor at the University of California, Berkeley, calls them.

22   "It's convenient," Mr. Hoofnagle said. "But do you want Facebook and Google to know where you're going?"

23   As for Facebook's crackdown on Mr. Rushdie, the company would not explain how it happened but admitted it was a mistake. "We apologize for the inconvenience this caused him," Facebook said in a statement.

24   Mr. Rushdie, who once lived incognito because of death threats, has more recently been busy revealing himself on Twitter. He had to fight for his online name there as well. An imposter was using the Twitter handle @SalmanRushdie earlier this year, and Mr. Rushdie had to ask the company for help reclaiming it. Now his page bears Twitter's blue "Verified Account" checkmark and quotes Popeye: "I yam what I yam and that's all that I yam."

Discussion Questions

1. What major strategies does the writer employ in this article? Which strategies did they find most helpful?
2. The article begins and ends with Salman Rushdie. What is the effect of this technique on readers? Why might the writer have used this approach?
3. In what ways did the writer use Facebook and Twitter in this article? In what ways is or isn't it effective?
4. What is the purpose of paragraph 6? Why might the reader have used the phrase "nym wars?"

Toward Key Insights

1. Should individuals be required to use real names or allow pseudonyms on social networks and why?
2. In what ways do we use names in our society, and when and why do we use made-up names?

Suggestions for Writing

1. Write an article to Facebook executives using multiple strategies to argue for or against their real-name policies?
2. Write an article on how names are managed in colleges, the gaming universe, or other areas of your life? You might consider the different ways people use the names, why they use the names that they do, the effects of such usage of names, and support your claims with illustrative examples.

Handbook

Sentence Elements

Learning the parts of English sentences won't in itself improve your writing, but it will equip you to handle errors at the sentence level. Before you can identify and correct unwarranted shifts from past to present time, for example, you need to know about verbs and their tenses. Similarly, recognizing and correcting pronoun case errors requires a knowledge of what pronouns are and how they are used. In this section, we first cover subjects and predicates, then complements, appositives, and the parts of speech, and, finally, phrases and clauses.

Subjects and Predicates

The subject of a sentence tells who or what it is about. A *simple subject* consists of a noun (that is, a naming word) or a noun substitute. A *complete subject* consists of a simple subject plus any words that limit or describe it.

Watch the Animation on Sentences

The predicate tells something about the subject and completes the thought of the sentence. A *simple predicate* consists of one or more verbs (words that show action or existence); a *complete predicate* includes any associated words also. In the following examples, the simple subjects are underlined once and the simple predicates twice. The subjects and predicates are separated with slash marks.

William/laughed.

Mary/has moved.

Sarah/painted the kitchen.

The student over there in the corner/is majoring in art.

Complex subjects can be very long; it is helpful to be able to pick the simple subject out of a complex subject.

The <u>storms</u> in March, which dropped a record rainfall in a week's time, <u>resulted</u> in fierce floods.

A sentence can have a compound subject (two or more separate subjects), a compound predicate (two or more separate predicates), or both.

The <u>elephants</u> and their <u>trainer</u>/<u>bowed</u> to the audience and <u>left</u> the ring.

Sentences that ask questions don't follow the usual simple subject-simple predicate order. Instead, the word order may be changed slightly.

When questions use forms of the verb *be* (*is, am, are*), the verb appears before the subject, while the rest of the predicate still follows the subject.

Is/<u>*Angela*</u>/ *an experienced mountain climber?*

When the sentences include auxiliary, or helping, verbs, the auxiliary is moved in front of the subject, while the rest of the predicate remains in the same place.

Has/<u>a package</u>/ *arrived yet for me?*

Sometimes a question word such as *when, why, who,* and *where* appears in front of the sentence with the helping verb.

When will/<u>*we*</u>/ *be allowed to park on campus?*

Sometimes certain types of phrases and clauses can fall between the subject and the predicate. These should not be confused with the subject. They are usually easy to detect since they can be moved elsewhere in the sentence. The subject is underlined.

<u>My dog</u>/ , *since he has gotten old,* simply lies around the house.

<u>My dog</u>/simply lies around the house *since he has gotten old.*

Sometimes a phrase that is not part of the subject can introduce the sentence. This phrase can also usually be moved.

After we have repaired the rock wall,/<u>*we*</u>/will begin to plant the new flowers.
<u>We</u>/will begin to plant the new flowers *after we have repaired the rock wall.*

Usage Considerations   Because subjects are such important sentence elements, think carefully about each one you write so that your sentences won't be vague or misleading. Read the example below:

Our government has failed to enact a national value-added tax.

This statement can be expressed more precisely:

Congress has failed to enact a national value-added tax.

The *president* has vetoed the proposed national value-added tax.

Paying close attention to subjects lets you present your ideas more accurately and clearly.

EXERCISE

Place a slash mark between the complete subject and the complete predicate; then underline the simple subject once and the verb(s) twice. If a subject comes between an auxiliary verb and the main verb, set it off with two slash marks. If a phrase that is not the subject comes between the subject and the predicate, set it off with two slash marks.

1. Boston is one of my favorite cities.
2. My brother built a barn for his horses.
3. The cup of coffee on the counter is mine.
4. Do you know how to design a Web page?
5. The driver of the pickup truck backed into my car and then sped away.
6. The psychology final, though it was very long, was not very hard.
7. Bulimia and anorexia are disorders that affect too many young women.
8. If you plan to make a purchase using the Internet, you should make sure that the site is secure.

Complements

A complement is a word or word group that forms part of the predicate and helps complete the meaning of the sentence. Anything that comes after the verb is usually a complement. There are many kinds of complements, including phrases and clauses, that will be reviewed later in this chapter.

- I think *that Copland was the quintessential American composer.*
- Robert hesitated *to trap the ground hog behind his house.*
- We were late *because our car would not start.*

Four common complements of traditional grammar are direct objects, indirect objects, subject complements, and object complements.

A *direct object* names whatever receives, or results from, the action of a verb.

The millwright repaired the *lathe.* (Direct object receives action of verb *repaired.*)

Hilary painted a *picture.* (Direct object results from action of verb *painted.*)

They took *coffee* and *sandwiches* to the picnic. (Direct objects receive action of verb *took.*)

An *indirect object* identifies someone or something that receives whatever is named by the direct object.

Doris lent *me* her calculator. (Indirect object *me* receives *calculator,* the direct object.)

Will and Al bought their *boat* new sails. (Indirect object *boat* receives *sails,* the direct object.)

An indirect object can be converted to a prepositional phrase that begins with *to* or *for* and follows the direct object.

Doris lent her calculator *to me.*

Will and Al bought new sails *for their boat.*

A *subject complement* follows a linking verb—one that indicates existence rather than action. It renames or describes the subject.

Desmond is a *carpenter*. (Complement *carpenter* renames subject *Desmond*.)

The lights are too *bright* for Percy. (Complement *bright* describes subject *lights*.)

An *object complement* follows a direct object and renames or describes it.

The council named Donna *treasurer*. (Object complement *treasurer* renames direct object *Donna*.)

The audience thought the play *silly*. (Object complement *silly* describes direct object *play*.)

If a word is an object complement, you can form a short test sentence using *is*.

Donna is *treasurer*.

The play is *silly*.

Usage Considerations   Like subjects, direct objects can be revised for greater precision, as these examples show:

John sent *a gift*.

John sent *a giant coloring book as a birthday gift*.

Often, you can carry the revision one step further by adding an indirect object, subject complement, or other complement to the sentence.

John sent his *niece* a giant coloring book as a birthday gift. (Indirect object added.)

Appositives

An appositive is a noun or word group serving as a noun that follows another noun or noun substitute and expands its meaning. Appositives may be restrictive or nonrestrictive. Restrictive appositives distinguish whatever they modify from other items in the same class. They are written without commas.

My sister *Heidi* is a professional golfer. (Appositive *Heidi* distinguishes her from other sisters.)

I have just read a book by the novelist *Henry James*. (Appositive *Henry James* distinguishes him from other novelists.)

Nonrestrictive appositives provide more information about whatever they modify. This sort of appositive is set off by a pair of commas except at the end of a sentence; then it is preceded by a single comma.

Anatoly Karpov, *the Russian chess player*, was interviewed on TV. (Appositive names *Karpov's* occupation.)

Todd plans to major in paleontology, *the study of fossils*. (Appositive defines *paleontology*.)

Usage Considerations   When a brief definition is necessary, appositives can help you improve your sentences.

> John Cage wrote hundreds of pieces for prepared pianos.

> John Cage, *a twentieth-century avant-garde composer,* wrote hundreds of pieces for prepared pianos, *instruments with odds and ends stuck between their strings to provide unusual effects.*

Don't, however, clutter your writing with appositives that provide unneeded information; the overload will impede and irritate your reader.

Identify each italicized item as a direct object (DO), an indirect object (IO), a subject complement (SC), an object complement (OC), or an appositive (AP).

1. The critics considered the movie *a masterpiece.*
2. Robert Heinlein, a science fiction *writer,* thought that writers should tell an interesting story.
3. Jasmine completed her research *paper* two weeks ahead of the due date.
4. John sent his wife *candy* and *flowers* for Valentine's Day.
5. My roommate, a terrible *procrastinator,* finally relaxed after he turned in his paper.
6. Mr. Hanley offered *me* a job.
7. Darrel is a fine young *man.*

Parts of Speech

Traditional English grammar classifies words into eight parts of speech: *nouns, pronouns, verbs, adjectives, adverbs, prepositions, conjunctions,* and *interjections.* This section discusses these categories as well as verbals, phrases, and clauses, which also serve as parts of speech.

◉⎯ Watch the Animation on **Parts of Speech**

It is important to recognize that words that may look like one part of speech can function as another part of speech. For example, the verb *swim* can function as a noun. *Swimming* is good for your health. To identify a word as a part of speech is to identify how it functions in a sentence.

Traditional grammar defined nouns as words that name persons, places, things, conditions, ideas, or qualities. Most nouns can take a plural (book, books), possessive (Andy, Andy's), or article (bench, the bench).

Proper Nouns

Some nouns, called *proper nouns,* identify one-of-a-kind items like the following and are commonly capitalized.

◉⎯ Watch the Animation on **Nouns**

France	New Years
Pacific Ocean	North Dakota
Pulitzer Prize	World Series
Spirit of St. Louis	Wyandotte Corporation
Declaration of Independence	Miami-Dade Junior College

Common Nouns

Common nouns name general classes or categories of items. Some common nouns are *abstract* and name a condition, idea, or quality that we can't experience with our five senses. *Abstract nouns* often cannot accept the plural; we cannot usually say we have *envys*. *Concrete nouns* identify something that we can experience with one or more of our senses and usually have plural forms.

Abstract Nouns	Concrete Nouns
arrogance	man
fear	bicycle
liberalism	desk
sickness	cartoon
understanding	smoke

Count and Non-Count Nouns

Most nouns identify things we can count and such nouns usually can take the plural form: *three bananas, a book, two children.* Some nouns, including many abstract nouns, cannot accept a plural: *coffee, water, bread.*

Usage Considerations Good writing demands precise, potent nouns. If you carefully select your nouns, you can sharpen your message. Ill-chosen nouns, on the other hand, suggest poor thinking. Note how the vague word *freedom* robs the following sentence of any specific meaning:

Our *freedom* needs to be protected.

What did the writer have in mind? Here are a few possibilities:

Our *right to own guns* needs to be protected.
Our *private behavior* needs to be protected.
Our *national sovereignty* needs to be protected.

Even when meaning does not present problems, sentences can be sharpened by careful attention to nouns. Note the greater precision of the second sentence below:

Our *dog* has a savage bite.
Our *pit bull* has a savage bite.

Identify the nouns in the following sentences. Indicate if they are proper nouns (PN) or common nouns (CN), count nouns (count) non-count nouns (non-count), or collective nouns (coll). Clearly, a noun can belong to more than one category.

1. Josh downloaded the new song by Rufus Wainwright from the Internet.
2. Americans want to be secure from terrorist attacks without surrendering their fundamental liberties.

3. Students quickly develop an addiction to coffee as they try to survive night-long cram sessions.

4. Our football team had an excellent season even if we didn't make it to a bowl game.

5. Math, especially algebra, is a subject that gives many students a fair amount of difficulty.

6. The water in the Gulf of Mexico can be uncomfortably warm by August.

7. Whether you agree or disagree with the views of the organization, the National Rifle Association has played an important role in the debate over how we should understand the Second Amendment.

Pronouns

Pronouns are a special class of words that can fit the place of nouns in a sentence and sometimes can be seen as taking the place of a noun in a sentence. Pronouns can help you avoid the awkward repetition of nouns.

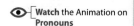 **Watch** the Animation on Pronouns

Personal Pronouns   Personal pronouns refer to identifiable persons or things. Personal pronouns have different cases. The subjective case is used when the pronoun serves as the subject of the sentence or clause. *I helped Steve.* The objective case is used when the pronoun is the object of a verb or preposition. *Steve helped **me**. We spoke about **him**.* The possessive case shows possession or ownership. *That is **my** briefcase. My, your, our,* and *their* always precede nouns, as in *their car. Mine, hers, ours, yours,* and *theirs* do not precede nouns, as in *That book is mine. His* and *its* may or may not precede nouns.

	Subjective	**Objective**	**Possessive**
Singular			
First person	I	me	my, mine
Second person	you	you	your, yours
Third person	he, she, it	him, her, it	his, her, hers, its
Plural			
First person	we	us	our, ours
Second person	you	you	your, yours
Third person	they	them	their, theirs

Relative Pronouns   A relative pronoun relates a dependent clause—a word group that has a subject and a predicate but cannot function as an independent sentence—to a noun or pronoun, called an antecedent, in the main part of the sentence.

The relative pronouns include the following:

who	whose	what	whoever	whichever
whom	which	that	whomever	whatever

Who in its various forms refers to people, *which* to things, and *that* to either people or things.

Mary Beth Cartwright, *who* was arrested last week for fraud, was Evansville's "Model Citizen" two years ago. (The antecedent of *who* is *Mary Beth Cartwright.*)

He took the electric razor, *which* needed a new cutting head, to the repair shop. (The antecedent of *which* is *electric razor.*)

David Bullock is someone *whom* we should definitely hire. (The antecedent of *whom* is *someone.*)

Montreal is a city *that* I've always wanted to visit. (The antecedent of *that* is *city.*)

Which typically introduces nonrestrictive clauses; that is, clauses that provide more information about whatever they modify (see page 672).

The palace, *which* was in bad condition a century ago, is finally going to be restored. (Clause adds information about palace.)

That is typically used in other situations, especially to introduce restrictive clauses: those that distinguish the things they modify from others in the same class (see page 672).

The used car *that* I bought last week at Honest Bill's has already broken down twice. (Clause distinguishes writer's used car from others.)

Page 665 explains the use of *who* and *whom.*

Interrogative Pronouns   Interrogative pronouns introduce questions. All of the relative pronouns except *that* also function as interrogative pronouns.

who	which	whoever	whichever
whom	what	whomever	whatever
whose			

What is the matter?

Who asked you?

Whatever do you mean?

When *what, which,* and *whose* are followed by nouns, they act as adjectives, not pronouns.

Which movie should we see?

Demonstrative Pronouns   As their name suggests, demonstrative pronouns point things out. There are four such pronouns.

this	these
that	those

This and its plural *these* identify recent or nearby things.

This is the play to see.

These are the times that try men's souls.

That and its plural *those* identify less recent or more distant things.

That is Mary's house across the road.

Those were very good peaches you had for sale last week.

Reflexive and Intensive Pronouns   A reflexive pronoun is used when the pronoun refers back to a noun in the same clause. An intensive pronoun lends emphasis to a noun or pronoun. The two sets of pronouns are identical.

myself	herself	ourselves
yourself	itself	yourselves
himself	oneself	themselves

My father cut *himself* while shaving. (reflexive pronoun)

The president *himself* has asked me to undertake this mission. (intensive pronoun)

Don't substitute a reflexive pronoun for a personal pronoun.

Faulty	*Jill and myself are going to a movie.*
Revision	*Jill and I are going to a movie.*
Faulty	*Give the tickets to John and myself.*
Revision	*Give the tickets to John and me.*

Sometimes you'll hear people say things like "He made it *hisself*," "They're only fooling *theirself*," or "They bought *theirselves* sodas." Such forms are nonstandard. Say "himself" and "themselves" instead.

Indefinite Pronouns   These pronouns refer to unidentified persons, places, or things. One group of indefinite pronouns consistently acts as pronouns.

anybody	everything	one
anyone	nobody	somebody
anything	no one	someone
everybody	nothing	something
everyone		

A second group may function as either pronouns or adjectives.

all	any	most	few	much
another	each	either	many	neither

Here are some examples:

Everyone is welcome. (indefinite pronoun)

Many are called, but *few* are chosen. (indefinite pronouns)

Many men but only a *few* women attend the Air Force Academy. (adjectives)

Pages 647–650 discuss indefinite pronouns as antecedents.

Reciprocal Pronouns   The two reciprocal pronouns show an interchange of action between two or more parties. *Each other* is used when two parties interact, *one another* when three or more do.

Pam and Patty accidentally gave *each other* the same thing for Christmas. (two persons)

The members of the football team joyfully embraced *one another* after their victory. (more than two persons)

Usage Considerations Many students handle pronouns carelessly, damaging the clarity of their writing. Problems include letting the same pronoun stand for different nouns or using a pronoun where detailed, vivid language would be more effective. The following passage illustrates poor pronoun usage:

> My brother loves fly fishing. He thinks *it* is the only way to spend a summer weekend. In fact, whenever he's off work, he'll do *it*.

Rewritten as follows, the passage has been notably improved:

> My brother loves fly fishing. He thinks that *wading in a stream and casting leisurely for trout* is the only way to spend a summer weekend. In fact, whenever he's off work, he *can be found up to his hips in water, offering his hand-tied flies to the waiting rainbows.*

Identify each pronoun in the following sentences and indicate its type (personal, relative, interrogative, demonstrative, reflexive, intensive, indefinite, reciprocal). If it is a personal pronoun, indicate if it is in the subjective (S), objective (O), or possessive (P) case.

1. Anyone who wants to be successful needs to be able to use the Internet.
2. John helped himself to my copy of *The Canterbury Tales*.
3. Which fraternity did he say he was considering joining?
4. The black Subaru that is parked at the back of the lot is mine.
5. This is the kind of day that I really enjoy.
6. The president himself will teach one of the classes in political science.
7. We will all be more likely to succeed as writers if we help each other by offering our honest responses to drafts.
8. Despite his bad back, Brian offered to help us move.

Verbs

A verb indicates action or existence. Main verbs fall into two classes: *action verbs* and *linking verbs*. A very different type of verb is the *auxiliary* (or *helping*) verb, which adds specific kinds of meaning to the main verb.

Action Verbs As its name suggests, an action verb expresses action. Some action verbs are transitive, others intransitive. A *transitive* verb has a direct object that receives or results from the action and rounds out the meaning of the sentence.

> The photographer *took* the picture.

Without the direct object, this sentence would not express a complete thought. In contrast, an *intransitive* verb requires no direct object to complete the meaning of the sentence.

> Lee Ann *gasped* loudly.
> Little Tommy Tucker *sings* for his supper.

Many action verbs can play both transitive and intransitive roles, depending on the sentences they are used in.

> Kari *rode* her bicycle into town. (transitive verb)
>
> Karl *rode* in the front seat of the car. (intransitive verb)

Linking Verbs   A linking verb shows existence or a state of affairs such as taste rather than action. Linking verbs are often followed by subject complements that reflect back on the subject of the sentence.

> Ms. Davis *is* our new director. (Complement *director* renames subject *Ms. Davis.*)
>
> The soup *was* lukewarm. (Complement *lukewarm* describes subject *soup.*)

The most common linking verbs are forms of the verb *to be (is, are, am, was, were, be, being, been.)* Likewise, verbs such as *seem, become, appear, remain, feel, look, smell, sound,* and *taste* function as linking verbs when they do not indicate actual physical action. In such cases, they are followed by adjectives (see pages 624–626). Here is an example:

> Harry looked *angry.*

When such verbs do indicate physical action, they function as action verbs and are followed by adverbs (see pages 627–628).

> Harry looked *angrily* at the referee.

Linking verbs can also be followed by adverb phrases of place or time.

> Your dinner is *on the table* (adverb phrase of place).
>
> The meeting will be *at 8:00* A.M. (adverb phrase of time).

Auxiliary Verbs   Auxiliary (helping) verbs accompany action or linking verbs and provide information about time, possibility, or obligation, or establish the passive. *Have, be,* and *do* can function as both auxiliary and main verbs.

The auxiliary verbs *have (has, had)* and *be (is, are, was, were)* can provide information about time.

> Carol has repaired your computer.
>
> Carol is reformatting your hard drive.

The auxiliary verb *do* is inserted to form the negative or a question when there is no other auxiliary.

> Ellen *did* not resign.
>
> *Did* Ellen resign?

Auxiliary verbs called modals show time, obligation, possibility, or ability: *shall, should, will, would, can, could, may, might.*

With questions, the auxiliary verb is often moved to the front.

> *Will* Ellen *resign?*

vbs

Identify each verb or auxiliary in the following sentences and indicate whether it is a main verb (MV) or auxiliary (AUX).

1. An explosion rocked the apartment building and scattered debris in all directions.
2. We should be considering ways that we can improve the quality of our lives.
3. Americans have been buying iPads at a surprising rate.
4. Did you ask Jennifer if she has her digital camera in her backpack?
5. With genetic screening, we can identify individuals who are at higher risk for many serious diseases.
6. An espresso doesn't always taste good, but it is always an eye-opener.
7. Beethoven's string quartets have stood the test of time as masterpieces that are rivaled only by Bartok's works in the genre.

Usage Considerations   Energetic writing requires precise verbs. Don't take verbs for granted; revise them as necessary to strengthen a sentence. Note the improved precision of the second example.

> I *gave* the maître d' a ten-dollar bill.
>
> I *slipped* the maître d' a ten-dollar bill.

Tense   Verbs change in form to show distinctions in time. Every main verb has two basic tenses: present and past.

The *present tense* shows present condition and general or habitual action, indicates permanent truths, tells about past events in the historical present, and sometimes denotes action at some definite future time.

Verbs in the present tense must agree with their subjects. If the subject of a verb is a singular noun or pronoun (*he, she, it*), add *s* or *es* (if the word ends with an *s* or *ch* sound, as in *talks* or *teaches*). If the subject is plural or a second-person pronoun (*you*), the verb takes no ending (*talk, teach*).

> Helen *looks* beautiful in her new gown. (present condition)
>
> John *works* on the eighteenth floor. (general action)
>
> I *brush* my teeth each morning. (habitual action)
>
> The earth *rotates* on its axis. (permanent truth)
>
> On November 11, 1918, the guns *fall* silent, and World War I *comes* to an end. (historical present)
>
> Monday, I *begin* my new job. (future action)

The past tense shows that a condition existed or an action was completed in the past. This verb tense leaves the time indefinite, but surrounding words may specify it. Most verbs are regular and form the past tense by adding *-ed: talk, talked.* Some verbs are irregular and form the past by changing the vowel: *stand, stood.* A very few verbs do not change forms at all in creating the past: *set, set.*

> Paul *was* angry with his noisy neighbors. (past condition, time indefinite)
>
> Sandy *received* a long letter yesterday. (past action, time specified by *yesterday*)

Past Participle   In addition to the basic tenses, there is a *past participle* form of the main verb that is used to form the perfect form of the verb phrase and the passive voice. For most verbs, the past participle form is identical with the past tense in form.

vbs

Watch the Animation on Regular and Irregular Verbs

Present	Past	Past Participle
talk	talk**ed**	talk**ed**
stand	st**oo**d	st**oo**d
set	set	set

Some verbs have different past forms and past participles. This can often lead to errors where less experienced writers often use the regular past (*He has* **swam** *this river before*) when the past participle form is required (*he has* **swum** *this river before*). Below is a table of many, but not all, of the irregular verbs for your reference.

Present Infinitive	Past	Past Participle	Present Infinitive	Past	Past Participle
arise	arose	arisen	blow	blew	blown
be	was, were	been	break	broke	broken
become	became	become	choose	chose	chosen
bite	bit	bitten	come	came	come
do	did	done	grow	grew	grown
draw	drew	drawn	hide	hid	hidden
drink	drank	drunk	know	knew	known
drive	drove	driven	ride	rode	ridden
eat	ate	eaten	see	saw	seen
fall	fell	fallen	shake	shook	shaken
fly	flew	flown	slay	slew	slain
freeze	froze	frozen	speak	spoke	spoken
get	got	gotten	spring	sprang	sprung
give	gave	given	write	wrote	written

Time and Verb Forms

In addition to the tenses in English, many other forms of the verb express time.

Watch the Animation on Time and Verb Forms

Future Time   *Future time* is frequently indicated by the auxiliary modals *shall* or *will* with the present tense form of the verb.

> You *will feel* better after a good night's sleep. (future condition)
> I *shall attend* the concert next week. (future action)

Perfect Verb Forms   The perfect form of a verb is formed by a form of the auxiliary verb *have* and the past participle of the verb.

The *present perfect* tense is formed with *has* or *have* and the past participle of the main verb. It shows that a past condition or action, or its effect, continues until the present time.

> The players *have been* irritable since they lost the homecoming game. (Condition continues until present.)

vbs

Juanita *has driven* a United Parcel Service truck for five years. (Action continues until present.)

William *has repaired* the snow blower. (Effect of action continues until present, although the action itself was completed in the past.)

The *past perfect* tense combines *had* and the past participle of the main verb. It refers to a past condition or action that was completed before another past condition or action.

He *had been* in the army two years when the war ended. (Past perfect condition occurred first.)

Vivian moved into the house that she *had built* the summer before. (Past perfect action occurred first.)

The *future perfect* tense is formed from the verbs *shall have* or *will have* plus the past participle of the main verb. It shows that a condition or an action will have been completed at some time in the future. Surrounding words specify time.

Our sales manager *will have been* with the company 10 years next July. (Condition will end.)

By the end of this year, I *shall have written* the great American novel. (Action will be completed.)

Progressive Verb Forms   Each verb form, including the basic tenses, has a *progressive form* that indicates action in progress. The progressive is always indicated by some form of the verb *to be* followed by a present participle (or progressive), a verb that ends in *-ing*.

Present progressive	I am running.
Past progressive	I was running.
Future progressive	I will be running.
Present perfect progressive	I have been running.
Past perfect progressive	I had been running.
Future perfect progressive	I will have been running.

Pages 657–658 discuss unwarranted shifts in tense and their correction.

An easy way to identify the form of the verb phrase is to use the following formula.

(modal) + (have + en/ed) + (be + ing) + main verb
        Perfect   *Progressive*

Simply read the first available tense. If the modal is *will,* then that designates future time. Then if *have, has,* or *had* is present, the verb phrase is *perfect.* If a form of *be* is present and the main verb ends with *ing,* then the verb phrase is progressive.

will	have	been	living
Future	*Perfect*	*Progressive*	

Usage   While most students use regular tenses and the progressive accurately, many less experienced writers do not always use the perfect verb form where appropriate. This is acceptable in informal writing; it is not acceptable for most formal writing.

Not acceptable Jim *studied* accounting for the last three years. (This suggests that the action is over and done with.)

Acceptable Jim *has studied* accounting for the last three years. (The present perfect verb form shows that the action comes right up to the present and may not be finished yet.)

Voice   Transitive verbs have two voices: active and passive. A verb is in the *active voice* when the subject carries out the action named by the verb.

Barry *planned* a picnic. (Subject *Barry* performs action.)

A verb is in the *passive voice* when the subject receives the action. The performer may be identified in an accompanying phrase or go unmentioned.

A picnic *was planned* by Barry. (The phrase *by Barry* identifies the performer.)

The picnic *was canceled.* (The performer goes unmentioned.)

A passive construction always uses a form of *to be* and the past participle of an action verb. Like other constructions, the passive may show past, present, or future time.

Amy *is paid* handsomely for her investment advice. (present tense)

I *was warned* by a sound truck that a tornado was nearby. (past tense)

I *will be sent* to Ghana soon by the Peace Corps. (future tense)

I *have been awarded* a sizable research grant. (present perfect tense)

The city *had been shelled* heavily before the infantry moved in. (past perfect tense)

By the end of this month, the site for our second factory *will have been chosen.* (future perfect tense)

To convert a sentence from the passive to the active voice, make the performer the subject, the original subject the direct object, and drop the form of *to be.*

The treaty *was signed* by the general. (passive)

The general *signed* the treaty. (active)

Technical and scientific writing commonly uses the passive voice to explain processes since it focuses on the objective observation or the action rather than the agent who can vary and should be irrelevant to the result. Other kinds of writing, however, avoid the passive voice except when it is desirable to not identify the one performing the action or when the action is more significant than the actor. See pages 112–113 for more information on usage.

((•— Listen to the Podcast on **Voice and Mood**

vbs

Identify each verb group in the following sentences, indicate its form (present, past, future, present perfect, past perfect, future perfect, and any of the progressive forms), and note any use of the passive voice.

1. Devon broke his leg when he was thrown from his horse.
2. Deidra has managed our money for the last several years.
3. The Chicago Symphony is performing Mahler's *Resurrection Symphony*.
4. We will have completed the repairs on your computer by next Friday.
5. Computers will be placed in every classroom as soon as the funds are available.
6. Maria has been acting in Shakespeare plays every summer since she first moved to Michigan.
7. At last the ceiling in the McCracken Building has been repaired.

Mood The mood of a verb shows whether the writer regards a statement as a

1. fact
2. command or request
3. wish, possibility, condition contrary to fact, or the like.

English has three moods: the indicative, imperative, and subjunctive.

A sentence in the *indicative mood* states a real or supposed fact or asks a question.

Nancy *graduates* from high school tomorrow.

We *lived* in Oakmont when Rachel was born.

He *had been* a sailor during the war.

Has Joe *asked* anyone to the prom yet?

Most verbs are used in the indicative mood.

A sentence in the *imperative mood* delivers a command or makes a request.

Leave the room immediately! (command)

Please *turn* the music down. (request)

The subject of a sentence in the imperative mood is always *you*. Although ordinarily unstated, the subject sometimes appears in the sentence.

You leave the room immediately!

The *subjunctive mood* is used

1. in *if*, *as if*, and *as though* clauses to express a wish, a possibility, or an action or a condition contrary to fact
2. in *that* clauses expressing orders, demands, requests, resolutions, proposals, or motions
3. with modal auxiliaries to express wishes, probability, possibility, permission, requirements, recommendations, suggestions, and conditions contrary to fact.

To express a present or future wish, possibility, condition or action in an *if*, *as if*, or *as though* clause, use *were* with any personal pronoun or noun serving as the subject of the clause.

If only Stan *were* less gullible! (present wish contrary to fact)

Even if Kay *were* to explain, Mary wouldn't believe her. (future possibility)

Arthur is behaving as if he *were* a millionaire (present condition contrary to fact)

To express a wish, possibility, or condition contrary to past facts, use *had been* or *had* plus the past participle of an action verb.

If the engine *had been lubricated*, the bearing wouldn't have burned out. (past condition contrary to fact)

Alice looked as if she *had lost* her best friend. (condition expressed in clause occurs before action of verb *looked*)

When writing *that* clauses expressing orders, demands, requests, resolutions, proposals, or motions, use *be* or the present plural form of an action verb.

I move that they *be* rewarded for their bravery.

The group proposed that Margaret *go* to the scene of the accident and *inspect* it personally.

In other *that* clauses, use the appropriate indicative form of the verb.

I know that they *were* rewarded for their bravery.

The group believed that Margaret *had gone* to the scene of the accident and *inspected* it personally.

The modal auxiliaries include the helping verbs *can, could, may, might, must, shall, will, would, should*, and *ought to*. The examples below illustrate the meanings they can express.

1. Wishes *(could, would)*
   I wish I *could* shimmy like my sister Kate.
   The Republicans wish the Democrats *would* go away and vice versa.
2. Probability *(should)*
   Because I've studied diligently, I *should* do better on my next chemistry test.
3. Possibility *(may, might, can, could)*
   Low inflation *could* cause our stock market to soar.
   I *might* stay up to watch the eclipse of the moon tonight.
4. Permission *(can, may)*
   The public *can* use these tennis courts every afternoon.
   You *may* leave as soon as you've finished filing these folders.
5. Requirements *(must)*
   The landlord has raised our rent again; we *must* find another apartment.
6. Recommendations, suggestions *(should, ought to)*
   Randy *should* see a doctor about his chest pains.
   All of us *ought to* exercise regularly.
7. Conditions contrary to fact *(could)*
   If only I *could* live my life over!

adj

For each of the following sentences, identify the mood as indicative (IND), imperative (IMP), or subjunctive (SUB):

1. See your doctor before starting a strenuous exercise program.
2. The tired runner staggered across the finish line.
3. These new cell phones should prove very popular.
4. Let me know what you think of this novel.
5. Hang gliding is a great sport for anyone unafraid of heights.
6. If you practiced more, you could become an outstanding pianist.
7. The latest unemployment figures should help calm inflation fears.

Adjectives

Watch the Animation on **Adjectives**

An adjective *modifies* a noun or pronoun by describing it, limiting it, or otherwise making its meaning more exact.

> The *brass* candlestick stood next to the *fragile* vase. (*Brass* modifies *candlestick*, and *fragile* modifies *vase*.)
> The cat is *long-haired* and *sleek*. (*Long-haired* and *sleek* modify *cat*.)

Common Adjectives   Most adjectives use the standard form of adjectives. Two or more adjectives may modify the same noun or pronoun.

> He applied *clear* lacquer to the tabletop.
> The *slim, sophisticated* model glided onto the runway.
> The child was *active, happy,* and *polite*.

Proper Adjectives   A proper adjective is derived from a proper noun and is always capitalized.

> The *American* principles of democracy have encouraged many living under tyranny.
> Kenneth Branagh started as a *Shakespearean* actor before branching out into television and directing.

Comparison with Adjectives   Adjectives can be used to show comparison. When two things are compared, shorter adjectives usually add *-er* and longer adjectives add *more*. When three or more things are compared, shorter adjectives usually add *-est* and longer ones add *most*.

> John is *taller* than Pete. (short adjective comparing two things)
> Sandra seems *more engaged* than Jill today. (long adjective comparing two things)
> John is the *tallest* of the three brothers. (short adjective comparing three things)

Sandra is the *most engaged* student in the class. (longer adjective comparing more than three things)

Some adjectives, like the examples below, have irregular forms for comparisons.

good—better—best
bad—worse—worst

Don't use the *-est* form of the shorter adjective to compare just two things.

Faulty This is the *smallest* of the two castles.

Instead, use the *-er* form.

Revision This is the *smaller* of the two castles.

Position of Adjectives   Most adjectives come immediately before the words they modify. In a few set expressions (for example, heir *apparent*), the adjective immediately follows the word it modifies. Similarly, adjective pairs sometimes appear in a follow-up position for added emphasis (The rapids, *swift* and *dangerous*, soon capsized the raft). Sometimes adjectives also serve as subject complements and follow their subjects (The puppy was *friendly*).

Usage Considerations   Some students overuse adjectives, especially in descriptions, but most underuse them. Review your sentences carefully to see where adding or cutting adjectives can increase the impact of your writing.

My Buick is the talk of my friends.
My *old, dilapidated, rusty, fenderless 1970* Buick is the talk of my friends.
My *rusty, fenderless 1970* Buick is the talk of my friends.

The first sentence lacks adjectives that show why the car is discussed. The second sentence overcorrects this fault by including two adjectives that repeat the information provided by the others. The final sentence strikes the proper balance.

Determiners   There is a category of words that are sometimes classified with adjectives that limit the noun or pronoun but do not name a quality or characteristic of the noun or pronoun.

Three sailboats raced around the island.

While we know how many sailboats are involved, there is no descriptive content added to the concept of sailboats.

There are many different kinds of determiners.

Determiners	**Name**
a, an	Indefinite article
the	Definite article
this, that, these, those	Demonstrative

adj

Determiners	Name
one, two, three, four, five	Cardinal number
first, second, third, fourth	Ordinal number
my, our, your, his, her, hers, its, their	Possessive pronoun
some, any, no, every, another, enough, either, neither, all, both, each, less, other, many, more, most, few, several	Indefinite pronoun
Tom's, Mary's	Possessive noun
which, whose	Interrogative or relative determiner depending on use

The most common determiners are the indefinite article a/an and the definite article *the*. These can give special difficulty to non-native speakers of English since it is not always clear when they are used and not used. While there are underlying rules for their use, these rules can be complex and beyond the scope of this book. With an indefinite article *a/an, a* precedes words beginning with consonant sounds; *an* precedes words with a vowel sound to make pronunciation easier.

A book is a great pleasure on *a* cold, winter night. (indefinite article *a before a* consonant)

An apple may be a nice snack, but I like apples better in a pie. (Indefinite article *an* before a vowel.)

Whose laptop was left is on the table? (interrogative determiner)

The student *whose* laptop was left in class must be frantic. (relative determiner)

Some people have no luck at all. (indefinite pronoun)

Lady Gaga got *her* start in a punk band. (possessive pronoun)

EXERCISE

Identify the adjectives and determiners in the following sentences.

1. The climbers seemed very tiny as they rappelled down the sheer cliff.
2. Janine's paper offered an insightful and well-supported argument.
3. Fresh grapefruit juice can be a tart but tasty breakfast beverage.
4. In some medieval cathedrals, there were statues representing the seven deadly sins.
5. Many expeditions to climb Mt. Everest were defeated more by the inhospitable environment than by the actual challenges of the climb.
6. A good educational environment can be made better by smaller classes.
7. After the chilly air-conditioning in the restaurant, Christy was grateful to step out into the warm, damp summer air.

Adverbs

adv

An adverb modifies a verb, an adjective, another adverb, or a whole sentence. Adverbs generally answer questions such as "How?" "When?" "Where?" "How often?" and "To what extent?"

👁 Watch the Animation on **Adverbs**

The floodwaters receded *very* slowly. (Adverb modifies adverb and answers the question "How?")

My sister will visit me *tomorrow*. (Adverb modifies verb and answers the question "When?")

The coach walked *away* from the bench. (Adverb modifies verb and answers the question "Where?")

The tire is *too* worn to be safe. (Adverb modifies adjective and answers the question "To what extent?")

The teller is *frequently* late for work. (Adverb modifies adjective and answers the question "How often?")

Unfortunately, the game was canceled because of rain. (The adverb modifies the whole sentence but does not answer any question.)

Formation of Adverbs   Most adverbs are formed by adding *-ly* to adjectives.

The wind is *restless*. (*Restless* is an adjective modifying *wind*.)

He walked *restlessly* around the room. (*Restlessly* is an adverb modifying *walked*.)

Many common adverbs, however (*almost, never, quite, soon, then, there*, and *too*), lack *-ly* endings.

I *soon* realized that pleasing my boss was impossible.

This movie is *too* gruesome for my taste.

Furthermore, some words such as *better, early, late, hard, little, near, only, straight*, and *wrong* do double duty as either adjectives or adverbs.

We must have taken a *wrong* turn. (*Wrong* is an adjective modifying the noun *turn*.)

Where did I go *wrong*? (*Wrong* is an adverb modifying the verb *go*.)

Comparison with Adverbs   Like adjectives, adverbs can show comparison. When two things are compared, adverbs add *more*. When three or more things are compared, *most* is used.

Harold works *more* efficiently than Don. (adverb comparing two people)

Of all the people in the shop, Harold works the *most* efficiently. (adverb comparing more than two people)

Some adverbs, like some adjectives, use irregular forms for comparisons.

well—better—best

much—more—most

prep

Position of Adverbs   Adverbs are more movable than any other part of speech. Usually, adverbs that modify adjectives and other adverbs appear next to them to avoid confusion.

> Her *especially* fine tact makes her a welcome guest at any party. (Adverb *especially* modifies adjective *fine*.)
>
> The novel was *very* badly written. (Adverb *very* modifies adverb *badly*.)

Adverbs that modify verbs, however, can often be shifted around in their sentences without causing changes in meaning.

> *Quickly*, he slipped through the doorway.
>
> He slipped *quickly* through the doorway.
>
> He slipped through the doorway *quickly*.

Usage Considerations   You can often sharpen the meaning of a sentence by adding a well-chosen adverb.

> The student squirmed in his chair.
>
> The student squirmed *anxiously* in his chair.

Including the adverb *anxiously* in the second sentence shows the mental state of the student.

Be careful, however, not to overuse adverbs because they can bog down your writing.

EXERCISE

Identify the adverbs in the following sentences:

1. Three friends slowly but steadily hiked up the mountain trail.
2. Everyone agreed that it was too hot to mow the lawn.
3. While the screenplay was exceptionally well written, the movie itself was poorly directed and badly miscast.
4. The violins entered too early, but no one but the conductor really noticed.
5. We should meet tomorrow to plan our camping trip.
6. Some people are strangely attracted to unusually dangerous activities.
7. The two planes came nearer to each other than anyone would like.

Prepositions

👁 **Watch** the Animation on **Prepositions**

A preposition links its object—a noun or noun substitute—to some other word in the sentence and shows a relationship between them. The relationship is often one of location, time, means, or reason or purpose. The word group containing the preposition and its object makes up a prepositional phrase.

> The new insulation *in* the attic keeps my house much warmer now. (Preposition *in* links object *attic* to *insulation* and shows location.)

We have postponed the meeting *until* tomorrow. (Preposition *until* links object *tomorrow* to *postponed* and shows time.)

The tourists traveled *by* automobile. (Preposition *by* links object *automobile* to *traveled* and shows means.)

Warren swims *for* exercise. (Preposition *for* links object *exercise* to *swims* and shows reason or purpose.)

The following list includes the most common prepositions, some of which consist of two or more words:

about	before	except	on
above	behind	for	onto
across	below	from	out of
after	beside	in	over
against	between	instead of	since
along with	by	into	through
among	by reason of	like	to
around	contrary to	near	toward
at	down	next to	under
because of	during	of	with
			without

Many of these combine to form additional prepositions: *except for, in front of, by way of, on top of,* and the like.

Some words that are usually used as prepositions such as *up, on,* and *in* can also function as a different part of speech called a *verb particle*. Here are two examples.

The instructor let Jeff make *up* the test.

The officer turned *in* his best friend.

The verb particle is closely associated with the verb and is a part of its meaning. If a word is a verb particle, it can usually be moved after the noun.

The instructor let Jeff make the test *up*.

The officer turned his best friend *in*.

Usage Considerations   It is easy to use a small group of prepositions over and over in your writing. This habit often results in imprecise or misleading sentences. To avoid this problem, think carefully about your choice of prepositions as you revise. Read the following example:

He walked *by* the railroad tracks on his way home.

Note that two interpretations are possible.

He walked *along* the railroad tracks on his way home.

He walked *past* the railroad tracks on his way home.

Clearly, you would use the preposition that conveys your intended meaning.

con

EXERCISE

Identify the prepositions (P) and their objects (O) in the following sentences:

1. Angela searched her house for a book of poems by Rilke.
2. Dave and Silvia traveled across America on a motorcycle.
3. Because of the hurricane, the causeway from the Florida Keys was closed.
4. Contrary to everyone's expectation, Barry decided to go into advertising instead of theater.
5. Before her first class, Carrie likes to swim 25 laps in the school's pool.
6. The two boys hid for several hours in the woods behind their house.
7. In his paper on cloning, James cut through the confusion about the topic and clearly presented the arguments for each side of the issue.

Conjunctions

Conjunctions serve as connectors, linking parts of sentences or whole sentences. These connectors fall into three groups: coordinating conjunctions, subordinating conjunctions, and conjunctive adverbs.

Coordinating Conjunctions   Coordinating conjunctions connect terms of equal grammatical importance: words, word groups, and simple sentences. These conjunctions can occur singly *(and, but, or, nor, for, yet, so)* or in pairs called correlative conjunctions *(either—or, neither—nor, both—and,* and *not only—but also)*. The elements that follow correlative conjunctions must be parallel; that is, have the same grammatical form.

> Tom *and* his cousin are opening a coffee shop. (Coordinating conjunction connects nouns.)
>
> Shall I serve the tea in the living room *or* on the veranda? (Coordinating conjunction connects phrases.)
>
> I am going to Europe this summer, *but* Marjorie is staying home. (Coordinating conjunction connects simple sentences.)
>
> Amy *not only* teaches English *but also* writes novels. (Correlative conjunctions connect parallel predicates.)
>
> You can study nursing *either* at Ferris State University *or* at DeWitt College. (Correlative conjunctions connect parallel phrases.)
>
> Friendship is *both* pleasure *and* pain. (Correlative conjunctions connect parallel nouns.)

Subordinating Conjunctions   Like relative pronouns, subordinating conjunctions introduce subordinate clauses, relating them to independent clauses, which can stand alone as complete sentences. Examples of subordinating conjunctions include *because, as if, even though, since, so that, whereas,* and *whenever.*

I enjoyed the TV program *because* it was so well acted. (Conjunction connects *it was so well acted* to rest of sentence.)

Whenever you're ready, we can begin dinner. (Conjunction connects *you're ready* to rest of sentence.)

Conjunctive Adverbs   These connectors resemble both conjunctions and adverbs. Like conjunctions, they serve as linking devices between elements of equal rank. Like adverbs, they function as modifiers, showing such things as similarity, contrast, result or effect, addition, emphasis, time, and example.

The job will require you to travel a great deal; *however,* the salary is excellent.

Sean cares nothing for clothes; *in fact,* all of his socks have holes in their toes.

The following list groups the most common conjunctive adverbs according to function:

Similarity: likewise, similarly

Contrast: however, nevertheless, on the contrary, on the other hand, otherwise

Result or effect: accordingly, as a result, consequently, hence, therefore, thus

Addition: also, furthermore, in addition, in the first place, moreover

Emphasis or clarity: in fact, in other words, indeed, that is

Time: afterward, later, meanwhile, subsequently

Example: for example, for instance, to illustrate

Conjunctive adverbs should not be confused with coordinating conjunctions. Unlike conjunctions and more like adverbs, conjunctive adverbs can move, often to create a specific emphasis.

The job will require you to travel a great deal; the salary, *however,* is excellent.

The job will require you to travel a great deal; *however,* the salary is excellent.

Sean cares nothing for clothes; all of his socks, *in fact,* have holes in their toes.

Sean cares nothing for clothes; *in fact,* all of his socks have holes in them.

Because conjunctive adverbs can move, the second independent clause must be treated as a complete sentence and either be joined to the previous independent clause with a semicolon or be separated by a period.

Usage Considerations   You can add variety and precision to your writing by varying the conjunctions you use. If you consistently rely on the conjunction *because,* try substituting *as* or *since.* Likewise, you may periodically replace *if* with *provided that.* The right conjunction shows the relationship among ideas.

When you have choppy sentences, try combining them by using a conjunction.

You can buy smoked salmon at Sally's Seafoods. You can buy it at Daane's Thriftland as well.

You can buy smoked salmon *either* at Sally's Seafoods *or* at Daane's Thriftland.

The revision is much smoother than the original sentence pair.

Interjections

An interjection is an exclamatory word used to gain attention or to express strong feeling. It has no grammatical connection to the rest of the sentence. An interjection is followed by an exclamation point or a comma.

Hey! Watch how you're driving! (strong interjection)

Oh, is the party over already? (mild interjection)

Identify the coordinating conjunctions (CC), subordinating conjunctions (SC), conjunctive adverbs (CA), and interjections (I) in the following sentences:

1. There is evidence that the polar ice caps are receding; however, scientists do not yet know the probable impact of this event.
2. Neither term limits nor campaign reform will take money out of politics.
3. Since there has been an increase in the alligator population, some lawmakers think the ban on alligator hide products should be lifted.
4. Rats! My computer ate my report.
5. Most companies work hard to secure their Internet sites, but hackers can usually find their way around these safeguards.
6. Extensive resources have been committed to the war on drugs; nevertheless, illegal narcotics continue to flow into this country.
7. After Barbara got the promotion, she took all her coworkers out to celebrate.

Phrases and Clauses

Phrases

A phrase is a group of words that lacks a subject and a predicate and serves as a single part of speech. This section discusses four basic kinds of phrase: *prepositional, participial, gerund,* and *infinitive.* The last three are based on participles, gerunds, and infinitives, which are verb forms known as verbals. A fifth type of phrase, the verb phrase, consists of sets of two or more verbs (*has fixed, had been sick, will have been selected,* and the like).

Prepositional Phrases   A prepositional phrase consists of a preposition, one or more objects, and any associated words. These phrases serve as adjectives or adverbs.

The picture *over the mantel* was my mother's. (prepositional phrase as adjective)

He bought ice skates *for himself.* (prepositional phrase as adverb modifying verb)

The toddler was afraid *of the dog.* (prepositional phrase as adverb modifying adjective)

Our visitors arrived late *in the day.* (prepositional phrase as adverb modifying another adverb)

Frequently, prepositional phrases occur in series. Sometimes they form chains in which each phrase modifies the object of the preceding phrase. At other times, some or all of the phrases may modify the verb or verb phrase.

John works *in a clothing store/ on Main Street/ during the summer.*

Here the first and third phrases serve as adverbs modifying the verb *works* and answering the questions "Where?" and "When?" while the second phrase serves as an adjective modifying *store* and answering the question "Where?"

On occasion, especially in questions, a preposition may be separated from its object, making the phrase difficult to find.

Dr. Perry is the person *whom* I've been looking *for.*

What are you shouting *about?*

Participial Phrases   A participial phrase consists of a participle plus associated words. Participles are verb forms that, when used in participial phrases, function as adjectives or adverbs. A present participle ends in *-ing* and indicates an action currently being carried out. A past participle ends in *-ed, -en,-e, -n, -d,* or *-t* and indicates some past action.

The chef *preparing dinner* trained in France. (present participial phrase as adjective)

The background, *sketched in lightly,* accented the features of the woman in the painting. (past participial phrase as adjective)

She left *whistling a jolly melody.* (present participial phrase as adverb)

A perfect participial phrase consists of *having* or *having been* plus a past participle and any associated words. Like a past participial phrase, it indicates a past action.

Having alerted the townspeople about the tornado, the sound truck returned to the city garage. (perfect participial phrase)

Having been alerted to the tornado, the townspeople sought shelter in their basements. (perfect participial phrase)

Some participial phrases that modify persons or things distinguish them from others in the same class. These phrases are written without commas. Other phrases provide more information about the persons or things they modify and are set off with commas.

The man *fixing my car* is a master mechanic. (Phrase distinguishes man fixing car from others.)

Mr. Welsh, *fatigued by the tennis game,* rested in the shade. (Phrase provides more information about Mr. Welsh.)

Gerund Phrases   A gerund phrase consists of a gerund and the words associated with it. Like present participles, gerunds are verb forms that end in *-ing*. Unlike participles, though, they function as nouns rather than as adjectives or adverbs.

> Kathryn's hobby is *collecting stamps.* (gerund phrase as subject complement)
> Kathryn's hobby, *collecting stamps,* has made her many friends. (gerund phrase as appositive)
> He devoted every spare moment to *overhauling the car.* (gerund phrase as object of preposition.)

Infinitive Phrases   An infinitive phrase consists of the present principal part of a verb preceded by *to (to fix, to eat),* together with any accompanying words. These phrases serve as adjectives, adverbs, and nouns.

> This looks like a good place *to plant the shrub.* (infinitive phrase as adjective)
> Lenore worked *to earn money for college.* (infinitive phrase as adverb)
> My goal is *to have my own business some day.* (infinitive phrase as noun)

Gerunds can often be substituted for infinitives and vice versa.

> *To repair this fender* will cost two hundred dollars. (infinitive phrase as subject)
> *Repairing this fender* will cost two hundred dollars. (gerund phrase as subject)
> At times the *to* in an infinitive is omitted following verbs such as *make, dare, let,* and *help.*
> Kristin didn't dare *(to) move* a muscle.
> The psychiatrist helped me *(to) overcome* my fear of flying.

Verbals Not in Phrases   Participles, gerunds, and infinitives can function as nouns, adjectives, or adverbs, even when they are not parts of phrases.

> That *sunbathing* woman is a well-known model. (participle as adjective)
> *Dancing* is fine exercise. (gerund)
> The children want *to play.* (infinitive as noun)
> If you're looking for a job, Sally is the person *to see.* (infinitive as adjective)
> I'm prepared *to resign.* (infinitive as adverb)

Usage Considerations   Phrases can often clarify or develop the information in a sentence or combine choppy sentences.

> *Original*   My brother is fishing.
> *Revision*   My brother is fishing *for trout just below Barnes Dam on Sidewinder Creek.* (prepositional phrases added)
> *Original*   The boat barely made shore.
> *Revision*   The boat, *listing heavily and leaking badly,* barely made shore. (participial phrases added)

cl

To avoid ponderous sentences, don't, however, weigh them down with phrases, as in the following example:

My brother is fishing for trout just below Barnes Dam on Sidewinder Creek *near Perry Pass in the mountains of Central Colorado.*

Testing a Phrase's Function

To determine whether a phrase is functioning as noun, adjective, or adverb, try a substitution test; if a common noun (something, someone, or it), adjective or adjective phrase, or adverb fits, that demonstrates the function of the phrase.

Walking at a brisk pace is excellent exercise. (gerund phrase)

Something is excellent exercise. (noun phrase)

I am prepared *to finish the job.* (infinitive phrase)

I am prepared *completely.* (adverb phrase)

He was a man *of unusual craftiness.* (prepositional phrase)

He was a *crafty* man. (adjective phrase)

Identify the italicized phrases as prepositional, participial, gerund, or infinitive and indicate whether each is used as a noun, an adjective, or an adverb.

1. *Sleeping in late* can be one of the great pleasures of a holiday.
2. The students waited *for 10 minutes* before they left.
3. *Racing around the corner,* Tim crashed into another student and sent her sprawling.
4. The employees were afraid that there was a plan *to lay off a third of the workforce.*
5. Our guest speaker has written a book about *kayaking around New Zealand.*
6. Most high school students cannot wait *to graduate.*
7. David broke his leg *skiing in Colorado.*

Clauses

A clause is a word group that includes a subject and a predicate. An *independent clause*, sometimes called a main clause, expresses a complete thought and can function as a simple sentence. A *subordinate clause*, or dependent clause, cannot stand by itself. Subordinate clauses may serve as nouns, adjectives, or adverbs.

Noun Clauses   A noun clause can serve in any of the ways that ordinary nouns can.

What the neighbor told John proved to be incorrect. (noun clause as subject)

The woman asked *when the bus left for Spokane.* (noun clause as direct object)

I'll give a reward to *whoever returns my billfold.* (noun clause as object of preposition *to*)

cl

Noun clauses normally begin with one of the following words:

Relative Pronouns		**Interrogative Pronouns**
who	whoever	when
whom	whomever	why
whose	that	where
what	whatever	how
which	whichever	whether

The complementizer *that* is sometimes omitted from the beginning of a clause that acts as a direct object.

> Dr. Kant thinks *(that) he knows everything.*

If a clause is serving as a noun, you can replace it with the word *something* or *someone*, and the sentence will still make sense.

> Dr. Kant thinks *something.*

If the clause is serving as an adjective or an adverb, making the substitution turns the sentence into nonsense.

> The person *who wins the lottery* will receive two million dollars.
> The person *someone* will receive two million dollars.

Adjective Clauses   Like ordinary adjectives, adjective clauses, often called *relative clauses*, modify nouns and noun substitutes.

> Give me one reason *why you feel the way you do.* (Adjective clause modifies noun.)
> I'll hire anyone *that Dr. Stone recommends.* (Adjective clause modifies pronoun.)

Generally, adjective clauses begin with one of the following words:

Relative Pronouns	**Relative Adverbs**
who	when
whom	where
whose	why
what	after
which	before
that	

Sometimes the word that introduces the clause can be omitted.

> The chair *(that) we ordered last month* has just arrived. (pronoun *that* omitted but understood)
> The man *(whom) we were talking to* is a movie producer. (pronoun *whom* omitted but understood)

Sometimes, too, a preposition comes ahead of the introductory pronoun.

> The grace *with which Nelson danced* made the onlookers envious.

An adjective clause may be restrictive and distinguish whatever it modifies from others in the same class, or it may be nonrestrictive and provide more information about whatever it modifies.

> Flora wiped up the cereal *that the baby had spilled.* (restrictive clause)
>
> Harriet Thomas, *who was born in Alaska,* now lives in Hawaii. (nonrestrictive clause)

As these examples show, restrictive clauses are not set off with commas, but nonrestrictive clauses are. See pages 672–673 for further information.

Adverb Clauses   These clauses modify verbs, adjectives, adverbs, and sentences, answering the same questions that ordinary adverbs do.

> You may go *whenever you wish.* (Adverb clause modifies verb.)
>
> Sandra looked paler *than I had ever seen her look.* (Adverb clause modifies adjective.)
>
> Darryl shouted loudly *so that the rescue party could hear him.* (Adverb clause modifies adverb.)
>
> *Unless everyone cooperates,* this plan will never succeed. (Adverb clause modifies whole sentence.)

The word or word group that introduces an adverb clause is always a subordinating conjunction. Here are the most common of these conjunctions, grouped according to the questions they answer.

> *When?* after, as, as soon as, before, since, until, when, whenever, while
>
> *Where?* where, wherever
>
> *How?* as if, as though
>
> *Why?* as, because, now that, since, so that
>
> *Under what conditions?* although, if, once, provided that, though, unless
>
> *To what extent?* than

Occasionally in an adverb clause, the omission of one or more words won't hurt its meaning. Such a construction is called an *elliptical clause.*

> *While (he was) making a sandwich,* Garth hummed softly. (*he was* omitted but understood)

Unlike noun and adjective clauses, adverb clauses can often be moved about in their sentences.

> Garth hummed softly *while (he was) making a sandwich.*

Usage Considerations   Like phrases, clauses can help develop sentences as well as smooth out choppiness.

> *Original*   The old grandfather clock ticked loudly through the night.
>
> *Revision*   The old grandfather clock *that my great-aunt gave me before she died* ticked loudly through the night. (Clause adds information.)

Original   The chemistry professor insisted on lab safety. He had been hurt in a lab explosion the previous year.

Revision   The chemistry professor, *who had been hurt in a lab explosion the previous year,* insisted on lab safety. (Clause adds smoothness.)

To avoid clumsiness, avoid overloaded sentences like the one below:

The old grandfather clock that my great-aunt gave me before she died *and that I took with me to England when my company transferred me there for two years* ticked loudly through the night.

EXERCISE

Identify the italicized clauses as noun, adjective, or adverb.

1. Brad pulled a muscle in his back *while he was lifting weights.*
2. The astronauts *who landed on the moon* should still be household names.
3. Some astronomers suggested *that Pluto should not be considered a planet.*
4. Jody Singleton was touched by the cards *her students sent her.*
5. *Although coffee shops would seem like the quintessential small business,* some companies have turned America's coffee habit into multimillion dollar chains.
6. *Whoever decorated this house* has an excellent eye.
7. Andrea was pleased to find out that her new employer used the kind of accounting software *on which she had been trained.*

Coordination and Subordination

Coordination and subordination are ways to rank ideas in sentences. Coordination makes ideas equal; subordination makes them unequal. To understand coordination and subordination, you need to know about four kinds of sentences: simple, compound, complex, and compound–complex.

Simple Sentences   A simple sentence has one subject and one predicate. Some simple sentences consist merely of a single noun and a single verb.

Millicent shouted.

Others include elements such as compound subjects, compound verbs, direct objects, indirect objects, and subject complements.

Jim and Sue have bought a car. *(compound subject, direct object)*

Lucretia Borgia smiled and mixed her guests a cocktail. *(compound verb, indirect object, direct object)*

Autumn is a sad season. *(subject, complement)*

Compound Sentences   A compound sentence contains two or more independent clauses, each holding the same (coordinate) rank. As a result, the idea in the first clause receives the same emphasis as the idea in the second.

In some cases, a comma and a coordinating conjunction *(and, but, or, nor, for, yet, so)* link successive clauses.

Name the baby Huey, *or* I'll cut you out of my will.

The audience was young, friendly, and responsive, *so* it cheered for each speaker.

In others, a semicolon and a conjunctive adverb *(for example, however, in fact, likewise, meanwhile, instead,* and the like) furnish the connection.

Tod wants to see the play; *in fact,* he's talked about it for weeks.

Today, many young women do not rush into marriage and motherhood; *instead,* they spend several years establishing careers.

Finally, a writer may omit any connecting word and separate the clauses with a semicolon.

The sky grew pitch black; the wind died; an ominous quiet hung over the whole city.

Be sure to read this Hemingway novel; it suggests how to cope gracefully with pressure.

As the preceding sentences show, compound sentences allow writers to express simple relationships among simple ideas. However, such sentences have one important limitation: It is impossible to highlight one particular idea. To do this, we need complex sentences.

Complex Sentences   A complex sentence has one independent clause and one or more dependent clauses. Relegating an idea to a dependent clause shows that the writer wishes it to receive less emphasis than the idea in the main clause. In the following examples, the dependent clauses are italicized.

Because the young, friendly audience was responsive, it cheered for each speaker.

After the dance was over, Arthur collapsed on the sofa.

Once they had reached the lakeshore, the campers found a level spot *where they could pitch their tent.*

Unlike compound sentences, complex ones allow writers to vary the emphasis of ideas.

While I watered the grass, I discussed stock options with Liz.

I watered the grass *while I discussed stock options with Liz.*

The first sentence emphasizes the talk with Liz, the second watering the lawn.

Compound–Complex Sentences   This type of sentence features two or more independent clauses and one or more dependent clauses. Here are two examples with the dependent clauses italicized:

Ms. Harris works as an investment manager, and Mr. Williams, *who lives next door to her,* owns a jewelry store.

If you are to communicate properly, your thoughts must be clear and correct; thoughts are wasted *when language is muddled.*

EXERCISE

Label the independent and dependent clauses in the sentences below. Then identify each sentence as simple, compound, complex, or compound–complex.

1. A career in broadcasting requires good verbal skills, an extensive wardrobe, and a pleasant smile.
2. Because its bag was too full, the vacuum cleaner backfired, leaving the room dirtier than it had been.
3. Leave your boots in the back hall, please.
4. When Tom arrived home, his roommate asked him where he had really gone; six hours seemed too long a time to spend in the library.
5. My orange tree blossomed last week; however, the grapefruit trees have withered, probably because of the freeze last month.
6. Kites make good gifts for children; even if a child already has a kite, a second one will come in handy if the first one becomes tangled in a tree.
7. It's risky to confide in a coworker because one can never be sure that the confidence will be kept.

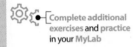

Complete additional exercises and practice in your MyLab

Editing to Correct Sentence Errors

Accepted usage improves the smoothness of your prose, makes your writing easier to understand, and demonstrates that you are a careful communicator.

When you've finished revising the first draft of a piece of writing, edit it with a critic's eye to ensure that you eliminate errors. Circle sentences or parts of them that are faulty or suspect. Then check your circled items against this section of the Handbook, which deals with the most common errors in college writing.

Revising Sentence Fragments

A sentence fragment is a group of words that fails to qualify as a sentence but is capitalized and punctuated as if it were a sentence. To be a sentence, a word group must (1) have a subject and a verb and (2) make sense by itself. The first of the following examples has a subject and a verb; the second does not. Neither makes sense by itself.

Watch the Animation on **Sentence Fragments**

> If you want to remain.

> His answer to the question.

Methods of Revision   Eliminating a sentence fragment is not hard. Careful reading often shows that the fragment goes with the sentence that comes just before or just after it. And sometimes two successive fragments can be joined. Note how we've corrected the fragments (italicized) in the following pairs:

Faulty	*Having been warned about the storm.* We decided to stay home.
Revision	Having been warned about the storm, we decided to stay home.
Faulty	Sally went to work. *Although she felt sick.*
Revision	Sally went to work although she felt sick.
Faulty	*That bronze clock on the mantel. Once belonged to my grandmother.*
Revision	That bronze clock on the mantel once belonged to my grandmother.

641

Joining a fragment to a sentence or to another fragment works only if the problem is simply one of mispunctuation. If the fragment stems from an improperly developed thought, revise the thought into correct sentence form.

Intentional Fragments   Fragments are commonly used in conversation and the writing that reproduces it. Professional writers also use fragments to gain special emphasis or create special effects. Pages 107–108 discuss these applications.

frag

EXERCISE

Ten main clauses paired with fragments are shown below. In each case, identify the sentence (S) and the fragment (F) and then eliminate the fragment.

1. I would like you to meet Janine Lee. One of my good friends from high school.
2. Jason and Steve bought several posters. To spruce up their dorm room walls.
3. In order to get tickets to the concert. We had to stand in line for hours.
4. After we finish studying for our math test. We plan to go out for pizza.
5. The road to Cedar Lake will be closed for months. Because the flood has washed away the bridge over the Rouge River.
6. There are several ways for companies to save on energy costs. One of them energy recycling.
7. Kristen first searched the library for information for her report. And then turned to the Internet for additional material.

Connected Discourse Exercise

Identify and correct the sentence fragments in the following letter:

My recent bill included $254 in charges for text messages. I do not understand these charges, Since my plan includes unlimited text messaging. In fact, the bill includes a charge for that very service. In addition, many of these text messages are unsolicited and come from companies selling products I don't want, Including several text messages from your company reminding me of your services. One company I contacted admitted that they got my name from a list they purchased from you, Without my granting permission for such a release. Because I pride myself on paying my bills on time. I am submitting payment for all but the $254. However, I expect you to appropriately adjust my bill, And fix this problem for future billing cycles.

Sincerely,

Texted Out.

Revising Run-On Sentences and Comma Splices

A run-on, or fused, sentence occurs when one sentence runs into another without anything to mark their junction. A comma splice occurs when only a comma marks the junction. These errors lead your readers to think that you are hasty or careless. Here are some examples:

Watch the Animation on **Run-On Sentences**

ro cs

Run-on sentence	Laura failed to set her alarm she was late for work.
Comma splice	Violets are blooming now, my lawn is covered with them.
Run-on sentence	Rick refused to attend the movie he said he hated horror shows.
Comma splice	Perry watched the road carefully, he still missed his turn.
Run-on sentence	Janet worked on her term paper her friend studied for a calculus test.
Comma splice	Janet worked on her term paper, her friend studied for a calculus test.

Testing for Errors   To check out a possible comma splice or fused sentence, read what precedes and follows the comma or suspected junction and see whether the two parts can stand alone as sentences. If *both parts* can stand alone, there is an error. Otherwise, there is not.

Darryl is a real troublemaker, someday he'll find himself in serious difficulty.

Examination of the parts preceding and following the comma shows that each is a complete sentence:

Darryl is a real troublemaker.
Someday he'll find himself in serious difficulty.

The writer has therefore committed a comma splice that needs correction.

Methods of Revision   You can correct run-on sentences and comma splices in several ways.

1. Create two separate sentences.

Revision   Violets are blooming now. My lawn is covered with them.
Revision   Rick refused to attend the movie. He said he hated horror shows.

2. Join the sentences with a semicolon.

Revision   Violets are blooming now; my yard is covered with them.
Revision   Rick refused to attend the movie; he said he hated horror shows.

3. Join the sentences with a comma and a coordinating conjunction *(and, but, or, nor, for, yet, so)*.

Revision   Laura failed to set her alarm, *so* she was late for work.

Revision   Perry watched the road carefully, *but* he still missed his turn.

4. Join the sentences with a semicolon and a conjunctive adverb (see page 631).

Revision   Laura failed to set her alarm; *consequently*, she was late for work.

Revision   Violets are blooming now; *in fact*, my yard is covered with them.

5. Introduce one of the sentences with a subordinating conjunction (see pages, 630–631).

Revision   *Because* Laura failed to set her alarm, she was late for work.

Revision   Janet worked on her term paper *while* her friend studied for a calculus test.

As our examples show, you can often correct an error in several ways.

Indicate whether each item is correct (C), is a run-on sentence (RO), or contains a comma splice (CS) and then correct the faulty items.

1. Our computer assistants have only had three weeks of training, you cannot expect them to know the answer to every technical question.

2. Ellen worked very hard on her report she really earned her A.

3. The research on the effect of television violence on children remains inconclusive, but still most of us would think that excessive exposure to images of violence would be harmful.

4. Alternative forms of punishment such as home incarceration have proven very effective, nevertheless prison is still the standard punishment for most nonviolent crimes.

5. The photographer accidentally exposed his film to the light as a result all our wedding pictures were ruined.

6. Jason got a terrific tan, he spent the winter break in Florida.

7. While tuberculosis is a terrible disease, it is rare and usually can be treated with antibiotics.

Connected Discourse Exercise

Identify and correct the comma splices and run-on sentences in the following message:

Text Message from the Cell Phone Company.

Thank you for your recent bill payment of eighty-five dollars, our records show that you still owe an additional $254. Given the significant volume of your text messaging, this is clearly a service that is valuable to you. You might consider paying an increased fee for unlimited text messaging this fee is significantly less than you are currently paying with a charge for each text message. We appreciate the permission you granted us to share your names with other companies. We have shared your name with a number of companies, you should be receiving even more text messages for new products and sales. This is another reason to change to our unlimited text-messaging plan for only $50 a month. You may pay the remaining $254 online using your credit card, this will allow you to continue to receive a service you so clearly value.

sv agr

Creating Subject–Verb Agreement

A verb should agree in number with its subject. Singular verbs should have singular subjects, and plural verbs should have plural subjects.

*Watch the Animation on **Subject-Verb Agreement***

Correct	My *boss* is a grouch. (singular subject and verb)
Correct	The *apartments have* two bedrooms. (plural subject and verb)

Ordinarily, matching subjects and verbs causes no problems. The following special situations, however, can create difficulties.

Subject and Verb Separated by a Word Group   Sometimes a word group that includes one or more nouns comes between the subject and the verb. When this happens, match the verb with its subject, not a noun in the word group.

Correct	Our *basket* of sandwiches *is* missing.
Correct	Several *books* required for my paper *are* not in the library.
Correct	*Mr. Schmidt*, along with his daughters, *runs* a furniture store.
Correct	The old *bus*, crammed with passengers, *was* unable to reach the top of the hill.

Two Singular Subjects   Most singular subjects joined by *and* take a plural verb.

Correct	The *couch* and *chair were* upholstered in blue velvet.

Sentences like the one above almost never cause problems. With subjects like *restoring cars* and *racing motorcycles*, however, singular verbs are often mistakenly used.

Faulty	*Restoring cars* and *racing motorcycles consumes* most of Frank's time.
Revision	*Restoring cars* and *racing motorcycles consume* most of Frank's time.

When *each* or *every* precedes the subjects, use a *singular* verb in place of a plural.

Correct   Every *book* and *magazine was* badly water-stained.

Singular subjects joined by *or, either—or,* or *neither—nor* also take singular verbs.

Correct   A *pear* or an *apple is* a good afternoon snack.

Correct   Neither *rain* nor *snow slows* our letter carrier.

Finally, use a singular verb when two singular subjects joined by *and* name the same person, place, or thing.

Correct   My *cousin* and business *partner* is retiring next month.

Cousin and *partner* refer to the same person.

sv agr

One Singular and One Plural Subject

When one singular subject and one plural subject are joined by *or, either—or,* or *neither—nor,* match the verb with the closer of the two.

Correct   Neither *John* nor his *parents were* at home.

Correct   Neither his *parents* nor *John was* at home.

As these examples show, the sentences are usually smoother when the plural subject follows the singular.

Collective Nouns As Subjects

Collective nouns (*assembly, class, committee, family, herd, majority, tribe,* and the like) are singular in form but stand for groups or collections of people or things. Ordinarily, collective nouns are considered to be singular and therefore take singular verbs.

Correct   The *class* is writing a test.

Correct   The *herd was* clustered around the water hole.

Sometimes, though, a collective noun refers to the separate individuals making up the grouping, and then it requires a plural verb.

Correct   The *jury are* in dispute about the verdict.

Sentences in Which the Verb Comes Ahead of the Subject

Sentences that begin with words such as *here, there, how, what,* and *where* fall into this category. With such sentences, the verb must agree with the subject that follows it.

Correct   Here *is* my *house.*

Correct   Where *are* my *shoes?*

Correct   There *is* just one *way* to solve this problem.

Correct   There *go* my *chances* for a promotion.

Choose the correct verb form from the pair in parentheses.

1. The library, along with many of the books, (*was, were*) severely damaged by the storm.
2. Congress (*retains, retain*) the right to control the country's purse strings.
3. A house with two baths and four bedrooms (*is, are*) for sale in my neighborhood.
4. What (*does, do*) these new printers cost?
5. A van or three cars (*is, are*) needed to drive the wrestling team to the meet.
6. Each of these suggestions (*has, have*) a lot of merit.
7. John Finch and his assistant (*plans, plan*) to review the contract with you next Friday.
8. There (*is, are*) a few advantages to carefully planning your work schedule.
9. Every piece of clothing and bedding (*has, have*) to be washed in scalding water.
10. Each of our employees (*knows, know*) the answer to the most common questions about our product.

pa agr

Connected Discourse Exercise

Identify and correct the subject–verb agreement errors in the following e-mail:

To: Cell Phone Service

From: Texted Out

Re: Phone Bill ID 754 657 8934 265

One of the phone representatives handling my case have seriously misunderstood my previous letter. My records show that I have paid for unlimited text messaging for the last three years; yet, I am still being charged a fee for individual text messages. Either your records or your billing system are faulty. Worse, each of the text messages listed are from a company that purchased my name from you without my permission. Your team of representatives are the worst that I have ever seen. This charge, along with any additional individual text messaging charges, need to be dropped from my bill immediately. If this problem, as well as the unwanted text messages, are not corrected immediately, I will have to change my cell phone provider.

Achieving Pronoun–Antecedent Agreement

The antecedent of a pronoun is the noun or pronoun to which it refers. Just as subjects should agree with their verbs, pronouns should agree with their antecedents: singular antecedents require singular pronouns, and plural antecedents require plural pronouns. Ordinarily, you will have no trouble matching antecedents and pronouns. The situations that follow, however, can cause problems.

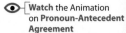
Watch the Animation on **Pronoun-Antecedent Agreement**

Indefinite Pronouns as Antecedents   Indefinite pronouns include words like *each, either, neither, any, everybody, somebody,* and *nobody.* Whenever an indefinite pronoun is used as an antecedent, the pronoun that refers to it should be singular.

Faulty   *Neither* of the actors had learned *their* lines.

Revision   *Neither* of the actors had learned *his* lines.

As the revised example shows, this rule applies even when the pronoun is followed by a plural noun.

When the gender of the antecedent is unknown, you may follow it with *his or her,* or if this results in awkwardness, rewrite the sentence in the plural.

Correct   *Anyone* who has studied *his or her* assignments properly should do well on the test.

Correct   *Those* who have studied *their* assignments properly should do well on the test.

Occasionally, a ridiculous result occurs when a singular pronoun refers to an indefinite pronoun that is obviously plural in meaning. When this happens, rewrite the sentence to eliminate the problem.

Faulty   *Everybody* complained that the graduation ceremony had lasted too long, but I didn't believe *him.*

Revision   Everybody complained that the graduation ceremony had lasted too long, but I didn't agree.

Two Singular Antecedents   Two or more antecedents joined by *and* ordinarily call for a plural pronoun.

Correct   Her briefcase and umbrella were missing from *their* usual place on the hall table.

When *each* or *every* precedes the antecedent, use a singular pronoun.

Incorrect   Every college and university must do *their* best to provide adequate student counseling.

Correct   Every college and university must do *its* best to provide adequate student counseling.

Singular antecedents joined by *or, either—or,* or *neither—nor* call for singular pronouns.

Correct   Neither Carol nor Irene had paid *her* rent for the month.

Applying this rule can sometimes yield an awkward sentence. When this happens, rewrite the sentence to avoid the problem.

Faulty   Neither James nor Sally has finished *his or her* term project.

Revision   James and Sally have not finished *their* term projects.

pa agr

Singular antecedents joined by *and* that refer to the same person, place, or thing use a singular pronoun.

> *Correct*   My *cousin* and business *partner is* retiring to *her* condo in Florida next month.

Singular and Plural Antecedents   If one singular and one plural antecedent are joined by *or, either—or,* or *neither—nor,* the pronoun agrees with the closer one.

> *Correct*   Either Terrence James or the Parkinsons will let us use *their* lawn mower.

> *Correct*   Either the Parkinsons or Terrence James will let us use *his* lawn mower.

Sentences of this sort are generally smoother when the plural subject follows the singular.

Collective Nouns as Antecedents   When a collective noun is considered a single unit, the pronoun that refers to it should be singular.

> *Correct*   The *troop* of scouts made *its* way slowly through the woods.

When the collective noun refers to the separate individuals in the group, use a plural pronoun.

> *Correct*   The *staff* lost *their* jobs when the factory closed.

EXERCISE

Choose the right pronoun from the pair in parentheses.

1. Company rules require every memo and letter to receive (*its, their*) correct authorization number.
2. Neither the Grangers nor Tom Cauldwell knew (*his, their*) lines by opening night.
3. After weeks of deliberation, the jury finally reached (*its, their*) decision.
4. Maria and Tim completed (*his or her, their*) project by the deadline.
5. Either Sally or the Randalls will lend us (*her, their*) punch bowl for our party.
6. Everybody has been assigned (*his or her, their*) own log-on name and password.
7. Every one of the women in our police force has proved that (*she, they*) can handle the duties of an officer.

Connected Discourse Exercise

Identify and correct the pronoun-antecedent agreement errors in the following e-mail.

To: Texted Out

From: Your Cell Phone Service

Re: Phone Bill ID 754 657 8934 265

Our team appreciates your kind compliments about their hard work.

Your phone representatives do the best they can to meet your needs. Any

of our representatives would have been glad to do their part to explain
your bill. You owe $254 for the text messages you received from numer-
ous companies and an additional $50 in late fees. Today every customer
and business does their best to reduce costs. You can reduce your costs
by either paying for unlimited texting or by limiting the number of texts
messages you receive. Either your local phone retailer or one of our many
representatives would be glad to offer you their assistance in promptly
resolving this matter before we have to discontinue your service.

Using Effective Pronoun Reference

Any pronoun except an indefinite pronoun should refer to just one noun or
noun substitute—its antecedent. Reference problems result when the pronoun
has two or more antecedents, a hidden antecedent, or no antecedent. These errors can cause mix-ups in meaning as well as ridiculous sentences.

More Than One Antecedent   The following sentences lack clarity because
their pronouns have two possible antecedents rather than just one:

Faulty	Take the screens off the windows and wash *them*.
Faulty	Harry told Will that *he* was putting on weight.

The reader can't tell whether the screens or the windows should be washed or
who is putting on weight.

Sometimes we see a sentence like this one:

Faulty	If the boys don't eat all the Popsicles, put *them* in the freezer.

In this case, we know it's the Popsicles that should be stored, but the use of *them*
creates an amusing sentence.

Correct these faults by replacing the pronoun with a noun or by rephrasing
the sentence.

Revision	Wash the windows after you have taken off the screens.
Revision	Take off the screens so that you can wash the windows.
Revision	Harry told Will, "I am (you are) putting on weight."
Revision	Put any uneaten Popsicles in the freezer.

Hidden Antecedent   An antecedent is hidden if it takes the form of an adjective rather than a noun.

Faulty	The movie theater is closed today, so we can't see *one*.
Faulty	As I passed the tiger's cage, it lunged at me.

To correct this fault, replace the pronoun with the noun used as an adjective or switch the positions of the pronoun and the noun and make any needed changes in their forms.

Revision   The theater is closed today, so we can't see a movie.

Revision   As I passed its cage, the tiger lunged at me.

No Antecedent   A no-antecedent sentence lacks any noun to which the pronoun can refer. Sentences of this sort occur frequently in everyday conversation but should be avoided in formal writing. The examples below illustrate this error:

Faulty   The lecture was boring, but *they* took notes anyway.

Faulty   On the news program, *it* told about a new crisis in the Persian Gulf.

To set matters right, substitute a suitable noun for the pronoun or reword the sentence.

Revision   The lecture was boring, but the students took notes anyway.

Revision   The news program told about a new crisis in the Persian Gulf.

Sometimes *this, that, it,* or *which* will refer to a whole idea rather than a single noun. This usage is acceptable provided the writer's meaning is obvious, as in this example:

Correct   The instructor spoke very softly, *which* meant we had difficulty hearing him.

Problems occur, however, when the reader can't figure out which of two or more ideas the pronoun refers to.

Faulty   Ginny called Sally two hours after the agreed-upon time and postponed their shopping trip one day. *This* irritated Sally very much.

What caused Sally to be irritated—the late call, the postponement of the trip, or both? Again, rewording or adding a clarifying word will correct the problem.

Revision   Ginny called Sally two hours after the agreed-upon time and postponed their shopping trip one day. *This tardiness* irritated Sally very much.

Revision   Ginny called Sally two hours after the agreed-upon time and postponed their shopping trip one day. Ginny's *change of plans* irritated Sally very much.

The first of these examples illustrates the addition of a clarifying word; the second illustrates rewriting.

pr ref

EXERCISE

Indicate whether each sentence is correct (C) or contains a faulty pronoun reference (F) and then correct the faulty sentences.

1. When the supervisor walked by the water cooler, they stopped talking.
2. I like trout fishing because it is very relaxing.
3. Since I knew that our employees found their chairs uncomfortable, I replaced them with new ones.
4. In the report, it suggested that we needed to be more attentive to employee suggestions.
5. Because the batting cap hurt his head, Fred removed it.
6. At Electronic City, they sell many brands of computers.
7. Janine asked Caroline if she could rewrite her paper for her English class.

shft

Connected Discourse Exercise

Identify and correct any faulty pronoun references in the following e-mail:

To: Cell Phone Service

From: Texted Out

Re: Phone Bill ID 754 657 8934 265

Given the erroneous charge for my phone service, I expect you to discontinue it immediately. Despite my attempts to resolve this problem with the company, they were unhelpful. As a result, I intend to change to a different carrier who promises a better one. I will also not pay it and will take legal action if you attempt to harm my credit rating. The mistake in the billing was yours, not mine, and I stand ready to prove it in court.

Managing Shifts in Person

Watch the Animation on **Shifts in Person**

Pronouns can be in the first person, second person, or third person. *First-person* pronouns identify people who are talking or writing about themselves (I). *Second-person* pronouns identify people being addressed directly (you), and *third-person* pronouns identify persons or things that are being written or spoken about (he). See page 613 for a list of pronouns with persons and cases.

All nouns are in the third person. As you revise, be alert for unwarranted shifts from one person to another.

Faulty	I liked *my* British vacation better than *my* vacation in France and Italy because *you* didn't have language problems.
Revision	I liked *my* British vacation better than *my* vacation in France and Italy because *I* didn't have language problems.
Faulty	Holidays are important to *everyone.* They boost *your* spirits and provide a break from *our* daily routine.
Revision	Holidays are important to *everyone.* They boost *one's* spirits and provide a break from *one's* daily routine.
Faulty	The taller the *golfer,* the more club speed *you* will have with a normally paced swing.
Revision	The taller the *golfer,* the more club speed *he* or *she* will have with a normally paced swing.

shft

As these examples show, the shift can occur within a single sentence or when the writer moves from one sentence to another.

Some shifts in person, however, are warranted. Read the following correct sentence:

Correct	*I* want *you* to deliver these flowers to Ms. Willoughby by three o'clock. *She* needs them for a party.

Here the speaker identifies himself or herself (*I*) while speaking directly to a listener *(you)* about someone else *(she).* In this case, shifts are needed to get the message across.

Indicate whether the sentence is correct (C) or contains an unwarranted shift in person (S). Correct faulty sentences.

1. After the teacher collected our essays, she told the students that she would return the graded papers on Wednesday.
2. For someone to be successful in today's marketplace, you need to have adequate technical skills.
3. If you each will bring the results of your assigned research to the next meeting, we will be ready to begin working on our collaborative report.
4. Anyone who would like to purchase the discounted Caribbean cruise tickets should place your order by May 15.
5. We enjoy living in the Grand Rapids area very much; you have access to theater, sporting events, and fine dining.
6. If you would like to learn to kayak, novices can usually get free lessons from the people who sell kayaks.
7. In our attempt to determine whether there has been an increase in tornado activity over the last 20 years, the researchers collected data on storm sightings and damage reports.

Connected Discourse Exercise

Identify and correct the unwarranted shifts in person in the following e-mail:

To: Texted Out

From: Cell Phone Service

Re: Contract Violation ID 754 657 8945 265

We are sorry to hear that you have decided to violate your contract. One has a responsibility to his contract, which is the customer's agreement with our company to pay for your services. In the small print at the bottom of the agreement you signed, one will notice that in case of cancellation of the contract they are required to pay $1,000 in cancellation fees. We will, however, allow one to reconsider canceling the service. To keep their service in place, one only needs to pay $154 for text messages and $100 in late fees. We value you as a customer, which is why we work hard to meet ones wireless needs.

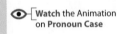

case

Using the Right Pronoun Case

Case means the changes in form that a personal pronoun (see page 613) undergoes to show its function in a sentence. English has three cases: the *subjective (I)*, the *nonsubjective* (objective) *(me)*, and the *possessive (my/mine)*.

The subjective case is used for subjects and subject complements, the nonsubjective for direct objects, indirect objects, and objects of prepositions. The possessive case shows ownership and is also used with gerunds.

The following pointers will help you select the proper pronoun as you revise.

We and Us Preceding Nouns Nouns that serve as subjects take the pronoun *we*. Other nouns take the pronoun *us*.

Correct	*We* tourists will fly home tomorrow. (*We* accompanies the subject.)
Correct	The guide showed *us* tourists through the cathedral. (*Us* accompanies a nonsubject.)

If you can't decide which pronoun is right, mentally omit the noun and read the sentence to yourself, first with one pronoun and then with the other. Your ear will indicate the correct form.

My mother made (*we, us*) children vanilla pudding for dessert.

Omitting *children* shows immediately that *us* is the right choice.

Correct	My mother made *us* children vanilla pudding for dessert.

Pronouns Paired with Nouns When such a combination serves as the subject of a sentence or accompanies the subject, use the subject form of the pronoun. When the combination plays a nonsubject role, use the nonsubject form of the pronoun.

⊙ Watch the Animation on **Pronoun Case**

Correct	Arlene and *I* plan to join the Peace Corps. (*I* is part of the compound subject.)
Correct	Two people, Mary and *I*, will represent our school at the meeting. (*I* is part of a compound element accompanying the subject.)
Correct	The superintendent told Kevin and *him* that they would be promoted soon. (*Him* is part of a compound nonsubject.)
Correct	The project was difficult for Jeffrey and *him* to complete. (*Him* is part of a compound nonsubject.)

Again, mentally omitting the noun from the combination will tell you which pronoun is correct.

case

Who and Whom in Dependent Clauses   Use *who* for the subjects of dependent clauses; otherwise, use *whom*.

Correct	The Mallarys prefer friends *who are interested in the theater.* (*Who* is the subject of the clause.)
Correct	Barton is a man *whom very few people like.* (*Whom* is not the subject of the clause.)

A simple test will help you decide between *who* and *whom*. First, mentally isolate the dependent clause. Next, block out the pronoun in question and then insert *he* (or *she*) and *him* (or *her*) at the appropriate spot in the remaining part of the clause. If *he* (or *she*) sounds better, *who* is right. If *him* (or *her*) sounds better, *whom* is right. Let's use this test on the sentence below:

The woman *who(m) Scott is dating* works as a mechanical engineer. Scott is dating (*she, her*).

Clearly, *her* is correct; therefore, *whom* is the proper form.

Correct	The woman *whom Scott is dating* works as a mechanical engineer.

Pronouns As Subject Complements   In formal writing, pronouns that serve as subject complements (see page 610 always take the subject form.

Correct	It is *I*.
Correct	It was *she* who bought the old Parker mansion.

This rule, however, is often ignored in informal writing.

> It's *her*.
>
> That's *him* standing over by the door.

Comparisons Using *Than* or *As...As*   Comparisons of this kind often make no direct statement about the second item of comparison. When the second naming word is a pronoun, you may have trouble choosing the right one.

Harriet is less outgoing than (*they, them*).

My parents' divorce saddened my sister as much as (*I, me*).

Not to worry. Expand the sentence by mentally supplying the missing material. Then try the sentence with each pronoun and see which sounds right.

Harriet is less outgoing than (*they, them*) are.

My parents' divorce saddened my sister as much as it did (*I, me*).

Obviously, *they* is the right choice for the first sentence, and *me* is the right choice for the second one.

Correct	Harriet is less outgoing than *they* are.
Correct	My parents' divorce saddened my sister as much as it did *me*.

Pronouns Preceding Gerunds   Use the possessive form of a pronoun that precedes a gerund (see page 634).

I dislike *their* leaving without saying goodbye.

Ted can't understand *her* quitting such a good job.

This usage emphasizes the action named by the gerund instead of the person or persons performing it. Thus, in the above sentences, the possessive form of the pronoun signals that it's the *leaving* the writer dislikes and the *quitting* that Ted can't understand. The persons involved are secondary.

When the pronoun precedes a participle (see pages 632–635), it should be in the nonsubject case. The emphasis is then on the actor rather than the action.

Jennifer caught *them* listening to records instead of studying.

In this example, Jennifer caught the listeners, not the listening.

If you have trouble deciding between the nonsubject and possessive forms of a pronoun, ask yourself whether you want to emphasize the action or the actor; then proceed accordingly.

Choose the right form of the pronoun for each of the following sentences. For the purpose of this exercise, assume that there would have been the appropriate pronoun antecedent in the sentence preceding the one that is shown.

1. No one is as pleased as (*I, me*) by John's recent promotion to assistant vice president.
2. There is no excuse for (*him, his*) yelling at us in public.
3. The newspaper's editor praised Marge and (*I, me*) for our coauthored article on women in the military.
4. Megan is one student (*who, whom*) I believe really understands the importance of writing well.
5. (*We, Us*) Americans pride ourselves on our individuality.
6. The conductor decided that Marie and (*I, me*) should sing a duet at the next recital.
7. Rilke is the poet (*who, whom*) I like best.
8. The judge told (*we, us*) contestants that we would be called when it was our turn.

Connected Discourse Exercise

Identify and correct the pronoun case errors in the following paragraph:

Between my best friend and I, there has always been a competition to see whom could participate in the most extreme sports. My friend took up extreme snowboarding, and him and some other nuts raced down a mountain just ahead of an avalanche. I didn't think I could try anything as crazy as him. However, someone who I had climbed mountains with gave me a chance to go hang gliding off the Grand Canyon. I jumped at the chance, literally, and broke both legs and four ribs. Who do you think won the competition?

time

Creating Consistency in Showing Time

Inconsistencies occur when a writer shifts from the past tense to the present or vice versa without a corresponding shift in the time of the events being described. The following paragraph contains an uncalled-for shift from the present tense to the past:

Watch the Animation on **Shifts in Tense**

> As *The Most Dangerous Game* opens, Sanger Rainsford, a famous hunter and author, and his old friend Whitney are standing on the deck of a yacht and discussing a mysterious island as the ship passes near it. Then, after everyone else has gone to bed, Rainsford manages to fall overboard. He swims to the island and ends up at a chateau owned by General Zaroff, a refugee from the Communist takeover in Russia. Zaroff, bored with hunting animals, has turned to hunting humans on his desert island. Inevitably, Rainsford is turned out into the jungle to be hunted down. There were [shift to past tense] actually four hunts over a three-day period, and at the end of the last one, Rainsford jumped into the sea, swam across a cove to the chateau, and killed Zaroff in the general's own bedroom. Afterward he sleeps [shift back to present tense] and decides "he had never slept in a better bed."

The sentence with the unwarranted shift in tense should read as follows:

> There are actually four hunts over a three-day period, and at the end of the last one, Rainsford jumps into the sea, swims across a cove to the chateau, and kills Zaroff in the general's own bedroom.

The time shift in the quotation part of the final sentence is justified because the sleeping has occurred before Rainsford's thoughts about it.

A second kind of inconsistency results when a writer fails to distinguish the immediate past from the less immediate past. The following sentence illustrates this error:

Faulty   Mary *answered* all 30 test questions.

This sentence indicates that Mary completed all 30 test questions during the final instant of the class, an impossibility. When you detect this type of error in your writing, determine which action occurred first and then correct the error by adding *had* to the verb. In this case, the first verb needs correcting:

Revision   Mary *had answered* all 30 test questions when the class ended.

Besides adding *had*, you may sometimes need to alter the verb form.

Faulty	Before he turned 20, John *wrote* two novels.
Revision	Before he turned 20, John *had written* two novels.

Indicate whether each sentence is correct (C) or contains an unwarranted shift (S) in tense. Then correct the faulty sentences.

1. A thin wisp of smoke drifts from under the hood, and then the engine burst into flames.
2. Jason took on many projects but finishes few of them.
3. As Charlie laid pieces of the model on the table, his wife picks them up.
4. As soon as the snow falls, we break out our cross-country skis.
5. David is building his own house but found it harder work than he anticipated.
6. While Robert applies the adhesive, David carefully positioned the floor tiles.
7. Although it started to rain heavily, Debbie continues to mow the lawn.

Connected Discourse Exercise

Identify and correct any inconsistencies in showing time in the following passage:

There is no better time to go swimming than at night. The summer after I had graduated from high school, I worked for a landscaping company. After a sweaty day mowing lawns and digging up gardens, all of us who worked there would jump into the back of Dick's old pickup and rattle out to Woods Lake. It is just dark as we arrive. The moon is beautiful, reflected in that black mirror set in a frame of hills. We stumble down a small, sandy hill to the beach, where we strip off our dusty jeans and sweaty shirts before plunging into the cool reflection of stars.

Using Adjectives and Adverbs Effectively

Watch the Animation on **Using Adjectives and Adverbs**

Inexperienced writers often use adjectives when they should use adverbs and also confuse the comparative and superlative forms of these parts of speech when making comparisons.

Misusing Adjectives for Adverbs   Although most adjectives can be misused as adverbs, the following seven, listed with the corresponding adverbs, cause the most difficulty.

Adjectives	Adverbs
awful	awfully
bad	badly
considerable	considerably
good	well
most	almost
real	really
sure	surely

The following sentences show typical errors:

Faulty   Bryan did *good* in his first golf lesson. (*good* mistakenly used to modify verb *did*)

Faulty   *Most* every graduate from our auto service program receives several job offers. (*most* mistakenly used to modify adjective *every*)

Faulty   The speech was delivered *real* well. (*real* mistakenly used to modify adverb *well*)

Because adverbs modify verbs, adjectives, and other adverbs (see page 627), and adjectives modify nouns and noun substitutes (see page 624), the above sentences clearly require adverbs.

Revision   Bryan did *well* in his first golf lesson.

Revision   *Almost* every graduate from our auto service program receives several job offers.

Revision   The speech was delivered *really* well.

In one notable case, an adverb is commonly misused as an adjective.

Faulty   I feel *badly* about providing the wrong phone number. (*Badly* is mistakenly used as a subject complement.)

Revision   I feel *bad* about providing the wrong phone number.

If you can't decide whether a sentence requires an adjective or an adverb, determine the part of speech of the word being modified and proceed accordingly.

Confusing the Comparative and Superlative Forms in Comparisons

The comparative form of adjectives and adverbs is used to compare two things, the superlative form to compare three or more things. Adjectives with fewer than three syllables generally add -*er* to make the comparative form and -*est* to make the superlative form (tall, tall*er*, tall*est*). Adjectives with three or more syllables generally add *more* to make the comparative and *most* to make the superlative (enchanting, *more* enchanting, *most* enchanting), as do most adverbs of two or more syllables (loudly, *more* loudly, *most* loudly).

When making comparisons, beginning writers sometimes mistakenly use double comparatives or double superlatives.

Faulty	Harry is *more taller* than James. (double comparative)
Faulty	The Chrysler Building has the *most splendidest* lobby I've ever seen. (double superlative)

The correct versions read as follows:

Revision	Harry is *taller* than James.
Revision	The Chrysler Building has the *most splendid* lobby I've ever seen.

mis adj/adv

In addition, writers may erroneously use the superlative form, rather than the comparative form, to compare two things.

Faulty	Barry is the *richest* of the two brothers.
Faulty	Jeremy is the *most talented* of those two singers.

Here are the sentences correctly written:

Revision	Barry is the *richer* of the two brothers.
Revision	Jeremy is the *more talented* of those two singers.

Reserve the superlative form for comparing three or more items.

Correct	Barry is the *richest* of the three brothers.
Correct	Jeremy is the *most talented* of those four singers.

EXERCISE

For each of the following sentences, choose the proper word from the pair in parentheses:

1. The milk in the refrigerator tastes (*bad, badly*).
2. Old science fiction movies can be (*real, really*) funny to watch because of the clumsy special effects and stilted dialogue.
3. Steve did (*good, well*) on his history project.
4. The Vandorns have the (*prettiest, most prettiest*) house in the development.
5. Terry hurt his knees (*bad, badly*) playing football.
6. The Mustang is the (*less, least*) expensive of the two sports cars you are considering.
7. (*Most, Almost*) all of our employees make use of the day care facility we provide on the premises.

Connected Discourse Exercise

Identify and correct the adjective–adverb errors in the following paragraph:

Roller Derby is back; and our team, the Crushers, is the better team in the league. We play to win, so we play real fierce, ready to crush the opposition. That is how we got our name. Our blockers show no mercy, smashing others to the rink so that our wild skating jammer can streak past for points. Seeing members of the other team sprawled helpless on the rink is a most wonderfulest feeling. It is an experience that we can sure plan on enjoying in future matches.

mm

Placing Modifiers Correctly

A misplaced modifier is a word or word group that is improperly separated from the word it modifies. When separation of this type occurs, the sentence often sounds awkward, ridiculous, or confusing.

Watch the Animation
on **Modifiers**

Usually, you can correct this error by moving the modifier next to the word it is intended to modify. Occasionally, you'll also need to alter some of the phrasing.

Faulty	There is a bicycle in the basement *with chrome fenders.* (The basement appears to have chrome fenders.)
Faulty	David received a phone call from his uncle *that infuriated him.* (The uncle appears to have infuriated David.)
Revision	There is a bicycle *with chrome fenders* in the basement.
Revision	David received an *infuriating* phone call from his uncle. (Note the change in wording.)

In shifting the modifier, don't inadvertently create another faulty sentence.

Faulty	Fritz bought a magazine with an article about Michael Jackson *at the corner newsstand.* (The article appears to tell about Jackson's visit to the corner newsstand.)
Faulty	Fritz bought a magazine *at the corner newsstand* with an article about Michael Jackson. (The corner newsstand appears to have an article about Jackson.)
Revision	*At the corner newsstand,* Fritz bought a magazine with an article about Michael Jackson.

As you revise, watch also for *squinting modifiers*—that is, modifiers positioned so that the reader doesn't know whether they are supposed to modify what comes ahead of them or what follows them.

Faulty	The man who was rowing the boat *frantically* waved toward the onlookers on the beach.

Is the man rowing frantically or waving frantically? Correct this kind of error by repositioning the modifier so that the ambiguity disappears.

Revision   The man who was *frantically* rowing the boat waved toward the onlookers on the beach.

Revision   The man who was rowing the boat waved *frantically* toward the onlookers on the beach.

dm

Indicate whether each sentence is correct (C) or contains a misplaced modifier (MM). Correct faulty sentences.

1. Jason handed his report to his teacher neatly tucked into a binder.
2. The girl driving past the school wildly waved at her friends.
3. The dancers practiced Swan Lake for a month before the performance.
4. I tossed the rainbow trout to my brother still hooked firmly in the mouth.
5. Most companies do not like placing managers in charge of employees who are inexperienced.
6. There is a computer in our classroom that beeps loudly at the most unexpected times.
7. Stacey found beautiful and inexpensive macramé wall hangings for her dorm room in the Bahamas.

Revising Dangling Modifiers

A dangling modifier is a phrase or clause that lacks clear connection to the word or words it is intended to modify. As a result, sentences are inaccurate, often comical. Typically, the modifier leads off the sentence, although it can also come at the end.

Sometimes the error occurs because the sentence fails to specify who or what is modified. At other times, the separation is too great between the modifier and what it modifies.

Faulty   *Walking in the meadow,* wildflowers surrounded us. (The wildflowers appear to be walking in the meadow.)

Faulty   Dinner was served *after saying grace.* (The dinner appears to have said grace.)

Faulty   *Fatigued by the violent exercise,* the cool shower was very relaxing. (The cool shower appears to have been fatigued.)

The first of these sentences is faulty because the modifier is positioned too far away from *us.* The other two are faulty because they do not identify who said grace or found the shower relaxing.

You can correct dangling modifiers in two basic ways. First, leave the modifier unchanged and rewrite the main part of the sentence so that it begins with the term actually modified. Second, rewrite the modifier so that it has its own subject and verb, thereby eliminating the inaccuracy.

Revision	*Walking in the meadow,* we were surrounded by wildflowers. (The main part of the sentence has been rewritten.)
Revision	*As we walked in the meadow,* wildflowers surrounded us. (The modifier has been rewritten.)
Revision	*Dinner was served after we had said grace.* (The modifier has been rewritten.)
Revision	*Fatigued by the violent exercise,* Ted found the cool shower very relaxing. (The main part of the sentence has been rewritten.)
Revision	*Because Ted was fatigued by the violent exercise,* the cool shower was very relaxing. (The modifier has been rewritten.)

Ordinarily, either part of the sentence can be rewritten, but sometimes only one part can.

Indicate whether each sentence is correct (C) or contains a dangling modifier (DM). Correct faulty sentences.

1. After listening to a tape of Orson Welles' radio broadcast of *The War of the Worlds*, I understood why many who tuned into the middle of the broadcast panicked.
2. The baseball game will start after singing *The Star-Spangled Banner*.
3. Looking at the night sky, a million stars seemed to smile down on us.
4. Having scored 100 percent on the pretest, the teacher placed two students in the next level math class.
5. Picasso was known to leave customers waiting for several days, painting furiously.
6. John cataloged his CD collection, listing each CD in a database.
7. Rushing over the banks, Main Street was soon under three feet of water.

Maintaining Parallelism

Nonparallelism results when equivalent ideas follow different grammatical forms. One common kind of nonparallelism occurs with words or word groups in pairs or in a series.

⊙ Watch the Animation on **Parallelism**

Faulty	Althea enjoys *jogging, biking,* and *to swim.*
Faulty	The superintendent praised the workers *for their productivity* and *because they had an excellent safety record.*
Faulty	The banner was *old, faded,* and *it had a rip.*

Note how rewriting the sentences in parallel form improves their smoothness.

Revision	Althea enjoys *jogging, biking,* and *swimming.*
Revision	The superintendent praised the workers for *their productivity* and *their excellent safety record.*
Revision	The banner was *old, faded,* and *ripped.*

Nonparallelism also occurs when correlative conjunctions *(either—or, neither— nor, both—and,* and *not only—but also)* are followed by unlike elements.

Faulty   That sound *either* <u>was a thunderclap</u> *or* <u>an explosion</u>.

Faulty   The basement was *not only* <u>poorly lighted</u> *but also* <u>it had a foul smell.</u>

Ordinarily, repositioning one of the correlative conjunctions will solve the problem. Sometimes, however, one of the grammatical elements must be rewritten.

Revision   That sound was *either* <u>a thunderclap</u> *or* <u>an explosion</u>. (*Either* has been repositioned.)

Revision   The basement was *not only* <u>poorly lighted</u> *but also* <u>foul smelling</u>. (The element following *but also* has been rewritten.)

EXERCISE

Indicate whether each sentence is correct (C) or nonparallel (NP). Correct faulty sentences.

1. The cause of the fire either was faulty wiring or an overloaded outlet.
2. After graduation, Marci will be moving to Chicago and work for a large public relations firm.
3. For spring break, Steve and his friends plan to visit either New Orleans or Orlando.
4. A good candidate for social work enjoys talking with people, helps solve problems, and seeing projects through to their conclusion.
5. This course will involve reading a number of short stories, and you will need to turn in weekly journal responses.
6. Although he was an excellent auto mechanic, Andy could neither repair air-conditioning units nor car stereos.
7. Canton chicken balls are sweet, tangy, and satisfying.

Revising Faulty Comparisons

A faulty comparison results if you (1) mention one of the items being compared but not the other, (2) omit words needed to clarify the relationship, or (3) compare different sorts of items. Advertisers often offend in the first way.

Faulty   Irish tape has better adhesion.

With what other tape is Irish tape being compared? Scotch tape? All other transparent tape? Mentioning the second term of a comparison eliminates reader guesswork.

Revision   Irish tape has better adhesion than any other transparent tape.

Two clarifying words, *other* and *else,* are frequently omitted from comparisons, creating illogical sentences.

Faulty   Sergeant McNabb is more conscientious than any officer in his precinct.

Faulty   Stretch French is taller than anyone on his basketball team.

The first sentence is illogical because McNabb is one of the officers in his precinct and therefore cannot be more conscientious than any officer in the precinct. Similarly, because French is a member of his basketball team, he can't be taller than anyone on his team. Adding *other* to the first sentence and *else* to the second corrects matters.

Revision   Sergeant McNabb is more conscientious than any *other* officer in his precinct.

Revision   Stretch French is taller than anyone *else* on his basketball team.

Comparing unlike items is perhaps the most common kind of comparison error. Here are two examples:

Faulty   The cities in California are larger than North Dakota.

Faulty   The cover of this book is much more durable than the other book.

The first sentence compares the cities of California with a state, while the second compares the cover of a book with a whole book. Correction consists of rewriting each sentence so that it compares like items.

Revision   The cities in California are larger than *those in* North Dakota.

Revision   The cover of this book is much more durable than *that of* the other book.

Connected Discourse Exercise

Identify and correct the misplaced modifiers, dangling modifiers, nonparallelism, and faulty comparisons in the following memorandum:

TO: Roger's Electronics Employees

FROM: Tim Colton, Sales Vice President

RE: Cell Phone Sales

I have received a report on our cell phone sales from our store manager that greatly disturbs me. Our cell phone sales still significantly lag the national average. Our sales numbers are even lower than Tidley Market. As an electronics store, we make our greatest profits from cell phone sales, signing up customers for wireless plans, and extended warranties. Working harder, cell phone sales should at least double next month. You must ask each customer if they are interested in a new cell phone with a wireless plan, regardless of the purchase. There is a sheet next to each register with the updated plan information. I look forward to a much better sales report next month.

Indicate whether each sentence is correct (C) or contains a faulty comparison (FC). Correct the faulty comparison.

1. *Death of a Salesman* is performed more often than any American play.
2. The power of today's laptop computers is much greater than the large defense department mainframes of the 1950s.
3. This quarter's earning report shows significantly greater net profits.
4. The Sunday brunch at the 1913 room is much more elegant than the Eatery.
5. Of the two quarterbacks, Allen has a stronger throwing arm than Tom.
6. In contrast to your car, I usually get 40 miles to the gallon.
7. The winters in North Dakota are much worse than Maine.

Complete additional exercises and practice in your MyLab

Handbook

Editing to Correct Faulty Punctuation and Mechanics

Punctuation marks indicate relationships among different sentence elements. As a result, these marks help clarify the meaning of written material. Similarly, a knowledge of mechanics—capitalization, abbreviations, numbers, and italics—helps you avoid distracting inconsistencies.

This part of the Handbook covers the fundamentals of punctuation and mechanics. Review it carefully when you edit your final draft.

Apostrophes

Apostrophes (') show possession, mark contractions, and indicate plurals that are singled out for special attention.

Watch the Animation on Apostrophes

Possession   Possessive apostrophes usually show ownership *(Mary's cat)*. Sometimes, though, they identify the works of creative people *(Hemingway's novels)* or indicate an extent of time or distance *(one hour's time, one mile's distance)*.

Possessive apostrophes are used with nouns and with pronouns like *someone, no one, everybody, each other,* and *one another.* The possessive form is easily recognized because it can be converted to a prepositional phrase beginning with *of.*

The collar of the dog

The intention of the corporation

The birthday of Scott

To show possession with pronouns like those above, singular nouns, and plural nouns that do not end in an *s*, add an apostrophe followed by an *s*.

Someone's car is blocking our drive. (possessive of pronoun *someone*)

The *manager's* reorganization plan will take effect next week. (possessive of singular noun *manager*)

The *women's* lounge is being redecorated. (possessive of plural noun *women*)

Sentences that make comparisons sometimes include two possessives, the second coming at the very end. In such cases, be sure to use an apostrophe with the second possessive.

Birmingham's football team is much better than *Central's*.

With singular nouns that end in *s*, the possessive is sometimes formed by merely adding an apostrophe at the end (*James' helmet*). The preferred usage, however, is *'s* (*James's helmet*) unless the addition of the *s* would make it awkward to pronounce the word.

Moses's followers entered the Promised Land. (awkward pronunciation of *Moses's*)

Moses' followers entered the Promised Land. (nonawkward pronunciation of *Moses'*)

Plural nouns ending in *s* form the possessive by adding only an apostrophe at the end.

All the *ladies'* coats are on sale today. (possessive of plural noun *ladies*)

The *workers'* lockers were moved. (possessive of plural noun *workers*)

To show joint ownership by two or more persons, use the possessive form for the last-named person only. To show individual ownership, use the possessive form for each person's name.

Ronald and *Joan's* boat badly needed overhauling. (joint ownership)
Laura's and *Alice's* term projects are almost completed. (individual ownership)

Hyphenated nouns form the possessive by adding *'s* to the last word.

My *mother-in-law's* house is next to mine.

Never use an apostrophe with the possessive pronouns *his, hers, whose, its, ours, yours, theirs*.

This desk is *his;* the other one is *hers*. (no apostrophes needed)

Contractions   Contractions of words or numbers omit one or more letters or numerals. An apostrophe shows exactly where the omission occurs.

Wasn't that a disappointing concert? (contraction of *was not*)

Around here, people still talk about the blizzard of *'79*. (contraction of *1979*)

Don't confuse the contraction *it's*, meaning *it is* or *it has*, with the possessive pronoun *its*, which should never have an apostrophe. If you're puzzled by an *its* that you've written, try this test. Expand the *its* to *it is* or *it has* and see whether the sentence still makes sense. If it does, the *its* is a contraction and needs the apostrophe. If the result is nonsense, the *its* is a possessive pronoun and does not get an apostrophe. Here are some examples:

> *Its* awfully muggy today.
>
> *Its* been an exciting trip.
>
> Every dog has *its* day.

The first example makes sense when the *its* is expanded to *it is*.

> *It is* awfully muggy today.

The second makes sense when the *its* is expanded to *it has*.

> *It has* been an exciting trip.

Both of these sentences therefore require apostrophes.

> *It's* awfully muggy today.
>
> *It's* been an exciting trip.

The last sentence, however, turns into nonsense when the *its* is expanded.

> Every dog has *it is* day.
>
> Every dog has *it has* day.

In this case, the *its* is a possessive pronoun and requires no apostrophe.

> Every dog has *its* day.

Plurals   To improve clarity, the plurals of letters, numbers, symbols, and words being singled out for special attention are written with apostrophes.

> Mind your *p*'s and *q*'s. (plurals of letters)
>
> Your *5*'s and *6*'s are hard to tell apart. (plurals of numbers)
>
> The formula was sprinkled with [Φ] 's and [σ] 's. (plurals of symbols)
>
> Don't use so many *however*'s and *therefore*'s in your writing. (plurals of words)

Apostrophes can be used, though they are not needed, to form the plurals of abbreviations.

> How many *CD*'s (or *CDs*) do you own? (plurals of abbreviation for *compact discs*)

When no danger of confusion exists, an *s* alone will suffice.

> During the late *1960s*, many university students demanded changes in academic life.

EXERCISE

Supply apostrophes where necessary to correct the following sentences:

1. This years winter promises to be significantly more severe than last years.
2. Everyones office will be furnished with the newest ergonomic chairs and work spaces.
3. Were attempting to determine how our students needs can best be met.
4. Somebodys purse was left in Dean Smiths office.
5. Cindys computer program was much more efficient than her peers programs.
6. There are two *Rs* and two *Ss* in the word "embarrassment."
7. Lets determine what caused the schools mainframe computer to fail before we panic.

Connected Discourse Exercise

Supply, delete, or relocate apostrophes as necessary in the following paragraph.

Its very important to understand todays media environment. The three major network's market share has decreased significantly over the year's as the number of cable channels increased. Now as people turn to services like Hulu and Netflix, the Internet's impact on entertainment consumption has become almost as great as televisions. The Internet provides viewers' with the programs they want when and where they want them. With the numerous wireless devices, it's portability makes the Internet services especially attractive to younger audience. Television has been a staple in many American homes since the 1950's; the question is whether television as we know it has a place in our future.

comma

Commas

 Watch the Animation on Commas

Since commas (,) occur more frequently than any other mark of punctuation, it's vital that you learn to use them correctly.

Commas separate or set off independent clauses, items in a series, coordinate adjectives, introductory elements, places and dates, nonrestrictive expressions, and parenthetical expressions.

Independent Clauses   When you link two independent clauses with a coordinating conjunction (*and, but, or, nor, for, yet,* or *so*), put a comma in front of the conjunction.

> Arthur is majoring in engineering, *but* he has decided to work for a clothing store following graduation.

> The water looked inviting, *so* Darlene decided to go for a swim.

Don't confuse a sentence that has a compound predicate (see page 608) with a sentence that consists of two independent clauses.

> Tom watered the garden and mowed the lawn. (single sentence with compound predicate)

> Tom watered the garden, *and* Betty mowed the lawn. (sentence with two independent clauses)

Here's a simple test. Read what follows the comma. Unless that part can stand alone as a sentence, don't use a comma.

2 Items in a Series

A series consists of three or more words, phrases, or clauses following on one another's heels. Whenever you write a series, separate its items with commas.

> *Sarah, Paul,* and *Mary* are earning *A's* in advanced algebra. (words in a series)

> Nancy strode *across the parking lot, through the revolving door,* and *into the elevator.* (phrases in a series)

> The stockholders' report said *that the company had enjoyed record profits during the last year, that it had expanded its work force by 20 percent,* and *that it would soon start marketing several new products.* (clauses in a series)

3 Coordinate Adjectives

Use commas to separate coordinate adjectives—those that modify the same noun or noun substitute and can be reversed without altering the meaning of the sentence.

> Andrea proved to be an efficient, cooperative employee.

> Andrea proved to be a cooperative, efficient employee.

When reversing the word order wrecks the meaning of the sentence, the adjectives are not coordinate and should be written without a comma.

> Many new brands of videocassette recorders have come on the market lately.

Reversing the adjectives *many* and *new* would turn this sentence into nonsense. Therefore, no comma should be used.

4 Introductory Elements

Use commas to separate introductory elements—words, phrases, and clauses—from the rest of the sentence. When an introductory element is short and the sentence will not be misread, you can omit the comma.

> *Correct*   After bathing, Jack felt refreshed.
> *Correct*   Soon I will be changing jobs.
> *Correct*   Soon, I will be changing jobs.
> *Correct*   When Sarah smiles her ears wiggle.
> *Correct*   When Sarah smiles, her ears wiggle.

comma

The first example needs a comma; otherwise, the reader might become temporarily confused.

>   After bathing Jack…

Always use commas after introductory elements of six or more words.

>   *Correct*   Whenever I hear the opening measure of Beethoven's
>   *Fifth Symphony*, I get goose bumps.

5 **Places and Dates**   Places include mailing addresses and geographical locations. The following sentences show where commas are used:

>   Sherry Delaney lives at 651 Daniel Street, Memphis, Tennessee 38118.
>
>   I will go to Calais, France, next week.
>
>   Morristown, Oklahoma, is my birthplace.

Note that commas appear after the street designation and the names of cities, countries, and states, except when the name of the state is followed by a zip code.

>   Dates are punctuated as shown in the following example:
>
>   On Sunday, June 9, 1991, Elaine received a degree in environmental science.

Here, commas follow the day of the week, the day of the month, and the year. With dates that include only the month and the year, commas are optional.

>   *Correct*   In July 1989 James played chess for the first time.
>   *Correct*   In July, 1989, James played chess for the first time.

◉ Watch the Animation on
Nonrestrictive
Expressions

6 **Nonrestrictive Expressions**   A nonrestrictive expression supplies added information about whatever it modifies. This information, however, is *nonessential* and does not affect the basic meaning of the sentence. The two sentences below include nonrestrictive expressions:

>   Senator Conwell, *the senior senator from this state,* faces a tough campaign for reelection.
>
>   My dog, *frightened by the thunder,* hid under my bed while the storm raged.

If we delete the phrase *the senior senator from this state* from the first sentence, we still know that Senator Conwell faces a tough reelection battle. Likewise, if we delete *frightened by the thunder* from the second sentence, we still know that the dog hid during the storm.

Restrictive expressions, which are written *without commas,* distinguish whatever they modify from other persons, places, or things in the same category. Unlike nonrestrictive expressions, they are almost always *essential* sentence elements. Omitting a restrictive expression alters the meaning of the sentence, and the result is often nonsense.

>   Any person *caught stealing from this store* will be prosecuted.

Dropping the italicized part of this sentence leaves us with the absurd statement that any person, not just those caught stealing, faces prosecution.

Parenthetical Expressions   A parenthetical expression is a word or a word group that links one sentence to another or adds information or emphasis to the sentence in which it appears. Parenthetical expressions include the following:

Clarifying phrases

Names and titles of people being addressed directly

Abbreviations of degree titles

Echo questions

"Not" phrases

Adjectives that come after, rather than before, the words they modify

The examples that follow show the uses of commas:

Myra Hobbes, *our representative in Seattle*, is being transferred to Spokane next month. (clarifying phrase)

I think, *Jill*, that you'd make a wonderful teacher. (name of person addressed directly)

Tell me, *Captain*, when the cruise ship is scheduled to sail. (title of person addressed directly)

Harley Kendall, *Ph.D.*, will be this year's commencement speaker. (degree title following name)

Alvin realizes, *doesn't he*, that he stands almost no chance of being accepted at West Point? (echo question)

Mathematics, *not home economics*, was Tammy's favorite high school subject. ("not" phrase)

The road, *muddy and rutted*, proved impassable. (adjectives following word they modify)

Punctuating Conjunctive Adverbs   Writers often mistakenly punctuate conjunctive adverbs with commas and create, as a result, a comma splice.

Floridians do not have the heating bills of their Northern neighbors, however, they do have extensive air-conditioning bills.

Conjunctive adverbs actually do not join sentences and can actually be moved, revealing the underlying comma splice.

Floridians do not have the heating bills of their Northern neighbors, they do, however, have extensive air-conditioning bills.

To fix such comma splices, join the sentences with a semicolon or punctuate with a period and start a new sentence.

Floridians do not have the heating bills of their Northern neighbors; however, they do have extensive air-conditioning bills.

Floridians do not have the heating bills of their Northern neighbors. They do, however, have extensive air-conditioning bills.

comma

EXERCISE

Supply commas as necessary to correct the following sentences:

1. Let us know Ms. Granger when you would like to enjoy your free stay at Rolling Hills Resort.
2. The landscapers killed the existing grass rototilled the ground added new topsoil and sprayed the prepared ground with hydroseed.
3. If you are interested in making a tax-deductible donation to the Stratford Festival please write Carla Darma treasurer at 165 University Avenue Suite 700 Toronto Ontario Canada M5H 3B8.
4. The day was unusually beautiful so Mr. Collins decided to hold his class on the Romantic poets outside.
5. Standing in the long winding line for hours on a hot muggy New York summer day Tom was able to get discount tickets to one of the most popular musicals.
6. Mr. Carlin was hired by our New York office on March 25 1997 and was supposed to report to work in our Nome Alaska office three months after his hiring date.
7. Before eating raccoons carefully wash their paws.

Connected Discourse Exercise

Add or delete commas as necessary in the following letter

comma

Grendel College Alumni

While it has only been a few years since you graduated from Grendel you have already joined a long history of proud capable Grendel graduates who have forged successful futures. That is why we are inviting you to join your fellow graduates, at a special alumni recognition weekend to be held from 6 PM Friday March 22 to 6 PM Sunday March 24 here in Bliss Michigan.

We would like you to join Dr. Jasmine Kleften our current president, and members of the board for a special dinner on Friday evening. After the gourmet meal served by dining services there will be a wine and cheese reception where you can reunite with your old friends and favorite faculty members. On Saturday there will be a breakfast buffet a home football game and a jazz concert on the quad. Sunday after a delightful brunch we would like to give you a tour of the campus, to show you many of the developments that are underway. In the afternoon you will have an opportunity to meet many of our current brilliant students, and attend a poster session that showcases their work.

No we are not going to ask you for money, however, if you feel at the end of the visit that you wish to make a contribution our Jim Beowulf Vice President for University Advancement will be available to speak with you. We want you back to visit us, because you are an important part of our family. Just send back the confirmation card with your signature and we will make all of the arrangements.

Semicolons

The main use of the semicolon (;) is to separate independent clauses, which may or may not be connected with a conjunctive adverb (see page 631). Other uses include separating

(see page 631)

((•—Listen to the Podcast on Semicolons

- two or more series of items
- items containing commas in a single series
- independent clauses that contain commas and are connected with a coordinating conjunction.

Independent Clauses The examples that follow show the use of semicolons to separate independent clauses.

> The fabric in this dress is terrible; its designer must have been asleep at the swatch. (no conjunctive adverb)

> Steve refused to write a term paper; *therefore*, he failed the course. (conjunctive adverb *therefore* joining independent clauses)

Conjunctive adverbs can occur within, rather than between, independent clauses. When they do, set them off with commas.

> Marsha felt very confident. Jane, *on the other hand*, was nervous and uncertain. (conjunctive adverb within independent clause)

To determine whether a pair of commas or a semicolon and comma are required, read what comes before and after the conjunctive adverb. Unless both sets of words can stand alone as sentences, use commas.

Two or More Series of Items With sentences that have two or more series of items, writers often separate the series with semicolons in order to lessen the chances of misreading.

> My duties as secretary include typing letters, memos, and purchase orders; sorting, opening, and delivering mail; and making plane and hotel reservations for traveling executives.

The semicolons provide greater clarity than commas would.

Comma-Containing Items within a Series When commas accompany one or more of the items in a series, it's often better to separate the items with semicolons instead of commas.

> The meal included veal, which was cooked to perfection; asparagus, my favorite vegetable; and brown rice, prepared with a touch of curry.

Once again, semicolons provide greater clarity than additional commas.

Independent Clauses with Commas and a Coordinating Conjunction
Ordinarily, a comma is used to separate independent clauses joined by a coordinating conjunction. When one or more of the clauses have commas, however, a semicolon provides clearer separation.

The long black limousine pulled up to the curb; and Jerry, shaking with excitement, watched the President alight from it.

The semicolon makes it easier to see the two main clauses.

Supply semicolons wherever they are necessary or desirable in the following sentences. You may have to substitute semicolons for commas. If a sentence is correct, write C.

1. When he visits the main office, Mr. Harmon would like to meet with the vice president of marketing, Carol Chaffe, the personnel director, Carl Hart, and the vice president of finance, Mary Angelo.
2. Donald Nathanson, a clinical psychologist, has written an insightful book on shame, and other psychologists, who at first were very critical of his work, have begun to use his ideas in their practice.
3. E-mail is a crucial part of most businesses; in fact, some companies have replaced all memos with electronic communication.
4. This year a number of new musicals have opened on Broadway, it promises to be an exciting theater season.
5. The reading for the course was eclectic, including *The Invisible Man*, a science fiction novel, *Shane*, a western, and *Antigone*, a classic Greek play.
6. Computers can crash at any time, therefore, it is important to back up your data frequently.
7. We will offer sales training this summer in Lansing, Michigan, Ames, Iowa, and Minneapolis, Minnesota.

Connected Discourse Exercise

Add and delete semicolons as appropriate in the following letter. You may have to substitute semicolons for commas.

To: All Students

From: John Bits; IT Manager

Re: Improving Our Online Learning Environment

As many of you have pointed out, there have been a number of problems with GrendelUP, our online learning platform, and those problems, President Kleften agrees, have been severe enough to warrant a new system.

You deserve a system that offers consistent, reliable service, is compatible with recent Java Script, allows you to easily view Internet links, and makes it possible for you to review your grades, without changing systems. We believe that you should have an opportunity to have a say in the system we select, therefore, you are invited to attend the demonstration sessions for the possible replacements.

We hope you will attend one or all of these sessions, the system we select should reflect your needs as students.

Periods, Question Marks, and Exclamation Points

Since periods, question marks, and exclamation points signal the ends of sentences, they are sometimes called *end marks*. In addition, periods and question marks function in several other ways.

Watch the Animation on End Punctuation

Periods   Periods (.) end sentences that state facts or opinions, give instructions, make requests that are not in the form of questions, and ask indirect questions—those that have been rephrased in the form of a statement.

> Linda works as a hotel manager. (Sentence states fact.)

> Please move away from the door. (Sentence makes request.)

> I wonder whether Ruthie will be at the theater tonight. (Sentence asks indirect question.)

Periods also follow common abbreviations as well as a person's initials.

Mr.	Sr.	P.M.
Ms.	B.C.	lb.
Jr.	A.D.	St.
Dr.	A.M.	Corp.

> Mark J. Valentini, Ph.D., has consented to head the new commission on traffic safety.

Writers today often omit periods after abbreviations for the names of organizations or government agencies, as the following examples show:

ABC	FBI	IRS
ACLU	FHA	NAM
AFL-CIO	GM	USAF

> Dr. Angela Fish has accepted the position as the CEO of BioMed Corp and will help make the company a leader in bioengineering technology.

An up-to-date college dictionary will indicate whether a certain abbreviation should be written without periods.

Periods also precede decimal fractions and separate numerals standing for dollars and cents.

0.81 percent	$5.29
3.79 percent	$0.88

Question Marks   A question mark (?) ends a whole or a partial sentence that asks a direct question (one that repeats the exact words of the person who asked it).

> Do you know how to operate this movie projector? (whole sentence asking a direct question)

> Has Cinderella scrubbed the floor? Swept the hearth? Washed the dishes? (sentence and sentence parts asking direct questions)

.?!

Dr. Baker—wasn't she your boss once?—has just received a promotion to sales manager. (interrupting element asking a direct question)

The minister inquired, "Do you take this woman to be your lawful wedded wife?" (quotation asking a direct question)

A question mark may be used to indicate uncertainty.

Jane Seymour (1509?–1537), third wife of Henry VIII, was a lady in waiting to his first two wives.

Exclamation Points   Exclamation points (!) are used to express strong emotion or especially forceful commands.

Darcy! I never expected to see you again!

Sam! Turn that radio down immediately!

Help! Save me!

Use exclamation points sparingly; otherwise, they will quickly lose their force.

EXERCISE

Supply periods, question marks, or exclamation points wherever they are necessary. You may have to change existing punctuation marks. If a sentence is correct, write C.

.?!

1. Be sure to proofread your paper before you submit it for a grade.
2. Sigmund Freud—isn't he now generally dismissed by many psychologists—really established the concept of the unconscious.
3. The sales tax in our state was raised to 65 percent.
4. Great we will have to buy another candle.
5. When you shopped for a new computer, did you consider what programs you wanted to run, set a budget for yourself, check the reliability of the different brands.
6. The engineer wanted to know how much stress would be placed on the beams.
7. Has Dr Stevens read the research on the most recent anti-clotting medication.

Connected Discourse Exercise

Add, change, or remove end marks as necessary. You may want to do some slight rewording.

Are you worried about being audited by the I.R.S. Stop worrying. Dr Carl Sly, a C.P.A. with a PhD in Accounting, will be available next Friday afternoon in the Chomsky room to answer all of your questions. Many often ask, "does using a tax preparation program protect you." No. Tax preparation software doesn't keep you from an audit. Only the kind of knowledge Carl Sly provides can make certain you avoid costly hours answering an audit! Learn how to itemize safely, how to avoid the dreaded alternative minimum tax, and how to even take off for home improvements?

Colons, Dashes, Parentheses, and Brackets

Colons, dashes, parentheses, and brackets separate and enclose, thereby clarifying relationships among the various parts of a sentence.

Watch the Animation on Other Punctuation

Colon   Colons (:) introduce explanations and anticipated lists following words that could stand alone as a complete sentence.

His aim in life is grandiose: to corner the market in wheat. (explanation)

Three students have been selected to attend the conference: Lucille Perkins, Dan Blakely, and Frank Napolis. (list)

Three factors can cause financial problems for farmers: (1) high interest rates, (2) falling land values, and (3) a strong dollar, which makes it difficult to sell crops abroad. (numbered list)

The first of the following sentences is incorrect because the words preceding the colon can't stand alone as a sentence:

Faulty   The tools needed for this job include: a hacksaw, a file, and a drill.

Revision   The tools needed for this job include a hacksaw, a file, and a drill.

Colons also frequently introduce formal quotations that extend beyond a single sentence.

The speaker stepped to the lectern and said: "I am here to ask for your assistance. Today several African nations face a food crisis because drought has ruined their harvests. Unless we provide help quickly, thousands of people will die of starvation."

In such situations, the material preceding the quotation need not be a complete sentence.

Colons also separate hours from minutes (8:20 A.M.), salutations of business letters from the body of the letters (Dear Ms. Stanley:), titles of publications from subtitles (*The Careful Writer: A Guide to English Usage*), numbers indicating ratios (a 3:2:2 ratio), and chapter from verse in biblical references (Luke 6:20–49).

Dashes   Like colons, dashes (—) set off appositives, lists, and explanations but are used in less formal writing. A dash emphasizes the material it sets off.

Only one candidate showed up at the political rally—Jerry Manders. (appositive)

The closet held only three garments—an out-at-the-elbows sports coat, a pair of blue jeans, and a tattered shirt. (list)

I know what little Billy's problem is—a soiled diaper. (explanation)

Dashes set off material that interrupts the flow of thought within a sentence.

> Her new car—didn't she get it just three months ago?—has broken down twice.

Similarly, dashes are used to mark an interrupted segment of dialogue.

> "I'd like to live in England when I retire."
>
> "In England? But what will your wife—?"
>
> "My wife likes the idea and can hardly wait for us to make the move."

Dashes set off parenthetical elements containing commas, and a dash can set off comments that follow a list.

> The comedian—short, fat, and squeaky-voiced—soon had everyone roaring with laughter. (parenthetical element with commas)
>
> A brag, a blow, a tank of air—that's what Senator Conwell is. (comment following a list)

Type a dash as two unspaced hyphens and leave no space between it and the words on either side of it.

Parentheses   Parentheses () are used to enclose numbers or letters that designate the items in a formal list and to set off incidental material within sentences. Except in the kind of list shown in the first example below, a comma does not usually precede a parenthesis.

> Each paper should contain (1) an introduction, (2) several paragraphs developing the thesis statement, and (3) a conclusion.
>
> Some occupations (computer programming, for example) may be overcrowded in 10 years.

If the material in parentheses appears within a sentence, don't use a capital letter or period, even if the material is itself a complete sentence.

> The growth of genetic engineering (one cannot foresee its consequences) worries some people today.

If the material in parentheses is written as a separate sentence, however, then punctuate it as you would a separate sentence.

> Paula's angry outburst surprised everyone. (She had seemed such a placid person.)

If the material in parentheses comes at the end of a sentence, put the final punctuation after the closing parenthesis.

> This company was founded by Willard Manley (1876–1951).
>
> In contrast to dashes, parentheses de-emphasize the material they enclose.

Brackets   In quoted material, brackets [] enclose words or phrases that have been added to make the message clearer. They are also used with the word *sic* (Latin for "thus") to point out errors in quoted material.

"This particular company [Zorn Enterprises, Inc.] pioneered in the safe disposal of toxic wastes," the report noted. (The bracketed name is added to the original.)

"[John Chafin's] expertise in science has made him a popular figure on the lecture circuit," his friend stated. (The bracketed name replaces *his* in the original.)

"The principle [sic] cause of lung cancer is cigarette smoking," the article declared. (the word *principal* is misspelled "principle" in the original.)

To call attention to an error, follow it immediately with the bracketed *sic.* The reader will then know that the blame rests with the original writer, not with you.

Supply colons, dashes, parentheses, and brackets wherever they are necessary.

1. Many former Presidents Millard Fillmore, for example have been largely forgotten by most Americans.
2. Our international sales have outperformed domestic sales by an 83 ratio.
3. The newspaper headline read, "Piece sic deal broken."
4. Among our social ills, one condition seems to be the source of many other problems poverty.
5. The new library better considered an information center will have over 50 computers with full Internet capability.
6. Our city area offers many advantages to businesses a skilled workforce, a well-developed infrastructure, and low taxes.
7. Mozart, Miles Davis, The Talking Heads his tastes certainly are eclectic.

Connected Discourse Exercise

Supply any necessary or appropriate colons, dashes, parentheses, and brackets in the following paragraph.

America's entitlement programs Medicare, Medicaid, and Social Security offer a serious challenge to our future budget. The recipients mostly the elderly, the poor, and the disabled are ones few would like to see harmed. However, with the national debt increasing to nearly 90% of GDP Gross Domestic Product, there are only a few option increase taxes a lot, cut spending deeply, or do some of both. As one pundit put it, "we ain't sic going to be able to have our cake for free and eat it too." There are only tough choices ahead of us. Let's hope we have the political will to make those choices.

Quotation Marks

Watch the Animation on Quotation Marks

Quotation marks (" ") set off direct quotations, titles of short written or broadcast works, subdivisions of books, and expressions singled out for special attention.

Direct Quotations   A direct quotation repeats a speaker's or writer's exact words.

> "Tell me about the movie," said Debbie. "If you liked it, I may go myself."

> The placement director said, "The recruiter for Procter and Gamble will be on campus next Thursday to interview students for marketing jobs." (spoken comment)

> "The U.S. trade deficit is expected to reach record levels this year," the *Wall Street Journal* noted. (written comment)

> Jackie said the party was "a total flop."

As these sentences show, a comma or period that follows a direct quotation goes inside the quotation marks. When a quotation is a sentence fragment, the comma preceding it is omitted.

When an expression like "he said" interrupts a quoted sentence, use commas to set off the expression. When the expression comes between two complete quoted sentences, use a period after the expression and capitalize the first word of the second sentence.

> "Hop in," said Jim. "Let me give you a ride to school."

> "Thank you," replied Kelly, opening the car door and sliding into the front seat.

> "I can't remember," said Jim, "when we've had a worse winter."

Titles of Short Works and Subdivisions of Books   These short works include magazine articles, essays, short stories, chapters of books, one-act plays, short poems, songs, and television and radio episodes.

> The article was titled "The Real Conservatism." (article)

> Last night I read John Cheever's "The Enormous Radio," "Torch Song," and "The Swimmer." (short stories)

> Many John Denver fans consider "Take Me Home, Country Roads" to be his greatest piece of music. (song)

> The unsuccessful TV show *Pursued* ended its brief run with a segment titled "Checkmate." (TV episode)

Here, as with direct quotations, a comma or period that follows a title goes inside the quotation marks.

Expressions Singled Out for Special Attention   Writers who wish to call the reader's attention to a word or symbol sometimes put it within quotation marks.

> The algebraic formula included a "π," a " Θ," and a "Δ."

> "Bonnets" and "lifts" are British terms for car hoods and elevators.

More frequently, however, these expressions are printed in italics (page 692).

Again, any commas and periods that follow expressions set off by quotation marks go inside the marks.

Quotation Marks within Quotation Marks

When a direct quotation or the title of a shorter work appears within a direct quotation, use single quotation marks (' ').

> "I heard the boss telling the foreman, 'Everyone will receive a Christmas bonus,'" John said.

> The instructor told the class, "For tomorrow, read Ernest Hemingway's 'The Killers.'"

Note that the period goes inside of both the single and double quotation marks.

Positioning of Semicolons, Colons, and Question Marks

Position semicolons and colons that come at the end of quoted material after, not before, the quotation marks.

> Marcia calls Francine "that greasy grind"; however, I think Marcia is simply jealous of Francine's abilities.

> There are two reasons why I like "Babylon Revisited": the characters are interesting and the writing is excellent.

When a question mark accompanies a quotation, put it outside the quotation marks if the whole sentence rather than the quotation asks the question.

> Why did Cedric suddenly shout, "This party is a big bore"?

Put the question mark inside the quotation marks if the quotation, but not the whole sentence, asks a question or if the quotation asks one question and the whole sentence asks another.

> Marie asked, "What college is your brother planning to attend?" (The quoted material, not the whole sentence, asks the question.)

> Whatever possessed him to ask, "What is the most shameful thing you ever did?" (The whole sentence and the quoted material ask separate questions.)

EXERCISE

Supply properly positioned quotation marks wherever they are necessary.

1. Some linguists think that the quintessential American ok may have come from the African waka.
2. My favorite piece of jazz music is St. James Infirmary.
3. What did Yeats mean by the line in his famous poem The Second Coming, Things fall apart, the center cannot hold?
4. Carl Thomas described the performance as extremely intense.
5. I managed to read Faulkner's short story The Bear, Jennifer sighed, but I don't really know what I want to say about it in my paper for English.

6. In response to the Great Depression, Franklin Roosevelt declared The only thing we have to fear is fear itself; however, many families who had lost their homes and couldn't even earn enough for food really did have something to fear.

7. In his closing argument, the defense attorney asked the jury, How would any one of us act if accused of a crime we knew we didn't commit?

Connected Discourse Exercise

Use quotation marks correctly in the following paragraph:

Mr. Silver recently lectured our class on Stephen Crane's The Bride Comes to Yellow Sky. One thing we shouldn't forget, Mr. Silver insisted, is that the town is deliberately named Yellow Sky. What is the significance of Crane's choice of the words Yellow Sky? Mr. Silver pointed out a number of possible associations, including cowardice, the setting sun, the open expanse of the West, freedom, the sand in the concluding passage. The story, Mr. Silver stated, is drenched in color words. For example, he pointed out, in the first three paragraphs alone Crane mentions vast flats of green grass, brick-colored hands, new black clothes, and a dress of blue cashmere.

Hyphens

((•—[Listen to the Podcast on Hyphens

Hyphens (-) are used to join compound adjectives and nouns, compound numbers and word-number combinations, and certain prefixes and suffixes to the words with which they appear. In addition, hyphens help prevent misreadings and awkward combinations of letters or syllables and are used to split words between two lines.

Compound Adjectives   Hyphens are often used to join separate words that function as single adjectives and come before nouns. Typical examples follow:

Howard is a very *self-contained* person.

The *greenish-yellow* cloud of chlorine gas drifted toward the village.

Betty's *devil-may-care* attitude will land her in trouble someday.

When the first word of the compound is an adverb ending in *-ly* or when the compound adjective follows the noun it modifies, no hyphen is used.

The *badly* burned crash victim was rushed to the hospital.

The color of the chlorine gas was *greenish yellow.*

When two or more compound adjectives modify the same last term, the sentence will flow more smoothly if that term appears just once, after the last item in the series. The hyphens accompanying the earlier terms in the series are kept, however.

> Many seventeenth-, eighteenth-, and nineteenth-century costumes are on display in this museum.

Compound Nouns   Hyphenated nouns include such expressions as the following:

secretary-treasurer	good-for-nothing
sister-in-law	man-about-town

Here is a sentence with hyphenated nouns:

> Denton is *editor-in-chief* of the largest newspaper in this state.

Compound Numbers and Word–Number Combinations   Hyphens are used to separate two-word numbers from twenty-one to ninety-nine and fractions that have been written out.

> Marcy has worked *twenty-one* years for this company.

> *One-fourth* of my income goes for rent.

Similarly, hyphens are used to separate numerals from units of measurement that follow them.

> This chemical is shipped in *50-gallon* drums.

Prefixes and Suffixes   A prefix is a word or set of letters that precedes a word and alters its meaning. A suffix is similar but comes at the end of the word. Although most prefixes are not hyphenated, the prefixes *self-* and *all-* do get hyphens, as does the suffix *-elect*. Also the prefix *ex-* is hyphenated when it accompanies a noun.

> This stove has a *self-cleaning* oven.

> Let Claire Voyant, the *all-knowing* soothsayer, read your future in her crystal ball.

> Ethel is the *chairperson-elect* of the club.

> Several *ex-teachers* work in this department.

A prefix used before a capitalized term is always hyphenated.

> The *ex-FBI* agent gave an interesting talk on the operations of that agency.

Preventing Misreadings and Awkward Combinations of Letters and Syllables   Hyphens help prevent misreadings of certain words and also break up awkward combinations of letters and syllables between certain prefixes and suffixes and their core words.

> The doctor *re-treated* the wound with a new antibiotic. (The hyphen prevents the misreading *retreated*.)

> The company plans to *de-emphasize* sales of agricultural chemicals. (The hyphen prevents the awkward repetition of the letter *e* in *deemphasize*.)

Between Syllables Whenever you have to split a word between two lines, place a hyphen at the end of the first line to show the division. The word is always broken, and the hyphen inserted, between syllables. (Any good dictionary shows the syllable divisions of each word it includes.) Never divide a one-syllable word or leave two letters to be placed on the second line, even if those two letters constitute a syllable.

EXERCISE

Supply hyphens wherever they are necessary. If the sentence is correct, write C.

1. The piece of music ended with bird like sounds made by the entire woodwind section.
2. In this brokerage firm we follow sound investment strategies rather than chase after will o' the wisp schemes.
3. It can be sobering for the president elect to learn the full requirements of the job.
4. The union negotiators were forced to retreat from their initial demands.
5. One fifth of the shipment of fresh tomatoes turned out to be spoiled.
6. The classical radio station can be received by anyone within a 100 mile radius of its broadcasting tower.
7. In this class, we will study nineteenth and twentieth century American authors.
8. Emerson thought that it was important for people to be self reliant.
9. Once the power came back on, I had to recreate the file.
10. The Gundersons have been married for thirty five years.

cap

Capitalization

Watch the Animation on Capitalization

Capitalize the first word in any sentence, the pronoun *I*, proper nouns and adjectives, titles used with names, and the significant words in literary and artistic titles.

Proper Nouns A proper noun names one particular person, group of persons, place, or thing. Such nouns include the following:

Persons

Organizations

Racial, political, and religious groups

Countries, states, cities, and streets

Companies and buildings

Geographical locations and features

Days, months, and holidays

Trademarks

Languages

Ships and aircraft

Abbreviations for academic degrees

Sacred writings and pronouns standing for God and Jesus

Titles used in place of names

The sentences below show the capitalization of proper nouns:

Sigmund works for the *National Psychoanalytical Institute*, an organization that has done much to advance the science of psychiatry.

How much does this roll of *Saran Wrap* cost?

Gwen Greene moved to *Paris, France*, when her father became the consul there.

On *Friday, December* 10, 1993, *Michael Jordan* visited our city.

Larry has a master of arts degree, and his sister has a *Ph.D.*

My father works for the *Ford Motor Company*, but I work for *Daimler Chrysler*.

Do not capitalize words like *institute, college, company,* or *avenue* unless they form part of a proper name. Likewise, do not capitalize the names of courses unless they start a sentence, are accompanied by a course number, or designate a language.

I have a 95 average in *Economics* 112 but only a 73 average in sociology.

Harry plans to take intermediate *German* in his junior year.

Do you plan to attend *Drew College* or some other college?

Proper Adjectives   Adjectives created from proper nouns are called proper adjectives. Like the nouns themselves, they should be capitalized.

Lolita Martinez, our class valedictorian, is of *Mexican* ancestry. (*Mexican* is derived from the proper noun *Mexico*.)

Abbreviations   As a general rule, capitalize abbreviations only if the words they stand for are capitalized.

Milton DeWitt works for the *IRS*. (*IRS* is capitalized because *Internal Revenue Service* would be.)

The flask holds 1,500 *ml* of liquid. (The abbreviation *ml* is not capitalized because *milliliters* would not be.)

A few abbreviations are capitalized even though all or some of the words they stand for aren't. Examples include TV (television) and VCR (videocassette recorder).

Personal Titles   Capitalize a personal title if it precedes a name or is used in place of a name. Otherwise, do not capitalize.

The division is under the command of *General* Arnold Schafer.

Tell me, *Doctor*, do I need an operation?

The *dean* of our engineering division is Dr. Alma Haskins.

Many writers capitalize titles of high rank when they are used in place of names.

The *President* will sign this bill tomorrow.

The *president* will sign this bill tomorrow.

Either usage is acceptable.

cap

Titles of Literary and Artistic Works   When citing the titles of publications, pieces of writing, movies, television programs, paintings, sculptures, and the like, capitalize the first and last words and all other words except *a, an, the*, coordinating conjunctions, and one-syllable prepositions.

> Last week I played *Gone with the Wind* on my VCR and read Christopher Isherwood's *Goodbye to Berlin*. (the preposition *with*, the article *the*, and the preposition *to* are not capitalized.)
>
> John is reading a book called *The Movies of Abbott and Costello*. (The preposition *of* and the coordinating conjunction *and* are not capitalized. *The* is capitalized because it is the first word of the title.)
>
> Although I'm no TV addict, I used to watch every episode of *Murder, She Wrote*. (All of the words in the title are capitalized.)

Note that the titles of literary and artistic works are italicized.

EXERCISE

Identify any word or abbreviation that should be capitalized in the following sentences:

1. Every friday at 1:00 P.M. the computer support team meets to review the problems that occurred during the previous week.
2. Any student of mexican history will soon see how radically different that history has been from american history.
3. Though many consider it a liberal organization, the aclu has actually protected the right to free speech of many extremely conservative groups.
4. Many students in the rotc choose to take history 321: american military history to satisfy their humanities requirement.
5. A student has a right to be proud upon earning an a.a.s. or a b.s. degree.
6. All requests for sabbatical leave must be submitted to dean Styron by october 1.
7. Though many consider latin a dead language, others continue to study it since so many great classical works were written in that language.
8. Your request for a leave of absence cannot be approved by professor Murphy.
9. Students of roman literature should be familiar with ovid's *metamorphoses*.
10. During World War II, dr. Johnson served on the u.s. submarine eel.

ab

Abbreviations

Watch the Animation on **Abbreviations** and **Numbers**

Items that are abbreviated include certain personal titles, names of organizations and agencies, Latin terms, and specific and technical terms.

Personal Titles   Abbreviate *Mister, Doctor*, and similar titles when they come just ahead of a name, and *Junior, Senior*, and degree titles when they follow names.

> Will *Mr.* Harry Babbitt please come to the front desk?
>
> Arthur Compton, *Sr.*, is a well-known historian; his son, Arthur Compton, *Jr.*, is a television producer.
>
> This article on marital discord was written by Irma Quarles, *Ph.D.*

Names of Organizations and Agencies   Many organizations and agencies are known primarily by their initials rather than their full names. Several examples follow:

AAA	FBI	NBC
CARE	FHA	NATO
CIA	IBM	UNESCO

Latin Terms   Certain Latin terms are always abbreviated; others are abbreviated when used with dates or times.

e.g. (*exempli gratia:* for example)

i.e. (*id est:* that is)

etc. (*et cetera:* and [the] others)

vs. or v. (*versus:* against)

A.D. (*anno Domini:* in the year of our Lord)

A.M. or a.m. (*ante meridiem:* before noon)

P.M. or p.m. (*post meridiem:* after noon)

The play starts at 8 P.M.

Many writers (*e.g.,* Dylan Thomas and Truman Capote) have had serious problems with alcohol.

For consistency with A.D., the term "before Christ" is abbreviated as B.C.

Scientific and Technical Terms   For brevity's sake, scientists and technicians abbreviate terms of measurement that repeatedly occur. Terms that the reader would not know are written out the first time they are used, and they are accompanied by their abbreviation in parentheses. Unfamiliar organizations and agencies that are mentioned repeatedly are handled in like manner.

The viscosity of the fluid measured 15 centistokes (cs) at room temperature. Common practice calls for writing such abbreviations without periods unless they duplicate the spelling of some word.

Standard dictionaries list common abbreviations. When you don't recognize one, look it up. Use abbreviations sparingly in essays. If you're unsure about what is appropriate, don't abbreviate.

EXERCISE

Supply abbreviations wherever they are necessary or are customarily used.

1. We are pleased that Mister Jones has decided to join our firm.
2. Dissolve 1 gram of NaCl in 20 milliliters of water.
3. The freezing point of water at sea level is 32° Fahrenheit (0° Celsius).
4. Since its start, the National Broadcasting Company has been strongly committed to its news programming.
5. Doctor Baxter has been doing extensive research on nanotechnology, supported by a National Science Foundation grant.

6. Carl Thorton, Junior, will offer a workshop on how to save for retirement.

7. Many composers who are now seen as giants of classical music (*exempli gratia*, Mozart and Beethoven) died paupers.

Numbers

Some instructors ask their students to use figures for numbers larger than ninety-nine and to spell out smaller numbers.

> Boise is *100* miles from here.

> Boise is *ninety-nine* miles from here.

Other instructors prefer that students switch to figures beginning with the number ten.

> My son will be *nine* years old on his next birthday.

> My son will be *10* years old on his next birthday.

With either practice, the following exceptions apply.

Numbers in a Series Write all numbers in a series the same way regardless of their size.

> Gatsby has *64* suits, *110* shirts, and *214* ties.

> In just one hour the emergency room personnel handled *two* stabbings, *five* shootings, and *sixteen* fractures.

> We have *150* salespeople, *51* engineers, and *7* laboratory technicians.

Dates Use figures for dates that include the year.

> February *14, 1985* or 14 February 1985 (not February 14th, 1985)

When the date includes the day but not the year, you may use figures or spell out the number.

> June 9

> June ninth

> the ninth of June

Page Numbers and Addresses Use figures for page numbers and street numbers in addresses.

> Check the graph on page *415*.

> I live at *111* Cornelia Street, and my office is at *620* Fifth Avenue.

Numbers Beginning Sentences Spell out any number that begins a sentence. If this requires three or more words, rephrase the sentence so that the number comes after the opening and numerals can be used.

> The year *1989* was a good year for this wine.

> *Sixty thousand* fans jammed the stadium.

> An army of *265,000* troops assaulted the city. (If this number began the sentence, five words—an excessive number—would be needed to write it out.)

Decimals, Percentages, Times   Use figures for decimals and percentages as well as for expressions of time that are accompanied by A.M. or P.M.

> The shaft has a *0.37-*inch diameter.
>
> Last year the value of my house jumped *25* percent.
>
> The plane leaves here at *9:50* A.M. and reaches New Orleans at *2:30* P.M.

One Number Following Another   When a number-containing term that de-notes a unit of weight or measurement comes immediately after another num-ber, spell out the first number, if smaller than 100, and use numerals for the second one. If the first number is larger than 100, use numerals for it and spell out the second one.

> We ordered *six 30-*gallon drums of solvent for the project.
>
> The supplier shipped us *600 thirty-*gallon drums by mistake.

Identify any miswriting of numbers in the following sentences and rewrite these numbers correctly:

1. The supermarket ordered five hundred five-pound bags of sugar.
2. The holes that the automated system drilled in the brackets were off by two hundredths of an inch.
3. The first memo warning the company of the problem was dated May fifteenth, 1993.
4. 8,000 people usually subscribe to our symphony orchestra series.
5. There are a number of serious editing errors on page thirty-nine of the report.
6. Over the last year, sales have increased by twenty-three percent.
7. We found that only 3 computers needed to be upgraded.

Italics

Italics are used for the titles of longer publications, the names of vehicles and vessels, foreign words and phrases, and expressions singled out for special atten-tion. Use underlining to represent italics when hand writing or typing papers.

Titles of Longer Publications and Artistic Works   These items may in-clude the following:

books	record albums	long musical works and poems
magazines	paintings	plays
newspapers	movies	sculptures

As noted on page 683, quotation marks are used for the titles of articles, short stories, short poems, one-act plays, and other brief pieces of writing.

Last night I finished F. Scott Fitzgerald's *The Great Gatsby* and read two articles in *The New Yorker.* (book, magazine)

Michelangelo's *David* is surely one of the world's greatest sculptures. (sculpture)

The *Detroit Free Press* had praise for the revival of Tennessee Williams's play *The Glass Menagerie.* (newspaper, play)

Stephen Vincent Benét's poem *John Brown's Body* won a Pulitzer Prize in 1929. (book-length poem)

Do not use italics when naming the Bible and its parts or other religious works such as the Torah and Koran.

Joanna's favorite book of the Bible is the Book of Ecclesiastes, part of the Old Testament.

Names of Vehicles and Vessels   Names of particular airplanes, ships, trains, and spacecraft are italicized.

The plane in which Charles Lindbergh flew over the Atlantic Ocean was named *The Spirit of St. Louis.*

Foreign Expressions   Use italics to identify foreign words and phrases that have not yet made their way into the English language.

The writer has a terribly pessimistic *weltanschauung.* (philosophy of life)

This season, long skirts are the *dernier cri.* (the latest thing)

When such expressions become completely assimilated, the italics are dropped. Most dictionaries use an asterisk (*), a dagger (†), or other symbol to identify expressions that need italicizing.

Expressions Singled Out for Special Attention   These include words, letters, numerals, and symbols.

The Greek letter *pi* is written π.

I can't tell whether this letter is meant to be an *a* or an *o* or this number a *7* or a *9.*

In England, the word *lorry* means truck.

As noted on pages 682–683, quotation marks sometimes replace italics for this purpose.

EXERCISE

Supply italics wherever they are necessary.

1. The British often use the word lift to refer to an elevator.
2. Arthur Miller's Death of a Salesman is considered by many critics to be the great American tragedy.
3. Given the quality of the movie version, it takes a considerable amount of courage to produce a stage version of the musical West Side Story.

4. The delight many people take in the discomfort of characters in situation comedies suggests that all of us may be subject to some schadenfreude.
5. The USS Enterprise was the first nuclear aircraft carrier.
6. I have always fantasized about taking a ride on the Orient Express, which figured so prominently in a mystery by Agatha Christie.
7. There has been a very conscious effort to make Scientific American available to a larger segment of the reading public.

Connected Discourse Exercise

Use hyphens, capitalization, abbreviations, numbers, and italics properly in the following passage:

Because I can speak Russian fluently, I was recruited by the central intelligence agency while still at Boston college. I suspected that it was professor Hogsbottom, a Political Science teacher, who had suggested that they consider me. After all, he had been a General during World War II and still had connections with the intelligence community. It turned out that my brother in law was responsible; he was an ex FBI agent. Soon I was an american spy located, of all places, in England. Who would suspect that we had to spy on the english? For 3 years I posed as a british aristocrat who was a general bon vivant and man about town. I went by the alias of Mister Henry Higgins, Junior. Everyone, of course, wanted to know if I had seen My Fair Lady. Personally I thought the whole thing was a monty python type of joke until I found a position in the british secret service. Who could have believed the british kept so many secrets from their american allies? For twenty one years I spied on the british without anyone suspecting that I was an all american boy. I did find out recently, however, that because of my fluent russian they had suspected me of being a russian spy and had been feeding me false information all along.

ital

Complete additional exercises and practice in your MyLab

Spelling and Word Usage

"Why the big deal about accurate spelling?"

"Does it really make that much difference if I have an *i* and an *e* turned around or if I omit a letter when spelling a word?"

Students frequently question the importance of proper spelling. Perhaps the answer is suggested by the following sentence, taken from a student essay:

I spent over seven hours *studing* one day last week.

The omission of a *y* in *studing* changes the person from one who is studious to one who is a dreamer. Not only does inaccurate spelling smack of carelessness, but also it sometimes drastically alters meaning.

Although there is no sure-fire way of becoming a good speller, you can minimize the difficulties by learning basic spelling rules, applying helpful spelling tips, and keeping a spelling log of your most common errors.

Spelling Rules

The following four rules should ease spelling pains.

Rule 1   If a word has the double vowels* *ie* or *ei* and the combination has a long *e* sound (as in *me*), use *ie* except after *c*. If the combination has an *a* sound, use *ei*.

ie (as long *e*)	*ei* after *c*	*ei* (as long *a*)
relieve	deceive	freight
belief	receive	neighbor
grieve	receipt	reign
piece	perceive	weigh

The main exceptions to this rule include *either, financier, leisure, neither, seize, species,* and *weird.*

---

*The vowels are *a, e, i, o,* and *u.* The consonants are the remaining letters of the alphabet.

Rule 2   If a one-syllable word (example: *sin*) ends in a single consonant preceded by a single vowel, double the consonant before adding a suffix (see page 685) that starts with a vowel. Apply the same rule with a word of two or more syllables (example: *admit*) if the final syllable is accented and ends with a single consonant preceded by a vowel.

Words with Single Syllables	Words with Two or More Syllables
rig—rigged	admit—admittance
sin—sinned	control—controller
stop—stopping	equip—equipped

If the accent does not fall on the last syllable, do not double the final consonant.

audit—audited	chatter—chattered
counsel—counselor	simmer—simmering

Rule 3   If a word ends in *y* preceded by a single consonant, change the *y* to an *i* unless you are adding the suffix *-ing*.

y changed to *i*	*y* retained
beauty—beautiful	copy—copying
fury—furious	defy—defying
easy—easily	dry—drying
vary—various	vary—varying

Rule 4   If a word ends in a silent *e*, the *e* is usually dropped when a suffix starting with a vowel is added.

blue—bluish	fame—famous
dense—density	grieve—grievous

In a few cases, the *e* is retained to avoid pronunciation difficulties or confusion with other words.

dye—dyeing (not dying)	singe—singeing (not singing)
shoe—shoeing (not shoing)	

The *e* is also retained when it is preceded by a soft *c* sound (pronounced like the letter *s*) or a soft *g* sound (pronounced like the letter *j*) and the suffix being added starts with an *a* or an *o*.

peace—peaceable	courage—courageous
change—changeable	manage—manageable

Helpful Spelling Tips

Here are some tips that can further improve your spelling:

1. Examine each problem word carefully, especially prefixes (*au*dience, *au*dible), suffixes (superintend*ent*, descend*ant*), and double consonants (sate*ll*ite, roo*mm*ate, and co*ll*apsible).

2. Sound out each syllable carefully, noting its pronunciation. Words like *height, governor,* and *candidate* are often misspelled because of improper pronunciation.

3. Make a list of your problem words and review them periodically. Concentrate on each syllable and any unusual features (ar*c*tic, ambig*uous*). There are online programs that help you build your spelling skills as well.

4. Use any crutches that will help: there is *gain* in *bargain;* to *breakfast* is to *break a fast;* a disease causes *dis-ease.*

5. When you copy anything from the blackboard or a textbook, copy it carefully. Writing a word correctly helps you to spell it correctly the next time.

6. Look up the words you don't know how to spell. (See pages 120–122 for more information on dictionaries, including online resources.)

7. If you have a word processor that has a spell checker, use it. But a word of caution: Don't rely exclusively on this tool. Your spell checker may not distinguish between *to* and *too, their* and *there,* and similar sound-alike words. The ultimate spell checker is you.

Common Troublesome Words and Expressions

Watch the Animation on
Easily Confused Words

The English language has many words and expressions that confuse writers. These troublesome items include the following:

Word pairs that sound alike or almost alike but are spelled differently and have different meanings

Word pairs that do not sound alike but still are often confused

Words or phrases that are unacceptable in formal writing

The following glossary identifies the most common of these troublemakers. Familiarize yourself with its contents. Then consult it as you revise your writing if you have even the slightest doubt about the proper use of a word, phrase, or expression.

usage

a, an   Use *a* with words beginning with a consonant sound (even if the first written letter is a vowel); use *an* with words beginning with a vowel or a vowel sound.

a brush, *a* student, *a* wheel, *a* risky situation, *a* once-in-a-lifetime opportunity

an architect, *an* apple, *an* unworthy participant, *an* interesting proposal, *an* honest politician

accept, except   *Accept* is a verb meaning "to receive" or "to approve." *Except* is used as a verb or a preposition. As a verb, *except* means "to take out, exclude, or omit." As a preposition, it means "excluding," "other than," or "but not."

She *accepted* the bouquet of flowers.

Linda *excepted* Sally from the list of guests. (verb)

All of Linda's friends *except* Sally came to the party. (preposition)

access, excess   *Access* is a noun meaning "means or right to enter, approach, or use." In the computer field it is a verb meaning "gain entrance to." *Excess* is an adjective meaning "too much; more than needed; lack of moderation."

> I have *access* to a summer cottage this weekend.
>
> The code permits users to *access* the computer.
>
> The airline booked an *excess* number of passengers on that flight.

adapt, adopt   To *adapt* is "to adjust," often by modification. To *adopt* is "to take as one's own."

> He *adapted* to the higher elevations of the Rocky Mountains.
>
> She *adopted* the new doctrine expounded by the prophet.

adverse, averse   *Adverse* is an adjective meaning "unfavorable." *Averse* is an adjective meaning "disinclined" or "feeling distaste for."

> *Adverse* circumstances caused the ceremony to be postponed.
>
> Martha was *averse* to naming all the guilty children.

advice, advise   *Advice* is a noun meaning "a recommendation about how to deal with a situation or problem." *Advise* is a verb meaning "to recommend or warn."

> The young man followed his sister's *advice*.
>
> Mr. Smith *advised* John to buy 10,000 shares of the stock.

affect, effect   Although both words may function as nouns and verbs, usually *affect* is a verb and *effect* is a noun. The verb *affect* means "to influence, cause a change in, or arouse the emotions of." The noun *affect* is a technical term in psychology and refers to feeling. The noun *effect* means "result or outcome." The verb *effect* means "to bring about or achieve."

> His speech *affected* me greatly. (verb)
>
> The *effect* of the announcement was felt immediately. (noun)
>
> The doctor was soon able to *effect* a cure. (verb)

aggravate   *Aggravate* is a verb meaning "to intensify or make worse" an existing situation. The use of *aggravate* to mean "annoy" or "anger" is colloquial.

Colloquial	Susan's behavior at the dance really *aggravated* me.
Standard	Marcy's interference only *aggravated* the conflict between Bill and Nadine.

ain't   This nonstandard term for *isn't, aren't, hasn't,* or *haven't* is unacceptable in college writing.

all ready, already   *All ready* means "completely prepared" or "everyone is ready." *Already* means "previously, even now, even then."

> The scouts are *all ready* for the camp out.
>
> When we arrived we found he had *already* gone.
>
> The report is *already* a week overdue.

usage

all right, alright   *Alright* is a nonstandard spelling of *all right* and is not acceptable in college writing.

all together, altogether   *All together* means "all in one place" or "in unison." *Altogether* is an adverb meaning "completely, entirely."

> The family was *all together* at the wedding.
>
> *All together*, men, push!
>
> Mr. Doe is *altogether* at fault for writing the letter.

allusion, delusion, illusion   An *allusion* is an indirect reference. A *delusion* is a mistaken belief, often part of a psychological condition. An *illusion* is a deceptive appearance presented to the sight or created by the imagination.

> In his sermon, the minister made many *allusions* to the New Testament.
>
> He suffers from the *delusion* that he is a millionaire.
>
> They wore makeup to give the *illusion* of beauty.

a lot, alot   *Alot* is an erroneous spelling of the two words *a lot*. The phrase *a lot* is usually colloquial; in formal writing replace it with "many."

already   See *all ready, already*.

alright   See *all right, alright*.

alternately, alternatively   *Alternately* means "occurring by turns, one after the other." *Alternatively* means "providing a choice between two items."

> The U.S. flag has seven red and six white stripes, arranged *alternately*.
>
> Highway 44 offers the most direct route to Junction City. *Alternatively*, Highway 88 is much more scenic.

altogether   See *all together, altogether*.

among, between   Use *between* when referring to two things and *among* when referring to more than two.

> He divided the candy *between* Allan and Stephanie.
>
> He divided the candy *among* the five children.

amoral, immoral   *Amoral* means "neither moral nor immoral; morally neutral." *Immoral* means "contrary to the moral code."

> The movie, which takes no clear position on the behavior it depicts, seems curiously *amoral*.
>
> Murder is an *immoral* act.

amount, number   *Amount* refers to total quantities, things in bulk, or weight. *Number* refers to countable things. Never use *amount* when referring to people.

> Cassandra inherited a large *amount* of money.
>
> Cassandra now has a large *number* of friends.

an, a   See *a, an*.

and/or   Although often used in commercial and legal documents, this combination should be avoided in other writing.

angry, mad   *Mad* means "insane," although it is often used colloquially to mean "annoyed" or "angry." To be precise, use *mad* only to mean insane.

Colloquial	I was *mad* at Debbie.
Standard	I was *angry* with Debbie.

any, any other   Do not use *any* when you mean *any other*. Using *any* in the following example would mean that Theresa is more qualified than herself:

Theresa is more qualified than *any other* candidate.

anyone, any one   *Anyone* means "any person." *Any one* means "any single person or thing."

I can whip *anyone* in this room.

I saw three movies last week but didn't like *any one* of them.

appraise, apprise   *Appraise* means "to determine the value of something." *Apprise* means "to notify" or "to tell."

The jeweler *appraised* the gold brooch at $1,500.

Having been *apprised* of the situation, the family priest was able to reconcile the parents and the children.

apt, liable, likely   Both *apt* and *liable* express a tendency or inclination. *Liable* suggests something unpleasant or likely to result in legal action. It should be used only when the event may have unpleasant consequences.

We are *liable* to miss the train.

My lawyer said that I was *liable* for the damage my car had caused.

If the probable consequences are not unpleasant, *apt* is the better word.

I am *apt* to buy books if we go to the shopping center.

Likely merely implies strong probability.

Sandra is *likely* to pass this course without difficulty.

around   *Around* is colloquial use for "approximately" or "about."

Colloquial	She arrived *around* 10:00 P.M.
	The blouse cost *around* $15.
Standard	She arrived at *approximately* 10:00 P.M.
	The blouse cost *about* $15.

as   *As* is frequently used as a weak substitute for *because, since, when,* and *while.*

Weak	She ran out of the house *as* it was on fire.
Better	She ran out of the house *because* it was on fire.

usage

As should not be used in place of *whether* or *that*.

| Nonstandard | I don't know *as* I like her. |
| Standard | I don't know *that* I like her. I don't know *whether* I like her. |

as, like   *As* may be used as a conjunction that introduces an adverb clause, but *like* should not be used this way.

| Unacceptable | *Like* my father always said, "You can fool some of the people all of the time." |
| Standard | *As* my father always said, "You can fool some of the people all of the time." |

Like may, however, be used as a preposition.

In times *like* this, it's hard not to despair.

Any woman *like* Sally can expect a successful career in business.

assure, ensure, insure   To *assure* is "to make safe from risk, to guarantee" or "to convince." *Ensure* and *insure* can be variant spellings meaning "to make certain." *Insure*, however, is now generally associated with the business of insurance.

The counselor tried to *assure* the students that they had made a wise choice.

The captain *assured* them that they would be rescued.

The father, wanting to *ensure* his son's college education, applied for a federally *insured* loan.

averse   See *adverse, averse*.

awful, awfully   In everyday speech, *awful* is used to describe things disagreeable or objectionable: "an *awful* movie," "an *awful* character." *Awfully* is used colloquially as an intensifier: "*awfully* nice," "*awfully* bad." Unless they are used to mean "solemnly impressive," however, both words should be avoided in formal writing.

The *awful* majesty of the cathedral silenced the chattering tourists.

awhile, a while   *A while*, consisting of the noun *while* and the article *a*, means "a period of time." *Awhile* is an adverb meaning "for a short time."

Dinner will be served in *a while*.

Sit *awhile* and tell me the latest gossip.

bad, badly   *Bad* is an adjective. *Badly* is an adverb. *Badly* is colloquial when used to mean "very much."

Unacceptable	She feels *badly* about her mistake.
	Tom behaved *bad* at the circus.
Collo-quial	I want a new car *badly*.
Standard	She feels *bad* about her mistake. (adjective as subject complement) Tom behaved *badly* at the circus. (adverb)
	I want a new car *very much*.

being as, being that   When used as substitutes for *because* or *since*, these expressions are nonstandard.

> | *Nonstandard* | *Being that* I was the first in line, I was able to purchase choice tickets. |
> | *Standard* | *Because* I was first in line, I was able to purchase choice tickets. |

beside, besides   Both words are prepositions, but they have different meanings. *Beside* means "at the side of," and *besides* means "in addition to."

> Sheila and Bill sat *beside* the trailer to eat their lunch.
>
> *Besides* Harvey, Seymour is coming to dinner.

between   See *among, between.*

breath, breathe   *Breath* is a noun and *breathe* is its verb counterpart.

> Nicole stepped outside the stuffy cabin for a *breath* of fresh air.
>
> The cabin was so stuffy that Nicole could hardly *breathe.*

broke   *Broke,* when used to mean "without money," is colloquial.

> | *Colloquial* | Because Shelley was *broke,* she had to miss the movie. |
> | *Standard* | Because Shelley *had no money,* she had to miss the movie. |

can, may   *Can* refers both to permission and to the ability to do something, while *may* refers to permission only.

> I think I *can* pass the exam on Friday. (ability)
>
> My mother says I *can* go to the movies. (permission)
>
> *May* I take the test next Monday? (permission)

When used to denote permission, *can* lends a less formal air to writing than does *may.*

cannot, can not   The use of *cannot* is preferred unless the writer wishes to italicize the *not* for emphasis.

> You *cannot* expect a raise this year.
>
> No, you can *not* expect a raise this year.

can't hardly   This nonstandard form for *cannot, can't,* or *can hardly* is unacceptable in college writing.

can't help but   In college writing, this colloquial phrase should be revised to the simpler *I can't help* or *I cannot help.*

> | *Colloquial* | I *can't help but* wish that I were going to the concert. |
> | *Standard* | I *can't help* wishing that I were going to the concert. |

usage

capital, capitol *Capital* means "a city that serves as a seat of government." *Capitol* means "a building in which a state legislature meets" or "the building in which Congress meets."

> Dover is the *capital* of Delaware.

> The *capitol* in Dover is popular with visitors.

Capital can also refer to wealth or assets, to an offense punishable by death, or to something excellent or first-rate.

> My *capital* consists entirely of stocks and bonds.

> Murder is a *capital* crime in this state.

> That's a *capital* suggestion!

censor, censure To *censor* is "to judge"—literature, movies, letters, and the like—and to decide what material is unfit to be read or seen. To *censure* is "to judge harshly" or "find fault with."

> The warden *censored* all the prisoners' mail.

> The judge *censured* Clyde's criminal behavior.

childish, childlike Both of these terms mean "like a child." *Childish*, however, has a negative connotation.

> He is fifty-two years old, but he behaves in a *childish* manner.

> Jon's face has a *childlike* quality that everyone likes immediately.

cite, sight, site *Cite* means "to mention or quote as an example," *sight* means "to see" or "a view," and *site* means "a location."

> Cheryl *cited* Abraham Lincoln's Emancipation Proclamation in her talk.

> He was able to *sight* the enemy destroyers through the periscope.

> The building *site* is a woody area south of town.

climactic, climatic *Climactic* is an adjective that means "of, being, or relating to a climax." *Climatic* is an adjective meaning "of or relating to a climate."

> Riding the roller coaster was the *climactic* event of Alice's day.

> The *climatic* features of Arizona are desirable to many people.

complement, compliment Both words can act as nouns or verbs. As a noun, *complement* means "something that completes or makes up the whole." As a verb, it means "to complete or perfect." As a noun, *compliment* means "a flattering or praising remark." As a verb, it means "to flatter or praise."

> A *complement* of navy personnel boarded the foreign freighter. (noun)

> This fruit will *complement* the meal nicely. (verb)

> Scott paid Sara Jane a lovely *compliment* at the time of her graduation. (noun)

> Mother *complimented* me for cleaning my room. (verb)

conscience, conscious *Conscience* refers to the sense of moral right or wrong. *Conscious* refers to the awareness of one's feelings or thoughts.

> Edgar's *conscience* forced him to return the money.

> Basil was not *conscious* of his angry feelings.

usage

Do not confuse *conscious* with *aware;* although these words are similar in meaning, one is *conscious* of feelings or actions but *aware* of events.

contemptible, contemptuous   *Contemptible* means "deserving of contempt." *Contemptuous* means "displaying contempt."

> Peter's drunkenness is *contemptible.*

> Mary is *contemptuous* of Peter's drunkenness.

continual, continuous   *Continual* means "frequently or regularly repeated." *Continuous* means "uninterrupted."

> The telephone's *continual* ringing made the morning a nightmare.

> His wound caused him *continuous* pain for a week.

could have, could of   *Could of* is an unacceptable substitute for *could have* because a preposition cannot substitute for a verb.

> *Nonstandard*   I *could of* gone with my parents to Portugal.

> *Standard*   I *could have* gone with my parents to Portugal.

council, counsel   A *council* is a group of people that governs or advises. *Counsel* can be used as both a noun and a verb. The noun means "advice," and the verb means "to advise."

> The city *council* meets on the second Tuesday of every month.

> The lawyer's *counsel* was sound. (noun)

> The psychologist *counsels* many abused children. (verb)

couple   *Couple* denotes two things and should not be used to refer to more than that number.

criteria, criterion   *Criterion* is always singular; *criteria* always plural.

> The primary *criterion* for performing this job is manual dexterity.

> Manual dexterity is but one of many *criteria* on which you will be judged.

cute   *Cute,* an overused colloquialism, should be avoided; it has too many connotations to be used precisely in writing.

data   *Data* is the plural of *datum.* Although *data* is sometimes used with a singular verb, this use is considered incorrect.

> *Standard*   These *data* are incorrect.

> *Unacceptable*   This *data* is incorrect.

definite, very definite   Since *definite* means "precise" or "unmistakable," *very definite* is repetitive. One really cannot be more definite than *definite.*

delusion   See *allusion, delusion, illusion.*

desert, deserts, dessert   *Desert* is land that is arid. With the accent on the last syllable, it is a verb meaning "to abandon." *Deserts* means "that which is deserved." *Dessert* is food served after dinner.

usage

The Sonoran *desert* is full of plant life.

You'll get your just *deserts* if you *desert* me now.

They had cheesecake for *dessert* every Thursday night.

device, devise   *Device* is a noun meaning "a mechanical contrivance, gadget, or tool." *Devise* is a verb meaning "to plan or invent."

This new *device* gives us better gas mileage.

We must *devise* a new approach to our problem.

different from, different than   *Different from* is preferred over *different than.*

His ideas on marriage were *different from* those of his wife.

Different than is accepted, however, when a clause follows and the *from* construction would be wordy.

Acceptable	Susan looks *different than* she did last summer.
Wordy	Susan looks *different from* the way she looked last summer.

discreet, discrete   To be *discreet* means to be "prudent, tactful, or careful of one's actions." *Discrete* means "distinct or separate."

Jack was always *discreet* when he talked to his grandparents.

When two atoms of hydrogen combine with one atom of oxygen, they are no longer *discrete* entities.

disinterested, uninterested   A person who is *disinterested* is impartial or unbiased. A person who is *uninterested* is indifferent or not interested.

We need a *disinterested* judge to settle the dispute.

Joe is completely *uninterested* in sports.

don't   This contraction for *do not* should never be used with singular subjects such as *he, she,* or *it.* Instead, use *doesn't,* the contraction for *does not,* with singular subjects.

Nonstandard	*Don't* he know how to spell?
	That mistake *don't* help your image.
	She *don't* think of anyone except herself.
Standard	*Doesn't* he know how to spell?
	That mistake *doesn't* help your image.
	She *doesn't* think of anyone except herself.

due to   *Due to* has always been acceptable following a linking verb.

Her success was *due to* hard work.

Purists, however, object to *due to* when it is used in other situations, especially in introductory phrases.

Due to the many requests we have had, not everyone who wishes tickets will receive them.

In such cases, you may wish to recast the sentence.

Because we have had so many requests, not everyone who wishes tickets will receive them.

effect   See *affect, effect.*

e.g.   This abbreviation, from the Latin *exempli gratia*, means "for example." Avoid using it except in comments in parentheses and in footnotes, and always follow it with a comma.

elicit, illicit   *Elicit* is a verb that means "to draw forth." *Illicit* is an adjective meaning "not permitted."

> A good professor can always *elicit* responses from students.

> He was engaged in many types of *illicit* activities.

emigrate, immigrate   When people *emigrate*, they move out of a country. When people *immigrate*, they move into a country.

> The family *emigrated* from Poland.

> Many Russians *immigrated* to America.

eminent, imminent   *Eminent* means "prominent," whereas *imminent* means "about to happen."

> Niels Bohr was an *eminent* physicist.

> Our instruments show that an earthquake is *imminent.*

ensure   See *assure, ensure, insure.*

enthused, enthusiastic   *Enthused* is a colloquial word and should not be used in place of *enthusiastic.*

> *Colloquial*   John was *enthused* about the prospects for jobs in his hometown.

> *Standard*   John was *enthusiastic* about the prospects for jobs in his hometown.

especially, specially   The term *especially* means "particularly, notably." *Specially* means "for a specific purpose."

> He is an *especially* talented pianist.

> He was *specially* chosen to represent his group.

et al.   This expression, from the Latin *et alia*, means "and others," referring to people. Ordinarily, the abbreviation should be used only in footnotes and bibliographic entries.

etc.   This abbreviation, from the Latin *et cetera*, means "and other things" and is used in reference to objects rather than people. It should be avoided except in comments in parentheses or in footnotes. It should never be preceded by *and.*

everyone, every one   *Everyone* means "every person." *Every one* means "every particular person or thing."

> *Everyone* who wants to go to the ball game should let me know today.

> If you carefully check *every one* of your paragraphs, you can improve your writing.

except   See *accept, except.*

usage

excess   See *access, excess.*

explicit, implicit   *Explicit* means "clearly expressed" or "straightforward." *Implicit* means "implied" or "understood without direct statement."

You must state your needs *explicitly* if you want them fulfilled.

When I took on the project, I made an *implicit* commitment to see it through.

extant, extent   *Extant* is an adjective meaning "still existing." *Extent* is a noun meaning "scope, size, range, limit."

The dodo bird is no longer *extant.*

From Nevada to Colorado is the *extent* of my travels.

farther, further   The traditional distinction is that *farther* refers to physical distance and *further* to distance in time. Only *further* should be used to mean "additional" or "additionally."

In the race for the Muscular Dystrophy Association, Janet ran *farther* than Cindy.

If you think *further* on the matter, I am certain we can reach an agreement.

Let me make one *further* point.

fewer, less   *Fewer* refers to countable items. *Less* refers to quantity or degree.

Mrs. Smith has *fewer* dogs than cats.

There is *less* money in Joan's checking account than in Stanley's.

Jack was *less* ambitious in his later years.

Never use *less* to refer to people.

Nonstandard	*Less* people were there than I expected.
Standard	*Fewer* people were there than I expected.

flaunt, flout   To *flaunt* is "to display in a showy way." To *flout* is "to express contempt" or "to show scorn."

Jay *flaunted* his handsome physique before all his friends.

Jerrold *flouted* the convention of dressing for dinner by arriving in tennis shoes.

formally, formerly   *Formally* means "according to established forms, conventions, and rules; ceremoniously." *Formerly* means "in the past."

The ambassador *formally* greeted his dinner guests.

Formerly, smallpox was one of our most serious diseases.

funny   *Funny* refers to something that is amusing. In college writing it should not be used to mean "odd" or "unusual."

Colloquial	I felt *funny* visiting my old fourth-grade classroom.
Standard	I felt *odd* visiting my old fourth-grade classroom.

further   See *farther, further.*

get   *Get*, in any of its many colloquial senses, should not be used in writing.

Colloquial	Her way of looking at a man really *gets* me.
	I'll *get* him if it's the last thing I do.
Standard	Beth will *get* at least a *B* in this course.

good and   Replace this colloquial phrase with *very*.

Colloquial	She is *good and* tired of the cafeteria food.
Standard	She is very tired of the cafeteria food.

good, well   Do not mistakenly use *good* as an adverb when an adjective is required.

Unacceptable	John did *good* on his first test.
Standard	John is making *good* progress on his report.
	John is a *good* student.

Well can be used as an adjective meaning "in good health." Otherwise it should always be used as an adverb.

Last week I had a bad cold, but now I am *well.* (adjective)

John did *well* on his first test. (adverb)

got, gotten   Both are acceptable past-participle forms of the verb *to get.*

had ought, hadn't ought   Both are incorrect in formal writing. The correct forms are *ought* and *ought not.*

I *ought* to start studying.

You *ought not* to cut class again.

hanged, hung   People may be *hanged.* Objects may be *hung.*

The prisoner was *hanged* at noon.

Mavis *hung* the picture in the dining room.

hisself, theirself, theirselves   These are nonstandard forms of *himself* and *themselves.*

hopefully   *Hopefully* means "in a hopeful manner." In informal speaking, it is used to mean "it is hoped" or "I hope," but this usage is not correct in formal writing. (Compare this with *carefully,* which means "in a careful manner"; no one uses *carefully* to mean "it is cared.")

Colloquial	*Hopefully,* it will not rain during the class picnic.
Standard	Sally walked *hopefully* into the boss's office to ask for a raise.

hung   See *hanged, hung.*

i.e.   This abbreviation, meaning "that is," comes from the Latin *id est.* Avoid using it except in comments in parentheses or footnotes, and always follow it with a comma.

usage

if, whether *If* is used to introduce adverb clauses, where it means "assuming that."

> *If* I finish my report on time, I'll attend the concert with you.

> *If* and *whether* are often used interchangeably to introduce noun clauses that follow verbs such as *ask, say, doubt, know,* and *wonder.* In formal writing, however, *whether* is preferred.

Less Desirable	I don't know *if* we'll be able to see the North Star tonight.
More Desirable	I don't know *whether* we'll be able to see the North Star tonight.

illicit See *elicit, illicit.*

illusion See *allusion, delusion, illusion.*

immigrate See *emigrate, immigrate.*

imminent See *eminent, imminent.*

immoral See *amoral, immoral.*

impact Although *impact* is sometimes used in colloquial speech as a verb meaning "affect," this use is unacceptable in college writing.

Colloquial	This new law will greatly *impact* political campaigning.
Standard	This new law will greatly *affect* political campaigning.

implicit See *explicit, implicit.*

imply, infer To *imply* is "to indicate indirectly or give implication." To *infer* is "to conclude from facts, evidence, or indirect suggestions."

> Jack *implied* that he wanted a divorce when he told his wife that all marriages come to an end.

> Doris *inferred* that Jack wanted a divorce when he told her all marriages come to an end.

As these examples indicate, speakers and writers imply; listeners and readers infer.

incidence, incidents *Incidents* are separate, countable experiences. *Incidence* refers to the rate at which something occurs.

> Two *incidents* during childhood led to her reclusiveness.

> The *incidence* of cancer in Japan is less than that in the United States.

incredible, incredulous *Incredible* means "fantastic, unbelievable." *Incredulous* means "skeptical, disbelieving."

> That she could run so fast seemed *incredible.*

> Why is Bill wearing that *incredulous* look?

infer See *imply, infer.*

ingenious, ingenuous   *Ingenious* means "clever and inventive." *Ingenuous* means "unsophisticated and innocent."

> Sue presented an *ingenious* solution to our problem.
>
> Mary's *ingenuous* comments amused everyone in the room.

in regards to   This is an incorrect use of *in regard to*.

insure   See *assure, ensure, insure*.

inter-, intra-   *Inter-* means "between or among." *Intra-* means "within."

> From Chicago to Milwaukee is an *interstate* drive of approximately ninety miles.
>
> From San Francisco to Los Angeles is an *intrastate* drive of about 400 miles.

in terms of   Avoid this vague, overused expression.

Vague	*In terms of* the price he is asking, I would not recommend purchasing Tom's car.
Preferred	*Because* of the price he is asking, I would not recommend purchasing Tom's car.

irregardless   This nonstandard form of *regardless* includes the repetitive elements of *ir* and *less*, both of which mean "without."

is when, is where   *Is when* properly refers only to time.

> April *is when* our lilac bush blooms.

Is where properly refers only to place.

> Athens *is where* I met him.

The following sentences are *faulty* because of poorly phrased predicates which indicate that muckraking is a place and an abscess is a time:

> Muckraking *is where* someone investigates corporate or governmental abuses of power.
>
> An abscess *is when* some spot in body tissue fills with pus.

These sentences should be rephrased to eliminate the faulty assertion.

> Muckraking is the investigation of corporate or governmental abuses of power.
>
> An abscess occurs when some spot in body tissue fills with pus.

its, it's, its'   *Its* is a possessive pronoun. *It's* is a contraction of *it is* or *it has*.

> The gold chair was ruined, for someone had torn *its* seat.
>
> *It's* all I have to offer. (It is all I have to offer.)
>
> *It's* been a difficult day. (It has been a difficult day.)

There is no correct use for *its'*.

usage

kind of, sort of   In college writing, these are unacceptable substitutes for *somewhat*, *rather*, or *slightly*.

Colloquial	She is *sort of* angry. I am *kind of* glad she went away.
Standard	She is *somewhat* angry. I am *rather* glad she went away.

When *kind* and *sort* refer to a type, use them with singular nouns and verbs. With their plural forms, *kinds* and *sorts*, use plural nouns and verbs.

Unacceptable	These *kind* of exams are difficult.
Standard	This *kind* of exam is difficult. These *kinds* of exams are difficult.

In such constructions, be certain that *kind of* or *sort of* is essential to your meaning. Otherwise, these phrases are unnecessary.

later, latter   *Later* refers to time; *latter* points out the second of two items. If more than two items are listed, use *last* to refer to the final one.

> He arrived at the party *later* than he was expected.
>
> Although Professors Stein and Patterson both lectured during the course, only the *latter* graded the final exam.
>
> Of my three cats, Sheba, Tiger, and Spot, only the *last* still needs the vaccination.

lay, lie   *Lie* means "to recline" or "to remain in a particular position." It never takes a direct object. *Lay* means "to place" and always takes a direct object. These verbs are often confused, in part because the past tense of *lie* is *lay*. (The past tense of *lay* is *laid*.)

> If I *lie* here a minute, I shall feel better.
>
> *Lay* the book on the table, please.
>
> As I *lay* asleep, a robber entered my apartment and stole my stereo.
>
> He *laid* a hand on her shoulder.

leave, let   *Leave* means "to depart," and *let* means "to allow." Never use *leave* when *let* is meant.

Nonstandard	*Leave* him figure it out alone.
Standard	*Let* him figure it out alone.

lend, loan   Traditionally, *loan* has been classed as a noun and *lend* as a verb. Today, the use of *loan* as a verb is so commonplace that it is accepted as colloquial English.

Standard	I have applied for a *loan* so that I can buy a car. (noun) Please *lend* me your class notes. (verb)
Colloquial	Please *loan* me your class notes. (verb)

usage

less   See *fewer, less.*

let   See *leave, let.*

liable   See *apt, liable, likely.*

lie   See *lay, lie.*

like   See *as, like.*

likely   See *apt, liable, likely.*

literally   The word *literally* means "restricted to the exact, stated meaning." In formal writing, use *literally* only to designate factual statements.

Colloquial	It was 65°, but I was *literally* freezing.
Standard	Our dog was *literally* foaming at the mouth.
	It was 65°, but I was *very* cold.

loan   See *lend, loan.*

loose, loosen, lose   *Loose* can be used as both a verb and an adjective. As a verb, it means "untie or unfasten"; as an adjective, it means "unattached, unrestrained, not confined." *Loosen* is a verb meaning "undo or ease." *Lose* can be used only as a verb meaning "mislay, fail to win, unable to maintain."

He *loosed* the restraints on the tiger. (verb)

One should wear *loose* clothing when bowling. (adjective)

When will Mrs. Brady *loosen* her control over young Tom? (verb)

You would *lose* your nose if it were not attached to your face. (verb)

lots, lots of   *Lots* and *lots of* colloquially mean "many, much, a large amount, or a great amount." Avoid these expressions in college writing.

Colloquial	I've spent *lots of* money in my life.
Standard	I have spent *much* money in my life.

mad   See *angry, mad.*

many, much   *Many* is used when referring to countable items; *much* is used when referring to an indefinite amount or to abstract concepts.

There are *many* students in the biology class.

How did Betty learn so *much* in so little time?

may   See *can, may.*

may be, maybe   *May be* is always used as a verb phrase. *Maybe* is an adverb meaning "perhaps."

I *may be* chairman of the board by next June.

Maybe we will see Jim at home.

usage

medium, media   *Medium* is the singular form of this word; *media* is the plural.

Television is the *medium* I use most to get the news.

The *media* have given extensive coverage to the brain transplant story.

much   See *many, much.*

myself   *Myself* is an intensive and a reflexive pronoun; it cannot substitute for a personal pronoun such as *I* or *me.*

Unacceptable   Four other students and *myself* founded the club.

Standard   Four other students and *I* founded the club.

nice   *Nice* is an adjective suggesting delicacy, precision, subtlety, accuracy, the ability to discriminate, or the need for great care.

These two seemingly identical proposals actually have several *nice* differences.

This author's short stories have a *nice* touch.

Nice as a term of approval meaning "pleasing, enjoyable, attractive" is too generalized for use in college writing.

not hardly   This is a nonstandard variation of *hardly* and is inappropriate in college writing.

number   See *amount, number.*

of between, of from, off of   Eliminate the unnecessary *of* from these colloquial phrases.

Colloquial   There was a crowd *of between* three and four thousand people at the contest.
Get *off of* my property!

Standard   The crowd at the contest numbered *between* three and four thousand people.
Get *off* my property!

on account of   When used to begin an adverb clause (see page 637), this is a nonstandard substitute for *because.*

Nonstandard   The team was unable to practice *on account of* everyone was still upset over Tuesday's loss.

Standard   The team was unable to practice *because* everyone was still upset over Tuesday's loss.

When *on account of* precedes a single word or a phrase, it is considered colloquial.

Colloquial   The game was called *on account of* rain.

over, more than   *Over* should not be substituted for *more than;* if *more than* fits the phrase, use it.

Nonstandard   My brother likes ice cream *over* cake.

Standard   My brother likes ice cream *more than* cake.

passed, past   *Passed* is a verb designating activity that has taken place. *Past* is a noun or an adjective designating a former time.

> The parade *passed* the reviewing stand at 10:30 A.M.
>
> In the *past*, few people were concerned about the environmental effects of pesticides.
>
> This *past* summer, I visited France.

patience, patients   *Patience* means "the ability to wait or endure without complaining." *Patients* are "people being treated by health-care professionals."

> Thad's *patience* was exhausted by the slow service in the restaurant.
>
> Following the tornado, doctors in the emergency room treated over 60 *patients*.

persecute, prosecute   *Persecute* means "to harass persistently because of race, religion, or belief." *Prosecute* means "to bring legal suit against."

> Ethnic groups are often *persecuted*.
>
> The company will *prosecute* anyone caught stealing.

personal, personnel   *Personal* is an adjective meaning "private, individual." *Personnel* are the people working in an organization.

> Religious preference is a *personal* matter that you do not have to reveal during a job interview.
>
> The *personnel* of the sanitation department will not be involved in the city workers' strike.

plenty   When used as an adverb, *plenty* should be replaced by *very*.

> *Colloquial*   That geology exam was *plenty* hard.
>
> *Standard*   That geology exam was *very* hard.

precede, proceed   *Precede* means "to go before or ahead of." *Proceed* means "to go on" or "to go forward."

> The ritual of sharpening his pencils always *preceded* doing his homework.
>
> The guide then said, "If you will *proceed*, I will show you the paintings by da Vinci."

predominant, predominate   *Predominant* is an adjective meaning "chief, main, most frequent." *Predominate* is a verb meaning "to have authority over others."

> The *predominant* European influence on South American culture was Spanish.
>
> In America, the will of the people should *predominate*.

presently   *Presently* means "soon" rather than "at the present time." *Currently* is correct for the second meaning.

> I will be there *presently*.
>
> *Currently*, I am otherwise engaged.

usage

principal, principle   *Principal*, which means "chief," "most important," or "the amount of money on which interest is computed," is used as both a noun and an adjective. *Principle* is used only as a noun and means "truths, beliefs, or rules generally dealing with moral conduct."

> The *principal* suspect in the case was arrested last Friday by the police.
>
> The *principal* of Lewiston High School is Alison Cooperstein.
>
> At this interest rate, your *principal* will double in ten years.
>
> His *principles* are unconventional.

proceed   See *precede, proceed.*

prosecute   See *persecute, prosecute.*

quiet, quite   *Quiet* is an adjective meaning "silent, motionless, calm." *Quite* is an adverb meaning "entirely" or "to a considerable extent or degree."

> The class grew *quiet* when the teacher walked in.
>
> He is *quite* wrong.
>
> The movie was *quite* good.

raise, rise   *Raise* is a transitive verb and therefore requires a direct object. *Rise*, its intransitive counterpart, takes no direct object.

> We plan to *raise* horses on our new farm.
>
> The temperature is expected to *rise* to 75°F tomorrow.

Raise can also be a noun meaning "an increase in pay."

> Tammy received a 25 percent *raise* last week.

real, really   *Real* is an adjective; *really* is an adverb.

> She had *real* plants decorating the bedroom.

When used as an adverb, *real* is a colloquialism and should be replaced with *really*.

> Colloquial   We had a *real* good time at the party.
>
> Standard   We had a *really* good time at the party.

reason is because, reason is that   The *reason is because* is colloquial and unacceptable in formal writing; the *reason is that* is the correct usage.

> Colloquial   The *reason is because* I love her.
>
> Standard   The *reason is that* I love her.

respectfully, respectively   *Respectfully* means "with respect." *Respectively* indicates that the items in one series are related to those in a second series in the order given.

> Joseph should treat his parents *respectfully*.
>
> Tom, Anna, and Susan were assigned *Bleak House*, *Great Expectations*, and *Dombey and Son*, *respectively*, for their reports.

usage

rise   See *raise, rise.*

sensual, sensuous   *Sensual* refers to bodily or sexual sensations. *Sensuous* refers to impressions experienced through the five senses.

> Singles bars offered *sensual* pleasures without emotional commitments.
> The Tivoli Garden provides many *sensuous* delights for visitors.

set, sit   Generally, *set* means "to place" and takes a direct object. *Sit* means "to be seated" and does not take a direct object.

> Alice *set* her glass on the mantel.
> May I *sit* in this chair?

When it refers to the sun, however, *set* is used without a direct object.

> As the sun *set*, we turned homeward.

shall, will   *Shall* is used in first-person (see page 613) questions and in specialized forms of writing such as military orders and laws. Otherwise, *will* is generally used.

> *Shall* we go to the movies tonight?
> The company *shall* fall into formation at precisely 12 noon.
> No family home *shall* be assessed at more than 50 percent of its actual value.

should have, should of   *Should of* is an unacceptable substitute for *should have* because a preposition cannot substitute for a verb.

> *Nonstandard*   I *should of* gone to the lake.
>
> *Standard*   I *should have* gone to the lake.

[sic]   This Latin word, always enclosed in brackets, follows quoted errors in grammar, spelling, or information. Inclusion of [sic] indicates that the error appeared in the original, which is being quoted exactly.

sight   See *cite, sight, site.*

sit   See *set, sit.*

site   See *cite, sight, site.*

so   *So* is an acceptable coordinating conjunction but tends to add an informal effect to writing and should therefore be used sparingly. For example, "Tom said he was divorcing me, *so* I began to cry" would be more effective if restated as follows: "When Tom said he was divorcing me, I began to cry." Do not use *so* as a substitute for *extremely* or *very* except with adverb clauses beginning with *that*.

> *Colloquial*   You are *so* careless in what you say.
>   The discussion was *so* informative that I took many notes.
>
> *Standard*   You are *very* careless in what you say.
>   The discussion was *extremely* informative.

some   *Some* is colloquial and unacceptable in writing when used as an intensifier (We had *some* time of it!) or an adverb (He'll probably pout *some* after you leave).

usage

sometime, some time, sometimes *Sometime* means "at a future unspecified time," *some time* means "a span of time," and *sometimes* means "occasionally."

We should get together *sometime* and play bridge.

The weather has been hot for *some time.*

Sometimes I go to dinner with Ethel.

sort of See *kind of, sort of.*

specially See *especially, specially.*

stationary, stationery *Stationary* means "not moving" or "fixed." *Stationery* means "paper for writing letters."

The circular part in the center must remain *stationary*, or the machine will not function.

Sue always writes on scented *stationery.*

such, such...that The use of *such* when it means "very" or "extremely" is unacceptable unless it is followed by a *that* clause completing the thought.

Colloquial	They were *such* good cookies.
Standard	They were *such* good cookies *that* I asked Steve for his recipe.

suppose to, supposed to *Suppose to* is the nonstandard form of *supposed to.* In speech, it is difficult to hear the final *d* on *supposed*, and one may say *suppose to* without being detected; however, the correct written form is always *supposed to.*

sure, surely *Sure* is colloquial for the adverb *surely.*

Colloquial	You *sure* know how to make good coffee, Mrs. Olsen.
Standard	You *surely* know how to make good coffee, Mrs. Olsen.

Although *surely* is correct, it may sound too formal and insincere. Therefore, *certainly* is often a better word to use.

take and, try and Avoid these expressions. Simply eliminate them from the sentence or substitute *try to* for *try and.*

Unacceptable	If you *take and* cover the tomato plants, they probably won't freeze. I think you should *try and* settle your differences.
Standard	If you cover the tomato plants, they probably won't freeze. I think you should *try to* settle your differences.

than, then *Than* is used to make comparisons; *then* means "at that time, in that case," or "after that."

Jill is taller *than* her brother.

First we will eat, and *then* we will discuss business.

usage

that, which   These two words have the same meaning. *That* may refer both to things and groups of people; *which*, only to things. When referring to things, *that* is generally used with clauses that distinguish the things they modify from others in the same class (restrictive clauses). *Which* is generally used with clauses that add information about the things they modify (nonrestrictive clauses). Note that clauses starting with *which*, unlike those starting with *that*, are generally preceded by a comma.

> Any book *that* she likes is certain to be trashy. (restrictive clause)
>
> The Winthrop Building, *which* cost two million dollars to construct, could not now be duplicated for 10 times that much. (nonrestrictive clause)

See pages 672–673 for a more comprehensive explanation of restrictive and nonrestrictive expressions.

their, there, they're   These three separate words are often confused because they sound alike. *Their* is the possessive form of *they*. *There* is an expletive that appears at the beginning of a sentence and introduces the real subject, or it is an adverb meaning "in or at that place, at that point." *They're* is a contraction of *they are*.

> It is *their* basketball.
>
> *There* are many reasons why I cannot come.
>
> Put the sofa down *there*.
>
> *They're* going to be here soon.

theirself, theirselves   See *hisself, theirself, theirselves*.

then   See *than, then*.

there   See *their, there, they're*.

thorough, through   *Thorough* means "careful, complete, exact, painstaking." *Through* means "in one side and out the other, from end to end, from start to finish, over the whole extent of, finished."

> Brenda has done a *thorough* job.
>
> Let's run *through* the plan again.

thusly   *Thusly* is a nonstandard form of *thus*.

to, too, two   *To* is a preposition meaning "as far as, toward, until, onto." *Too* is an adverb meaning "excessively" or "also." *Two* is a number.

> I'm going *to* the store.
>
> Are you going *too*?
>
> This car is *too* expensive for me.
>
> There are *two* characters in the play.

toward, towards   Both forms are correct. *Toward* generally is used in the United States and *towards* in England.

usage

try and See *take and, try and.*

two See *to, too, two.*

uninterested See *disinterested, uninterested.*

unique *Unique* means "without an equal" or "extremely unusual" and thus should not be modified by an adverb such as *very.*

use to, used to *Use to* is the nonstandard form of *used to.* In speech it is difficult to hear the *d* on *used,* and one may say *use to* without being detected; however, the correct written form is always *used to.*

used to could This phrase is nonstandard for *used to be able to.*

>   *Nonstandard*   I *used to could* run 10 miles.
>
>   *Standard*   I *used to be able to* run 10 miles.

very definite See *definite, very definite.*

wander, wonder *Wander* is a verb meaning "to move about without a plan or set destination." *Wonder* is a noun meaning "something causing surprise, admiration, or awe" or a verb meaning "to be curious about."

>   Some people like to *wander* through shopping malls for recreation.
>   That child is a *wonder* at mathematics.
>   I *wonder* whether I have received an *A* on that test.

way, ways *Ways* may be used to refer to two or more means or methods but not to time or distance.

>   *Unacceptable*   Timbuktu is a long *ways* from the United States.
>
>   *Standard*   There are two *ways* of thinking about that issue.
>   Timbuktu is a long *way* from the United States.

well See *good, well.*

were, where *Were* is the past form of the verb *to be. Where* is an adverb or a pronoun meaning "in, at, to, from a particular place or situation" or "which or what place."

>   I'm sorry that you *were* ill yesterday.
>   Mr. Morris will show you *where* to register.

where...at, to, from *At, to,* and *from* are unnecessary after *where.*

>   *Wordy*   *Where* are you taking the car *to*?
>   *Where* does she live *at*?
>   *Where* did you get the book *from*?
>
>   *Standard*   *Where* are you taking the car?
>   *Where* does she live?
>   *Where* did you get the book?

whether   See *if, whether*.

which   See *that, which*.

who, whom   In formal writing, *who* should be used only as a subject in clauses and sentences and *whom* only as an object.

> *Unacceptable*   *Who* are you taking to dinner on Friday?
> I know *who* the boss will promote.
> John is the candidate *whom* I think will be elected.
>
> *Standard*   *Whom* are you taking to dinner on Friday?
> I know *whom* the boss will promote.
> John is the candidate *who* I think will be elected.

See page 655 for a fuller discussion of *who* and *whom*.

who's, whose   *Who's* is a contraction of *who is* or *who has*, and *whose* is the possessive form of *who*.

> *Who's* coming to see us tonight?
> I would like to know *who's* been dumping trash in my yard.
> *Whose* book is that?

will   See *shall, will*.

wise   Do not randomly add *wise* to the ends of nouns. Such word coinings are ineffective.

> *Ineffective*   Personality *wise*, Sheila is ideal for the job.
>
> *Standard*   Sheila has an *ideal personality* for the job.

wonder   See *wander, wonder*.

would have, would of   *Would of* is an unacceptable substitute for *would have*. A preposition cannot substitute for a verb.

> *Nonstandard*   I *would of* enjoyed seeing the Picasso exhibit.
>
> *Standard*   I *would have* enjoyed seeing the Picasso exhibit.

would have been, had been   When *would* occurs in the main part of a sentence, use *had been* (not *would have been*) in an "if" clause.

> *Nonstandard*   If the engine *would have been* lubricated, the bearing *would not have* burned out.
>
> *Standard*   If the engine *had been* lubricated, the bearing *would not have* burned out.

your, you're   *Your* is a possessive form of *you; you're* is a contraction of *you are*.

> Where is *your* history book?
> Tell me when *you're* ready to leave.

usage

Complete additional
exercises and practice
in your MyLab

Credits

Maya Angelou, "Momma's Encounter" from *I Know Why the Caged Bird Sings* by Maya Angelou, copyright © 1969 and renewed 1997 by Maya Angelou. Used by permission of Random House, Inc.

Marti Bercaw, "Krumping" Socal.com Writer. Reprinted by permission of the author.

Maressa Brown, "Teacher Natalie Munroe Has a Right To Call Kids Lazy and Rude" from *The Stir*, February 16, 2011. This was originally posted at CafeMom's blog, The Stir.com, written by Maressa Brown.

Bruce Catton, "Grant and Lee: A Study in Contrast" from *The American Story*, ed. Earl Schenck Miers. Reprinted by permission of U.S. Capitol Historical Society.

James Bucky Carter, "Going Graphic", 2009, *Educational Leadership*, 66(6), pp. 68–72. Copyright © 2009 by ASCD. Reprinted with permission. Learn more about ASCD at www.ascd.org.

Shari Caudron, "Can Generation Xers Be Trained?" *Training and Development Magazine*, v. 51, March 1997, pp. 20–4. Copyright © 1997 from T&D by Shari Caudron. Reprinted with permission of American Society for Training and Development.

Countee Cullen, "Yet Do I Marvel." Used by permission of Amistad Research Center, Tulane University.

Michel Foucalt, "Las Meninas" from the book *Valezquez's Las Meninas*, Chapter 1, by Michel Foucault, Cambridge University Press, 2002.

Conor Friedersdor, "Immigration Policy Gone Loco" from *The Daily Beast On Line*, Apr 17, 2010. Copyright © 2010 The Daily Beast. Reprinted by permission.

Bruce Jay Friedman, "Eating Along in Restaurants," from *The Lonely Guy's Book of Life*, 1978. Reprinted by permission of the author.

Amy Gross, "The Appeal of the Androgynous Man" from *Oprah Magazine*.

Dan Greenburg, "Sound and Fury." Reprinted by permission of the author. All rights reserved.

Marianne Halavage, "Turn Down Your iPod Volume (Or Go Deaf)." Used by permission of the author.

Henry Jenkins, "Art Form for the Digital Age." *Technology Review* Sept 2000 v. 103 i5 p. 117. Copyright © 2000 by MIT Technology Review. Reproduced with permission of MIT Technology Review in the format Electronic via Copyright Clearance Center.

Kevin Johnson, "For Cops, Citizen Videos Bring Increased Scrutiny" from *USA Today*, October 15, 2010. Copyright © 2010. Used by permission.

Martin Luther King, Jr., "I Have a Dream." Copyright © 1963 Dr. Martin Luther King, Jr., copyright renewed 1991 Coretta Scott King. Reprinted by arrangement of the Estate of Martin Luther King, Jr., c/o Writers House as agent for the proprietor New York, NY.

Caroline Knapp, "Why We Keep Stuff" from *The Merry Recluse*, pp. 195–199. Counterpoint Press. Reprinted by permission of Perseus Books Group.

Chris Lee, "Invasion of the Bodybuilders" from *Newsweek*, June 5, 2011. Copyright © 2011 Newsweek. Used by permission.

Belinda Luscombe, "The Science of Romance: Why We Flirt" from *TIME Magazine*, January 17, 2008. Copyright TIME Inc. Reprinted by permission. TIME is a registered trademark of Time Inc. All rights reserved.

Bernice McCarthy, "A Tale of Four Learners." *Educational Leadership* v. 54 March 1997, pp. 46–51. About Learning, Excel, Inc. 1996. Reprinted by permission.

From Merriam Webster's Collegiate® Thesaurus © 2012 by Merriam Webster, Incorporated (www.Merriam Webster.com) By permission.

Chris Mooney, "The Science of Why We Don't Believe Science" from *Mother Jones*, May/June 2011. Copyright © 2011, Foundation for National Progress.

Patrick Moore, "Going Nuclear" from Sunday, April 16, 2006 in *Washington Post* online. Used by permission of Patrick Moore.

Judith Newman, "If You're Happy and You Know It, Must I Know Too?" from *The New York Times*, October 23, 2011. Copyright © 2011 The New York Times. Reprinted by permission.

Perfect Home HVAC Design, "Ground Source Heat Pumps: Mother Earth Will Wrap You in Warmth" courtesy of Perfect Home HVAC Design.

Michael Pollan, "Supermarket Pastoral" from *The Omnivore's Dilemma: A Natural History of Four Meals*. New York: Penguin Books, 2006. pp. 134–139. Reprinted by permission.

Richard Rodriguez, "Private Language: Public Language," from *Aria: A Memoir of a Bilingual Childhood* by Richard Rodriguez. Copyright © 1980 by Richard Rodriquez. Originally appeared in American Scholar. Reprinted by permission of Georges Borchardt, Inc., on behalf of the author.

Alexis Rowell, "Ten Reasons Why New Nuclear Was a Mistake Even Before Fukushima" from *Transition Culture*, March 15, 2011. Also available at www.cuttingthecarbon.co.uk/resources/why nuclear is not the answer. Reprinted by permission of Alexis Rowell.

Sabrina Erdely Rubin, "Binge Drinking: A Campus Killer." Reprinted by permission of the author.

Marta Salinas, "The Scholarship Jacket" from *Nosotras: Latina Literature Today*, edited by Maria del Carmen Boza, Beverly Silva, and Carmen Valle, Bilingual Press/Editorial Bilingue, 1986, Tempe, Arizona.

Scott Russell Sanders, "The Men We Carry in Our Minds," copyright © 1984 by Scott Russell Sanders; first appeared in Milkweed Chronicle; reprinted by permission of the author and Virginia Kidd Agency, Inc.

John Phillips Santos, "Back to the Future" from *Texas Monthly* , Vol 38, No 11, 2010. Reprinted with permission from the November 2010 issue of Texas Monthly.

Somini Sengupta, "Rushdie Runs Afoul of Web's Real-Name Police" from *The New York Times*, November 14, 2011. Copyright © 2011 The New York Times Co. Used with permission.

John Shepler, "What Thoreau Knew: Walden and the Meaning of Voluntary Simplicity," http://www.johnshepler.com/articles/thoreau.html. Reprinted by permission of the author.

James Alexander Thom, "The Perfect Picture." Reprinted with permission from the August 1976. issue of Reader's Digest. Copyright © 1976 by The Reader's Digest Association, Inc.

Beth Wald, "Let's Get Vertical!" from *Listen: Journal of Better Living*, June 1989. Reprinted by permission.

Douglas Alden Warshaw, "Pulling Off the Ultimate Career Makeover" from *Fortune*, July 4, 2011. Copyright © 2011 Fortune. Used by permission.

Marion Winik, "What are Friends For?", from *Telling* by Marion Winik, copyright © 1994 by Marion Winik. Used by permission of Villard Books, a division of Random House, Inc.

Byron York, "A Carefully Crafted Immigration Law in Arizona" from *The Washington Examiner* (online), April 26, 2010. Reprinted by permission of Universal Uclick.

John V. Young, "When the Full Moon Shines Its Magic" from *The New York Times*, March 16, 1969. Copyright © 1969 The New York Times Co. Reprinted by permission.

Jonathan Zimmerman, "When Teachers Talk Out of School" from *The New York Times*, June 3, 2011. Copyright © 2011 The New York Times. Reprinted by permission.

Marc Zwelling, "The Blended Economy" from *The Futurist* v. 36 no. 1 (Jan–Feb 2002) pp. 12–13. Used by permission.

Index

Editing Symbols

Symbol	Problem	Page	Symbol	Problem	Page
ab	improper abbreviation	688–689	*no*	new paragraph not needed	
agr pa	faulty agreement of pronoun and antecedent	647–650	⊙	period needed	677
agr sv	faulty agreement of subject and verb	645–647	*// or para*	nonparallelism	663–664
∨ or apos	missing or misused apostrophe	667–670	*? or ques*	missing or misused question mark	677–678
awk	awkward phrasing		*"/" or quot*	missing or misused quotation marks	682–684
bib	faulty bibliographic form	396–434	*ref*	unclear reference of pronoun to antecedent	650–652
cap	capital letter needed	686–688	*ro*	run–on sentence	643–645
case	wrong case	654–657	*; or sem*	missing or misused semicolon	675–676
cl	cliché	137–138	*sp*	spelling error	694–696
∧ or com	missing or misused comma	670–674	*shift p*	shift in person	652–654
cs	comma splice	643–645	*shift t*	shift in tense	657–658
comp	faulty comparison	664–666	*sq*	squinting modifier	661–662
dm	dangling modifier	662–663	*t or tense*	wrong tense	619–622
… or ellip	missing or misused ellipsis	373	*trans*	poor transition	
frag	sentence fragment	641–642	*vb*	wrong verb form	
ital	missing or misused italics	691–693	*wdy*	wordiness	135–136
lc	lowercase (small) letter needed	686–688	*ww*	wrong word	
// or lev	wrong level of usage	124–128	ℛ	delete (omit)	
log	faulty logic		^	material omitted	
mm	misplaced modifier	661–662	⟨?⟩	meaning unclear or word illegible	
num	use numerals	690–691			
nsu	nonstandard usage new paragraph needed				